The Lessons of History

LECTURES ON MODERN HISTORY
AND THE FRENCH AND AMERICAN REVOLUTIONS

BY

William Smyth

ABRIDGED AND EDITED BY

WALLACE BROCKWAY

WITH A FOREWORD BY

BERNARD M. BARUCH

SIMON AND SCHUSTER · NEW YORK · 1955

FIRST PRINTING
LIBRARY OF CONGRESS CATALOG CARD NUMBER: 55-6955
DEWEY DECIMAL CLASSIFICATION NUMBER: 042
MANUFACTURED IN THE UNITED STATES OF AMERICA
BY VAIL-BALLOU PRESS, BINGHAMTON, N. Y.

Foreword
by BERNARD M. BARUCH

BROWSING *through old forgotten books—especially when I am oppressed by the confusion and clamor of our times and surfeited with contemporary writing—is one of my favorite forms of relaxation. A stroll down some deserted lane of literature or history, like a walk along a secluded country road, clears my mind and helps restore my perspective.*

To be sure, not every excursion along the less traveled byways of books ends in some neglected garden of literature. But often enough I come upon some battered old volume which has survived damp and rats and the neglect of generations and which is still interesting and even exciting. Then I know the pleasure of discovery and the satisfaction of recovering from discard a work which, at least in my opinion, deserves to be read again.

Such a book is The Lessons of History. *Some years ago at an auction I chanced upon it in five formidable-looking volumes under its original title of* Lectures on History. *Struck by the author's felicity of language and his apparent erudition, I took it with me to my South Carolina home. There, where the distractions of the city do not intrude and I feel no compulsion to keep abreast of the latest books, I read it. I have been reading in it ever since. I know of no book which has given me more instruction and more pleasure.*

I doubt whether there are half a hundred copies of Smyth's work in print or a score of men in England and America who are familiar with it. Yet the few persons to whom I have shown the book have unanimously applauded it. When I called it to the attention of the perceptive M. Lincoln Schuster, he enthusiastically suggested that it be reclaimed from obscurity. In the present one-volume abridgment, edited by Wallace Brockway, readers now have the opportunity to make the acquaintance of this forgotten historian.

Although Smyth wrote more than a century ago of the long history of the Western world culminating in the American and French revo-

lutions, time has not impaired the real value of his work. This con-
sists not of the routine chronicle of events, most of which the editor
has wisely excised. Modern scholarship has superseded Smyth in this
respect. The significance of Smyth's work lies in his reflections on
human nature and on the character and conduct of men—the great
and the not so great, the thinkers and the doers—such as Cromwell,
Pitt, Godwin, Burke, Voltaire, Robespierre, Washington, to name
a few at random. It lies in his observations on the enduring problems
of the world—on war and peace, liberty and tyranny, reform and
revolution, poverty and wealth, and chiefly on the use and abuse of
power. It lies in brief in his attempt to read the lessons of history.

Neither human nature nor the fundamental problems of man-
kind have changed since Smyth's time. Nor can it be said that we
have learned much from history. But since it is always possible to do
so, and since wisdom and understanding are never obsolete, Smyth
may still be read with profit.

The lessons of history which Smyth discerned a century ago have
been underscored by events since then. They will be underscored
again, to our sorrow, unless we learn to apply them. What are some
of these lessons which we would do well to consider?

History teaches that liberty is among the most priceless possessions
of men and indispensable to just government. It teaches also that in
undisciplined, unpracticed hands it is incompatible with govern-
ment and capable of abuses as evil as those of any tyranny.

History teaches the danger of unrestricted authority. "The more
unlimited the power, the greater the abuse," Smyth observes. Yet if
men are to maintain an ordered society, they must learn to handle
power, Smyth remarks, as they learn to handle money. I like the
analogy. It may be said that men handle money no better than they
handle power. That is their fault. Just as it is not money that is the
root of all evil, it is not power that corrupts, Lord Acton to the con-
trary notwithstanding. It is the lust for them which does the damage.
Men may possess both money and power to the benefit of them-
selves and their fellows. It is when money and power possess men
that the harm ensues.

History teaches that progress comes in slow stages and only through
reason and moderation. When men set out to remake the world,

when they permit the demagogue to incite their passions and the Utopian to seduce their reason, they must not only fail, but the world must suffer. Surveying the history of noble causes lost, of idealism gone astray, Smyth concludes that "elevated sentiment is no basis for the conduct of human affairs." The only basis lies in reason and realism. This, to Smyth, is the cardinal lesson of history.

"Those who cannot remember the past," Santayana said, "are condemned to repeat it." There is good reason to doubt that the world could survive a repetition of its recent history. If it is to avoid that test it must begin to learn the lessons of history. One may find many of those lessons catalogued and explained in Smyth's book. Some books, he remarks, are to be tasted, others digested. Whether one merely tastes his or digests it thoroughly, it will, I am sure, yield both pleasure and nourishment.

Contents

Lectures on Modern History

Lectures on the History of the French Revolution

Supplementary Lectures

William Smyth

A BIOGRAPHICAL NOTE

GEORGE I, a personage neither respected nor indulged by historians of any stripe, in 1724 founded professorships of modern history at Oxford and Cambridge. What should have constituted a telling attack on the obsolete curriculum had no effect at either university, for the king's fiat, that the professors "Shall be obliged to read Lectures in the Publick Schools, at Such times as shall hereafter be appointed," was tacitly ignored. Nothing disturbed the snores of the "mostly die-hard, port-drinking dons"—tories even at Cambridge—who continued to provide the intellectual pabulum for many a year to come. Of the two universities Cambridge was slightly less sunk in lethargy, and it was here that some respectable conception of the role to be played by the regius professor of modern history was first realized.

In view of the founder's explicit instructions that the professorships were designed to qualify young men for the public service, the indifference of the early holders of the chairs borders on the scandalous. Beyond an inaugural lecture couched in the vaguest terms, they drew their sine-cures of £400 a year, wholly theirs but for a pittance divided between "two persons . . . well qualified to teach and instruct in writing and Speaking . . . Modern Languages" (usually French and Italian, the staples of the Grand Tour). It is no guess that these poor hirelings, with possibly £40 a year between them, worked harder than the regius professor.

Four of the first five holders of the chair at Cambridge may be described, not unfairly, as nonentities. Samuel Harris, the first of them, not unnaturally tended to exaggerate the greatness of the house of Hanover in his inaugural lecture. Of Shallet Turner, regius professor for more than a quarter of a century, good or ill fame says nothing: he is a foot-note, and an uninteresting one. Laurence Brockett, the next incumbent (1762–68), "died by a fall from his horse, being (as I hear) drunk, & some say, returning from Hinchinbroke," the seat of that brilliant rake-hell, the fourth earl of Sandwich. The words are those of the poet Gray, who succeeded to the easy chair after yearning for it a good twenty years. Unquestionably the most learned of the poets, Gray did not bother to lecture, though he hints, in his letters, at occasional twinges of conscience. Apparently, conscience caught up with John Symonds, whose interests were colonization, agriculture, and theology—certainly a mixed bag. The first and second topics may well have figured in the lectures, the extent and effectiveness of which are not recorded. Symonds died in 1807, having held his chair for thirty-six years, and was succeeded by William Smyth, the subject of this note.

Smyth was lucky in his father, a Liverpool banker whose wide intellectual interests may have been overindulged. William, born in 1765, was the eldest of nine children and, until his father's bank failed in 1793, enjoyed the advantages of a son of a prosperous middle-class family with good connections. He went to Eton for three years, where with half a dozen friends he formed a poetry society. He found exclusive emphasis on the classics somewhat irksome, and made the wise choice of reading mathematics with a tutor before going on to Cambridge in 1783. Graduated eighth wrangler in 1787, he was made a fellow of his college—Peterhouse—the same year. During holidays in London, Smyth haunted the House of Commons whenever Parliament was in session, drinking in the eloquence of Fox, Sheridan, and the younger Pitt—an admirable discipline for the future historian. (He listened to Burke but noted that he was past his prime.) At Liverpool he cultivated the friendship of William Roscoe, whose famous volumes on the Medici were still to be written.

After his father's financial ruin Smyth was uneasily circumstanced for some years. He was lucky—or unlucky—enough to secure the post of tutor to Tom Sheridan, son of Richard Brinsley Sheridan. Pay was slow, uncertain, and yet not meager when Sheridan had the wherewithal. Smyth spoke of his dealings with the great man as "one eternal insult, mortification, and disappointment," but with a certain detachment he made himself the laughingstock in this tragicomedy. Sheridan's fascinating manner could always win Smyth over. At a typical interview with his employer, Smyth wrote that "I had come into the room like a lion and went out like a lamb . . . and after a few paces down the street I made one discovery more—what a fool am I." Fortunately, some of Sheridan's powerful political friends liked Smyth, and the ministry of "All the Talents" (in which Sheridan held a noncabinet post) gave him preferment. In 1807, just before the ministry fell, Smyth became Cambridge's sixth regius professor of modern history. He held the chair until his death, forty-two years later, and appears to have been active as a lecturer until 1840.

Except for his professorial activities, the rest of Smyth's long life was almost eventless, and he died unmarried in 1849 at a very advanced age. Its sole major annoyance occurred in 1825, when, in deference to the current college statutes, he was forced to relinquish his fellowship upon inheriting real estate. He continued to occupy his rooms in Peterhouse, a "comfortable bachelor establishment," as George Ticknor described them in 1838, then, as before, the meeting place of a large circle of friends, which eventually included the geologist Sedgwick, Whewell, the massively learned master of Trinity College, and George Thomson, the untiring collector of the melodies of Scotland, Wales, and Ireland. A minor poet whom Byron condescended to except (very lukewarmly, it is true) from his general censure of Cambridge poets in *English Bards and Scotch Reviewers*, Smyth had a positive genius for sociability. Without a trace of the romantic fervor and exaggerated sentimentality that were then coming into fashion, he had a benevolent attitude toward those of decent character but mediocre intellectual qualifications, and whose sole remaining qualification appears to have been a desire for the pleasure of his conversation. Among these was Mary Ann Kelty, who recorded the charms of the concerts in Smyth's rooms, and sang—one wonders how well—songs by Corelli, Scarlatti, Germiniani, and Handel. Among his better-known female friends were Mrs. Barbauld, Joanna Baillie, Lucy Aiken, the Misses Berry (the special friends of Horace Walpole's old age), Mrs. Opie, and Lady Dacre. Smyth's grandniece, Dame Ethel Smyth, claimed that he was an intimate friend of Jane Austen, but this claim seems to have been put forward without foundation.

As is clear from Smyth's literary and musical tastes, as well as from his political opinions, he had a good deal of the eighteenth century about him to the last. This made him appear a trifle conservative to the rather self-conscious romantics of later generations, but fortunately what he kept of the eighteenth century was a serene and urbane liberalism. The best portrait of Smyth represents him at the ripe age of seventy, and comes from the careful pen of George Ticknor: "Tall and somewhat awkward, dressed like a *marquis de l'ancienne régime*, and looking like one, with his earlocks combed out and his hair powdered, but still with an air of great carelessness, he moved about in that brilliant assembly, hardly spoken to by a single person . . . as if he belonged not to it; and yet, when there was a fine passage in the music, seeming to enjoy it as if he were all ear." The "brilliant assembly," be it noted, was held at Samuel Rogers' famous house overlooking the Green Park. Ticknor continues: "He talked well, and not much, and some of his remarks had great beauty as well as great truth and originality; now and then he showed a striking eagerness in manner which contrasted strongly with his usual modesty and reserve. On the whole, I think he justified his reputation as a man of genius, and as one of the finest men now at Cambridge."

Such was the man who was certainly the first holder of the regius professorate at Cambridge to fulfill his academic duties and to do so with scholarly thoroughness. Possibly, had he not been limited to a single course of lectures every third term, he would have left a greater name as a historian—one, in short, not in need of resuscitation. His historical work is by no means negligible, but in the context of his life it seems not to have been so old or so deeply a cherished interest as others.

He was, as they used to say, a man of parts, and could have made his mark at almost anything. History must be considered one of the accidents, nonphilosophically speaking, of his life. The regius professoriate came his way as a political plum, but he did not treat the office as a mere sinecure. As soon as he felt himself ready, he gave his first course of lectures. There is evidence that he was an inspired and popular teacher, and we know of at least one of his students who came back, years after his graduation, to hear Smyth lecture again.

The preparation of his lectures must have been more than ordinarily difficult for Smyth, who throughout his life suffered from eye trouble, being subject to a most painful inflammation of the retina. This situation forced him to budget his reading time with more than usual care. He once said that if all the time he had spent quietly in a darkened room were added up, it would come to a considerable portion of his life. Yet there is little evidence that he skimped the vast amount of reading that went into the fabric of his two large historical courses. He poked wry but respectful fun at some of the longer chronicles—rather, he groaned at their longueurs. Yet throughout, the refrain is ever much the same: they must be read. Such obvious secondary sources as Gibbon and Hume, for example, he had at his memory's need, but he did not neglect other writers whose crowded pages have been superseded by the products of the modern schools of historical study, one of the most famous of which was nurtured at Smyth's own university.

Some of Smyth's power as a historian—perhaps even more so as a teacher—lay in his ability to relate the past to the present without straining precedent. He wrote, at his best, with the mature wisdom of a man who knew the world. His fine summations bespeak the careful observer of all around him and the happy intimate of the best minds of the day. During his visits to London, Smyth dined with Francis Horner, Sir Samuel Romilly, Bobus Smith (credited with as much wit and conversational brilliance as his brother Sydney), and the many-faceted Brougham. In later years he came to know David Ricardo and Tom Moore, and was especially close to Sir James Mackintosh and Malthus, both his precise contemporaries. To know these last two was to know the most advanced thought of the day.

Smyth first lectured in Michaelmas term, 1809. He regretted that only one term in every year was allowed him for his course, "in order not to interfere with other public lecturers who take their particular term in like manner." This condition of lecturing made difficulties for him, especially after 1837 when half his audience was lost to him because of curricular prerequisites. Only undergraduates of at least two years' standing could attend his courses, so that none but third- and fourth-year men and their private tutors ever got a chance to hear Smyth's entire course. In his first two series of lectures (from the origins to 1688, and from 1688 to the war between Great Britain and her colonies), Smyth gave a concluding lecture for the first, and an introductory lecture for the second, which summarized both series. He experimented in different years with various kinds of abridgments and introductions, and "In some years . . . he actually abbreviated the two parts sufficiently to get both into one term."

In preparing his lectures on the French Revolution, Smyth had the advice of John Lewis Mallet, a son of Jacques Mallet du Pan, the Royalist agent, "a pioneer of modern political journalism." He was given access to the father's important papers and obtained for the university library a complete set of the *Mercure historique et politique* (1788–92), edited by Mallet du Pan and vital to any true understanding of the French Revolution. When Smyth was repeating his course on these events in 1831, he stated in his introductory lecture that he would not read a line from the chair (without express notification in writing) that had not been written and spoken in the same lecture before 1830. Similarly, despite many requests to do so, he refused to extend his lectures to include Bonaparte, preferring to leave this task to his successor. He probably did not lecture often after 1840, the date of publication of both series of lectures.

It was inevitable that Smyth—"a Whig of the old school," as he was proud to call himself—would be compared to Macaulay, particularly after 1855, when the last volumes of Macaulay's great *History of England from the Accession of James II* had appeared, and Smyth's own lectures had achieved a semiclassical status by inclusion in Bohn's Standard Library. It was inevitable that the comparison would be made, and it was inevitable that Smyth would eventually be submerged. There is no use pretending that posterity did not make the right verdict, though in recent years Macaulay has lost some of his stature. The truth is, comparing the two was frivolous and impertinent. Quite apart from the fact that the first (and better-known) series, *Lectures on Modern History*, is a rapid survey, only a small portion of which is devoted to the events that Macaulay covered in detail, their methods were quite different. Smyth's modest aim, even in the *Lectures on the French Revolution*, where he is often both diffuse and swamped by detail, was to provide food for thought. A *Westminster Review* writer makes this point well, even though his words suggest a keepsake school of criticism—it was, after all, 1855: "Mr. Macaulay understands nothing of varieties of sentiment, Professor Smyth knows that there lies between man and man constitutional differences which can find no meeting ground. Mr. Macaulay exhausts his subject, leaving no place nor room for obscurity, and nothing to be

supplied by the reader's meditation. Professor Smyth so marshals his subject as not to leave it unexhausted but to show that, in its full significance,
it is inexhaustible."

When the *Lectures on Modern History* first appeared, Smyth sent the
volumes to Ticknor. He pronounced it "a genial work, like himself, and,
if not a regular abstract of dates and events, a work as well fitted as any
I have ever seen to rouse up the minds of young men and induce them
to inquire and learn for themselves."

The task of making a book out of the *Lectures on Modern History*
and *Lectures on the French Revolution* has involved two criteria: retaining Smyth's best thoughts and what, in older days, used to be called
"beauties," and achieving some sort of continuity. This latter desideratum
has been less successfully achieved than the other, partly because Smyth,
particularly in the *Lectures on Modern History*, had a tendency to choose
what he considered to be important lessons, and partly because the editor
had to omit much that has been more thoroughly illuminated by the
painstaking studies of the modern historical schools.

WALLACE BROCKWAY

Lectures on
Modern History

FROM

THE IRRUPTION OF THE NORTHERN NATIONS TO

THE CLOSE OF THE AMERICAN

REVOLUTION

INTRODUCTORY LECTURE

My FIRST impressions . . . with respect to a scheme for Lectures on Modern History, were these—

That, in the first place, all detail, all narrative were impossible.

That the great subject before me was the situation of Europe in different periods of these later ages—the progress of the human mind, of human society, of human happiness, of the intellectual character of the species for the last fifteen centuries. Every thing therefore of a temporary nature was to be excluded; all more particular and local history; all peculiar delineations of characters, revolutions, and events, that concerned not the *general* interests of mankind. That the history of France or Spain or England was not to be considered separately and distinctly, but only in conjunction, each with the other; each, only as it affected by its relations the great community of Europe. That, in short, such occurrences only were to be mentioned, as indicated the character of the times—such changes only, as left permanent effects. That a summary, an estimate of human nature, as it had shown itself, since the fall of the Roman empire, on the great theatre of the civilized part of the world, was, if possible, to be given.

I must confess that this still appears to me to be the genuine and proper idea of a course of lectures on modern history. But to this plan, the obvious objection was, its extent and its difficulty.

The great Lord Bacon did not find himself unworthily employed when he was considering the existing situation, and contemplating the future advancement of human learning; but to look back upon the world and to consider the different movements of different nations, whether retrograde or in advance, and to state the progress of the whole from time to time, as resulting from the combined effect of the failures and successes of all the parts—to attempt this, is to attempt more than was effected even by the enterprising mind of Bacon; for it is to appreciate the facts as well as to exhibit the theory of human society—to weigh in the balance the conduct, as well as the intelligence of mankind, and to extend to the religion, legislation, and policy of states, and to the infinitely diversified subject of their political happiness, the same inquiry, criticism, and speculation which the wisest and brightest of mankind had been content to extend only to the more particular theme of human knowledge. . . .

A plan of this sort, though rejected by me as a lecturer, should always be present to you as readers of history. By no other means can you derive the full benefit that may and should be derived from the annals of the past.

Large and comprehensive views, the connexion of causes and effects, the steady, though often slow and, at the time, unperceived influence of general principles; habits of calm speculation, of foresight, of deliberative and providing wisdom, these are the lessons of instruction, and these the best advantages to be gained by the contemplation of history; and it is to these that the ambition of an historical student should be at all events directed.

The next scheme of lectures, that occurred to me, was to take particular periods of history and to review and estimate several of them, if possible, in a connected manner. The period, for instance, of the Dark Ages, of the Revival of Learning, of the Reformation, of the Religious Wars, of the power and enterprises of Louis the Fourteenth, of the prosperity of Europe towards the close of the last century. . . .

But after some deliberation, this plan, also, I have thought it best to reject; chiefly, because to attempt it, would be rather to attempt to write a book, than to give lectures. I do not say that those pages, which now make a good book, can ever have made bad lectures. But a lecture is, after all, not a book; and the question is whether the same lecturer might not have improved his hearers more by a less elaborate mode of address.

Instead, then, of endeavouring to draw up any general history of Europe since the overthrow of the Roman empire in the west, and instead of attempting any discussion of different periods under the form of regular treatises, I at last thought it best to fix my attention on my hearers only and to confine my efforts to one point. The object, therefore, which I have selected is this, to endeavour to assist my hearers in reading history for themselves. . . .

Turning now from the consideration of the plan of the lectures, to the mode in which I have endeavoured to execute it, as my object was to assist my hearers in reading history for themselves, my first inquiry was this—What course of historical reading it would be fittest to recommend —what were the books, and how were they to be read. . . .

The first advice then which I shall take upon me to give, as the result of my experience, is this—not to read general histories and abridgments of history, as a more summary method of acquiring historical knowledge. There is *no* summary method of acquiring knowledge. Abridgments of history have their use, but this is not their use nor can be. When the detail is tolerably known, the summary can then be understood, but not before. Summaries may always serve, most usefully, to revive the knowledge that has been before acquired, may throw it into proper shapes and proportions, and leave it in this state upon the memory, to supply the materials of subsequent reflection. But general histories, if they are read, first, and before the particular history is known, are a sort of chain of which the links seem not connected; certain representations and statements, which cannot be understood, and therefore cannot be remembered; and exhibit to the mind a succession of objects and images, each of which appears and retires too rapidly to be surveyed, and when the whole vision has passed by, as soon it does, a trace of it is scarcely found to remain. . . .

General histories may be considered as of great importance, and *that*, even *before* the perusal of the particular histories to which they refer, but they must never be resorted to, except in the instances and for the purposes just mentioned—they must not be used as substitutes for more minute and regular histories; not as short methods of acquiring knowledge—they are meant to give (and they may most usefully give) commanding views, comprehensive estimates, general impressions; but these cannot supersede that labour which must be endured by all those, who would possess themselves of information.

If, therefore, general histories and summaries of history are not to be read, as a short way of acquiring historical knowledge, and if history, when it is of importance, must be read in the detail, a most melancholy prospect immediately presents itself; for the books of historical detail, the volumes which constitute modern history, are innumerable. Alps on Alps arise. This is a difficulty of all others the most invincible and embarrassing. I must endeavour to consider it with all possible attention.

The great authority on a subject like this, is Dufresnoy—Dufresnoy's Chronology. After laying down a course of historical reading such as he conceives indispensably necessary, and quite practicable, he calmly observes that the time which it is to take up is ten years; and this too upon a supposition, that much more of every day is to be occupied with study than can possibly be expected, and that many more pages shall be read in the twenty-four hours than can possibly be reflected upon.

I remember to have heard that a man of literature and great historical reading * had once been speaking of the great French historian Thuanus in those terms of commendation which it was natural for him to employ, when alluding to a work of such extraordinary merit. A youth who had listened to him, with all the laudable ardour of his particular time of life, had no sooner retired from his company than he instantly sent for Thuanus, resolving to begin immediately the perusal of a performance so celebrated, and from that moment to become a reader of history. Thuanus was brought to him—seven folio volumes. Ardent as was the student, surprise was soon succeeded by total and irremediable despair. Art was indeed too long, he must have thought, and life too short, if such was to

---

* Jacques Auguste de Thou (1533–1617), the great French lawyer who helped to draft the edict of Nantes. The work referred to is the *Historia sui temporis*.—ED.

be his entrance to knowledge, and not indeed to knowledge, but to one department among many others of human inquiry.

Now this effect was certainly not the effect which was intended—all risk of any event like this must be most carefully avoided. And on the whole it is sufficiently evident, that any lecturer in history cannot be better employed than in studying how to render the course of reading, which he proposes, as short, i. e. as practicable, as it can possibly be made. Such, as amid the natural occupations of human life, may be accomplished. It is in vain to recommend to the generality of readers books, which it might be the labour of years to peruse; they will certainly not be perused, and the lecturer, while he conceives that he has discharged his office, has only made the mistake so natural to his situation, that of supposing that there is no art or science or species of knowledge in existence, but the one he professes, and that his audience are, like himself, to be almost exclusively occupied in its consideration.

But evils are more easily described than remedied. What is in this case to be done? Are the great writers of history not to be read? What is the study of history, but the reading of them?

The first object therefore, of my anxieties, in consequence of this difficulty, has been, through the whole of my lectures to recommend, not as many books as the subject admitted of, but as few.

And I am the more at ease while I do this, because the best authors in every different part of history have their margins crowded with references to other books and to original authorities; and such readers, as are called upon to study any *particular* point or period of history more minutely than can in *general* be necessary, need be at no loss for proper materials on which to exercise their diligence, and cannot want to receive from me an enumeration of those references and means of information, which they can in this manner so readily find.

But I have ventured to do more than this—for I have not only recommended as *few* books as possible, but I have recommended only parts of books, and sometimes only a few pages in a volume. . . .

He knows little of human learning or of himself who venerates not the scholars of former times—the great intellectual labourers that have preceded us. It would be an ill interpretation indeed, of what I shall recommend, if it be concluded that because I think their volumes are often to be read in parts only, that I do so from the slightest feeling of disrespect to authors like these, or to the great literary works that they have so meritoriously accomplished.

But the condition of society is continually changing, and the situation of our ancestors is no longer ours. In no respect has it altered more than in the interior economy of the management of time—more especially of a student's time. Avenues of inquiry and knowledge have been opened to us that were to them unknown. The regions of science, for instance, may be considered as a world lately found, hitherto but partially explored, and in itself inexhaustible.

What are we to say, in like manner, of the avocations, and even amusements, of social life, which have every where been multiplied by the growing prosperity of mankind—many of them not only intellectual, but intellectual in the highest sense of the word? The patient and solitary student can never be a character without its value and respectability; but the character can no longer be met with, as it once was, now that the genius of men is attracted to the inventions of art, the discoveries of science, and the various prizes of affluence and of honour, that are more and more held up to ambition, as a country more and more improves in civilization and prosperity.

There is another consideration which must not be forgotten, when this method which I have mentioned, of reading books in parts, is considered.

Literature, like society, advances step by step. Every treatise and book of value contains some particular part that is of more value than the rest— something by which it has added to the general stock of human knowledge or entertainment—something on account of which it was more particularly read and admired while a new book, and on account of which it continues to be read and admired while an old one. Now, it is these different portions of every different volume, that united form the effective literature or knowledge of every civilized nation; and when collected from the different languages of Europe, the literature and knowledge of the most civilized portion of mankind. It is by these parts of more peculiar and original merit, that these volumes are known. It is these to which every man of matured talents and finished education *alone* adverts. It is these which he endeavours chiefly to remember. It is these that make up the treasures, and constitute the capital, as it were, of his mind—the remainder of each volume is but that subordinate portion which has no value but as connected with the other, and is often made up of those errors and imperfections which are in fact the inseparable attendants of every human production, which are observed and avoided by every writer or reasoner who follows, and which gradually become in *one* age only the exploded characteristics of *another*.

It is thus that human knowledge becomes progressive, and that the general intelligence of society gains a new station in advance, from the reiterated impulses of each succeeding mind. It therefore by no means follows, when books are read in parts, that they are therefore read superficially. Some books (says my Lord Bacon), are to be tasted, some few to be chewed and digested: that is, some books are to be read only in parts: others to be read, but not curiously; and some few to be read wholly, and with diligence and attention. The same may be pretty generally said of the different portions of the same work. Much care and circumspection must undoubtedly be used in selecting and discriminating the parts to be tasted, to be chewed, and to be digested. The more youthful the mind, the less skilful will be the choice, and the more hazardous the privilege, thus allowed, of reading pages by a glance, and chapters by a table of contents. But the mind, after some failures and some experience, will materially improve in this great and necessary art, the art of reading much, while reading little. Now if there be any department of human inquiry into which this very delicate, difficult, and dangerous mode of reading may be introduced, it is surely that of history. Whatever may be thought of books of science or of knowledge, in books of history at least there is every variety in the importance of different passages. Neither events, nor characters, nor periods of time, are at all the same, or of equal consequence. Nor are the writers of like merit with each other, or of like authority, or have they written with the same views, or are they to be consulted for the same purposes. There is ample room, therefore, for the exercise of judgment in the preference we give to one writer above another, and in the different degrees of attention which we exercise upon one event or character or era, rather than another; and as the powers as well as the opportunities of the human mind are bounded, it behooves us well to consider what is the nature of the burthen we impose upon our faculties, for assuredly he who is very anxious to load his memory with much, will in general have little which in the hour of need he can produce, and still less of which his understanding has ascertained the value. . . .

It cannot but be supposed, that he who reads and retains the most, will always have a superiority over those whose talents or diligence are in truth inferior. But this only renders it a point of prudence the more pressing upon every man to inform himself thoroughly of the nature of his own capacity, particularly of his memory, and to provide accordingly. It is peculiarly so on an historical student. After having considered what he may pass over slightly and what he must regularly read, he may next consider what he is to remember minutely, what generally; and what, for the purpose of remembering better things, he may suffer himself to think of no more.

Now what I would wish to suggest to my hearers, more especially to those whose memories are either of a common or of an inferior description, is this, that general impressions, that general recollections, are of far greater importance than might be at first supposed.

General impressions will enable us to treasure up in our minds all the great leading lessons, all the philosophy of history. . . .

General impressions are sufficient to prevent us from making positive mistakes ourselves, and even from suffering them to be made by others.

We are aware that there is something which we have read on the point at issue, though we do not precisely recollect it. But the apprehension that is left on the mind, obscure and imperfect as it may be, still suffers a sort of violence, when any statement positively inaccurate is presented to it. We at least suspend our judgment. We require that the question may not be determined till after proper examination.

General impressions, indeed, will not furnish a reasoner in conversation, an advocate at the bar, or a debater in parliament, with proper authorities, at the very moment of need, to establish his statements and illustrate his arguments; or with all the proper materials of wit and eloquence. A weak memory can never afford to its possessor the advantages which result from a memory capacious and retentive; yet may it still be very adequate, by careful management, to many of the most useful purposes of reflection and study; it may still enable a man to benefit himself and to administer to the instruction of others.

And now, before I turn away from this particular part of my prefatory address, I must confess to you, that after all the expedients I have resorted to for the purpose of abridging your labours, I am well aware that many of you will still be disheartened and repelled by the number of books which you will hear me quote and refer to, before my lectures are brought to a conclusion. . . .

Your time will not be entirely thrown away while you are listening to the references I make and the descriptions I give, even though you should not always turn to the particular books and passages I thus recommend. You will at least know, after a certain indistinct manner, what history is, and this is the great use of all public lectures; for public lectures may give you a general idea of any science or subject, but can never of themselves do much more—they can never put you in possession of it. . . .

And now I must call the attention of my hearers to a difficulty which belongs to all public lectures on history, and which I conceive to be of considerable importance. It is this. A lecturer must refer sometimes to books which have not been read at all by his hearers; and perpetually to those that have not been read lately, or with very minute attention. He must presuppose a knowledge which has not been acquired, or not retained. He must therefore often make remarks which cannot be judged of,—deliver sentiments and opinions which must necessarily be unintelligible,—and make frequent allusions which cannot be felt or comprehended by those whom he addresses. The truth is, that a lecturer arranges and writes down what he has to deliver while full of his subject, with all the information he can collect fresh and present to his mind; and he then approaches his hearers, who have in the mean time undertaken no labour of the kind, and are furnished with no equal advantages. The lecturer is in one situation and the hearer in another. And this is the reason why lecturers on the subject of history must always be found, at the time of delivery, more or less inefficient, and therefore unsatisfactory; why they must be even listened to with difficulty, certainly not without an almost continued effort of gratuitous attention. . . .

There is one point . . . which is so material that, though I have alluded to it before, I must again recall it to your attention. . . . The great use, end, and triumph of all lectures is to excite and teach the hearer to become afterwards a lecturer to himself—to facilitate his progress, perhaps to shorten his course—to amplify his views—to make him advance to a subject, if possible, in the united character of a master and a scholar. A hearer is not to sit passive, and to expect to see performed for him those tasks which he can only perform for himself. It is from a mistake of this nature that they who attend public lectures often retire from them with strong sensations of disappointment. They have sought impossibilities. They who listen to lectures must be content to become wise, as men can only become wise,—by the exercise—the discipline—the warfare, and the fatigue of their own faculties, amid labours to be endured, and difficulties to be surmounted. The temple of wisdom, like that of virtue, must be placed on an eminence. . . .

Curiosity is natural, and therefore history will be always read, and as he who has any thing to relate becomes immediately of importance to others and to himself, history will be always written.

History is a source of pleasure; a piece of history is at least a sort of superior novel; it is at least a story, and often a busy one; it has its heroes and its catastrophes; it can engage attention, and though wanting in that force and variety and agitation of passion, which a work of imagination can exhibit, still as it is founded in truth, it can in this manner compensate for the calmer nature of its materials, and has always been found capable of administering amusement even to the most thoughtless and uninformed.

But as others will read, when, even the thoughtless read, and as history is generally read in early life, it has always been one instrument, among others, of education; it is not too much to say, that the whole character of the European nations would have been totally different, if the classic histories of antiquity had not come down to them; and if their youth had not been, through every succeeding generation, animated and inspired by the examples which are there displayed of integrity and patriotism, of eloquence and valour.

But every nation has also its particular annals and its own models of heroism and genius.

The political influence of history may therefore often be of inestimable value: it may tell a people of their ancestors, of their freedom and renown, their honourable struggles, sacrifices and success, and it may warn them not to render useless, by their own degeneracy, the elevated virtues of those who went before them.

But history may do more than this, it may exhibit to a people the rallying points of their constitution, the fortresses and strong holds of their political happiness; and it may teach them a sort of wisdom un-bought by their own dreadful experience, a sort of wisdom which shall operate at the moment of need with all the rapidity and force and ac-curacy of instinct.

History is of high moral importance; for the wise, the good, and the brave can thus anticipate and enjoy the praise of ages that are unborn, and be excited to the performance of actions, which they might not other-wise have even conceived.

It is probable too, that men of bad passions and certainly men of doubt-ful character, are sometimes checked by the prospect of that awful cen-sure which they must endure, that lasting reproach and detestation with which their memories must be hereafter loaded by the inevitable judg-ments of mankind.

Undoubtedly too the man of injured innocence, the man of insulted merit, has invariably reposed himself with confidence on the future jus-tice of the historian; has often spoken peace to his indignant and afflicted spirit by dwelling in imagination on the refuge, which was thus to be afforded him, even on the theatre of *this* world, from the tyranny of fortune or the wrongs of the oppressor. . . .

Unless the past be known, the present cannot be understood; records therefore and memorials often form a very material part of professional study.

To the philosopher, history is a faithful mirror which reflects to him the human character under every possible variety of situation and colour, and thus furnishes him with the means of amplifying and confirming the knowledge of our common nature.

But history also exhibits to the philosopher the conduct and fortunes of mankind continued through many ages, and it therefore enables him to trace the operation of events, to see the connexion of causes and effects, and to establish those general principles, which may be considered by the statesman, if not as axioms, as the best guides at least, that can be found, for his conduct, in his management of the affairs of mankind.

It is the misfortune in general of the man of reflection, and always of the intelligent statesman, that he has to combat with the prejudices of those around him, and as arguments can be always produced, on each side of a question, while he has only reasoning to oppose to reasoning, he is little likely to succeed; but an example properly made out from history assumes the appearance of a fact, and embarrasses and silences opposition, till all further resistance is at length, in some succeeding generation, with-drawn. It is thus that a Montesquieu, a Smith, or a Hume, by their appli-cation of general principles, exemplified by facts, to systems of national policy, may be sometimes enabled, however slowly, to expand and rectify the contracted and unwilling understandings of mankind.

Such are the uses of history, the uses which it has always served.

There are others to which it *might* be made subservient.

It *might* teach lessons of moderation to governments, and when the lesson is somewhat closely presented, it sometimes does; but cabinets are successive collections of men whose personal experience has not been long continued; and they therefore act too often with the blind passions of an individual, and are so habituated to temporary expedients, to making provision for the day which is going over them, and to the rough manage-ment of mankind, that when they are approached by the man of reflection and prospective wisdom, they are not sufficiently disposed to listen to what he has to suggest or to object; they are too apt to dismiss with little ceremony his admonitions and his plans; and when they speak of them, it is for the most part in some language of their own, under some general appellation of "theory and nonsense," or perhaps of "metaphysics."

History, by its general portraits of different states and kingdoms, might teach any particular people the infinite diversity of human characters and opinions, and inspire them with sentiments of general kindness and toler-ation abroad and at home.

But history is, on the contrary, generally converted by a people to the purpose of perpetuating religious or political dissensions, and of harden-ing those antipathies which it should rather remove or soften; its examples are appealed to; the characters of offence and blood, that were obliterated or grown faint by age, are traced out and coloured anew; and it is for-gotten, that such unhappy animosities have no longer any proper object or reasonable excuse.

Having thus endeavoured to give some general idea of the purposes and value of history, it is necessary, before I conclude, to observe, that there is one objection to history, too imposing and too weighty not to be alluded to and examined. It is no other than this; that history, after all, is not truth; that it neither is nor ever can be; that the affairs of the world are carried on by a machinery known only to the real actors in the scene, the rulers of kingdoms and the ministers of cabinets—a machinery which must for ever be concealed from the observation of the public; particu-larly of historians, men of study and retirement, who know nothing of that business of the world, which they are so ready to describe and to ex-plain.

This is not unfrequently the language of ministers themselves, at least of those who are somewhat of an ordinary cast—practical men, as they are called: more distinguished for their talents in the dispatch of business than for their genius. "Do not read history to me," said Sir Robert Walpole, one of the best specimens of them—(his son, it seems, had hoped, in this manner, to amuse the languor of a man, who, because he was no longer in office, knew not how to employ himself)—"Do not read history, for that I know must be false."

Lord Bolingbroke, on the contrary, a statesman also, writes letters in his retirement on the study and use of history, and even discusses the very point before us, and maintains the credibility of history.

Ministers, like Sir Robert Walpole, may on these occasions be not a little suspected of something like affectation: of being dupes to their art. Our own king, James the First, was the most egregious pedant of this kind on record; the mysteries of his state-craft, as he called it, were deemed by him to be so profound, that they were not to be comprehended even by the houses of parliament or men of any ordinary nature; and Walpole himself might have been thought by this royal trifler, as unfit, as the historian was thought by Walpole, to penetrate into the secrets of the world.

The short state of the question seems to be, that history consists of the narrative of facts and of explanations of those facts—that the facts and events are points which are perfectly ascertainable; nor will this indeed be denied—but with respect to the explanations, how the events related came actually to take place, points of this kind must be always matters of investigation, to be traced out by the same processes of reasoning, which are applied on all similar occasions through life; from a comparison of events and of appearances with the acknowledged principles of human actions. Mistakes may sometimes be made (as by juries on a trial), but this is not a sufficient reason for concluding that no judgment can be formed.

It is impossible to say in general that explanations always can be given, or never can be given; each particular point becomes a particular question to be decided on by its own merits; in every instance the proper inquiry is, whether the explanation offered be or be not sufficient.

Historians have always affected, and have generally exercised, great circumspection in their decisions. It must be remembered what the merits of an historian are supposed to be; not eloquence, not imagination, not science,—but patience, discrimination, and caution—diligence in amassing his materials, strict impartiality in displaying them, sound judgment in deciding upon them.

Mankind endeavour, in the same manner, to judge, in their turn, upon their historians; their sources of intelligence, their industry, their candour, their good sense,—all these become the subjects of the public criticism; and at last a decision is pronounced, a decision that is not likely to be ultimately wrong.

It is not pretended, that history, if written at the time, can be in all points depended upon; or that truth can become entirely visible till some interval has elapsed, and the various causes, that are always operating to produce the discovery of it, have had full opportunity to act.

And lastly, there are facts and events that have occurred in the world, of which history does not undertake to give any solution: and historical writers are certainly not guilty of the folly of professing to explain every thing.

Were one of these ordinary ministers to be asked what means they always employed in the management of mankind, they would answer, without hesitation, their leading interests and passions; and they would laugh at any of their associates in a cabinet who depended upon the more delicate principles of individual character.

Would it not be strange, then, that such leading interests and passions, as they have made use of, should not be afterwards visible to the eyes of an historian? Are they not themselves, though sitting in a cabinet, collections of men influenced by their own leading interests and passions like their fellow-mortals without? How are these, in like manner, to remain for ever impenetrable and unintelligible?

Finally, it must be observed that the writers of history are by no means to be considered as excluded from all knowledge of those petty intrigues, on which so much is supposed to depend; private memoirs and the letters of actors in the scene are very often referred to by historians—they are sought for with diligence, they are always thoroughly sifted and examined. In the course of half a century after the events, the public are generally put into possession of such documents as even the objectors to history ought to think sufficient to explain the mysteries of intrigue, and therefore even in *their* view of the subject, the transactions of the world.

On the whole, therefore, to call history a romance, and to say that it must necessarily be false, is to confound all distinctions of human testimony, criticism, and judgment: sweeping positions of this kind occur in other subjects as well as this of the study of history; and after a little examination may quietly be dismissed, as the offspring of indolence or spleen; or that love of paradox, which may sometimes assist the sagacity, but more often misleads the decisions of the understanding.

One word more in reference to this objection, and I have done. Something may perhaps be conceded to it.

It is always difficult to estimate, with perfect accuracy, the moral characters of men; i. e. to compare exactly the temptation that has been incurred with the resistance that has been made—the precise motives of the agent with his actual conduct.

And this, which is so true in private life, may be still more so in public. It may not be always easy to determine, in a minister or a party, what there was of mistake, what of good intention, what of uncontrollable necessity, in their apparent faults.

It may be allowed, therefore, that the moral characters of statesmen may not always be exactly estimated: but it must be observed, at the same time, that in many instances these moral characters are appreciated differently by different historians, and are confessedly a subject of historical difficulty. That here, therefore, no mistake is made; and that mankind, though very likely to praise or censure too vehemently at first, are not likely to be materially inaccurate at last.

Add to this, that statesmen, who perceive that their conduct may hereafter be liable to misrepresentation, have it always in their power, and have in general been induced, to leave documents to their family for the purpose of explaining their views, and justifying their measures; and as they know beforehand the nature of that tribunal of posterity, which is to determine on their merits, the conclusion is, if they refuse to plead, that they foresee a verdict, against which they have nothing satisfactory to urge, and which is therefore right.

But I must now conclude. . . .

Though the more minute peculiarities of history may cease to engage our attention; its graver subjects may have now, more than ever, a claim upon our powers of reflection and inquiry. History may have less of amusement for our leisure, but may offer much more of instruction for our active thoughts. The mere relator of events may be now less fitted to detain us with his details; but to the philosophic historian we shall henceforward be compelled to listen with a new and deeper anxiety. If history be the school of mankind, it must be confessed that its lessons are at length but too complete; and that states and empires may now be considered in all their positions and relations, from the commencement to the termination of their political existence. We may see what have been the causes of their prosperity; we may trace the steps by which they have descended to degradation and ruin.

1. BARBARIANS AND ROMANS

OF THE ancient world we derive our knowledge from the sacred Scriptures and the writings of Greece and Rome. We have no other sources of information on which we can well depend; but every such information must be at all times interesting. There is no nation, however removed from us by distance or by time, whose history will not be always a subject of rational curiosity to a reflecting mind: yet the student of ancient history will find his attention irresistibly drawn to three particular nations—

the Greeks, the Romans, and the Jews: these are names for ever associated with our best feelings and our first interests: the poets and the orators, the sages and the heroes of Greece and Rome still animate our im-
aginations and instruct our minds; and the law-giver of Israel led his
people from Egypt to give birth to the prophets of our religion, and when
the fulness of time was come, to the SAVIOUR of the world.

Ancient history is not excluded; a knowledge of it is presupposed in
the study of modern history; a knowledge, at least, of those events, which
can now be ascertained, and of those nations more particularly whose
taste, philosophy, and religion are still visible in our own. Ancient history
at last conducts us to the exclusive consideration of the Romans. Rome
is the only figure left in the foreground of the picture; but in the distance
are seen the northern nations, who are now to come forward and to share
with the Romans our curiosity and attention.

These nations had already been but too well known to the Roman people. They had destroyed five consular armies—encountered Marius—contended with Julius Cæsar—annihilated Varus and his three legions, and
given the title of Germanicus to the first Roman of his age.

In the time of Marcus Antonius a general union was formed by the
Barbarians, and they were not subdued till after a long and doubtful conflict.

About the middle of the third century, under the reign of Valerian
and Gallienus, they began every where to press forward, and were seen
fairly struggling with the Romans for the empire of Europe.

Here then we are to make our first pause; we are to stop and reflect
upon the scene before us. We have the civilized and uncivilized portions
of the world contending—we have the two great divisions of mankind,
which then existed, drawn up in array. What were the exact characters
of each?—which was likely to prevail?—what was to be the result of this
strange and tremendous collision? These are the great questions that occur at this remarkable juncture, at this critical interval between the ancient
and modern history of the European nations. We are not without our
means of inquiry into this interesting subject. We will take each of these
questions in their order. 1st, What were the exact characters of the Barbarians and the Romans at this extraordinary crisis? With respect to the Barbarians—fortunately for us they fell under the observation first of one of
the most celebrated men, and afterwards of one of the most celebrated
writers of antiquity—of Cæsar and of Tacitus: to them we must refer. I
will say a word of each in their order. The Commentaries of Cæsar must be
consulted, not only in the sixth book, but in the first and fourth. And here
I must observe, that though the Celts or Gauls are not to be confounded
with the Gothic nations, who finally overran the Roman Empire, still
there is not a part of the work that is not connected with the general

subject; the whole is a picture of the two great portions into which mankind might be then divided (the civilized and the barbarians), while it professes to be only an account of the campaigns of Cæsar in Gaul. . . .

More than a hundred years after the Germans had attracted the notice of Cæsar, they were delineated by the masterly pencil of Tacitus, and that in a professed work on the subject, *De moribus Germanorum.*

The figures are still bold and savage, but something of a more soft and agreeable light is diffused (however faintly) over the picture. In our estimation of the whole, some allowance must be made for the great historian himself. We may remember in our times how the eloquent Rousseau, amid the vices of civilized life, could sigh for the innocence and the virtue—"the sublime science of simple souls"—which he conceived could be found only amid the rocks and the forests of uncultivated man.

The sensibility of Tacitus—a man of imagination also—exasperated by the licentiousness of Rome, may be suspected, in like manner, of having surveyed these unpolished Barbarians with considerable indulgence. The manly virtues were undoubtedly to be found among them; but to the perfection of the human character it is necessary that these should be softened by humanity and dignified by knowledge.

I stop to observe that savage and civilized life may each exhibit the disgusting extremes of opposite evil: but the one uniformly, the other only partially. It is in vain to fly from one, to be lost in the still more frightful degradation of the other; and the propensities and capacities of our nature seem clearly to indicate that we are intended not for solitude and torpor, but for society and improvement.

Whatever value we may justly affix to the account of Cæsar, the Treatise of Tacitus is still more distinct, complete, and important. There is no work of profane literature that has been so studied and discussed. . . .

After such writers, as I have mentioned or alluded to, the three first chapters of Mr. Gibbon's History, and the ninth, must be most diligently studied. These chapters may serve to point out more particularly the classical authors that should be consulted—they are very comprehensively and powerfully written; nothing more can be wanted to give the most lively and complete idea of the Romans and the Barbarians, and to enable us to understand and sympathize with the great contest that was to ensue. I must again suppose this done; and the student having thus acquainted himself with the state of the barbarous and civilized nations of Europe, at this remarkable epoch, may be next employed in considering our second question—Which of the two descriptions of combatants was likely to prevail—what were the natural and acquired advantages and disadvantages of each?

When we read the account of the hardiness and fierce courage of the

Barbarians, it seems impossible that they should be, by any other human beings, resisted; and yet still more impossible to suppose, that the Roman legions can be overcome, when we consider, on the other hand, their skill, their courage, and their discipline; the long result of many ages of experience and victory: arms, science, and union are on one side; savage nature and freedom on the other. The ultimate success, however, of the Barbarians could not well be doubted: every change, it was clear, would be in their favour; it was the contest of youth against age, of hope against fear.

In the civilized state the government had degenerated into a military despotism: the vital principle was in decay; the freedom, the genius of Rome was gone for ever. Discipline, it was evident, would in the Barbarians continually improve—among the Romans gradually disappear. The jealousies and dissensions of the Barbarians on one side might delay the event; as might, on the other, great ability and virtue in the Roman emperors. But a succession of such merit could not be expected. Under the military government of the army (a government of anarchy and licentiousness) the character of the Roman people, and of the army itself, would eventually sink and perish: and a few Barbarian chieftains arising at different periods, of sufficient ability to combine and direct the energies of their countrymen, would, it was evident, at first shake and at length overwhelm the licentious affluence, the relaxed discipline, the broken, the wasted, the distracted powers of the empire of Rome. Such, indeed, was the fact. The particular events and steps of this great revolution are to be seen in the history of Gibbon. . . .

The fall of the empire of the West was evidently to be expected for the reasons we have mentioned; but to these might have been added, by any reasoner at the time, the possibility that a new torrent of Barbarians might rush into Europe from the northeast and the plains of Scythia. The empire had never been undisturbed, and had often suffered very severe defeats in that quarter; such a calamity might not prove fatal, though dreadful, even to the Germans: but there was every probability that it would complete the destruction of Rome. Such an irruption did in fact take place; the nation of the Huns suddenly appeared, savages still more odious and terrific than had before been experienced. From the north of China they had passed or retreated to the confines of the Volga, from thence to the Tanais, and after they had defeated the Alani, they pressed onward to the conquest of Europe.

The Goths themselves, on whom they first descended, considered them as the offspring of witches and infernal spirits in the deserts of Scythia; an opinion that forcibly expressed, how unsightly was their appearance, and how tremendous their hostility.

An account of this invasion, and of the nation itself, may be read in the twenty-sixth, thirty-fourth, and thirty-fifth chapters of Mr. Gibbon: and notwithstanding the range of knowledge displayed, and the masterly compression of the subject, the reader will be often reminded, but too painfully of the simplicity of Hume and the perspicuous though somewhat laboured elegance of Robertson.

This dreadful visitation of the Huns did not, after all, destroy the Roman empire, or leave that impression on the face of Europe, which might have been expected. When the fierce Attila was no more, the force of his nation gradually decayed: Attila himself retreated from Gaul, which in the progress of his conquests he had attacked; and this whole irruption of the Huns must be considered chiefly as a sort of temporary interruption to the great contest between the northern nations and Rome. To this contest our attention must again return, and we must pursue the fall of the Western Empire, as shown in the stately and brilliant narrative of Gibbon. The northern nations we shall now see every where triumphant: distinct divisions of them taking their station; the Franks in Gaul, the Visigoths in Spain, the Burgundians on the Rhone, the Austro-Goths in Italy: and the western empire, at last, sinking under the great leader of his nation, Odoacer, who was himself subdued by the renowned Theodoric.

And now a second epoch is presented to us,—the fall of the western empire of Rome and the rise of the different empires of the Barbarians; and therefore now comes the third and the last question which we have mentioned; What was to be the result of this tremendous collision between the civilized and uncivilized portions of mankind, and of this ultimate triumph of the Barbarians?

Could we suppose a philosopher to have lived at this period of the world, elevated by benevolence and enlightened by learning and reflection, concerned for the happiness of mankind, and capable of comprehending it, we can conceive nothing more interesting, than would to him have appeared the situation and fortunes of the human race. The civilized world, he would have said, is sinking in the west before these endless tribes of savages from the north. The sister-empire of Constantinople in the east, the last remaining refuge of civilization, must soon be overwhelmed by similar irruptions of Barbarians from the northwest, from Scythia, or the remoter east. What can be the consequence? Will the world be lost in the darkness of ignorance and ferocity? sink, never to emerge? Or will the wrecks of literature and the arts, that may survive the storm, be fitted to strike the attention of these rude conquerors, or sufficient to enrich their minds with the seeds of future improvement? Or, lastly, and on the other hand, may not this extended and dreadful convulsion of Europe be, after all, favourable to the human race? Some change is necessary; the civilized world is no longer to be respected; its manners are corrupted, its literature has long declined, its religion is lost in controversy, or debased by superstition. There is no genius, no liberty, no virtue; surely the human race will be improved by the renewal which it will receive from the influx of these free-born warriors: mankind, fresh from the hand of nature, and regenerated by this new infusion of youth and vigour, will no longer exhibit the vices and the weakness of this decrepitude of humanity: their aspect will be erect, their step firm, their character manly. There are not wanting the means to advance them to perfection; the Roman law is at hand to connect them with each other: Christianity to unite them to their Creator: they are already free. The world will, indeed, begin anew, but it will start to a race of happiness and glory. Such, we may conceive, *might* have been the opposite specu-lations of any enlightened reasoner at that critical period. But with what eagerness would he have wished to penetrate into futurity! how would he have sighed to lift up that awful veil which no hand can remove, no eye can pierce! with what intensity of curiosity would he have longed to gaze upon the scenes, that were in reality to approach! And could such an anticipation of the subsequent history of the world have been in-deed allowed him, with what variety of emotions would he have surveyed the strange and shifting drama that was afterwards exhibited by the conflicting reason and passions of mankind. The licentious warrior, the gloomy monk, the military prophet, the priestly despot, the shudder-ing devotee, the iron baron, the ready vassal, the courteous knight, the princely merchant, the fearless navigator, the patient scholar, the munifi-cent patron, the bold reformer, the relentless bigot, the consuming mar-tyr, the poet, the artist, and the philosopher, the legislator, the statesman, and the sage, *all* that were by their united virtues and labours to assist the progress of the human race, *all* that were at last to advance society to the state which, during the greater part of the last century, it so happily had reached, the state of balanced power, of diffused humanity and knowl-edge, of political dignity, of private and public happiness.

There are periods in the history of mankind, when wishes like these to look into futurity, strange and unmeaning as to colder minds they may at first sight appear, vain, as to minds the most ardent and enlightened we must confess them to be, are still natural and inevitable; and are felt, and deeply felt, by all intelligent men, to the very fatigue and sickening of curiosity. Such a period has been our own; it continued to be so for more than twenty years, from the breaking out of the French revolution in 1789. Such a period was found in the days of Columbus, and of Luther. Such, lastly, was the period which we are in this lecture more immediately considering, the period when the northern nations were every where pre-vailing; and the question was, what were to be the future fortunes of the world,—to what changes were to be exposed the knowledge and civilization of the human race?

I must recommend it to you to take every opportunity to pause in this manner, and to indulge any effort of the imagination by which you can suppose yourselves for a time transported into distant ages, taking part with the actors in the scene, animated with their hopes, alarmed by their fears, oppressed by their anxieties, their apprehensions for the future, their regrets for the past. For it is only by this plastic power of the mind, and these voluntary delusions, that either the instruction or the entertainment of history can be realized; that history can be thoroughly understood, or properly enjoyed.

We return, then, to that memorable epoch in the history of Europe, to which I have endeavoured to direct your reflections.

The Barbarians have every where broken down the Roman empire, and have established their own; they have taken their different stations.

What then was the result? To what degree, on the one hand, was the independent ferocity of the Barbarians softened, by that Christianity and those laws which were at the time in the possession of the Romans; and to what degree, on the other, was the degeneracy of the Romans elevated? What purity did their controversial religion, what freedom did their courtly jurisprudence, derive from the bold and native virtues of the Barbarians?

In a word, what were the fortunes of the human race? What impression, what direction, did the happiness of mankind receive?

The answer to these questions is not at first as favourable as might be wished: it is for some time contained in the history of the Dark Ages. The Dark Ages were the more immediate result of this memorable crisis of the western world.

And it is thus that the Dark Ages are almost the first subject that is to be encountered by the student of modern history.

This is unfortunate—unfortunate more especially for the youthful student. Look at the writers that undertake the history of these times. They oppress you by their tediousness; they repel you by their very appearance, by the antiquarian nature of their researches, and the very size of their volumes. You recoil, and very naturally, from events and names, which you have never heard of before, which you do not expect to hear of again, and which, above all, it is impossible to remember.

Were you to fly to the general history of Voltaire, you might be able to read indeed the page, from the occasional sprightliness of the remarks; but you would not be able to understand the events and characters, which you would there see pass before your eyes, in a succession far too shadowy and rapid; nor would you be able more than before to remember what you had read. The only benefit that you would appear to derive would be this, that you would think you had learnt from the perusal, that though you remembered nothing, there was nothing worth remembering; that savages, under whatever name, were only fitted to disgust you; and that you had better hasten to parts of history more authentic and more instructive.

The same conclusion you would see drawn by Lord Bolingbroke in his Letters on History.

Conclusions, however, like these, are not the proper conclusions.

The history of the Dark Ages, for all philosophic purposes, is neither without its authenticity nor its value, and you must, in some way or other, acquire some knowledge of it; some knowledge of these barbarous times, and these our barbarous ancestors; because you must, by some means or other, see the manner in which the European character was formed; and from what elements the different governments of Europe have originally sprung.

The European character, you must be aware, is not the Asiatic character, nor the native American character, but one singularly composed, and one that has been able to subjugate every other in the world. Nor is the European form of government like the Asiatic, nor is that of England like that of France, nor either, like that of Germany; and it is these differences and their origin—these differences both in the personal character of the individual of Europe, and in the general character of the constitution under which he lives—that are the first objects which present themselves to your diligence; and to trace them out and to understand them, must constitute your entertainment and support your diligence, while you are labouring through the history of the Dark Ages. . . .

II. LAWS OF THE BARBARIANS

THE FEUDAL System is one on which the student may exhaust his time and exercise his diligence to any extent he pleases: it has employed the penetration and industry of innumerable antiquarians, philosophers, and lawyers, in whose inquiries and dissertations he may, if he pleases, for ever wander. . . .

No doubt the state of anarchy from which the feudal system saved society must be duly considered. Whatever was fitted, as was the feudal system, to bind men together by any sense of protection, of gratitude, of fidelity, of reciprocal obligation; whatever was likely to create or uphold any generous feelings or milder virtues among them; whatever had a tendency to protect Europe from any one great conqueror; whatever introduced or maintained among men any notion of legal or political right, was during a long interval (such was then the unhappy state of the world) of the greatest consequence to the world. But when this office had been rendered to mankind, the feudal system became in its turn a source of the most incessant, vexatious, unfeeling, and atrocious oppression, and a great impediment to all prosperity and improvement. These two different situations of the system and of the world must be kept distinctly in remembrance.

iii. MAHOMET—PROGRESS OF SOCIETY, ETC.

I HAVE HITHERTO directed your attention to the Romans and Barbarians, their collision, the fall of the Western Empire, the settlement of the Barbarians in the different provinces of Europe, and the dark ages that ensued.

On these dark ages the light gradually dawned, till at length appeared the Revival of Learning and the Reformation.

It is in this manner, therefore, that you have presented to you, by the addition of this last circumstance, a subject that is a sort of whole.

You begin with marking the decline and depression of society, and you then watch its progress to a state of great comparative elevation.

But instead of conducting your thoughts onward from the one to the other, in this natural succession, I must now interrupt them, because the great concerns of Europe were in fact thus broken in upon and interrupted; and though the whole of this interruption may be almost considered as a sort of episode to the main subject, I have no alternative but to produce it now, in its real place, and you must join the chain hereafter yourselves; the links of which must be considered as thus for a certain interval separated from each other. . . .

An individual had started up amidst the sands of Arabia, had persuaded his countrymen that he was the prophet of God, had contrived to combine in his service two of the most powerful passions of the human heart; the love of glory here, and the desire of happiness hereafter; and triumphant in himself and seconded by his followers, had transmitted a faith and an empire, that at length extended through Asia, Africa, Spain, and nearly through Europe itself; and had left in history a more memorable name, and on his fellow creatures a more wide and lasting impression, than had ever before been produced by the energies of a single mind. This individual was Mahomet.

We are invited to examine and estimate a revolution like this by many considerations. I will mention some of them. The learning of the disciples of Mahomet is at one particular period connected with the history of literature. The Saracens (for this is their general, but not very intelligible appellation) contended with the Franks and Greeks for Europe, with the Latins for the Holy Land, with the Visigoths for Spain. The Caliphs, or successors of the Arabian Prophet, were possessed of Syria, Persia, and Egypt, and through different eras of their power exhibited the most opposite prodigies of simplicity and magnificence; these are powerful claims on our attention. The Turks, who became converts to the religion of Mahomet, gradually swelled into a great nation, obtained a portion of Europe, and have materially influenced its history.

If we turn from the descendants of Mahomet to Mahomet himself, we must observe that his religion professed to be derived from divine inspiration; and is, from its very pretensions, entitled to the examination of every rational being. To be unacquainted with this religion, is to be ignorant of the faith of a large division of mankind. An inquiry into the rise and propagation of it will amplify our knowledge of human nature; and an attention to the life of the Prophet may enlarge our comprehension of the many particular varieties of the human character. The religion of Mahomet has, in the last place, been often compared with the religion of Christ; and the success of the Koran has been adduced to weaken the argument that is drawn from the propagation of the gospel.

If such, therefore, be the subject before us, it is evidently sufficient to awaken our curiosity, and we may be grateful to those meritorious scholars, who have saved us from the necessity of pursuing our inquiries through the volumes of the original authors. The Arabic writers have been translated; and the interesting occupation of a few weeks, or even days, may now be sufficient to satisfy our mind on topics, that might otherwise have justly demanded the labour of years.

With respect then to the books, that are to be read, I would propose to you, in the first place, to turn to the work of Sale—Sale's Koran—read the preface and his preliminary dissertation, consulting, at the same time, his references to the Koran. Of the Koran you may afterwards read a few chapters, to form an idea of the whole. And, as it is a code of jurisprudence to the Mussulman, as well as a theological creed, you may easily, by referring to the index, collect the opinions and precepts of Mahomet on all important points. . . .

These works, however, will but the better prepare you to discern the merit of the splendid and complete account which Mr. Gibbon has given of the Arabian legislator and prophet. The historian has descended on this magnificent subject in all the fulness of his strength. His fiftieth chapter is not without his characteristic faults, but it has all his merits: and to approach the account of Mahomet and the Caliphs, in Gibbon, after travelling through the same subject in the volumes of the Modern History, is to pass through the different regions of the country, whose heroes these authors have described; it is to turn from the one Arabia to the other; from the sands and rocks of the wilderness to the happy land of fertility and freshness, where every landscape is luxuriance, and every gale is odour. . . .

I had intended to have briefly stated the leading points of the life and religion of Mahomet; but I had rather, that the guides I have mentioned should conduct you through the whole of a subject, which is in fact too interesting and important to be touched upon in a general or summary manner. The effect of inquiry will be materially to diminish the general impression of wonder, with which every reflecting mind must have originally surveyed a triumph of imposture so extensive as that of Mahomet. The causes of his success have been well explained by the authors I have mentioned. Yet gifted as he was with every mental and personal qualification, and highly assisted in his enterprise by the moral and political situation of his countrymen, the student cannot fail to observe, how slow and painful was the progress of his empire and religion. After becoming affluent at an early period of life, he continued fifteen years in habits of occasional solitude and meditation. He was three years in effecting the conversion of his wife, his slave, his cousin, and eleven others; he was ten years employed in extending the number of his disciples within the walls of Mecca. This long interval (twenty-eight years) had elapsed, before the guardians of the established idolatry were duly alarmed, and proceeded, from opposition, at last to attempt his life. After flying from Mecca, and being received and protected at Medina, it was six years before he could again approach his native city; two more before he could establish there his sovereignty and his worship; and two more, before the various tribes of Arabia could be brought to acknowledge him for their prophet. On several occasions the fate of himself and of his religion hung on the most wavering and doubtful balance. It was not Mahomet, who conquered the east, but his successors; and had he not attached to his fortunes and faith a few men of singular virtues and extraordinary military talents, his name and his religion might have perished with him, and the Arabians at his death might have relapsed into their former habits of loose political association, and of blind, unthinking idolatry.

To Mahomet, indeed, his success must have appeared complete. Arabia must have been the natural boundary of his thoughts, and every thing in Arabia he had conquered, and it was his own: he was become the great chief of his nation, and he held a still dearer empire over their feelings and their faith: he was the leader of an invincible army, but he was more than an earthly conqueror; he was considered as the prophet of God; mere humanity was below him. It was at this moment of his elevation, when he was preparing to extend his temporal and spiritual dominion to Syria, that the angel of death was at hand to close his eyes for ever on the prospects of human greatness, and to remove him to the presence of that awful Being whose laws he had violated, whose name he had abused, and whose creatures he had deceived. . . .

Of Mahomet, as of others, it is often asked whether he was an enthusiast or an impostor. He was both. In men like him the characters are never long separated. It is the essence of enthusiasm to overrate its end, to overvalue its authority; all means are therefore easily sanctified, that can accomplish its purposes. Imposture is only one amongst others: and as it is the nature of enthusiasm at the same time to overlook the distinctions of reason and propriety, what is, or what is not imposture, is not always discerned; nor would be long regarded, if it were.

The designs of Mahomet are often supposed to have originated early in life, and to have been formed from a long, comprehensive, and profound meditation on the situation of his countrymen, and the nations of the east.

It is not thus, that great changes in the affairs of men are produced; it is not thus, that the founders of dynasties, the authors of revolutions, and the conquerors of the world proceed: men like these are formed not only by original temperament and genius, but by situation and by the occasion; their ideas open with their circumstances, their ambition expands with their fortune; they are gifted with the prophetic eye, that can see the moment that is pregnant with the future; they are distinguishable by the faculty, that discerns what is really impossible from what only appears to be so; they can avail themselves of the powers and capacities of every thing around them; the time, the place, the circumstances, the society, the nation, all are at the proper instant understood, and wielded to their purpose. They are the rapid, decisive, fearless, and often desperate rulers of inferior minds; not the calm reasoners or profound contrivers of distant schemes of aggrandizement, seen through a long series of concatenated events; events which, as they well know, are ever liable to be disturbed by the ceaseless agitations and business of human life, and the unexpected interference of occurrences, which it may be their fortune indeed and their wisdom to seize and employ, but which they cannot possibly produce or foresee. . . .

The empires of the east bowed before the concentrated tribes of Arabia, who passed over them with all the force and rapidity of a whirlwind; these new centaurs it was equally impossible to face, as they advanced, or pursue, as they retreated. It is true that these eastern empires were at the time particularly unfitted to sustain any powerful attack; but what could have been opposed to the natives of the desert, educated in the most tremendous habits of privation and activity, and in habits, still more tremendous, of fanaticism and fury? . . .

The transmission of the faith of Mahomet pure and unadulterated, the same faith which he originally delivered, is no doubt remarkable; and the absence of any clerical order among the Moslems, and the union of the regal and sacerdotal characters in the commanders of the faithful, may perhaps explain this striking phenomenon. But the continuance of the religion at all, as it is not founded in truth, is deserving of regard. It must be remembered, that it gained possession of the eastern nations and subsisted several centuries under the caliphs, with whose power it was identified. It was easily propagated among the wandering conquerors of the east; men without knowledge and without reflection, whose religious creeds were readily formed, slightly considered, and loosely held; and whose military and arbitrary government indisposed and disabled them from all exercise of their reason in the search of truth. The Koran must also be considered as not only a religious but a civil code. To alter therefore the religion of a Mahometan is to alter his opinions, habits and feelings, to give him a new character, a new nature: add to this, that the intolerant expressions and precepts of the Koran have been so improved upon by the followers of Mahomet, that the great characteristic of their religion is, and has been long, a deadly hostility and fixed contempt for the professors of every other belief. The Koran therefore, when once established, was (humanly speaking) established for ever; and it has now for eleven centuries occupied the faith of a large but unenlightened portion of mankind.

But this permanency of the religion and institutions of Mahomet has been in every respect a misery to his disciples and a misfortune to the human race. It might have been possible for Mahomet to have moulded the simplicity and independence of the Arabians into some form of government favourable to the civil liberty of his followers and to the improvement of their character and happiness; but no speculations of this kind seem ever to have approached his mind; all civil and ecclesiastical power was united in his own person, and he left them without further reflection to be the portion of his successors. The result has been fatal to his disciples; their caliphs and sultans have been the leaders of fanatics, or the now arbitrary, now trembling, rulers of soldiers and janizaries; but they have never enjoyed the far more elevated distinction of the limited monarchs of a free people. The east has therefore made no advance; it is still left in a state of inferiority to Europe, and it has derived from Mahomet no accession of wisdom or vigour to regenerate its inhabitants or save them from the enterprise and plunder of the west. In vain did he destroy the idols of his countrymen and sublime their faith to the worship of the one true God; in vain did he inculcate compassion to the distressed, alms to the needy, protection and tenderness to the widow and the orphan. He neither abolished nor discountenanced polygamy, and the professors of his faith have been thus left the domestic tyrants of one half of their own race. He taught predestination, and they have thus become by their crude application of his doctrine, the victims of every natural disease and calamity. He practised intolerance, and they are thus made the enemies of the civilized world. He permitted the union of the regal and sacerdotal offices, and he made the book of his religion and legislation the same. All alteration therefore among the Mahometans must have been thought impiety; lost in the scale of thinking beings, they have exhibited families without society, subjects without freedom, governments without security, and nations without improvement. For centuries they have continued the destroyers of others, and been destroyed themselves; the ministers and the victims of cruelty and death; and even when appearing in their most promising form of an established European empire, such has been their bigoted attachment to their Koran, that they have been contented to decline and fall with the progress of improvement in surrounding nations, to see their military science become contemptible, their strength unwieldly, their courage stagnate without hope or effort, and even their virtues languish, if possible, without respect or use.

The student may now once more make a pause, and return to consider the state of Europe at this particular period. The nations of the west have been the objects of his attention, and he has been called aside to observe the appearance of a great revolution that had taken place in the east; and supposing him now to renew his speculations with respect to the happiness of mankind, there seems little to afford him any pleasure for the present, or any hope for the future. This interference of the followers of Mahomet from the east in the affairs of Europe can only give the prospect a new and additional gloom; their religion is not true, their civil polity destructive to liberty. Most fortunately they have indeed been driven back by Charles Martel and the Franks; but they may ultimately make some permanent and considerable settlement in the western world, which can in no case be favourable to its interests.

But what, in the meantime, has been the fate of Europe itself? The student will recollect the hopes with which we entered on its history at the accession of Clovis: the Christian religion, the Roman arts, literature, and law, might have tempered and improved, it had been fondly supposed, the bold independence and simple virtues of the barbarian character; and the result might have been that mixture of freedom and restraint, of natural reason and divine illumination, which gives the last finish and perfection to the dignity and happiness of human nature. How different, how melancholy has been the event! We are now supposed to have travelled through five centuries, and there is no liberty, no knowledge, and no religion. Instead of liberty, there has grown up the feudal system; instead of knowledge, darkness has overspread the land, and thick darkness the people; and instead of religion, there has arisen a long train of ceremonies and observances; and the empire of the priest, in the odious sense of the word, has been established over the conscience and the happiness of his blind and unresisting votaries.

All this is surely mournful to behold, yet it is all in the natural order of things; the speculation that hoped otherwise, was inattentive to the great laws of human nature. A state of natural liberty, for example, implies a state of ignorance; and the result of both cannot, in the first instance, be civil liberty. Of the same ignorance, in like manner, the result cannot be religion; the result can only be superstition. Religion, even if, by peculiar interposition, it had been received pure, would soon be disfigured and corrupted, and become a gross and comfortless system of blind devotion. It must be ever thus. They who would indispose men to all restraint, prepare them, not for civil liberty, but for mutual violence; to end at length in submission to some military leader, or in the tyranny of a few. They, in like manner, who would keep men in ignorance, the better to incline them to the observances of religion, prepare them for superstition, and not for the reasonable sacrifice of the heart; and as ignorance in the hearer must be followed by ignorance and usurpation in the teacher, the priest and the people will each in their turn contribute to the debasement of the other.

Abandoning, therefore, all our former expectations of the happy effects that were on a sudden to arise from that new mixture of civilized and uncivilized life, which took place in Europe on the conquest and settlement of the northern nations, we must now be only anxious to observe how the evils that had been established *gradually* softened, or were at length counteracted, by *attendant* causes of good; how the clouds cleared away that overhung these middle ages; how the interests of society became at last progressive, lost and hopeless as at this melancholy period they certainly appeared.

The great evils that existed, the great objects of attention, are the feudal system and the papal power. As we read the facts of history, we may be enabled to observe the more obvious effects of these two great calamities by which mankind were oppressed; but we must carefully recollect, that far more was suffered than history can possibly express. History can exhibit an emperor, like Henry IV of Germany, barefooted and in penance for three winter days before the palace of the pope; or a feudal lord, like Earl Warren [Warenne], producing his sword as the title-deeds of his estate; but history cannot enter into the recesses of private life, and can by no means delineate what was daily and hourly suffered by the inhabitants of the towns or country from the unrestrained and uncivilized usurpation of the feudal lords, from the 'oppressor's wrong, the proud man's contumely.' Still less can history describe the more obscure and silent, but not less dreadful, effects of ecclesiastical despotism; the hopeless yet protracted languor of some mistaken victim of credulity in the odious cell of a monastery; or all that was suffered by the terrified imagination of him, who had incurred the censures of the church or the overwhelming evils of excommunication. Even if we suppose the slave no longer to complain, and the monk no longer to feel, still that destruction of the faculties, that debasement of the nature, which is so complete as to be unperceived by the individual himself, is on that very account but a more deserving object of our compassion: the maniac who dances heedless in his chains, but awakens our pity the more. . . .

I shall venture . . . to propose once more to the consideration of my hearers the still more contracted estimate of this great subject, which I have already mentioned. The leading and important evils of mankind, I must still contend, became at last the feudal system and the papal power; the attention, therefore, may be fixed, as I conceive, chiefly on these. Whatever had a tendency to break up and dissipate the power so collected was favourable to the interests of mankind, and the contrary: all healthful motion and activity were, by these two great causes of evil, excluded from society: military exercises and church ceremonies were the only result; and whatever withdrew the human mind into any new direction, could not fail to assist the progress of general improvement. I will say a word, and but a word, on each.

With respect then, first, to the feudal power. This feudal power lay in the great lords, and in the king, as the greatest of those lords. In England the situation of things was not exactly the same as in the rest of Europe, from the greater influence of the crown: but in general it may be said, that whatever shook and scattered the power of the great barons was favourable to civil liberty; even if the power was, in the event, to be transferred entirely to the king; it was less injurious thus single, than when multiplied among the lords; and there was always a probability that in the course of the struggle the commons might come in for a part, if not the whole, of the share that belonged to them.

The great cause, then, of the improvement of society during these centuries was the rise and progress of Commerce. For the great point to be attained was the elevation of the lower orders.

Both the crown and the barons were sufficiently ready each of them to employ the lower orders against the other. Consequence was therefore given to this oppressed race of men, and immunities and privileges afforded to them, more particularly in the towns and cities. The result was commerce, which again added to the consequence they had before acquired.

As the towns and cities were on various accounts materially leagued with the crown, the power of the barons was thus on the whole assaulted from without.

But it was also attacked and wasted from within. A taste was gradually introduced for the more elegant and expensive enjoyments of life, and the barons could not spend their revenues on themselves, and at the same time on their retainers—at once on articles of luxury and in rude hospitality. The number of their retainers was therefore diminished; that is, their power and political importance. The whole subject has been admirably explained by Smith in his third book of the Wealth of Nations, and I depend on your reading it; leaving here a blank in my lectures, which you must yourselves fill up. It would be an improper use of your time to offer you here, in an imperfect manner, what can be afforded you, and far better afforded you, by the study of this very masterly part of his celebrated work. . . .

With respect to the causes which shook the ecclesiastical power of Rome, the second great evil of society, they may be comprised in two words, that at this period of the world were of kindred nature—Heresy and Knowledge.

The gradual progress of these causes, and their final success, may be hereafter considered. The student may, however, look upon either of them whenever it appears in the history of these times, as the symptom and harbinger of the subsequent reformation.

Ignorance and superstition are naturally allied; their cause is common, their friends and enemies the same. The opposers of a barbarous philosophy are soon entangled in the misapprehensions and corruptions of an abused religion; the spirit of inquiry which struggles with the one is immediately suspected of a secret hostility to the other. The student, as he proceeds in his historical course, will soon be called on to observe the Albigenses, the Lollards, and the Hussites, with our earlier sages and philosophers exhibiting amid the chains and dungeons of the inquisition or of the civil power, the melancholy grandeur of persecuted truth, and insulted genius.

These first but unfortunate luminaries of Europe were, however, not lost to the world: the Reformation and the revival of learning at last took place; the pillar of light continued to march before mankind in their journey through the darkness of the desert, and it was in vain that the oppressor would have prevented their escape from their houses of bondage, or denied them the possession of the promised land of religion, liberty, and knowledge.

I conclude this general subject with observing, that the Crusades, while they so happily dispersed the possessions and influence of the great lords, and therefore so materially assisted the progress of society, contributed to the influence of the clergy, and that in the most unfavourable manner, by furnishing them with relics and miracles, and with new and multiplied modes of extending and confirming the superstition of the age; but I must at the same time remark, once for all, that the power, which the clergy enjoyed, was not always exercised to the injury of society; in many most important respects materially otherwise. They shook the power of the barons by contriving to draw within their own jurisdiction the disputes and causes which had belonged to the feudal courts—they had always kept alive in society whatever knowledge amidst such rapine and disorder, could be suffered to exist—they were the instructors of youth—they were the historians of the times—they maintained in existence the Latin language—they were the only preservers of the remains of Greek and Roman literature—they everywhere endeavoured to mitigate and abolish slavery—they were the most favourable landlords to the peasantry; to the lower orders the mildest masters—they laboured most anxiously and constantly to soften and abolish the system of private war by establishing truces and intermissions, and by assisting the civil magistrate on every possible occasion—they were every where in those times of violence, a description of men whose habits and manners were those of peace and order—they could not profess such a religion as Christianity without dispensing, amidst all their misrepresentations, the general doctrines of purity and benevolence, and without being, in a word, the representatives of what learning and civilization, moderation and mercy, were yet to be found. These were great and transcendent merits.

That their power was inordinate, and that they abused it most grossly, is but too true; a strong proof, if any were wanting, that power should be always suspected, and should be checked and divided by every possible contrivance. In this instance it was capable of converting into the rulers, and often into the tyrants of the earth, men who breathed the precepts of meekness and lowliness of heart, and who continually affirmed that their kingdom was not of this world.

Such are the general views which I have been enabled to form of the situation and prospects of society during these middle ages, and such are the writers on whom I have depended for instruction, and to whose labours I must now finally refer you.

But before I conclude my lecture, I must make a particular remark. It cannot have escaped your observation how often I have mentioned the historian Gibbon; how much I leave entirely to depend upon him; the manner in which I refer to him as the fittest writer to supply you with information in all the earlier stages of modern history, and, indeed, as the only writer that you are likely to undertake to read; add to this, that I have already had occasion, and shall often hereafter have occasion, to mention his history in terms either of admiration or respect.

Yet I cannot be supposed ignorant of the very material objections which exist to this History; and I am certainly not at ease in recommending those parts of the work which I do approve, while I know there is so much both in the matter and manner of the whole, and of every part of it, which I cannot approve. . . .

In the chapters which I in the first lecture referred to, the faults of this great historian do not appear. In the earlier part of his work he respected the public, and was more diffident of himself. Success produced its usual effects; his peculiar faults were more and more visible as his work advanced, and in his later volumes he seems to take a pride, as is too commonly the case among men of genius, in indulging himself in liberties which he would certainly have denied to others. And as the powers of the writer strengthened, as he went on, and kept pace with his disposition to abuse them, the History of the Decline and Fall became at last a work so singularly constituted, that the objections to it are too obvious to escape the most ordinary observer, while its merits are too extensive and profound to be fully ascertained by the most learned of its admirers.

These faults will only be the more deeply lamented by those, who can best appreciate such extraordinary merits. Men of genius are fitted by their nature not only to instruct the understanding, but to fill the imagination and interest the heart. It is mournful to see the defects of their greatness; it is painful to be checked in the generous career of our applause. With what surprise and disgust are we to see in such a writer as Gibbon the most vulgar relish for obscenity! With what pain are we to find him exercising his raillery and sarcasm on such a subject as Christianity! How dearly shall we purchase the pleasure and instruction to be derived from his work, if modesty is to be sneered away from our minds, and piety from our feelings! There seems no excuse for this celebrated writer on these two important points: he must have known, that some of the best interests of society are connected with the respectability of the female character; and with regard to his chapters on the progress of Christianity, and the various passages of attack with which his work abounds, it is in vain to say, that, as a lover of truth, he was called upon to oppose those opinions, which he deemed erroneous; for he was concerned, as an historian, only with the effects of this religion, and not with its evidences; with its influence on the affairs of the world, not with its truth or falsehood.

It would be to imitate the fault, to which I object, were I now to travel out of my appointed path, and attempt to comment upon these parts of his work. But as they who hear me are at a season of life, when liveliness and sarcasm have but too powerful a charm, more particularly if employed upon subjects that are serious, it may not be improper to remind them, how often it has been stated, and justly stated, that questions of this nature are to be approached neither by liveliness nor by sarcasm, but by calm reasoning and regular investigation; and that to subject them to any other criterion, to expose them to any other influence, is to depart from the only mode we possess of discovering truth on any occasion; but more especially on those points, which youth, as well as age, will soon discover to be of the most immeasurable importance.

If we pass from the matter to the manner of this celebrated work, how are we not to be surprised, when we find a writer, who has meditated the finest specimens of ancient and modern literature, forgetting the first and most obvious requisite of the composition he is engaged in —simplicity of narrative. In the history of Mr. Gibbon, facts are often insinuated, rather than detailed; the story is alluded to, rather than told; a commentary on the history is given, rather than the history itself; many paragraphs, and some portions of the work, are scarcely intelligible without that previous knowledge, which it was the proper business of the historian himself to have furnished. The information which is afforded is generally conveyed by abstract estimates: a mode of writing which is never comprehended without an effort of the mind more or less painful; and when this exertion is so continually to be renewed, it soon ceases to be made. The reader sees, without instruction, sentence succeed to sentence, in appearance little connected with each other; cloud rolls on after cloud in majesty and darkness; and at last retires from the work, to seek relief in the chaster composition of Robertson, or the unambitious beauties of Hume.

On this account it is absolutely necessary to apprize the student of what it might, at first, seem somewhat strange to mention, that he will not receive all the benefit, which he might otherwise derive from the labours of this great writer, unless he reads but little of his work at the same time. It is not that his paragraphs, though full and sounding, signify nothing; but that they comprehend too much: and the reader must have his faculties, at every instant, fresh and effective, or he will not possess himself of the treasures, which are concealed, rather than displayed, in a style so sententious and elaborate. The perversity of genius is proverbial; but surely it has been seldom more unfortunately exercised than in corrupting and disfiguring so magnificent a work.

For the moment we reverse the picture, the merits of the historian are as striking as his faults.

If his work be not always history, it is often something more than history, and above it: it is philosophy, it is theology, it is wit and eloquence, it is criticism the most masterly upon every subject with which literature can be connected. If the style be so constantly elevated as to be often obscure, to be often monotonous, to be sometimes even ludicrously disproportioned to the subject; it must, at the same time, be allowed, that whenever an opportunity presents itself, it is the striking and adequate representative of comprehensive thought and weighty remark.

It may be necessary, no doubt, to warn the student against the imitation of a mode of writing so little easy and natural. But the very necessity of the *caution* implies the attraction that is to be resisted: and it must be confessed, that the chapters of the Decline and Fall are replete with paragraphs of such melody and grandeur, as would be the fittest to convey to a youth of genius the full charm of literary composition, and such as, when once heard, however unattainable to the immaturity of his own mind, he would alone consent to admire, or sigh to emulate.

History is always a work of difficulty, but the difficulties, with which Mr. Gibbon had to struggle, were of more than ordinary magnitude. Truth was to be discovered, and reason was to be exercised, upon times where truth was little valued and reason but little concerned. The materials of history were often to be collected from the synods of prelates, the debates of polemics, the relations of monks, and the panegyrics of poets. Hints were to be caught, a narrative was to be gathered up, from documents broken and suspicious, from every barbarous relic of a barbarous age: and, on the whole, the historian was to be left to the most unceasing and unexampled exercise of criticism, comparison, and conjecture. Yet all this, and more than all this, has been accomplished.

The public have been made acquainted with periods of history which were before scarcely accessible to the most patient scholars. Order and interest and importance have been given to what appeared to defy every power of perspicacity and genius. Even the fleeting shadows of polemical divinity have been arrested, embodied, and adorned: and the same pages which instruct the theologian, might add polish to the liveliness of the man of wit, and imagery to the fancy of the poet.

The vast and the obscure regions of the middle ages have been penetrated and disclosed; and the narrative of the historian, while it descends, like the Nile, through lengthened tracts of present sterility and ancient renown, pours, like the Nile, the exuberance of its affluence on every object which it can touch, and gives fertility to the rock and verdure to the desert.

When such is the work, it is placed beyond the justice or the injustice of criticism; the Christian may have but too often very just reason to complain, the moralist to reprove, the man of taste to censure, even the historical inquirer may be fatigued and irritated by the unseasonable and obscure splendour, through which he is to discover the objects of his research. But the whole is, notwithstanding, such an assemblage of merits so various, so interesting, and so rare, that the *History of the Decline and Fall* must always be considered as one of the most extraordinary monuments, that has appeared, of the literary powers of a single mind; and its fame can only perish with the civilization of the world.

iv. THE DARK AGES

THE CHIEF object of St. Louis [Louis IX] seems to have been to prepare his people for the adjustment of their quarrels, not by private combat but by the decisions of law after an examination of witnesses. At the same time it must be observed, that most of the great objects of civil and penal jurisprudence appear to have occupied his attention; and it is not very possible now to understand all the meaning, and therefore all the merit of his provisions; but the great design of the whole must have been to soften and modify the jurisprudence of the baronial courts, and to have placed the whole within the reach of improvement by opening the way to the paramount jurisdiction of the courts of the sovereign.

France in the time of St. Louis was divided into the country under the king's obedience, and the country under the obedience of the great barons. It was not possible for St. Louis to embody his own opinions of equity and law, and then enforce a new system of jurisprudence. He attempted to reform existing systems by introducing one more improved within his own dependencies, and holding it up to the observation of the other parts of the kingdom. He seems every where to struggle with difficulties, to modify and to balance, to capitulate with the evils which he could not remove, evils on which by any other conduct he could have made no impression. Such must ever be the true reformer; ardour may animate his mind, but patience must be his virtue. The true reformer is the philosopher who supposes no wonders in himself, and expects them not in others; and is rather the sower who goes forth to sow his seed, than the lord who comes to gather into barns. The result was what might have been expected, the labours of St. Louis were successful, and he exhibited the great criterion of genius, that of advancing his countrymen in improvement a step beyond the point at which he found them.

Again and as another specimen of subjects to be further considered. The reign of Philip le Bel is remarkable for the struggle between the pope and the king, and still more for the first assembly of the states general, summoned by this prince for his defence and justification; but which must however not be confounded or thought the same with the national assemblies in the times of Charlemagne. These events are very important and may be considered in Velly. The commons formed a distinct part of this assembly, and they took their share in animating the king to defend the rights of his kingdom; but their language spoke an infant power, and breathed no longer the independent fierceness of the soldier who resisted Clovis:—"Be pleased [they said] to guard the sovereign freedom of your kingdom, for in temporal matters the king can acknowledge no sovereign on earth but God alone."—"We own no superior in temporals but the king," said the nobles. The clergy hesitated, but at last confessed their duty to their temporal sovereign. The failure of such a pope as Boniface on this occasion shows clearly that the power of the see had already in 1303 passed its meridian.

Again 3rdly. The French parliaments are a proper subject of inquiry. Philip proposed to make the parliaments or courts of justice stationary; this afterwards took place. The account given by Velly should be consulted. The student is no doubt aware that the dispensers of justice should be few in number, and neither be removed nor advanced at the mere pleasure of the executive power, that is, neither be exposed to be corrupted nor terrified.

You will do well to observe the changes that took place with respect to this part of the French constitution, a part so important to the happiness of every community.

Indeed one of the great subjects of this early period of modern history is the constitution of France, or rather, the fortunes of the constitution of France. . . .

I must now make a pause. I must consider myself as having passed through the first and most repulsive portion of modern history. . . .

The great conclusions to be drawn from these Dark Ages are, as I conceive,—

1st. That civil liberty cannot result, in the first instance, from the rude, natural liberty of barbarous warriors.

Again, that religion, in like manner, cannot consist with uncivilized ignorance.

The power of the sword and of superstition, of the military chief and of the priest (of the priest in the unfavourable sense of the term), must at first follow, and may continue for ages.

But, in the next place, the great lesson which the Dark Ages exhibit is also that which human life is unhappily at every moment and on every occasion exhibiting—the abuse of power.

The great characteristics of the Dark Ages are the feudal system and the papal power; but consider each; the incidents as they are termed, of the feudal system—that is, the practices that obtained under the feudal system; and again the doctrines and the decrees of the papal see.

Outrageous as many of these may seem, they were still but specimens of the abuse of power.

The Dark Ages show human nature under its most unfavourable aspects, but it is still human nature.

We see in them the picture of our ancestors, but it is only a more harsh and repulsive portrait of ourselves.

Observe, for instance, the feudal system, its origin, its results. Among a set of independent warriors, the distinctions of the weak and the strong naturally arose, the leader and the follower, the military chief and the dependent. Society necessarily fell into little knots and divisions; in the absence of all central government, of all more regular paramount authority, each military chief in extensive conquered countries necessarily became a petty sovereign; the petty sovereign a despot.

When lands were once received on the general principle of homage, the natural course of the abuse of power was inevitable; the incidents, that is the oppressions, of the feudal system followed; but for all these disgusting specimens of legal outrage and licensed wrong a sort of reason may be always found to have existed, when the incident is traced up to its first elements and original introduction.

Consider, in like manner, the Ecclesiastical Power.

The priests of the Dark Ages proceeded only, as did the barons, with the same unchecked and therefore insatiable selfishness, to subjugate every thing to their will. The ecclesiastical tyrants, like the civil tyrants, only converted the existing situation of mankind and the genuine principles of human nature to their own gratification and aggrandizement. That they should attempt to do so is not wonderful, nor is it wonderful that they succeeded.

Our barbarian ancestors, ignorant themselves, confided in men whom they considered as wise, and learned, and who comparatively, were wise and learned; this was natural, it was even reasonable; they had no other resource but to confide, and they had no means of learning how to measure their confidence.

It should not be forgotten, that the distinguishing doctrines of the Roman Catholic communion were all addressed to the most established feelings of the human heart: absolution, confession, prayers for the dead, penance, purgatory. Their rites and ceremonies not less so. Not to mention that their tenets were, and are still fortified by texts more numerous, and even more weighty (I do not say conclusive), than we of the Protestant communion are now in the habit of condescending to consider or even to know. The great doctrine of all, the paramount authority of the pope, as the genuine successor of St. Peter, was always supported, when necessary, by the words of our Saviour to that apostle; even his infallibility was sufficiently proved to our rude ancestors by the obvious argument, that Christ would not leave His church without a guide, to whom recourse might be had under all those difficulties, which must necessarily arise among the contradictory views of contending sects; in a word, those doctrines of the Roman Catholic communion, which, at a very late period, could subdue for a time even the learning and understanding of a Chillingworth, may readily be supposed to have obtained an easy victory over the unlettered soldiers of the Dark Ages.

Whatever may be said of the thoughtlessness of mankind amid the occupations of civilized life, their apprehensions for the future are unceasing, the moment that the great truth of their immortality is properly announced to them in their ruder state. These apprehensions, in themselves so just and natural in every period of society, when united to ignorance so great as that which existed in Europe at this particular period, produced effects, which at *first sight* may appear, but cannot on *reflection* appear, astonishing. The most fierce and savage soldier became docile and submissive; the most powerful monarch trembled in secret on his throne, and found his knights and his vassals a pageant and a show.

But the single terror of excommunication, and all the preparatory processes of spiritual punishment, were perfectly adequate to produce these intellectual and political wonders. No one in our own happier times can form an idea of what was then a sentence of excommunication. It was to live alone in the midst of society, to be no longer human, to be without the character of man here, and to be without hope hereafter. The clergy of the Dark Ages (to adopt *in part* the striking illustration of Hume, suggested, indeed, by a passage in Dryden's [*Don*] *Sebastian*), the clergy of the Dark Ages had obtained, what only Archimedes wanted: they had got another world on which to rest their engines, and they moved this world at their pleasure.

The inquisition itself had its origin in the most acknowledged feelings of our nature. Its advocates and its ministers could always appeal in its support to the most regular conclusions of the human mind.

The reasoning was then, as would be now to the generality of mankind, perfectly intelligible and convincing. Truth, it was said, could only be on one side; by error we may destroy our own souls and those of others. Error must, therefore, be prevented, and if not by gentle means, on account of the greatness of the object, by other means, by any means, by force. This is the creed of intolerance to this hour.

The tribunal that appeared with all its tremendous apparatus of familiars, inquisitors, and executioners, was but a consequence which, in an unenlightened period, followed of course.

The great and only difficult victory of the papal see was over the clergy themselves—the law of celibacy. When this triumph, that had been long in preparation, was once obtained by the renowned Gregory

VII, towards the close of the eleventh century, the ecclesiastics then became a sort of regular army, with a dictator at their head, to which nothing could be successively opposed.

But even this, the most extraordinary phenomenon of the whole, may still be traced up, as well as the existence of the various monastic orders, with all their extravagant and at first sight unnatural observances, to principles that are, notwithstanding, the genuine principles of the human heart, and inseparable from our nature.

The *esprit de corps*—the merit of the severer virtues, of self-denial, of self-abasement—these, united with the religious principle, gave occasion to the monastic character and all its observances, and they form at once a solution of all these outrageous deviations from the more calm and ordinary suggestions of the common sense and common feelings of mankind.

Observances of this kind have, in fact, existed among the nations of every clime and age; they exist in India at this moment. But consider the principles we have mentioned. This *esprit de corps* is founded on the sympathies, on some of the most effective sympathies of the human mind; and the severer virtues of self-control, of self-denial, of self-abasement, of chastity, and again the virtues of humility and of piety, are all virtues in themselves so awful and respectable, that they have always, even in their excesses, received the admiration of mankind, and they are the highest and the best praise of man, when well directed and attempered; that they should not be so in times of ignorance can be matter of no surprise; these are subjects which are often misunderstood even among ourselves.

Pursue the same train of reasoning to the less fatal, less degrading extravagances of this dark period—the institution of Chivalry, for instance —the expeditions to the Holy Land.

Chivalry, if considered in its original elements, is only a very striking testimony to those more generous principles of the human heart, which, it should seem, can never be separated from our nature under any, the most disorderly state of society. The same testimony seems to have been offered in times the most remote.

The knights of the Middle Ages were not a little the counterparts, however improved, of the fabled gods and heroes of antiquity, of Hercules and Theseus; and have been celebrated in the same romantic manner. They were the redressors of oppression; the moral benefactors of the community in which they lived; the mirrors of the noblest qualities of the human character; the exhibitors of those two great virtues of tenderness and courage, which were then so peculiarly necessary to society. The foundations of the chivalrous character were laid in human nature, in the consciousness that belongs to good actions, and in that sensibility to the applause of others, from which those who can really perform good actions, neither can, nor need be exempt.

Original principles like these could easily be associated in a religious age with the religious principle, more especially with Christianity, the religion of benevolence: the religion which, of all others, teaches us to think most of those around us, and least of ourselves.

The only part of the chivalrous character, which it is somewhat difficult to account for, is that delicate devotion to the fair sex by which it was so strongly and often so whimsically distinguished.

This devotion must be traced up to the woods of Germany; where, however, it may be explained, it appears from Tacitus, that the other sex had even more than their natural share of importance and respect. This natural importance and respect could not but be materially strengthened and improved subsequently, by the influence of the Christian religion, which still existed amidst the confusions of Europe, and survived them. This religion could not but have made the weaker sex more worthy of the estimation of the stronger, and the stronger in its turn more fitted to comprehend and relish the more gentle virtues of the weaker. . . .

Humanity and courage are the virtues which the softer sex must from their very nature be always most disposed to patronize. The knight and his lady were thus formed in their characters for each other. Jousts and tournaments still further contributed to animate all the natural sentiments with which both were inspired; and these trials of skill and spectacles of magnificence were the necessary exhibitions of the merits of both, of beauty on the one side, and military prowess on the other; and were the obvious resources of those, who must otherwise have been without occupation and amusement, and whose minds could not at that period be diversified by all the intellectual pursuits of modern and more civilized life.

On the whole, there was in chivalry much which the natural ardour and enthusiasm of the human character might convert into the extravagant, and sometimes into the ridiculous, and in this state it might be seized upon by a man of genius like Cervantes, and when arrayed in the colours of his own pleasantry and fancy, be transmitted to the amusement of posterity; but the virtues of the knight, of the hero of chivalry, were real and substantial virtues. Courtesy to the low; respect to the high; tenderness to the softer sex, and loyalty to the prince; courage and piety; gentleness and modesty; veracity and frankness; these after all are the virtues of the human character; and whatever appearances they might assume under the particular circumstances of these ages, they are still the proper objects of the love and respect of mankind under every circumstance and in every age.

The knights, it must be confessed, received an education that was too military to be favourable to knowledge; they were not the scholars or the men of science of their day, but they contributed, notwithstanding, to elevate and to humanize the times in which they lived, and they transmitted, and they indeed thoroughly engrafted upon the European character, the generous and manly virtues.

Lastly, to take the other specimen, which we have mentioned, of these Middle Ages, the crusades.

These are, according to Mr. Hume,* the most durable monuments of human folly: it may be so; but whatever may have been the less worthy motives, that contributed to carry such myriads to the Holy Land, no warriors would have reached it, if a piety, however unenlightened, if a military spirit, however rude, that is, if devotion and courage had not been the great actuating principles of the age; but courage and devotion are still virtues, however unfortunately exercised; the difference between these crusaders and ourselves is still only that of a more intelligent faith in us, and better regulated feelings. Piety and magnanimity are still our virtues, as they were theirs.

The crusaders, indeed, were inflamed by the images of the Holy Land; for they saw, and they were overpowered with indignation, when they saw the sacred earth, which had been blessed by the footsteps of our Saviour, profaned by the tread of Barbarians, who rejected His faith, and outraged His pious and unoffending followers: but in this the crusaders submitted only to the associations of their nature. The same power of association is still the great salutary law by which we, too, are animated or subdued, by which we, too, are hurried into action, or moulded into habit; and it is as impossible for us now, as it was to the crusaders of the Middle Ages, to behold, without affection and reverence, whatever has been once connected with objects that are dear and venerable in our eyes.

It is thus that things, in themselves the most inanimate, are every day seen to assume almost the nature of life and existence. Is there at Runnymede (for instance) to be found nothing more than the beauty of the scene? Do we walk without emotion amidst the ruins of ancient Rome? Is Palestine a land, and Jerusalem a city, like a common land and a common city? Far different is the answer which nature has unalterably given to appeals of this kind in every climate and in every heart. And if, indeed, the sepulchre in which our Saviour was inurned; if indeed the cross on which He expired, could be presented to our eyes; if we could indeed believe that such were in truth the objects actually exhibited to our view, assuredly we should sink in reverence as did our forefathers, before

* David Hume (1711–76), Scottish philosopher, whose *History of England* was still highly regarded.—ED.

such affecting images of the past; assuredly with the sufferer Himself we should identify these visible instruments of His sufferings; and the sacrifice of our hearts would not be the idolatry of blindness, but the natural effusion of irresistible devotion and awe.

It is not the sentiments by which these heroes were impelled that we can bear to censure; it is the excess to which they were carried; it is the direction which they took; it is piety preposterously exercised; it is courage unlawfully employed; the extravagancies to which virtue and religion may be made subservient, not virtue and religion.

So natural indeed are such sacred principles, so attractive, so respectable even in their excesses, that we willingly allow to our imagination the facility, which it loves, of moulding into visions of sublimity and beauty the forms and the scenes which time has now removed within its softened twilight, and in some respects secured from the intrusions of our colder reason.

Who is there that can entirely escape from the delusion and the charm of pilgrims grey and redcross knights, the fights of Ascalon and the siege of Acre, the prowess and the renown of our lion-hearted Richard? It is by an effort, an unwilling effort, that we turn to think of the bloodshed and desolation, the disease and famine, the pain and death, by which these unhappy enterprises were accompanied.

Little need be said of the custom of duelling by which these ages were so distinguished. The custom is founded too evidently on some of the most powerful principles of our nature, particularly that of resentment; given us for the wisest purposes, and necessary to our well being, but of all others the principle, that has been most abused by the folly of mankind.

The practice has even descended to our own times, though we have no longer the reasons or the excuse which our forefathers had for such nefarious or ridiculous or misguided excesses of just and honourable sentiment. In the absence of all general law, men were, in former times, naturally a law unto themselves. These appeals, too, were considered, at that period, as appeals to heaven; there was here something of necessity, something of reasonableness. With respect to ourselves, on the contrary, experience has taught us no longer to expect these extraordinary interpositions to defend the right: a more enlarged philosophy has served to show us the impropriety of supposing, that the general laws of the Creator should be continually suspended for the adjustment of our quarrels, or that the rewards and punishments, which are to await innocence and guilt hereafter, should be regularly expected and realized in our present state; but customs remain, when the reasons of them have ceased. In the midst of our lawyers, our sages, and our divines, we violate every precept of law, morality, and religion; in the midst of civilization, improvement, and social happiness, we suffer our comforts and our peace, here and hereafter, to hang upon the chance of an angry look or word; and we retain the preposterous folly, while we have lost the ignorance; the bloody ferocity, but no longer the humble piety of our ancestors.

It is thus that the history of the Dark and Middle Ages, like every other part of history, is still but a representation of human nature, and as such deserving of our curiosity and examination.

The poet may no doubt find the richest materials amid transactions, where the passions were so violently excited, and in a period when human manners were cast into forms so striking and so different from our own; and the antiquarian, the constitutional lawyer, and the philosopher must find, amid the opinions and practices of these illiterate Barbarians, the origin and foundation of the laws, the sentiments and the customs, that distinguish Europe from the other quarters of the world, and the different kingdoms of Europe from each other.

But to the moralist and the statesman the great reflection is every where the same; the deplorable nature of ignorance; the value of every thing which can enlighten mankind; the merit of every man who can contribute to open the views or strengthen the understanding of his fellow creatures. It is but too evident from the history of these periods of darkness, that we have only to suppose a state of society, where the general ignorance shall be sufficiently complete; and impossibilities themselves seem realized; men may find degradation in the most ennobling sentiments of their nature, and destruction and crimes in their best virtues.

v. ENGLAND

I HAVE HITHERTO said nothing of England. Yet has England a dearer claim on our curiosity and attention, and its history, and more particularly its constitutional history, must be considered with more diligence and patience, than can possibly be directed to those of any other country.

The first authentic notice which we have of the inhabitants of this island, is honourable to their memory: they were attacked by the first man of the first nation in the world; they resisted, and were not subdued. The account is given by Cæsar himself, and what Cæsar delivers to posterity, however short, cannot but be deserving of our observation.

Further information with respect to the Britons may be afterwards collected from Suetonius; and the gradual successes of the Roman commanders will be found in Tacitus. In his life of Agricola the subject is closed; all further contest is at an end. But the speech which is there attributed to Galgacus, when once read, can never be forgotten: the great historian has here displayed the rare merit of a mind elevated in the cause of justice above every domestic partiality and national prejudice. When he exhibits the cause which called the Caledonians to the field, he is no longer the son-in-law of the Roman general, nor the countryman of the Roman people; he is the assertor of all the generous principles of our nature; he is the protector of humanity, and he discharges with fidelity and spirit the noble office, the great duty of the historian, by exhibiting to our sympathy the wrongs of unoffending freedom.

The Romans were indeed successful, and the independence of Britain was no more. But the sentiments which must have animated these last defenders of their country still breathe in the immortal pages of this celebrated writer; and the virtues of the Caledonians are now for ever united to the taste and feelings of mankind.

Another melancholy scene succeeds. The Romans retire from the island, and the Britons, deprived of their protection, are insulted and overpowered by every invader. The Romans had long inured them to a sense of inferiority. The country had been partly civilized and improved, but the *mind* of the country had been destroyed. The Britons had lost the rude virtues of barbarians, but had not acquired that sense of honour and consciousness of political happiness, which do more than supply their place in the character of civilized man. They had not felt the influence of a government which themselves could share. They were unable to make head against their enemies; and they exhibited to the world that lesson, which has been so often repeated, that a country can never be defended by a population that has been, on whatever account, degraded; that they who are to resist an invader must first be moulded by equal laws and the benefits of a free government into a due sense of national pride and individual importance; and that men cannot be formed into heroes on the principles of suspicion and injustice. . . .

The next era in our history exhibits the total subjugation of Britain by the Angles, Jutes, and Saxons. These were northern nations; and we are thus brought, with respect to England, exactly to the same point from whence we set out in examining the history of Europe, the conquest of the northern nations.

Again, we must observe the particular circumstances of the Norman Conquest which followed. This conquest gave occasion to the establishment of the feudal system in all its rigours. The pope had also extended his empire to this remote island. So that in England, as in the rest of Europe, we have the feudal system and the papal power; and these were, in the instance of our own country, as in the rest of Europe (without stopping to notice some fortunate peculiarities in our case, or some advantages concomitant with these evils), the great impediments to the improvement of human happiness.

The subject of English history now lies before us from the expulsion of the Romans to the time of Henry VIII. . . . There are before you the facts of the history, and the philosophy of the history. You will soon learn the one, but you must endeavour to understand the other.

Having thus given you my general notion of what you are to attempt to do, I will describe to you the best and shortest means you can use for the purpose. You must read, then, and compare Hume and Rapin, and study Millar on the English Constitution. . . . I must now add the invaluable History of Mr. Hallam,* and that no one who has been admitted to the benefits of a regular education, can be pardoned if he do not exert himself at least to this extent.

But when England is the subject, most of you may be disposed to take any pains, that can be thought necessary, to inform yourselves of its constitutional history; and it is to those, therefore, that I shall now, for some time, address myself; to those who are ready to study the constitutional history of their country more thoroughly. . . .

You must come to no decision on any point connected with this subject, without first turning to this chapter of Mr. Hallam. He thinks for himself; and he is a critic and examiner of the labours of those, who have gone before. Since this lecture was written, his *Constitutional History* † has also appeared; a work, as I have already said, quite invaluable.

Dr. Lingard has lately published a *History of England*; and we have now, therefore, the views and reasonings of those, who are members of the Roman Catholic communion, presented to us by a writer of great controversial ability. Dr. Lingard also consults records, and judges for himself, and his book must therefore be always referred to on every occasion of importance. He tells the story of England in too cold a manner, and it is truly the Roman Catholic History of England; but his work is interesting, because the reader knows that the writer is not only an able writer, but a man of research and of antiquarian learning, and it therefore never can be conjectured beforehand, what may be the information which he will produce, nor the sentiments that he will adopt. . . .

You may easily consult the monkish writers; you will find them edited in a form by no means repulsive, Rerum Anglicarum Scriptores decem, &c.

You will not probably turn to read works of this kind in any very regular manner; but I would advise you to consult them at particular periods

---

* Henry Hallam's *Constitutional History of England* first appeared in 1827.—Ed.

† This work, by the English historian and antiquary John Lingard (1771–1851), was for many years the chief history of England from a Roman Catholic point of view. It was published 1819–30.—Ed.

of our history: periods, where their representations are likely to be instructive. When popular commotions, for instance, occur; changes of the government; any transaction that may be connected with general principles. . . .

It is totally impossible to convey the impression which is given by these original documents [of parliamentary history] in any words but their own; nothing can be more curious and striking than their language to our modern ears, particularly where the Commons are mentioned: when we consider what, very happily for the community, that assembly now is, it is perfectly amusing to observe the submissive approaches, which they long made, not only to the king, but to the lords and prelates; their alarm, their total despondency, when they see any tax impending over them.

It is in these original documents that their early insignificance, and the slow but accelerated growth of their power, can best be seen: and how idle is the declamation which would refer us to these times, as the best times of our parliaments. Most of the valuable privileges, which the House of Commons enjoys, most of the important offices which that house now discharges for the community, may be there traced up to all their rude beginnings; sometimes visible in the shape of pretensions and assumptions, sometimes of claims and rights, and all or any of them, with the exception of the right to give away their own and the public money, waived or asserted, or modified according to the circumstances of their situation. So much has liberty owed to perseverance, and to the vigilant improvement of opportunity; not to any original contract or adjustment between the elementary powers of the constitution, the monarch, the aristocracy, and the commonalty. . . .

Turn, for instance, to the *History* of Hume. We are scarcely entered upon the work and referred to the notes, before we see the symptoms of some contrariety of opinion between the historian and other writers with respect to the original nature of our constitution. If we have recourse to the authors whom he quotes or alludes to, the shades of controversy soon thicken around us, and we perceive that the same dispute exists among our own writers that will be found among the historians and antiquarians of the French nation; between those who insist upon the popular, and those who contend for the aristocratic and monarchical nature of the original constitutions and governments of Europe.

Controversies of this kind have arisen not only from the curious and disputable nature of these topics, but from a difference of sentiment, which has always existed among the writers and reasoners that have lived under the mixed governments of Europe; secretly or avowedly they have always fallen into two divisions—those who think the interests of the community are best served by favouring the monarchical part of a

constitution, and those who think the same end is best attained by in-
clining to its popular privileges. The result has been that writers of the
first description have been eager to show that the prerogatives of the
monarch were from the earliest times predominant: and that those of the
last description have been equally earnest to prove that all power, not
only in theory but in fact, was first derived from the people.

Such discussions may be thought by many little more than the natural,
though unimportant, occupation of speculative writers and antiquarians; for the real question (it will be said) must always be, by what form
of government the happiness of the community is best secured,—not,
what was in fact the form that happened to exist among our ancestors a
thousand years ago; their mistakes or misfortunes can be no rule or
obligation to us; we may emulate or avoid their example, but cannot be
bound by their authority.

All this must be admitted, yet it must be remembered that the affairs
of men are not disposed of by the rules of logic or the abstract truths
of reasoning: these may remain the same, and may always exhibit to
the monarch and to the people, to the courtier and the patriot, those
principles and maxims, which are best fitted to promote the happiness
of the community. Neither the one nor the other are, however, likely
to see such truths very clearly, or to examine them very accurately. It is
by a certain loose and coarse mixture of right and wrong in the reasoning,
and of selfishness and generosity in the intention, that the *practical*
politics of mankind are carried on according to the varying circumstances
of the case; not only, therefore, are the reasonings of philosophy produced, but arguments are urged, drawn from precedent and ancient
usage, which thus appear to moderate, as it were, between the contending
parties, and to be unaffected by the heats and prejudices of the moment.
It seems, for example, more reasonable to insist upon privileges which
have been *before* enjoyed, more reasonable to maintain prerogatives
which were *originally* exercised. Topics of this nature, which can in no
respect be slighted by any sound philosopher, much the contrary, are
perfectly adapted to the loose, sweeping, and often irrational decisions
of the generality of mankind; and, therefore, the discussions of antiquarians and philosophic historians, with respect to the original state of
prerogative and privilege, can never be without their interest and importance. In the practical politics of mankind, usage, prescription, custom, are everything, or nearly so, but in this country, such discussions
are fitted to excite a more than ordinary degree of interest. The language
of the statesmen and patriots, to whom we are so much indebted for
our constitution, has always been, that they claimed their undoubted
rights and privileges, their ancient franchises, the laws and liberties of
the land, and their immemorial customs. One monarch has been obliged

to capitulate with his subjects, and acknowledge their immunities and franchises formally by charter; one has perished on a scaffold; another been exiled from the throne. Revolutions and a civil war have marked the influence of opposite opinions with respect to the popular nature of our constitution. These dreadful and perilous scenes could not fail to transmit this original division of sentiment to us their posterity. The distinction between those who incline to the popular part of the constitution and those who incline to the monarchical exists to this hour, and can only cease with the constitution itself.

The great leading idea which should be formed of our constitutional history is that there has always been a constant struggle between prerogative and privilege. . . .

Grievances like these continually occurred from the irregular nature of government and society, in such barbarous times; but the natural feelings of mankind, operating upon the example transmitted by more ancient times, continually revived the spirit of resistance. This virtuous spirit found in the House of Commons a regular and legal organ through which the rights of the community could be asserted; and this is the struggle and this the merit of our ancestors—this the inherited duty (if necessary) of ourselves.

Now, such being the real picture of our constitutional history, the student is in the next place to be reminded of . . . the natural divisions, not only of mankind, but of philosophers, on political subjects; and the manner in which they separate into two classes: those, for instance, who are anxious first and principally for the prerogative of the crown; and those, on the other hand, who are zealous first and principally for the privileges of the people.

It may be very true, that could the selfishness and the irritability of men allow them to weigh and consider the reasonings of each other, the real interests of both crown and people would be found to consist in their mutual support, and are always in truth the same; but the rude warfare of human passions admits not of such salutary adjustments, and as mutual offences are in practice constantly given and received, men who naturally kindle at the sight of what they conceive to be insolence and usurpation on the one side, or on the other to be cruelty and wrong, are not only inflamed, when they live at the time, and are witnesses of the scene, but they are unable to give an accurate representation even of the transactions of the past; they cannot consider them, with proper calmness, even when they observe them, in a subsequent period, at a secure distance of time and place; so true is this, that not one thoroughly impartial historian of our annals can be mentioned; and it is necessary to warn my hearers that they are to adopt no train of reasoning, nor even the narrative of any important proceeding without a due examination of

different writers, and a careful consideration of their particular prejudices. . . .

It is Hume who is read by every one. Hume is the historian, whose
views and opinions insensibly become our own. He is respected and admired by the most enlightened reader; he is the guide and philosopher of
the ordinary reader, to whose mind, on all the topics connected with
our history, he entirely gives the tone and the law. . . .

It is impossible, indeed, that the confidence of a reader should not be
won by the general air of calmness and good sense, which, independent of
other merits, distinguishes the beautiful narrative of Hume. If he should
turn to his authorities (speaking first on the favourable side of the question), he will then, and then only, be able to perceive the entire merit of
this admirable writer: the dexterity and sagacity with which he has often
made out his recital, the ease and grace with which it is presented to the
reader, and the valuable and penetrating remarks by which it is enriched.

But to speak next on the unfavourable side, by turning to the same
authorities, we shall then only perceive the entire demerit of his work.
It is understood, indeed, by every reader, it has been proclaimed by many
writers, that Hume always inclines to the side of the prerogative; that in
his account of the Stuarts his history is little better than an apology; his
pages are therefore read, in this part of his work at least, with something
of distrust, and his representations are not considered as decisive. But
what reader turns to consult his references or examine his original authorities? What effect does this distrust after all produce? Practically
none. In defiance of it, is not the general influence of his work, on the
general reader, just such as the author would himself have wished; as
strong and as permanent as if every statement and opinion in his history
had deserved our perfect assent and approbation?

I must confess that this appears to me so entirely the fact, judging
from all that I have experienced in myself, and observed in others, that
I do not conceive a lecturer in history could render (could offer at least)
a more important service to an English auditory than by following Mr.
Hume, step by step, through the whole of his account; and showing what
were his fair, and what his unfair inferences; what his just representations, and what his improper colourings; what his mistakes, and above all,
what his omissions; in short, what were the dangers, and what the advantages, that must attend the perusal of so popular and able a performance.

But such lectures, I apprehend, could not be listened to. Were they
even formed into a treatise, they would only be in part perused by the
general reader; nor would they be properly and thoroughly considered,
by any but the most patient inquirers. . . .

When Mr. Hume comes to comment upon the title of Henry IV to the crown, he attributes a speech to the king, and properly, for he can extract from the rolls of parliament the very words which the king made use of. This Mr. Hume does, and this is to write history.

The words extracted are certainly very remarkable, and very descriptive of the scene and the age; but it is relics of this kind, that an historian should produce and make the subject of the philosophic meditation of his reader, not offer him modern views and sentiments of his own.

A few barbarous words or any distinct fact, that can be shown to be authentic, are worth volumes of reasonings and conjectures of a thinking mind; or rather it is, on such relics and facts that the student must in the first place *alone* depend when he collects materials for his instruction, and he must never lose sight of them, when he comes afterwards to build up his political reasonings and conclusions. . . .

But to return to Hume. Gilbert Stuart,* a very able though somewhat impetuous inquirer into the earlier parts of our history, has pronounced his opinion upon the work of Mr. Hume in the following words: "From its beginning to its conclusion, it is chiefly to be regarded as a plausible defence of prerogative. As an elegant and spirited composition, it merits every commendation. But no friend to humanity, and to the freedom of this kingdom, will consider his constitutional inquiries, with their effect on his narrative, and compare them with the ancient and venerable monuments of our story, without feeling a lively surprise, and a patriot indignation." . . .

One word more and I conclude, one word as an estimate of the whole subject between Mr. Hume and his opponents.

In the first place, we may agree with Mr. Hume, that the whole of our history during the period from Edward I to Henry VIII was a scene of irregularity and of great occasional violence; that the laws could neither be always maintained, nor could the principles of legislation be ever said to be well understood; we must admit, therefore, that it is not fair to imagine, as Mr. Hume complains we do, that all the princes who were unfortunate in their government, were necessarily tyrannical in their conduct, and that resistance to the monarch always proceeded from some attempt on his part to invade the privileges of the subject. This we must admit.

But, in the second place, it must be observed that the struggle between the subject and the crown was constantly kept up in the times of the most able, as well as of the weakest monarchs: that they who resisted the prerogative never did it, without producing those maxims and without asserting those principles of freedom, which are necessary to all rational government; which are by no means fitted in themselves to produce anarchy, and by no means inconsistent with all those salutary prerogatives

* Scottish historian and reviewer (1742–86).—Ed.

of the crown which are requisite to the regular protection of the subject. In the third place, that if these maxims and principles had not been from time to time asserted, and sometimes with success, that the result must have been, that our constitution would have degenerated, like that of France and of every other European state, into a system of monarchical power, unlimited and unrestrained by the interference of any legislative assemblies.

And that therefore in the last place, Mr. Hume tells the story of England without giving sufficient praise to those patriots who preserved and transmitted those general habits of thinking on political subjects, which have always distinguished this country, and to which alone every Englishman owes, at this day, all that makes his life a blessing and his existence honourable.

vi. ENGLAND

IT IS WONDERFUL to see men like Mr. Hume, of peaceful habits, and of benevolent affections, men at the same time of improved minds and of excellent sense, it is wonderful to see them so indifferent to the popular privileges of the community.

Yet is this a sort of phenomenon that we witness every day. Such men would not in practice vindicate themselves from oppression, by rising up in arms against their arbitrary governors; they are not of a temperament to set their lives upon a cast. What possible chance, then, have *they* for the security of their property, for the very freedom of their persons, above all, for the exercise of their minds, but the existence of popular privileges? To them, above all men, civil freedom is everything.

Civil freedom cannot indeed exist without the existence at the same time of executive power, that is, of prerogative. Men must be protected from the multitude. But surely it can still less exist, without the existence of popular privileges; because society must be protected from the few, as well as from the many; from the insolence, injustice, and caprice of the high, as of the low. The mistake that is made seems to be, that it is supposed popular privileges will always lead to disorder, and render the government insecure.

The very reverse is the fact; so much so, that certain privileges may be trusted, not merely to legislative bodies, men of property and education (which is the first and main point to be contended for), but even to the lowest orders of the people; the very rabble can learn to know how far they are to go, and with this as with their right, to be content, and advance no further.

The advantages obtained in the cheerfulness and vigour, that are thus imparted to the whole political system of a country, are above all price, and the occasional excesses of a mob are an evil trifling, and in comparison of no account.

Men of arbitrary or timid minds WILL not understand this, and men bred under arbitrary governments never *can*.

Foreigners who survey, for instance, one of our popular elections at Brentford or Westminster, generally suppose that our government is to break up in the course of the week, and have been known to announce to their correspondents on the continent, and even to their courts, an approaching revolution. The mob, in the meantime, know very well the limits within which they may for a time disturb the peace of the community, and they therefore sing their ballads, hoot their superiors, remind them (very usefully) of their faults and follies, parade the streets, and brandish their bludgeons, but as to an insurrection or revolution, no enterprise of the kind ever enters into their thoughts; certainly it makes no part of their particular bill of the performances.

In a word, power is like money; men should be accustomed, as much as possible, as much as they can bear, to the handling of it, that they may learn the proper use of it: they are so, more or less, in free governments; not so in arbitrary: and this is the circumstance which always constitutes the insecurity of arbitrary governments, while they stand, and the difficulty of improving them, when they can stand no longer.

Where popular privileges exist, the monarch can always distinguish between the characters of a lawful sovereign and an arbitrary ruler; so can his counsellors, so can his people, these are advantages totally invaluable. The world has nothing to do with certainty and security; but popular privileges afford the best chance of real tranquillity, strength, and happiness to all the constituent parts of a body politic, the monarch, the aristocracy, and the people. . . .

When we look into these charters [Magna Charta and similar documents wrested from the sovereign by the barons and, later, the commons] for those provisions of civil liberty which the enlarged and enlightened view of a modern statesman might suggest, we forget that they who obtained these charters were feudal lords, struggling with their feudal sovereign; and that more was, in fact, performed than could be reasonably expected; at all events they had the obvious merit of resisting oppression; a conduct that is always respectable, as it always indicates a sense of right and courage.

The exertion of such qualities is of use generally to the existing generation, and still more to posterity. No such steadiness and spirit was shown by the barons of other countries; and this of itself is a sufficient criterion of the merit of the English barons. The plain narrative of these transactions is, of itself, the best comment on their conduct, and its highest praise. That the barons should be jealous of their own powers and comforts, when they found them trenched upon by the monarch, may have been natural; that they should assert their cause by an appeal to arms, may have been the character of the age; that they should resist and overpower such princes as Henry or John, was perhaps what might have been expected. In all this there may possibly not be thought any very superior merit; but there is still merit, and merit of a most valuable kind. To maintain, however, a struggle systematically, and for many succeeding ages, was neither natural, nor the character of the age; and to have encountered and overpowered the rage, the authority, and the ability of a prince like Edward I, so fitted in every respect to dazzle and seduce, deceive and subdue them, this constitutes a merit which in other countries had no parallel, and which leaves us no sentiment but that of gratitude, no criticism but that of applause.

But in addition to these general remarks, one more particular observation must be left with you, and it is this,—that in the course of these charters (if they are properly examined), it will at length be seen, that *all* the leading objects of national concern were adverted to; that the outlines of a system of civil liberty were actually traced. Provision was made for the protection and independence of the church; the general privileges of trade were considered; the general rights of property; the civil liberties of the subject; the administration of justice.

It may indeed be remarked, that the provisions for general liberty in these charters were few, short, indistinct, and that it is impossible to suppose, that a few words like these could in any respect embrace all the multiplied relations of social life and regular government; and that much more must be done before the liberties of mankind can be secured, or even delineated or described with proper accuracy and effect. Where then, it may again be urged, where is now the value of these celebrated charters? To this it must be replied, that a rude sketch was made according to the circumstances of the times; and that nothing more could be accomplished or expected; that a reasonable theory, that the right principle, was everywhere produced and enforced; and that this was sufficient. Posterity was left no doubt to *imitate* those who had gone before them, by transfusing the general meaning of the whole into statutes, accommodated to the new exigencies that might arise. It was not necessary that they who were to follow should tread precisely in the same steps; but they were to bear themselves erect, and walk after the same manner. The track might be altered, but the port and the march were to be the same. Such indeed was the event. In Hampden's cause of ship money, and on every occasion, when the liberties of the subject were to be asserted—in writing, in speeches, in parliament, in the courts of law

—these charters were produced, examined, and illustrated; and they supplied the defenders of our best interests at all times with the spirit and the materials of their virtuous eloquence. Civil liberty had got a creed which was to be learnt and studied by its votaries, a creed to which the eyes of all were to be turned with reverence; which the subject considered as his birthright; which the monarch received from his predecessors as the constitution of the land; which the one thought it his duty to maintain, and which the other thought it no derogation to his dignity to acknowledge.

"It must be confessed," says Hume, "that the former articles of the great charter contain such mitigations and explanations of the feudal law as are reasonable and equitable; and that the latter involve *all* the chief outlines of a legal government and provide for the equal distribution of justice, and the free enjoyment of property; the great objects for which political society was at first founded by men; which the people have a perpetual and unalienable right to recall, and which no time, nor precedent, nor statute, nor positive institution ought to deter them from keeping ever uppermost in their thoughts and attention."

At the close of the subject, though he resumes his natural hesitation and circumspection, he seems considerably subdued by the merit of the actors in these memorable transactions.

"Thus," says he, "after the contests of near a whole century, and those ever accomplished with violent jealousies, often with public convulsions, the great charter was finally established, and the English nation have the honour of extorting by their perseverance, this concession from the ablest, the most warlike, and the most ambitious of all their princes. Though arbitrary practices often prevailed, and were even able to establish themselves into settled customs, the validity of the great charter was never afterwards formally disputed; and that grant was still regarded as the basis of English government, and the sure rule by which the authority of every custom was to be tried and canvassed. The jurisdiction of the star-chamber, martial law, imprisonment by warrants from the privy council, and other practices of a like nature, though established for several centuries, were scarcely ever allowed by the English to be parts of their constitution. The affection of the nation for liberty still prevailed over all precedent, and even all political reasoning. The exercise of these powers, after becoming the source of secret murmurs among the people, was in fulness of time abolished as illegal, at least as oppressive, by the whole legislative authority."

These appear to me remarkable passages to be found in the history of Hume, and I therefore offer them to your notice.

You will find Hallam very decisive in his opinion of the value of this great charter. He considers it as the most important event in our history, except the Revolution in 1688, without which its benefits would rapidly have been annihilated.

Before I conclude, I must once more remind you that it is the general spirit and habits of thinking in a community that are all in all; that charters, and statutes, and judges, and courts of law, are all of no avail for perpetuating a constitution, or even for securing the regular administration of its blessings from time to time,—are all of no avail, if a vital principle does not animate the mass, and if there be not sufficient intelligence and spirit in the community to be anxious about its own happiness and dignity, its laws and government, and those provisions and forms in both, which are favourable to its liberties. When this vital principle exists, every defect is supplied from time to time by those who bear rule, and who can never be long or materially at a loss to know, what either Magna Charta or the free maxims of our constitution require from them. However complicated may be the business, however *new* the situations for which they have to provide, the outline of a free constitution, though rude and imperfect, can easily be filled up by those who labour in the spirit of the original masters.

When this is honourably done, and when the spirit and vital principle of a constitution are faithfully preserved, those who rule and those who are governed, may and do sympathize with each other. They are no longer drawn out and divided into ranks of hostility, open or concealed; there is no storm above ground, no hollow murmuring below. The public good becomes a principle, acknowledged by the monarch as his rule of government, and loyalty is properly cherished by the subject, as one of the indispensable securities of his own political happiness. Men are taught to respect each other and to respect themselves. The lowest man in society is furnished with his own appropriate sentiment of honour, which in him, as in his superiors, is to protect and animate his sense of duty: he, too, like those above him, has his degradations of character, to which he will not stoop; and his elevations of virtue, to which he must aspire.

This is that real protection to a state, that source of all national prosperity, that great indispensable auxiliary to the virtue and even the religion of a country, which may well be considered as the mark of every good government, for it constitutes the perfection of the best.

But all this must be the work, not of those who are placed low in the gradations of the social order, but of those who are destined, by whatever advantages of property, rank, and particularly of *high* office, to have authority over their fellow creatures; of such men (men like yourselves) it is the bounden duty to cherish the constitutional spirit of their country, and, in one word, to promote and protect the respectability of the poor man. When those who are so elevated use to such purposes the influence and the command which do and ought to belong to them, they employ themselves in a manner the most grateful to their feelings, if they are men of benevolence and virtue; the most creditable to their talents, if they are men of genius and understanding.

VII. FRANCE

I HAVE ALREADY endeavoured to draw your attention to this great subject—the constitutional history of France. There are few that can be thought of more consequence in the annals of modern Europe. Had France acquired a good form of government, while the feudal system was falling into decay, the character of the French nation would have been very different from what, in the result, it afterwards became. All the nations on the continent would have been materially influenced in their views and opinions by such an example. The whole history of France and of those countries would have been changed, and the private and public happiness of the world would have been essentially improved.

The first and great subject of inquiry, therefore, in the French history is this,—What were the circumstances that more particularly affected the civil liberties of France?

It is quite necessary to remark, that this subject is never properly treated by the French historians. They never seem to feel its importance; to understand its nature. When they advert to the state of France; when they endeavour to consider how the country is to be improved, how advanced to perfection, they content themselves, as their orators seem to have done in the States-General, with vague declamations about order and virtue, and the discharge of the duties of life: a love of his people must, they think, be found in the sovereign, purity of morals in his subjects. These are the topics on which they harangue. Every political good, they suppose, is to result from the private and individual merits of the monarch and those whom he is to govern. They look no further. It seems never to have occurred to them, that the virtues which they wish for, both in the prince and the subject, are generated by a free government, and that it is in vain to expect them under any other. . . .

With respect to the constitution of France, the great point in that constitution was, as it has been in all the European constitutions, simply this,—whether the national assemblies could maintain their importance, and above all, preserve their right of taxation. On this right of taxation every thing depended.

To the general principles of liberty, a nation is easily made blind, or can even become indifferent. Such principles are never understood by the multitude; and the interest they excite is of a nature too refined and generous to animate the mass of mankind either long or deeply. But fortunately for them, they who trample upon their rights, generally (as it would be expressed by the people themselves) want their money; and here at least is found a coarser string, which can always vibrate strongly and steadily. The tax-gatherer can at all events be discovered by the people to be an enemy, as they suppose, to their happiness. Popular insurrections have seldom had any other origin; and the unfeeling luxury of the great is thus sometimes most severely punished by the headlong and brutal fury of the multitude. Patriots and legislators are, therefore, the most successfully employed when they are fighting the ignorant selfishness of the low against the vicious selfishness of the high; when they are exchanging tax for privilege, and purchasing what is, in fact, the happiness of both, by converting the mean passions of each to the purpose of a generous and enlightened prudence. But to do this, it is necessary that some body of men who can sympathise with the people should have a political existence, and that their assent should be necessary to make taxation legal. Of peaceful, regular, constitutional freedom, which is the only freedom, this is the best and the only practical safeguard. . . .

The contest in the reign of King John of France has distinct stages, in some of which it resembles the struggle between our own King John and the barons: in others, the struggle between Charles I and his parliament; and, at length, it assumes an appearance precisely the same, which it did in the frightful and disgraceful periods of the late French revolution; every thing at the disposal of the multitude; and even the outrages carried on in a manner very similar. The dauphin's officers murdered in his presence, and the party-coloured cap placed upon his head, as was in a similar irruption into the palace, the *bonnet rouge* on the head of the late most amiable and most unfortunate monarch, Louis XVI. The result was but too certain; either the erection of some military despotism, or the restoration of their ancient government, returning with all its abuses, and more than ever confirmed in its faults and errors.

Either event would necessarily have been destructive of all rational liberty; the latter took place. And here may be said to have ended all the more regular, and therefore more hopeful, efforts for the constitution of France.

The great mistake seems to me to have been that charters were not continually obtained (one was obtained), but I mean continually obtained or renewed, from time to time, as was done in England. It is impossible that a constitution should be established, or even very thoroughly improved *at once*, by the law or provisions of any *one* body of men: and the provisions that were made for this purpose by our own ancestors at

Runnymede, seem to have been for a long time but too ineffectual. But a charter, often renewed or improved, may long remain and always be remembered, and in this manner teach those, who succeed, the duties that have been performed by those who went before them, till freedom becomes at last interwoven with the general habits of thinking in a community, and may then be converted into the effective law of the land.

We cannot now, as I have just observed, trace all the causes of this calamitous alteration in the prospects of France. The kingdom was most dreadfully situated; in a state of hostility with a victorious enemy; troops of soldiers, who acknowledged no law and no country, pillaging what the ravages of war had not entirely swept away; and, soon after, the horrible insurrection of the *Jacquerie*, described by Froissart, the peasants against the nobles; all uniting to complete a combination of horrors which no civilized country ever before or since exhibited.

That the deputies from distant parts should, in circumstances like these be unwilling or unable to meet in the capital; that the moderate and the good should no longer be disposed to projects of reform, should easily fall away from their more ardent associates, should be even wanting in their duties as patriots and as men, should no longer prosecute the tasks of hope amid the scenes of despair; all this can surely be surprising to no one. Nor can we wonder, in a country thus situated, at the failure of any generous experiment for its liberties, when such experiments, it is but too evident, must always depend for their success, not only on the merit of those who engage in them, but on something of good fortune in the conjuncture of circumstances in which they are attempted.

It is impossible, therefore, to read this particular portion of the French history without sensations of the most painful kind. However imperfect might be the character of Marcel * and his associates, some great effort was on this occasion evidently made for the democratic part of the constitution of France—it failed; and as we read the history, we are left with an impression on our minds, that the French sovereigns will, from this time, endeavour to carry on the administration of the government without the assistance of any representative assemblies, i. e. without any control or check on their own power; or, in other words, that the people are henceforward to be oppressed, and the sovereign to be, by his very situation, corrupted; a state of things disgraceful to both, and even dangerous; dangerous because whenever any system of policy is arranged in any manner directly opposed to the reason and feelings of mankind, it can never be in a state of safety. Nothing is really secure that is not in

* Etienne Marcel (d. 1358), provost of the merchants of Paris. His efforts at reform came to an end when he was murdered by an agent of the dauphin, later Charles V.—Ed.

harmony with the great and established moral feelings of the human heart. The slightest accident may give occasion to the most violent efforts for its overthrow; and such efforts are likely to be attended with the destruction of, at least, all those who were too exclusively benefited by a disposition of things, in itself, unnatural and unjust.

Considerations, indeed, of this remote and contingent nature, I grieve to say, are little likely to influence the rulers of mankind, or the higher orders. General principles like these may slumber (if I may be allowed the expression) for centuries, and then be roused into action in an instant.

Mankind, on these occasions, stand astonished at what has been long foreseen to be very possible by every intelligent reasoner; just as they stand amazed at the first eruption of a volcano, which the philosopher has from physical appearances always predicted, in vain protesting against the erection of palaces and villas in situations where they are every moment exposed to be buried in ashes, or annihilated by lava.

In this manner, in France, the great national bodies which had existed under Charlemagne, the assemblies of the fields of March and May, were succeeded by no adequate representation of the force of the community; and the States-General that were convened by Philip le Bel and the house of Valois, were but imperfect and fading images of their greatness.

In England, on the contrary, the national assemblies never lost their importance; the witenagemots were succeeded by parliaments, these by assemblies of the lords and commons in two distinct houses, and the civil liberties of the community were thus, and thus only, saved from destruction.

The States-General of France had been, as we have already intimated, resisted, overcome, and, in fact, disposed of by John and the Dauphin. The latter mounted the throne with the title of Charles the Fifth.

In consequence of the late contest, every thing was submitted to his will. But what was the result? What use did he make of his power? Did it occur to him that he ought to be a patriot as well as a king; that he should endeavour not to extinguish, but rather to modify, the power of the States-General; that he should endeavour to establish by a proper mixture of royal and popular authority, the glory of his own name and the happiness of his subjects; that he should labour to elevate them from the state of ignorance and ferocity in which they were evidently sunk; that he should allow them, if not to exercise power themselves to delegate their power to others; that he should teach them the feelings of humanity, by admitting them to the exercise of the rights of it; did considerations of this reasonable nature occur to him? Was it in this manner that this renowned politician was employed from his first accession to power? Far otherwise. His wisdom was exclusively exerted in confirm-

ing and extending the prerogative of the crown, in labouring to destroy
that authority of the States, and in deceiving his subjects into the most
fatal of all political delusions, that "whatever is best administered is best";
in persuading them, in contriving that they should persuade themselves,
that as he had foiled and overpowered the English by the prudence of
his military operations, as he had swept away from the country the
banditti by which it was pillaged, as there was no point which he seemed
to carry by cruelty or by force, that therefore, in this happier state of
things, it was he, the king, who was assuredly the father of his country;
and that it was of no consequence what became of the States-General,
the right of taxation, the principles of the constitution, or any other right
or principle whatever, while Marcel and his Parisian mob were not destroying the public peace, nor the English, the peasants, or the banditti,
the public prosperity; while, in short, all the *effects* of the happiest form
of government and the most legitimate authority were produced by the
easier exercise of his individual wisdom and experience, benevolence and
justice.

Let no nation presume to blame the French for submitting to considerations or acquiescing in reasonings like these. No nation has ever risen
superior to delusions so natural and soothing. It is scarcely necessary to
say, that Charles succeeded in all the objects of his administration; and
he and his courtiers contemplated, no doubt, with the most sincere
complacency and applause, the dexterity with which he wielded the
minds of men to his purposes, and the gradual decay of all those forms
and principles in their government which were likely to be offensive or
troublesome (as they would have called it) to the influence and authority
of the wearer of the crown. Was it, however, virtuous, was it, after all,
wise in the king and his courtiers, thus to deceive their country and destroy its constitution? The history of the succeeding reign is no testimony
in their favour. And as Charles the Wise (for *such* he was denominated)
—as Charles the Wise approached that melancholy period of decay and
death, when worldly wisdom is but too apt to appear mistaken folly, the
politician discovered that his son was a minor, that the princes of the
blood were disunited and ambitious, that the general prosperity of the
nation and of his royal house had been left totally to depend on his own
personal management and prudence, and that therefore, every interest
that was dear to him, as a father or a king, would in the event be thrown
into a situation of perplexity and danger, from the moment that he himself expired.

With what sentiments are we to see him summoning his brothers
around him, portioning out his authority among them, labouring to provide for the welfare of his child and his kingdom by the vain expedient
of promises and oaths?

He had no States-General, no legislative assemblies, whom he had familiarized to their own particular duties, whom he had allowed to exercise along with himself the administration of the public happiness, whom he had taught to see in the royal authority the best security and protection of their own; he had no guardians like these to whom he could entrust his son; or the helpless, hopeless expedients of oaths and promises had been unnecessary. . . .

On what principle was it that Charles . . . remitted his taxes when sinking into the grave? Was he conscious, when too late, of the injury he had done his country by imposing them on his own authority? Did he wish in this manner to attach the people to his child [Charles VI]? On either supposition, what a lesson to those who favour the maxims of arbitrary power!

The genius of Charles had been devoted to the establishment of the power of the crown; and the nation who called him *wise*, and the prince to whom he was a father, were soon to reap the effects of what was esteemed his policy, in seeing their country without order and without law, destroyed by the factions of the royal family, and subdued by a foreign invader. . . .

From whom, it may be asked, were they [the princes of the blood] to have learnt this love of their country? From the deceased monarch?—He had taught no lessons but those of arbitrary power. From the free constitution of their country?—It had been corrupted till it was unfit for the production of patriots. . . .

I have already intimated to you the inference that is to be drawn from all the past transactions between the crown and the people of France. The same is the inference from all that you are to approach. The difference between cunning and wisdom; between paltry policy and liberal prudence; between mean, jealous, contracted, tricking sagacity, and a pure, enlarged, enlightened benevolence; the difference between these, and the superiority of the latter to the former, even upon the principles of mere selfish policy, and though the calls of humanity and duty had no claim to be heard. . . .

After the decease of the unhappy Charles VI whom we have just mentioned, the English were expelled by his son Charles VII. Charles VII is the monarch who was crowned by the Maid of Orléans, an heroine, in the recital of whose noble and matchless exploits history appears to be converted into romance, and whose merits were so great, as to be thought supernatural by her contemporaries. But the enemies of France were no sooner driven from her fields, than the prerogatives for the crown were necessarily strengthened, and a far more fatal, because a far more lasting enemy, than the English, succeeded in the person of the sovereign himself, in the person of Charles VII. Here was again another instance of the still recurring ill fortune of the constitution of France. How was the nation to resist a prince whom they had themselves rescued from the English, and whom *they*, rather than any spirit of enterprise in his own nature, had enabled to win his crown? What blessing could now be made either desirable or intelligible to Frenchmen, but that of peace and repose? What could there be of alarm or terror in the prerogative of the crown to those, who had seen an invader on the throne? Before the ministers of the power of Charles, to the afflicted imagination of the French people, must have walked the spectres of their slaughtered countrymen, and the frowning warriors of England; and slavery itself, if it was not foreign slavery, must to *them* have appeared a state of happiness and triumph.

That fatal measure, fatal for the liberties of his country, was now taken by Charles VII, by which his reign must be for ever distinguished, the establishment of a military force, and the allotment of a perpetual tax for the support of it, unchecked by any representative assembly.

This military force and tax might not be formidable in their first appearance; but, the principle once admitted, both the force and the tax were easily advanced step by step, to any extent that suited the views of each succeeding monarch. Excuses, and even reasonable considerations (reasonable to those who see not the importance of a precedent and a principle), can never be wanting on these occasions; they were not wanting on this.

It should be observed that this vital blow to the real greatness of France was introduced as a reform. If any of those who were living at the time had spoken of the probable *consequences* of such a precedent, and had insisted upon its danger to the best interests of their country, they would only have been disregarded or suspected of disloyalty. But no stronger instance can be given, if any were necessary, of the importance of a principle at all times; a precedent may not be often carried into all its consequences when *favourable* to the liberties of a country, but it always is, when it is otherwise. . . .

When this military force and tax had been once established, and both removed (which is the important point) entirely from all check and control by any other legitimate authority in the state, the power of the crown had no more tempests to encounter; no further contest appears in the succeeding reigns; the person of the king might be insulted or endangered, but not the royal authority. We hear of no more struggles for the privileges of the people, and for the right of taxation; no more important meetings of the States-General: all hope, at least all assertion of constitutional liberty was at an end: and the contentions of the great, who were alone left to contend, were directed solely to the questions of their own personal ambition.

If any hope for France yet remained, it expired under the reign of Louis XI, the son and successor of Charles. This prince was of all others the most fitted to destroy the liberties of his country; penetrating, sagacious, cautious, well considering the proportion between his means and his ends; a finished dissembler of his own interests and passions, and a skilful master of those of others; decisive, active, and entirely devoid of principle and feeling. The nobles made an ineffectual effort to retain some of that political power, which, if they lost it, was destined, all of it, to fall entirely into the possession of the crown, and this effort was made in the war, for the public good, as they affected to call it. But Louis contrived to cajole, overpower, or wield to the purposes of his ambition the king of England, the duke of Burgundy, and the Swiss. He increased the standing army, raised the taille to the most enormous amount, made this tax a step to the introduction of other imposts, reunited many important fiefs to the crown; and if men could acquire glory by the successful enterprises of ungenerous ambition; if happiness could be the consequence of cruelty and oppression, deceit and fraud; if any treasures or any possessions could be compared with the consciousness of being loved and respected, then, indeed, Louis XI might have been thought the renowned, the powerful, and the happy; and this detestable tyrant might have been held up by courtiers and courtly writers, as the envy of all succeeding monarchs. A different conclusion is, however, to be drawn from the picture of his life and character, which fortunately has been exhibited to us by Philippe de Commines, a faithful and confidential minister, who knew him thoroughly, and who appears even to have been attached to his person and memory, in defiance of his better judgment, by the influence of the kind treatment which he had personally received from him, as his master.

The king, it seems, successful in his intrigues, unresisted in his oppressions, and with nothing further to apprehend from his rivals or his enemies, was at last admonished of the frailty of all human grandeur by messengers far more ominous and dreadful, than the couriers and officers that announce the miscarriage of ambitious projects or the defeats of invading armies: he was seized by a first and then a second fit of epilepsy, so violent and long, that he lay without speech, and apparently without life, till his attendants concluded that he was no more. To life, indeed, he returned, but all the comforts of existence were gone for ever. "He came back to Tours [says the historian Commines, I quote his own artless words], where he kept himself so close, that very few were admitted to see him; for he was grown jealous of all his courtiers, and afraid they would either depose or deprive him of some part of his royal authority: he did many odd things, which made some believe that his senses were impaired; but they knew not his humours. As to his jealousy, all princes are prone to it, especially those who are wise, have many enemies, and have oppressed many people, as our master had done. Besides, he found that he was not beloved by the nobility of the kingdom, nor by many of the commons, for he had taxed them more than any of his predecessors, though he now had some thoughts of easing them, as I said before; but he should have begun sooner. Nobody was admitted into the place in which he kept himself but his domestic servants and his archers, which were four hundred, some of which kept constant guard at the gate, while others walked continually about to prevent his being surprised. Round about the castle he caused a lattice, or iron gate, to be set up, spikes of iron planted in the wall, and a kind of crow's feet, with several points to be placed along the ditch, wherever there was a possibility for any person to enter. Besides which he caused watchhouses to be made, all of thick iron, and full of holes, out of which they might shoot at their pleasure, in which he placed forty of his crossbows, who were to be on their guard night and day. He left no person of whom he had any suspicion either in town or country, but he sent his archers not only to warn but to conduct them away. To look upon him, one would have thought him to be rather a dead than a living man. No person durst ask a favour, or scarce speak to him about any thing. He inflicted very severe punishments, removed officers, disbanded soldiers." . . .

By clothes more rich and magnificent than before; by passing his time in subjecting those around him to every variety of fortune, to the changes of his smile and of his frown; by filling distant countries with his agents, to purchase for him rarities, which, when brought to him, he heeded not; by every strange and ridiculous expedient that his uneasy fancy could devise; by all this idle bustle and parade of royalty and power, did this helpless, wretched man endeavour to conceal from the world and himself the horrid characters of death which were visible on his frame; the fearful handwriting which had told him, that his kingdom was departing from him. In vain did he send for the holy man of Calabria, and on his approach "fall down," says the historian, "on his knees before him, and beg him to prolong his life." In vain was the holy vial brought from Rheims; the vest of St. Peter sent him by the pope. "Whatever was thought conducible to his health," says Philippe de Commines, "was sent to him from all corners of the world. His subjects trembled at his nod," he observes, "and whatever he commanded was executed; but it was in vain. He could indeed command the beggar's knee, but not the health of it"; and suspicious of everyone, of his son-in-law, his daughter, and his own son, having turned his palace into a prison for himself; into a cage, not unlike those which in his hours of cruelty he had made for others; insulted by his physician, and considered by his faithful minister, as expiating by his torments in this world, the crimes,

which, as he says, would otherwise have brought down upon him
the punishments of the Almighty in the next, this poor king, for
such we are induced to call him, expired in his castle, a memorable example, that whatever be the station or the success, nothing can compensate for the want of innocence, and that amid the intrigues of cunning
and the projects of ambition, the first policy which is to be learned,
is the policy of virtue.

VIII. SWITZERLAND

SWITZERLAND IS A name associated with the noblest feelings of our nature, and we turn with interest to survey the rise and progress of
countries which we have never been accustomed to mention, but with
sentiments of respect. In the history of the world, it has been the distinction of three nations only, to be characterized by their virtue and
their patriotism—the early Romans, the Spartans, and the Swiss. We
speak of the splendour of the Persians, of the genius of the Athenians;
but we speak of the hardy discipline and the inflexible virtue of Sparta,
and of ancient republican Rome; "the unconquerable mind, and freedom's holy flame." So in modern times we speak of the treasures of
Peru, of the luxuries of India, of the commerce of Venice or of Holland,
and of the arts of France; but it is to Switzerland that we have been
accustomed to turn, when as philanthropists or moralists, we sought
among mankind the unbought charms of native innocence, and the
sublime simplicity of severe and contented virtue.

More minute examination might possibly compel us to abate something of the admiration which we have paid at a distance: yet our admiration must be ever due to the singular people of Switzerland; and
it must always remain a panegyric of the highest kind, to owe renown
to merit alone; to have earned their independence by valour, and to
have maintained their prosperity by virtue; to be quoted as examples of
those qualities by which men may be so ennobled, that they are respected, even amid their comparative poverty and rudeness; to be described as heroes who, though too few to be feared by the weak, were too
brave to be insulted by the strong. The student, while he reads the history of Switzerland, finds himself, on a sudden, restored to his earliest
emotions of virtuous sympathy, and he will almost believe himself to be
once more surrounded by the objects of his classical enthusiasm; the
avengers of Lucretia, and the heroes of Thermopylae. Insolence and brutality he will see once more resisted by the manly feelings of indignant
nature. A few patriots meeting at midnight, and attesting the justice

of their cause to the Almighty disposer of events, the God of equity and mercy, the protector of the helpless: calm and united, proceeding to the delivery of their country; overpowering, dismissing, and expelling their unworthy rulers, the agents and representatives of the House of Austria, without outrage and without bloodshed: retaining all the serene forbearance of the most elevated reason, amid the energies and the fury of vindictive right; and magnanimously reserving the vengeance of their arms for those of their rulers who should dare to approach them in the field, with the instruments of war, and the bloody menaces of injustice and oppression.

Such a trial indeed awaited them; but these inimitable peasants, these heroes of a few valleys, were not to be dismayed. They united and confirmed their union by an oath; and if their enemy, as he declared, was determined to trample the audacious rustics under his feet, they would unawed (they said) await his coming, and rely on the protection of the Almighty. Their enemy came; and he came according to his language, in his council of war, to take some by surprise; to defeat others; to seize on many; to surround them all, and thus infallibly extirpate the whole nation. Three separate attacks were prepared, and the Duke Leopold himself conducted the main army; but he was met at the straits of Morgarten by this band of brothers. Like one of the avalanches of their mountains, they descended upon his host, and they beat back into confusion, defeat, and destruction, himself, his knights and his companions; the disdainful chivalry, who had little considered the formidable nature of men, who could bear to die, but not to be subdued; men, whom nature herself seemed to have thrown her arms around, to protect them from the invader, by encompassing them with her inaccessible mountains, her tremendous precipices, and all her stupendous masses of eternal winter.

The Three Forest Cantons, five and twenty years after the assertion of their own independence, admitted to their union a fourth canton; eighteen years after, a fifth; and soon a sixth, seventh, and an eighth.

These eight ancient cantons, whose union was thus gradually formed and perfected in the course of half a century from 1307, were afterwards joined by five other cantons; and the Helvetic confederacy was thus in the course of two centuries finally augmented to a union of thirteen.

But many were the difficulties and dangers through which the cantons had to struggle for their independence, and the strength of the oppressor was more than once collected to overwhelm, in the earlier periods of its existence, this virtuous confederacy. Seventy-one years after the defeat at Morgarten, another Duke of Austria, a second Leopold, with a second host of lords and knights, and their retainers, experienced once more a defeat near the walls of Sempach; but the battle was long suspended:

these Austrian knights were unwieldy indeed from their armour, but they were thereby inaccessible to the weapons of the Swiss; and as they, too, were brave, and deserved a better cause, they were not to be broken.

"I will open a passage," said the heroic Arnold, a knight of Underwalden: "provide for my wife and children, dear countrymen and confederates, honour my race." At these words he threw himself upon the Austrian pikes, buried them in his bosom, bore them to the ground with his own ponderous mass, and his companions rushed over his expiring body into the ranks of the enemy; a breach was made in this wall of mailed warriors, and the host was carried by assault.

Such were long the patriots of Switzerland; such they continued to the last. They received privileges and assistance from the empire, while the empire was jealous of the House of Austria. The paucity of their numbers was compensated by the advantages of their Alpine country. Their confederacies were artless and sincere; their lives rural and hardy; their manners simple and virtuous; eternally reminded of the necessity of a common interest, every peasant was a patriot, and every patriot a hero. Human prosperity must be always frail, human virtue imperfect; yet we can long pursue their history, though with some anxiety and occasional pain, on the whole, with a triumph of virtuous pleasure.

The most disagreeable characteristic of the people of Switzerland is their constant appearance as mercenaries in the armies of foreign countries.

In excuse of the Swiss, from the natural reproaches of the reasoners and moralists of surrounding nations, it may be observed, that in a poor country emigration is the natural resource of every man, whose activity and talents are above the ordinary level; that the profession of arms was the obvious choice of those who could pretend to no superiority but in the qualities that constitute the military character.

That, with respect to the Swiss magistracies they could have no right to prevent their youth from endeavouring to better their condition; and that, while part of the population was employed in the service of the different monarchies of Europe, a part which could always be recalled on any urgent occasion, Switzerland supported, in fact, at the expense of those monarchies, not at its own, the disciplined troops, which were necessary to its security, and might otherwise have been dangerous to its liberties. It may be added, that their fellow-citizens, who remained at home, were thus saved from all the vices and calamities which result from the redundant population of every bounded community.

No great legislator ever appeared in Switzerland. The speculatist will find no peculiar symmetry and grace in their systems, and may learn not to be too exclusive in his theories. Times and circumstances taught their own lessons; civil and religious establishments were imperfectly produced, roughly moulded, and slowly improved; and whatever might be their other merits, they were perfectly adequate to dispense the blessings of government and religion to a brave and artless people. The great difficulty with the inhabitants of Switzerland was at all times, no doubt, to judge how far they were to mix, on the principles of their own security, with the politics of their neighbours.

A second difficulty, to keep the states of their confederacy from the influence of foreign intrigue and private jealousy. A third, to make local and particular rights of property and prescription conform to the interests of the whole. And finally, to preserve themselves simple and virtuous. In a word, publicly and privately "to do justice, and to love mercy"; and again, "to keep themselves unspotted from the world." This was indeed a task which, perfectly to execute, was beyond the compass of human virtue. But with all their frailties and mistakes, their faults and follies, they existed for nearly five hundred years in a state of great comparative independence and honour, security and happiness; and they only perished amid the ruthless and unprincipled invasions of revolutionary France, and the general ruin of Europe.

IX. REFORMATION

You will be brought down to the history of the fourteenth and fifteenth centuries, and this era, you will perceive, was the era of inventions and discoveries.

I allude more particularly to, first, the art of turning linen into paper. Secondly, The art of printing. Thirdly, The composition and application of gunpowder, more especially to the purposes of war. Fourthly, The discovery, or at least the general application of the strange property of the magnetic needle to the purposes of navigation. The importance of such discoveries will be sufficiently obvious to your own reflections.

To each of these inventions and discoveries belongs an appropriate history highly deserving of curiosity (of more curiosity indeed than can now be gratified), and each strongly illustrative of the human mind; creeping on from hint to hint, like the Portuguese mariner from cape to cape, owing something to good fortune, but far more, and even that good fortune itself, to enterprise and perseverance.

As the study of the Dark Ages conducts us to the ages of inventions and discoveries, so do these last to the era which was marked by the Revival of Learning and the Reformation. All these periods mingle with each other, the prior with the succeeding one, and no line of demarcation can be traced to separate or define them; yet may they be known, each by its more prevailing characteristic of darkness, discovery, and progress; and as we are now supposed to have passed through the first two, we must next proceed to the last, the era of the Revival of Learning and the Reformation.

To this era we shall be best introduced by adverting to the general situation of Europe; more particularly by turning to the eastern portion of it: for we shall here be presented with a train of events, which, if we could but transport ourselves in imagination to this fearful period, would almost totally overpower us, by appearing to threaten once more, as in the irruption of the barbarians, the very civilization of society. For what are we here called to witness? The progress of the Turks; the terror of Bajazet; the danger of Constantinople; and then again the unexpected appearance of savages still more dreadful than the Turks, Tamerlane and his Tartars; the extraordinary achievements of these tremendous conquerors; afterwards the revival of the Ottoman power; and at last the destruction of the Eastern Empire, of Constantinople itself. . . .

In contemplating the final extinction of the Eastern Empire, it may be some consolation to us to think that Constantinople did not fall without a blow; that the city was not surrendered without a defence, which was worthy of this last representative of human greatness; that the emperor was a hero, and that amid the general baseness and degeneracy, he could collect around him a few at least, whom the Romans, whom the conquerors of mankind, might not have disdained to consider as their descendants.

Some melancholy must naturally arise at the termination of this memorable siege: the extinction of human glory, the distress, the sufferings, the parting agonies of this mistress of the world.

But such sentiments, though in themselves neither useless nor avoidable, it is in vain entirely to indulge. The Grecian as well as the Roman empire, and Constantinople, the last image of both, must for ever remain amongst the innumerable instances presented by history, to prove that it is in vain for a state to expect prosperity, in the absence of private and public virtue; and that every nation where the honourable qualities of the human character are not cultivated and respected, however fortified by ancient renown, prescriptive veneration, or established power, sooner or later must be levelled with the earth and trampled under the feet of the despoiler.

The fall of Constantinople became, when too late, a subject of the most universal terror and affliction to the rest of Europe.

Yet such is the intermingled nature of all good and evil, that some benefit resulted to the world from the calamities of the empire. Constantinople had always been the great repository of the precious remains of ancient genius. The Greeks had continued to pride themselves on their national superiority over the Barbarians of the west, and they celebrated, as exclusively their own, the great original masters of speculative wisdom and practical eloquence, the dramatists who could awaken all the passions of the heart, and the poets who could fire all the energies of the soul; Plato and Demosthenes, Sophocles and Euripides, Pindar and Homer. But though they admired, they could not emulate the models which they possessed. Century after century rolled away and these inestimable treasures, however valued by those who inherited them, were lost to mankind.

Yet as the fortunes of the Greek empire declined, the intercourse between Constantinople and the rest of Europe long contributed to the improvement of the latter; and the splendour of the Greek learning and philosophy, even as early as the thirteenth century, had touched with a morning ray the summits of the great kingdoms of the west. In the public schools and universities of Italy and Spain, France and England, distinguished individuals, like our own Bacon of Oxford, applied themselves with success to the study of science, and even of the Grecian literature. In the fourteenth century the generous emulation of Petrarch and his friends gave a distinct promise of the subsequent Revival of Learning. While the Turks were encircling with their toils, and closing round their destined prey, the scholars of the east were continually escaping from the terror of their arms or their oppression, and after the destruction of the metropolis of the east, it was in the west alone they could find either freedom or affluence, either dignity or leisure.

In the sack of Constantinople, amid the destruction of the libraries, one hundred and twenty-thousand manuscripts are said to have disappeared; but the scholars, and such of the manuscripts as escaped, were transferred to a new sphere of existence; to nations that were excited by a spirit of independence and emulation, and to states and kingdoms that were not retrograde and degenerating, as was the empire of the Greeks. The result was favourable to the world; like the idol of a pagan temple, the city of the east, though honoured and revered by succeeding generations, was still but an object of worship without life or use. When overthrown, however, and broken into fragments by a barbarian assailant, its riches were disclosed, and restored at once to activity and value.

This great event, the Revival of Learning, is a subject that from its importance and extent, may occupy indefinitely the liberal inquiry of the student. . . .

The leading observations on this subject will not escape your reflections. That Constantinople was attacked by the Arabs in the seventh and eighth centuries, and might have been swept away from the earth by any of the various Barbarians that infested it at an earlier time; when her scholars and her manuscripts could have had no effect on the rest of mankind, and when the seeds of future improvement would have fallen on a rocky soil, when no flower would have taken root, and no vegetation quickened. It is not easy to determine how long the darkness of Europe might in this case have continued, and how little we might have known of the sages, the poets, and the orators of antiquity.

Even the Latins themselves, after besieging and capturing Constantinople at the beginning of the thirteenth century, were in possession of the city, and of all that it could boast and display for sixty years, and in vain. Their rude and martial spirits were insensible to any wealth which glittered not in their garments or on their board; and warriors like these could little comprehend the value of those intellectual treasures that can give tranquillity to the heart and enjoyment to the understanding. But at a still later period, when the same city was once more and finally subdued by the Turks, the same western nations had been *prepared* for the due reception of what had to no purpose been placed within the reach of their more uncivilized forefathers; and then followed what has been justly denominated the Revival of Learning.

We may congratulate ourselves that the fall of the empire was postponed so long, and observe on this, as on other occasions, how different is the effect of the same causes and events at different periods of society.

Again, we may observe with admiration and with gratitude the curiosity and zeal of the human mind at this interesting era. The munificence of the patron and the labour of the scholar, the wealth of the great and the industry of the wise could not then have been more usefully directed; and if the readers of manuscripts are now more rare; if the rivals of the great scholars of the fifteenth and sixteenth centuries now seldom appear, and if our late Greek professor, the celebrated Porson, for instance, could no longer see the princes and potentates of the earth contending for the encouragement of his genius, it must be remembered that though men like these can never be without their use or their admiration, much of the service which they offer to society has been already rendered; that their office has been already, to a considerable degree, performed; that we have been for some time put in possession of the great classical authors; of the models of taste and the materials of thought, and that we must now labour to emulate what sufficiently for our improvement we already understand. We must reflect that were mankind not to exercise their unceremonious and often somewhat unfeeling criticism upon merit of every description, and applaud it precisely to the extent in which it contributes to their benefit, society would be soon retrograde, or at best but stationary, and each succeeding age would no longer be marked by its own appropriate enlargement of the boundaries of human knowledge.

A concluding observation seems to be that an obvious alteration has been made in the situation of men of genius. They need no longer hang upon the smiles of a patron; they need no longer debase the muses or themselves; the progress of human prosperity has given them a public who can appreciate and reward their labours; and even from that public if too slow in intellect, or too poor in virtue, an appeal has been opened to posterity by the invention of printing; and a Locke may see his volumes stigmatised and burnt, or a Newton the slow progress of his reasonings, with that tranquillity which is the privilege of genuine merit, and with that confident anticipation of the future, which may now be the enjoyment of all those, who are conscious that they have laboured well, and that they deserve to be esteemed the benefactors of mankind.

But you will not long be engaged in the histories I have mentioned, before you will perceive that, at the opening of the sixteenth century, a new and indeed fearful experiment was to be made upon mankind; a spirit not only of literary inquiry, but of *religious* inquiry, was to go forth; the minds of men were everywhere to be agitated on concerns the most dear to them, and the church of Rome was to be attacked, not only in its discipline, but in its doctrine; not only in its practice, but in its faith.

Opposition to the papacy in these points, or what was then called heresy, had indeed always existed. The student will be called upon, as he reads the preceding history, to notice and respect the more obvious representatives of this virtuous struggle of the human mind, the Albigenses, our own Wycliffe and the Lollards, as well as the Hussites in Bohemia. But as it was in vain that the works of literature were placed within the reach of the Franks, who first captured Constantinople, so the doctrines of truth, and the rights of religious inquiry were to little purpose presented to the consideration of the nations of Europe by the more early reformers; "the light shone in the darkness, but the darkness comprehended it not." At the opening, however, of the sixteenth century, the condition of Europe was in some respects essentially improved; and it now seemed possible that they who asserted the cause of the human mind in its dearest interests might at least obtain attention, and probably see their laudable exertions crowned with success.

But whatever might be the virtues or the success of distinguished individuals in establishing their opinions, it was but too certain that a reformation in the doctrines of religion could not be accomplished without the most serious evils; these might be indeed entirely overbalanced by the good that was to result, but the most afflicting consequences must necessarily in the first place ensue. . . .

Whenever the human mind exercises its powers with freedom, different men will take different views of the same subject; they will draw different conclusions, even where the materials presented to their judgment are the same. Not only this, but in points of religious doctrine, from the very awfulness of the subject, the mind scarcely presumes to exercise its faculties; and in *these* disquisitions men have no longer the chance (whatever it may be) which they have on *other* subjects, of arguing themselves into agreement. Again, the evidence which the reformers had to produce to each other for their respective opinions was their respective interpretation of one or many different texts of Scripture, of one or many different passages in the writings of the fathers.

Now, of all such evidence it must be observed, that it never, from the very nature of it, could be demonstrative. In mathematical questions, where the relations of quantity are alone concerned, a dispute can be completely terminated; because from wrong premises or false reasoning, a contradiction can be at last shown to result; some impossibility appears; the greater is equal to the less, or the less to the greater.

The same may be said of many parts of the sciences, because a question can here always be asked which admits of a precise answer, and is, at the same time, decisive of the contest—What is the fact?—what says the experiment?

But when a question is to depend on the interpretation of texts and passages in Scripture, the case is totally altered; for of the different meanings that can be affixed, no one can be shown to be (strictly speaking) impossible. They may be shown to be more or less reasonable, but no more: the scale of evidence here is reasonableness; metaphysically speaking, is probability. Men cannot be proved in these, as in mathematical disquisitions, to be totally right or totally wrong; they cannot be left at once without an argument or without an opponent. A reasoner on such subjects may from inferiority of judgment, or what is called perversity of judgment, or any other cause, adopt that meaning which is the less sound and just of any two that may be proposed to him; but if he does, he can never, by any consequent impossibility, be absolutely compelled to admit the more reasonable opinion of his opponent.

It is very true that this probable evidence is sufficient for men to reason and act upon; but it is not sufficient to preclude the possibility of dispute; and this is all that is here contended for. When the nature of the evidence is this of probability, the varying powers of judgment and the ready passions of mankind have full liberty to interfere; men may be more or less reasonable, as these causes direct. No such interference is possible in discussions that concern matters of experiment and fact, and the relations of quantity.

We have, therefore, no sects or parties in mathematics, but they abound in every other department of human opinion.

We have now therefore, to present to the consideration of the student two observations; they are these: not only, in the first place, that the human mind was naturally intolerant; but that, in the second place, the evidence that could be laid before it never, from the nature of it, could be demonstrative; and that, therefore, this intolerance had full opportunity to act. . . .

It was not only that disputes could not be necessarily terminated even when exercised upon the great and proper topics of debate, but it was clear, both from the nature of the human mind and from the testimony of history, that men, when awakened to the consideration of religious subjects, would assuredly engage in the most subtle metaphysical inquiries, and, by their vain efforts to know and to teach more than the Scriptures had taught them (or than, it may be presumed, the Almighty Creator intended their faculties to comprehend), would involve themselves and their followers in disputes, which it would be more than ever impossible to set at rest by reasoning, and which, on that very account, would be only the more calculated to exasperate their passions.

In addition to these considerations, there is another; we must reflect on the situation of the world at this particular epoch.

Europe had no doubt improved during several of the preceding centuries, and was even rapidly improving at the time. But it must still be noted, that literature had made as yet little progress, science still less; men had not been softened by the fine arts, and the peaceful pleasures which they afford; they had not been humanized by much intercourse with each other; martial prowess was their virtue; superstitious observances their religion. In this situation, they were on a sudden to have their passions roused, and their intellectual talents exercised upon subjects which require to their adjustment all the virtues and all the improvement of which the human character is capable.

On these accounts the prospect for mankind on the opening of the Reformation was very awful; it was evident much misery must result from the natural intolerance of the mind, from the materials with which that intolerance was now to be supplied, and from the general ignorance and rudeness of society. . . .

We have hitherto endeavoured to estimate the evils to which the breaking out of the Reformation would give occasion, by stating its more natural and appropriate effects upon the human mind; but the religious principle which was thus to be awakened was sure to intermingle itself in all *earthly* concerns; it was sure to give names to parties, to multiply afresh the causes of irritation and offence, and to add new restlessness and motion to the politics of the world.

Again, there was even an inherent and inevitable difficulty in the subject, by whatever unexpected influence of moderation and reason mankind had chosen to be controlled. The Roman hierarchy were the spiritual instructors of the people, and as such had ecclesiastical revenues. But it was evident, that if there arose a set of men who disputed the doctrines of that hierarchy, these last would no longer think it reasonable that such revenues should be so applied; they would represent them as devoted only to the unrighteous purposes of superstition and error; they would insist upon at least a share, if not the whole, for the support of themselves, while engaged in the propagation of truth and genuine Christianity. The established teachers would, therefore, be disturbed in their possessions, deprived of their benefices, some perhaps thrown naked and defenceless into the world at advanced periods of age and infirmity. Such mutations of property, it was but too clear, could neither be attempted nor executed without violence: and violence so exercised, could not but be attended by the most furious animosities, disturbance, and calamity.

Again, when these revenues had been converted to the support of the first reformed preachers, these were likely to be in their turn opposed by new and succeeding descriptions of religious inquirers; the same reasoning would, therefore, again be urged, the same struggle be repeated, the same force be employed. On the whole, therefore, statesmen, and princes, and warriors were sure from the first, to be engaged in all these disputes, and to kindle in the general flame; and controversies of religion were sure to be decided, like the ordinary contests of mankind, by the sword—by the sword, indeed, but amid a conflict of passions rendered more than ever blind and sanguinary from the materials which were now added of more than human obstinacy, intrepidity, and rancour.

Such were the evils that were to be expected at the breaking out of the Reformation, from the intolerance of men, from the nature of the evidence that could be produced to them in their new subjects of dispute, from the particular metaphysical turn which these disputes would probably take, from the unimproved state of society in Europe, from the intermixture of the earthly politics of the world with religious concerns, and from the inevitable and difficult question of the disposal of the ecclesiastical revenues.

But what was then the benefit that mankind was likely to receive which might compensate for the evils to which they were to be thus exposed? The benefit that it was probable would result was above all price; it was this: that they who disputed the doctrines of the Romish church, however they might for a time appeal to the pope or general councils, must at length appeal to the Bible itself; that the sacred text would be therefore examined, criticised, and understood; that however violent or unjust the force which the hierarchy or the civil magistrate might attempt to exercise, still, as the human mind was capable of the steadiest resistance, when animated by the cause of truth; as men were equal to the contempt of imprisonment, tortures, or death, for the sake of their religious opinions; as history had borne sufficient testimony to the exalted constancy of our nature in these respects;—*that therefore,* the reformers must in all probability *succeed* in establishing a purer faith, and must at all events contribute to improve both the doctrines and the conduct of their opponents; that from the general fermentation which would ensue, it could not *but* happen that the *Bible would be opened*; that doctrines would no longer be taken upon authority; that religion would no longer consist so much in vain ceremonies and passive ignorance; that devotion would become a reasonable sacrifice; and that the gospel would, in fact, be a second time promulgated to an erring and sinful world.

Now, what further benefit might attend this emancipation of the human mind from its spiritual thraldom, it might have been difficult at the time properly to estimate. But this new gift of Christianity to mankind was a blessing in itself sufficient to outweigh all temporal calamities, of whatever extent. To be the humble instruments, under Divine Providence, of imparting such a benefit to the world, was the virtuous ambition, the pious hope, of the early reformers. It was this, that gave such activity to their exertions, such inflexibility to their fortitude. This sacred ardour, this holy energy in the cause of religious truth, is the remaining principle which, in conjunction with those I have mentioned, will be found to have actuated mankind during the ages we are now to consider. As the principles before mentioned gave occasion to all that was dark and afflicting in the scene, so did the principle *now* mentioned give occasion to all that was bright, and cheering, and elevating to the soul; united, they may serve, when followed up through their remote as well as immediate effects, to explain, as I conceive, the events of the Reformation, and for some ages all the more important part of the history of Europe.

x. REFORMATION

"THE ROMAN CATHOLICS," says Robertson,* "as their system rested on the decisions of an infallible judge, never doubted that truth was on their side, and openly called on the civil power to repel the impious and heretical innovators, who had risen up against it. The Protestants, no less confident that their doctrine was well founded, required, with equal ardour, the princes of their party to check such as presumed to impugn or to oppose it. Luther, Calvin, Cranmer, Knox, the founders of the reformed churches in their respective countries, inflicted, as far as they had power and opportunity, the same punishments, which were de-

* William Robertson (1721–93), Scottish historian, whose long-enduring fame dates from *The History of Charles* V (1769).—ED.

nounced against their own disciples by the church of Rome, upon such
as called in question any article of their creed. To their followers, and
perhaps their opponents, it would have appeared a symptom of diffidence
in the goodness of their cause, or an acknowledgment that it was not well
founded, if they had not employed in its defence all those means which
it was supposed truth had a right to employ."

This passage from Robertson I conceive to be, in the main, just, though
I think Luther might have been favourably distinguished from Calvin
and others. There are passages in his writings, with regard to the interference of the magistrate in religious concerns, that do him honour; but
he was favourably situated, and lived not to see the temporal sword at his
command. He was never tried. . . .

Calvin, too, must be thought a man of religion and goodness, according to his own melancholy notions of religion and goodness; yet could
this celebrated reformer, as is well known, cause Servetus to be condemned to death for heresy; and because the unhappy man had reiterated his shrieks, when condemned, at the very idea of the fire, in
which he was to perish, Calvin could find, when writing in the retirement of his closet, a subject not only for his comment, but his censure
and even his ridicule (at least his contempt), in these afflicting agonies
of affrighted nature. . . .

I cannot enter into any discussion of the different degrees of intolerance which different sects have exhibited. It is possible, it might be
naturally expected, that the Protestant would be less deeply criminal
than the Roman Catholic, or rather the papist; but I cannot now stay
to appreciate this relative criminality, or point out its causes. I speak of the
guilt of all, of mankind, of human nature, of the inherent intolerance
of the human heart, be the bosom in which it beats, of whatever character or description, pagan or Christian, Protestant or Roman Catholic.

Much improvement has no doubt taken place in society on this
momentous subject; much, since the first breaking out of the Reformation. . . .

The misfortune still is that men honour the doctrines of toleration with
their lips, while they seem not aware that their heart is far from them.*
The principles of intolerance, that is, the principles of their nature, still
maintain their hold, though they may be awed and tamed and civilized,
and reduced to assume forms less frightful and destructive in these later
ages. . . .

I must now recur to the second observation which I proposed to your
consideration. It was this, not only that disputes would necessarily arise

* Smyth was doubtless thinking of the civil disabilities imposed on English Catholics
and Jews. Catholic emancipation came in 1829; not until 1858 were the Jews relieved
finally of all civil disabilities.—ED.

from the particular constitution of the human mind, but that from the very nature of the evidence on which points of doctrine must necessarily rest, they never could be expected to appear exactly terminated; that this evidence could never, as in mathematical subjects, be demonstrative; that it might be fitted to convince a candid inquirer after truth, but could never bear down the mind and insuperably extort conviction. The history of the Reformation, like all prior ecclesiastical history, confirms this remark. . . .

My third observation was, that it might be expected that the disputes of mankind would immediately involve them in the most inextricable labyrinths of metaphysical subtlety, and that most serious evils must inevitably be the consequence.

Before the time of the Reformation, the religious animosities of mankind had always turned on speculative points of doctrine; they did so afterwards.

The first reformers had scarcely attacked with success such doctrines and corruptions of the church of Rome as were more or less destructive of morality and real religion, but they plunged into discussions of the most mysterious and impenetrable nature. This will be but too obvious to those who read even the history of the Reformation; it will be only the more obvious to those who make themselves acquainted with the theological writings of the reformers.

The celebrated book written by Father Paul,* the History of the Council of Trent, . . . may serve as a general specimen of this part of the subject. It may not be possible to read the whole of it, but of the eight books which constitute the work, the second more particularly, and the latter part of the eighth, should at least be read. Observation should be made on the nature of those Protestant tenets, which were drawn out for examination, or rather for condemnation by the Roman Catholic Fathers. Their abstruse nature will be very apparent, and the reader cannot but be reminded of the controversial discussions that he has before seen in Ecclesiastical history.

The tendency, therefore, of theological inquiries and disquisitions, to run into the speculations of metaphysical divinity, is thus visible, both before and after the Reformation, and may now be considered as quite a characteristic of the human mind.

I observed, too, that disputes of this nature were not the more likely, on account of their real difficulty, to be treated with calmness and pronounced upon with hesitation; but that the contrary would be the event; and that these very points of difficulty were those for which men would contend with the greater fury, and on which they would decide with the more ready dogmatism.

* Paolo Sarpi (1552–1623), Italian historian; he was a Servite friar.—ED.

Now, on looking at the history of the Reformation, abundant evidence will be found to substantiate this assertion. By whatever mysterious abstractions, by whatever controversial subtleties, by whatever unaccountable observances and ceremonies the faith of any sect was distinguished, followers were never wanting to glory in those particular characteristics of discipline or doctrine; for the sake of them to submit to any privations, to march to battle, to languish in imprisonment, or to expire in the flames.

The great orator of Rome was compelled to sigh over the inanity of all human contentions. Something of a similar sentiment may, perhaps, pass across the mind, when we survey the volumes of the Council of Trent; the monument of the unavailing warfare of the learning and ability of the times; but we may sigh more deeply when we consider, that among the thousands and the ten thousands, that suffered persecution and death, most of them were guilty only of some supposed error in speculative doctrine; of taking the literal, or figurative sense, of some passages in Scripture; of interpreting a text in a manner different from its accepted sense; or of drawing, from a comparison of several texts, a different conclusion from that which they were understood to warrant. The real presence in the Eucharist, for instance, was the great point on which the lives of men depended. . . .

A due sense of religion with *us*, takes a different, and surely a more reasonable direction; and the awful *reserve* which it prescribes, in every public allusion to such sacred subjects, and to the mysteries of our faith, the Incarnation for instance, it can be no wish of mine, even for a moment, or however innocently, to violate or offend. But to return. Men, it will be said, are not now tormented, or deprived of life, for metaphysical distinctions in divinity. It may be so: we shall, however, do well to note, as I have before observed, what the nature of the human mind really is. Thus much may be certainly affirmed, that there never was, and there never will be, a time when the multitude will not suppose that all these questions are perfectly intelligible. The real and matured scholar, indeed, may hesitate, while he assents to particular points, but the multitude have no difficulties: the mazes which look intricate and dark to the man of sense and learning, are to them without a thorn, and even arrayed in all the sunshine of heaven.

Such was, indeed, the spectacle sometimes displayed during the progress, and long after and before the Reformation. Erasmus might distinguish and refine, the excellent Chillingworth might debate and decide, decide and debate again, and lose and disquiet himself in the shifting and uncertain shadows of his learning. St. Augustine might confess with what labour, with what sighs, the truth could be at last elicited. No such unintelligible embarrassments disquieted the vulgar, or men who were like the vulgar; to be dogmatic it was only necessary *then*, as it is *now*, to be sufficiently ignorant or unfeeling; and Europe every where exhibited a proof, which will on every occasion be repeated, that the mass of mankind, though they understand not the controversies of theologians, can easily be inflamed about them, can readily seize upon badges of distinction, and invent terms of reproach for the purposes of mutual hostility; find no difficulty in associating with their own vindictive passions, the cause of the Most High; and in this frightful state of presumption and blindness, stand prepared for any outrage that can be proposed to them, and bid defiance alike to every expostulation of reason, and precept of religion.

It is on these accounts that the statesmen of the world are always so justly alarmed, when they foresee the interference of the religious principle in the concerns, over which they preside; and the true Christian is more than ever compelled to examine the religious spirit, and the practical precepts of any denomination of Christians, by the great criterion, of their consistence with morality; and if he once discerns that this spirit, and these precepts, oppose themselves to our moral feelings, to that great religion which the Almighty has, from the first, written upon the hearts of all men, that great original code of mercy and justice, to which our Saviour Himself so constantly appeals in His parables and discourses; if he once discovers that there are any speculative, or practical conclusions, which clash with these great laws of the Moral Governor of the world, such conclusions will need with him no further refutation: he will be at no loss to determine from their very nature, that they must be derived from some misapprehension, or some exaggeration, or some exclusive consideration of particular passages in Scripture, and that, assuredly, they are not sanctioned by the authority of revelation. . . .

I am now arrived at the last of the observations which I proposed to your consideration—That to compensate for these evils, particular benefits might probably result to mankind from the rise and progress of the Reformation.

On recurring to the history, and to the facts, these benefits will be found such as might have been expected; such as have been already described as likely to ensue. The Bible was opened; those particular pretensions and doctrines of the Roman Catholic Church, which were so destructive of the morality and religion of mankind, were successfully combated; the chain of authority was broken, and the appeal was transferred, from popes and general councils, to the Scriptures themselves.

Such were the immediate, the invaluable blessings that resulted. But a distinction is now to be made between those good effects that more immediately, and those that more *remotely* followed the Reformation; between those that Luther and the first reformers *meant* to produce, and *saw* produced, and those which they did not see, and might not perhaps mean to produce.

Now the first we have already mentioned—the opening of the Bible —the establishment of a purer faith. We must therefore next advert to the latter. The first reformers, while they were struggling to deliver themselves and mankind from the authority of the church of Rome, asserted the right of private judgment.

When this emancipation from the authority of the pope was once effected, it was natural for them to lay down, in their turn, what they believed to be the doctrines of religious truth. It was natural for them to conceive, that those who opposed their new creeds, so evidently deduced as they thought, from the sacred Scriptures, misused, and dangerously misused, that right of private judgment which had thus been procured. It was natural for them to call for the interposition of legislative authority, for the assistance of the secular arm, and to endeavour to become, in their turn, a new church of Rome; though certainly very distinguishable in religious doctrine, and in moral practice.

But when the right of private judgment had been, by the reformers, once happily exerted, it was in vain to prescribe limits to its activity. A spirit of inquiry had arisen, and who was to stay its progress? Who was to define the boundaries within which the human heart was to hope and fear—within which the human understanding was to doubt and discover? The earthly means by which this second emancipation of the human mind was effected, this second emancipation which the first reformers did not mean to produce, are sufficiently evident. They were found in the Revival of Learning and the invention of printing: these secured the victory that had been obtained over the Roman see. The reformers had every where encouraged the study of the Greek language, and the meaning of the texts of the New Testament was thus brought within the comprehension of the more intelligent part of society. Men of education (though laymen) could no longer distinguish between themselves and their spiritual teachers. With the same longings after immortality, the same terrors of the future, the same revelation proposed to them, and the means of interpreting its doctrines and its precepts now common to both, no further distinction remained between them—between the laymen and the priest—none but that of superiority of learning in the clerical character, or greater purity of manners; no further spiritual influence but such as did and ought to belong to more regular and extensive erudition, and more settled and anxious piety.

The action and reaction of this freedom of private judgment has been productive of the most salutary consequences both to the clergy and the laity. The two characters have been more assimilated to each other, materially to the benefit of both. This is that silent and still more important reformation which slowly succeeded to the more visible, and to the important Reformation in the days of Luther, of Calvin, and of Cranmer; and it is not the less real because it may or may not stand acknowledged in the creeds or legislative acts of the different churches or states of Christendom.

But the same freedom of the mind which had been successfully asserted by the reformers in religious subjects extended itself afterwards to every department of human inquiry. The nature and different provinces of civil and ecclesiastical power were examined and ascertained; and the temporal as well as spiritual concerns of mankind were delivered from their long and injurious bondage.

The world of science too was now thrown open, and men had no longer to be checked in their curiosity or debarred the exercise of their natural faculties, while investigating the laws of nature, by the terrors of the Inquisition or the disapprobation of their temporal and spiritual rulers. The same right of private judgment came at length to be exercised on the more abstruse subjects of speculative inquiry, on the original principles of metaphysics and morals. Even the evidences of religion itself became subjects of discussion, and they who had not the means of investigating truth themselves, the illiterate and the busy, might be consoled by perceiving that such means were amply in the possession of others, and that belief in authority might now be reasonable, when no authority was evidently acknowledged but the authority of truth.

Lastly, it must be observed, that although the religious principle mingled itself most unhappily with the temporal politics of Europe, its interference was in some respects productive of the most permanent and beneficial effects. The reformers, through all their different varieties of opinion, were necessarily (till they became themselves the established sect) the friends of religious liberty. But with the rights of religious liberty, the rights of civil liberty were naturally connected; the cause, therefore, of civil freedom was always the cause of the reformers; a cause most dear to them while they were the inferior sect, and more congenial to them, whenever they became the superior.

It is not easy to estimate the salutary influence that came thus to operate upon the different constitutions of civil polity in Europe, particularly in our own island. It is not too much to say, that had it not been for this animating spark, the civil rights of mankind, on the decline of the feudal system, would have expired under the increasing power which the sovereign at that critical period every where obtained.

The Reformation, when considered as it ought to be, in all these points of view, may be reasonably represented as one of the greatest events, or rather as *the* greatest event, in modern history. To the Reformation we

owe, not only the destruction of the temporal and spiritual thraldom of
the papacy, the great evil with which Europe had to struggle, but to the
Reformation we may be said to owe all the improvements which afterwards took place, not only in religion, but in legislation, in science, and
in our knowledge of the faculties and operations of the human mind;
in other words, all that can distinguish the most enlightened from the
darkest periods of human society.

xi. FRANCE—CIVIL AND RELIGIOUS WARS

THE LESSON which may, on the whole, be derived from this first half of
the sixteenth century, is the folly, the crime, of attempting foreign conquest: this is the leading observation I have to offer. Charles VIII of
France had descended into Italy, Louis XII must therefore do the same;
so must Francis I and Henry II. The honour of the French nation was, it
seems, engaged.

But Spain, which was becoming the great rival state in Europe, chose
also, like France, to be, as she conceived, powerful and renowned; Ferdinand therefore, and Charles V and afterwards Philip II, were to waste,
with the same ignorant ferocity, the lives and happiness of their subjects: and for what purpose? Not to keep the balance of Europe undisturbed; not to expel the French from Italy, and to abstain from all projects of conquest themselves; but on the contrary, by rushing in, to contend for the whole, or a part of the plunder.

The Italians, in the meantime, whose unhappy country was thus made
the arena on which these unprincipled combatants were to struggle with
each other, adopted what appeared to them the only resource,—that of
fighting the one against the other—if possible to destroy both; leaguing
themselves sometimes with France, sometimes with Spain, and suffering from each power every possible calamity; while they were exhibiting, in their own conduct, all the degrading arts of duplicity and intrigue.

A more wretched and disgusting picture of mankind cannot well be displayed. All the faults of which man, in his social state is capable; opposite
extremes of guilt united; all the vices of pusillanimity, and all the crimes
of courage.

The miseries and degradation of Italy have never ceased since the fall
of the Roman empire. The great misfortune of this country has always
been its divisions into petty states, a misfortune that was irremediable.
No cardinal made into a sovereign could ever be expected to combine its
discordant parts into a free government; and unless this was done, nothing

was done: could this, indeed, have been effected, the Italians might have been virtuous and happy.

Artifice, and a policy proverbially faithless, were vain expedients against the great monarchies of Europe. But while Italy was to be thus destroyed by these unprincipled despoilers, what in the meantime was to be the consequence to these very monarchies? In *Spain*, the real sources of power neglected; immense revenue and no wealth; possessions multiplied abroad, and no prosperous provinces at home; the strength of the country exhausted in maintaining a powerful army, not for the purposes of defence, but of tyranny and injustice; and the whole system of policy, in every part, and on every occasion, a long and disgusting train of mistake and guilt.

In France, the same neglect of the real sources of strength and happiness; the produce of the land, and labour of the community employed in military enterprises; the genius of the nobles made more and more warlike; military fame, and the intrigues of gallantry (congenial pursuits), converted into the only objects of anxiety and ambition; licentiousness everywhere the result, in the court and in the nation; the power of the crown unreasonably strengthened; the people oppressed with taxes, their interests never considered; the energies of this great country misdirected and abused; and the science of public happiness (except, indeed, in the arts of amusement and splendour) totally unknown or disregarded.

France and Spain, therefore, concur with Italy in completing the lesson that is exhibited to our reflection: ambition and injustice have their victims in the countries that are invaded and destroyed; and have alike their victims in those very invaders and destroyers. Better governments in all, or in any, would have made these evils less; and good governments are thus, in all times and situations of the world, the *common* interest of every state, as connected with its neighbours, and of every prince and people, as concerned in their own individual happiness.

I now proceed to make some general remarks on the latter part of the century. The remaining half comprehends, in French history, the era of the civil and religious wars, an era that is peculiarly interesting; and the great difficulty is to prevent our minds from being overpowered and bewildered by the variety of subjects which present themselves to our examination.

The events are striking; the actors splendid; the interests important; and could we see and understand the scene, with the rapidity with which we do the dramas of Otway or of Shakespeare, the effect would be even more powerful, and the impression more lasting. . . .

I have first to remark, that these dreadful wars of the latter half of the sixteenth century were of a civil as well as of a religious nature; they are called the Civil and Religious Wars.

I mentioned, in my lecture on the Reformation, how easily the concerns of religion would mingle with the politics of the world; how readily each would act and react upon the other; the rage and rancour that must ensue. This was so much the case in the instance of France, that men appeared almost to lose the common attributes of their nature. Some of the leading particulars seem to have been as follows.

The great families in France, though their free constitution was no more, though they might now be controlled by any prince of ability, who dispensed his favours with care, and suffered none to become too powerful, were still in themselves perfectly able to disturb the state and to shake the monarchy, whenever a man of great enterprise and genius appeared among them, or whenever a weak prince was seated on the throne.

Francis I, though formed to be the idol of Frenchmen, still carried on a regular system of inspection over his nobles and their proceedings in every place and province of France. "Beware," he said, on his death-bed, to his son, Henry II,—"beware of the Guises!" His sagacity was but too well shown by subsequent events. The historians . . . give a very clear description of the court and of the great men who were ready to contend for power immediately on his decease, and during the reign of his successor, Henry II. The chances of confusion were already very sufficient, but they were still further increased when Francis II came to the throne, who was not only a minor and of no capacity, but the queen-mother was Catherine de Medicis. Charles IX was, again, a minor, and again, her son; and she was mother even to Henry III, who next mounted the throne after Henry II and Francis II.

The family of Guise, connected by marriage with the reigning family, produced distinguished men, two more particularly of great genius, and of the most aspiring ambition. These were the two men whom Francis I had dreaded. The Prince of Condé, as a prince of the blood, conceived that the administration naturally belonged to him; the Constable Montmorency, with the ancient families, had the same pretensions; and the queen-mother had unhappily resolved to hold the reins of government herself, and therefore endeavoured to rule all competitors for authority by dividing and opposing them to each other.

As Catherine was a woman of great natural ability, and as Charles IX and Henry III were far from being devoid of it, it is probable that the authority of the crown might still have maintained itself, and preserved a tolerable state of peace and order; but it happened most unfortunately that the Prince of Condé was a Protestant, the constable a Roman Catholic; the court and the Guises were of the Roman Catholic persuasion also; and the people had been inflamed against each other by the natural progress of religious differences. The Prince of Condé, therefore, had only to state the grievances of the Calvinists, and to be their leader, the Duke of Guise to assert the supposed rights of the Roman Catholics, and to declare himself their chief, and long wars of the most exterminating fury were sure to be the consequence. . . .

The contests, therefore, of civil and religious hate were now to begin. I cannot relate the facts; I have to observe, therefore, generally,—first, that the commencement of wars, particularly of civil wars, must always be interesting to every reader of reflection. We may turn away our eyes, when the sword has been once drawn, from the crimes and the horrors that ensue; but till the first fatal act of hostility has been committed, we examine with care, we follow with anxiety, the steps of the contending parties, and we bless in silence those real patriots, if any there be, who have breathed, however vainly, the sounds of forbearance and kindness; who have expostulated, explained, conciliated, and laboured, if possible, to procure a pause. . . .

If there be any principle necessary to mankind, it is that of the civil obedience of the subject, that principle by which the single mind of the ruler is able to direct and control the physical strength of millions: if there be any one good that is totally invaluable to our helpless condition, it is religion. But there are seasons in the history of mankind when we are tempted almost to wish that men could be disrobed at once of all the distinctions and ties which belong to their social state, and thrown again into the woods to take the chance of savage existence, rather than be suffered so frightfully to abuse, so intolerably to waste, the best materials of their happiness, and the first blessings of their nature.

It is on this account that the wars of faction, and more particularly, as in this case, of religious faction, should be most thoroughly studied; that, as much as possible, not only the nature of ambition should be known, but the temptations of the religious principle, when interfering in the affairs of the world, should be understood; that, as much as possible, mankind may be put upon their guard, not only against their rulers, but against themselves; not only against their own vices, but against the most virtuous tendencies of their nature. . . .

The great leading conclusions to be deduced from these wars are much the same as have been already drawn from the prior history of the Reformation; as,

1st. The slowness with which the doctrines of toleration are comprehended even by the best men.

Forbearance to the Protestants is never argued upon any general principles, such as the right of private judgment; but upon the inefficacy of force and punishment to convince men of their errors. Good men, even if sufficiently enlightened, could probably then venture on no other language, and indeed naturally adopted the argument that admits of no answer.

The parties themselves seem always to have supposed each that the other was abominable in the sight of the Creator, and that as such they were to be punished and subdued by all who had any proper sense of religion. . . .

2ndly. The difficulties in the way of concord were the same as they have always been.

The questions to be settled were the exercise of public worship, the payment of tithes to the ministers of the prevailing communion, the admission to places of honour and influence; and in these civil wars the Calvinists were so inferior in strength to their opponents, that even the education of their children, the rites of burial and marriage, the equal participation of the laws, and other similar considerations, were all subjects of contention. But though always defeated in the field, though always inferior in number and resources to their opponents, they were never totally subdued. It is said that in number they were not above one-tenth of the whole.

Before the civil wars began, they were dragged to the stake; but during them, they continually obtained edicts which rendered their existence more tolerable. Like their gallant and virtuous leader, the Admiral Coligny, they never despaired of the common cause, and were thus enabled to procure something like forbearance and respect from their unenlightened opponents. The sort of success that they obtained, and the injuries they inflicted on their adversaries, are calculated to teach mankind not only that men cannot be influenced in their religious opinions by force, but that every sect is to be managed (even on the mere principles of worldly policy) with proper deference and kindness; that the objects clamoured for by the bigoted are not worth the risk of such contention as they might occasion; that men, whether right or wrong, and with or without success, will die in support of what they think the truth; and that they may often be enabled thus to die, amid the calamities and slaughter of their persecutors.

3dly. There were conferences of divines to settle religious differences, as in other countries, during and after the Reformation, and with the same ill success. . . .

When indeed Henry IV afterwards announced that he was ready to be converted, if proper arguments could be afforded to him, the reasonings of the Roman Catholic Divines were successful, and they demonstrated to him the doctrines of auricular confession, the invocation of saints, and the spiritual authority of the Papal see. These it seems were the points on which the scruples of the king had happened to fall. On the doctrine of transubstantiation he had no difficulty.

All history thus shows, what all theory announces, that speculative truth, particularly in religious questions, can be left with best advantage to the silent influence and ultimate decision, not of creeds and councils, but of free inquiry.

Again, there appeared in these religious wars the same want of good faith that has so often marked the conduct of the ruling sect; the same inextinguishable resentment; the same unwillingness to be satisfied, while their opponents were suffered to appear in any state, but that of total degradation and submission; and then the next lesson is this, that the whole of the history bears testimony to the impolicy of a temperament so unjust and so irreligious.

Even the massacre of St. Bartholomew extinguished not the evil which the court meant to remedy; it only made their anxieties, and perhaps even their dangers, the greater.

Thus far the religious wars of France seem to exhibit the same features and lessons of instruction that are presented by other religious wars, whatever be the ruling sect, the Roman Catholic or the Protestant; but in one respect these were distinguishable from all others that Europe has witnessed; their more than usual horrors; their singularly atrocious crimes; in none others were all the charities and obligations of mankind so violated, and all the common principles of mercy and justice so outraged and set at nought. This seems to indicate not only the necessity of a free government to humanize men, but also that the members of the Roman Catholic communion are of all other sects the most intolerant and cruel.

The reason is that they are more under the influence of their spiritual guides; and every sect will be found more or less intolerant and cruel, as this is more or less the case. A spiritual director, like every human being, abuses the power that is given him. The more unlimited the power, the greater the abuse; and whether it be the Brahmin of the east, the Calvinistic preacher in Scotland, or the Roman Catholic priest in France and Spain, the effect proceeds from the same cause, and is proportioned to it.

The spiritual guide, in these cases, generally deceives himself, and always deceives his follower, by considering the cause in which his passions have got engaged as the cause of the Deity. And yet strange as it may seem, it appears from this very history that men may sometimes teach themselves the same identification of their own religious opinions with the cause of the Deity, by the workings of their own mind, even *without* the interference of any spiritual instructor. . . .

Generally with the sanction of the deliberations and reasonings of some priest, or confessor, was the life of Henry III taken away, and that of Henry IV several times attempted.

Even the enthusiasm of Ravaillac, who at last assassinated Henry IV, though it reached insanity, was religious insanity; so careful should all religious men be never to lose sight for a moment of their moral obligations; if they once do, it is impossible to say what point of enthusiasm, or even of guilt, they may not reach.

But not only were murders of this nature committed, but a massacre (I allude to the massacre of St. Bartholomew), a massacre of every person of consequence that belonged to the inferior sect, under cover of a reconciliation, was actually both conceived, and almost entirely perpetrated; and that, by the first people of rank in France, regularly deliberating, contriving, and executing, slowly and systematically, what is not pardoned to human nature even in her wildest transports of sudden fury and brutal folly.

With all the latitude that can be imagined for civil and religious hatred, nothing but evidence totally irresistible could reconcile the mind to the belief of such an astonishing project of guilt and horror.

The entire and total separation and hatred that existed between the two religious sects must have been carried to an extent now inconceivable, or such a scheme could never have been devised, and still less executed. . . .

The Protestant part of Europe at the time, and posterity ever since, have vindicated the rights of insulted reason and religion. It is some melancholy consolation to observe, that even the abominable court itself was, *at first*, obliged to pretend, and their apologists since, that they only anticipated a projected insurrection of the Huguenots. Charles IX seems never to have known health or cheerfulness again: he had pages to sing him to sleep; and he at last died, ere his youth had well passed away, lost and destroyed in body as in mind, and, if possible, an object of compassion. . . .

Such seem the general reflections that may occur to us while we are engaged in earlier parts of the annals of this period. But in reading the history of these civil and religious wars, you must observe, that though for *some* time the Roman Catholics are united with the court in opposition to the Protestants, yet at length a *new* scene opens, and the contest is carried on against the Protestants, by the Roman Catholics *themselves*, with, or *without* the assistance of the court. The celebrated combination, called the "League," makes its appearance (a combination independent of the crown); and the result is, that the throne itself is at last shaken, and the crown nearly overpowered by positive rebellion. . . .

Here . . . is one of those instances in history, which are to teach men very carefully to watch over the erection of any power unknown to the constitution of their country—any power which may be brought into competition with the existing authorities. How careful they must be on this point, if they really mean only to improve that constitution, and do not mean eventually to overthrow it. This is my first observation, but the history of this League exhibits, among many lessons, another that may be mentioned.

The intolerance of the Roman Catholics, and the zeal of their preachers, was of great and indeed of indispensable service to the Duke of Guise, in the gradual prosecution of his ambitious designs. During the first part of the history of these civil wars, the Roman Catholic clergy enforced the doctrines of intolerance against the Protestants, and united with the court; that is, they inflamed the animosities of the parties, and, in fact, did every injury to the state and to religion, that was possible. During the latter part, the same clergy were employed in the cause of the League, opposed to the Protestants indeed, and engaged in support of the supposed cause of religion, but opposed to the king also.

"The king is no good Catholic," said the preachers. "Religion will be destroyed among us." I quote from the historian. Examples of this kind in history have taught statesmen most anxiously to deprecate, at all times, the interference of the ministers of religion in the politics of the state.

Their zeal may be virtuous, and often is, but they see every thing through the mist of that zeal; they exaggerate, they inflame the people, they inflame themselves; they set into motion a principle (the religious principle), against which, if it once becomes inflamed, no other principle of reason or propriety can be successfully opposed. They have been naturally accustomed to look in one direction, and they are therefore, though men of education, seldom able to take a view, sufficiently extended, of the general interests of the community. This was the opinion even of Lord Clarendon.

Such statesmen, therefore, as have meant ill, have often converted men of this sacred character into instruments to serve their own political purposes; and such statesmen as have endeavoured well, have but too often found them impediments to their designs. All history enforces upon the attention disagreeable conclusions of this nature, and pious and good men should be aware of it; though I cannot mean that men, because they are clergymen, should cease to be citizens. I state the lessons and monitions of history, more particularly of this period of history. The impression which it had left on the mind of Mr. Burke must have been of this kind; for when the late Dr. Price,* about the beginning of the French Revolution, preached a sort of political discourse at the Old Jewry, which he afterwards published, Mr. Burke was immediately reminded of

---

* In Smyth's pages Mr. Burke and Mr. Hume refer respectively to Edmund Burke and David Hume, dead in 1797 and 1776 respectively. Dr. Price was Richard Price (1723–91), an English nonconformist minister and supporter of the French Revolution.—Ed.

the very times we are now considering—the times of the League in
France. He mentions them along with the solemn League and Covenant,
so memorable in the history of Scotland and England; and he admonishes
the doctor, that men like him, men of his sacred profession, were unacquainted with the world, and had nothing of politics but the passions
they excite.

Another observation must also be made. The Duke of Guise found a
no less effective, though more unworthy support in the king and in the
court itself, than he did in the clergy; that is, he found a support in their
profligacy, their waste of public money, their scandalous disposal of
places of trust and honour, and their total disregard of public opinion.

These vices produced in the people that effect, which they have invariably done, and which they can never fail to do. It is possible that circumstances may not be sufficiently critical to produce, exactly at the
time, insurrections and revolutions, but the materials for these most
dreadful calamities are always ready, when such flagitious conduct has
been at all persevered in.

The great on these occasions have no right to blame the populace;
they have themselves first exhibited the vices and crimes, to the commission of which they were more particularly liable; and the vulgar do
no more, when they break out, in their turn, into acts of brutality and
ferocity. Manners and principles are propagated downwards, and on
this account the lower orders, to a considerable extent, become what they
are made by the examples of their superiors. This example may be vicious,
or may be virtuous; in either case, it cannot but have influence. . . .

The theatre of the world is not the place where we are to look for
religion; her more natural province must ever be the scenes of domestic
and social life: too elevated to take the lead in cabinets and camps, to
appear in the bustle and ostentation of a court, or the tumults of a
popular assembly, amid the struggles of political intrigue, or the vulgar
pursuits of avarice and ambition, Religion must not be judged of by the
pictures that appear of her in history. The form that is there seen is an
earthly and counterfeit resemblance, which we must not mistake for the
divine original.

XII. HENRY IV AND THE LOW COUNTRIES

THE SITUATION of Henry, while mounting the throne of France, was so
beset with difficulties, that as we read the history, we can scarcely imagine
how he is ever to become successful, though we already know that such
was the event. He was a Huguenot, and the nation could not there-

fore endure that he should be king; he had been leagued with Henry, the former king, while that prince was stained with the blood of the Duke of Guise, the great object of national admiration; he had a disputed title; an able and experienced general to oppose him in Mayenne, the brother of the murdered Guise, backed by a triumphant party, and by the furious Parisians. Lastly, he was exposed to the hostile interference of one of the most consummate generals that ever appeared, the Duke of Parma, at the head of the Spanish infantry, then the first in the world.

It must be confessed that Henry, with some assistance from fortune, fairly, slowly, and laboriously, won and deserved his crown. . . .

But Henry had not only to win the crown, but to wear it; not only to acquire, but preserve it.

Now the great lesson to be drawn from Henry's life is the wisdom of generous policy, the prudence of magnanimity. To these he owed his success. There was nothing narrow in his views, no ungovernable animosity that rankled in his memory; he forgot, he forgave, he offered favourable terms, he negotiated with all the fearless liberality of an elevated mind. The path of honourable virtue was here, as it always is, that of true policy, that of safety and happiness. The result was, that he was served by men who had been opponents and rebels, more faithfully than other princes have been by their favourites and dependents.

Henry has always been, and with some justice, the idol of the French nation. But in his private life two fatal passions reduce him (great as he was in public) to a level with his fellow mortals, and sometimes far below them.

It was in vain that the virtuous Sully remonstrated against his passion for play. Again, Henry seems never to have suspected that domestic comfort was only to be purchased by domestic virtue. In respect of the Princess of Condé such was his licentious nature, such the result, as is always the case, of the long indulgence of his passions, that he is, in this affair, as far as I can understand the history, very little to be distinguished from a mere violent and unprincipled tyrant.

The name of Henry IV may remind us of a celebrated work, the *Henriade* of Voltaire. This extraordinary writer was allowed to be a poet by Gibbon, and an historian by Robertson. The poem will exhibit him in both capacities. It should be read immediately after reading the history of these times. Thus read, it will strike the judgment, and refresh the knowledge of the student, while it exercises his taste, and to a certain degree, animates his imagination. The work was considered by its author merely as a poem, and not a history; but it is now chiefly valuable for the descriptions which it gives of the great characters and events of these times, drawn with great beauty and force, and evidently by the pencil of a master. It will be found very entertaining, read in the way I propose. On the whole, the striking scenes of this celebrated period in French history (the period of the sixteenth century), attach powerfully on our attention; but we must never forget to remark those incidents which paint the manners, laws, and constitution of any people whose annals we are reading. . . .

After the personal character of Henry, the events of his reign, and the manners of the times, have been considered, the last and great object of inquiry is the constitution of France. If this had received any improvement, however dreadful might have been the effects of these civil and religious wars in other respects, the prospect of future happiness to this great kingdom, would have been still open.

What, therefore, we ask, had been the fortunes of the States-General? The answer may, unhappily, be given in the description in the *Henriade*:—"Inefficient assemblies where laws were proposed, rather than executed, and where abuses were detailed with eloquence, but not remedied."

The public seem, indeed, to have felt the weight of taxes; and complaints and representations were made in these assemblies, which in this manner occasionally reached the throne itself. At two different periods, in 1576, and still more in 1588, an opportunity was offered of at least some effort for the general good, but in vain. The images of liberty had been too long withdrawn from the eyes of the nation; and no reasonable ideas on the subject seem to have been entertained by any leader or description of men in the state.

Even the religious reformers seem not in France to have felt in themselves, or to have endeavoured to excite in the minds of their countrymen, any of those principles of civil liberty, which so honourably distinguished them in other parts of Europe.

In the constitution of France, the only part of the system which the reader can fix upon, as yet of consequence to the cause of civil liberty, the only body from which anything could yet be hoped, was the parliaments. These assemblies, particularly that of Paris, seem continually to have offered a sort of yielding resistance to the arbitrary power of the crown; to have been ever ready to assert privileges (to assert or create them) which might eventually be of decisive importance to the nation; for instance, they acquired, or retained, the prerogative of registering the edicts of the king. In the exercise of this prerogative, a most important one, it is true they always accommodated themselves to the wishes of the monarch, whenever he insisted upon their compliance: still the prerogative itself remained in existence; royal edicts after all, were not exactly laws: they became so, only when the parliaments had given them a last sanction, by consenting to *register* them.

Here, then, lay the great secret of the constitution; how far the king could legally compel this acquiescence; and here was fixed the proper engine of constitutional control or resistance. You will see its importance when you come to read the history of the French Revolution. . . .

The value of a national representation, as an instrument of taxation, even to the crown itself, may be seen in the history of France. The monarch, it is true, could issue edicts, but the taxes were intercepted by the collectors of them; though the subject paid much, the crown received little. Arbitrary power is not favourable to the real affluence of the sovereign. For the same notions in the people and in the monarch that lead to arbitrary power, lead to abuses of every description; compulsory loans, venality of offices, demands of free gifts, rapacious exactions from opulent traders, destructive impositions, and anticipations of revenue; habits of expense, improvident management, and a universal system of waste and peculation.

But it is in this manner that all the sources of national revenue are destroyed; and if the revenue be not produced, the monarch cannot have a part of it.

It was in vain for the prince, even if patriotic, to endeavour to introduce economy into his household and expenses: a large sum might be collected in such a country as France, by a minister like Sully, under a king like Henry IV; but the memoirs of Sully himself resound with the king's embarrassments and poverty.

The whole organization of society, from the throne down to the cottage, if the government be arbitrary, is always to the purposes of a royal exchequer, unfavourable; every instrument that the monarch can employ is, more or less, a bad one. The monarch and court, by the absence of all apparent criticism from public assemblies, themselves lose the necessary discipline and support of virtue. They become themselves, and everyone around and below them, expensive and depraved, profuse and needy.

The great accusation to be brought against Henry is that he did nothing for the liberties of France, nothing for its constitution. He never attempted to turn to the best advantage such a means of improvement as might still have been found in the States-General. He laboured to be a father to his people, but only because it was his own good pleasure to be so; he forgot that the power which he directed to the benefit of his subjects was to descend to others; and that it was one thing for a nation to have a good king, and another to have a good constitution.

There are two services, however, which he rendered to the constitution of France, and that by his own merits. First, he prevented the renewal of the government of the fiefs. The great nobles were made so powerful by the civil wars, their followers so familiarized to arms, all order and law so banished from the kingdom, and the governors of provinces were possessed of powers so vast and dangerous, that independent sovereignties might probably have been established if Henry IV had not been on the throne during the first very critical years that succeeded to the assassination of Henry III. Considerable efforts were made by some of the great leaders to have their governments made hereditary, even while Henry IV was their monarch, armed with all his advantages of talents and success. The hereditary governments, if once established, might readily have assumed the nature and privileges of independent sovereignty, and the country been broken up and ruined.

Secondly, he procured for the Protestants the Edict of Nantes. The promulgation of this edict must be considered as a sort of conclusion of the religious wars; wars which, for nearly forty years, desolated France, and had more than realized the dreadful pictures of Tacitus, even when describing the worst times of the worst people. . . .

The humanity and philosophy of the Abbé de Mably * take fire when he comes to notice this celebrated edict. To establish (he observes) a solid peace between the two religions, there ought to have been established between them a perfect equality.

If the Protestants were feared, no exercise of their religion could have been, he contends, too public. Their preachings were otherwise to be rendered always the hotbeds of intrigue, cabal, and fanaticism. Henry, he adds, should have called the States-General; made the parties produce and discuss their claims; then have mediated between them and formed a law—the law of the whole nation.

To views and observations like these, the history itself, and all history, is a melancholy but sufficient answer. It is only astonishing that after such scenes as had taken place, Henry could accomplish what he did. Insufficient as it may seem to the Abbé de Mably, it was not effected without the most meritorious exertions on his part, and the assertion of all his authority, with both laity and clergy, particularly the latter.

Had he called the States-General he would only have dignified and organized the opposition which he could scarcely with the assistance of the most favourable circumstances overpower. Like a real statesman he was resolved to do something for the benefit of his country, but was contented, when he had done what seemed practicable; when, in short, he had made the best of his materials. It was sufficient for him, as it must often be for others, to have laid the germ of future improvement, which was to ripen, if succeeding times were favourable; if otherwise to perish. . . .

The merits of Henry IV had an easy conquest over the French nation; for he restored them to peace after the calamities not only of civil war, but of civil and religious war. Favoured by fortune, and recom-

* Gabriel Bonnot de Mably (1700–85), French historian and philosopher.—ED.

mended by great merit, Henry became at once, and has always remained, the object of universal admiration.

It seems but too generally forgotten that Henry made no attempt to revive the constitution of his country. The people of France themselves seem never to have objected to this most important fault in him.

Mankind, it must be confessed, are ever running headlong in their feelings of praise and censure, and they seem almost justified, when they give the free reins to their confidence and affections in favour of princes, who have been their deliverers and protectors.

But it is unhappily on occasions like these, after revolutions or great calamities, that a nation loses, as did the French, as did the English at the restoration of Charles II, all care of its laws, its privileges, and its constitution. It thinks only of the horrors of the past, and of the comparative enjoyments of the present; slavery itself is a comfort when compared with the miseries that have been endured; and good princes as well as bad princes have converted to the purposes of their own power these thoughtless but natural sentiments, in a fatigued, terrified, and scarcely yet breathing people. . . .

We must now turn to a scene that will have been often presented to us indirectly during our perusal of these evils and religious wars in France, the contest between Philip II and his Dutch and Flemish subjects; the progress of the Reformation in the Low Countries. . . .

There seem to me two principal lessons to be drawn from this part of the history of the Low Countries.

First, the unhappy effects of intolerance. In this respect the facts and the conclusions to be derived from them are the same as in other countries, and such as we have already noticed.

Secondly, the impolicy of all harsh government. The Netherlands were dependencies of the Spanish monarchy. It has never yet been possible to teach any country, nor even any cabinet, the wisdom of governing its colonies or dependencies with mildness.

The first portion of this history, while Margaret of Parma was in authority, is therefore particularly to be studied; the portion I have already mentioned. She endeavoured to govern mildly.

The system of Philip II was no doubt the most violent specimen of harsh government that has yet been exhibited among mankind. But the system of all other mother countries has been similar; and what difference there may be is in degree, and not in kind.

A distinction is here to be made. Philip II has always been considered, and justly, as the most perfect example of bigotry that history supplies; and to this must be imputed much of the abominable tyranny which he exercised over the Low Countries.

But the love of arbitrary power is always found where bigotry is found. The human mind, amid its endless inconsistencies, is indeed capable of being animated with a love of religious liberty, and yet of being at the same time ignorant of the nature, or somewhat indifferent to the cause, of civil liberty. Instances of this kind, though very rare, have sometimes occurred, but the converse never has; no man was ever a religious bigot, and at the same time a friend to civil liberty; and it was perfectly consistent for Philip not only to introduce the inquisition into the Low Countries, but also Spanish soldiers into the fortified towns; to deprive the Flemings of the free exercise of their religious opinions, and at the same time of the laws and privileges of their states and assemblies; to leave, in ecclesiastical matters, no visible head but the Pope, and in civil affairs no real authority but his own. These were parts of a system of conduct that perfectly harmonized with each other: each took its turn as the occasion required.

The favourite instruments of his tyranny were men of like nature with himself; foes equally to civil and religious liberty—Cardinal Granvelle and the Duke of Alva.

Bigotry and the love of rule had so conspired even in Charles V, his father, that he had paved the way, by his edicts, for all the subsequent proceedings of Philip; and was, perhaps, only saved from similar enormities by a partiality which he had contracted for Flanders in his early years; those years when his mind was in its natural state, could be capable of attaching itself to the objects that surrounded it, and of tasting a happiness, which it is probable no subsequent splendour could ever afterwards bestow.

The object contended for by Philip was that the religious persuasion of these countries should be the same as his own. "You may lose them if you persist," said one of his officers. "I would rather be without kingdoms," he replied, "than enjoy them with heresy."

Now, on all occasions when harsh government is to be the means, it will always be found, as in this instance, that, in the first place, the end to be accomplished is not worth the risk of the experiment, to say nothing of the injustice of the experiment itself.

Next, it will be found that some statesman like Cardinal Granvelle always makes his appearance; very violent and very able; qualities not incompatible; skilled in business, and perhaps acquainted with the inferior country that is to be ruled; distinct, decisive, and consistent in his opinions; whose counsels therefore have an air of wisdom which does not belong to them, and acquire irresistible authority in the superior or mother country, with the monarch and his cabinet, because they are not well informed themselves, and are already sufficiently disposed to such counsels from the prejudices of their own situation.

Again—the Roman Catholic historians are satisfied in imputing all the turbulence, as they would call it, of the Prince of Orange and the Flemish leaders to disappointed ambition. But it is always forgotten that such disappointment is reasonable. When authority and influence are generally conferred, not on the natives of the country governed, but on those who in comparison are considered as aliens, it is impossible that men should be satisfied with the government which robs them of their natural consequence in their own land. This is a very common species of impolicy and injustice. . . .

Lastly, the student will observe, on the other side, great irregularities committed by the people in their mode of resistance to Philip; the symbols of the Roman Catholic worship insulted with great violence and outrage; and an intolerance displayed by *them,* precisely of the same nature with the intolerance of Philip himself.

Excesses of this kind always occur and are instantly seized upon in argument, by those who govern, as justifying the harsh measures that in fact led the way to them; they are brought forward as demanding fresh applications of force and severity.

But the very contrary of all this is the proper conclusion; it is the total inability of the people to govern for themselves; it is their inevitable fury, ignorance, and brutality, when once roused, that renders mild government so indispensable a duty in their rulers. Their faults are a part of the very case: temper, moderation, reasonable views, it is ridiculous to expect from them; but in cabinets they may and ought to be found: if they are not found somewhere, what must be the consequence? . . .

Reason and history are equally unavailing to teach the wisdom of temperate and healing counsels to a brave and prosperous people, as were the Spaniards in the first instance and the English in the second. Such a people and their rulers inflame each other, and every thing is to be submitted to that irritable jealousy and high sense of national importance which their courage and their power so inevitably produce.

It was in vain that Margaret of Parma had, in the mean time, very tolerably composed the troubles of the Netherlands. The imperious nature of Philip and his counsellers was to be gratified, the Flemings were to be taught what it was to resist authority, and Alva was to be dispatched to enforce that obedience by arms, which it suited not, it seems, the dignity of the monarch to deserve by humanity and justice. . . .

The resistance of the Prince of Orange and of some of the Flemish nobles will be found . . . to have been as temperate and regular as the calmest speculator could require. And the whole of the proceedings between them and the regent Margaret, and between both and the Spanish court, are very instructive.

But when we come to the next part of the subject, the resistance that in fact was made, it must surely be a matter of great surprise to us to find, that no general effort of this kind seems to have been made against the Duke of Alva when he at length appeared.

He came into the Low Countries, and with an army of about fourteen thousand men he disposed of the lives and privileges of the Flemings of all ranks at his pleasure, imprisoned two of the most popular and meritorious noblemen, erected a Council of Tumults, or, as it was more properly called, a council of blood, and destroyed, in the course of a few months, by the hands of the executioner, more than one thousand eight hundred different individuals; while more than twenty thousand persons fled into France, Germany, and England, without the slightest attempt having first been made, either by themselves or others, for their common safety and protection. . . .

"The danger is common," says the Prince of Orange, "so should the cause be. The Spanish forces, once in Flanders, will be always ready to enter Germany; and you will have new taxes, new customs, severe laws, more severely executed; heavy yokes upon your persons, and more heavy upon your consciences. I am held," said he, "to be the contriver of conspiracies; but what greater glory can there be than to maintain the liberty of a man's country, and to die rather than be enslaved?"

William and his brother led separate armies against the Duke of Alva, but were obliged, the one to fly, and the other to disband his troops. The want of the means to pay them proved equally fatal in different ways to the enterprises of each commander; and neither proper funds nor adequate assistance were supplied by the Flemings themselves.

This is one instance among many which it is melancholy to observe, of the difficulty with which the regular troops of an unprincipled tyrant can be resisted, or at least ever are resisted, by an insulted and oppressed people.

The principal cities became sensibly thinner in population; whole villages and small towns were rendered almost desolate. Still no resistance, that is, no resistance from the Flemings themselves.

But it fortunately happened that Alva was not only made more arbitrary and insolent by success, but he began himself to feel the same want of money for the payment of his troops, which had been so fatal to the Protestant leaders.

Philip was supposed at the time to possess all the wealth of the world, and he certainly did possess a large portion of the gold and silver of it; but it was now to be shown that ambition and harsh government could exhaust even Mexico and Peru.

Alva found himself obliged to have recourse to taxation, and to require from the industry and wealth of the Flemings themselves that constant supply which all the mines and slaves of his master were insufficient to afford him.

And now for once it happened, that a total ignorance of the principles of political economy in the rulers was eventually favourable to the happiness of the people. . . .

It is not very agreeable to observe, that every where through all history, the most sensible nerve that can be touched is this of taxation. Privileges may be taken away, laws violated, public assemblies discontinued, no *distant* consequence is regarded, no common principle seems as yet sufficiently outraged: the community are silent, or only murmur for a short season and submit; but if a tax is to be levied, every man feels his interest at issue, every man starts up in arms, every man cries with Shylock—

> *"Nay, take my life, and all; . . . .*
> *. . . . . You take my life,*
> *When you do take the means whereby I live."*

Observe the facts in these Low Countries.

The Flemings had seen their fellow-citizens executed by the Duke of Alva, had seen all the principles of their civil and religious liberty destroyed; had suffered the Prince of Orange and their patriot leaders to fight their battles by means of German Protestants, whom he was to pay in any manner he could devise, a task to which it must have been known that his funds were totally unequal: all this they had seen, and all this pusillanimous guilt they had incurred; but the moment that the loss of their civil liberty was to produce *one* of its many injurious effects, the moment that the duke's tax-gatherers were to interfere with their manufactures and with the sources of their opulence, then, and not till then, combinations could be formed, a universal sensation take place, and resistance to the Spanish tyranny every where assume a visible form, and become a regular system.

But our mortification is not yet to end. We might wish to see mankind always ready to kindle with a generous and rational sympathy. We might wish to see them act with some reasonable consistency and courage when oppressed; but what was the fact? The Walloon or southern provinces, being not so entirely commercial as those that were more maritime, will be found on that account (for no other reason can be given) to have resisted the taxes of Alva *less* firmly.

It is painful to follow the subject through all the more minute but important particulars that belong to it, and to observe the manner in which so many of the provinces could be practised upon and gained over; could be soothed, deluded, or terrified; could basely consent to submit to a certain part of the proposed requisitions, that is, to fit on such of the chains as they thought might possibly be borne, while the rest were to be left still hanging in the hands of their oppressors, ready to be applied on the first occasion, an occasion which they might be certain would so soon and so inevitably follow.

Had it not been for the resistance of Brabant, and the still more intelligent and invariable firmness of the single province of Utrecht, all might have been lost, and the bigoted, unfeeling Philip, though his subjects might no longer have been worth his ruling, would at least have had the gratification of seeing them bound and prostrate at his feet.

The example, however, of Utrecht was not without its effect, and its resistance was fatal to the Spanish system of taxation; a distinction, it is true, may always be perceived between the seven northern, more commercial provinces, and the rest. The more southern and less commercial often observed a cold neutrality, and were even guilty of a species of hostility to the Prince of Orange and the patriotic cause that was often but too convenient and favourable to the Spanish arms.

Cruelty and oppression were, however, destined at last to receive some lessons. Holland, Zealand, and five other of the more bold and virtuous provinces of the Low Countries which with Brabant must be always distinguished from the rest, openly and steadily resisted. It is consoling to observe, that even the exiles, men whom Alva had reduced, as he supposed, to the condition of mere outcasts and pirates, too contemptible to interest his thoughts for a moment, were in fact the very men who gave strength and animation to the revolt; and by their armed vessels, their enterprises, their extraordinary exertions by sea as well as by land, so shook, and injured, and endangered the Spanish greatness, that the entire independence of a part at least of the Low Countries was at last formally asserted.

The military conduct of Alva is remarkable. In the field he was as calm and considerate, as he was rash and intemperate in the cabinet; that is, he understood the science of war, but not of politics. Yet still he could not, even in arms, succeed. The opportunities for resistance afforded by the singular situation of the maritime provinces, the consummate prudence, the zeal, and the tolerant spirit of the Prince of Orange, were obstacles which he could not entirely overcome. The great towns in Holland, Haarlem, and others, were besieged, taken, and outraged by the most extraordinary excesses of cruelty and rapine; but there were other towns that could not be taken. Holland, Zealand, and five other provinces acknowledged the authority of the Prince of Orange, not of Philip; and Alva at last retired, though the rebellion in the Low Countries was not put down, and neither his own vengeance, nor that of his master, as yet satiated. He consoled himself, we are told, with the reflection, that eighteen thousand heretics had suffered by the hands of the executioner, and a much greater number fallen by famine or the sword.

It appears from this history, that concessions were made by the Spanish court; but, as is usual in such contests, made too late: orders had been sent by Philip to remit the taxes of the ten and twenty per cent, but not till the maritime provinces had already revolted. After Alva, with his soldiers and executioners, had been let loose upon the provinces for nearly six years together, Philip began at last to doubt a little the efficacy of force. . . .

To advert, therefore, to the final result of this great struggle, and to finish my lecture.

The Prince of Orange, notwithstanding the defection of some, and the mutual jealousies of too many of the provinces, had contrived to form the Union of Utrecht—a combination of seven of them; and this union may be considered as the first foundation of the republic of Holland.

It is difficult for unprincipled ambition to be prudent. Philip had not only schemes of tyranny in the Low Countries, but of invasion in England, and of aggrandizement in France. The multiplicity of his designs exhausted even his American treasures: the impossibility of his wishes squandered away even the resources of the genius of the Duke of Parma. The United Provinces were not subdued, England not overcome, France not united to his crown, and Europe not subjected to the domination of the House of Austria.

We have at last the satisfaction to see the seven maritime provinces at least, treating with their oppressors as sovereign states; and not only their independence admitted, but their trade with the Indies allowed, and their cause completely triumphant. . . .

On the whole of this memorable contest—a contest of half a century—the great hero was the Prince of Orange, the great delinquent was Philip II. The one may be proposed as a model, in public and in private, of every thing that is good and great; and the other (with the exception of attention to business), of every thing that is to be avoided and abhorred.

To Europe and mankind, in the meantime, the success of the maritime provinces was of the greatest importance. The power of the House of Austria was for ever prevented from gaining too dangerous an ascendancy.

Resistance to those who were controlling religious opinions by fire and sword, and trampling upon constitutional privileges, had been successfully made.

An asylum was opened for all those, of whatever country, who fled from persecution—from persecution of whatever kind. The benefit thus accruing to mankind cannot now be properly estimated, for we cannot now feel what it is to have no refuge and no means of resistance, while men are ready to punish us for our opinions, and are making

themselves inquisitors of our conduct. It is known to have been one of
the severest miseries of the later Romans, that they could not escape from
their government; that the world belonged to their emperors.

It was in the Low Countries that the defenders of civil and religious
liberty found shelter. It was there that they could state their complaints,
publish what they conceived to be the truth, and maintain and exercise
the privileges of free inquiry. These were the countries to which Locke
retired, and where William III was formed.

But this was not all. The wonders that can be effected by commerce
and the peaceful arts were displayed, and, on the whole, a practical example was held up to the princes and statesmen of every age and nation,
well fitted to teach them many of those great truths which every friend
of humanity would wish always present to their minds: that ambition
should be virtuous and peaceful, that religious feelings should be tolerant, that government should be mild.

XIII. THE THIRTY YEARS' WAR

[THE] THIRTY YEARS' WAR is a memorable era in history, and I must
therefore allude to the conduct of it, and to the great hero of the Protestant
cause on this occasion, Gustavus Adolphus. . . .

I may, however, select what I consider as the leading events, and recommend you to fix your attention upon them. They are the following:

First, the denial of the authority of the pope by Luther.

Secondly, the total intolerance of Charles V, avowed in the Edict of
Worms.

Thirdly, the resistance of the Protestants, and the exhibition of their
own faith in the confession of Augsburg.

Fourthly, their appeal to arms from the injustice of Charles—the
league of Schmalkalden.

Lastly, after the various events of unrighteous warfare, the religious
peace concluded at Passau, in 1555, about the close of his reign.

These are the principal events. You must consider them, particularly
the peace of Passau.

On this last, as it is so important, I will stop to make a few observations.

It was the first great adjustment of the contending religious interests
of Germany. It was extorted from Charles V, and, on the whole, it was
favourable to the great cause of religious freedom, and the welfare of
mankind.

Those of the inferior sect were no longer to be insulted, dispersed, or exterminated: they were to exist in society as their Roman Catholic brethren, erect and independent: they were to worship their God in the manner they thought most agreeable to his word. Human authority in matters of religious faith was avowedly cast off by a large and respectable part of the continent; and neither the magistrate nor the soldier were any longer to unsheath the sword, to imprison, to massacre, or to drag to the stake.

In practice, therefore, some progress had been made; some progress in practice, but little in the understandings or feelings of mankind. The parties abstained from mutual violence because they were well balanced, and feared each other; not because they discerned and acknowledged their mutual rights and duties. Not only were the Roman Catholics separated from the Protestants, but the Lutherans had separated themselves from the Zuinglians, afterwards called the Calvinists; and had endeavoured to stigmatize them with the name of Sacramentarians. That is, the Roman Catholics, the Lutherans, and Calvinists, were all equally ready to believe, that every religious opinion but their own was sinful, and therefore that their own, upon every principle of piety and reason, was at all events to be propagated, and every other repressed.

Again. We have already observed that one of the great difficulties on the subject always must be the disposal of property to the ecclesiastic: to which sect it is to be given by the state; to one, or to all, and upon what conditions.

This difficulty necessarily appeared at the pacification which was attempted at Passau.

It was insisted by the Protestants, that all those who separated from the church of Rome should, nevertheless, retain their ecclesiastical emoluments; emoluments it must be observed, which had been received originally from the Roman Catholic establishment.

By the Roman Catholics it was contended, on the contrary, that every such separatist should immediately lose his benefice.

This point could not at the peace of Passau be carried by the Protestants. They seem to have sullenly submitted, and to have virtually acquiesced in what was called the ecclesiastical reservation. This reservation secured the benefice, and he left it to remain with the Catholic establishment when the holder turned Protestant.

The Protestants were consoled on the other hand, by a declaration, securing liberty of conscience to those who adopted the confession of Augsburg—a declaration which the Roman Catholics as little relished as the Protestants did the reservation just mentioned.

The parties were therefore not as yet sufficiently religious and wise to settle the real subjects of contention. Then followed, after this peace of Passau, a sort of interval and pause. After this interval, all Germany was laid waste and convulsed by the Thirty Years' War.

We naturally turn to ask what were the causes of so dreadful an event —Thirty Years' War! the very term is a disgrace to humanity. To this the answer will, I think, be found to be, first, the intolerant conduct of the Protestant princes to each other; second, the bigotry, ambition, and arbitrary politics of the princes of the House of Austria.

I will say a word on each. First, with regard to the conduct of the Protestant princes, Lutheran and Calvinistic. It will appear to those who examine the history that the Protestant cause was well established at the peace of Passau, and at the death of Charles V; but that it was afterwards nearly lost by the advantages which the Roman Catholic arms and politics derived from the dissensions which existed between the Lutheran and Calvinistic princes.

Though these princes had the most palpable bond of union (their wish to exercise the right of private judgment)—though they were both equally opposed to the Catholic powers who would have denied them this inestimable privilege, yet was it impossible for them to differ in some mysterious points of doctrine without a total disregard to mutual charity; and each sect, rather than suffer the other to think differently from themselves, was contented to run the chance of being overpowered by the Catholics, that is, of not being suffered to think at all.

The Lutherans might have been possibly expected to be the most rational, that is, the most tolerant of the two, but they were not so; they were in reality more in fault than the Calvinists; being not only the first aggressors in this dispute with their fellow Protestants, but the more ready to temporize, to betray and desert the common cause.

You will perceive that I am here obliged to leave great blanks behind me as I go along, and you will perceive the same through every part of this lecture. These blanks must be hereafter filled up by your own diligence. I cannot expect to make the steps I take through my subject very intelligible at present.

But you will be able to judge of my arrangement, my statements, and my conclusions hereafter, when you come to read the history.

I must, then, for the present, content myself with repeating to you that the Protestant princes were themselves very faulty, more particularly the Lutheran princes; their intolerance to each other most unpardonable; and that the conduct of some of the electors of Saxony was very despicable, and most injurious to the Protestant cause; and finally, that all this folly and intolerance led to the Thirty Years' War.

My next statement was that the Thirty Years' War, and all its dreadful scenes, were occasioned, in the second place, by the civil and religious politics, the bigoted and arbitrary conduct of the princes of the House of Austria. . . .

There is no period connected with these religious wars that deserves more to be studied than these reigns of Ferdinand I, Maximilian, and those of his successors who preceded the Thirty Years' War. We have no sovereign who exhibited that exercise of moderation and good sense which a philosopher would require, but Maximilian; and he was immediately followed by princes of a *different* complexion, and as all the various sects themselves were ready from the first to display at any moment those faults which belong to human nature, when engaged in religious concerns, the whole subject of toleration and mild government, its advantages and its dangers, and the advantages and dangers of an opposite system, are at once presented to our consideration; and the only observation that remains to be made is this, that the difficulties and the hazards of the harsh and unjust system are increased and exasperated by their natural progress, while those that belong to the mild system are chiefly to be expected at first; that they gradually disappear, and become less important, particularly as the world advances in civilization and knowledge, and as the thoughts of men are more diversified by the active pursuits and petty amusements which multiply with their growing prosperity.

Nothing could be more complete than the difficulty of toleration at the time when Maximilian reigned; and if a mild policy could be attended with favourable effects in his age and nation, there can be little fear of the experiment at any other period.

No party or person in the state was then disposed to tolerate his neighbour from any sense of the justice of such forbearance, but from motives of temporal policy alone. The Lutherans, it will be seen, could not bear that the Calvinists should have the same religious privileges with themselves. The Calvinists were equally opinionated and unjust; and Maximilian himself was probably tolerant and wise, chiefly because he was in his real opinions a Lutheran, and in outward profession, as the head of the empire, a Roman Catholic.

For twelve years, the whole of his reign, he preserved the religious peace of the community, without destroying the religious freedom of the human mind. He supported the Roman Catholics, as the predominant party, in all their rights, possessions, and privileges; but he protected the Protestants in every exercise of their religion which was then practicable. In other words, he was as tolerant and just as the temper of society then admitted, and more so than the state of things would have suggested. Now, more than this, no considerate Christian or real philosopher will require from the sovereign power at any time; not more than to countenance toleration, to be disposed to experiments of toleration, and to lead on to toleration, if the community can but be persuaded to follow. More than this will not, I think, be required from the rulers of the world by any real philosopher and true Christian; and this is not because the great cause of religious truth and inquiry is at all indifferent to them (it must be always most dear to them), but because they know that mankind on these subjects are profoundly ignorant, and incurably irritable. The merit of Maximilian was but too apparent the moment that his son Rodolph was called upon to supply his place.

The tolerance and forbearance of Maximilian had been favourable, as it must always be, to the better cause; but the Protestants, instead of being encouraged by the visible progress of their tenets, and thereby induced to leave them to the sure operation of time, and the silent influence of truth, had broken out with all the stupid fury that often belongs to an inferior sect, and indulged themselves in the most public attacks and unqualified invectives against the established church. The gentle but powerful hand of Maximilian was now withdrawn; and he had made one most fatal and unpardonable mistake: he had always left the education of his son and successor too much to the discretion of his bigoted consort. Rodolph, his son, was therefore as ignorant and furious on his part as were the Protestants on theirs; he had immediate recourse to the usual expedients—force, and the execution of the laws to the very letter. It is needless to add, that injuries and mistakes quickly multiplied as he proceeded; and Maximilian himself, had he been recalled to life, would have found it difficult to extricate his unhappy son and his unfortunate people from the accumulated calamities which it had been the great glory of his own reign so skilfully to avert. After Rodolph comes Matthias, and unhappily for all Europe, Bohemia and the empire fell afterwards under the management of Ferdinand II. Of the different Austrian princes, it is the reign of Ferdinand II that is more particularly to be considered.

Such was the arbitrary nature of his government over his subjects in Bohemia, that they revolted. They elected for their king the young Elector Palatine, hoping thus to extricate themselves from the bigotry and tyranny of Ferdinand. This crown so offered was accepted; and in the event, the cause of the Bohemians became the cause of the Reformation in Germany, and the Elector Palatine the hero of that cause. . . .

The Elector Palatine, by accepting the crown of Bohemia, became . . . the chief of the Protestant cause; but he undertook a cause so important, and he suffered the lives and liberties of thousands to depend on his firmness and ability, without ever having properly examined his own character, or considered to what situations of difficulty his powers were equal. When, therefore, the hour of trial came, when he was weighed in the balance, he was found wanting, and his kingdom was divided from him. Had he himself been alone interested in his success, his subsequent sufferings might have atoned for his fault; but the kingdom of Bohemia was lost to its inhabitants, the Palatinate to its own subjects, and the great cause of religious inquiry and truth might have also perished in the general wreck of his fortunes.

But in the reign of the same Ferdinand II there arose, in the same cause in which the Elector Palatine had failed, a hero of another cast, Gustavus Adolphus.

And now, to recapitulate a little, that you may see the connecting links of this part of the subject, in which I am obliged to leave such blanks; you will have understood in a general manner, and I must now remind you, that the House of Austria was the terror of the Protestants of Germany; that Ferdinand II oppressed by his tyranny and bigotry his Protestant subjects, more particularly in Bohemia; that their cause became the cause of the Protestant interest in Germany; that the Elector Palatine was the first hero of this great cause, and that he failed; that the illustrious Swede was the second, and that he deserved the high office which he bore—that he deserved to be the defender of the civil and religious liberties of Europe, and that he was the great object of admiration in the Thirty Years' War. . . .

As it must needs be that offences will come, as violence and injustice can only be repelled by force, as mankind must and will have their destroyers, it is fortunate when the high courage and activity of which the human character is capable, are tempered with a sense of justice, wisdom, and benevolence; when he who leads thousands to the field has sensibility enough to feel the nature of his awful office, and wisdom enough to take care that he directs against its proper objects the afflicting storm of human devastation. It is not always that they who have commanded the admiration of mankind have claims like these to their applause. Courage and sagacity can dignify any man, whatever be his cause; they can ennoble a wretch like Tilly, while he fights the battles of a Ferdinand. It is not always that these great endowments are so united with other high qualities as to present to the historian at once a Christian, a soldier, and a statesman; yet such was Gustavus Adolphus, a hero deserving the name, perfectly distinguishable from those who have assumed the honours that belong to it, the military executioners, with whom every age has been infested. . . .

The great question which it is necessary for the fame of Gustavus should be settled in his favour is the invasion of Germany. Sweden, the country of which he was king, could, at the time, furnish for the enterprise only her two great products, "iron and man, the soldier and his sword"; and with these a leader like Gustavus, some centuries before, might have disposed of Europe at his pleasure; but, happily for mankind, the invention of gunpowder and the progress of science had made war a

question, not merely of physical force, but of expense. The surplus produce of the land and labour of the snowy regions of Sweden were little
fitted to support a large military establishment either at home or abroad,
little fitted to contend with the resources of the House of Austria. It
was therefore very natural for the counsellors of Gustavus to represent
strongly to their sovereign the expenses of a war on the continent, the
great power of the emperor, and the reasonableness of supposing that the
German electors were themselves the best judges of the affairs of the
empire, and the best able to vindicate their own civil and religious
liberties.

But it was clear, on the other hand, that the power of the House of
Austria, which had already distantly menaced, might soon be enabled
to oppress, the civil and religious liberties of Sweden: it was impossible to
separate the interests of that kingdom from those of the Protestant
princes of Germany; and, therefore, the only question that remained was
whether Gustavus should come forward as a leader of the combination
against Ferdinand II, or wait to be called in, and join the general cause
as an auxiliary.

Now the prince, who was naturally the head of the Protestant union,
was the Elector of Saxony, a prince whose politics and conduct at the
time could only awaken, in the minds of good men, contempt and abhorrence. If, therefore, no one interfered, and that immediately, all was
lost; and the very want of a principal, and the very hopelessness of the
Protestant cause, must have been the very arguments that weighed most
with a prince like Gustavus, and were indeed the very arguments that
would have influenced an impartial reasoner, at the time, in favour of
this great attempt, provided the abilities of Gustavus were clearly of a
commanding nature.

On this last supposition, it must also be allowed that the case, when
examined, supplied many important probabilities to countenance the
enterprise. Speculations of this kind you should indulge, as much as
possible, while you are engaged in historical pursuits; it is the difference
between reading history and studying it.

After all, it is often for genius to justify its own projects by their execution; and such may, if necessary, be the defence of Gustavus.

If any war can be generous and just, it is that waged by a combination
of smaller states against a greater in defence of their civil and religious
liberty. Such was the contest in which Gustavus was to engage. Nothing,
therefore, could be wanting to him but success. He won it by his virtues
and capacity, and his name has been justly consecrated in the history
of mankind.

It sometimes happens, that when the master hand is removed, the
machine stops, or its movements run into incurable disorder; but Gus-

tavus was greater than great men: when Gustavus perished, his cause did not perish with him. The mortal part of the hero lay covered with honourable wounds and breathless in the plains of Lützen; but his genius still lived in the perfect soldiers he had created, the great generals he had formed, the wise minister he had employed, and the senate and people of Sweden, whom he had elevated to his own high sense of honour and duty. Neither his generals, his soldiers, his minister, nor his people, were found so unworthy of their sovereign as to be daunted by his loss, and they were not to be deterred from the prosecution of the great cause which he had bequeathed them. The result was, that sixteen years afterwards, at the peace of Westphalia, Sweden was a leading power in the general settlement of the interests of Europe; and if Gustavus had yet lived, he would have seen the very ground on which he first landed with only fourteen thousand men to oppose the numerous and regular armies of the House of Austria publicly ceded to his crown, the power of that tyrannical and bigoted family confessedly humbled, and the independence and religion of his own kingdom sufficiently provided for in the emancipation and safety of the Protestant princes of Germany.

In considering the reign and merits of Gustavus, our attention may be properly directed to the following points:—the invasion of Germany, the improvements which the king made in the military art, the means whereby he could support his armies, the causes of his success, his conduct after the victory of Leipzig, his management of men and of the circumstances of his situation, his private virtues and public merits, his tolerance, and the nature of his ambition—how far it was altered by his victories—the service he rendered Europe. . . .

The extraordinary character of Wallenstein—the great general who could alone be opposed by Ferdinand to Gustavus—was sure to catch the fancy of a German dramatist like Schiller. Here, for once, were realized all the darling images of the scene: mystery without any possible solution; energy more than human, magnificence without bounds, distinguished capacity; gloom, silence, and terror; injuries and indignation; nothing ordinary, nothing rational; and, at last, probably a conspiracy, and, at least, an assassination.

The campaigns of Gustavus, and the military part of his history, will be found more than usually interesting. . . . The continuance of the contest after his death under the generals and soldiers he had formed, which becomes another; and in this manner we are conducted to the settlement of the civil and religious differences of Germany by the Treaty of Westphalia, more than one hundred years after the first appearance of Luther, which treaty is thus left, as the remaining object of our curiosity and examination, for it is the termination of the whole subject.

This celebrated treaty has always been the study of those who wish to understand the history of Europe and the different views and systems of its component powers and states. . . .

As a great record . . . in the history of Europe; as a great specimen of what human nature is, when acting amid its larger and more important concerns, it must ever remain a subject of interest to the politician and philosopher. This treaty was the final adjustment of the civil and religious disputes of a century.

In examining the Treaty of Westphalia, the first inquiry is with respect to its ecclesiastical provisions.

After the Reformation had once begun, the first effort of the Protestants was to put themselves into a state of respect, and to get themselves acknowledged by the laws of the empire. In this they succeeded at the peace of Passau.

But the ecclesiastical reservation, as I have before mentioned, had then ordained that if a Roman Catholic turned Protestant, his benefice should be lost to him.

Truth, therefore, had no equal chance: a serious impediment was thrown in the way, not only of conviction, but of all avowal of conviction, and even of all religious inquiry. For with what candour, with what ardour, was any ecclesiastic to inquire, when the result of his inquiry might be, that he would have to lose not only his situation in society, but his accustomed means of subsistence? This point, however, could never be carried by the Protestants.

The Roman Catholics considered the reservation as the bulwark of their faith, and found no difficulty in persuading the people, and more particularly the rulers of the people, that their cause was the cause of all true religion and good government. At the peace of Westphalia, therefore, it was agreed, that if a Catholic turned Protestant, he should lose his benefice as before, and the same if a Protestant turned Catholic. But it will be observed, that to make the last provision was, in fact, to do nothing; for the Protestant was the invading sect. There was no chance of the Protestant's turning Roman Catholic, and the only question of practical importance was whether the Catholic might be allowed to open his eyes, and, if he thought good, turn Protestant without suffering in his fortunes. This he could not; the eyes of the Protestant were already opened.

The great cause, therefore, of religious inquiry at least (there was no doubt a great difficulty in the case) failed, but not entirely. For the inroads that the Protestants had made on the Catholic ecclesiastical property, during the first century of the Reformation, down, for instance, to the year 1624, were not inconsiderable; and in the possessions which they had thus obtained, they were not to be disturbed; a certain progress —an important progress—was therefore made and secured.

Again (what is very remarkable) the *civil* rights of the Protestants, their equality with their Catholic brethren on all public occasions, in the diet and other tribunals, were allowed.

This was an important victory; far more than inferior sects have been always able to obtain, more than they have obtained for instance, in our own country; far more than can be accounted for by any influence which moderation and good sense could have had upon the contending parties.

Another result took place; the Calvinists and Lutherans contrived at last to consider themselves as one body, whose business it was, during the negotiations of the peace and ever after, to provide for their common security, while equally resisting the authority of the Church of Rome.

This too, was an important victory, a victory which the two sects obtained, not over their enemies, but over themselves, partly in consequence of their past sufferings, still more from the influence of their own worldly politics; above all, from the master interference of France, whose ministers, equally disregarding the distinctions between Lutheran and Calvinist, and the cause of Protestant and Papist, wished only to subdue the House of Austria, and to combine and manage every party so as to produce this grand effect, the object of all their politics—the humiliation of the House of Austria.

The future progress of religious truth seems to have been but loosely provided for. A prince was allowed to change or reform the religion of his dominions in all cases not limited by the treaty, or settled by antecedent compact with the subject.

The truth is that a question like this last was too delicate to be adjusted by any formal ordinance in an age of religious wars, or indeed in any age.

The general principle adopted by the treaty seems to have been to confirm everything in the state it was left by the year 1624, an arrangement that must, on the whole, be considered favourable to the Protestants, far more so than could have been expected, if we reflect on their own unfortunate intolerance of each other, and the difficulty, at all times, of sustaining a combination of smaller powers against a greater.

The great gainer in this contest was France; the great sufferer the House of Austria. The grandeur of the one was advanced, and the ambition of the other was for ever humbled.

A combination against the House of Austria had been long carried on with more or less regularity and effect, but chiefly by the influence of France. The result of this united effort, was seen in the peace of Westphalia.

It is painful to think that the establishment of the civil and religious liberties of Germany was owing, not to the generous, rational, steady resistance of the Protestant princes, but much more to the anxiety of France to depress the House of Austria; and again, to the check which that House of Austria continually experienced to its designs, and was still likely to experience, from the arms of the Ottoman princes.

In this manner it happened that for the religious part of the great Treaty of Westphalia; for such toleration, good sense and Christianity as are to be found there, mankind were, after all, indebted principally to such strange propagators of the cause of truth and free inquiry, as Richelieu and the Mahometans.

By the Treaty of Westphalia, the apprehensions which Europe had so long entertained of the power of the House of Austria were, as I have just mentioned to you, removed.

But it is the great misfortune of mankind that the balance is no sooner restored by the diminishing of one exorbitant power than it is again in danger by the preponderancy of another. From this epoch of the peace of Westphalia the real power to be dreaded was no longer the House of Austria, but France; and the ambition of her cabinets, the compactness of her possessions, the extent of her resources, and the genius of her people, soon converted into the enemy of the happiness of the world, that very nation which at the peace of Westphalia appeared, and but *appeared*, in the honourable character of the protectress of the civil and religious liberties of Germany, and the mediatrix of the dissensions of a century. In the empire, the different states and princes were now more protected than before from the emperor, but they were not harmonized into a whole, nor was it possible that a number of petty sovereigns should be influenced by any general principle. It was impossible that they should form themselves either into any limited monarchy, or fall into any system; which, however it might have advanced the substantial greatness of all, would have diminished the personal splendour and fancied importance of each individual potentate.

They therefore continued in their common form of union and law, and endeavoured to maintain the independence of the several princes and states by a league for their common interest; but this league could not possibly be made sufficiently binding and effective to secure that common interest, while they were exposed to the practices of foreign intrigue, not only from their situation, but from the improvident selfishness which belongs as well to states as to individuals. Thus it happened that France, or any other power, found it easy at all times to convert a portion of the strength of Germany to its own purposes. Thus it happened that this immense division of the most civilized portion of the world never rose to that external consequence, and what is more, never to that state of internal improvement and happiness, which, under favourable circumstances, it might certainly have realized.

xiv. HENRY VIII, ELIZABETH, JAMES I, CHARLES I

WE MUST NOW turn to England. During the reign of a prince so respected for his courage and understanding, and so tyrannical in his nature as Henry VIII, in the interval between the decline of the aristocracy and the rise of the commons, the constitution of England seems to have been exposed to the most extreme danger, and if Henry had lived longer, or if his successor had resembled him in capacity and disposition, this island, like France, might have lost its liberties for ever.

It appears that the slavish submission of parliaments had proceeded at length to allow to the proclamations of the king an authority, which, notwithstanding the remarkable limitations annexed to it, might eventually have been extended, in practice, to the destruction of all other authority in the realm. . . .

With respect, however, to the great point of the very existence of our legislative assemblies, it is to be observed, that from the violent, cruel, and unprincipled measures into which Henry was so repeatedly hurried, he had continually to apply to his parliaments, which kept up the use of them at this most critical era in our constitution.

In France, on the contrary, Francis I could always contrive to do without his national assemblies; a circumstance which most unhappily, and most materially, contributed to their decline and fall. . . .

I hasten to the reign of Elizabeth. . . . Whatever concerned the royal prerogative was considered by Elizabeth as forbidden ground, and she included within this description, in a religious age, every thing that related to the management of religion, to her particular courts, and to the succession to the crown; she insisted in her own words, "that no bills touching matters of state, or reformation in concerns ecclesiastical, should be exhibited." . . .

Not a session took place in the reign of Elizabeth which does not present some speech or motion, or debate, characteristic of the times, and of the undefined nature of the constitution; and we have repeated specimens of the same sort of constitutional questions, the same sort of state difficulties that took place in the subsequent reigns of James and Charles.

But there is this important difference invariably to be observed: Elizabeth could always give way in time to render her concessions a favour. Unlike other arbitrary princes, and unlike chiefly in this particular, she did *not* think it a mark of political wisdom always to persevere when her authority was resisted. She did not suppose that her subjects, if she yielded to their petitions or complaints, would necessarily conclude that she did so from fear; she did not conclude, that if she became more reasonable, they must necessarily become less so.

With as high notions of her prerogative as any sovereign that can be mentioned, in her own nature most haughty and most imperious, she had still the good sense not only to perceive, but to act as if she perceived, that it was her interest to be beloved as well as respected; and her reign, if examined, shows a constant assertion and production of the powers of the prerogative, but still the most prudent management of it, and the most careful attention to public opinion. This last is a great merit in all sovereigns and their ministers, and indeed somewhat necessary to the virtue of all men, in private life as well as public.

Now the question is, successful and able as she was, what was it that imposed any restraint upon her disposition? Why did she so respect and abstain from the privileges which she might or might not think belonged to the commons? Why did she temper the exercise of what she judged her own prerogative, make occasional concessions, and, after all, not be that arbitrary sovereign, which, according to Hume, the constitution rendered her? There seems no answer but one; that such was the spirit of the constitution (whatever might be its letter), such was the effect it produced on the minds of her people, and of her houses of legislature, that, on the whole it was not prudent, it would not have been thought sufficiently legal, for her to be often or systematically that absolute sovereign which the historian supposes her to be. The conclusion, therefore, is, that the constitution was not, in fact, what *he* imagines. There is certainly some confusion in Hume; he does not distinguish between the constitution as originally understood before Henry VII, and the constitution as it afterwards obtained in practice under the Tudors. Add to this, that it is in vain to look entirely at statutes and at courts, whether equitable or oppressive. The general spirit of the whole, the notions of it that are inherited and transmitted, the effect produced on the opinions and temperament of the public and of the rulers themselves—*these* are the great objects to be considered when we speak of a constitution.

It is but too obvious to remark the superiority of Elizabeth over her successors, particularly the unhappy Charles, in one most important requisite, the art of discovering the state of the public mind, the art of appreciating well the nature of the times in which she lived.

The fact seems to have been that the great merit, the sole merit of this renowned queen was this; with great faults, bad passions, and most female weaknesses, she had still the spirit and the sense so to control her own nature, that, with the exception of her appointment of Leicester to charges the most critical, she never, like other sovereigns of similar faults, neglected the interests of her kingdom, or by the indulgence of her own failings brought calamities on her subjects. This is an honourable distinction. If princes and ministers, in their real disposition as reprehensible and odious as Queen Elizabeth, would in practice become rulers as prudent and patriotic, the affairs of mankind would present a very different and far more pleasing appearance. . . .

The same interest which belongs to the reign of Elizabeth belongs still more to the parliamentary proceedings in the reign of James I.

The commons and the sovereign seem of like disposition with their predecessors; but the former far more advanced in wisdom, and the latter in folly.

The great contest between prerogative and freedom may be seen still ripening into fatal maturity; and the parties and maxims which so distinguished the reign of Charles I are clearly visible.

The proceedings in parliament, and the speeches of the king, are most of them marked by expressions and reasonings, the perusal of which can alone convey an adequate picture of the times, and the revolution which was approaching. . . .

The king appears to have formed one idea of the constitution, and the commons another. Before the end of his reign he was brought to express himself in a manner somewhat more agreeable to the general spirit of the laws and customs of the realm, yet his reign was marked by a continual state of warfare, and an open rupture was at last the result.

Understanding that a protestation had been drawn up by the house on the subject of their privileges, he sent for their journal book, and tore it out with his own hand.

This protestation had affirmed that the liberties, franchises, privileges, and jurisdiction of parliament are the ancient and undoubted birthright and inheritance of the subjects of England; had asserted the competence of parliament to consider such affairs as the king thought exclusively the objects of what, in the pride of his folly, he called his *statecraft*; had laid down the freedom of speech, the immunity from arrest, and the illegality of the king's giving credence (as it was called) with respect to the conduct of the members. . . .

On the decline of the feudal system, the king was left to depend for the support of his own state, and even for the expenses of foreign war,— first, on the claims of his feudal rights, and on the exercise of his prerogative; and secondly, on the supplies of parliament. These feudal claims and exercises of the prerogative were daily becoming, from the changes that had taken place in the world, less valuable to the crown, and yet more injurious and offensive to the subject.

But if these were entirely to be withdrawn, the sovereign was then to be left totally dependent on the favour of the commons. It was neither in itself just, nor in any respect agreeable to the best interests of the people, that the sovereign should be thus deprived of all proper funds for the maintenance of his personal dignity and constitutional importance. The only expedient for avoiding all the evils that might ensue, was, that the king should give up the feudal rights and prerogatives which his predecessors had exercised; and the commons in return secure him an adequate revenue, a revenue which might be collected from the subjects with less injury to their civil freedom and growing prosperity.

In a few years after the king's accession, a scheme of this sort was actually in agitation.

The Lords mediated, as usual, between the king and commons. Even the terms of the bargain, or, what was then very properly called, of the great contract, were all adjusted.

The parliament was prorogued in the summer to October; and all that remained was that they should state the manner in which the sum agreed upon (two hundred thousand pounds per annum) was to be secured. But though the conferences and committees were resumed, no effectual progress was made, and the parliament was dissolved in December—nothing done. This great chance for avoiding all the evils that were impending was thus lost for ever. We in vain inquire by whose fault, by what unhappy train of circumstances, this golden opportunity was lost.

The journals of the commons are here wanting; the journals of the lords give little or no information, nor do the contemporary historians assist us. The king in his proclamation, after alluding to the affair, says only, "that for many good considerations known to himself, he had now determined to dissolve the parliament." When he called a new one, four years afterwards, he only observes in his speech, that "he will deal no more with them like a merchant, by way of exchange," that "he shall expect loving contribution for loving retribution"; "that to come to account with them how and what, was too base for his quality." In another speech he alludes to some who had done ill offices between him and his commons. The probability seems that the higgling manner of the commons had naturally disgusted the king: and that two hundred thousand pounds per annum was a sum larger, at that time, than they on their part durst commit to the exclusive disposal of the crown; and this conjecture is confirmed by a few words which I observed in a passage of one of Sir John Eliot's speeches, made some time after.

In a few months this new parliament was likewise dissolved, and in great ill-humour; yet nothing occurs in the speeches of the members, or elsewhere, with the casual exception just mentioned in Sir John Eliot's hint, that throws any light on this important transaction. Neither the leaders, therefore, of the commons, with all their real ability, nor the king, with all his "statecraft," nor the historians at the time, much less the people, appear to have seen the crisis in which the realm was already placed, or that the best, perhaps only, system had been struck upon, and yet abandoned, for saving alike the people and the monarch from the dangers to which they were exposed. These dangers were now inevitable. The commons had publicly stated the maxims of their conduct—the principles, as they conceived, of the constitution. The king had indignantly torn them from their journals, as inconsistent with his rights and the honour of his crown. The great question of prerogative on the one side, and of privilege on the other, was therefore at issue; and it would have required far other abilities and virtues than those which his successor Charles possessed, to have been a guardian minister of good to his unhappy country, in a situation so little understood, and however understood, so encompassed with difficulties.

Making every allowance for the imperfection of human judgment, making every allowance for the impossibility which seems always to exist either for king or people properly to comprehend their situation, when these dreadful revolutions are approaching, still the conduct of Charles appears totally infatuated.

Admit that he entertained the same notions of the royal prerogative which his father had done, that he thought himself bound in honour to defend it, was it not clear that he must then adopt a system of economy, and avoid expense at home and wars abroad?

If his parliaments differed with him about his rights, could he on any other system do without them? Admit, again, that he lived in a religious age, when Papist and Protestant, when Roman Catholic, Lutheran, and Calvinist, gave each of them the most unreasonable importance, as they are always disposed to do, to their own particular doctrines and ceremonies, had not the nature of the religious principle sufficiently displayed itself? Had not the transactions in Germany, from the beginning of the Reformation, been a subject of the most *recent* history? Had not the efforts which the Calvinists made in France, had not the wars in the Low Countries, had not the success of the Hollanders, been exhibited immediately before his eyes? Could he draw no lesson for his own conduct from instances like these? Could all that he had even then witnessed in what is now called the Thirty Years' War in Germany produce no effect upon his understanding; and as if the ability and spirit of his English parliaments were not sufficient for his embarrassment, was he still further to increase his difficulties, was he to go on and summon to his destruction all the furies of rage and fanaticism from Scotland? The wisest monarch, in the situation of Charles, might, no doubt, have failed; but it seems scarcely possible for his worst enemy to have advised more obvious and fatal mistakes than those, which, with all our compassion for his fate, we must allow that he committed. . . .

All that I can attempt in the ensuing lectures is this, to offer a few observations, such as I conceive may possibly be of use to those who undertake the perusal of all or any of the books I have recommended; such as may, perhaps, enable them to exercise their own diligence and their own powers of reflection with the better effect.

In the first place, then, I would suggest that there are two leading considerations in this subject which should be always kept in view. The first is this:—*What* was the effect of these transactions on the constitution *ultimately—on the whole?* Secondly, What were the comparative merits and demerits of the contending parties?

The first consideration must of course be suspended till we can turn and look back from a very distant point of view, such as the revolution of 1688, when these disputes were brought to a species of close.

It is the second consideration, the merits and demerits of the contending parties, which is more within the reach of our attention at present. And even in this last question, the first will be found continually implicated.

With respect to this last inquiry, the comparative merits and demerits of the parties, what I would recommend is that the whole of the reign of Charles should be separated into different intervals, and an estimate and comparison made of the conduct of the parties during each of these intervals.

This estimate may be very different during different intervals; and it is from a consideration of the whole that a verdict must at last be pronounced.

I shall in this and the ensuing lectures endeavour to give you a more distinct idea of what I have just proposed, and I shall attempt to do in a summary manner what, as I conceive, you may with some advantage execute hereafter more regularly for yourselves, as you read the history and the proper documents connected with it.

The first period which I select as an interval is from the accession of Charles to the dissolution of his third parliament in 1629, an interval of four years.

But before this interval or any part of the question be examined, one observation must be made; it is this, that in appreciating the comparative merits of the two contending parties, it is most important to consider what was their conduct at the commencement of their differences, and before the rupture actually took place: that is, which was *at first* the offending party. *Afterwards* it is *too late* for either of them to be wise. Offences and injuries generate each other from the very nature of human infirmity; the decision is soon committed to violence and force; and those are the most guilty who have been the original means of reducing themselves or their opponents to such dreadful extremities.

This being premised, we are to examine, in the next place, this short, but, for the reason I have just mentioned, this most critical period, this first interval of four years.

And to me it appears that it would be difficult to say how the king could have conducted himself in a manner less deserving of our approbation. Read the history, and then consider, were not his notions inconsistent, not only with the civil liberty which belongs to a free monarchy, but with the measure of civil freedom which at that time belonged to the English monarchy? Again, had his people any other hold upon him but their House of Commons? Had the commons any, but his necessities? Did they, therefore, in the last place, push their power of extorting concessions in return for their supplies to any extent not required by the public good, or rather, to any extent not required by the constitution, even as then understood?

Take, for a specimen of the whole subject, the proceedings on the famous Petition for Right.

When we, in the first place, read the history, and observe all the shifts and efforts of the king to evade it, and all the anxiety and labour of the commons to prepare it; and when we afterwards come to read the petition itself, the first sensation is surely that of extreme surprise, for it actually appears to contain no declaration and no provision that we should not have hoped that Charles, or any other English monarch from the time of Magna Charta, would have assented to with cheerfulness.

One observation, however, is to be made; the Petition of Right did in fact endeavour to settle or rather to confirm for ever one particular point, which may not, at the first reading of the petition, sufficiently occur to you; this point was the personal liberty of the subject. . . .

There is a political difficulty, no doubt, in the question. Thus, it is fit that every government should have a power of imprisonment, even *without shewing cause;* because very extraordinary occasions may arise: a rebellion, for instance, may be reasonably apprehended. But this Petition of Right gives *no* such occasional power, allows of no exceptions in any supposed case, but lays down the personal freedom of the subject in *all situations* but those in which the subject has already become obnoxious to the existing laws. This, therefore, does not seem a proper adjustment of the great question of the personal liberty of the subject.

It must, however, be observed, that it was on account of no theoretical objection of this kind that Charles was resolved, if possible, not to assent to the Petition of Right. The real reasons of his opposition were these:

because he had no means of raising money by the exertions of his prerogative, unless he could throw men into prison (without showing cause)
if they resisted his requisitions; and because he had no expedient for
controlling the freedom of speech in the houses of parliament, unless it
was, on the whole, understood, that the members were within reach of
what he and the lords called his sovereign power.

There can surely, therefore, be no doubt that if the commons had
not made provision against this claim of the crown, it would soon have
been totally unsafe and impossible for any member in parliament, or
any subject out of it, to have offered any legal resistance to the arbitrary
measures of the king; and the contest must at length have terminated
entirely against the constitution.

Charles had exercised a power of imprisonment on pretences and for
purposes totally incompatible with all liberty; what was left for the
commons but to insist upon it, as a fixed principle, that no man should
be imprisoned without a cause shown?

But what are we to say, when we find that this has been always the
language of the constitution, from Magna Charta down to that moment? "The truth is," says Mr. Hume, "that the great charter and the
old statutes were sufficiently clear in favour of personal liberty. But as
all kings of England had ever, in cases of necessity or expediency, been
accustomed at intervals to elude them; and as Charles, in a complication of instances, had lately violated them; the commons judged it
requisite to enact a new law, which might not be eluded or violated by
any interpretation, construction, or contrary precedent. Nor was it sufficient, they thought, that the king promised to return into the way of
his predecessors. His predecessors in all times had enjoyed too much
discretionary power, and by his recent abuse of it, the whole world had
reason to see the necessity of entirely retrenching it." These are the words
of Mr. Hume.

But upon this statement of Mr. Hume, does not the conduct of the
commons appear perfectly constitutional and perfectly reasonable? With
what propriety is Mr. Hume, at the close of this subject, to use the following expressions:

"It may be affirmed, without any exaggeration, that the king's assent
to the Petition of Right produced such a change in the government as
was almost equivalent to a revolution."

How could this enactment of the Petition of Right, this confirmation of
Magna Charta and the old statutes, which were already so clear in favour of personal liberty, how can this new assertion of what had been
always asserted, this new assertion in times of such extreme peril to the
constitution—how can this be represented as equivalent to a revolution? The great political difficulty of the personal liberty of the subject,

which was thus decided by the commons *entirely* in favour of the subject according to the ancient laws and constitution of the realm, was not settled with philosophical accuracy by the Petition of Right. To have expected this in such times was to expect too much. Afterwards, it was more skilfully provided for, as is well known, by making effective the writ of habeas corpus, in the first place; and by the occasional suspension of the writ, in the second. In consequence of this writ, made at last available, no man can be now kept in prison without cause shown; and when the writ is to be suspended, and men are to be kept in prison without cause shown, the suspension is asked for by the executive power, and is assented to by the legislative power for a time specified, and on reasons first produced and deemed sufficient.

The general freedom of the subject is thus secured, and the very necessary interference of government in an arbitrary manner occasionally to protect the community from the concealed practices of foreign or domestic traitors, is thus admitted.

This is, I conceive, a very happy adjustment of one of the greatest difficulties that belong to the science of government.

Observe, however, it is quite clear, that from the moment the writ of habeas corpus is suspended, and the executive power can throw men into prison without showing cause, the government is at once changed from a free to an arbitrary government; and that the liberties of the country are, from that instant, left to depend on the spirit of freedom, and on the habits of right thinking, that have already been generated by that free constitution; not only in the houses of parliament, the judges of the land, and the people, but even in the executive power itself. The question therefore that remains is whether this justly celebrated writ of habeas corpus would now have existed in our constitution, if it had not been for the exertions of the commons in the reign of Charles I, and more particularly on this occasion of the Petition of Right, and whether, if it had not been for these exertions, an order from a secretary of state, and the Tower, might not have been as common in England, as *lettres de cachet* and the Bastile were once in France. . . .

The second and next interval which I would select, is from the end of the first four years of Charles's reign, from 1629 to 1640; a most remarkable interval of eleven years, and which is extremely important.

Here a new scene opens:—we have no longer, as hitherto, the king calling parliaments, and then demanding the grant of supplies, as the condition of his favour; and the commons, in their turn, requiring the admission of constitutional claims, as the condition of their subsidies. We have no longer prorogations, dissolutions, imprisonment of the members, and during the intermission of parliament, loans and benevolences; but we have now a resolution to call parliaments no more; we have what were before occasional expedients, converted into a system of regular government; we have every effort exerted to make the prerogative of the crown *supply the place* of parliaments; and this plan of government persevered in for eleven years together.

Now it is very evident, that if this experiment had succeeded—if Charles I could have ruled without parliaments, as he was to be followed by such princes as his sons really were, and must necessarily have been made, no difference could have long remained between the English monarchy and the French; and Charles I, though amiable in private life, a man of virtue and of religion, would, in fact, have been the destroyer of the liberties of his country; and in this important respect, precisely on a level with the perfidious and detestable tyrant of France, Louis XI. . . .

What I have to press upon your reflections is this:—If men like these, a calm, deliberating philosopher like Hume (though favourable to monarchy, yet certainly not meaning to be unfavourable to the interests of mankind), if Hume, at the distance of more than a century in the security of his closet; and Clarendon, a lover of the constitution, of his country, a patriotic statesman, while delivering, as he rightly conceived, a work to posterity: if such men could think that *these* were observations on the subject, too reasonable to be withheld from the minds of their readers, how difficult it must have been for men at the time, to have escaped from the soothing, the fatal influence of such considerations; this supposed prosperity of their country, this peace, this order, these domestic virtues and piety of their king, their safety under his kind protection; how difficult to have been generous enough to think of those Englishmen who were to follow them, rather than of themselves; how difficult to have encountered the terrors of fines and imprisonments, for the sake of any thing so vague, so abstract, so disputed (such might have been their language), as the constitution of their country; how difficult to have resisted all those very prudent suggestions with which sensible men, like Hume and Clarendon, not to say, the minions of baseness and servility, could have so readily supplied them; how difficult, when all that was required of them was a little silence, and the occasional payment of a tax of a few shillings!

Yet if our ancestors had not escaped from the soothing, the fatal influence of such considerations; if they had not thought that there was something still more to be required for their country, than all this peace, and industry, and commerce, this calm of felicity, this protection and repose, under the most virtuous and merciful of kings; if they had not resisted with contempt and scorn all the very prudent suggestions with which their minds might have been so easily accommodated; if they had not been content to encounter the terrors of fines and imprisonments, the loss of their domestic comforts, the prospects of lingering disease and death, for the sake of their civil and religious liberties; if they had not had the generosity and magnanimity, the virtue and the heroism, to think of their descendants as well as themselves, what, it may surely be asked, would have been *now* the situation of those descendants, and where would have been now the renowned constitution of England?

xv. CHARLES I

CHARLES HAD been persevering in this faulty, or rather criminal course, for some time after the fourth year of his reign; but as he added folly to his political transgressions, he at last supplied his subjects with that "striking motive" which the historian justly represents as so necessary to rouse a people into rebellion.

Unfortunately for his royal house, both he and his father lived in a religious age; and their particular temperaments impelled them to introduce the religious principle into politics; an unworthy direction, which, of itself, it would have been but too apt to take in the existing circumstances of the world.

James I had pronounced the celebrated maxim of "No bishop, no king." The divines of the church of England were in these times not wanting in their endeavours to establish the doctrine of passive obedience; it was indeed supposed to be the unqualified doctrine of the Scriptures. A sympathy and a supposed bond of interest, to be carried blindly to any unconstitutional length, was thus unhappily formed between the regal and episcopal power. Add to this that the religion of Charles and the famous Laud was narrow and intolerant; and in a fatal hour it was resolved to introduce the canons and liturgy of the church of England, or rather a modification of them, that was even more offensive, into Scotland. . . .

It was in vain that Charles at length made concessions to his Scottish subjects; these concessions were never made in time, nor ever sufficient for the occasion. They never deserved the praise of magnanimity; and they therefore never reaped the benefit of it. From the first, his cause in Scotland was continually verging to defeat and disgrace. However necessary he and Laud might conceive their own ecclesiastical institutions to be, the Covenanters were equally clear that such relics and images of Popery were quite fatal to all rational hopes of acceptance with the Deity. The king drew the sword; the obvious consequence, but the last fatal consummation of his impolicy and intolerance. On the one hand, contributions were levied, by the influence of Laud, on the ecclesiastical bodies of England; while, on the other, the pulpits of Scotland resounded with anathemas against those, who went not out to assist the Lord against the mighty. . . .

The result was, as it is desirable it may always be, that the cause of intolerance was successfully resisted.

But the effects of this attempt of Charles and Laud were not to end with Scotland.

The king could not wage war without expense, nor encounter expense without pressing upon his English subjects.

After having made a pacification with the Scots, the king could not persuade himself fairly to give up the contest; and he therefore once more collected an army: an army which he could not pay; and for the purpose of paying it, he was at last obliged to summon once more an English parliament, and this after an intermission of eleven years, and after all his tyrannical expedients to do without one.

And here commences a third interval, which I should propose to extend only to the king's journey into Scotland in the August of 1641. This interval includes the *whole sitting* of the parliament now called, and the *first period* of the proceedings of the next, the noted parliament, afterwards called the long parliament; it is a short interval of about a year; but it is clearly to be distinguished from the two former intervals, when the conduct of the king was so deserving of reprobation, and again from the fourth or last interval, when the conduct of the parliament was unequivocally wrong. Even in this third, this intermediate interval, the king was still, as I conceive, to be blamed, and the parliament to be praised; but this blame and this praise become now more questionable, and not to be given without some hesitation and reserve.

When the parliament met, it was soon evident that the king only wanted money; while the commons, on *their* part, were chiefly anxious for proper admissions on *his*, to secure the liberty of the subject. He could not wait, he said, for the result of discussions of this nature; and desired to be supplied, in the first place, and to be trusted on his promise for a subsequent redress of their grievances. The parliament civilly evaded his request, and would not comply, i. e. would not in fact trust his promise; they were, therefore, dissolved in haste and anger.

This important measure, which was decisive of his fate and of the peace of the community, will be found, on examination, though it may not at first sight appear so, impolitic and unjustifiable. "The vessel was now full," says Lord Bolingbroke, "and this last drop made the waters of bitterness overflow."

It was the subject of the most sincere lamentation, and evidently a measure much disapproved by Lord Clarendon, then Mr. Hyde, and a most valuable member of the House of Commons, valuable both to the king and people.

This unfortunate prince seems to have been, even at this advanced period of these dissensions, totally unable to comprehend his own situation, or make the slightest provision for future contingencies.

As money could not be raised by parliament, the former illegal expedients were renewed; and we are here to consider what was the object, all this time, which the king was so resolved to accomplish. Was it justifiable, the introduction of Laud's canons and liturgy into Scotland?

The event was, that an army undisciplined and ill-paid was led against the Scots, and found unfit to contend with them; and every thing being reduced to a state of exasperation and despair, the king, after calling a council of the peers at York, once more thought proper to summon a parliament.

It was the last he ever did summon; it was the long parliament.

Hitherto the feelings of Englishmen will sufficiently sympathize with the proceedings of the commons. But as the contest between prerogative and privilege was longer continued, and grew more and more warm, it must necessarily be expected that the hazards and perplexities of the great leaders of the House of Commons were to increase, and that right decisions were to be attained with more difficulty. After having been tried in the perilous warfare of doubtful and dangerous contest, a severer trial yet remained, that of success. They were now, if possible, though successful, to be wise and moderate.

In civil dissensions it is quite impossible to suppose that misconduct shall be found only on one side. Outrage and folly in the one party are necessarily followed by similar offences in the other; and from the condition of human infirmity, it must inevitably happen, that in examining the merits and demerits of actors in scenes like these, the question is soon altered; and ceasing to be, an inquiry of which is in the right, becomes rather an investigation of which is least in the wrong.

To the lasting honour of the long parliament, and by implication of the parliaments that preceded, it does not appear that its measures were, for a certain period, with one exception, the attainder of Lord Strafford, and perhaps also the vote for their own continuance, at all censurable; on the contrary, that they were highly laudable. The members of the long parliament would surely have been unworthy of their office if they had not provided for the meeting of parliaments, the integrity of the judges, the extinction of monopolies, and the abolition of the council of York, and the courts of Star Chamber and high commission.

Lord Falkland and Lord Clarendon concurred, for a time, with the measures of the popular party of this long parliament; and the major part of the house is stated by the latter to have consisted of men who had no mind to break the peace of the kingdom, or to make any considerable alteration in the government of church and state.

Mr. Hume himself, in his fifty-fourth chapter, gives the following opinion: observe the very considerate candour of his remarks. "In short, if we take a survey of the transactions of this memorable parliament [that is, the long parliament], during the *first* period of its operation [the period we are now considering], we shall find that, excepting Strafford's attainder, which was a complication of cruel iniquity, their merits in other respects so much outweigh their mistakes, as to entitle them to praise from all lovers of liberty. Not only were former abuses remedied, and grievances redressed; great provision for the future was made by law against the return of like complaints, and if the means by which they obtained such advantages savour often of artifice, sometimes of violence, it is to be considered that revolutions of government cannot be effected by the mere force of argument and reasoning; and that factions being once excited, men can neither so firmly regulate the tempers of others, nor their own, as to ensure themselves against all exorbitances." The admissions of Mr. Hume are often very striking.

Down, therefore, to the king's journey into Scotland in August, 1641, the student will find that, with the exceptions before stated, the attainder of Lord Strafford, and perhaps the vote for their own continuance, he may consider his country as for ever indebted to those who thus far resisted the arbitrary practices of prerogative; that thus far they are perfectly entitled to the highest of all praise—the praise of steady, courageous, and enlightened patriotism.

The next interval that may be taken is, the period that elapsed between the king's journey to Scotland in August, 1641, and the commencement of hostilities.

During this, the fourth interval, the measures of the commons became violent and unconstitutional. That this should be the case may be lamented, but cannot, for the reasons already mentioned, excite much surprise.

There were, however, various circumstances which still further contributed most unhappily to produce these mistaken and blameable proceedings. I will mention some of them; they must be considered as explanations and palliatives of the faults that were committed.

For instance, and in the first place, Lord Clarendon, after giving the testimony which I have quoted, to the general good intentions of the long parliament, distinguishes the *great body* of the house from some of the great leaders of the popular party. . . . That men, like these, men of great ability, should be found in an assembly like the House of Commons, is not to be wondered at; nor that such men should be of a high and impetuous nature, or should succeed in their endeavours to lead the rest—men of calmer sense and more moderate tempers.

Finally, we cannot be surprised, that moderate men of this last description should be deficient in their attendance on the house, should be wanting in activity, and above all, in a just confidence in themselves. That all this should happen, as, according to the noble historian, seems to have been the case, may readily be supposed. This inactivity, however, this want of confidence in themselves, was fatal to the state; and it is from circumstances like these that this period of our history is only rendered still more deserving of the study of every Englishman, and of all posterity. That men of genius who are the more daring guides, may learn the temptations of their particular nature, and that men of colder sense, who are the more safe guides, should be taught their own value— should be made to feel that it is they alone who ought not indeed to propose, but ultimately to decide; and though they may not apparently lead, at least determine, and in fact prescribe the course that is to be pursued; that it is their duty in this, their proper province, to exert themselves manfully and without ceasing.

For instance, the great occasion on which the moderate party failed was in the prosecution of Lord Strafford. That he was to be impeached by the leaders must have been expected; that he deserved it may be admitted; but that, when the existing laws did not sentence him to condign punishment, when no ingenuity could prove that he had capitally offended, then for the leaders to bring in a bill of attainder, that is, a bill to execute him with or without law, by the paramount authority of parliament, or rather of the House of Commons, acting merely on their own moral estimation of the case, all this was what no moderate, reasonable men should ever have admitted; and they ought surely to have considered that if they were once to be hurried over an act of injustice—a real crime against the laws like this—it was impossible to say into what offences they might not afterwards be plunged, by the violence of which they saw their leaders were certainly capable on the one part, and by what they already knew of the indiscretion and arbitrary nature of the king, on the other. . . .

The multitude, ever clamourous for punishment and public executions—ever careless for those forms of law in which they are of all others so deeply interested, might well have terrified even the commons themselves, and made them pause; a very little self-examination might have enabled these legislators to discover that they saw displayed in the furious looks and voices of the mob only a ruder image of their own intemperate thirst for vengeance, and dangerous disregard of the established principles of justice.

But to proceed with my subject. I will now mention another reason to account for the unconstitutional proceedings of the commons in addition to the reason just alluded to, the inertness of the moderate men. It is this: the peculiar nature of the times in which the great leaders of the commons happened to live. The age of the long parliament was a religious age. . . .

Again, and in the third place, it must be observed that various incidents occurred of the most untoward nature (the Irish rebellion for instance), all contributing to mislead those who directed the patriotic party, and to increase the perplexities and calamities of the scene.

But I will mention one circumstance more, in the fourth and last place, to account for the mistakes and faults, and unconstitutional proceedings of the long parliament. It is this: the conduct of the king himself. This conduct was marked with such a total want of foresight and prudence as made all reasonable system in his opponents impossible. To adopt, for the sake of illustration, a familiar illusion, you cannot play a game if your opponent observes not the common rules of it. The student may take, as an instance, his visit to the House of Commons to seize the five members.

Such are the four heads, under some of which may be included all those very peculiar events and circumstances which I conceive should be taken into consideration, when we decide on the blameable proceedings, and objectionable temper of the long parliament. They will certainly explain and extenuate all, excuse, perhaps, if not justify *much* of their conduct:—1. The inertness of the moderate men. 2. The peculiar nature of the times, and the religious nature of them. 3. The various untoward incidents that occurred; the Irish rebellion, e. g. 4. The totally unreasonable conduct of the king, which made any reasonable system in his opponents so difficult and impossible.

The result of the whole was that the parliamentary leaders did not choose to trust the king; and they required from him, for their own security, and the security of the subject (which, it must be observed, was now identified with their own, for if they had failed, no further resistance could have been again expected), they required, I say, such concessions as trenched on the prerogative of the crown, more than any precedents warranted; more than any constitutional view of the subject would have authorized in any ordinary situation of the political system; more than would have been favourable to the interests of England at any subsequent period. The question, therefore, which we have at length to decide is this: whether these leaders were justified in this distrust of the crown, or not? Whether they demanded more than was necessary for their own security, and the security of the constitution, which, as I have before observed, were now identified; for if they failed, as I must repeat, no subsequent effort could have been expected from others.

And this question ought, in candour, to be argued on the supposition that the king was in reality as deeply impressed with the rights of his prerogative as ever; as little disposed as ever to rule by parliaments, if he could do without them; as little disposed as ever to consider the exertions of the leaders of the commons in opposition to his authority, as any other than disobedience and rebellion, which ought to be punished according to its various degrees, by fine, imprisonment, or death; for these are the inferences that may clearly be drawn from his character, his education, and all the speeches and actions of his reign, down to the very period to which we now allude.

But though this appears nothing more than a fair statement of the case, it does not follow that the parliamentary leaders should therefore not have trusted the king, or should not have thought themselves sufficiently safe and successful, after they had once secured by law and by his public concessions, such material points as the calling of parliaments, the right of taxation, and the abolition of the courts of Star Chamber and high commission.

We are called upon to examine whether they did not underestimate their own strength; whether they appear to have considered how great was the victory which they had obtained; whether they seem to have asked themselves the reason of it; whether, in short, they did not make the same mistake which is so naturally, so constantly made by all who engage in contests of this or any other kind, the mistake of never supposing that an opponent has been sufficiently depressed.

The same mistake was made in the late revolution in France. The patriotic party of that country, the leaders of the constituent assembly of 1789, could never bring themselves to believe that they were sufficiently secure from the court and their opponents, that the executive power was sufficiently weakened, and the same difficulty or error operated, as in our own country, to the destruction of the king and themselves.

It is scarcely to be expected that in these dreadful conjunctures of human affairs, this particular mistake should not often be made. So many are the causes which concur to produce it; but I think it must be allowed that the mistake was committed by the parliamentary leaders.

The mistake, however, be it made when it may, is sure to be attended by the most fatal effects. The old system, which those who have loved their country meant only to improve, is inevitably destroyed; and the early patriots, the men of sense and virtue, are overwhelmed in the general calamity. They have grasped the pillars of the temple; the temple falls, and, like the strong man of Holy Writ, they bury in the ruins themselves as well as their opponents.

After all, there can be no doubt that if the question had been a question of prerogative and privilege only, the proceedings of the commons

would have been far more, and perhaps sufficiently moderate and constitutional; but the misfortune was that these dissensions were not
merely of a civil, but also of a religious nature. How, and to what extent,
they were of a religious nature, should be now explained to you. . . .

There were, more particularly, four different descriptions of religious
opinion—the Roman Catholics, the members of the Church of England,
the Presbyterians, and lastly, the Independents; that of the four descriptions of religious opinion that existed in the country at the time, the
Presbyterians and Independents were naturally separated from those
of the Roman Catholic and Church of England communion; and however differing from each other in the most important points, were united
in their common hatred to the hierarchy, and in their common wish for
a form of worship more simple than that established; at all events, they
were both resolved to have no bishops.

As Charles and Laud could not be satisfied unless they attempted to
introduce Episcopacy into Scotland, the puritanical interest in England
thought their labours and patriotism in the House of Commons imperfect, unless they, in like manner, improved, according to their own particular notions, the church government of England. In their debates,
therefore, their petitions and their remonstrances to the king, instead of
finding the great principles of civil government, and those *only*, insisted
upon, we are totally fatigued and overpowered by eternal complaints and
invectives against popish priests; the non-execution of penal laws; diabolical plots, and malignant counsellors. It is not only Strafford that is impeached, but also Laud; it is not only the right of the commons to concur
in the taxation of the people that is to be asserted, but the bishops are
to have no vote in the House of Lords; and when the mobs assemble
about the doors of the houses of parliament, the streets resound not with
the cry of parliament and privilege, but of "No popish prelates; no rotten-
hearted lords," &c. &c.; and it is not corrupt counsellors or arbitrary
judges, but it is the *bishops* that escape with difficulty from the fury of
this theological populace.

We must therefore consider whether the long parliament would have
acted, as they did, in any ordinary state of their minds and feelings;
whether the king would have found it so difficult to satisfy, at least to
appease them; whether their jealousy would have been so sensitive; their
dissatisfaction so constant; their complaints so ceaseless, captious, and
unreasonable, if they had not been, in a word, sectarians as well as
patriots.

The celebrated remonstrance, which was at last presented to the king,
and was so fitted by its tedious ill-humour to drive him to any possible
extremity, was with great difficulty carried, and if it had not been carried,
Cromwell told Lord Falkland, he would have quitted the kingdom:

that is, in other words, this manifesto upon which subsequent events so materially turned, was vitally dear to the Independents; and would probably not have been proposed, much less voted, if the great constitutional question of prerogative and privilege had not been interwoven with others of a theological nature; questions by which, it unfortunately happens, that the minds of men may, at any time, be exasperated and embittered to any possible degree of fury and absurdity.

It remains, therefore, to consider lastly, how far the Presbyterians are to be censured for this, their resolution to have the government altered in church, as well as in state.

Those among ourselves living in a subsequent age, who have been properly enlightened by the past, who not only see the duty of mutual tolerance, but act upon it, and who do not think it necessary that our own particular notions in religion or politics should be established and made to take the lead, merely because we believe them true,—such of us who so properly understand the principles of Christianity, and the duties of civilized society; such of us, if any there be, may perhaps have some little right to censure the Presbyterian faction. But no such censure could be exercised, at that unhappy period, by any of the actors in the scene. Not by Charles himself, nor Laud, nor the Episcopalian party, for they had attempted the same in Scotland. Not by any church or sect then existing, for it was an age of religious wars and mutual persecution.

In our moral criticisms, therefore, on the parties of these times, when we are speaking, it is to be remembered, not of the early patriots, but of the members of the long parliament, we have some, and yet but little preference to make. Charles and the Episcopalians were guilty of the first act of hostility—at least of the first violent, and even cruel proceedings—the Presbyterians, of urging their victory too far. If Charles and Laud had succeeded, the civil and religious liberties of England would have perished; and subsequently the Presbyterians could not succeed, but by such measures as rendered a civil war inevitable. It may be possible to determine which alternative is the worst, but mankind can have no greater enemies than those who reduce them to either.

Charles was guilty of a great want of political sagacity, in not perceiving the growing strength of the commons; and when he saw the increasing number of the sectaries, in not considering well the cautious and moderate system which he was to adopt when such men were to be opposed to his designs.

But the Presbyterians, in like manner, seem inexcusable for not taking into their account the growing strength and the increasing numbers of the Independents. The most violent of the Presbyterians had no intentions to overthrow the monarchy. But when they ceased to act *on a system of accommodation* with the king, they exposed every thing to the ultimate decision of violence. They might themselves wish only for a limited monarchy, and for Presbyters in the church instead of bishops; but a set of men remained behind them, the Independents, indisposed to all monarchy and ecclesiastical government whatever; and they were guilty of the fault, either of not properly observing the numbers and tenets of such men, or of not perceiving that, if they urged their differences with the king to the decision of the sword, or even to the immediate chance of it, men of this violent, unreasonable character must multiply, and be produced by the very urgencies of the times, and could not fail of ultimately overpowering the king, the parliament, and all who differed with them.

It must at the same time be confessed that it is the great misfortune of all critical periods like these, that parties cannot very immediately be distinguished from each other. They advance together under the same standards to a certain point, and then, and not before, they separate and take different directions: and as fury and absurdity are sure to be the most relished by the multitude, and at some time or other to have the ascendant, moderate men perceive not *in time*, that, on public, as well as on private grounds, there is more danger to be apprehended from many of those who appear to *go along* with them, than from those, who are their visible, decided, and declared opponents.

Observations of this kind have been again illustrated by the late revolution in France, and may therefore seem to indicate principles in human nature, that on such dreadful occasions will always exhibit themselves.

The vote of the remonstrance is an epoch in this calamitous contest. The commons are not to be justified in presenting this remonstrance, nor to be justified in their subsequent measures. It may be very true, that their proceedings, till the king's departure into Scotland in 1641, with the exception of Lord Strafford's attainder, and perhaps the vote for their own continuance, were (more particularly in the more early periods of the contest) most laudable and patriotic, but that they never were so afterwards. . . .

I would therefore fix the attention of the student on the famous remonstrance, and the proceedings relating to it, as the particular point where his opinion must, as I conceive, begin most materially to alter. . . .

XVI. CIVIL WAR

THE ENTERTAINMENT and instruction of history can never be properly felt or understood, as I cannot too often remark, unless you meditate upon the existing circumstances of the scene; suppose them before you, and estimate the probabilities that they present; then marking the events that really take place, thus derive a sort of experience in the affairs of mankind, which may enable you to determine with greater precision and success, on occasions when you may yourselves be called upon to act a part, and when the happiness of your country and your own may, more or less, be affected by the propriety of your decisions. . . .

The king seems to have been every way unfortunate. With sufficient courage and ability to make him the proper general of his own forces, he was still not possessed of that military genius which is fitted to triumph over difficulties, which can turn to its own purposes the dispositions of men, and the opportunities and unsuspected advantages of every situation: which can seem by these means to control the decisions of chance, and to command success. That a soldier, however, of this description, should arise against him on the popular side, was to be expected; a captain like Cromwell was sure to appear, at least to exist, in the ranks of his opponents. But that such a general as Fairfax should be found among the men of distinction in the country, and yet be opposed to his cause, this might surely be considered by the king as a hard dispensation of fortune. Still harder, if it be considered, that Fairfax was, of all other men that history presents, the most fitted for the purposes of a soldier like Cromwell: too honest to have criminal designs of his own: too magnanimous to suspect them in those around him; superior to every other in the field; inferior in the cabinet; enthusiastic enough to be easily deceived, but not enough to be a hypocrite and to deceive others.

The character of Cromwell seems the natural production of the times, though, it must be confessed, the most complete specimen of their influence that can well be imagined; still, the character itself consists but of the common materials—courage, fierceness, decisive sense, clear sagacity, and strong ambition; all, no doubt, given in a very eminent degree, added to such qualities as resulted from an age of religious dispute; and the whole nourished and drawn out in the most extraordinary manner, by the temptations and urgencies of a revolutionary period. Hampden early predicted his future eminence, on one supposition— the breaking out of a civil war.

From the moment that the sword was drawn, all wise and good men must, with Lord Falkland, have been overpowered with the most afflicting expectations. One of two alternatives, equally painful, could alone have occurred to them as probable; either that the king would conquer, and the privileges of the subject, and all future defence of them, be swept away in his triumph: or that the parliament would prevail, and the result would be, that the whole government, for want of some proper constitutional head, would fall into the disposal of the army, and be seized upon by some of its great captains, to the total degradation, and probably to the destruction of the existing monarch; perhaps even of the ancient forms of monarchy itself. . . .

In this calamitous state of things, the famous Prynne rose up in his place, and delivered a speech in defence of the king's answers to the propositions of parliament. Long as it is, I cannot but recommend it to an entire and attentive perusal. Allowance must be made for the violence of the author's prejudices in favour of Presbytery and against popery, and when this allowance has been made, it will be found that a train of persuasion more fairly drawn out and more clearly conducted to effect a particular purpose has seldom been produced before a public assembly. You will see it in Cobbett. Certainly a more striking exhibition of principle never occurred. Prynne was speaking in an assembly overawed by soldiers, in a situation that might have made a Roman shrink. Every reason that could irritate the heart of man concurred to render him inveterate against the king. He had to preface his arguments with relating what he had endured from him. He said "that at two different times he had suffered mutilations in the most barbarous manner [these are specimens, it is to be observed, of the conduct of Charles and Laud—note them]; that he had been set upon three several pillories: that his licensed books had been burnt before his face by the hangman; that *two* fines each of five thousand pounds [what a sum in those days!] had been imposed upon him; that he had been expelled out of the Inns of Court and University of Oxford, and degraded in both, that he had lost his calling almost nine years' space; that his books had been seized, and his estate; that he had been eight years imprisoned in several prisons; that four of these years had been spent in close imprisonment and exile, at Carnarvon, and in the Isle of Jersey, where he was debarred the use of pen, ink, paper, and all books almost but the Bible, without the least access of any friend, or any allowance of diet for his support; and all this for his good service to the state in opposing popery and regal tyranny."

Yet did this virtuous man continue to reason out his conclusion, hour after hour, with the most patient and penetrating sagacity—continue to show himself superior alike to the meanness of fear from Cromwell and the soldiers, and the remembrance of all the ferocious insults and all the abominable pains and penalties which he had endured from Charles and his advisers; in defiance of all, he continued to enforce upon the house, by the exertion of every faculty he could command, his own upright declaration, that they were bound in honour, prudence, justice, and conscience, to proceed upon the king's propositions to the speedy settlement of the peace of the kingdom.

Still further to the credit of human nature, it is to be mentioned, that this speech had a most clear and positive effect, that many members were converted to his side, that his opinion prevailed, and would probably have prevailed by a far larger majority, if nearly one-third of the house, from age and infirmities, had not been obliged to retire.

The debate had lasted without intermission for a day and a night.

The subsequent events are but too well known. Cromwell and the army sent Colonel Pride to clear the house of all who were disposed to an accommodation with the king. The public execution of the sovereign followed.

This cruel and dreadful outrage has given occasion to much reasoning with respect to the nature of government, and the original grounds of civil obedience. No subject can be more interesting, and it may very properly employ your meditations when you arrive at an event so afflicting and so awful as the public execution, in the midst of a civilized community, of the great and high magistrate of the realm. . . .

Government is no doubt instituted for the restraint of the people, but it is also instituted for the promotion of their happiness; and while obedience is the duty that should be inculcated on the people, resistance is the doctrine that should be ever present to the rulers. There may be intervals between resisting, dethroning, and executing a sovereign, and the last may be an extremity which ought never to be supposed possible; but there is a wide interval, in like manner, between rational obedience and servile submission; and though rational obedience be necessary to all human society, servile submission is inconsistent with all its purposes and enjoyments. No people can be long happy that do not reverence authority; but no governors will long do their duty who do not respect the public.

"Obedience," says Mr. Hume, "is the doctrine to be alone inculcated; nor is there any danger that mankind should degenerate into a state of servitude: when the exception occurs, it will overpower the restraint imposed by the general doctrine."

But it is no resistance to begin till such extremes of oppression arise, as create an exception to all general rules. If such is to be the nature of resistance and obedience, as Mr. Hume seems to suppose, it will then be found that resistance, when it does come, has come too late; it will then be found that the people can seldom resist their governors without fatally injuring themselves.

This therefore, is neither the resistance, nor the obedience that is wanted, and something very different from either must be generated by some means or other in a community, or the great political problem of the public happiness and security is neither solved, nor its solution in any reasonable degree even approached. It can only be solved by one expedient.

Some power of criticism must be given to the people upon the conduct of their rulers; must be introduced into the political system, to be so reasonably and yet so constantly exercised, that it shall be respected in time by those rulers, and be so taken into their account, while they are forming their measures, that it shall always have an effective tendency to render their proceedings sufficiently agreeable to the public good. Some power of criticism like this, if by any machinery of government, by representative assemblies for instance, it can be made to exist, can never exist without being a cause of the most complete improvement and advantage to both parties, to those who are to command, and to those who are to obey. The constitution, therefore, of a country is good exactly in proportion as it supplies this power of peaceable yet operative criticism; it cannot be good without it, and the reasons for civil obedience are so many, and so powerful, that the rulers of mankind are always secure, in their honours and their situation, while they administer the high office which they bear, with any tolerable portion of wisdom and integrity.

The character of Charles has been drawn by the first masters, and may be now considered as sufficiently understood. The truth is that his situation at successive periods of his reign was so different, that we view him with sentiments the most different, though his character was always intrinsically the same. He is no object of our affection and respect, but of reprehension, and almost of contempt, while we observe him in the early part of his life, though a prince destined for empire, finding the friend of his bosom in Buckingham, the unworthy favourite of his father, without capacity as a minister, or virtue as a man.

For the first few years after his accession, his conduct is only fitted to create in us very warm disapprobation, strong dislike of his measures, and suspicion of his intentions.

Afterwards, from the years 1629 to 1640, while endeavouring to rule without parliaments, he appears before us in no other light but in that of a prince of narrow mind and arbitrary nature; incapable of respecting the civil and religious liberties of his country; hurrying on to the destruction of them; and the proper object of our unequivocal hatred and indignation.

These emotions, however, gradually subside, soon after the meeting of the long parliament, as he gradually relinquishes, though by compulsion, the dangerous prerogatives he had attempted to establish.

But when a still further change of situation takes place, and when the parliament, in its turn, becomes unreasonable and bigoted, his offences are forgotten, for he ceases to be the offender; and as we begin to dislike the parliament, he is necessarily considered, first, with complacency, and then with favour.

But yet another change, still more affecting, is to be witnessed; and we do not deny him, we willingly offer him, our esteem, when we survey him at last supporting, with firmness and courage in the field, the honour of his crown against men, whom it was impossible to satisfy by any fair concessions in the cabinet.

Once more are our sentiments altered; and this esteem is softened into kindness when his fortunes lour; when the battle of Naseby is lost, and when the sword which he has drawn in vain must be at last thrown down and abandoned.

But scenes still more gloomy and affecting are to be opened. He is to be a monarch "fallen from his high estate"; he is to fly he knows not whither, to try expedients without hope, and plans without a meaning; to negotiate with his conquerors; to be called upon to proscribe his friends, and to stigmatize his own cause; to be required by formal treaty, and in the face of the world and of posterity, to be his own accuser—his own accuser, and the accuser of everything he holds venerable and dear; to be passed from prison to prison, and from enemy to enemy. We are to see him solitary and friendless; his "grey discrowned head, with none to reverence it," and, alone and unprotected, left to expostulate with enthusiasts, no longer within the reach of the common workings of our nature, or with ferocious soldiers, who call aloud, they know not why, for justice and execution; arraign him before a court of their own formation, and proclaim him a traitor to his country, and a murderer of his people!

With what sentiments are we now to behold him? With our former suspicions and dislike, indignation, and terror? Is it Charles that is before us; the friend of Buckingham; the patron of Laud; the opponent of Hampden; the corrupter, the encourager, the deserter of Strafford; the dissolver of parliaments; the imposer of liturgies; the violator of privileges? These are images of the past no longer to be recalled; these are characters of offence with which he has now no concern. It is the monarch unsubdued by adversity; it is the hero unappalled by death; it is the Christian sublimed by piety and hope; it is these that occupy our imagination and our memory. It is the tribunal of violence, it is the scaffold of blood, that banish from our minds all indignation but against his destroyers; all terrors but of the licentiousness of the people; that render all regular estimation of his character odious and impossible; and that leave nothing in the heart of the generous and humane, but compassion for his misfortunes, and reverence for his virtues.

Sentiments like these, so natural at any period, so powerful at the time as to have produced almost his deification, it is not the province of true philosophy to destroy, but rather to temper and enlighten.

It is turning history to no adequate purpose, if we do not accept the instruction which it offers. The lives and actions of men have been in vain exhibited to our view, if we make not our moral criticisms, even when to make them is a task painful and repulsive to our nature. The early part of the reign of Charles must be remembered as well as the close; the obscure as well as the brighter parts of his imperfect character. His faults should be studied, that there never may again be a necessity for the display of his virtues. Those faults were the faults of all those sovereigns who, though men of principle, have involved themselves and their country in calamities. Such sovereigns have always wanted, as did Charles, that simplicity and steadiness which could afford good men the means of understanding and depending upon their conduct; the en-lightened benevolence which could make them think more of their people than of themselves; that magnanimity which might enable them to call to their councils statesmen who would announce to them the real sentiments of the community, not echo and confirm their own; and lastly, and above all, that political sagacity, which could discern the signs of the times, the new opinions that had arisen, and which could draw forth, with equal wisdom and benevolence, such principles of improvement as the constitution of the country contained, and adapt-ing them according to the justice of the case, ere it was too late, to the ever shifting scene before them, save the state and themselves alike from the fury of the passions of the people, and the treachery of their own. . . .

XVII. CROMWELL, MONK, REGICIDES

TOWARDS THE conclusion of my last lecture, we had arrived at the usurpa-tion of Cromwell; and this usurpation of a military chief, I then observed, has been always considered as the natural issue of any successful appeal to arms on the part of the people.

This position, it appears to me, has been always laid down too broadly and indiscriminately. The question seems to admit of a distinction, and it is this:—

If a people have been long subject to all the evils of an arbitrary gov-ernment, and at last break out into insurrection, it is to be expected, no doubt, that the last favourite of the army, who survives the contest, will gradually procure for himself the power which the former sovereigns had abused and lost. There is no material shock here given to those habits of thinking and feeling, which, notwithstanding all the intermediate troubles, must still form the genuine character of the great body of the nation; but the case is materially altered, if we suppose a people, *before*, possessed of constitutional rights, and endeavouring to defend or enlarge them, in opposition to those who would limit or destroy them. Here the event, if the popular party succeed, seems more naturally to be, the ultimate strengthening and enlarging of the prior constitutional privileges, under some form of government similar to the former one.

In this case an usurpation is either not attempted, as in the instances of Switzerland and Holland, and in our own times, of America, or if attempted, the usurper finds himself impeded with such political difficulties, at every movement which he makes, that the continuance of his power is always a matter of uncertainty; and the original and irremediable disposition of the people, the result of their former better government, is sure at last to prevail, either over himself, or over his successors.

In illustration of this general reasoning may be cited the difficulties which Cromwell had to overcome, while he was endeavouring to seize the power of the state, and still more while he was labouring to retain it.

I will give a general representation of them. Together they form a strong testimony to the permanent nature of the English mixed constitution, particularly of the monarchical part of it; and they go far to prove that the usurpation of Cromwell was not, as has been generally supposed, a successful one. . . .

Cromwell had to subdue not only the royalists, but the Presbyterians; and this, not merely by force, but by the most extraordinary performances of cant and hypocrisy that human nature ever yet exhibited.

But why? Because these descriptions of men bore fresh upon their minds the impression of the constitution of England, and were only solicitous, according to the best of their judgment, to support or improve that constitution.

By the same arts and means were the Independents, the Republicans, to be overpowered by the usurper, and for the same reason. They too were impressed with the original stamp which had been received from the popular part of this constitution; and they had only deviated from it, because they thought that the monarchical part had been found, from trial, incompatible with the interests of the country.

That a military usurper, that any single person should rule, was not in the contemplation or wishes, probably, of any one disinterested Englishman at the time.

And it is here that may be found the great proof of the talents of Cromwell, which is not only, as Mr. Hume states, that he could rise from a private station to a high authority in the army; but still more, that he could afterwards bend the refractory spirits, and direct the disordered understandings of all around him, to the purposes of his own ambition, to the elevation of himself to the protectorate, in violation of all his former professions and protestations, public and private, and in defiance of all the men of principle and intrepidity, who had been so long his associates and friends in the parliament and in the army.

The gross and ignorant soldiers might, indeed, be well content, that he who gave them pay and plunder, should have every thing to dispose of: and in their idolatry of a successful general, they might, for a time, forget their country, and those forms of established authority to which they had once been accustomed. But still, it was these coarse and brute instruments upon which Cromwell could *alone* depend; and, after all, as the mass of an army must always be managed through the medium of its officers, it was here (in this management of the officers) that his extraordinary powers were exhibited in a manner so striking. Some he could make his creatures by mere bribery, by lucrative posts and expectations: but the rest, and not unfrequently many of the common soldiers themselves, he was obliged to cajole, by every art and labour of hypocrisy; to surround and bewilder them with a tempest of fanaticism, of sighs and prayers, of groans and ejaculations; in short, to elevate and involve his heroes and himself in a cloud, till he was able there to leave them, and himself to descend and take undisturbed possession of the earth.

Whoever reads the history of these times cannot well believe that this military usurper, daring and powerful as his abilities were, both in the cabinet and in the field, could possibly have succeeded, if the religious principle had not unfortunately found its way into every part of the dispute between the king and his people, and so disturbed the natural tendency of things, as to render any achievement practicable, which could well be conceived by a man of military skill and fanaticism united. But observe his progress.

When the young king had been finally defeated at Worcester, when the Republicans had been turned out of the House of Commons, when Cromwell, with his council of officers, was left alone on the stage, and when it would generally be said, that the natural termination of the contest had arrived, and Cromwell had now only to enjoy what he had acquired; his difficulties, on the contrary, seemed rather to multiply than to cease. Cromwell, though triumphant, and without a rival, could never be at ease, and he was continually labouring to make his government approach, as much as possible, to the model of the old one, and to those forms which he knew could alone be considered as legitimate.

He was now himself precisely in the situation in which the Independents (the Republicans) had lately been. He, like them, durst not appeal to a full and fair representation of the people, yet it was necessary to have a parliament; he could not otherwise colour his usurpation; he therefore proceeded to manufacture one with all expedition.

But as he had violated the feelings and opinions of every man of principle and consideration, he could trust no one who possessed much of either; and his parliament contained, though with a mixture of others of a superior class, men of low condition and foolish fanaticism.

The parliament which he collected and made was the parliament known by the ludicrous appellations which were gravely assumed by many of its members, "Praise God Barebones," &c. &c.

These creatures he seems to have let loose upon the courts of law, probably for the sake of terrifying the lawyers. Courts of law are never very popular with the vulgar; and, therefore, senators like these soon proceeded to the attack of the Court of Chancery, *nem. con.* If you look into Cobbett, their language will amuse you. They showed a rapidity of movement which must have appeared not a little marvellous to the court itself; certainly the court could not have been taught to comprehend it from any experience in its own proceedings.

But a parliament of this kind, so little fitted to be a part of an English government, was found by Cromwell, after a few months' trial, unfit to answer his purposes; so their power was partly resigned and partly taken from them, and they returned to their more natural occupations in private life.

Still a parliament and a constitutional government of some kind or other was necessary. Cromwell, therefore, and his council of officers drew up an instrument of government, spread the power of representation over the whole of England and Wales very fairly, and began again.

Even in this instrument it is observable that the supreme legislative authority is made to reside in one person and in the people, assembled in parliament; that is, in a king and House of Commons; and that the provisions are far more unfavourable to the executive power than those in the English constitution, with one exception. This exception is contained in those articles on which, no doubt, Cromwell depended for his own protection, the twenty-seventh and three following. These provided for the maintenance of a standing military force of ten thousand horse and twenty thousand foot. The powers, however, that were given to the parliament might soon have been converted to the destruction of any protector who was not a favourite with the army.

Three hundred members assembled, and Cromwell was soon obliged, on account of the freedom of their debates, to make them a long harangue, and to declare that, "after seeking counsel from God, he must prescribe to them a test to sign." The debates still continued disagreeable to him. At length, after the manner of the very king whom he had dethroned, he dissolved them.

After an interval of two years and a half, he still thought it expedient to call once more a parliament (the third); and every effort was made to pack together an assembly devoted to his designs; but all in vain. He had to deny particular members admittance, was resisted by a large portion of the house, assailed by a spirited remonstrance, and felt in his turn, like his misguided master, that it is in vain to expect sufficient countenance to illegal proceedings from any tolerable representation of the people of England.

Still anxious and dissatisfied, still desirous to rest his authority upon some established principle, he meditated the assumption of the title of king.

He got the affair put into motion in the house. The lawyers told him, and probably with great sincerity, that this title of king, to use their own words, was a wheel upon which the whole body of the law was carried: that it stood not on the top, but ran through the whole veins and life of the law; that the nation had ever been a lover of monarchy, and of monarchy under the title of king; that, in short, this title of king was the title of the supreme magistrate, which the law could take notice of, and no other.

Cromwell desired time to "seek God for counsel"; that is, he wished to know the opinions of the army; and while he was ascertaining them, he hesitated from day to day, and renewed from day to day his long replies —replies which gave no answer, and were full of broken sentences, interrupted conclusions, doubts and insinuations, perplexity and more than Egyptian darkness; but having at length satisfied himself that the measure was disagreeable to his *army*, his elocution cleared up in an instant, and nothing can be more distinct than his short final speech, "that he could not undertake the government with the title of king."

Legitimate authority, or even the appearance of it, was now impossible; a new settlement of the government was therefore adjusted, under the form of a petition and advice, in its articles still very favourable to the liberties of the subject, but with the same material exception of the grant of a revenue to maintain the army of the executive power. Cromwell was to be solemnly inaugurated Protector; a second house was to be added to the House of Commons. Lords were to be called to it by Cromwell; that is, the form of government was thus made still more and more to approach to the model of the original constitution.

Cromwell, however, was still overpowered with impossibilities. The few real peers that he summoned to his upper house, with one base exception (Lord Eure), forbore to take their places; the commons relished not their title and questioned their authority; and the protector, enraged at their impracticable behaviour, dissolved them. This was the last experiment in the way of a parliament that he made: having dissolved the assembly in February, he died in September.

Now this after all is not a specimen of successful usurpation. He maintained his power for five years, but it seems very doubtful whether he could have done it much longer; his friend Monk thought not; his power still continued to be, as it began, merely that of the sword; no appearance of legitimate rule could be contrived for him; there was no principle existing in the English constitution which he could work up to accomplish his designs; there was no train of habits in the minds of the people of England which could afford him any foundation on which to build authority for himself; he was not assassinated, but he lived in continual apprehensions of it; he was not hurled from the government by his soldiers, but it was the labour of his life to prevent it. Abroad was the young king; at home were the Royalists, the Presbyterians, the Republicans, and enthusiasts of every description, the most insane and dangerous; most of whom he had in turn deceived, and therefore exasperated. Even in the bosom of his family, the great questions of religion and politics had interfered to disturb his peace; and his example seems to show, as far as the example of so extraordinary a character in times so extraordinary can afford any general conclusion on such points, that amid a people whose constitution has been free, a brave and able man may sometimes seize upon the chief executive power, and even possess it for some time, but that he will neither be able to enjoy it, nor engraft it upon the former constitution of the kingdom; that he will not be able to introduce a new line of arbitrary sovereigns (himself the first); and on the whole, that in public as well as private, success, as it is called, will be forever fatal to all ideas that even an ambitious man can entertain of happiness and repose.

If this reasoning be just, and the facts, at least, I have not misstated, the conclusion is—first, a strong testimony to the permanency of the monarchical part of our constitution, arising from the steadiness and intelligence of the English character; and again, that when freedom has been at all enjoyed in any country (for this is the supposition), resistance to arbitrary encroachments is not necessarily followed, even if a revolution is to be endured, by any military usurpation that will be ultimately successful.

Cromwell, I must contend, did not succeed; he could not become the peaceful and acknowledged sovereign of his country. He did, however, what alone it was in his power to do. He was a good discerner of character, and he therefore selected lawyers of ability from the profession, and persuaded them to administer to the people, though he might sometimes disregard them himself, the known laws of the country; he employed offi-

cers of courage and capacity by land and sea; he wielded with effect the
formidable energies of a people that had been lately and might still
be considered as in a state of revolution; and, like other usurpers, he endeavoured to hide in a blaze of glory a throne that was defiled with
blood. . . .

Upon the death of Oliver, the protectorate was quietly transferred to
his son, and he received addresses from all quarters, that left him to expect the peaceable possession of his honours. But the sky was soon
overcast; he had fallen upon evil days; was unfit to control the soldiery;
and, after consulting with Thurlow and other experienced counsellors,
to learn how he could best maintain his authority, too amiable to contend for power by the sanguinary measures which were proposed to
him, and too rational, perhaps, to be much concerned about the loss of
it, he dissolved the parliament which he had assembled, the only civil
authority that existed, and therefore the only power that could be friendly
to him. . . . Monk was in Scotland with an army, and nothing very certain was known about him but that Lambert and he were no friends.

And now it was that the nation very narrowly escaped the greatest of
all evils—the contentions of rival generals at the head of their armies,
the *plusquam civilia bella*.

Happily the officers that Cromwell left behind him were none of them
like himself, fit to rule the world when it was wildest. . . .

Monk must have been also aware that not only the Cavaliers, but all
the Presbyterians, constituting together, as he must have suspected, a
large majority of the nation, longed ardently for the restoration of the
monarchy. His own opinions, or, at least, ideas of interest, probably inclined the same way. . . .

The result was that with far less difficulty than could possibly have
been expected, he restored the young king to the throne of his ancestors.

Monk was a leader of armies and of fleets, and upon every occasion
displayed the most consummate valour: yet is he never considered as a
hero, so inseparable from our idea of heroism is that *fearless sincerity*,
that open, *impetuous generosity*, which formed, in fact, no part of his
character.

The services of Monk were of the most solid and striking nature; he
rescued his country from the domination of an army that had grown invincible among the civil wars, and that lived upon her ruin.

Yet has Monk never been honoured with the appellation of a patriot,
for he interested not himself in her laws and liberties, and temporized
till he seemed to follow rather than to lead the current of public sentiment.

Monk was originally the friend of Cromwell. He was employed by the

Republic; he received their pay, and led their armies; he has been therefore denied even the common praise of a gentleman and a soldier—integrity and honour. So deep a shade will always involve the fame of him, who has ever, in politics, obviously shifted his ground, and at last adopted, whether from a real change of principle or not, the side which was favourable to his interest.

These sweeping decisions of mankind, on the characters of public men, are not to be regretted; public men should be taught that their virtues are at all events to be clear and intelligible; that their conduct is to explain itself.

Such expectations in the community are the best discipline that public men can conform to. Even when this discipline has had its full effect, under every form of government, the public men will be always too much disposed to sink themselves beneath their own natural standard of excellence, to be satisfied with wishes and intentions, rather than positive exertions and acts of service, and to be too ready unworthily to yield to the suggestions of shuffling meanness and ingenious self-interest. . . .

His [Monk's] great praise was his advice to the king from the first to pass an act of indemnity on the past offences of his subjects; but even this advice, it must be confessed, was at the time, both for himself and the sovereign, the best policy; as the soldiers and officers who had dethroned Charles I might have been otherwise rendered desperate. . . .

On the restoration of the king, as public opinion is ever in extremes, the probability was that the liberties of the country would have been laid by the parliaments at the feet of the monarch. But this cannot with any propriety be said of the first parliament—the convention or restoration parliament. They sat from May to the end of the year. They passed an act, or rather confirmed an act of the long parliament, for taking away the courts of wards and liveries, together with tenures in capite, knights' service, tenures in purveyance. This was the great legislative merit of the long parliament. . . .

The king and parliament met and parted with mutual expressions of kindness. And after we have travelled through the horrors of a civil war; through all the ill-timed perseverance of the one party, the deplorable cant of the other, and the intolerance of all; it is very pleasing to us to hear at last the parliament claiming to themselves the title of the "healing parliament": and the Chancellor Clarendon, in one of his speeches, declaring that "the king was a suitor to them; was a hearty suitor; that they would join with him in restoring the whole nation to its primitive temper and integrity; to its old good manner, its old good humour, and its old good nature."

It is on occasions like these that the character of this minister is so attractive and respectable. It is understood that, even during the sitting of this parliament, he dissuaded the king from an attempt to procure an independent revenue for life. And, on the whole, it sufficiently appears that he never failed, while he possessed any influence, to use it to purposes the most noble, by recalling his sovereign's mind, whenever a fair opportunity offered, to those great principles and free maxims of the English constitution, which as the chancellor's good sense and bitter experience had told him, were not only the safeguard of the liberty of the subject, but the best security of the crown.

The mind of the chancellor was ardent; and when the punishment of the Regicides came to be decided upon, his own sufferings, and those of his first unhappy master, made him, and still more the court and the lords, but too much forget the recommendations he had so well expressed in his speeches. . . .

With respect to the number that were put to death, the conclusion is on the whole, considering the nature of these times and the occasion, tolerably favourable to the court and to the kingdom. About thirteen were executed; but most of the Regicides lost their estates; and of those who did not fly, many were kept to die in imprisonment, and very improper cruelty seems here to have been exercised.

Men must, no doubt, be deterred from crimes against the state by positive punishments; but the more complete and wide the acts of indemnity and oblivion are made in national dissensions, the better. The rancour of contending parties is thus softened. What is of still more consequence, the returns to peace in the course of national contests are afterwards more practicable. The great impediment to conciliation is always that the parties dare not trust each other.

He who draws his sword against the prince, must throw away the scabbard. The steps between the prisons and graves of princes are few. These maxims, the dreadful maxims of civil dispute, have been the cause of more misery and destruction to sovereigns and their subjects than all the real causes of contention that ever existed between them.

The history of our country during these wars was not defiled by those massacres, assassinations, proscriptions, or, with the exception of the execution of the king, with those outrages which have marked the progress of civil and religious fury in other countries and ages: a striking testimony to the merits of the English constitution, which could have alone infused into all ranks those manly feelings which are so indispensably necessary to the maintenance of honourable warfare; an indirect proof, at the same time, that the constitution had not been of the arbitrary nature that was by some supposed. . . .

XIX. CHARLES II

I MUST NOW allude to what I consider as the remaining part of this contest between Charles and the friends of civil freedom, when the patriotic leaders had to contend, not only with the king, but also with the Duke of York, and when, on account of the arbitrary nature of the religion of the latter, they were at last driven to the resolution of endeavouring to exclude him from the throne.

During the first period of their contest with the crown, the patriotic leaders must be considered as successful. The king, we may remember, broke the seals of his declaration and gave way.

But during this second period, the event was otherwise; the king could neither be persuaded nor intimidated into any compliance with the wishes of his opponents; and the struggle ended at length in the execution of some of their leaders, and in the ruin of all.

Whatever difference of opinion there may be respecting their intentions and conduct during this latter period (during their struggle with the king on the subject of the exclusion of the Duke of York from the throne), there can be none respecting the merit of their exertions during the former period. Had the king then succeeded, the liberties of England might have perished.

On the whole, the contest by which the reign of Charles II is distinguished, can be considered as inferior in interest and importance only to that which immediately preceded it, during the era of the great rebellion; and such was the necessity of resistance to the son, as well as to the father, that the same Englishmen who have loved and revered the memory of Hampden, have never ceased to venerate the virtue and respect the patriotism of Sidney and Lord Russell. . . .

As far as principle is concerned, it is the Duke, not Charles, who appears to be the man of principle; it is he who is a bigot to his opinions, religious and political; to popery and arbitrary power. These, with Charles, were rather the instruments than the objects of his designs; but the duke really had opinions that were dear to him; and he thoroughly and from his heart did detest and abjure all men, principles, and parties that presumed to interfere with the powers that be, either in church or state.

When the duke speaks of the proceedings of parliament, his expressions are, "His Majesty was forced to prorogue them; I fear they will be very disorderly. They will leave the king nothing but the empty name of king; no more."

He and the king had now to meet the due punishment of their conduct, the just consequences of their conspiracies against the laws and constitution of their country; and their perplexities and anxieties can be no proper subject of the slightest sympathy or compassion.

But questions like those comprehended in the Exclusion Bill (whether the regular and presumptive heir shall or shall not ascend the throne), must always be considered as the greatest calamities that can befall a nation; and their very agitation is a complete proof of criminality having existed somewhere, either in those who have administered the government, or in those who are opposed to them, and generally in the former.

Nothing can be more easy, and nothing can be more true, than to say that all government being intended for the good of the whole, the community have a right to deviate from the line of succession when the presumptive heir is a just subject of their apprehension. But what, in the mean time, are to be the sentiments of the existing government and of that presumptive heir? What sort of acquiescence or degree of patriotism is to be expected from them? It is in vain to suppose that questions of this tremendous nature can be decided by the mere reasonableness of the case, or either settled or discussed without the imminent hazard of the peace and prosperity of the country.

The popular leaders contend for the exercise of this great right of society, for entire exclusion; the king proposed the most reasonable limitations; the question was, therefore, rendered as fit a subject for debate as it could possibly become; and as there were men of the greatest ability in the houses, no proceedings in parliament can be more interesting than these must always be to every Englishman who has reflected upon the critical nature of our own mixed and of all mixed governments.

On whatever side the question could be viewed, the difficulties were very great. The popular part of the constitution was almost as much asserted by the limitations as by the exclusion, since the right of the community to interfere and control the executive power was acknowledged in either case. In argument, however, the exclusionists had the advantage over those who were contented with limitations, because their measure was evidently in practice the only complete remedy for the evil supposed, and the only remedy which could provide at the same time (a most material consideration) for the safety of those who were to administer it.

Still it was, on the whole, impossible that the exclusion could be carried while the king proposed limitations.

The character of the king led the exclusionists to suppose that, if they remained firm, he would give way. This was their great political mistake. For once in his life, as the point of duty was at least dubious, he was steady to his supposed principle; he kept his word. Had the exclusionists

turned short, and accepted his limitations, he had been indeed embarrassed.

It is now clear . . . that not only the Duke of York reprobated the
scheme of limitations, but that the king himself was not sincere in his
offers; and this must indeed have been suspected by the popular leaders.
But the truth is, that their cause (as it could not be carried without the
full co-operation of the public) was from the first not a little hopeless.
The nation had but just escaped from all the sufferings of civil war,
from anarchy, usurpation, and military despotism; it is naturally, from
the general sobriety of its habits both of speculation and conduct, duti-
ful and loyal; is always very properly attached to the hereditary nature of
the monarchy; nor is it ever the natural turn of men, more especially of
bodies of men, or a whole nation to provide against future evils by extraordinary expedients, in themselves a sort of evil, in themselves exposed
to objection, and in every respect difficult and disagreeable. The conduct,
therefore, to be pursued by the king was plain, and the result much what
might have been expected. He kept at issue with his parliaments, making
to them reasonable though not sincere offers, and addressing them with
temper and dignity; till at last the public, as will always be the case when
there is a proper exercise of skill and prudence on the part of the sovereign, sided with him, and left the constitution (as usual) to its fate,
and the patriots to their fortunes. . . .

Whatever difficulty may belong to the question of the Exclusion Bill,
and whether it might or might not be necessary at the time, still if we
consider what had long been the known characters of Charles and James,
the licentiousness of the court, its connection with France (which had
been publicly proved in the course of Danby's impeachment), its measures through the whole of the reign, and the idea then entertained of the
deadliness of the sin of popery, it must be confessed that the manner in
which the community totally deserted the leaders of the House of Commons on this occasion was not very creditable to the national character.
The result was a new temptation to the political virtues of the king, in
which, as usual, he failed. Instead of justifying the unbounded and headlong attachment of his people, by showing in his turn a due care and
veneration for their constitutional rights, a dishonest advantage was taken
of their blind partiality, and the administration of the government became, in every point, as arbitrary and unprincipled, as brutal judges, dishonourable magistrates, and wicked ministers, under the patronage and
protection of the court, could possibly render it.

And then commenced, in like manner, the temptation of the popular
leaders; they had been defeated—what were they to do? The measures of
the court were detestable; this must be allowed. The constitution of

England seemed to be certainly for a season, perhaps for ever, at an end. Charles might live long, or, as James II was to succeed, the violations of the law might by prescription become the law. All this was true, and might very naturally affect the popular leaders with sentiments of the deepest mortification and sorrow; more especially, as they saw, that the public had abandoned them, and, with some few exceptions, every where continued to abandon them. But what then was the effect produced on the minds of the patriotic leaders? Instead of reflecting how capricious a master they served, when the public was that master; how prone to run into extremes, how easily deceived, how little either able or disposed to take care of itself, how pardonable in its follies, because always honest in its intentions; instead of meditating on topics so obvious as these, most of the popular leaders, particularly Shaftesbury, seemed to have lost on this occasion all temper and prudence, and to have thought of nothing but an insurrection and force; an insurrection which was only called for by the rabble in London—force, which can never be justified, even with right, but under the strongest assurance of success.

And in this manner are we conducted to the last important transaction of the reign, known under the general name of the Ryehouse Plot; a plot, as it was supposed, of the patriotic leaders against the king.

It appears, however, to have been rather a treasonable plot and insurrection intended by the lower and more desperate members of the party, and countenanced by Shaftesbury, than a regular project formed by the whole party, the more respectable leaders included.

But these machinations, however various their description, were fatal to many who were connected with them—they were fatal to Algernon Sidney and Lord Russell. These distinguished men were tried for treason, and found guilty, with what propriety I cannot now discuss. Sidney marched to the scaffold as to a victory, displaying at his execution, as on his trial, all the bold and sublime traits of the republican character. The steady step, the serene eye, the untroubled pulse, the unabated resolve, "the unconquerable mind, and freedom's holy flame"; the memory, that still lingered with delight on the good old cause, as he termed it, for which he was to shed his blood; the imagination, that even in the moments of death, disdainful alike of the government, its judges, its indictments, and its executioners, soared away to some loftier code of justice and of right, and hung enamoured on its own more splendid visions of equality and freedom.

The spectators presumed not to shed tears in the presence of Sidney, but their tears had bedewed the scaffold of Lord Russell; Lord Russell, the amiable and the good; the husband with whom the bitterness of death was past, when the partner of his bosom had looked her last farewell; the friend, whom the faithful Cavendish would have died to save; the lover of truth, the lover of England; the patriot who had laboured to *assert, not* change her constitution; filled with no images of liberty, as Sidney had been, drawn from the imperfect models of Greece and Rome, but intent on a monarchy, restrained by popular freedom, and on popular freedom civilized by a monarchy; imprudent, rather than criminal; a memorable instance to show, that they who would serve their country, are not to mix their own good intentions and virtuous characters with those of men of doubtful principles, irregular and violent in their spirit; men whom it is idle for them to suppose they can long control, and whose faults they may discern clearly, but by no means their ultimate designs.

Such was the termination of the struggle between prerogative and privilege, which, after all the horrors of the civil war, it is most afflicting and mortifying to observe, had, in the first place, once more to be renewed during the reign of the restored monarch, and in the second, to terminate entirely against the patriotic cause. . . .

Instead of labouring to investigate what the fury of those times leaves us little chance of understanding, there is much remains which may be perfectly understood, and to which it may be far more important for you to direct your reflections: I mean the consequences of the plot, the consequences of the alarm excited by this plot. The rage, for instance, and stupidity of which a community are capable when their religious prejudices are worked upon; the outrages that may be committed by judges, juries, and all the regular authorities of a state, the moment that the great maxims and established forms of equity and law are dispensed with; the melancholy excesses of injustice, cruelty, and absurdity, that in times of public alarm may disgrace the most civilized society.

When the more enlightened part of a nation share, for a time, the same violence of prejudice or terror, which more naturally belongs to the blind and precipitate passions of the populace, they themselves become populace; like the very mob, senseless and ferocious, and are actually not to be appeased without the shedding of blood.

Lord Stafford and others (supposed conspirators in this Popish plot) were therefore formally murdered. The king durst not interpose, nor was he of a temper to disturb his own security in the cause of insulted humanity. It is here that is to be found the unpardonable violence, the criminality of the popular leaders. The penetrating Shaftesbury becomes either an atrocious statesman, or a blind and vulgar demagogue; and even the amiable and virtuous Russell is, for a season, no longer to be loved. . . .

I must lastly introduce my hearers to what I will call, for the sake of distinction, the moral part of the history of this period.

All wars destroy the morals of mankind, by habituating them to refer everything to force, and by necessitating them so often to dispense with the ordinary suggestions of sympathy and justice. But this is peculiarly the effect of civil wars, where the moral obligations, before the contest, have been more completely established, and are yet during the contest, with more than ordinary violence, torn asunder; that regular occupation of the mind, amid the common pursuits of life, those peaceful habits of thought which are so nutritive, so necessary to most of the virtues of the human character, all these, on occasions of civil war, are most materially disturbed, and even sometimes destroyed; and the military virtues, high virtues no doubt, but which have been always found compatible with the greatest licentiousness, seem alone to survive.

It is therefore probable that England, on the Restoration, would have exhibited these unhappy effects of the past disorders, under whatever circumstances the kingdom had been placed: but still more unfortunately, to complete the general dissolution of manners after this event, the vanquished party, the Puritans and Presbyterians, had been always distinguished not only, many of them, for the real exercise of the severer virtues, but most of them for a ridiculous affectation of a piety and perfection more than human.

Men always in extremes upon other occasions were equally so on this; and because the Puritans mistook the true nature of virtue and religion, and rushed headlong in one direction, the Cavaliers could do no less than offend every reasonable precept of both, by hurrying away as violently in the other; because the most sacred and awful terms which our religion affords were used by the one party on the most unworthy occasions, and to purposes the most familiar, their opponents could do no better, it seems, than become scoffers at all religion, and could find no substitute for cant, hypocrisy, and nonsense, but profaneness and infidelity.

These great features of the times have not escaped the notice of our historians and moral writers. On this subject I must refer you to their observations.

I may, however, remark, that if any of my hearers should become very conversant in the history and in the writings of this singular period, he will soon, as I conceive, be but too conscious that the very actors in the scene often impart to it an unworthy charm, from the liveliness of their licentiousness, from the variety, the brilliancy, the strength, of their restless and striking characters.

It is one, and not the least, of the many trials which virtue has to encounter, that she is liable to be seduced from her more tranquil, but happier path, by the imposing bustle, the entertaining whims, the ever changing, careless, animating revelry, which may generally be found in the haunts of her most fatal enemies.

Such was the effect of the fascinating manners and specious qualities of Charles, that he was never hated or despised in the degree which he deserved. Even at this distance of time we may not readily bring ourselves to entertain sentiments sufficiently severe against the king, the courtiers, and all the considerable personages, that appeared during these critical times. The truth is that this period was marked by a sort of conspiracy against all sobriety and order, against all liberty and law, against all dignity and happiness, public and private; and we must not suffer our taste for pleasantry, and our admiration of shining talents, to betray us into a forgetfulness of every graver virtue, which can seriously occupy our reflection, or engage our respect.

But I must be allowed to make one observation more, which I shall leave to your own examination.

The writers on morals have always insisted that vice has at least no advantage over virtue, but the contrary, even in this life.

The period of history now before us is enlivened by the most striking and the most profligate characters, and will, as I conceive, abundantly illustrate this position—a position certainly founded in nature and truth, and which no man ever acted upon—and repented.

The Buckingham, for instance, of these times, the author of *The Rehearsal* and the delight of the court; "the life of pleasure and the soul of whim," but the most unprincipled of men, was the Villiers of Pope; the great Villiers, who, though he died not "in the worst inn's worst room," died "victor of his health, his fortune, friends, and fame," and well fitted

To point a moral and adorn a tale.

Rochester, at the early age of three and thirty, when his talents might have been ripening into strength, and his virtues into usefulness, sunk into the grave amid the wild waste of his existence and his advantages, and discovered how mistaken had been his estimate of happiness, when it was too late.

In a grander style of misconduct appears the celebrated Shaftesbury. Of powers as universal as his ambition was unbounded; the idol of the rabble at Wapping, the wit and man of fashion among the courtiers at Whitehall; and a statesman in the House of Lords, whom the king, after listening to him in a debate, pronounced fit to teach his bishops divinity and his judges law; a minister, a patriot, a chancellor, and a demagogue. In whatever direction he moved, the man on whom all eyes were to be turned; to whom nothing was wanting but virtue,—Shaftesbury, died at last an exile from his country, seeking protection from that very republic of Holland, which in the hour of his corruption and prosperity he had denounced; towering with all the consciousness of genius, yet humiliated by the triumphs of opponents, whom he must have despised even more than he hated, and no longer able to hope, as the scene for ever closed around him, either for the gratification of success, or the comforts (for such to his unchastened mind they would have been thought) of vengeance.

Compare with the lives of these men the life of Sir William Temple, the man of cultivated mind; the man of sense and humanity: of civilized passions, and well-directed aims; the philosopher and the statesman, appearing on the stage of public affairs only to be honoured; retiring to the shade only to be more loved and applauded; the minister who could speak the language of patriotism and truth to his corrupted, dissembling sovereign, nor yet suffer himself, by disappointment at his sovereign's subsequent conduct, to be hurried into projects of dangerous experiment and doubtful ambition; and who, on every occasion, converted all the advantages which he had received from nature and from fortune, to their noblest purposes; the fair fame and happiness of himself, the honour of his country, and the benefit of mankind.

Take again an instance of virtue in a form more severe, and apparently less fitted for happiness—the patriot Andrew Marvell.

Of this man it is well known that the Treasurer Danby once made his way to his garret, and, under a proper disguise of courtly phraseology, offered him a bribe. It was refused, and this virtuous representative of the people, when he had turned away from the thousand pounds of the minister, was obliged to dine a second time on the dish of the former day, and borrow a guinea from his bookseller. But which of the two are we to envy?

> *Count what the advantage prosperous vice obtains,*
> *'Tis but what virtue flies from and disdains.*

Pursue the same train of inquiry into the recesses of the cabinet. The king had deceived his ministry, the Cabal; Arlington (one of them) betrayed the king; the Duke of York and the king had cajoled Shaftesbury; and Shaftesbury, at the moment he was most wanted, turned short on his deceivers. Danby had preferred his place to his honour, and had committed himself to Montague. At that time they were friends; soon after, enemies; each wished the ruin of the other; but the ambassador (Montague) was more adroit, and the treasurer Danby was lodged in the Tower. What friendship, what happiness, have we here among men like these?

The members of the Cabal gained little by their baseness but disgrace and impeachments. Charles himself was occupied all his life in extracting money from Louis, and in deceiving him for that purpose; but Louis was equally employed in deceiving Charles, and in carrying on counter intrigues with his subjects. Two years before his death, Charles came to the knowledge of all the French monarch's proceedings; he received, says Dalrymple, a yet more mortifying stroke; he found that the court of France had been capable of intending (though the design was at last laid aside) to make public his secret negotiations with the Duchess of Orleans. What was the result? Conscious that he could no longer be either respected or loved by the intelligent part of his subjects; that he was distrusted and despised by every court in Europe, and that he had been all his life betrayed by the very prince to whom he had sold the immediate jewel of his soul, his secret chagrin became at length visible on his countenance, and for two years before his death, he had ceased to be the merry monarch, who could laugh at the virtues, and triumph in the vices of mankind.

Charles, in the earlier part of his reign, had seen Clarendon stand before him the representative of English good sense and English good feelings. He had been afterwards exhorted by Temple to be the man of his people; for such a king, the patriot minister told him, to use his own words, "might in England be any thing, and otherwise nothing"; but from the first, Charles had traced out another path of happiness for himself, and in the event, as we may collect from the historians, he found he had judged but ill; he is even understood to have formed serious resolutions of retracing, if possible, his steps, and of acting up to the model which had vainly been presented to his view. But life admits not of this neglect of opportunities: he was struck by the hand of death, and what, then, is his history? The history of a man of pleasure; a fine understanding converted to no useful purpose, and at last, as is always the case, not convertible to any; the common feelings of our nature corrupted into total selfishness by sensual indulgence; the proper relish of the gratifications of our state worn down by abuse into a morbid indifference for every thing; with no friendship that he thought sincere; with no love that he did not hire; without the genuine enjoyment of one social affection, or of one intellectual endowment but his wit; floating helplessly on from one amusement to another; oppressed with the burden of time, yet ashamed of his expedients to get rid of it; living and dying, Charles is the proper object of our indignation or contempt; through life a conspirator against the liberties of his people, or a mere saunterer amid his courtiers and his mistresses; and on his death-bed delivering himself over to his stupid brother and a popish priest. Such is the history of Charles; but what is there here which the meanest of his subjects could have to envy? what to envy in the monarch, however he may be himself, in his humbler station, submitted to the tasks of daily labour, to the duties of self-denial, or the necessities of self-exertion?

But whatever may be our decision with respect to the great position of the moralists (that vice has no advantage even in this world, but the contrary), it must at least be admitted that men like these, whether or not they procure happiness for themselves, undoubtedly produce misery to every one around them; in private life they injure, distress, or corrupt whatever is within their influence, and in public they are yet more injurious to society, by disposing of their talents and integrity under some form or other, to the best bidder. . . .

In an age of such depravity, the great minister Clarendon was not unconscious of what was due to his sovereign, to his country, or to his own character; and he resisted, by every effort in his power, the immoralities of his master, and the licentiousness of the court. His gravity, as it was called, was the great object at which the ridicule of Buckingham and the wits was eternally levelled; but the chancellor was of a temperament too dignified to be faced out of his principles either by the frowns of the king or the grimaces of his companions. He would never suffer his wife to visit the lady, as he calls her, that is, the king's mistress; and he continued, as he began, the champion of the ordinary duties of life.

In our own times, the great upholder of the domestic virtues has been, not any particular minister, but the monarch himself [George III]. To whatever variety of criticism a reign like his, so long and so eventful, may be hereafter exposed, this praise—this solid praise—will never be denied him: and it will remain, while the story of England remains, an honour to his memory. His people, in the meantime, have never been backward in acknowledging their obligation. His conduct in this respect has always been the theme of their loud and just panegyric; and they have never ceased to look up to the throne, not only with sentiments of loyalty to the high office, but with feelings of gratitude and respect for the person of their sovereign. . . .

xx. JAMES II, REVOLUTION

ON THE DEATH of Charles II, the Duke of York took as peaceable possession of the throne as if no effort had ever been made to debar him from the succession.

If the exclusionists had carried their measure, James would have been always represented by a very large and respectable description of writers, as, on the whole, a victim to party rage.

Without perhaps denying exactly the right of a community to provide for its own happiness, they would have contented themselves with observing that religious opinions were in themselves no just disqualification; that it by no means followed that James, though a Papist himself, would have violated the constitution of his country, rather than not make his subjects the same; that the conduct of men altered with their situation; and that, at all events, the patriotism and good sense of James were not fairly tried.

But happily for one of the most important of all causes, the cause of civil liberty, the experiment was really made; and all that the exclusionists had foreseen, all that with very manly wisdom they had endeavoured to prevent, actually took place.

When, however, the expectations of the exclusionists were verified, and the arbitrary and bigoted nature of James was inflamed rather than pacified by the possession of power, it by no means followed that the community would be then able to relieve itself from the calamity which it had incurred. It is very easy for a theorist to say that a nation has only to will to be free, and to be so. The affairs of mankind proceed in no such manner.

On such a subject as the Revolution in 1688, the student will surely think that no pains he can bestow are too great. But he will rise from the whole with very different impressions from what I have done, if he does not entitle this Revolution not only the *glorious*, but, in the first place, the *fortunate* Revolution of 1688. If he can but place himself in the midst of these occurrences, and suppose himself ignorant of what is to happen, it is with a sort of actual fear and trembling that he will read the history of these times; let him consider what his country has become by the successful termination of these transactions, and what it might have been rendered by a contrary issue; how much the interests of Europe were at this juncture identified with those of England; and what a variety of events, the most slight and the most natural, might have thrown the whole into a state of confusion and defeat.

The first question to be examined is the conduct of James, his unconstitutional measures, his arbitrary designs. . . .

When the crown was afterwards offered to William and Mary, both houses prefaced their offer by declaring the reasons that compelled them to adopt a measure so extraordinary. They were these; and they form a sort of summary of the reign of James II, and therefore I shall read them to you; in every word they deserve attention; they are the case of the people of England on this great occasion.

"Whereas the late king, James II, by the assistance of divers evil counsellors, judges, and ministers employed by him, did endeavour to subvert and extirpate the Protestant religion, and the laws and liberties of this kingdom; by assuming and exercising a power of dispensing with, and suspending of laws, and the execution of laws, without consent of parliament; By committing and prosecuting divers worthy prelates, for humbly petitioning to be excused from concurring to the said assumed power; By issuing and causing to be executed, a commission under the great seal, for erecting a court called 'the Court of Commissioners for Ecclesiastical Causes'; By levying money for and to the use of the crown, by pretence of prerogative, for other time and in other manner than the same was granted by parliament; By raising and keeping a standing army within this kingdom, in time of peace, without consent of parliament, and quartering soldiers contrary to law; By causing divers good subjects, being Protestants, to be disarmed, at the same time when Papists were both armed and employed contrary to law; By violating the freedom of election of members to serve in parliament; By prosecutions in the Court of King's Bench for matters and causes cognizable only in parliament; and by divers other arbitrary and illegal courses: And whereas of late years partial, corrupt, and unqualified persons have been returned, and served on juries in trials, and particularly divers juries on trials for high treason, which were not freeholders; and excessive bail hath been required of persons committed in criminal cases, to elude the benefit of the laws made for the liberty of the subject; and excessive fines have been imposed, and illegal and cruel punishments inflicted; and several grants and promises made of fines and forfeitures, before any conviction or judgment against the persons upon whom the same were to be levied: all which are utterly and directly contrary to the known laws, and statutes, and freedom of this realm." . . .

Having now, in a general manner, considered the nature of the attack that was made by James on the constitution of the country, which is the first part of the subject, we may next turn to examine the nature of the resistance that was opposed to him; which is the second part.

And when this part is considered, the conclusion seems to be, and it is a melancholy conclusion, that if James had not violated the religious persuasions of his subjects, he would have met with no proper resistance whatever, and that the English nation, after all the sufferings and exertions of their ancestors, would at this period have submitted to such violations of their civil liberties, and would have allowed such precedents to be established, that in the event these liberties might very probably have been lost, like those of the other European monarchies.

The natural guardian of the community was, in the first place, the parliament. But so successful had been the practices of the king, and of his predecessor, Charles, that when he looked over the lists of the returns, he declared "that there were not more than forty names which he could have wished not there."

The parliament was only suffered to sit a year. Some proper feeling was indeed shown, when the king intimated to them (clearly enough) that he meant to maintain a standing army. But their expostulations with the crown in this last address were merely directed against his suspensions and violations of the law in favour of the papists. . . .

The king immediately prorogued the parliament, and never suffered it again to assemble; and here, for any thing that can be discovered to the contrary, in the honest unpremeditated effusion of a single representative of the people, might have ended all the efforts that could be made in the cause of the civil liberties of the country.

For from what quarter comes the next resistance to the illegal proceedings of the crown? From the ecclesiastical bodies—the Charter House, the University of Cambridge, the colleges of Oxford, and the seven bishops, the representatives of the English clergy; that is from men who had been so lately, at the close of the reign of Charles II, the addressers of the crown in the language of servility, and the preachers and the propagators of the doctrine of passive obedience.

Happily for the nation, the clergy at this period venerable in their characters and situation, however mistaken in their political theories, however the teachers of passive obedience, could after all resist, when their own acknowledged rights, when their own established opinions in religion were endangered: and the community on their part, could be roused into some sense of their danger when they saw the most dignified ministers of their religion, even the prelates of the land, hurried away by officers of justice and consigned to imprisonment in the Tower.

The king's own standing army, and the very sentinels who had to guard these peaceful sufferers, participated with the multitude in their sense of religious horror at the king's intolerable violation of all law, privilege, and security; of every thing that was dear and respectable in the eyes of his subjects.

The fact was that the age still continued to be an age of religious dispute. In the former part of the century, we saw the sectaries, animated by the religious principle, enter into a contest with the Church of England and the crown; we now see, by the unexpected direction of the same religious principle, the Church of England itself slowly and heavily moved onward into an opposition to the monarch.

Not that the church had begun to entertain more enlightened notions on the subject of civil obedience, but that the crown had most fortunately allied itself to popery; and the church, though it abjured the doctrines of resistance, however modified, abominated with still greater earnestness the tenets and superstitions of the Roman Catholic communion.

It is not too much to assert that the resistance of the people of England to James was *universally* of a religious nature; of a very large portion of the country, the high Tory and ecclesiastical part, exclusively so.

But besides these, there was another great division of the nation, of which the resistance was not exclusively of a religious nature. The resistance here was compounded; it was not only of a religious, but also, and very properly, of a civil nature. This party was the Whig party, the exclusionists, who, like Coke of Derby, were not to be put down by high words; these, however fallen and trampled upon since the victory of Charles II and the accession of James, still existed, though discountenanced and in silence; and they must no doubt have observed, with pleasure, their cause strengthening as the king proceeded, and new prospects arising of civil happiness to their country from the religious fury of their arbitrary monarch, the very prince whom they had endeavoured, from anticipation of his character and designs, to exclude from the throne.

So much for the resistance which the king experienced at home. The next great division of the subject is the resistance which James experienced from abroad.

Charles II, in a most fortunate moment of improvidence, had suffered his minister Danby to connect the Prince of Orange with the royal family of England. If James had no male children, the wife of William thus became first in succession. Even if he had, she remained so, in case the direct male line was to be departed from.

The great enemy of the civil and religious liberties of Europe was, at that time, Louis XIV; their great hero, William. William had seen his own country nearly destroyed, when he had to defend it or perish in the last dyke. The great assistants of Louis had been Charles and James. Between William and Louis there could be no peace, and only the appearance of amity between William and his father-in-law, James.

In the situation of England, all eyes were naturally turned upon this great and hitherto successful assertor of the rights of mankind.

William on his part could not but be perfectly alive to any representations that reached him from a country like England. . . .

But here we ought certainly to ask, how, after all, was the Prince of Orange to attempt any regular enterprise against the crown of England? Observe his difficulties, and you will then understand his merit. He was only at the head of a small republic; that republic had been reduced, but a few years before, to the very last extremities by the arms of Louis. How was William to prepare an expedition, and not be observed by the French and English monarchs; how to prosecute it, and not be destroyed by their power? If he attacked England with a small force, how was he to resist James? if with a large one, how was Holland in his absence to resist Louis? In either case, how was he to extricate himself from the English and French fleets, which might prevent his landing in the first place, or at least render his return impossible in the second? How could he expect that the English who had so long contended for the empire of the seas, with their great rivals, the Dutch, would forego the triumph of a naval victory, if it was once put within their reach? How was William to trust to the representations of the English patriots, who might be suspected of judging of their countrymen, through the medium of their own wishes and resentments? How was he to expect, even if he landed, that the gentry and nobility would hazard their lives and fortunes by appearing in arms, when only seven of them had as yet ventured, by any distinct act, to incur the guilt of treason? What spirit of freedom, much less of resistance, had the nation shown, now for seven years, since the political victory of Charles II over the exclusionists? Monmouth, the idol of the English populace, had just been destroyed by James without difficulty; so had Argyle. What was to be expected from a country that was loud indeed in their abuse of popery, but whose pulpits, and public meetings, and courts of justice, resounded with the doctrines of passive obedience, and whose very parliaments seemed to admit the same fatal principles?

Put the case that William should even succeed so far as to oblige James to call a parliament, give up his illegal pretensions, and promise conformity to the laws in future. To what end or purpose, as far as William was himself concerned, what benefit was to accrue to *him*, but the mere liberty of returning; while James was to be left in silence and at his leisure, to wait for more favourable times, watch his opportunities, recover his authority, and persecute or destroy, one by one, all who had contributed to resist or modify his prerogative.

It is by reflections of this kind, I must repeat, that we can alone be taught duly to estimate the merits of William. The difficulties of the enterprise show the greatness of his genius, and the extent of our obligation. . . .

Had James stood firm and called a parliament, and abided by the event, it is difficult to say what material advantage could have ultimately resulted to the constitution of the country; but most happily the same civil wars that so impressed upon the people of England the terrors of anarchy and military usurpation, contributed no less forcibly to impress on the mind of James the images of the trial and execution of the monarch. By a most fortunate want of political sagacity, he thought it his best policy to fly from the country and leave it in confusion, the more complete, he thought, the better. The result, he supposed, would be, that he should be recalled to settle it, or that at all events he might thus preserve himself and the royal family, and by the assistance of Ireland, Scotland, and Louis, be hereafter in a condition to return to it. . . .

The prudence and skill of William continued as perfect as they were in James defective. A House of Commons was peaceably formed, and the convention of the two estates assembled.

And now begins the last and not the least curious scene of all—in some respects the most so; for what was now the result? The church party and the Tory party, when James was gone and the danger removed, renewed their doctrines of passive obedience and the indefeasible tenure of the crown; Scripture, law, custom, seemed equally to confirm their tenets. "Be subject to the higher powers"; "the king can do no wrong"; "the crown of England never was nor ever can be considered as elective";—these were their positions, and these the Whig party and the friends of the prince knew not well how to deny; but they could see plainly that all was lost, if they were acted upon.

From the first, therefore, they had seized upon the mistake of the king, his departure from the country, and they converted it into an argument, which upon every hypothesis they might as they conceived, fairly urge. They insisted that it was an abdication of the crown, and that no expedient remained but to fill up the throne, which had thus become vacant.

Most fortunately it happened that the gentry of England had their understandings less bewildered by the abstractions of divinity and law than the nobility and bishops. In the commons, the Whig party were nearly two to one; however, after a very curious debate, they thought proper to produce only the following heterogeneous and inconsistent vote:—

"That King James II, having endeavoured to subvert the constitution of the kingdom by breaking the original contract between king and people, and by the advice of Jesuits and other wicked persons having violated the fundamental laws, and, having withdrawn himself out of his kingdom, has abdicated the government, and that the throne was thereby vacant."

We will observe for a moment the words here used:—"That King James II, having endeavoured to subvert the constitution of the kingdom by breaking the original contract between king and people," (so far we have the great interests of civil liberty and the Whig principles making their appearance,) "and by the advice of Jesuits and other wicked persons having violated the fundamental laws," (here we have the religious part of the contest,) but in consequence of all this—what? that his majesty had forfeited his right to the crown? that the next in the Protestant succession should be called to the throne? are these the words that follow? (as apparently they ought). No; the words that follow are these: "and having withdrawn himself out of this kingdom [not voluntarily, as every one knew], has abdicated the government," meaning by the word "abdicated" to imply, that he had done a legal act, that he had formally divested himself of the crown; and then and at last came the necessary conclusion of the whole, "that the crown was thereby vacant."

As the Whigs were, in the House of Commons, the stronger party, and, after asserting their principle of the original contract, had not chosen to push it to its logical conclusions, which would have been so offensive to the Tories, but to rest the vacancy of the throne on the departure of the king, the Tories of the lower house probably thought that no better terms were to be had; and, after a debate of four hours, the motion which the Tories made was only for an adjournment, and this was with some hurry and noise overruled, and the original vote, without a division, was carried, and sent up to the Lords. . . .

On the next sitting, the lords debated, in the first place, the great Whig doctrine of the original contract between the king and people, and the affirmative (that there was such an original contract) was carried by a majority of seven; fifty-three to forty-six. The Whigs, therefore, were gaining ground.

But here their triumphs ended; they could not get the word "abdicated" carried; nor, the next day, that the Prince and Princess of Orange should be declared king and queen, which was lost by five, forty-seven to fifty-two; nor, "that the throne was vacant": lost by eleven (forty-four to fifty-five, not forty-one to fifty-five, as it is in Lord Clarendon, probably by a mistake of the figure). The word "deserted" was substituted for the word abdicated; the clause about the vacancy of the throne omitted; and in this state the vote returned to the commons.

But the commons could not see the propriety of these alterations; a *conference*, therefore, took place.

The discussion which took place on this remarkable occasion is represented by some writers, and even by Hume, "as turning [to use his own words] upon frivolous topics, and as more resembling the verbal disputes of the schools than the solid reasoning of statesmen and legislators."

They who are at all acquainted with the very metaphysical nature of Mr. Hume's most favourite compositions will be somewhat surprised at this sudden impatience and dislike of those verbal disputes, as he terms them, or rather, as he ought to think them, of those explanations and distinctions of words and phrases, without which no subject of importance ever was or can be thoroughly examined. . . .

The value of this conference appears to consist in this, that it is a development of those principles which must always more or less exist in a mixed monarchical government—of the principles, and of their consequences when applied to practice; and such a development is and must ever be of importance, not only to ourselves, but to all who are ever to live under any reasonably mixed form of government; because the laws and ordinances of any such form of government can never speak, any more than our own do, of resistance to authority, of dethroning of kings, of trying, of punishing them, of the paramount authority of the public, and other political positions and maxims of the same kind. Such can never be the *language* of the constitution of a country; but if it be from thence inferred, that no language but the ordinary language of the constitution is ever to be used, that no maxims but the ordinary maxims of the laws are ever to be proceeded upon, *then* these memorable debates, and above all this memorable conference, will be of value, to show in what inextricable, what fatal perplexity, a nation and its statesmen must be left, if, when its liberties are invaded, they will not submit to acknowledge, that however sacred the general rules of hereditary monarchy or civil obedience may be, exceptions must be sometimes admitted, and whether admitted or not in theory, must at all events be sometimes proceeded upon in practice. . . .

Great bodies of men seldom understand very thoroughly those principles of religion and politics which they profess, or rather never understand the real value of the difference that exists between them and their opponents on these subjects; but they can always comprehend fully that it is dishonourable for them to desert, in time of trial, what they have been accustomed to profess, and therefore, right or wrong, *this* they will not *do*.

Here lay the great merit of the Whigs; their temper, their spirit of conciliation, their practical philosophy, their genuine wisdom, so different from the wisdom of those, who, on occasions of political or other weighty discussion, ignorant of the business of the world, and unfitted for it, bustle about with importance, displaying all the triumphs of their logic, and hurrying their opponents and themselves into difficulties and disgrace from the very offensiveness of their manner, and from their vain and puerile confidence in what they think the cogency of reason and the evidence of truth.

And now comes forward the great merit of William himself. William had done every thing from the first which he understood to be consistent with the liberties and laws of the country; he then waited the event: but he perceived that the parties were far more nearly balanced than he had probably at first supposed; that if either of these parties insisted on their own opinion in defiance of the other, a civil war might ensue; that the Tories were, in practice at least, indifferent to the service he had rendered them, now that they were safe from popery; that the Whigs themselves seemed to be thinking more anxiously of the maxims of the constitution of England than of what was due to the great cause of civil and religious liberty, not only in England, but in Europe; and that no one could be found who appeared sufficiently impressed with what was owing both to the states of Holland and to himself, for embarking in an enterprise originally so unpromising, always so perilous, and hitherto so unsuccessfully conducted.

That William had a perfect right to be considerably out of humour cannot be doubted; and if he had not expressed his own sentiments at a proper juncture, and given the weight of his decision to the arguments and expostulations of the Whigs, it is impossible to say how long and how preposterously the Tories might have persevered in their most impracticable opinions, and again, how long the moderation and caution of the Whigs might have been able to sustain itself, and might have continued to maintain the peace of the community; in other words, whether a civil war might not have been the result, or at least the return of James. What passed on this occasion between William and the Whig leaders is well known. "They might have a regent," he told them, "no doubt, if they thought proper, but he would not be that regent; they might wish him, perhaps, to reign in right, and during the lifetime of his wife, but he would submit to nothing of the sort; and he should certainly, in either case, return to Holland, and leave them to settle their government in any manner they thought best."

The conclusion from all this was plain, that he and the princess were to be raised to the throne, and that he chose himself to possess the crown, as if it had regularly descended to him, or not at all.

This conduct in William was at the time, and has often since been branded by many reasoners and writers as not a little base and criminal, —criminal from the violation of duty to James, his father-in-law, whom he was accused of having thus dethroned; base, from the proof thus exhibited, that from the first he had been actuated merely by selfish ambition; that from the first he had but dissembled his real designs on the crown; that from the first everything he had been doing was in direct contradiction to all he had professed and avowed in his own declaration.

To consider this subject for a moment—In his first declaration he had said that his expedition was intended for no other design but to have a free and lawful parliament assembled as soon as possible; "that he had nothing before his eyes in this undertaking but the preservation of the Protestant religion, and the securing to the nation the free enjoyment of their laws, rights, and liberties under a just and legal government"; and again, in his additional declaration, "that no person could have such hard thoughts of him as to imagine he had any other design in this undertaking than to procure a settlement of the religion and of the liberties and properties of the subject, upon so sure a foundation that there may be no danger of the nation relapsing into the like miseries at any time hereafter; that the forces he brought over were disproportioned to the design of conquest, and that of those who countenanced the expedition, many were known to be distinguished for their constant fidelity to the crown." This last is the strongest expression to be found, the only one where the crown is exactly mentioned.

To representations of this nature it may be briefly answered that it is mere mockery to speak of William's duty as a son, to one who never was or wished to be his father-in-law in any sense of the word, and that whatever construction might be given, by the Tories or by the Whigs, to the terms of the prince's declaration, it was quite idle to suppose that he and the states of Holland would embark in an enterprise like this, and put every interest that was dear to them into a situation of the most imminent danger, for the sake alone of the good people of England. What was England to either of them but as a member of the great community of Europe; as a country that might be Protestant or popish, that might concur to protect or destroy them, merely as James did or did not succeed in his designs upon its liberties and constitution? Their civil and religious interests, and those of England, thoroughly coincided, and the whole cause was the most generous and noble that could well be proposed to the human imagination; but when it had succeeded, and succeeded so completely—when without disturbance or bloodshed the whole force and energies of such a country as England were within the reach of William, to be turned to the defence of every interest of his own country, of Europe, and of England itself, when this could only be done by his requiring for himself the executive administration of the government, when every other expedient could only have served to renew the designs and power of James and Louis, and must have ultimately ended in the ruin of the civil and religious liberties of mankind; in this situation of things, was it for William to have disappointed the reasonable expectations of his own country, and of every intelligent man in Europe; to have been wanting to his own glory, and to have shown himself incapable of discharging the high office of humanity, to which, in the mysterious dispensation of events, he had been called? Was it for William to have abandoned all the great pretensions and honours of his life, embarked, as he had been from the first, in opposition to Louis, and placed on the theatre of Europe in a situation of all the most elevated—that of the champion, and hitherto the successful champion, of the civil and religious liberties of mankind?

The fact is that what was required or expected from William by the moralists and statesmen who criminated or even censured his conduct then or afterwards, was in itself inconsistent and impossible.

No man with the views or feelings of such moralists or statesmen would have ever engaged in such an enterprise at all, much less have conducted it with success.

Enterprises like these that produce an epoch in the annals of the world, and give a new career of advancement to society are neither approached nor comprehended at the time, but by men of a more exalted order like William. Even to such men the latent possibilities of such enterprises, from the uncertain nature of every thing human, can only be apprehended, dimly and at a distance, and suspected rather than seen; the prospect clears or darkens as they proceed; it opens at last, or shuts for ever; but if the moment of visible glory once presents itself, it is then that these heroes of the world march on as did William, and decide for themselves and for posterity the happiness of kingdoms and of ages. . . .

And now began the benefits of this successful enterprise. First, the line of succession was departed from, and it was declared that no papist should reign; popery was therefore escaped. Secondly, William was made king, though it was his wife, not himself, who was next in succession; William therefore was considered as elected. The right, therefore, of the community, in particular cases, to interfere with the disposal of the executive power, and even of the crown itself, was exercised and admitted. Thirdly, before the crown was conferred, as a preliminary part of the ceremony, the opportunity was taken, which had not been taken at the Restoration, of making some provision for the future security of the constitution, and certain rights and liberties were claimed, demanded, and insisted upon, as the undoubted rights and liberties of the people of England. The constitution was therefore renewed and confirmed. The prince and princess, when they received the crown, which was after this declaration tendered to them, in their turn declared, that they thankfully accepted what was offered them. . . .

It may be asked what were the alterations which the patriots in 1688 really did make in the constitution?

These will be found very much to disappoint the expectations of all such reasoners as suppose that constitutions of government are in the first place to be planned out, according to the suggestions of deliberative wisdom, and when reduced to shape and order and perfection, *then* to be proposed and accepted by a people, and the people thus made to grow up and fashion themselves to their prescribed model.

There is certainly little in these transactions to countenance any experiments or reasonings of this nature.

The same rights and liberties which had been claimed, demanded, and insisted upon, when the crown was tendered, were afterwards converted into the materials of an act, which was presented to the king, and received the royal assent, and the whole was then "declared, enacted, and established by authority of that present parliament, to stand, remain, and be the law of the realm for ever." This was done, and no more; this was all that, apparently at least, was attempted; no pretences were made to any merit of salutary alteration or legislative reform; the original declaration, the subsequent Bill of Rights, were each of them expressly stated to be only *declarations* of the old constitution; they were each an exhibition of the rights and liberties of the people of England, already undoubted and their own; experiment, innovation, every thing of this kind, is virtually disclaimed, for nothing of the kind is visible in the style or language of these singular records.

It must, however, on the other hand, be carefully noticed, that though the Bill of Rights might not propose itself as any alteration, it was certainly a complete renovation of the free constitution of England; the abject state to which the laws, the constitution, and the people themselves, had fallen, must never be forgotten; and it then can surely not be denied that this public assertion on a sudden, this establishment and enactment of all the great leading principles of a free government, fairly deserves the appellation which it has always received of the Revolution of 1688.

It is very material to observe that the declaration and enactment were totally on the popular side, were declaratory entirely and exclusively of the rights and liberties of the people, in no respect of the prerogatives of the crown; the Bill of Rights was, in fact, a new Magna Charta; a new Petition of Right; a new enrollment of the prerogatives, if I may so speak, of the democratic part of the constitution, which, though consented to by William, an elected prince, and perhaps even thought necessary to his own justification and security, could only have been extorted by force from any reigning hereditary monarch, and, in point of fact, was certainly not procured by the English nation on this occasion, till the regular possessor of the crown had ceased to wear it, and till the country had appeared in a state of positive and successful resistance to his authority.

It must be always remembered that through the whole of these proceedings there was an acknowledgment, and a practical exhibition, of the great popular doctrine that all government, and all the forms and provisions which are necessary to its administration, must ultimately be referred to the happiness of the people. This is supposed at every moment from the first resistance of the measures of James, to the last act of the ceremony of crowning the Prince of Orange; and it is this acknowledgment, and this practical exhibition of a great theoretical truth, which constitute the eternal value and importance of these most remarkable transactions. The caution, the moderation, the forbearance, the modest wisdom with which leading actors in the scene conducted themselves, are the proper subjects of our panegyric, but must never be so dwelt upon, that we are to forget the real meaning of these proceedings, their positive example, their permanent instruction, transmitted practically and visibly not only to the sovereign, but to the people. . . .

XXII. WILLIAM III

To ALL REASONERS at the time, the ultimate success of the Revolution must have appeared very doubtful. The student cannot have reflected upon the history of this Revolution in 1688, without observing the fortunate manner in which it was accomplished; that the success of it was owing, not only to the great prudence and merit of William, but the great mistakes and faults of James, and above all to the zeal of the latter for the Roman Catholic religion. The church party, and the Tory party, comprehending so large a portion of the nation, always looked upon the crown as really belonging to the Stuart family. France was, in the meantime, considered not only as pledged to the cause of James, but as a power not easily to be resisted. Charles II, it could not but be remembered, though long a wanderer on the continent, had been at last most triumphantly restored. Any good fortune or good management in James, the want of them in William, the death of either, a thousand contingencies, such as often take place in the affairs of the world, might obviously be sufficient to reinstate the Stuarts in their hereditary right. They had been driven away by a movement, forced and unnatural to the English nation: their return was therefore, on the whole, very probable; and while this probability continued, the cause of the Revolution must all along be considered as still at issue.

The very doubtful nature of the success of the Revolution will appear, not only from a consideration of the state of opinions in England, and the general instability of every thing that relates to the politics of kingdoms; but from a due reflection on the intrigues that were carrying on; and it was but too natural to expect would continue to be carried on, between the exiled family and many individuals of great power and consequence in England, Scotland, and Ireland. . . .

During the whole reign of William, his person and government were exposed to extreme danger; that from his coronation, till his title was acknowledged by the French king at the peace of Ryswick, a correspondence was carried on by King James, and many persons in England of the first rank and consequence; that individuals of every party, and even some of those who had been the most zealous agents in the Revolution, were accessory to that correspondence; that many conspiracies were formed, and very considerable preparations made for restoring the authority of James, and that even the most base and atrocious designs were set on foot to put an end, not only to the power, but the life of William.

But there were some circumstances that operated most happily to assist and support the establishment of the new government. For instance, it was difficult under the vigilant administration of William, possessed of the military force of the kingdom, to erect the standard of revolt without the protection of a French army. It was difficult in the meantime for Louis to see a sufficient chance of success, unless some insurrection first encouraged his interference. It was not easy for the parties to combine their measures and views. The personal character of James was ill-fitted to recommend his cause. The character of William, on the contrary, was marked by great qualities which were worthy of the confidence of brave and intelligent men. The friends of James were even divided in their political sentiments: some who were friends to him meant, (so endless are the mistakes of men on political subjects) to be friends (can it be believed?) to the constitution, and by no means to establish arbitrary power. William was often absent from England, and the regency of Queen Mary was, on these occasions, conducted with a prudence and moderation that gained friends among every party in the nation, not to mention that she was the eldest daughter of the exiled monarch; and her rule was, therefore, more agreeable to the prejudices of the Tories. Her death only united the interests of William and the Princess Anne; and set the exiled family at a greater distance by intercepting their more immediate return, and giving an opportunity of securing the descent of the crown in a line of Protestant successors. Lastly, as the constitution improved, all orders in the state became more and more alienated from the maxims of arbitrary prerogative, and were more and more disposed to a settlement, which gave them a greater share and interest in the constitution of their country.

On the whole, the Revolution in 1688, while William lived, appeared to succeed; and on his death-bed, he had the gratification of reflecting, not only that he had maintained this great cause during his reign, but that he saw, through his exertions, the crown descend to Anne on the principles of the Revolution, and provisions made for its subsequent transmission to the Protestant line, in exclusion of the exiled family.

The next question therefore is to whom are we indebted for the happy issue of so doubtful an experiment during this most critical period of the reign of William?

On inquiry it will, I think, be found that the greatest share of the merit must be allotted to William himself; but much will still remain to the great Whig leaders, and to their friends and adherents in the parliament and the nation; very little to the Church and Tory party, who acquiesced in the new order of things, and nothing more; and who negatively, rather than positively, contributed to its establishment. It was on the whole very fortunate for these kingdoms that the growing prosperity of the community had multiplied a description of men in the great cities and commercial and manufacturing towns, who were active, independent, and intelligent; who were therefore favourable to the Whigs, and could be successfully opposed to the landed proprietors; persons of great natural consequence and power, who in general had inherited, with their estates, opinions and feelings unfavourable to the civil and religious interests of mankind, derived from their too literal interpretation of particular texts in the Epistles. . . .

William endeavoured to balance between the two parties; to retain the affections of the Whigs, and yet acquire those of the Tories; to give his favour to the one, but not to exclude the other from his kindness. . . .

On the whole he failed, and the failure of such a man is an example to show the difficulty of mediating between two parties, and the impossibility of receiving the proper benefit of the talents and virtues of both. No monarch ever possessed more knowledge of human nature, more equanimity, more elevation of mind, than William: yet he found it impracticable to harmonize to the purposes of his government, men animated by principles and interests so discordant.

But the king, though failing in the manner and to the degree I have noticed, was successful in the main. He so triumphed over the difficulties of his situation, violent passions on the one side, and unfortunate opinions on the other, that he at least supported the cause of the Revolution; and though his own personal comforts and composure of mind were continually disturbed, and sometimes destroyed, the civil and religious liberties of a great people and of the continent were, with whatever sacrifices, embarrassments, and dangers to himself, asserted and maintained. . . .

On the whole, the first parliament in King William's reign was the conventional parliament, which legalized the Revolution, and enacted the Bill of Rights. But this was the work of the Whigs; and if they had done nothing more, they might, by these merits, have compensated for any subsequent faults, any faults but that of undoing their great work, and bringing the Stuarts back to the throne. This last crime, however, to the liberties of their country they neither did commit, nor endeavour to commit. It is painful, it is disgusting, it is astonishing, to find individuals among them corresponding with the exiled monarch, as if they were disposed to propitiate him, at least, and be considered as his friends rather than as his enemies, if fortune, by any of her unworthy caprices, placed him once more upon the throne. Of this baseness there were too many of them guilty, guilty as individuals; but as a body and as a party, they were never guilty. They were faithful to England and the best interests of mankind; and they never failed to show a lively sense of the great cause which was at issue, whenever the personal safety of William was in danger, or his throne was seen, as it sometimes was seen, really to shake under him. This is their paramount merit to all succeeding generations: they were the authors, the conductors, and the maintainers of the Revolution. . . .

The liberty of the press is . . . one of the subjects belonging to this remarkable period. I will dwell a little on the subject, on account of its importance.

The first measure which a country naturally adopts is to take the regulation of the press into its own hands, or rather to leave the executive magistrate to do so. It was therefore, with us, at first regulated by the king's proclamations, prohibitions, charters of privilege and licence, and finally by the decrees of the Star Chamber. A licenser is among the first expedients resorted to by a government, and beyond this stage in France the state seems never to have advanced.

So slow is the progress of mankind on such subjects, that even the long parliament, while it demolished the Star Chamber, assumed the very powers which the Star Chamber had exercised with respect to the licensing of books; and as if the constitution was in this point to be benefited by *no* variety of change, a licenser was still the expedient *after* the Restoration. This appears from the act made in the year 1662, when the subject fell again under the consideration of the legislature, or rather of Clarendon. The act itself should be perused. It is in the eighth volume of the statutes. A licenser, I must repeat, was still the expedient.

The language of the preamble is the natural language of mankind on these occasions; it is this, "that by the general licentiousness of the late times many evil-disposed persons have been encouraged to print and sell heretical, schismatical, blasphemous, seditious, and treasonable books, &c. &c., for preventing whereof no surer means can be advised than by reducing and limiting the number of printing presses," &c.

And what then is to follow? First, that no person shall presume to print any heretical, seditious, schismatical, or offensive books or pamphlets wherein any doctrine or opinion shall be asserted or maintained, which is contrary to the Christian faith, or the doctrine or discipline of the Church of England, or which shall or may tend, or be, to the scandal of religion or the church, or the government or governors of the church, state, or commonwealth, or of any corporation or particular persons or person whatsoever, nor shall import such books, &c. &c. These are very general and comprehensive terms.

What then were the printers or authors to do? As the terms were so general and comprehensive, how were they to be secure from offending?

Why, by the next clause, all books concerning the common laws of this realm were to be printed by the special allowance of the Lord Chancellor, the Lords Chief Justices, &c. or one of their appointment. All books of history and affairs of state, &c. by the licence of the Secretaries of State, &c.; books of divinity, physic, philosophy, &c. by the licence of the Archbishop of Canterbury.

The penalties of the act were that the printer for the first offence should be disenabled from exercising his respective trade for the space of three years, and for the second be disenabled for *ever*, with further punishment of fine and imprisonment to any degree not extending to life and limb, at the pleasure of the judges.

Now, here we have the first movement that is made by a state on this momentous subject. It wishes for knowledge, for inquiry, for literary exertion, for government, and for religion, but for no knowledge, and no inquiry inconsistent with the interests of either that government, or religion, which are actually established at the time. It therefore denounces every thing that is in its opinion heretical and seditious, and produces its licensers. And this I conceive to be the first stage of legislation on the subject.

The next stage is to lay aside the expedient of a licenser, to have no previous restraint on publications, but to give a general description of such books or writings as are illegal, and then to punish the author or printers of any publications that come under such general description.

This is the second stage, and one of great improvement; that to which you will see Blackstone allude, and in which he seems to rest content. But much remains to be discussed and determined; for instance, what really are the general terms which the state makes use of? for if general terms are to be used, there is no work where the slightest freedom of thought is exercised, that may not be brought within their meaning. Here there is a great difficulty; and yet how is this difficulty to be avoided? What terms but *general* terms *can* be adopted? No other certainly; it is therefore of very great importance what the general terms are; and this reflection will immediately lead to another inquiry,—Who are to decide whether the publication in question fairly comes within the general description of the law or not? The judges of the land, it will be answered, on the first view of the subject; for such men can alone know what is the exact meaning of the general terms made use of from their long familiarity with the phraseology of the laws; and they must, from their situation, necessarily possess minds more enlightened, and understandings more powerful, than can be expected to fall to the lot of ordinary jurymen.

And thus we arrive at the completion of the second stage of legislation on the subject; no longer a licenser as in the first, but a law made in general terms, and the judges of the land left to decide whether an author has offended against the law or not. This is a situation of things much more favourable to the interests of mankind.

But at length men will reason thus:—What is it that the laws mean?

Only to prevent and punish such writings as are injurious to morals and religion or dangerous to the state? They mean nothing more; they *ought* to mean nothing more. If therefore the writings are such that twelve ordinary men can see neither injury to morals and religion, nor danger to the state, in any reasonings or expressions which they contain, what can in fact be the injury or the danger?

The province, therefore, of deciding upon such cases, it will be argued, ought to be withdrawn from the judges, who are not, on the whole, sufficiently unprejudiced and disinterested, and should be transferred to twelve ordinary men, to whom no such objection, and certainly no very reasonable objection, can be made.

Here we seem to have the third and last stage to which this most important subject can be brought; a law in general terms, and a jury to decide whether the law has been broken.

One point still remains—the penalty. When the NATURE of the penalty has been previously described by the law in general terms—imprisonment and fine for instance—the DEGREE of it must be left to the discretion either of the jury or of the judges; to which, then, of the two?

With whatever hesitation, we must intrust it to the latter—to the judges; that is, to those who are accustomed to the *use* of power, to the exercise of their judgments on different cases, and who decide, happily for their country, in the face of the bar and of that country. To men like these rather than to successive bodies of men like jurymen, who would each act upon views of their own; whose punishments would therefore be capricious, and not to be calculated upon beforehand, and who being liable to be affected, still more than judges, by the passions of the hour, would make their decisions sometimes improperly lenient, and at other times preposterously severe.

Here I must leave the subject, but I must leave it with addressing three observations to those who wish to make it, what it highly deserves to be, a subject of their meditation.

The first is this, that the law must unavoidably make use of some general terms to describe what it prohibits. The difficulty then is to determine what those general terms shall be; what words and phrases will best allow to society all the means of information, and yet secure to it the peaceable enjoyment of some of its most important interests.

The difficulty is very great; and it will be found more and more great, the more it is considered; at the same time, that it is the very point which must be laboured, whenever any improvement in any existing system is thought of.

My next observation is that as the jury is to decide whether the law has been violated, it is of great consequence how that jury is composed;

who is the officer that selects them; in what manner, &c. Discretion must be lodged somewhere, no doubt; but here is another point in itself difficult, and that should be well considered.

My last observation is that we have been obliged to leave the *degree* of penalty to depend on the good pleasure of the judges, and that therefore the subject of the liberty of the press cannot be considered as one that can ever be dismissed from public anxiety; because, though judges are men who go through the duties of their situation with more uniform accuracy, integrity, and intelligence than perhaps any other description of public functionaries that can be mentioned, still it must be observed that they are not likely to be of themselves very favourable to the liberty of the press. They are men accustomed to observe the benefits, not of criticising the laws and government of a country, but of administering them;—peace, order, precedent, usage, these are the objects that naturally excite their respect; the necessity of control, of punishment, of reverence for established laws and institutions, these are the considerations that are alone familiar to their minds. The habits of their lives, the learning they possess, lead to no other trains of thinking or sympathy; and they are not likely to be very indulgent critics of popular feelings or even popular rights. Whatever be their personal integrity or professional ability, they are clearly distinguishable from the philosopher or patriot, who may be speculating both on them and the laws they administer and the government they serve; and the extent and ultimate wisdom of whose opinions they are never very willing to examine and understand.

They are not therefore very eligible dispensers of the penalties of the law, if any less objectionable could be found; but none can, and here therefore is a difficulty not entirely to be overcome—the unfavourable temperament of the judges. But the temperament of the judges will sympathize with the temperament of the surrounding society, the bar in whose presence they act, the houses of legislature, and every intelligent man in the kingdom.

Discretion must always be lodged somewhere, but the manner in which it is exercised will always depend on the habits of thought and feeling known at the time to exist in the community; so little can a constitution provide for its own administration and security.

The liberty of the press is therefore a very faithful index of the state of the public mind and of the public happiness; for the press is more or less restrained (it can never be left without some restraint, from the very nature of some particular subjects), but it is more or less restrained, as a country enjoys more or less a pure religion, and a reasonable government, a wide circulation of knowledge, and a general diffusion of commercial and manufacturing prosperity. . . .

With regard to the religious liberties of the country, progress had like-wise been made by the passing of the Act of Toleration.

The king's efforts in this great cause I have already noticed—his some-what unsuccessful efforts. No brighter part of his character can be found. Of the Whigs, the best panegyric, as far as relates to this subject, may be seen in the accusations of their political opponents, the Tories; who always called them Dissenters, and represented them as indifferent to the real interests of religion. This, however, was not their fault. They were guilty of no indifference to religion, but of a base fear of such accusations, and of a disgraceful compliance with the intolerant measures proposed to them; proposed to them by those who were not unfrequently, on these occasions, their rivals for popularity; that doubtful criterion of public merit on many subjects, but above all on religious subjects; for on re-ligious subjects popularity can always be acquired by stigmatizing with terms of reproach or pursuing with penalties or restrictions, any opposers to the established system. . . .

Before I conclude my lecture, I must allude, however shortly, to the second object of inquiry which I originally proposed; the foreign politics of William, or the history of the civil and religious liberties of Europe.

The general description of this part of our labours may be short. Louis was every where the enemy of mankind; William their defender. His campaigns against the celebrated Luxembourg, the peace of Ryswick, the two partition treaties and the renewal of the general confederacy against France, just before the death of William, form the chief topics of exami-nation and reflection. . . .

Macpherson has written a history of Great Britain from the Restoration to the accession of the House of Hanover. This history may always be resorted to whenever an unfavourable representation is wanted of the conduct or character of William. Yet, even with respect to that part of our subject which is at present before us, the foreign politics of William, Macpherson is obliged to allow that William was placed at the head of his native country as the last hope of her safety from conquest and a foreign yoke; that he was raised to the throne of Great Britain under the name of her deliverer from civil tyranny and religious persecution; that he was considered in the same important light by the rest of Europe; that the Empire, Spain and Italy looked up to his counsels as their only resource against the exorbitant ambition and power of Louis XIV; and that France herself, when she affected to despise his power the most, owned his importance by an illiberal joy upon a false report of his death.

Higher praise than this cannot possibly be received. Men who engage in the affairs of the world, and have talents sufficient to influence and control them as William did, can neither appear to be nor can really be without decided faults. But if such be the bright side of any human character, we may turn away from its obscurities.

William was a patriot and a hero, but not a successful warrior. It was said that he had raised more sieges and lost more battles than any general of his age. But he was opposed to the most consummate commanders that even France has produced; and his own armies were composed of the officers and soldiers of different nations. "His defeats," says Bolingbroke, "were manifestly due, in a great measure, to circumstances independent on him; and that spirit which even these defeats could not depress, was all his own. He had difficulties in his own commonwealth; the governors of the Spanish Low Countries crossed his measures sometimes; the German allies disappointed and broke them often; and it is not improbable that he was frequently betrayed."

The peace of Ryswick was loudly censured by the French politicians. It may be considered, on the whole, as a monument to the glory of William.

XXIII. ANNE

THE REIGN of Anne may be considered as a continuation of the reign of William. The great features are the same: national animosity against France; resistance to the aggrandizement and the ambition of Louis; contending parties, the Whigs and Tories; the constitution settling; and the great question of the return of the exiled family, i. e. the success of the Revolution, i. e. the cause of the civil and religious liberties of England still suspended on a shifting, doubtful balance. . . .

The reign opens with the great War of the Succession.

I have already observed that questions of peace and war are peculiarly deserving of attention. They cannot be made too often or too much the subjects of your examination. No more valuable result can be derived from the meditation of history than habits of dispassionate reflection, of caution, foresight, a strong sense of the rights of independent nations, of justice and of humanity on such momentous topics. It is on these occasions more particularly that the philosophic statesman is distinguished from the ordinary politician; and when we suppose a minister in a cabinet, a member of either of the houses in his place, an individual at a public meeting, or an intelligent man in the private circles of social life, contributing to make his countrymen more upright, reasonable, conciliatory, patient, while the tremendous issues of war are dependent, are hanging on the balance of words and expressions; are dependent, not merely on the wisdom or the folly, but the good and ill humour of the parties, we, in fact, suppose a man elevated to something above his nature, and for a season assuming the character and office of a superior being, one whose voice breathes the heavenly accents of peace on earth, and good will towards men.

In a government that is free, where every individual is educated upon a system, not of servility and baseness, but of personal dignity and independence, of submission to no power but the laws; in such a government, one like our own, there is no fear on these occasions of any want of sensibility to national honour, or of any contemptible sacrifice to present ease and short-sighted policy. The danger is on the other side, and the habits of thought to be cherished in free and powerful countries are entirely those of a deliberative, cautious and pacific nature.

The opening of this reign of Anne affords an opportunity to the student, such as I have described. One of these great questions is before him, that of the War of the Succession, a long and dreadful contest. . . .

At the peace of the Pyrenees, Mazarin united the royal family of France with that of Spain. As this union might eventually make the princes of the House of Bourbon heirs to the crown of Spain, this was always looked upon as a masterpiece of policy.

The first question which I would propose to the student is whether it was so? The King of Spain was at the time sufficiently aware of the possible consequences, and he therefore took due care that all title to the future succession to the crown of Spain, of whatever kind, should be publicly and for ever renounced.

This is a part of the case, and being so, the policy of the whole transaction, as far as Mazarin is concerned, may, I think, be proposed as a question.

Among other considerations that will occur to the student when he looks at the history, I would wish to leave the following more particularly to his examination.

First, whether the avoidance of all causes of war, and all temptations to war, is not the first point of policy to be secured?

Secondly, whether the union of the families was likely to influence materially the future intercourse of the two nations, and make it more friendly than hitherto it had been? If so, this was a most weighty consideration in favour of the measure. But on the other side, and

Thirdly, whether the union of the families did not rather hold up to the ambition of all succeeding princes of France the most tempting object, the succession to the crown of Spain; and yet the renunciation render that ambition totally unlawful; and whether the result was not therefore sure to be, that France would be engaged in a series of dishonest intrigues for the accomplishment of this object; and afterwards

in a war with the powers of Europe for the maintenance of this unlawful object, if those intrigues were successful; for the acquiescence of the
powers of Europe, without a struggle, could not possibly be expected.

Now, if this last question be answered in the affirmative, as well as
the first, where was the policy of Mazarin?

The event turned out to be that the prospect of the succession kept
continually opening to Louis, and that his family at last became the
regular heirs to the Spanish monarchy.

But it must not be forgotten that they were incapacitated by their renunciation. This renunciation was the very condition of their birth, for
it was the condition on which Louis was married to the infanta of Spain,
in right of whom they claimed.

I must now recommend the sixty-seventh chapter in Coxe's [*House of*]
Austria, where the subject of the Spanish succession is concisely and
clearly stated, and on the proper authorities. The claimants were the
Dauphin of France, the Emperor Leopold, who had married the next
sister of the infanta, and the Elector of Bavaria, who had espoused the
issue of this last marriage, and was the son-in-law of Leopold.

The father, Leopold, it must be observed, had induced his daughter, on
her marriage with the elector, to renounce her claims to the Spanish succession; but this renunciation was considered invalid, as not having been
approved by the King of Spain, nor ratified by the Cortes. In this state
of things, the second question that I should wish to propose to the
student, is this: What was our own King William to attempt to do? How
was he to prevent the succession from devolving on Louis; a prince
who was not likely to adhere to his original renunciations? . . .

William made a partition treaty with Louis; i. e. he compounded with
him. He consented that *part* of the Spanish possessions should be transferred to France, the better to secure the remainder from the ambition
of Louis; and to this end, that the elector might receive, undisturbed, the
main part of what by inheritance, devolved upon him; that in this manner the balance of Europe might be tolerably well preserved, and yet a
war avoided. These were his objects. . . .

Unfortunately the elector died, and a second partition treaty was therefore to be made: the archduke was substituted for the elector, and the
terms made more advantageous to France. Now the point I would submit to your consideration is this: whether, besides the alternatives which
Lord Bolingbroke enumerates as all that the case admitted of, whether
another did not remain, that of doing nothing at all; not abandoning all
care of the succession, but taking no distinct measure; certainly none but
with the privity, and in conjunction, with the court of Spain?

To parcel out the dominions of an independent kingdom, however
agreeably to the general interests of Europe, and from the best of motives,

without the interference or consent of that kingdom, was in itself un-just, and therefore not to be thought of; and was at the same time so offensive to Spain, that it could not possibly have any other effect but that of throwing her into the arms of France, for the sake of preserving the integrity of her empire and the dignity of her crown.

What line of policy in the meantime was the emperor to pursue? Of this there can be little question; he was to send to the court of Spain a minister of attractive manners, and by conciliating at the same time his own Hungarian subjects, to leave himself in possession of the full force of his empire, in case he had to contend with France.

The emperor did neither: he neither sent a minister of an agreeable accommodating temper, nor did he relax his harsh, severe system of policy to his Hungarian subjects.

It seems impossible for the haughty and ceremonious ever to think there is any thing of value in the world, but dignity and form; and the policy of mild government is a secret which, on some account or other, can never be discovered by those who have an opportunity of exercising it.

But to return to the succession: the King of Spain died, and, most un-fortunately, at last made a will in favour of the French line.

Here comes the next question; was Louis to accept the testament? On this point must be read, not only Lord Bolingbroke, but that part of the works of St. Simon which relates to the succession. It is not long.

In De Torcy's *Memoirs* will be found the defence of Louis, who *did* accept the testament; and in Mably's *Droit de l'Europe* (not his history), an argument in opposition to the reasoning of De Torcy, and in favour of adhering to the treaty of partition. . . .

In the third volume of St. Simon's *Memoirs* and in De Torcy will be found accounts of the debate that actually did take place in the presence of Louis. There is some little difference in the representation of these two authors with respect to the part which the speakers took; and Madame de Maintenon was consulted, according to St. Simon, which is positively denied (though it is somewhat impossible to suppose that she was not) by De Torcy.

The question debated was whether the king should accept the testa-ment, or adhere to the second partition treaty; and the case supposed was (which was indeed the fact) that the succession was to be offered instantly to the House of Austria, if declined by the French monarch. On the one side it was observed (even in the cabinet of Louis), "the national faith is pledged [I translate from the French writers]; and even in point of mere advantage, more will in fact be gained by the partition treaty than by placing the French line on the throne of Spain; the princes of which will soon lose their partiality to France, and become as jealous of her power, as have hitherto been the princes of the House of Austria. If we accept the testament, a war must follow; Europe will necessarily oppose itself to what will then be thought the colossal power of France. We have already had one war; we are only now taking breath; we are ourselves exhausted, so is Spain; of a new war it will be for us to support all the charge. We have here, therefore, before us, a train of consequences, of which the final issue no one can presume to tell; but in the gross, and at once, it is easy to pronounce, that it is but common prudence to avoid them, by adhering to the partition treaty. France, by this proof of her good faith, will conciliate all Europe—Europe which she has seen leagued against her because she has been considered as aspiring, like the House of Austria, to universal monarchy; and if she now accept this testament, will the truth of these accusations admit longer of a doubt?"

Such was, according to the more probable account of St. Simon, the statement of De Torcy himself; offered by him as the statement of *one* side of the question. But such were entirely, and stated as a proper estimate of the whole of the case, the sentiments of the Duc de Beauvilliers, the tutor of the Duke of Burgundy, the discerning and good man who had selected Fénélon to assist him in his momentous office; and similar to these are always the sentiments of discerning and good men on all such occasions. These are the natural and weighty topics that are insisted upon by all such reasoners, when peace and war can be made a question: national faith, the opinions of surrounding nations on our conduct; what there is, or what there may be, of justice in their accusations; the advantages that may assuredly be derived from peace; the evils that inevitably result from war; the calamities that will certainly, the very serious ruin that (it is possible at least) *may* result from dangerous experiments.

In the instance before us, the successes of Marlborough, the appearance of such a commander among the enemies of France, could not indeed have been expected by Louis or his counsellors. But even according to the ordinary nature of events, there were not only possibilities, but there were probabilities, and there were certainties sufficient to induce the Duc de Beauvilliers to insist, as he did insist, on the solid wisdom of the counsels which he recommended.

The chancellor, on the contrary, too much disposed, as it is thought by St. Simon, to sacrifice to the wishes of his master (such men will always be found among the counsellors of princes), presented to Louis views more splendid, and reasonings more attractive. He found it easy to show how fitted were the kingdoms of France and Spain to constitute a great empire under the dominion of the House of Bourbon.

There was no difficulty in depreciating the advantages presented by the treaty of partition, or in rendering suspected the policy of any system to which William, the great enemy of France, had become a party.

It was not difficult to show that it must always make a very material difference to France, whether there were seated on the throne of Spain princes of the House of Bourbon, or princes of the House of Austria, however interested the former might at length become, in the prosperity of the particular kingdom which they governed.

These were topics of fair debate, provided the question could ever have been brought to a point where it was proper to discuss them. The chancellor also insisted, that since the treaties of partition were made, new circumstances had occurred which rendered them no longer binding: the testament, for instance, had been made in Louis's favour.

This is the sort of dishonest reasoning that on all such occasions is produced, and it is therefore universally instructive. For the chancellor omitted to state, that the testament had been procured by the intrigues of France, and that Louis was thus to profit by his own wrong.

Again: "France," said the minister, "by refusing the testament, will gain, *not* the character of moderation, but, that of pusillanimity; will become an object of ridicule, not of respect, to surrounding nations, as was our good Louis XII and Francis I, to Ferdinand, Charles V, the pope, and the Venetians: not indeed that the point of honour is against us," said the chancellor. "Can it be supposed that such a succession as that of Spain is ever to fall into our hands without a war? Even to the treaty of partition the emperor will not assent: and then if we are, on every supposition, to have a war, is it not better to fight for the proper benefits of success, after first possessing ourselves of what is already within our grasp? Let us at least contrive not to show ourselves to the world unworthy of the high fortune to which we are so unexpectedly called."

These also are, I think, arguments universally instructive; for it is by considerations of this kind that nations are always inflamed, their passions excited, and their judgments betrayed by their orators, statesmen, and princes. It is even by considerations of this kind, that they who should counsel others are themselves led astray; and these therefore, as they continually occur in history, become the genuine instruction of history. . . .

The politicians of the world have never ceased on these subjects to commit, as did first Mazarin, and afterwards Louis, the most cruel mistakes. The gain of one country has always been supposed the loss of every other: colonies are to be fought for, and commerce is to be fought for, and kingdoms are to be fought for, and all for the sake of prosperity and power. Human life is to be wasted, all the proper materials of strength and accumulation to be dissipated and annihilated, to be directed to the purposes of destruction, and every experiment is to be attempted but one, the only proper and rational experiment, that of making governments gradually more free, the laws more equal, and the maintaining of peace. . . .

Marlborough seems to tower above all praise. It would be difficult to find any commander in any age or country to whom he can be thought inferior; he might rather seem to have united the merits of them all. He had the praise of Hannibal, for he had to oppose the armies of one great military nation by armies composed of many different nations. He had the praise of Cæsar, for though an enterprising, he was a safe commander; he lost no battle; he failed in no siege; he was no desperate knight-errant like Alexander in ancient story, or Charles XII in modern. He lived not like Attila, or Tamerlane, among barbarous nations, when the event of a single battle decided the fate of an empire, and when, if fortune once smiled, her smiles were afterwards superfluous: nor did he live like the great conqueror in our own times—the Emperor of France, in a revolutionary age, when the new and dreadful energies of a particular nation could be seized upon and directed against surrounding nations; against armies formed on a different model, statesmen obliged to deliberate under a different system, and governments submitted to different habits and principles of action.

The Duke of Marlborough was in no favourable situation like any of these creators of dynasties or destroyers of kingdoms; much the contrary; he flourished when war had been reduced to a science, and when likewise it could be waged in no sweeping or convulsive manner; he had to do with regular governments, orderly statesmen, soldiers animated by no fury of enthusiasm, political or religious; princes, magistrates, financiers, officers civil and military, individuals in all their divisions and departments, moving, each of them, after the prescribed rate and fashion of society in its most civilized and appointed state; nay more, he had to sway the factions of England, to animate the legislative bodies of Holland, to harmonize the members of the Germanic body; and all to the one single purpose of overpowering on the continent the vast, concentrated, prompt, and matured strength of France (an object this which no human art or genius could ever, before or since, be properly said to have, by regular military warfare, accomplished). Even the great William, trained up amid a life of difficulties and of war, with an intrepid heart and a sound understanding, was only able to stay the enterprises of Louis; successfully to resist, but not to humble him. It was for Marlborough to teach that unprincipled monarch the danger of ambition and the instability of human grandeur; it was for Marlborough to disturb his dreams of pleasure and of pride, by filling them with spectres of terror and images of desolation. Of Marlborough might be said, in a far more extensive sense of the words, what was afterwards said of Lord Chatham, that with one hand he wielded the aristocracy of England, and with the other he smote the House of Bourbon.

The great praise of Marlborough is that his glory was reached step by step, by no sudden indulgence of fortune, by no single effort of military skill and valour. Enterprise succeeded to enterprise, campaign to campaign, and the result was always the same; progressive fame, and victories and triumphs either accomplished or prepared. If commanders were sent against him who made the slightest mistake, victories like Blenheim and Ramillies were the consequence. If a man of consummate skill like Vendome was opposed to him, he consented to attempt nothing impracticable. No success improperly inflamed his expectations, yet could he show, as in his campaign with Villars, that no necessity of caution, no respect for his opponent, excluded from his mind the chances at least of success, and he could seize them with effect, and prove that, whatever might be his circumspection, he was equally gifted with the powers of military invention, and the spirit of military enterprise.

The career of other great generals has been always marked by varieties of chance and change, of light and shade, of success and defeat. But the panegyric of Marlborough is contained in a single word—he was always right; that is, he proportioned well his means to his ends, and did not, like other statesmen and generals, mistake passion for wisdom, wishes for possibilities, and words for things. On the whole, though, in his character as a man, some failings must be allowed, parsimony for instance (the result so often of the necessity of economy in early life), and the fault, the crime, of corresponding with the exiled family, on the whole, a degrading and a most unworthy attention to his own interest; such was his good sense, his military genius, the charms of his address and appearance, and his high and commanding qualities of every description, that he must even now be considered, what Lord Bolingbroke was compelled to call him in his day, the greatest of generals and of ministers.

Turning now from the character of the Duke of Marlborough, who won the victories that distinguished this reign, to the use that was made of them, though no difference of opinion can exist with regard to the first, much may with regard to the second question:—

How far the allies were or were not unreasonable in their demands; which of the parties was most in fault during the negotiations for peace, particularly during the first, that at the Hague?

I cannot repeat too often that questions of this sort are among the most profitable portions of study which can belong to the readers of history. We may not be able always to understand by what varieties of character or of personal interest, in the agents or in the principals, negotiations break off or terminate with success; but by being removed to a distance, we can take a commanding view of what were the *real* interests of the parties at the time. Such speculations are well fitted to prepare us for the discussion of similar subjects when we come to be ourselves concerned, to save us from unreasonable terrors or extravagant hopes, and above all to prevent us from magnifying points, for which we have been contending, into an importance which does not belong to them, and which temporary importance becomes to succeeding politicians not unfrequently a subject of surprise, compassion, or even contempt. . . .

I must now remind you, as I apprized you I should, of the reasons for the war, which were given when it first broke out. It is curious to remark the manner in which the tone of the allies *altered*, and their views enlarged, with their victories. This may be very *natural*, but it is not entirely and ultimately wise. A war is not to be entered upon without a grave and specific object; but when success has enabled a nation to obtain that object, and this had surely been effected by the great battles just alluded to, upon every principle of wisdom as of humanity, the war must close. If new objects are to arise and to be considered as indispensable to peace, the system of warfare is then converted into a system to each nation the most protracted possible, and therefore the most ruinous possible; a system more protracted than the passions of our nature, violent as they are, at all require. Peace is the great cause of human nature; it is the great secret of prosperity to all nations, collectively and individually. It is, therefore, the common policy of all; not to say, that even according to the short-sighted notions of rivalry and selfishness, a successful nation often carries on a war too long; more is lost by the expense of an additional campaign, than the advantages of a campaign do or can repay; and what is of still more consequence, the fortune of the contest may alter.

Again, it should have been considered that those who propose fair terms of peace, as Louis did, never fail of securing a most advantageous alternative. They obtain either a peace or a just cause. Louis, for instance, could not bring the allies to grant him honourable conditions (hard terms are never the true policy); he therefore published those which they had insisted upon, and he had it then in his power to say, as he did say, to his subjects, in a public address, "If it had depended on me, you should have enjoyed this blessing which you so earnestly desire, the blessing of peace; but it must be procured by new efforts; the immense sacrifices I have offered are of no avail; I can perfectly sympathize with all that my faithful subjects must endure, but I am persuaded they would themselves recoil from conditions of peace as repugnant to justice as to the honour of the French name." . . .

The Whigs ought surely to have been eager to have made the best bargain for Europe which they could, from the obvious probability that the queen, who always hated and feared them, as they well knew, would contrive to get other ministers, and the consequences be, a peace on terms much less advantageous to England and the continent than they could themselves obtain. They might easily see how difficult it was to keep up a combination of powers against France, and how many chances and how many reasons might make a war unpopular. . . .

In every free government it is the interest of the members of a cabinet, even with a view to their own personal aggrandizement, to proceed as much as possible on a system of peace, for the uneasiness which is occasioned by the pressure of war is very easily converted, by their political opponents, into the means of dislodging them from their power. In all free governments, those who make a war, as was the case in the present instance, seldom make a peace; war comes at last, with or without due reason, to be unpopular; and the war and its advisers are discarded together. . . .

Their interests, or at least their own views of their interests, are seldom the same while the war is carried on, still less, when peace begins to be thought of. It is very difficult to combine them so as to render them successful for any long period. Prosperity disunites them, from jealousy; adversity still more, from views of self-preservation.

In combinations of different powers, the great duty of all is disinterestedness. In this respect the Whig ministry of England set an example highly creditable to their characters as wise and honourable statesmen. They might mistake (it is a great question) the wisdom of the case at the proper season; but their language and their views were, resistance to the ambition of France—the establishment of the general interests of Europe.

But the question is, whether they suffered not the justice of the cause at last to be transferred to the French monarch. He had recourse to negotiation, was unsuccessful, and then appealed to his people and to the world.—I must ask again—

Were the allies and their ministers sufficiently attentive to the claims of humanity and to all the suggestions of sober policy at home and abroad on this occasion and in the course of these successes? To me it appears not.

If the rulers of mankind would not mix their own passions in the contests of nations, it is impossible that these appeals to negotiation should not be more frequent; it is impossible that wars should be drawn out to the protracted period we so often witness. All parties would be thrown more and more into a state of deliberation; would be reminded of the desirableness of peace; that it was the proper and only end of all war: that the real causes of hostility were always exaggerated; that in these cases there was nothing to be met with but misapprehension, fury, and absurdity.

But the whole system of national policy is mistaken, and cabinets, instead of considering how their own nation may be extricated from a contest with safety and honour, think only how the enemy may be reduced to the lowest possible state of depression, how their own views of political aggrandizement may be realized, how their own particular nation may be left hereafter without an equal, and the rest of mankind be taught to fall down and worship themselves and their countrymen.

xxiv. ANNE

THE REIGN of Anne is distinguished, even in the annals of England, for the violence of its politics. Party violence has been not uncommonly a topic of censure and lamentation with good men, and their accusations and reproaches have been urged often with sincerity, and sometimes with reason; but care must be taken on these occasions both by those who are disposed to make these indiscriminate indictments, and those who are disposed to listen to them. It is in itself rather a suspicious circumstance, when men who are at all conversant with the business of the world are found expressing themselves very strongly or very often against the violence of parties or the fury of factions. In a mixed and free government, there will naturally arise, as I must for ever repeat, two great and leading divisions, those who lean to the side of *authority*, and those who lean to the side of *privilege*. Questions, unlike in name and form, will often involve the same general principles, and men are not, therefore, always as inconsistent as they seem. Trains of measures will often emanate from one point, and proceed in the most strictly logical succession, and must be therefore supported and resisted always by the same men. It is, therefore, not possible that those who are really independent and sincere should not often in free legislative assemblies, vote in sets and parties, and it is equally impossible that they should not become inflamed by sympathy and collision. Read the works of Soame Jenyns, and of Locke. Would not each of these men, for instance, while they retained their integrity, have been seen always on the opposite sides of any question that could affect the constitution and government of a free country?

The real and proper topic for lamentation and reproach, is not, exactly, that men are often violent and systematic in their opposition to each other, but that they do not adopt their principles with sufficient care, and then follow them up with sincerity and honour. Moderate men, as they call themselves, and men of no party, as they profess themselves to be, will generally be found to be men who take little concern, or are but ill informed, on political subjects; and if they are members of the legislature, they are pretty uniformly observed, as they are of no party, forsooth, to take care to be of that party which is the strongest—to be of the minister's party (be he who he may), and to benefit by their neutrality. It is possible, indeed, for men to be of no party, and to assume the high station of real patriots; and even when they are of a party, to remain patriots, by refusing to sanction those measures of the party which they disapprove. This is, perhaps, the highest possible ambition of an intelligent and virtuous man, but such an eminence can only be attained on one hard condition, that of never receiving a favour from those in power. . . .

The causes of political animosity were, in these times, very peculiarly weighty and animating. The questions that lay often between the parties were, in reality, what family was to possess the throne; whether the title of the crown was to be founded on divine and hereditary right, or on the principles of an original contract, that is, whether on arbitrary or free principles; whether the religion established in the country was to be certainly Protestant, or probably Roman Catholic; in a word, whether principles decidedly favourable, or principles clearly hostile, to the civil and religious liberties of the country, were to be maintained and established.

But in a sort of connexion with this subject, I may mention, that in a mixed government like this, the attention of those who wish well to the popular part of it, has been always very naturally directed to the influence which the executive power can directly exercise on the legislative bodies, by means of posts, places, and pensions, given to their members. . . .

In a mixed and free government like our own, all questions that either occupy, or deserve to occupy attention, have a reference either to the prerogative of the crown, or privileges of the people, to religious toleration, to mild or harsh government, to peace and war, or finally, to some of the more important subjects of political economy; that suspense in all these cases is impossible, that honest men therefore vote with those who best promote such *systems* and principles as they approve; that in this manner are disposed of, and ranged on *different* sides, the men of *political integrity*; and that the remainder are those who are in the habit of thinking all questions matters of indifference, and of joining the men or the ministers, who are most likely to furnish their relations or themselves with emoluments and offices; but that such men are, and always have been, the proper objects of the suspicion and contempt, not only of the public, but of the very house itself; and it is impossible to suppose that they can be necessary to the stability of any good government; certainly not in any greater number than the infirmity of human nature will always produce them, after every possible political expedient and contrivance has been resorted to, for the purpose of diminishing their number, and weakening their efficiency.

I have now another topic to propose in like manner to your reflections.

The reign of Anne is remarkable as exhibiting in a very strong point of view one of those peculiarities in the constitution of a government which can only occur in a free and mixed form, like our own. I allude to the manner in which the executive power can be restrained, and even controlled by machinery not *avowedly* provided by the constitution for the purpose, and yet acting with far more certainty and success than any that could be devised by the most skilful contriver of political systems.

For instance, Queen Anne carried on the war against France when neither her wishes nor her opinions were favourable to its continuance. The Whig administration remained in power long after they had become disagreeable to her, and Marlborough was her general, and even the arbiter of her councils at the conferences for peace, when neither he nor his duchess any longer possessed her favour.

Louis XIV, in the meantime, had always understood that it was the acknowledged prerogative of the crown in this country to determine the questions of peace and war; that it was equally so to choose its own ministers; and though he must have known that these prerogatives, however acknowledged by the constitution, were, after all, not exercised in the manner they were done by himself, still he had learnt that the Duchess of Marlborough was supplanted, that Harley and Mrs. Masham were the real favourites; that the Whigs were on the decline, and the Tories preparing for their political triumph; and what difficulties, he must have thought, were left, and what was he now to fear?

All this is made very apparent by a few pages in the Duchess of Marlborough's *Apology*, describing the situation of things so early as in the winter of 1706 and spring of 1707, about a year after the battle of Ramillies, the great battle which seemed to decide the fortunes of the war. Yet all through the war of 1708, the war, and the great supporters of it, the Whigs, were still highly popular. At the end of this year, 1708, November 25, a new parliament met, in which the Whigs had, as before, a decided ascendancy, and they were possessed of a power that was still firm, and as yet not to be shaken. The nation and the houses of parliament were still in their favour, and though the queen longed for their dismissal almost as impatiently as did her secret counsellors and the rival party of the Tories, it required a certain lapse of time, and a continuance of mistake and infatuation on the part of the Whigs, to produce the great political events, which Louis perhaps expected to have taken place long before, without difficulty or delay.

When the Whig administration was at last fairly swept away, the queen was felicitated on her success, and even in express words, congratulated as being again a queen.

Instances of this sort of control over the wishes of the sovereign sometimes occur in our history since the restoration of Charles II, and they deserve attention. While the government remains mixed and free, they will never cease at particular periods to occur.

As on these occasions it is always said that the sovereign has assuredly a right to appoint his own ministers, and as this observation is generally considered as decisive, a few remarks may not be entirely without their use to those who would study these, the most critical portions of our annals, and certainly by far the most important peculiarities of our constitution.

To consider them a little. The great problem of government is to make the executive power sufficiently strong to preserve the peace and order of society, and yet not leave it sufficiently strong to disregard the wishes and happiness of the community. When this point is attained, every thing is attained that the nature of human society admits of.

But referring to our own history, we may say that this was not done in our own country before or during the reign of Elizabeth, nor yet during the reign of Charles I; a crisis of the most melancholy nature ensued. From this time, however, what had always been more or less the doctrine became at last the practice of the English constitution, and while the executive power was, in the person of the king, considered as incapable of doing any wrong, the ministers of that executive power were considered as its advisers, and therefore very capable of doing wrong, and as the proper and only subjects of national censure or punishment.

It is not easy to discover a more happy expedient than this for solving the great political problem which I have just mentioned; certainly no better has ever appeared in any government that has hitherto existed among mankind. The regular growth and final maturity of this expedient, if I may so speak, among all the changes and chances of the events of our history, may assuredly be esteemed one of the greatest blessings by which this country is distinguished; but the original difficulty is so very great, that it is scarcely possible for human beings entirely to escape it; and it is not escaped, but much the contrary, if it be once considered as a political maxim, that the sovereign can appoint his own ministers, and that no further debate is necessary.

I will now put two cases: one to show, in the first place, the impropriety of this political maxim, that the king can appoint, and that nothing more is to be said; and another, in the second place, to show the impropriety of any maxim directly the contrary; that the sovereign, for instance, should be always controlled in this point. Lastly, I will propose a conclusion from the whole.

And first, to show the impropriety of the maxim, that the sovereign can choose his own ministers, and that no further debate is possible.

Suppose, for instance, that Queen Anne, during the administration of the Whigs, had satisfied herself that the war ought to be terminated, and yet found her ministers of a different opinion; suppose in this case she had dismissed them, and appointed others; suppose that the houses of parliament were unfavourable, agreeing with her own ministers, and refusing her new ministers their support, that she therefore dissolved the parliament, and appealed to the people. Now, if on this occasion her people had returned her such representatives as were favourable to the new ministers, merely because the queen was vested by the constitution with the prerogative of making peace, and of choosing her own ministers, what difference would there in fact have been between her and Louis XIV? None but this, that the sovereign in this country had to go through the *ceremony* of dissolving an existing parliament and calling a new one, and that Louis could follow his own opinion without any such delay.

Or to put a still stronger case to the same purpose: suppose Queen Anne had resolved if possible to restore her brother and her family to the throne, she had found, we will imagine, her Whig ministers impracticable on this occasion; she had perceived that Bolingbroke and others on the contrary would try the experiment, if sure of her support. Bolingbroke, therefore, is made minister; her intentions, and those of her new adviser, become manifest; the houses of parliament, as before, thwart her measures, and the votes necessary for her purpose cannot be carried; she therefore dissolves the parliament, and appeals to the people. Now, if in this case also the electors return a House of Commons friendly to the new ministers, merely because those new ministers are the objects of the queen's choice, and because the constitution has given her the power of choice, if such had been the reasoning considered as final on the occasion, what would have been the result? That the Protestant succession would not have taken place; that the Stuarts would have been recalled; the Revolution failed; and more than this, all these events would have happened contrary to the real opinion and wishes of the community.

That is, in other words, this single maxim, if it should really obtain and be acted upon, would at once make the sovereign arbitrary, whenever any personal pique with his ministers, any particular views of his own in politics, or any great projects with respect to the descent of his crown, or to the constitution of the country, inspired him with a wish to become arbitrary; that is, to do what he thought best.

We will now change entirely the aspect of the reasoning; to show, in the second place, the impropriety of any maxim, exactly the contrary to that we have noticed. We will suppose that an appeal on some account or other had, as before, been made by the sovereign from the parliament to the people, and that the maxim in the mind of the electors had no longer been such as we have hitherto supposed, but that the reasoning had been of a nature totally different; for instance, that the legislative bodies, more particularly the House of Commons, were the natural protectors of the community; that the sovereign in a free government was not to do whatever he thought good; that the liberties of the country had always owed their existence to the control which the houses had exercised upon the executive power; that a free constitution in reality meant this, and meant little else, and that therefore the people should ALWAYS support their parliaments, who could not be expected to bear up against the executive power without the most ready sympathy and protection; without the most implicit confidence on the part of their constituents.

Now, it is evident that if reasonings like these were supposed to be *always decisive*, and to preclude, as in the first cases, *all further discussion*, that then the executive power would be a mere cipher, would be always at the mercy of those, who by whatever means had possessed themselves of the confidence of the houses.

I do not say that even this would be a bad species of government, or at least that it would not be the best alternative of the two; but I may safely say that it is not properly the constitution of England, and that therefore, as before, this must not be the maxim, viz. that the houses, or perhaps, as the case may more probably be, that the House of Commons is at all events to be supported.

Taking, therefore, the difficulties on each side of the question into account, I now proceed, in the third place, to propose a conclusion drawn from the whole, and it is this, that whenever an appeal is made by the executive power from the House of Commons to the nation by a dissolution, the veil of the constitution is for a time drawn aside; the personal conduct, the political wisdom not only of each representative of the public, but even of the high and supreme magistrate of the realm himself, is for one short interval brought before the consideration of the public, and is even subjected to their decision. The most important question that can possibly be proposed is then, in fact, proposed to every individual of intelligence or influence; for it is this—to which of the two parties (however elevated in the view of reason and the constitution one of these high parties may be)—to which of the two parties he is to give his support? And the result of the whole is this, that this support is to be given not in compliance with any pre-established maxims either of a monarchical or democratical nature, but after the most careful deliberation on the merits of the precise case before him; for it is by these merits he is to be decided, and not by any sweeping general preconceptions on the one side or the other, such as preclude at once all further discussion; he is to be determined, on the contrary, by a deliberation careful, honest, and independent; a deliberation which is the very virtue and the very office that on this occasion is required from him; he is to deliberate as having now become for a season the guardian and the arbiter of the British constitution, of the happiness of his country, of the rights and welfare of the existing generation and posterity. According to the issue of his inquiries and meditations, he is bound to return to parliament those who would be most likely to favour those views of the case which he himself entertains; and a greater fault—I had almost said a greater crime—can scarcely be committed, than for any man to suffer himself to be swayed on great occasions like these by any motives of base and detestable self-interest: by any hopes of preferment for himself or his relatives, or even by regard to his family connexions, his personal friendships, his obligations of kindness, or in short, by any motive even generous and virtuous, but the sole and proper motive which can alone in this particular instance be generous and virtuous, his real view of the case, the calm, plain, honest, unsophisticated decision of his judgment.

If ever the constitution of England is to be admired, it is on occasions like these; in every crisis of this nature, when the supreme executive power was in fact to be criticised and publicly controlled, at Rome a tribune was to appear on the part of the people with his veto; in Aragon a justiza was to be a sort of representative and guardian of the community. These are but very indifferent expedients; such as have appeared in Grecian or other republican forms of government are little better; in arbitrary governments there are none; but in our own happy country civil wars, violence, and bloodshed, those contests so disgraceful to humanity, so fatal but too often to the interests of the people, are avoided; they have now been so for a century and a half, and all this by the regular and orderly exercise of the different functions that belong to the sovereign, the houses of legislature, and the people. In England, if the great magistrate of the realm is at issue with other powers in the state, the question is for some time kept in suspense; the public attention is excited, and then, before either of the parties is irrecoverably committed or irreconcilably inflamed, the parliament is dissolved, a third party is called in, and that third party is the nation itself; not acting in any tumultuous or extraordinary manner; not exerting any physical force; not called upon to show any giddy rudeness, any vulgar insolence, any upstart airs of authority over their sovereign, to whom they owe a general obligation of duty and obedience; and on the contrary, not called upon to show the slightest disrespect or indifference to the office of that part of the legislature, their houses of parliament, to which they owe a general sentiment of confidence and affection, but called upon gravely and peaceably to furnish a new representative; a new special reporter of their opinion to their sovereign; one with whom he may again consult, and again propose his own particular views of the nature of his prerogative or of the national interest. If the sovereign should have lent too willing an ear to counsels unfavourable to the constitution or the welfare of his people, he may be thus warned of his mistake in time, by the opinions of the representatives which the people have returned to him, and be warned in a manner the most respectful, the most gentle, the most consistent with the high reverence that is due to his exalted station; and if, on the contrary, the people themselves mistake or betray their own interests, and send an improper representative, they must suffer, and they deserve to suffer (as men must always do in every concern and situation of human life), the natural consequences of their own servility, inattention, or ignorance.

xxv. ANNE—UNION OF ENGLAND AND SCOTLAND

THE GREAT domestic event by which the reign of Anne was distinguished was the union of the two kingdoms of England and Scotland. I am very desirous to recommend this subject to your diligence and reflection.

I will make a few observations, and endeavour to convey to you some general idea of the interest which belongs to it.

England has been connected with Scotland, with Ireland, with America. In each of these relations a sort of termination and crisis has at last taken place. In Scotland we adopted the measure of an union under the immediate apprehension of a rebellion; in Ireland, after a rebellion, which had but too nearly torn the two countries asunder; in America the rebellion was successful, and we lost the country for ever. We have still another country with which we are connected on the other side of the globe, the immense continent of India.

The political questions that arise from the connexion of nations with each other seem to me among the greatest that history or that human affairs can ever present to you. Such connexions of different nations have often occurred, and will never cease to occur in the annals of mankind. Spain has been connected with Portugal; both kingdoms with South America; France with America and the West Indies; the House of Austria with the Netherlands and Italy. By proximity of situation or by colonization kingdoms have been, and always will be, vitally dependent on the conduct of each other. The duties that hence arise are often very difficult, the best systems of policy not obvious. Happy would it have been and would it still be for mankind, if something more of good sense and good feeling either had been or could yet be introduced into the cabinets of their rulers, and into their own misguided understandings and selfish minds.

It is very true that when philosophy has exhibited all its reasonings and exhausted all its efforts, it is very true that the most serious difficulties will still remain on subjects like these; that the interest of connected nations cannot be entirely reconciled, nor their separate wishes be gratified. Nations must often be reduced to compound with evils, and at last to make such sacrifices as are necessarily accompanied with mortification and regret; but it is for political wisdom to encounter and reconcile men to these evils, to proclaim aloud that on these occasions nothing has happened at variance with the common necessities of our imperfect state.

The misfortune is that nations can never submit to the circumstances of their situation in time, or with any grace or good humour. Human life, however, at every turn, and in every stage of it, is continually requiring from us a wisdom of this melancholy cast. It is the great discipline to which the Almighty Ruler of the world has subjected us through all the successive changes of our state, and all the affecting relations of our domestic feelings, from infancy to the grave. On all such occasions, on the small scale of our social connexions, and in what relates to ourselves, we submit to necessity; we compound, we balance, we understand what is our best wisdom, and we endeavour to practise it; the father expects not that his son shall for ever remain dependent on his kindness, and moulded by his directions; men with their inferiors, neighbours with each other, act always on a system of mutual sacrifices, reciprocal duties, and interchanged offices of sympathy and good will.

But on the larger scale of the intercourse of nations, particularly of connected nations, the same moral truths, though equally existing, are not so obvious, and when apparent, not so impressive. We are therefore fretful, ill-humoured, outrageous; we contend against reason, philosophy, and nature itself; forget the great rule of doing to others as we would they should do unto us: and after wasting our blood and treasure to no purpose, we at last sit down faint and exhausted, abandon our vain projects only because it is impossible to pursue them, and then leave it to the reasoners of a succeeding age to show how egregious has been our folly, and how blind our fury.

The leading principles that belong to subjects of this nature have been introduced to the notice and to the assent of the more intelligent part of mankind in two different modes, by experience and by the reasonings of philosophers.

When nations are connected with each other, they can find causes of offence and hostility in three different points: in their religion, their laws and customs, their trade and manufactures.

Now experience has tolerably well taught mankind (however slowly), that with respect to the two former, toleration is the best and only policy; that it is best to suffer colonies or inferior nations to retain their own particular creeds and rites and ceremonies in religion, and their own particular modes of administering justice in civil or criminal matters; that improvements may be proposed to them, but not enforced; that till they can be properly enlightened, they must be left to indulge their own particular notions.

But on the last question, of trade and manufactures, the world is entirely indebted to the labours of the French writers on political economy, and to the works of Hume and Adam Smith. . . .

It is now admitted that the whole doctrine of the balance of trade is a mistake, and that nations are necessarily benefited by any commercial intercourse, of whatever kind, provided it is not artificially produced by the mere operation of laws or any species of extraneous necessity and force.

We have now, then, an adjustment of the whole of the case. What difficulty, it might be said, can remain? If nations are to be connected together, let the one allow to the other its own religion, its own laws, and the most free and unrestrained imports and exports; what cause of contention can remain? Let the supreme legislature be the same; and the countries being thus in every respect identified, the interests of both will be entirely served and secured, and every thing that philosophy can prescribe, or human affairs admit of, be at once accomplished.

But the conduct and even the reasonings of mankind have on all such occasions been widely different, and the result has been at all times fatal to their happiness.

We will take the simplest case, that of a mother country and her colonies. The religion has been here generally the same, and laws and customs similar; in these points there was little room for mistakes. But in questions of trade and commerce greater opportunity for errors was afforded, and the mistakes committed have in fact been very numerous and important. The most narrow jealousy, the most blighting systems of superintendence and control, have been continually exercised; no market allowed to the colonies till the supposed interests of the mother country were first secured; no manufactures to be imported, nor even to be used, but those that came from the land and labour of the parent state; and if ill-humour in the colonies was the consequence, troops were to be sent, and a policy, ultimately injurious to both countries, was to be supported by force.

In other cases that have occurred, cases of connected nations, as the real difficulties have been greater, the mistakes have been still more multiplied and fatal. For instance:—

Two nations may be completely connected together by proximity of situation, and yet be, by fortune, placed under different governments; England and Scotland, for instance: each kingdom possessing an independent sovereignty, and therefore each strongly affected by all those associations of national dignity and ancient renown which are so immediately derived from the noblest and best feelings of our nature. This is the most difficult case of all. Nations thus situated are of all others the most unfortunately situated, particularly the inferior nation; and what a reasoner would even now, at the present day, propose, would, in a case like this, be accompanied with the most intolerable difficulties,—difficulties such as the worst passions and the best passions of our nature would equally conspire to render almost insurmountable.

In the first place, nations so situated will be in a state of eternal hostility with each other; not only of hostility, but of petty warfare; and they will not only have their own quarrels to adjust, but the inferior state will attach itself to some third state for the benefit of its assistance; and thus become the tool of the one, and the victim of the other.

For evils like these, the first remedy that might be attempted would be a federal union; that is, each country to retain its own legislature, but both to have the same king or executive power. This sort of federal union took place by the union of the two crowns of England and Scotland under our James I. The same was in later years understood to be the situation of England and Ireland, but admitted by our government only at a very late period. Now this alteration, this federal union, will be on the whole beneficial, but not a remedy. In the first place, the two legislatures may disagree, and it will always be, therefore, the labour of the superior or more powerful country to influence by bribes the legislature of the inferior, to render all such disagreement impossible; and this will be the source of eternal indignation to all the intelligent and independent men of the state that is thus corrupted and ruled.

Again: the inferior country (meaning by superior and inferior the more or less powerful) will appear to itself of less consequence than it was before. It will see its nobles and its aristocracy move away to the seat of government, its rents follow them; its agriculture and manufactures will seem deprived of their natural encouragement and protection; dissatisfaction, jealousy, hatred, will be deeply felt; and as the inferior country will always compare itself with its more fortunate neighbour, such unhappy effects can never cease.

In the mean time the superior country will exercise no arts of conciliation, and adopt no measures of general policy. It will draw a fence around its own trade and manufactures; admit the inferior state to no markets, no colonies, no sources of affluence which are within its own influence; neglect the laws of the inferior state, corrupt its statesmen, perhaps interfere with its religion, and in short exhibit an abuse of power in every possible mode and direction.

Of this situation of things the natural crisis is either a sort of civil war and a total rupture, or the application of a new remedy, the measure of an incorporating union.

This last would have been always the best expedient, but it would not have appeared so to those concerned. The superior state would have conceived that it was thus called upon to give away its affluence, and injure the sources of its own prosperity; the inferior, that it was to lose its sovereignty, independence, and dignity; see its nobles and aristocracy resort to the capital; and feel most of the evils which have been already mentioned, as inseparable from a federal union, without any adequate return. A century would probably elapse before time had produced its happy effects on both kingdoms; and, depriving the one of its insolence, and the other of its unreasonableness, put each into possession of all the benefits which nature, from their different soil and climate, evidently intended for both.

Of principles like these, and of situations like these, we see a full exemplification, as I have already intimated, in the relative history of Scotland and England. Nothing can be more afflicting than the evils of the first situation, that of entire *independence* of each other. Tyranny, injustice, lawless ambition in the superior state, as in the instance of our Edward I, on a large scale; on a smaller, devastations, cruelties, unceasing alarm, malignity, and revenge, as in the instances of the border laws and the border wars. Nothing can be more dreadful than both these consequences, particularly the latter, the border wars. Never sure was the art by which poetry is distinguished, the art of withdrawing the repulsive and presenting the attractive parts of a picture, displayed in a manner so striking, as in reconciling to our imagination, as the great minstrel of the north has done, the marauders and moss troopers, the inroads and outrages of these unhappy times.

These evils of eternal warfare and ferocious depredation could not but be deplored even by our fierce ancestors at the time, and through the whole history of England and Scotland there seems to have been a series of negotiations, with an intent, if possible, to terminate such calamities by an union of the two crowns.

The marriage of the two royal families was frequently proposed; sometimes the union of the two kingdoms. But after all, the union of the crowns took place not till the reign of our James I, a late period; and the union of the kingdoms not till the reign of Queen Anne. It was then only accomplished by force and fraud; so incurable are the bad passions, so impracticable are sometimes the good passions, of our nature; so perverse are the selfish interests and temporary reasonings of mankind. . . .

The crown of England, on the demise of Anne, was to be transferred from the Stuart to the Protestant line: but as Scotland was not exactly obliged to adopt the views of England, and was competent to dispose of her own crown in whatever manner she thought best, the present was the moment, in the apprehensions of Fletcher * and the Scotch patriots, for some decisive effort to be made in favour of their country; the moment when an opportunity was offered to assert their rights, and either to be independent, and have a king of their own, or to make such provisions for its commercial interests, and such alterations in its constitution, that even if the king were the same, its counsels should no longer be guided by the English ministry, and Scotland be no longer neglected, as they thought, insulted, and sacrificed on every occasion to her more powerful neighbour.

It is the struggles of men acting with views like these, and in times like these, that form the most interesting and instructive portion of this subject of the Union. . . .

It is quite necessary that you should form some notion of Fletcher of Saltoun, the complexion of his mind, the nature of his views, the description of his elegance. Men like Fletcher of Saltoun, the same in kind, though different in degree, are always existing in society; they are always to be found armed with more or less ability and influence in every inferior country; criticising the conduct of the superior country; explaining, discussing, and aggravating its oppressions; brooding over the wrongs and insults of their native land, and warmed and exasperated to madness, by a comparison of the advantages and disadvantages of the two kingdoms; the wretchedness and poverty of the country they love, and the affluence and happiness of the country they hate. Ready, therefore, to propose or adopt any system of policy or line of conduct, if it seem (however slightly) to remove from their eyes that odious dependency which they consider as the obvious cause of all the evils they deplore. Men of this character should be studied by statesmen; but statesmen and men in authority are very apt entirely to neglect and even despise them and their efforts, and very often to confound them with others, daring and bad men, who have all their faults, but who have not their virtues; others with whom they are frequently associated, and into whose company and even friendship they are but too easily hurried by their own enthusiasm, and still more often driven by the violent measures and insulting menaces of the rulers of the superior country. The nature of every thing human is so mixed and blended, the good with the evil, that we are not to be surprised if we should find, that it is to men of this description, to men of these ardent and irregular minds, that society has been indebted, imperfect as are their characters, and doubtful and dangerous and calamitous as are very often their projects, for many of its favourable changes. There is a cer-

* Andrew Fletcher of Saltoun (1655–1716), Scottish patriot.—ED.

tain impracticableness in their temperaments and superficial dogmatism
in their understandings, with a certain fearlessness as well as generosity in
their dispositions, by which they may be known; but with all their faults
they would not be perhaps ill described by the expressions of the poet,
while, giving not only a character, but, as he conceived, a most honourable character of the English nation:

> Stern o'er each bosom Reason holds her state,
> With daring aims irregularly great;
> Pride in their port, defiance in their eye,
> I see the lords of human kind pass by;
> Intent on high designs, a thoughtful band,
> By forms unfashioned, fresh from Nature's hand,
> Fierce in their native hardiness of soul,
> True to imagined right, above control.

Such was the celebrated Fletcher of Saltoun, and as his country was
the inferior country; as England had conducted herself with the usual
harshness, ignorance, and illiberality of the superior country, and as the
times in which he lived happened to be of a critical nature, his powers
were called forth, his heart was animated, and his genius was kindled. He
became the hope, the pride, and the director of a small but popular party,
and neither regarding England nor France, nor the Protestant succession, nor the succession of the House of Stuart, but in relation to the
interests of Scotland; it was to that Scotland, his poor, oppressed, unfortunate, native country, to its prosperity, happiness, and glory, that he dedicated every passion of his soul, and every faculty of his being. . . .

Fletcher and the patriots had no sooner perceived that the court of
England had an object which must at all events be accomplished—the
proper adjustment of the succession to the crown, that the king of the
two countries might be the same—than they instantly set about forming
provisions for the interests of Scotland, and they proposed what they
called an Act of Security. . . .

This intended act was of no ordinary nature. It is sufficiently descriptive of the crisis I have spoken of. It was meant, and it was indeed avowed
by Fletcher in his speeches to be meant, to effect the following consequences: "They are not limitations," said Fletcher, "upon any prince
who shall only be king of Scotland, nor do they any way tend to separate us from England, but they are calculated merely to this end, that
so long as we continue to be under the same prince with our neighbour
nation, we may be free from the influence of English counsels and ministers; that the nation may not be impoverished by an expensive attendance
at court, and the force and exercise of our government may be as far as
is possible, within ourselves, by which means, trade, manufactures, and

husbandry will flourish, and the affairs of the nation be no longer neglected, as they have been hitherto. These are the ends to which all the
limitations are directed, that English counsels may not hinder the acts
of our parliaments from receiving the royal assent; that we may not be
engaged without our consent in the quarrels they may have with other
nations; that they may not obstruct the meeting of our parliaments, nor
interrupt their sitting; that we may not stand in need of posting to
London for places and pensions, by which, whatever particular men may
get, the nation must always be a loser, nor apply for the remedies of our
grievances to a court where, for the most part, none are to be had; on the
contrary, if these conditions of government be enacted, our constitution
will be amended, and our grievances be easily redressed, by a due execution of our own laws, which to this day we have never been able to obtain." . . .

You will easily see that it is such an act as could not be agreeable to
the government or people of England; such an act as made the connexion
between the two countries frail and slight; such an act as tended to rob
the superior country of most of the advantages that were supposed to result from the connexion between them. . . .

The English ministry had therefore now to determine whether they
should advise the queen to assent to this act, and make it law, or refuse
her assent; risk a total breach with the parliament of Scotland; receive no
more supplies, and have the act returned upon her in different shapes, if
the parliament was sitting; perhaps have the country in a state of rebellion
on the very first opportunity, if the parliament was dissolved. Such was
the crisis I have been speaking of. . . .

The English minister, Godolphin, in the absence, as he thought, of
every other alternative, at last advised the queen to give the royal assent
to this Act of Security, and it was accordingly passed. Wharton, his political opponent, now triumphed. "I have now then," said he, to quote
his own expression, "I have now the treasurer's head in a bag." Godolphin
was probably much of the same opinion, and even the English nation,
unfeeling as they had been to the interests and happiness of Scotland, and
selfish and stupid as they were, and always will be, to the claims and
merits of every other nation, when their own trade to their colonies, and
their own manufactures are concerned, could at length, and for once in
this critical emergence, perceive that sacrifices must be made, and at all
events that such questions as had lately been agitated in Scotland, nearly
amounting to a revolution and a civil war, must be avoided.

There seemed no other way of attempting to avoid them but by an
union of the two kingdoms, complete and entire; and in this manner the
English nation, as well as the English ministry, were at last rendered no
longer the coy and supercilious parties with whom Scotland had before to

treat, but the ardent proposers and claimants of a measure, without which, as they represented, and truly represented, all chance for the tranquillity and prosperity of both countries was at an end.

I stop to observe, that when the Act of Security was known in England, a *retaliating act* was passed by the English parliament; i. e. a proper spirit, as it was called, was shown, and the breach in fact made wider, and the crisis more dangerous. This sort of spirit, or rather of folly, on such occasions is always shown. What was the result? Before the Scotch parliament could be brought to treat of the union *at all*, the English parliament were obliged to repeal their act.

The point of interest that next presents itself is, *how* the union was carried.

This is a part of the subject which cannot be contemplated without pain. It was carried by force and fraud. The victories of the Duke of Marlborough left England with a strong military force at her disposal; and the Duke of Hamilton proved at last a traitor to his country; so did others. This foul name must belong to him, and must always more or less belong to all men who on great public occasions pursue even the right measure *only* because they are corrupted, who act upon any motives but those of the good of their country. Men may mistake the interests of their country; this is very pardonable; they cannot engage to be wise, but they may to be honest. It is of no consequence in what manner the bribe that makes them otherwise is administered; a place to their friends, a purse thrown to themselves, or a coronet to their descendants: the business is the same; and this deflection from virtue, this sacrifice of principle, is in no way to be distinguished from the acts of dishonesty, from the mere picking and stealing, of the vulgar, but that there is no personal risk incurred by the great, and that the consequences are far more important to society.

This part of the subject is painful on another account.

The union was a measure clearly conducive to the happiness of both kingdoms. The English ministry and nation had been thoroughly frightened, and they therefore made the terms of the union as reasonable and as advantageous as they could, the better to preclude opposition.

It is, therefore, very melancholy to observe, in the first place, that a great nation like England could never adopt a proper system of policy *before*, and never behave with proper liberality and prudence, till both were extorted from her by the ungenerous motives of selfishness and fear.

It is again very mortifying to observe how little the affairs of nations are affected by the influence of any calm and deliberating wisdom. The real merits of the measure seem to have had but little effect with the generality of those concerned; a sort of opposition resounded from every quarter. The meanness, ignorance, and cowardice of it are instructive.

We shall have our religion, said the Presbytery of Scotland, destroyed by the bishops in the English house. How can our sixteen peers oppose them?

The church, said the English bishops, on the contrary, the Church of England will be swept away, as it has before been, in the time of Charles I, by this new influx of Presbyterians.

Our manufactures will move away to the poor country where labour is cheap, said the English artists.

We shall be ruined, said the Scotch, by the superior articles of the English, if they are allowed to bring them into our markets, how can we contend with their advantages of skill and capital?

What security for our country or our constitution, said the Scotch politicians, when the union has been once made? We have only forty-five members in the one house, and sixteen in the other; how can these oppose the whole English legislature? We are destroyed, and that for ever.

What will become of us, said the English, when this new northern hive is allowed to swarm and settle upon our country and upon our houses of legislature? These are invaders that are hungry, intelligent, and servile; neither post nor place will be left for any of us.

> *The prostrate south to the destroyer yields*
> *Its purple harvests and its golden fields.*

Such are always, on great occasions like these, on subjects of great national concern (unions of kingdoms, for instance, treaties of commerce, treaties of peace, abolitions of slavery), such are always the contracted, wretched arguments and pretences which men make use of when they affect to debate, and are in fact not debating, but thinking only of themselves and their own supposed interests. . . .

And now I must digress for another moment, to observe, that eloquence and wisdom are by no means the same thing. They are sometimes united, but not necessarily; perhaps never when eloquence is the *mere* gift of nature rather than the slow result of nature and art conjoined. A ready supply of glittering language and an ardent conception, i. e. a fertile imagination, and quick feelings, united to a retentive memory—these are together quite sufficient to make an orator, but by no means to make a wise man; to make a speaker or even a leader in a popular assembly, but not necessarily a statesman. Amplification, for instance, is the great business of eloquence, while the first occupation of wisdom is to reduce every thing, if possible, to its original elements. The one distinguishes not, examines not, hesitates not, reflects not; the other is cautious, scrupulous, precise, patient, and deliberative. Enthusiasm is the soul of the one, calmness the essence of the other. . . .

xxvi. SIR ROBERT WALPOLE

ONE OF THE most striking circumstances in the administration of Sir Robert Walpole was the conduct of the nation on the subject of the excise scheme. It was a very striking exemplification of the constitutional jealousy which animated our ancestors at this particular period. The minister found himself at last obliged to abandon his measure, and the opposition to the bill owed its success entirely to the sensation that was excited in the community on that general ground of constitutional jealousy. "Liberty, property, and no excise," was every where the cry, and the cry that triumphed. The sentiment, whether in this instance judiciously applied or not, did the community honour. It was a sentiment received from earlier times, and was then, even in its application on this occasion, neither so unreasonable nor so unnecessary, as by some may have been pretended. Summary convictions before commissioners or justices of the peace, without the intervention of juries, were very properly considered by Englishmen at all times as a subject of alarm and aversion. Equally so, and with equal justice, the entry of a king's officer into the dwelling of a private man by day or by night at his pleasure. That every Englishman's house is his castle has been always a favourite maxim in this happy island; "and when I speak of a castle," said once the great orator of England, Lord Chatham, he who loved to produce and cherish these honourable feelings of his country, "I speak not of a mansion, the abode of some potentate or baron, surrounded with fortifications and towers, and garrisoned with soldiers, but I speak of a tattered and wretched hovel, the dwelling of some labourer or peasant, which the wind and the rain can enter, but the king *cannot* enter."

We may ourselves be obliged to submit to the necessities of our situation, and be satisfied to obtain revenue in the best manner we can, but the notions of our ancestors should never be forgotten; still less should it be forgotten, that among many other unhappy effects that accompany a system of taxation, one, and not the least melancholy, is, the tendency that every such system has to destroy more or less, as it is more or less urged, the free spirit, the free laws, and the free men of every regular and civilized community. . . .

It will, however, be an eternal honour to the memory of Sir Robert Walpole, that when his friends wished him to persevere, to despise what they, no doubt, called popular clamour, and show that government was not to be awed, this reasonable minister thought it more becoming to give way, to pay respect to public opinion, as he forfeited no moral duty by doing so, and not to suppose, that government has no other and no better attributes under which to be presented to the community, than those of force and terror.

I would now wish to draw your attention to another subject, one connected with the character of Sir Robert Walpole, with the history of these times, and with the history of our constitution; I mean the manner, or rather the means, by which Sir Robert Walpole so long conducted the administration of government in this country. These means, it was always objected to him by his opponents, were bribery and corruption, the power of the purse: such is the phrase continually occurring in the writings of Bolingbroke. This representation is considered by Burke as unjust: he considers Sir Robert as having ruled by party and family connexions. On the whole, the student may fairly suppose this celebrated minister to have ruled by the powers of his own sound and clear understanding, the effect of his amiable and social qualities; and in conjunction with these, by what is called the influence of government, no longer appearing, as formerly, in the palpable and offensive forms of the prerogative, but in the natural and peaceful agency of all the posts and employments under the disposal of the crown, in a highly prosperous and civilized state of society.

This influence, it is to be observed, is not at all inconsistent with the agency of the party and family connexions mentioned by Mr. Burke. Sir Robert Walpole availed himself of both; so have other ministers. The one is, indeed, to a certain extent, connected with the other; for it is by this influence of posts and places, that a minister can be assisted in attaching to himself party and family connexions, and they their dependants. . . .

Lord Bolingbroke is one of the classics of our literature: but he was also one of the great political characters of this period, the opponent and inveterate enemy of Walpole; and his personal qualities and his writings (his political writings, which are all I am now concerned with), may be said to be in reality subjects of history.

His *Dissertation on Parties,* and (out of deference to the opinions of others who admire it) I must also mention his *Patriot King,* will, I conceive, be quite sufficient for your perusal.

From Lord Bolingbroke's *Dissertation on Parties,* I would next recommend you to turn to the works of Mr. Burke; to his "Thoughts on the Present Discontents," particularly the latter part. These compositions of Lord Bolingbroke and Mr. Burke seem to me connected together; for instance, we have said that Sir Robert governed this country by his personal qualities, and by party and family connexions, in conjunction with the influence of the crown. To this system of government Lord Bolingbroke objects. But it is explained and commented upon, and defended by Mr. Burke.

Again: Lord Bolingbroke conceives the proper effect of the Revolution to be defeated by the powers of corruption which every minister has since enjoyed, and which he derives from the crown.

Mr. Burke thinks, with Lord Bolingbroke, that this influence of the crown is, and may be too great, but he views the subject in a new and different light, and in fact conceives that this influence of the crown can now be only opposed in practice by those very party connexions which it is the object of Lord Bolingbroke's *Dissertation* to discountenance and destroy. This is a very curious question, and one which can never be without its interest while our free and mixed constitution survives.

There is an air of freedom and purity of principle about such sentiments as are uttered by Lord Bolingbroke (not indeed the most exemplary of characters himself), well fitted to captivate the minds of men of virtue and public spirit. Corruption is the great topic of his lamentations and invectives; his great hope is a House of Commons that in some way or other shall be elevated above all sinister views; the members of which, unlike the members of any other body that ever appeared in society, are to be influenced by no consideration but the mere merits of the question before them. Views of this kind are always very animating and attractive to those who, like Lord Bolingbroke, can write or speak beautiful sentences, or think they can, and to many a youthful patriot, whose heart is sufficiently good, and understanding sufficiently somnolent, to dream over the visions of superficial or designing men. Statesmen of any sense or experience look not for such prodigies; they know, as Mr. Burke has observed, what stuff all supernatural virtue is made of; and when the corruption of parliament is represented as the beginning, middle, and end of all our grievances and calamities, they only see in a talker of this kind an artist who knows not the nature of his materials, or a future courtier at present in disguise; they know that men are in public, as in private life, some good, some bad, and that to depend on the *unmixed personal* virtue of men in the formation of a government, as a principle and a foundation on which to rest the public weal, is puerile and ridiculous in the extreme; that in a constitution, as in a machine, the question always is, does it work well? and finally, that there is no hope that it should do so, unless the great leading interests, and selfish passions, and *ordinary* virtues of our nature are so mingled, and opposed, and directed, as in the result to operate pretty steadily to the advancement and security of the public prosperity; that unless this is done, nothing is done, and that this is done in a most remarkable manner, notwith-

standing all its anomalies, in the British constitution. Something is indeed
said when useless places in the disposal of the crown are pointed out, and
it is proposed to abolish them; remove temptations from men, and you will
contribute to make them more victorious, but nothing can be a more
miserable waste of public talents in the speaker or writer, or of public virtue in the patient hearer or reader, than those vague and flowing harangues
on the subject of corruption. There are seasons, indeed, when they may
fall innocent on the ear, but there *are other* seasons when writings or
speeches of this kind are clearly of the nature of sedition, and become
perfect treason to the practical liberties and prosperity of the realm;
they may be at one time the mere mewlings and wailing of the cradle
(such they appear to me), they may be at another the thunders and light-
nings that issue from the tribune. . . .

The merit of every man, and of every body of men, must be estimated
with a reference to the times in which they lived. Since the administration of Sir Robert, a new system of political economy has been regularly presented, and successfully presented, by Adam Smith, to the consideration of the rulers of mankind; and we have a right to blame those
ministers of our own age, who seem ignorant of its principles, though
not on this account the ministers of former times.

The good sense of Sir Robert on particular occasions, enabled him to
discover the science of human prosperity; but no enlarged views on the
East India question, for instance, on the question of Ireland, or of any
other of this nature, appear to have made a part of his ordinary habits of
reflection.

"He was not," says Burke in his masterly character of him, "a genius
of the first class, but he was an intelligent, a prudent, and a safe minister."

This praise, and this abatement of it, we shall find just, even when
surveying him as a minister sincerely interested in the commercial advancement of his country. This intelligence, this prudence, still enabled
him, without the assistance of the more divine influence of genius, to
see and to provide for the interests of a commercial nation; without an-
ticipating the system of Adam Smith, he could, by the operation of his
own excellent understanding, perceive that he should assist the prosperity
of his country effectually by clearing away, as much as possible, the duties
and impositions by which he found our commerce incumbered and impoverished. It is said that he found our book of rates the worst, and left
it the best in Europe—a most important eulogium. We have here merit,
and of a most solid nature; a man in a high station going through minute
details and tedious, disgusting examinations, and exerting his patience,
his industry, and his talents in a sort of silent and obscure drudgery,

where, though they were exerted highly to the benefit of the community, they could not be exerted with that eclat to which they most assuredly were entitled.

But his panegyric must not stop here. He not only did every thing in his power, and according to the lights which he then possessed, for the emancipation of our commerce from vexatious interruptions and impolitic charges, but above all, he was the anxious friend, not only of order and mild government at home, but of peace abroad. This is his commercial panegyric, the highest and the best that any minister can aspire to. Men will better their condition, i. e. the prosperity of their country will advance, without the assistance of the state, if their exertions are only not interrupted, and their labours not destroyed, by the interference of laws at home, and the calamities of war abroad. Political economists require no more from princes, or ministers, or cabinets, or houses of assembly, than *that* praise, which they so seldom deserve, the praise of being very cautious how they suffer themselves to be involved in war, of being very cautious how they destroy, in a few years or months, what no efforts of theirs will repair in ages. . . .

In the course of these discussions Sir Robert had not done the Spanish cause justice: he had not told his own country the whole truth. (This I have already observed.) His excuse might be, and it may be admitted, that this was not the way to procure peace; that there was no chance for peace but his own continuance in power. Yet his patience, his good temper, his reasonableness, his exertions, great and meritorious as they were, in the cabinet and in the senate, were all unavailing. He found them to be so. In defiance of every effort he could make, his eloquence, his influence, his management, his sacrifices of every kind, the event turned out to be, that the two nations were hurried into a war, and that he had no comfort left but that of having strenuously laboured to prevent so fatal a termination of their differences.*

There is even more than this to be considered. It appears that the king was eager for the war; that Sir Robert was counteracted by the cabinet, blamed by many of his personal friends, reviled by the nation. The question, therefore, which is asked by Coxe should be asked by every reader, —Why did he not resign? Why did he not endeavour to make some impression upon his countrymen by throwing up his emoluments and his honours? This argument, at least, they could not but have felt. Why was not his own honest fame as a statesman, and his character with posterity, as dear to him as they ought to have been? Why did he not refuse his

---

* In 1739 Walpole was forced to abandon his peace policy, and embark on a war with Spain. George II wanted the war, and though Walpole did not want it, he shilly-shallied to his downfall.—ED.

sanction to a system of conduct which he thought precipitate, violent, and unreasonable?

It cannot be necessary, it cannot be proper, that a minister should have recourse to so strong a measure as the resignation of his office on light grounds and at every turn. Others are to have their opinions as well as himself; mutual concessions and sacrifices may be made by honourable men faithfully co-operating in the administration of a government. But when points of principle in themselves sacred, when questions of importance, like the alternatives of peace and war are at issue, then indeed it is not possible for a man of intelligence or spirit to proceed longer in his doubtful path amid the blended confines of right and wrong; he must no longer assent to what he does not approve. He can discharge no more necessary duty to his country than to avow his opinion and act upon it. It may be that his opinion is right, and a salutary effect may be produced. But on every supposition, one good will at least be attained—he will give an example of public virtue.

The path of honour is always the path of wisdom; and they who survey the situation of Sir Robert from the moment that he suffered himself to be persuaded by the king to continue in office (for he had the merit of proffering his resignation), will see no reason to call in question this great and universal maxim of human conduct. Sir Robert retained his place but two years, his place rather than his power, without comfort to himself or advantage to his reputation. Life itself he retained but a few years longer; what, then, were his gains in return for the mortifications he endured?

It is difficult, indeed, for men properly to engage in the affairs of mankind without being deeply interested in them. It is still more difficult to be thus interested, and at the same time to view them from that commanding height, and with those sentiments of philosophic criticism with which they will come at length to be surveyed by posterity. Yet such is the magnanimity, such the comprehensiveness of judgment which are, and which ought to be, expected from the rulers of mankind, and it is therefore with no pleasure that we observe the character of Sir Robert so strongly marked by the great fault of all statesmen—an inordinate love of power; that we observe him clinging to office, till he was torn and driven from it, and even in his fall, casting on it that longing, lingering look which was unbecoming him as a man of spirit, and unworthy of him as a man of virtue.

XXVIII. GEORGE II, REBELLION OF 1745

PULTENEY * . . . SEEMS to have made, when in opposition, a very improper declaration that he would never take office. A public man may certainly propose himself as a sort of inquisitor of all other public men; but on one supposition, that he takes no favours from any administration; this is a necessary proviso. He then may occupy a very elevated situation, and deserve and obtain the applauses of his country, for this is a sort of merit that is very great, and is intelligible. But men of talents, as well as good sense and honesty, may even more materially contribute to the service of their country, by going into office, and advancing its interests, foreign and domestic, civil and religious, by becoming such ministers as the former (the men of honesty and good sense), may safely patronise. This is a merit of a still higher nature, and for a virtuous and intelligent statesman to exclude it from his view is in fact to abandon the government of a country to every presumptuous, self-interested man that will undertake it. Pulteney, however, seems to have attempted to adhere (when power was within his reach) to the ill-judged declarations which he had made when in opposition; and when it was his business to form an administration, he seems to have entertained the unreasonable expectation, that he could still keep his consequence without being seen in any one responsible situation or post; not in opposition; not in office; not even as a neutral critic; but merely as a commoner made into a peer; placed calmly to survey the proceedings of the administration he had constructed, without any means of influencing their movements; without any duty to discharge to the public; i. e. in other words, without any right to receive their praises.

What was the result? He had scarcely finished his negotiations with the court when he found too late that he had attempted impossibilities. He was almost insulted with his insignificance, even by the Duke of Newcastle. He was so mortified as to have meditated a renewal of his opposition. This indeed would have crowned his mistakes; and he is said, in the agonies of his shame and disgust, to have trampled the patent of his peerage under his feet.

The most edifying part of these transactions is the view which Pulteney had himself formed of his plans and situation. "If," says he, "avarice, ambition, or the desire of power had influenced me, why did I not take (and no one can deny that I might have had) the greatest post in the kingdom?

* William Pulteney (1684–1764), English statesman, created Earl of Bath in 1742.—ED.

But I contented myself with the honest pride of having subdued the great author of corruption; retired with a peerage which I had at three different periods of my life refused; and left the government to be conducted by those who had more inclination than I had to be concerned in it. I should have been happy if I could have united an administration capable of carrying on the government with ability, economy and honour."

Public men are not to indulge themselves in dreams like these: they are not to suppose that they subdue a bad minister, or a set of bad men, unless they do their best to form a better administration; unless they hazard their own characters, and embark their own labours in a new system: bad ministers and bad measures are not so readily cleared away and disposed of. Pulteney knew very well, no one could know better, the discordant materials of which the opposition had been composed; and it was his business, as the great leader and soul of the whole, by disinterestedness, openness, and an adherence to the great constitutional points for which he had contended, to have united as many of them as possible, and to have made no bargain with the court that could leave the reasonable part of the public any cause of complaint. . . .

When Charles * first reached the Highlands, in a small ship, with no other means than a few muskets and about four thousand pounds in money, and proposed to some of the chiefs to march to England and dethrone George II, heroic as were their natural sentiments, they resolutely declined all share in so wild an undertaking. Charles talked to two of them who had come on board his vessel; he persuaded, argued, and explained; and as he walked backwards and forwards on the deck, he was overheard by a Highlander, who had come on board with his leader, and who had no sooner gathered from the discourse that the stranger was the Prince of Wales, and that the chief and his brother refused to take arms, than his colour went and came, his eyes sparkled, he shifted his place, he grasped his sword. "And will not *you* assist me?" said Charles, who had observed him. "I will, I will," said Ronald; "though no other man in the Highlands should draw a sword, I am ready to die for you." "I only wish that all the Highlanders were like you," said Charles. Without further deliberation the chief and the brother, the two Macdonalds, declared that they also would join and use their utmost endeavours to engage their countrymen to come forward in his cause.

Now such was the first extraordinary step in this extraordinary enterprise. Another remained. Lochiel, then the head of the powerful clan of the Camerons, was yet to be gained over. He was coming to Charles to give his reasons for not joining him—reasons, as he had told his brother,

* Charles Edward Stuart (1720–88), known as the "Young Pretender."—ED.

which admitted of no reply. "But that is of no consequence," said his wiser brother. He was no doubt very right; they certainly admitted of no reply, and had received none when urged to the prince. But as the conference was closing, Charles, in his despair, declared that he would erect the royal standard even with the few friends he had; proclaim to the people of Britain that Charles Stuart was come over to claim the crown of his ancestors—to win it, or perish in the attempt. "You, Lochiel," said he, "who my father has often told me was our firmest friend—you, Lochiel, may stay at home, and learn from the newspapers the fate of your prince." "No," said Lochiel, "I will share the fate of my prince, and so shall every man over whom nature or fortune has given me any power."

It is a point agreed amongst the Highlanders, that if Lochiel had persisted in his refusal to take up arms, the other chiefs would not have joined the standard of Charles; and the spark of rebellion must have instantly expired.

Such were the chances and turns of elevated sentiment on which this enterprise depended; such were the grounds on which these bands of brothers were to descend from their mountains, at every step they took incur the penalties of treason and death, lift up their eyes and gaze unappalled on the colossal power of England!—never pause for a moment to contrast the simple target and claymore of Scotland with her mighty lance and ægis—the artillery at her feet, and her fleets in the distance; but at all events precipitate themselves forward, and ask from their chief no question but—"Was it his will?" and from their prince no signal but— "Did he lead?"

It may be doubted whether the history of the world ever exhibited a stronger instance of the triumph of heroic sentiment over the calmer suggestions of reason. But when our first impression of surprise and indeed of admiration is passed away, we must look upon this as a very striking instance to prove the indispensable necessity of the general diffusion of political knowledge among all ranks and descriptions of men. A mistake was now made merely from the want of political knowledge; and on this account, and on no other, brave men were to perish in the field, and the great cause of civil and religious liberty was to be endangered to the utmost, the cause of the Revolution of 1688, the cause of England and of mankind, and endangered by the most noble and generous of men. I say, endangered to the utmost; for had the northern parts of England been as magnanimous in sentiment as they, too, were mistaken in opinion: had they been, like the Highlanders, not only ignorant and misled in their political notions, but generous and fearless in their characters, it is scarcely too much to affirm that the rebellion of 1745 would have been successful, the Brunswick family driven from our land, and freedom would have lost her boast (a boast so cheering to a philosophic mind), that she, too, had placed a monarch on a throne, and, in England at least, was had in honour in palaces and courts.

The sentiment on which the Stuart family had to depend, from the first, was merely an over-statement of an acknowledged principle in political science, the principle of hereditary right. It was this sentiment, and this alone, that now armed the clans of Scotland in their cause, and so prejudiced Wales and the northern counties of England in their favour.

I will not insult, as some seem ready to do, the memory of these heroes of the Highlands (for such they were) by supposing that either plunder or power was their object; far higher and more noble were the feelings of their hearts. It was loyalty to the chief in the follower; it was loyalty to the prince in the chief; it was in *all* the indefeasible nature, as they supposed, of hereditary right, that made the cause of Charles Stuart, in their opinion, the good cause and the true, whatever might be its issue, however discountenanced and abandoned by the time-serving sycophants of the Lowlands and of the south.

The king shall have his own again,

was the language of the popular ballads of the time. . . .

It is impossible not to respect men who could thus devote themselves, from principle, to an unprotected adventurer like Charles. It may be useful for us to meditate upon these examples of elevated sentiment, that we may catch a portion for our own hearts of the divine flame which we are admiring. But we must be admonished, at the same time, by examples like these, that heroism in the sentiment, and generosity in the feeling, are not *alone* sufficient; that these are the lights, which "though lights from heaven, *may* lead astray"; that principles, however elevated, must be properly estimated, their bounds ascertained, their value compared with that of other principles, and, in a word, that sentiment alone must not actuate the man, till it has *first* been shown its course and taught its limits by the superintending power of the understanding. . . .

The Highland clans, you will observe, were not all disaffected: far from it. There were Whigs as well as Jacobite clans. The government, therefore, of George I issued out its orders to disarm the Highlanders. This is always a very favourite measure of lazy and arbitrary, and I may add, ignorant legislators. They seize the arms, and leave the hearts of a people to be seized by others. But what was the result? The common one—that the well affected gave up their arms at the time appointed, and the rest concealed them, or took some subsequent opportunity of providing themselves afresh. . . .

Lord Chatham, who, with all his faults, had that elevation in the character of his mind without which no minister can ever be great,

made it his boast (and it was an honest boast) that he had been the first
to take advantage of the noble qualities of the Scottish nation. "I was the
first minister," said he, "who looked for merit, and found it in the mountains of the north. I called it forth, and drew into your service a hardy
and intrepid race of men; men who, when left by your jealousy, became
a prey to the artifices of your enemies, and had gone nigh to overturn
the state in the war before the last." His example stands alone. Nothing
is ever done by cabinets in the way of conciliation or timely and prospective wisdom; they live upon expedients, and provide only for the day that
is going over them. . . .

xxx. GEORGE III

IT IS ALWAYS to be remembered that it is the spirit with which a constitution is in practice administered, that is the great point of consequence, far more than the letter of the law. It was therefore very properly
specified by George II, in his speech at the breaking out of the Rebellion in 1745, that the "*maxims* of the constitution should ever be the
rule of his conduct." That sort of discretionary power, which must at
every turn be lodged somewhere or other, becomes the safeguard or
the enemy of the civil freedom of the community, just as it is, or is
not, exercised in a constitutional manner, in favour of the subject. What
then is to be the consequence, if every thing is to be administered in
that spirit which would be approved of by a monarch and his courtiers,
such as monarchs and courtiers, without the slightest disrespect to
them, may generally be expected, on the common principles of our
common nature, to be found, and gifted with whatever measure you
please of natural good sense and benevolence; what is to be the consequence (as every topic that respects either the polity or the affairs of
a nation admits at least of a debate) if in every question the king and
his friends are to give the tone, and if they who differ from the court
side of the question are to be esteemed no longer the friends of their
king, and are to be set apart from their fellow subjects as those who are
the last to be honoured with the royal favour? i. e. according to the new
system of government the last who are to appear in the cabinet, or the
great offices of state, or are to become king's counsel, or post captains,
or officers of excise or customs, or rise in the army, or receive ecclesiastical patronage, or have chancellor's livings, or be elevated to the bench;
to be the last themselves who are to be so promoted; and to find the
same system of silent discountenance extended to their relations and dependents, their friends and connexions. In the meantime, no complaint

can be made, and there is no one to accuse. The king has a right to appoint his own ministers and his own officers through every department of the state; one man can discharge an office as well as another; reasons of preference may exist, but of these the constitution has left the king the sole judge. We may say that he is ill advised; that the men preferred are not the best; that they have won their situations not so much by their known merits as by their known servility: all this we may say, and say truly, and the only answer returned will be, that we want the office for ourselves, and perhaps that we are factious and disloyal.

In the meantime, while the country becomes more and more civilized, it becomes more and more difficult for every man to provide for a family without sinking his rank in society. Professions are more and more preferred for the younger branches. The candidates for patronage continually increase; and if no patronage is to descend but through the medium of the king's friends; if none is to be gained but by those who profess and support high maxims of government on every occasion, what is to be the result?

Perhaps a word may not be uttered all this time by the court, or its friends, or its partisans, apparently unfavourable to the constitution of the country; certainly not a word contradictory to the letter of its laws, or the form of its institutions. Government must be supported; who can doubt it? The crown must have its weight in the system; assuredly—if not by prerogative, as in former times, by influence; by posts, places, and even sinecures. The friends of a limited monarchy are not very well prepared to deny this, and speak rather of the measure of these things than of the things themselves; and thus it happens, that well meaning, independent, and even sensible men either adopt, or do not oppose the new system, and do not perceive that the vital principle by which the constitution of these kingdoms, though always in its letter a strong arbitrary monarchy, was heretofore in its practice rendered a benign limited monarchy, and to all essential purposes a free government; that this vital principle is in truth endangered to the utmost; that it must gradually decline, as the new system grows up in strength and maturity, and the event ultimately be the appearance in our own government of that torpor and general servility which mark a government more or less arbitrary like the old government of France under Louis XIV. All this, or some recoil of a furious nature directly the reverse, from the supposed peril and despair of the case.

Extremes can be right on no side. The king is not to be a cipher in the state; he is to select his ministers and servants from the public men which the country supplies; but it is *the proper exercise of this discretionary power* that is the question before us; and this should become the subject of your reflections as you read the history of this country from the Revolution downwards; for it is this that is the hinge (if I may be allowed the expression) on which the constitution of the country really turns; this proper exercise of the discretionary power lodged by the constitution in the great executive magistrate to choose his ministers and servants; and as it would be one extreme to leave him no exercise of his judgment, or no powers of choice, on the one hand: so is it, on the other hand, *another* extreme to lay down, and have it avowed as a system, that the government shall always be carried on by those whom he or the court think proper to denominate his friends.

Times and circumstances, the nature and characters of public men, must teach their own lessons; a subject of this singular, delicate, and impalpable nature cannot be marked out by the line and the rule; but we may say, and cannot say it too often, that if the only road to honours and power is the mere personal favour of the sovereign, then, that those men alone will be found from time to time possessed of honours and power who are favourable to the maxims of prerogative—to the principles of harsh government; who are very indulgent critics of the measures of ministers; who are very careless auditors of the public expense; who are not made very uneasy by sinecures, jobs, and pensions; who are not very ready to try or punish public defaulters, unless they be indeed the writers of libels; who are, in a word, always unwilling to assist, or rather who are always willing to impede in its operations the democratic part of our mixed constitution. Whether it be by such men and such principles that the constitution of these kingdoms has been saved (not to speak of our Plantagenets, our Tudors, and our Charleses), but saved from James II, from Lord Bolingbroke, from the Jacobites of 1715 and 1745, and above all, from that silent tendency to deterioration which belongs to every thing valuable among mankind; whether it is to such men and such principles that we are to ascribe the freedom of this country at this moment, must be left to the consideration of those who can push their inquiries beyond the forms of things into their principles and essence; and who will soon perceive that however necessary to every civil polity must be its ranks and establishments, its officers and magistrates, and above all, its great magistrate the king as supreme; that all this is but an inferior and even (if I may use such an expression) but a vulgar part of the whole, for it is what has been accomplished by France and Austria, and every other monarchy in Europe; and that the real and rare, and above all price inestimable peculiarity of our constitution, is that democratic principle which can pervade and influence the whole, and yet not produce (its more natural fruits) confusion, disorder, and folly, but act in perfect consistence with the peace and best interests of the state; and which, whenever it becomes extinct, and can no longer thus influence and pervade the whole (from whatever cause the extinction may take place), a new system that has betrayed the constitution, the necessities of the times which have destroyed its maxims, either or both; whatever be the cause or the system that, in a word, leaves men of talents and property without popular motives of action, will assuredly, sooner or later, leave this great kingdom no longer to be distinguished from others that do, or have existed, on the continent or elsewhere; its lower orders without spirit, its middle ranks without opinions, its public assemblies without weight, and its kings without a people.

Before the Revolution, the favourites of our monarchs were often driven away from the sovereign, fined, imprisoned, or executed; and the democratic part of our constitution, on these occasions, rushed forth (if I may be allowed the expression) to teach the monarchical part its proper duties in its own rude and unceremonious manner. But these were, in fact, more or less, revolutions in the government. It is not thus that we can wish, in our own times, the personal character of our sovereign to be humbled, or the faults and failings, that may be more or less inseparable from any hereditary wearer of a crown, to be brought before the tribunal, and visited by the direct censure of the community. To set in array democracy against monarchy, and merely to leave the one to correct the mistakes and punish the offences of the other, is no very refined or rational expedient for the management of a state. It is every thing the reverse. It may have been resorted to by men who were hurried on by the torrent of circumstances, like our ancestors in the time of Charles I, or the patriots of Greece and Rome, who conceived they had no other resource against tyranny and oppression; but the politicians of a highly civilized and intelligent country will always consider any open collision in the state as the greatest of all calamities, unless it be the absence of civil freedom itself; and they will therefore look round very carefully to find, if possible, some expedient for the proper management of a community under a mixed monarchical system of government, the representative assembly having the power of taxation, and the king the power of dissolving them.

Now to those who are meditating the subject of a good constitution of government in this elementary manner, an aristocracy would first present itself; and at length an aristocracy with popular feelings would appear, as I conceive, the great desideratum. From such an aristocracy men might be chosen who might be ministers, not favourites; who could sympathize with the democratic part of the constitution, yet be naturally attached to the office and prerogative of the sovereign, might be themselves objects of love and respect to the one, and of kindness and esteem to the other; of confidence to both.

But how is such an aristocracy—an aristocracy with popular feelings, to be found? It could not well be generated by mere institution; none such has ever appeared in the world. A monarch may be easily created; the people we have already; but where is to be found such a cement of the two, as an aristocracy with popular feelings? Set an order of men apart, give them privileges and titles of honour, and you raise up a nobility: but it will only be to leave them to unite with the sovereign at all times against the public, to render them insolent and unfeeling to their inferiors. The patricians of Rome, the nobles of Venice, even the feudal nobility of Germany and France, none of these are the exact description of men we wish for.

Now I must confess it appears to me, that we were furnished very tolerably with what we could desire, when we had the aristocracy of England such as it existed during the reigns of George I and George II. Consider it in all its functions, relations, opinions, feelings; a nobility who were graced with privileges and honours; armed with property and power; who had placed the reigning family on the throne, but who had done this on popular principles; who were thus bound to the king, but were also pledged to the people; who were connected with the sovereign by the enjoyment and expectation of titles and offices, and yet united to the people, first, by a common resistance to an arbitrary power, then by common laws, common maxims and opinions, religious and political, mutual respect, common interests of property and security; and were even allied and interwoven into the mass of their fellow-citizens by mingling through the medium of their dearest relations, in the democratic branch of the legislature. A more favourable situation of things could not well be supposed by the most sanguine speculator on the social union of mankind. The misfortune would undoubtedly be that even this aristocracy might not be sufficiently jealous of the prerogative of the crown, not sufficiently alive to the claims and rights of the subject. But on the whole, a considerable approach would be made to secure, in a peaceful and steady manner, the main interests of all the constituent parts of the community.

Here we must come to a pause. It is now that the new system of Lord Bute presents itself. It was the very end and aim of this new system to destroy this very aristocracy, at least that part of this aristocracy with which we are at present concerned; that part more particularly distinguished for its more popular principles, receiving confidence alike from the favour of the sovereign, and the approbation and gratitude of the people. Far from turning it to the great purposes to which it might have been applied, far from bringing it forward to the discharge of all the high and healing offices of which it was capable, it was the immediate effect of the new system to counteract all such purposes, to disregard all such offices, to entertain far other views of the constitution of England, or of the benefits to be derived from any constitution of government; to provide in a manner totally different, for the dignity and happiness of the sovereign, for the respectability of the aristocracy, and for the welfare of the people.

According to the new system, the king was to be as independent of his aristocracy, and not as intermingled as possible in all their interests and sympathies; to be rescued from the necessity of sharing his consequence with any order, or any individuals of that order. He was to rule by men who looked only to the throne, not by the Whig families who had some respect for themselves, as well as reverence for the monarch; and who looked also to the people. He was to choose his ministers, and that entirely as his own partialities directed him; that is, "favourites," under the title of friends, were to be preferred as fit objects of his confidence, to men who had characters and opinions of their own, and who therefore could operate with a salutary influence on his. But this was not all. Great efforts were to be made to accomplish this destruction of the political influence and popular feelings of the Whig families; a miserable system of intrigue was to be entered upon. The least honourable men of each knot and division of the aristocracy were to be brought over to the court party, the better to destroy all confidence and union among those who remained; to divide, and therefore rule; to degrade, and therefore render insignificant, was the very scheme and essence of the plan, involved in the very supposition of it. And these new converts, these deserters and stragglers from their family and party attachments, from the notions of their ancestors, from the popular sympathies by which they had hitherto been so honourably distinguished, these were the men who were to be associated as friends and familiars to the bosom of their sovereign. The people in the meantime were to lose their former respect for public men, whom they were now to see mutually betraying and accusing each other; and even for the sovereign himself, whom they were *also* to see, as far as they could judge, practising upon the mean and selfish passions of his aristocracy.

I confess that it appears to me, a more unhappy expedient than the new system could not well have been devised, for procuring the extinction of every thing rare and precious in the constitution of our government, for destroying the British patriotism of the monarch, the British spirit of the nobility, the British loyalty of the people. Prerogative was to remain, and privilege was to remain, and obedience was to remain; but all these necessary elements of government were to lose their former sympathies, limits, and nature: they were no longer to be what they were made by the Revolution of 1688.

The maxims of a court are not the security of a court; servility is not loyalty; and attachment to civil freedom not republicanism. It may answer well to the designing on each side, to confound principles and characters in themselves distinct. But when proper allowance has been made, and pardon extended to the unavoidable faults and mistakes of public men and private men of every description, of parties and of their leaders, it will always be competent for any one who really understands the mixed and free constitution of this country, if he pleases, to distinguish from each other those who think too exclusively of the king, those who think too exclusively of the people; and those who are not only virtuous, but wise enough to think of the best interests of both. I condescend not to speak of those, who think only of themselves, who have no political principle at all, who mean only to get place or preferment in their profession.

Here I had been accustomed to end the lecture, after I had referred my hearers to Burke's *Thoughts on the [Cause of] Present Discontents*, to other pamphlets of the time, and to the general principles of Lord Bolingbroke's writings, as contrasted with those of Mr. Burke; but in the year 1823, I had been struck with certain appearances that I had observed in and out of parliament, and I from that time always ended the lecture, by subjoining what I shall now read, written, you will remember, in the year 1823.

This new system had a tendency to increase servility in the nation in the way I have suggested; but it did not follow, though it should succeed, as it did succeed in a most unfortunate manner, still it did not follow, that it should extinguish, in a country like this, the spirit of freedom; the spirit that naturally belongs to the commercial and manufacturing classes, as they rise into affluence and importance. But in this case it will have, undoubtedly, an effect in giving to this spirit, as exhibited in these classes, a more republican tone and feeling. The new system has gone far to destroy the Whig families and their influence. It is possible also that the great events of modern times, that mistakes of the Whigs themselves, that the fickle nature of human opinions, that all, or any of these, may have contributed to the same effect; but any change of this kind will be, to all who love the constitution of their country, and who, I must presume to add, have examined and understand it, a circumstance deeply to be lamented. For a fearful void, an arena that may very easily be covered with tumult and bloodshed, is immediately disclosed when the monarch is set on one side, and the people on the other, and an aristocracy with popular feelings is withdrawn from between them. It can never have been the interest of the people, still less of the crown, to have any alteration like this in our political system. What may not be the fortunes of our constitution, and the experiments to which it may be exposed, if the ancient friends of liberty, the friends of liberty upon the ancient and tried model, are no longer to be treated with confidence and respect?

When Mr. Burke had to defend his country, as he conceived, from the democratic principles of France, it was to the Whigs and their principles, and the Revolution of 1688, that he appealed. Mr. Sheridan, in like manner, with directly opposite opinions, did the same; and it was for the people of England to decide between them. Nothing could be more valuable to a community than to have, at any crisis like this, a common test and standard to which they could refer. Nothing can be so important to a nation already possessed of prosperity and freedom to so remarkable a degree; nothing so important, as a ready means like this, of protecting themselves from the heats and delusions of particular seasons, as a ready means, at all times, of distinguishing from each other the man of speculation and the man of sense.

In a word, they who have proposed and patronised the new system have been preparing the people of England, more or less, for that species of monarchy which has been represented by Hume as the euthanasia, the natural and tranquil death, of the British constitution; or they have been preparing us, on the other hand, for the influence of those who are desirous to refer every thing to the people, to their public meetings, their resolutions and addresses, their will, in short, and their wisdom, when enlightened by the press, to be produced on every occasion, and to be considered as a specific for every political disease that can approach us. But such an order of things is republicanism, under whatever name it may be disguised.

Such a government may be better for America: by some it may be thought better for England; but it is not the constitution of England, and on this head, at least, let no mistakes be made.

xxxi. AMERICAN WAR

I hasten to the subject which I always proposed to myself as the proper termination of these lectures—the American War.

Prior to the French Revolution, this subject could not have been well presented to you; for the passions that it had excited could scarcely have been said to have properly subsided. But at the very name and sound of the French Revolution, every other revolution and event loses its first, and even proper interest; and we now discuss the measures and administration of Lord North, or the conduct of the American congress, the claim of the right of taxation on the one part, and the resistance to that claim on the other, *almost* with the same impartiality which would be felt by the reasoners of after ages. Such sentiments therefore as occur to me, and as occur to others, I shall lay before you in the most unreserved manner; considering the whole as now become entirely a portion of history, which I may fairly attempt to convert, as I would any other, to the proper purposes of your instruction.

The American War must immediately appear to you a subject of historical curiosity. By the event of that war, an independent empire has arisen, boundless in extent, and removed from the reach of the arms— secure at least from the invasions of Europe; beginning its career with such advantages as our communities in the old world never possessed; beginning almost from the point, to which they have but arrived in the progress of nearly two thousand years. It is even possible that what England once was may have to be traced out hereafter by the philosophers of distant ages, from the language, the customs, the manners, the political feelings of men inhabiting the banks of the Mississippi, or enjoying the benefits of society amid what may be now a wilderness, inaccessible to the footsteps of every human being.

Such is the American War as a subject of historical curiosity to the readers of whatever clime or nation. But to ourselves it is even more attractive and important: one half of our empire has been violently rent from the other. We no longer in case of a war shut out that long line of harbours from the ships and fleets of our enemies; we no longer let loose the privateers of America upon their trade; we no longer man our fleets with her strong and skilful seamen: all these advantages are no longer exclusively our own; they may even be turned against us. Great Britain seems no longer to overshadow the globe, the west as well as the east, with the image of her greatness. Assuredly at the peace of 1763, the power and empire of this country seemed to the nations, and might have appeared even to the philosophers of Europe, above all ancient, and above all modern fame. To what extent that power and empire might have been carried by the interchange of the natural productions of America, with the manufactures of Britain, by the proper application and sympathy of youthful and matured strength, it is indeed difficult for us to determine; but the subject of the possible greatness of Great Britain did not a little disquiet, as it appears, the speculations of our enemies, whether feeling for their posterity, or attentive to their own advantages.

How then was it, or why that this promising appearance of things was, on a sudden, to cease? How was it that this great empire was to be torn asunder? that France, and other unfriendly powers on the continent, had no longer to dread the united strength of England and America; but could even please themselves, like Tacitus of old while in terror of the enemies of Rome, with the spectacle of a civil war, and employ themselves in turning the force of the one to the destruction of the other?

You may be told, indeed, in a word, that Great Britain wished to tax America, and that America successfully resisted. But how, may you reasonably think, could such things be? Could not a dispute about revenue have been composed without an open rupture and a separation; without the shedding of blood; without the horrors and calamities of a civil war? And again, if arms were to be resorted to, how could it happen that Great Britain could fail in the contest, that the same power which had just humbled the House of Bourbon should not be a match for her own colonies? should not be able, after overpowering the fleets and armies of the first nations of Europe, immediately to discomfit the farmers and merchants of America? How are such events to be explained? What demon of folly got possession of our councils? What malignant star shed its influence on our arms? Where were our statesmen, and where were our generals? . . .

North America, as you know, was peopled and civilized chiefly by adventurers from this country; that is, in a word, England was the parent, and America the dependent state. I have already made observations on the connexions of different states with each other; I did so in my lecture on the Union with Scotland. These observations it would be very convenient to me, if I could on this occasion recall to your recollection.

The sum and substance, however, of them was, that, in such a case as this before us, in the case of a mother country and colonies, an ultimate separation of the *two* was the result to which the progress of the prosperity of the dependent state naturally tended; that, as in the relation of parent and child, helplessness is to be succeeded by strength, strength by maturity, maturity by independence, so in states and empires issuing from each other, new sentiments and new duties are to arise from the changing situation of the parties; and that it is the business and the wisdom of the parent state, more particularly, to conform without a murmur to those eternal laws which have ordained a constant progress in all things, and which have decreed that nations, like individuals, are no longer to require from youth and from manhood the blind and unconditional submission which is connected with the imbecility and inexperience of the infant and the child; that by skill and forbearance this ultimate separation may be protracted to the benefit of the mother country, but that the separation itself must be always kept in view as an issue at length inevitable, and that the euthanasia of the connexion is an affectionate intercourse of good offices, an alliance of more than ordinary sympathy and sincerity, and a gradual transmutation of the notions of protection and submission, of supremacy and allegiance, into those of interchanged regard and respect, into those of a sense of common interest in the friendship and kindness and growing prosperity of each other.

Such must always be the philosophy of the case when the colonies can ever, by their extent and natural fertility, be advanced into any situation imitating that of the son to the father in the relations of social life. In the one case as in the other, much unhappiness may be caused, much injury may arise both to the parent and to the child, by a want of good temper and compliance with the ordinances of nature; but the wisdom which these ordinances point out is at all times the same, equally obvious and indispensable.

Now the case of America and England was one precisely of this nature. America, in extent boundless, in natural advantages unexampled, removed to a distance from the mother country, how was it possible that the natural tendency of things, in all other cases, should in this particular case of America and England, cease to operate? To what end, indeed, or purpose, as far as the best interests of either, or the good interests of humanity and the world were concerned? Why was a great continent, a country of lakes, into which our island might be thrown and buried; of forests, which might overshadow our principalities and kingdoms; of falls and cataracts, which might sweep away our cities; and of descending seas, to which our noblest streams might in comparison be thought but rivulets and brooks; why was such a country which the God of nature had clothed with all his highest forms of magnificence and grandeur; why was such a country, though in the mysterious dispensations of his providence it was to be raised into existence by an island in the old world; why was it to be impeded in its career by the manacles that were to be thrown over its giant limbs by the selfishness of its parent—why prevented from rushing on in its destined race, to become itself the new world, as Europe had been the old, teeming with the life and glowing with the business of human society, and doubling, trebling, multiplying to an indefinite extent the number of sentient beings, to which our planet may give support; why prevented from journeying on with all the accumulating resources of its independent strength, till the same progress of things which had thus ripened the colony into a kingdom, and a kingdom into the new Europe of the western hemisphere, should have advanced the planet itself to its final consummation, and the labours and the grandeur and the happiness of man, on this side the grave, should be no more.

There surely could be no reason, either on any general system of benevolence or on any practical scheme of human policy, why these great laws of our particular portion of the universe should not be cheerfully acquiesced in by any intelligent statesman, should not be patiently submitted to as a matter of necessity by every practical politician in the parent state. What other hope, what possible alternative, presented itself? Stay the sun in its course, because he has warmed the nations of the Atlantic till they are no longer dependent on our bounty!—arrest the principles of increase and decay, because they no longer appear to operate to our particular aggrandizement! Vain and hopeless efforts! Rather turn the opportunities and indulgences of nature which yet remain to their best advantage; far better to be grateful to the Author of all good for blessings past and to come, and, not from a blind, preposterous, unschooled, and irreverent ambition, fret and struggle where it is in vain to contend, and perhaps hurry on, a century or two before their time, all those evils of comparative decline and decreasing power which are now terrifying your imagination, and interrupting all the regular conclusions of the understanding. Pro-tract, if you please, by all the expedients of mild government, the day of separation; but to endeavour to adjourn it for ever, and that by force, is ridiculous, for it is in the very nature of things impossible.

Views of this kind should certainly have presented themselves to our statesmen soon after the middle of the last century. It was not necessary that they should be displayed in their speeches in parliament, or in their conversation in private society. But assuredly they should have been pres-ent to their minds when they came to speculate in their closets, and still more when they came to advise their sovereign in his cabinet.

Great caution, and a most conciliatory system of government from England to America, would no doubt have been the result; no high asser-tions of authority, either in theory or in practice; no search into dormant claims; no statements and adjustments of rights and duties, before un-certain and undefined; no agitation of perilous questions of supremacy and obedience; no experiments of legislation for the exclusive benefit of the parent state; in short, nothing that should disturb that general tend-ency which may be observed in mankind to retain their habits of think-ing and acting (all these would have been in favour of the mother coun-try), long after the reasons in which they originated have ceased to exist.

Had sentiments of this kind influenced the councils of Great Britain soon after the accession of his present majesty to the throne, it is impos-sible to say how long the two countries might have slumbered on in a long established system of generous superintendence on the one side, and habitual confidence and duty on the other. Many think the French Revo-lution would not have happened, had not the American preceded it; but at all events the connexion between England and her colonies might have been long protracted by a philosophic policy of the kind I have described; we should at least have avoided the folly of an opposite system, and of producing before its time the event we dreaded.

But we must now turn aside from those general views and great laws and principles of nature, which statesmen, amid their humbler details and more minute contrivances for the interest of their communities, ought never to lose sight of, and we must descend all at once to the miserable, mortifying, melancholy facts of our dispute with America.

I will describe this dispute in a few sentences.

We conclude a triumphant peace with the House of Bourbon in 1763. The French are obliged to abandon America, and all Europe is jealous of our present, and apprehensive of our future prosperity; and this happy state of things no sooner takes place, America and ourselves are no sooner in a situation to enjoy and urge to the utmost the prosperity of each other, than what is the consequence? Acts are drawn up by the British parliament to enforce restrictions on the trade of the colonies; to put an end to what was denominated their smuggling trade. The greatest irritation and considerable injury are thus occasioned; the mother country appears no longer the protectress and nurse of their prosperity. This is the first specimen I have to mention of our statesmen, and the next is this:— A resolution is actually formed to draw a revenue from America by the authority of the British parliament, which revenue, however small on its first introduction, might afterwards, when the precedent was once established, be increased, as it was very obvious, to any extent which the same British parliament might think proper. This is the second specimen; the rest is in due order. When this measure is resisted by America, as might have been expected, troops are sent from England to insist upon obedience. The sword is actually drawn; from year to year the contest is maintained; our rivals and enemies at length openly join the cause of the Americans, and the result of the whole is, that after a bloody and most perilous struggle, we are obliged to acknowledge the independence of our colonies, and be very well satisfied that we have been able to maintain our own independence, and support our own national consequence against the world.

But what a drama, what a tragedy, what a long spectacle of impolicy, is thus in a few words described. What solution are we to produce for such miserable infatuation in the most enlightened nation on earth, at the close of the eighteenth century?

"The whole of your political conduct," said Lord Chatham when addressing the ministers of the country in February, 1775, "has been one continuous series of weakness, temerity, despotism, ignorance, futility, negligence, blundering, and the most notorious servility, incapacity, and corruption."

"These ministers," said his son, the late Mr. Pitt, at a subsequent period, "will destroy the empire they were called upon to save, before the indignation of a great and suffering people can fall upon their heads, in the punishment which they deserve. I affirm the war to have been a most accursed, wicked, barbarous, cruel, unnatural, unjust, and diabolical war."

Yet were these ministers, the advisers and supporters of this war, as individuals, men of education and ability. Lord North was the delight of every private society which he honoured with his presence, and in the senate appeared in every respect fitted for his situation as far as natural talents were concerned; second to none in the powers of conducting a debate, unrivalled in the possession of a most inexhaustible fund of elegant pleasantry, and of a temper that was always the last to be ruffled, and the first to be appeased. In both houses they who resisted the impolitic system of American coercion were for several years left on every occasion in the most insignificant minorities, and the war was supported by a clear and ardent majority of every division of the community, with perhaps the exception for some time of a part of the manufacturers and merchants, those who found their trade interrupted, and were afraid of losing what they had lent to the American merchants.

Now, this on the whole appears to me a case well fitted to excite your inquiries. What are the causes that can be mentioned as having produced such unhappy effects on this side of the Atlantic?

I will offer to your consideration such as have occurred to me. I will mention first those that were natural and not discreditable to us, then those that *were* discreditable.

Of the first kind, then, was a general notion in the English people that their cause was just. The sovereignty was supposed to be in the parent state; in the rights of sovereignty were included the rights of taxation: England, too, was considered as having protected the Americans from the French in the war that had been lately concluded. The Americans therefore, when they resisted the mother country in her attempt to tax them, were considered on the first account as rebellious, and on the second as ungrateful.

The sentiment, then, of the contest, as far as it was honourable to the inhabitants of this country, originated in the considerations just mentioned. But this sentiment would have produced no such effect as the American War, had it not been excited and exasperated by other considerations which I shall now lay before you, and which were not creditable to us.

These I shall endeavour to illustrate in the ensuing lectures, because they were such as I think you may be exposed to the influence of yourselves hereafter, and their operation can never be favourable to the interests of your country. Of the first which I have mentioned, the supposed right of taxation, I shall now say no more, but shall allude finally to it before I advert to the conduct of the war. The ministers and people of England might neither *mean* to be, nor *be*, the tyrants and oppressors which they were thought by the people of America, but whether they were as reasonable and prudent, or even as well justified in their measures of taxation, much less of coercion, as they supposed, is quite another question.

It is this last part of the general subject, that which is discreditable to us, that I shall for some time more particularly place in your view. I may thus appear to some only an advocate for the American cause. I am not so; but I am anxious to show you the unpardonable mistakes that were made by the statesmen and people of Great Britain, that you may be the better able to avoid such mistakes yourselves.

Turning then, at present, from the causes first mentioned, an opinion in the people of England that the Americans were rebellious and ungrateful, and alluding to the causes that were less honourable in the sentiment, and that were discreditable to us, and that operated so fatally to the reduction and exasperation of the American contest, the first was, I think, a deplorable ignorance or inattention to the great leading principles of political economy.

The result of this ignorance or inattention was an indisposition to listen to the arguments of those who laid down from time to time, and explained the proper manner in which colonies might become sources of revenue to the mother country, not by means of taxes and taxgatherers, but by the interchange of their appropriate products, and by the exertions of the real revenue officers of every country, the merchants, farmers, and manufacturers. This was one of what I consider as the discreditable causes of the war on our part.

Secondly, a very blind and indeed disgraceful selfishness, in the mere matter of money and payment of taxes; this was another.

It was hence that the country gentlemen of the House of Commons, and the landed interest of England, had actually the egregious folly to support ministers in their scheme of coercing America, from an expectation that their own burdens, their land tax, for instance, might be made lighter, or at least prevented from becoming heavier.

Thirdly, an overweening national pride, not operating in its more honourable direction to beat off invaders, or repel the approach of insult or injustice, but in making us despise our enemy, vilify the American character, and suppose that nothing could stand opposed to our own good pleasure, or resist the valour of our fleets and armies.

Fourthly, very high principles of government; a disposition to push too far the rights of authority; to insist too sternly on the expediency of control; to expect the duty of submission to laws without much inquiry into the exact reasonableness of their enactments. These high principles of government operated very fatally, when the question was, whether Great Britain could not only claim, but actually exercise, sovereignty over the colonies of America: whether the people of America could be constitutionally taxed by the parliament of Great Britain, a parliament in which it could have no representatives.

Fifthly, a certain vulgarity of thinking on political subjects; narrow, and what will commonly be found popular notions in national concerns. In these last few words I might perhaps at once comprehend all the causes I have already mentioned. It was thus that men like Mr. Burke, who drew their reasonings from philosophic principles of a general nature, were not comprehended or were disregarded, while the most commonplace declaimer was applauded, and decided the different issues of the dispute.

Such were, I think, the causes (discreditable to us) which, without entering into any metaphysical niceties, may be said in a general manner to have led to the destruction of the British empire in America, as far as the legislators and people of England were concerned. I will recapitulate them, because I mean to illustrate them in the ensuing lectures, on account of what I fancy to be their importance, and I shall illustrate them not by selecting and endeavouring to discuss and decide upon the different arguments and events that this contest produced (this you must do yourselves), but by reading passages from speeches and pamphlets, so as to give you, if possible, in a very short compass, the spirit of the whole; but you must have the causes I have mentioned well infixed in your memory, that you may continually see the application of what I am reading, for I cannot stay to point it out. The causes, then, that I have mentioned, were (those that were *discreditable* to us, I mean) an ignorance of political economy; a mere blind, disgraceful money selfishness: an overweening national pride: high principles of government; and a certain vulgarity of thinking on political subjects.

XXXIII. AMERICAN WAR

FOR LORD NORTH on this occasion [the war between Great Britain and the American colonies], a man of fine talents and mild temper, there can be no excuse. He must have been guilty of acquiescing in measures, the general folly of which he must have resolved to shut out from his view. Either this, or he is an example to show that wit and eloquence, and acuteness and dexterity in debate are one thing, while decision, elevation, strength, and clearness of understanding, such as are indispensable in the rulers of mankind, are quite another. He slumbered on, amid the downy pleasures of patronage and social regard; amid shifts and expedients, and discreditable failures, vernal hopes, and winter disappointments; uniformly a year too late in every project he formed, and while he talked of having followed up the system of his predecessors, of not being the original author of a dispute from which he could not disengage himself, and of having pursued the conduct recommended to him by the advice of parliament and the wishes of the nation (the unfair excuses these, the palliatives of bad ministers at all times), he saw the empire gradually dismembered, his administration ending in defeat and disgrace, and his character and fame as a statesman in the opinion of posterity, lost for ever. This is not to pass too harsh a judgment upon him, nor is it to judge after the event; nothing is now known that was not then known, and nothing happened that was not repeatedly predicted. It was known, for instance, that the Americans were, on their first settlement, republicans; that the Pelhams and the Walpoles, had carefully abstained from stirring the critical question of American taxation; the difficulties and irritations connected with the restraint of the contraband trade of the colonies were also known. The spirit shown on the subject of the Stamp Act, both on its enactment and on its repeal, was a matter of the most perfect notoriety. Lord North, and his predecessors, Lord Grenville and Charles Town-shend, had nothing to learn with respect to the influence of posts and places on the minds of men; and it was known very well, that the crown had *no* very extensive or effective influence, arising from its patronage in North America. It was clear, therefore, that the precise *merit* of every measure, and its *agreeableness* to the notions, habits, and interests of the people, were points of the utmost consequence. These ministers were aware, or might have been, that this right of taxation was the particular point on which the Americans were sensitive. Fanaticism, as it is well known, made a part of the national character of America. Its transition from religious to civil liberty was very intelligible; it was part of the in-struction even of our own history, in the times of Charles I. It was known that a state of independence from the mother country was (at least might very possibly be) the ambition of many bolder spirits in America: again, that this was even the state to which the prosperity of large and distant colonies naturally tends. Every one was aware, that different opinions ex-isted in America on the justice of the claims of Great Britain; it was there-fore the obvious policy of the rulers of Great Britain so to deport them-selves, that those who in America undertook their defence, should have as good a case as possible against the opposite party. All these things were or might have been known and understood, and when all that was re-quested by the petitions from America was, in a word, only the renewal of their situation at the peace in 1763, only a return to the old system; what are we to say, when we see these petitions disregarded, troops sent to Boston, soldiers hired from Germany to force into submission such an immense continent as America, situated on the other side of the Atlantic!

There is a progress in these things, but it is from mistake to folly, from folly to fault, from fault to crime; it is at least from fault, to the shedding of blood in a quarrel, of which the theoretical justice must have been confessed by every one to have been a matter of some debate, but of which the issue, whatever direction it might take, could not have been well expected by *any one* to be favourable to the real interests of the mother country, if the question was once reduced to a question of arms.*

* I had observed, in the above Lecture, "that for Lord North there could be no excuse"; what excuse there is, I have lately, many years after, had an opportunity of ascertaining. I have seen papers which show that Lord North, after the affair at Sara-toga, from the beginning of the year 1778, made every effort to procure from the king permission to resign. These efforts were continually repeated for a long period, but in vain: the king could not give up the idea of coercing America, and therefore could not part with the only man who was, he thought, fit to manage the House of Com-mons.

xxxiv. AMERICAN WAR

THE LESSONS of history are neglected by those who are too intemperate to listen to any admonition, from whatever quarter it may come, and by those who have not philosophy enough either to relish historical inquiries, or to separate principles from the particular circumstances by which they may be surrounded.

To mark, however, the common appearance of any great principles in the case that is past, and in the case before us, is to read history with proper advantage; and to see, or not to see, instruction of this kind, is the great distinction between the statesman who may be trusted in critical times, and the mere man of office, who, in all such critical times, is more likely to injure than to serve the country. . . .

Passing now from the first part of the general subject, the origin of the dispute, the second seems to be the conduct of it.

The student will be already impatient to know how it could possibly happen that the fleets and armies of this country could be successfully resisted by those who had neither; why Howe did not drive Washington from the field; why regular armies of acknowledged skill and bravery did not disperse every irregular combination of men whenever they appeared; support the governors of the provinces in the enforcement of British acts of parliament, and by the assistance of the loyalists, partly by persuasion and partly by force, assert and establish the sovereignty of the mother country.

Now, to answer this general question, it is necessary to read the history of the American War. The authorities you must more particularly consult are Washington's Letters, and the *Life of Washington*, by Marshall; Stedman's *History of the American War*, and the examination into the conduct of Sir William Howe by the House of Commons, which you will find given in the debates.

I will allude to this general subject of the conduct of the war in the case of Sir William Howe, not only to exhibit to you the proper means of answering to yourselves a very natural question, but for the sake of drawing your attention to other topics perhaps still more important. For instance, I shall refer to the Letters of Washington, and to the *Life of Washington*, and the extracts I shall produce in the first place will enable you, and can alone enable you, to judge of the merit of Washington himself, the great character of the last century. In the next place, they will still further substantiate several of the points I have already been endeavouring to establish—the faults and follies, I mean, of England: you will see the most constant and extreme distress exhibited by Washington in these letters. The great inference you are to draw is therefore not only how great must have been the want of enterprise in Sir William Howe, but how great must have been the original impolicy and subsequent mismanagement of the quarrel on our part, so to exasperate the Americans that they should think of beginning, of prosecuting, of persevering in a system of resistance under difficulties so serious, distresses so painful, and privations so intolerable.

There are other conclusions to be drawn from these documents—the superiority, I am sorry to say, of regular armies over all and every description of militia: conclusions, too, with respect to the republican character, and those very unfavourable to it; its ridiculous jealousy, its impracticable nature, its coarseness, its harshness. Lastly, you will observe that while you are reading these accounts of the distresses and difficulties of Washington, you are, in fact, passing over, in your perusal, the materials of the most serious charge that I think can be brought against the American leaders in this dispute, because it is not quite enough that there should be right on the side of those who mean to resist; there should also be a fair, and indeed more than a fair, chance of success. Men cannot be otherwise justified in leading on their countrymen into measures which will be considered by their rulers, or oppressors, if you please, as rebellion, and punished as such by fire and sword. Of all the questions that occur in the whole of this dispute, this seems to me one of the most difficult, whether the very able men who composed the congress (admitting the justice of the cause), did or did not hurry on the resistance of their countrymen at too great a rate, and embark in the fearful enterprise of open rebellion to the mother country, with means far too disproportionate to the occasion. Of this it will be said the actors in the scene were the best, and can be the only judges, and that at least they were justified by the event.

Perhaps not—the difficulties they had to struggle with were all most obviously to be expected; while the causes of their success, some of them (and those very important), were not so: no one, for instance, could have presupposed such a want of skill and enterprise in the British ministers and generals.

On the whole, though the attempt of Great Britain permanently to establish a system of taxation by force was, from the first, not a little hopeless, from the distance and impracticability of the country, and the spirit and unanimity of the inhabitants; and though it was an attempt that could not *ultimately* be successful; still it must be allowed on the other side, that the American leaders won the independence of their country at a much *less* expense of carnage and desolation (long as the war lasted) than they had any reason to expect. . . .

His [Washington's] letter of 8th September, 1776, is very important, and contains his ideas on the late and future operations of the war, but it is too long to quote. "We must on all occasions," says he, "avoid a general action, nor put any thing to the risk unless compelled by a necessity into which we ought never to be drawn. The war must be defensive, a war of posts. I have never spared the spade and the pickaxe."

He never did afterwards spare them. The affair at Bunker's Hill had shown what it was to fight from behind intrenchments. The country gave opportunities of this species of defence, and the war was thus protracted by Washington till the irregular and undisciplined troops of America became in time fit to be opposed, in pitched battles, if necessary, to the regular troops of England and Germany. But Washington had no proper powers intrusted to him by the congress. These jealous republicans hazarded their cause to the utmost, rather than give their general the means of saving them from their enemies. This sort of impracticable adherence to a principle is always the characteristic of democratic men and democratic bodies. It is sometimes their praise, but more often their fault. The respectful patience with which Washington waited for the influence of his representations on his constitutional rulers exceeds all description, and certainly far exceeds the patience of those who read his letters. The lowest point of depression was at this moment, December, 1776. But the enterprise at Trenton, where he surprised a part of the British army, and which was the great achievement of the military life of Washington, then followed: the achievement that inspired with some hope the despairing friends and armies of America, and which enabled him to maintain a show of regular resistance to the superior forces of the British commanders. His own account of this affair, December 27th, is singularly modest and concise.

The year 1777 opens with a letter, in which he evidently expects very favourable effects from the ill conduct of the British in the Jerseys. "If what our countrymen have suffered in the Jerseys does not rouse their resentment, they must not possess the common feelings of humanity. To oppression, ravage, deprivation of property, insult has been added. We keep up appearances," says he, "before an enemy double to us in number. Our situation is delicate and truly critical, for want of a sufficient force to oppose to the enemy."

Now it was about this time, and in this situation of things, that the congress expressed to him their wishes (such was their reasonableness) that "he would confine the enemy within their present quarters, prevent their getting supplies from the country, and totally subdue them before they were reinforced." They do not exactly desire him to step over to London, and send them Lord North and Lord George Germaine in irons, but I really have quoted the very terms in which they expressed themselves.

The good temper of Washington is astonishing. "The enclosed return," says he, "comprehends the whole force I have in Jersey; it is but a handful, and bears no proportion in the scale of numbers to that of the enemy; added to this, the major part is made up of militia. The most sanguine in speculation," says he, "cannot deem it more than adequate to the least valuable purposes of war."

These notices, drawn from different letters (they proceed in the same strain to the end), will give you some idea of the work before us. The letters, you will see, however cold and formal, may serve to afford you a proper notion of the contest, and more particularly of the merit of Washington. You will scarcely be able regularly to read them, though you will easily perceive that they must be read very patiently by any historian of these times, and that if particular points are to be settled they must be referred to. You will remember that I have already announced to you that these letters may supply many more conclusions than such as relate to the merit of General Washington. . . .

It was during the campaign of 1776, and at the close of it, when it was for Sir William Howe to have struck some important blow. The enemy were unable to stand before the British troops in the field; the American army had diminished from thirty thousand almost to three thousand; Washington was scarcely able to maintain the appearance of a regular force; . . . the congress had retired into Maryland; Philadelphia only awaited the arrival of the British army to submit to the mother country; other parts would have done the same; New York was already in Howe's possession. These advantages were neglected, and other material errors, which he states, were in his opinion committed. I cannot enter into the details in this and in other parts of his work. You will consider also his twentieth chapter, where he finds another opportunity of renewing his censures when the general takes leave of his command.

The blame that belonged to the failure of our arms in America became of course a subject of dispute between the general and the secretary of war, Lord George Germaine.

In this question is involved, as I have already intimated, more than the character of either; and they who examine it will be continually led away to the more important question of the original probability of conquering America by any force which it was competent for this country to have sent across the Atlantic. On this account, and on account of many curious particulars which appeared in the course of the examination, I would recommend it to you to consult the debates. The labour will not be great. You will find General Howe, on his return, declaring in the house that he had resigned his command (I quote his words) "in consequence of a total disregard to his opinions, and to his recommendations of meritorious officers; that the war had not been left to his management, and yet when he applied for instructions, he frequently could not get them." Lord George Germaine expressed some surprise at so unexpected an attack; said his recommendations had been complied with, except in three instances, which he explained; declared that he had always seconded the plans of the general; and that if the general had not instructions when he called for them, it was because every thing depended on unforeseen circumstances, and it was impossible to send letters every day across the Atlantic; that the general must necessarily, in many respects, be left to his own discretion. . . .

If the general on the one hand supposed, that unless he was left entirely to his own discretion, he could not overpower Washington and the congress; or if, on the other hand, the secretary imagined, that while sitting at Whitehall, he had the slightest chance of conquering the continent of America, or even of materially assisting those whom he sent for the purpose, it was evident at once, that neither the general nor the secretary had genius enough to execute, or even properly to comprehend, the enterprise which was before them.

An inquiry took place to satisfy General Howe, and not Lord George Germaine. The general entered on his defence, and insisted that the papers before the house made out for him four points: first, that he supplied the ministry, from time to time, with proper information; secondly, that he gave his own opinion on what was practicable with the force on the spot, and with such succours as he expected; thirdly, that his plans were carried into execution with as little deviation as could have been expected; and, fourthly, that he never flattered the ministry with improper hopes of seeing the war terminated in any one campaign, with the force at any one time under his command.

The general then proceeded to his defence, and the student, as he reads it, will find himself silenced, if not satisfied, and that to a much greater degree than he could have expected. The great question is why the general did not attempt some decisive enterprise at the close of the campaign of 1776, about the time of the surprise at Trenton. The general seems always to have respected his enemy more than the student might think necessary: but it would be rather presumptuous to judge for him in this point. Instead of immediately making any important effort, he wrote for a reinforcement of fifteen thousand men and a battalion of artillery. The force could not be sent, and this opportunity (which was in fact a striking one) was lost.

You will see the defence of Lord George Germaine * . . . the main point of which is, that "he admitted that the general had demanded a large reinforcement of fifteen or twenty thousand men, but that it was after the affair at White Plains, in 1776, when the rebel army was all one as annihilated; and that for his part, against an enemy flying on every side, scarcely a battalion in any one body, and at the head of a victorious, well-disciplined army, combined with the information of persons well informed on the spot, and on his own judgment, he thought then, and now, that such a requisition on the part of the commander in chief ought not to be complied with."

Now here appears to me to turn the main hinge of the question between the secretary and the general, and the answer of the secretary seems not sufficient: it was for the general to judge of the quantity of force, not for him; and the better answer would have been, not that he *would* not, but that he *could* not comply with the requisition, and this answer would probably have been the real truth. To have said *this*, however, would have been to suggest to the opposition the incompetence of Great Britain to make a sufficient effort to conquer America at all, and the original folly of attempting it; and this therefore could not be said. . . . Much is made to depend on the evidence of Galloway, by the historian Adolphus; but you will see such conversation taking place in the House of Commons, with respect to Galloway's memory, situation, and other particulars, that you will receive with great hesitation any representations founded on his opinions.

At last you will find that the inquiry suddenly stops short. The general is absent, and the committee breaks up and expires. The general says, the next day, that his absence was no proper reason why it should do so. The two brothers ask the secretary whether, after having heard the evidence, he has any accusation to make. He is silent, and the whole business is at an end; not very intelligibly, or much to the credit of any of the parties concerned—the general, the secretary, or the house.

On the whole the conclusion seems to be that success could not have been accomplished, unless Howe had been more enterprising, or England more powerful. That America was a country so impracticable and so distant, that, considering the spirit of resistance which had been shown, no reasonable hope could be entertained of ultimately controlling the inhabitants by force of arms.

Marshall, in his *Life of Washington*, probably speaks the general opinion of intelligent men in America. He conceives that Sir William Howe might, on some occasions, have acted more efficiently, but in doing so that he would have risked much. Victories like those of Bunker's Hill,

---

* The detailed discussion of Lord George Germaine's defence has been omitted.— ED.

or that claimed by Burgoyne in September, 1777, would have ruined the royal cause. Howe's system he conceives to have been, to put nothing to hazard, and to be very careful of his troops. "Howe probably supposed," he says, "that the extreme difficulties under which America laboured, the depreciation of the paper money, the dispersions of the army on the expiration of the terms of enlistment, the privations to which every class of society had to submit, would in themselves create a general disposition to return to the ancient state of things, if the operation of these causes should not be counteracted by brilliant successes obtained over the British by Washington."

Now it is very possible that Howe did reason in this manner; but the train of reasoning would have been more solid, if it had concluded in a manner exactly opposite: for instance, that these causes would not create a general disposition in the Americans to return to the ancient state of things, *unless* he could assist their operation by obtaining some brilliant successes over Washington. . . .

I must now repeat that I have adverted to this subject on the merits of General Howe, not only to furnish some general answer to one of the first questions which the student will naturally ask, but to remind him, that while he is gratifying his curiosity, he must necessarily place before his view (and that he ought to observe them) two of the most important points connected with the American dispute: whether, for instance, the original idea of conquering America by force, was ever reasonable on our part; and again, whether the resolution of the principal men of America, at all events to hazard rebellion against the mother country, was properly justified at the time by their probable means of resistance. Finally, it is in this manner that the student can best be taught, in some degree, to comprehend the extraordinary merit of Washington.

xxxv. AMERICAN WAR

HITHERTO I HAVE alluded chiefly to the origin of this unhappy civil war: the causes of which, as they operated on each side of the Atlantic, you will even now be able, in a general manner, to estimate. Of these general causes, too many of those that operated with us, those that I have enumerated, for instance, may, I think, be held up to the censure and avoidance of posterity. The more they are analyzed, the less can they be respected; and it was very fit, and even desirable, that the haughty and selfish sentiments, the unworthy opinions, by which the people of Great Britain and their rulers were led astray, should not only be resisted, but successfully resisted.

And yet it is not so easy to come to a decision on the American part of the case. The colonies were from the first connected with the British empire. They had grown up under its influence, to unexampled strength and prosperity; a principle was no doubt on a sudden brought forward by the British minister, which might have been carried to an extent, and, if unresisted, would probably have been carried to an extent materially injurious to their liberties; but it had not been carried to any such extent when acts of fury and outrage were committed in the province of Massachusetts; and we assent to rather than enter into the reasonings of the Americans. We are surprised and struck with the fervour of their resistance rather than sympathize with it; certainly we do not feel the glow of indignation against the mother country which, on other occasions, of Switzerland and the Low Countries for instance, we have felt against the superior state. That the British nation was wrong, and deserved to be severely punished, must be allowed; but to lose half its empire, and to have America and Europe rejoicing in its humiliation and misfortunes, as in the fall of tyranny and oppression, is more than a speculator on human affairs (in this country at least) can be well reconciled to. The punishment seems disproportioned to the fault—the fault, however, must not be denied. It was one totally unworthy of the English people, the very essence of whose constitution, its safeguard, its characteristic boast, its principle from the earliest times, the very object of all its virtuous struggles, and for which its patriots had died on the scaffold and in the field, was this very principle of representative taxation. I must now, therefore, recall to your minds my observation, that the causes which led to the American War were not all of them, in their feeling and principle, discreditable to our country. For instance; a particular notion of political right had a great effect in misleading our ministers and people, and hurrying them into measures of violence and coercion. It was of the following nature: all general principles of legislation and national law seem to lead to the conclusion, that the sovereignty must remain with the parent state, and that the power of taxation was involved in the idea of sovereignty. Even Burke seems to have been of this opinion, and the Rockingham part of the Whigs. But this was a point much contested at the time. The reverse was loudly insisted upon by Lord Chatham and his division of the Whigs; that the general powers of sovereignty were one thing, and the particular power of taxation another— that this species of sovereignty, taxation, could not be exercised without representation.

And thus much must at least be conceded to Lord Chatham, that, in practice, this distinction had always existed in the European governments, derived from the barbarian conquerors of the Roman empire. This power of taxation was always supposed to be the proper prerogative of the people, or of the great assemblies that were quite distinct from the wearer of the crown. The granting or refusing of supplies was always considered as a matter of grace and favour to the sovereign—not of duty; and as something with which they were enabled to come (if I may so speak) into the market with their rulers, and truck and barter for privileges and immunities. But however this original point of the right of taxation being included in sovereignty be determined; whether it be admitted, or not, in the abstract and elementary theory of government, which is the first question; and whether it be admitted, or not, in any ideas we can form of our feudal governments of Europe, which is the second question; still the same point assumed a very different appearance, and became another and a third question, when this sovereign right of taxation was to be practically applied to colonies, situated as were those of America, and by a mother country, enjoying the kind of free constitution which Great Britain at the time enjoyed. The question of taxation, under these circumstances, became materially and fundamentally altered; and for the rulers and people of Great Britain to set up a right, one, if it existed at all, certainly of a very general and abstract kind; and even to carry it into practical effect, without the slightest accommodation to the feelings of freemen, and the descendants of freemen—without offering the slightest political contrivance, the slightest form of representation, by which the property of the Americans could be rendered as secure as is the property of the inhabitants of Great Britain; without the slightest attempt to avail themselves of the colonial governments existing in America at the time; for the rulers and people of Great Britain to be so totally deaf and insensible to all the reasonings and feelings which had dignified the conduct of their ancestors from the earliest period, and which at that moment continued to dignify their own—was to show a want of genuine sympathy with the first principles of the English constitution, and the first principles of all relative justice; was to show such carelessness of the happiness and prosperity of others, and such haughty contempt and disregard of the most obvious suggestions of policy and expediency, that it is not at all to be lamented, that the ministers and people of this country should fail in their scheme of unconditionally taxing America; should be disgraced and defeated in any such unworthy enterprise. And it is ardently to be hoped, that all nations, and all rulers of nations, and all bodies of men, and all individuals, should eternally fail and be discomfited; and, according to the measure of their offences, be stigmatized and made to suffer, whenever they show this kind of selfish or unenlightened hostility to such great principles as I have alluded to—the principles of civil freedom, of relative justice, and of mild government.

After having thus considered the original grounds of the war, when I came in the last lecture to advert to the conduct of the war, I pointed out to you the most curious and difficult question which the whole contest affords: whether the American leaders did not hurry into positive rebellion, before they had sufficient grounds to suppose they could resist what was then the greatest empire on earth.

The fact seems to have been that resistance ripened gradually and insensibly into rebellion. The leaders had incurred the penalties of treason, before they could well have asked themselves to what lengths they were prepared to go. They always debated with closed doors, so that what were their exact views, and the progress of their opinions, cannot now be known. But the strange, incoherent manner, in which both they and the people of America seemed to have supposed that the dispute would be terminated each year, in the course of that year, or the next, is very striking, and shows how little they were aware of the magnitude of the enterprise in which they had engaged. This is true in general; but particular individuals were more wise. Instances certainly did occur, and some are on record, of men who were aware how perilous was the course, which at the opening of the dispute, the patriots were pursuing. "We are not to hope," said Mr. Quincy, to the meeting assembled at Boston in 1774, "that we shall end this controversy without the sharpest, sharpest conflicts. We are not to flatter ourselves, that popular resolves, popular harangues, popular acclamations, and popular vapour will vanquish our foes: let us consider, before we advance to those measures, which must bring on the most trying and terrible struggle this country ever saw."

But on the whole, the general enthusiasm that was excited by this single principle, the fundamental principle of the American controversy, that the parliament of Great Britain had no right to tax them, is quite unexampled in history; and that men should act on the foresight and expectation of events, just as if the events were present, and should endure as much to avoid the approach of oppressive taxgatherers, as if they were already in their houses, is a perfect phenomenon in the records of the world, and a very curious specimen of that reasoning, sagacious, spirited, determined attachment to the principles of civil liberty, which so honourably distinguished the ancestors of these Americans, the very singular men who flourished in the times of Charles I, and who, whatever may be their faults, did certainly rescue from imminent danger the civil liberties of these islands.

I have hitherto, through all these lectures on the subject of the American dispute, been obliged to direct your attention to the ill effects of harsh government, to the unfortunate nature of high and arbitrary notions, when the interests of mankind are concerned; their civil liberties at home; their sense of relative justice to other states abroad: but the lessons I am now called upon to offer you, through this and the ensuing lecture, are of a different kind; and it will be now my business continually to remind you that though government ought not to be harsh, still that government must exist; and that whatever may be the temptations to which all executive power is exposed, still that somewhere or other executive power must be found, or there will be no chance for the maintenance of justice and right among mankind.

For as we proceed to consider still further the conduct of the American leaders, the principal, and I had almost said the only remaining observation I have to make, is this; that through the whole course of the accounts, as given by the American writers, the reflection that is continually presenting itself is the objectionable nature of the purely republican form of government; the total inadequacy of all forms strictly democratical for the management of mankind, where any management is required; their management, I mean, according to the proper principles of equity and wisdom. I do not think that any sober-minded speculator on government could have ever had much doubt on the subject, yet I conceive that any such doubt will be entirely at an end with those who peruse the volumes of Marshall, or even of Dr. Ramsay; for we are continually led to remark, through every stage of the contest, the want of a proper executive government on the part of the Americans, and the evils that hence ensued; and though the case before us is the case of a country at war, where the difficulties must necessarily be not of an ordinary nature, and the executive government ought to be particularly strong, still the conclusion is inevitably transferred to a country in a state of peace, so strong are the instances every where displayed of the impracticable nature of the human character, of the entire necessity that exists in every community for some controlling, superintending, executive power; some power that shall bind up, and bring into proper effect, and reduce to the proper standard of equity and reason, all the divided, dispersed, ardent, and often very ill-directed energies of the individuals that compose any society of human beings. Freedom must be enjoyed and men must not lose their nature, and be driven by their keepers like the beasts of the field, but neither must they be so enamoured of self-rule as to admit of no paramount directors and governors. The public rights and privileges for which they should contend are not the power of self-rule, nor even the immediate and palpable direction of the measures of their government, the great aim and boast of purely republican forms; but the privileges of peaceful criticism on their government, the power of subsequent censure, the acknowledgment in the rulers of a delegated, rather than an original authority, and a reference of their measures to the interest of the community. These are the points for which they should contend, the points which, as a government is more or less perfect, are more or less accomplished and secured. . . .

An English reader, when he comes to the history of the American

War, as given by the American writers, hears of nothing at first but fury
and resistance to the British ministers; resolutions to defend the liberties
of America; public meetings, patriotic sacrifices and exertions of every
description; and yet when congress is assembled, an army collecting, and
a general appointed, this congress, army, and general, these defenders of
their country, and representatives of the public will meet with nothing
but difficulties and distresses; no supplies for the troops, no pay for the
soldiers and officers, the paper money issued for the purpose intolerably
depreciated, and at last even a mutiny among the troops, and this repeated at different periods of the contest.

But whence could arise all these difficulties? Why did not the congress lay at once the necessary taxes on the people of America, and with
the produce of these taxes procure the necessary supplies; or if they
issued paper money, why not with the same produce of the taxes keep
their paper from being depreciated?

The fact was that the congress had it not in their power to tax America, and they had no real securities within their reach on which to rest
their paper; the different governments of the different provinces of
America were all separate and independent of each other; they were all,
in truth, separate and independent republics; congress was only a delegation from each province or republic, and was assembled merely for the
purpose of considering the situation, of representing the claims, and at
last of conducting the resistance of the whole continent; but no powers
were given to the congress of taxation; the utmost they could do was to
recommend it to the separate provincial legislatures to levy taxes; they
could not levy any taxes themselves, and so preposterous was the jealousy
in the mind of the Americans of all power, that many years elapsed before any authority existed that could *legally act for* the whole continent.
Thus the first thing that reason required to be done was the last thing
that could be admitted; no proper executive power could be suffered to
exist, and the fortunes of the contest, and indeed of America, after the
contest, were put to the most extreme hazard from this very circumstance; and it is this unreasonableness, and this consequent hazard, that
become the very lesson which I would now impress upon your minds;
for all arose from the want of an executive government. . . .

In every case, I must repeat (for I must repeat my principle), where
taxes cannot be laid, or some expedient resorted to of the same nature
and effect with taxes, it certainly does not seem possible to carry on any
system of resistance against invading armies. It is in vain to say that the
food and clothing exists in the country, if the state cannot by some mode
of taxation, or seizure, or confiscation, get possession of them, and convert them to the use of the soldier who wants them. Certainly the pages
of the American historians, and the letters of Washington himself show

very plainly how extreme is the hazard, how cruel are the difficulties, to which every cause must be exposed, when the executive government is too weak, when the leaders of the general emotion are not intrusted with proper powers to supply those who fight in the public cause with the proper means of fighting—with tents, with clothing, with ammunition, and food; and when such men, in those ebbings of the spirit and fluctuations of the resolution, to which all men must be exposed who have been highly wrought up by their feelings, when such men have to compare their own forlorn, desolate, helpless, and unworthy situation with all the pride, and pomp, and circumstance which may in the meantime belong to the armies of their enemy. I need not allude further to the letters of Washington, to make out to you the extent and intolerable nature of these privations and difficulties. The truth is that a considerable portion of the very extraordinary merit of Washington, as I have before stated, depends on this very point, and how he could keep his officers and his men in any tolerable state of good humour, or spirits, or discipline, amid the privations and wretchedness they had to suffer, in such a climate as that of America; how he could maintain even the appearance of an army before an army so accommodated and appointed as was that of England, must appear perfectly inexplicable to those who consider what the human mind is, and what the circumstances were by which not only the courage of the American soldier, but qualities of the mind and temper far more rare than courage, and of more difficult attainment, were tried to the utmost, day after day, and year after year.

Famine . . . was more than once in the camp. Washington saw his best officers throwing up their commissions; troops that could not be tempted by the enemy to desert were yet in a state of mutiny; all were suffering and all were complaining. If they met the enemy in the field, they were for a long period necessarily beaten; if they kept behind their entrenchments, they had no comfort or support but the looks of their general, and their consciousness of the high principles of liberty which ennobled their cause: they must, in the meantime, have supposed the congress totally inattentive to their distresses, totally regardless of those brave men for whose wants it was their proper duty to provide. The real difficulties of the case, the real impossibilities which their legislators were expected to accomplish, were not of a nature to be readily explained to their understandings, even if their minds had been in a state of tranquillity, much less when the result of the explanation was to show them that they were necessarily to be left in a state of nakedness and hunger.

But all these difficulties arose, in the instance before us, from the want of a proper executive power in the state; for this is the lesson to which I must now return, and which you must not forget.

There was no executive government to levy general taxes and convert the produce of the taxes to the proper purpose, nor was there any executive government to seize, as in France, on every thing that was wanted, nor any neighbouring nations on which the armies could be quartered.

But this want of a proper executive government was to be exhibited in a still more striking manner than has yet been alluded to.

Those meritorious and gallant men who successfully resisted the British armies were not only paid in a constantly depreciating paper while the war lasted, but they were never, even in the event, and *after* the war had ceased, properly paid their arrears; and the reader has to take up and lay down the subject of these arrears again and again, as he reads the history of Marshall, to peruse the expostulations of Washington to congress, and then ultimately to see the army break up and dissolve, and the general retire to his farm; to see the poor soldier, impatient to revisit his family and friends, dismissed on his furlough with only some slight portion of his arrears; dismissed never after to return to a state where he could demand his right; the reader is to witness all this till his feelings are wound up to such a pitch of indignation that he is ready to execrate and devote to eternal abomination all the legislators and legislative assemblies, the whole country and continent together, where such base, selfish, faithless ingratitude could be endured for a moment.

It is, however, to be supposed, that no such disgrace to the American name could have sullied the annals of the revolution, if there had existed at the time a proper executive power in the general government, or if it had ever existed afterwards, at any point of time sufficiently near the termination of the war. . . .

xxxvi. AMERICAN WAR

CONGRESS WAS at first only a committee, as I have already noted, an assembly of men delegated from the different states of the American union. They could only *recommend* whatever measures they thought expedient, they could *enforce* none.

For some time these recommendations were received as laws, but at length you will see, as you read the history (you will have collected even from the notices I have been able already to afford you), how miserable were the effects produced by the want of all proper executive power in the government.

At last a sort of confederation was agreed upon, and the congress was avowedly considered as the head of the whole union, acting for and representing all the different states of the continent. This confederation may be called the second stage of the revolutionary government of America.

But still no proper executive power was given even to this confederation, and nothing could be more unfavourable to the best interests of the country than to leave the confederated government so weak in executive power, and in fact thus to set up an assembly to act the part of a government, and leave it in the meantime at the mercy of thirteen other distinct sovereigns, each exercising the real powers of government in different provinces of the same country.

Yet such was the fact, and for some years continued to be the fact, in a manner that really exercises not a little the patience and good humour of any one who sits at a distance and reads the history of these events.

To any such person, this celebrated question of the federal government, that is, the question whether there should be a general government for the whole continent, appears, I had almost ventured to say, no question at all; however, it must have agitated America at the time, and continued to agitate America long after. To suffer thirteen republics to arise, to quarrel among each other, to destroy each other's interests, to be incapable of any connexion with the rest of the world, rather than combine the whole, by some general government, into a great community that might, in the progress of things, become a mighty nation, is a proposition so monstrous and extravagant, that I know not how it is to be looked upon as any other than the most important specimen which the history of the world affords of the influence of local feelings, long-established associations, and all those partial views and jealousies which in parishes, corporations, and public meetings we see so often occur, and which are always so justly the ridicule and scorn of every intelligent member of the community.

It must be supposed, indeed, out of that common respect which is always due to the opinions of others, that the principles of liberty were, somehow or other, considered as involved in the question: and this was certainly the case. The antifederalists reasoned, for instance, each in their particular state, after the following manner: that the liberties of that state would be endangered by being committed to the guardianship of a general legislature, acting at a distance, and with no particular regard for its criticisms or complaints; that this general legislature must have a president, this president a senate, and that he must even have a court, executive officers, &c. &c.; that, in short, the continent of America would be exposed to all the calamities (such they thought them) of a king, an aristocracy, a regular army, as in the old governments of Europe.

But if such be their reasonings, as they certainly were, this I hold to be of itself a lesson for all those who love liberty, and who would extend its blessings to their country. Men are not to be pedants in liberty, any more than in virtue. Though they are not to be oppressed by tyrants, they must at least be governed by their fellow-men. The great principles of independence in the heart of man are to be cherished and upheld; but order, prosperity, the purposes of society, must be accomplished. The many must delegate the government of themselves to the few. Control, executive power, must be lodged somewhere; and the question is not, as the friends of liberty sometimes suppose, how the executive power can be made sufficiently weak, but only how it can be made sufficiently strong, and yet brought within the influence of the criticism of the community; i. e. in other words, how it can secure the people from themselves, and yet be rendered properly alive to feelings of sympathy and respect for them, and alive also to the obligations of justice and good faith, and to sentiments of honour.

This, indeed, is a problem in the management of mankind not easily to be solved; but it is the real problem—the proper problem, to exercise the patriotism of wise and virtuous men; and such men are not, from the difficulty of it, to rush headlong into any extremes, either of authoritative, arbitrary government on the one hand, or mere democracy on the other.

It was so late almost as the year 1789, before the people of influence in America could be brought even by all their experience of the evils of inefficient government, properly to interest themselves in, what was to them, the most important question of all others—the formation of some general government for the whole continent. The confederation, it was seen, came not sufficiently within this description (the confederation to which I have just alluded, and called the second stage of the revolutionary government of America).

The mind of Washington had evidently been long agitated upon the subject. It appears from his letters, that at one period he was in a state of considerable despair at the situation of his country; and "it was painful to him," he said, "in the extreme, to be obliged to think, that after the war had terminated so advantageously for America, wisdom and justice should be still wanting to its people; that after they had confederated as a nation, they should still be afraid to give their rulers sufficient powers to order and direct their affairs—rulers placed in such very particular circumstances of transient, delegated, and responsible authority."

At length an effort was made, and this effort was ultimately successful. You will see the particulars in Marshall. But the difficulties that opposed themselves are very edifying; a few of these particulars are the following:—

It happened in 1785, that the provinces of Virginia and Maryland had to form an agreement relative to their own commercial interests; and from the settlement of these, they proceeded to propose, to all the states of America, the consideration of their *joint* interests as a *commercial* nation. This at length ripened into a scheme for assembling a general convention to revise the Articles of Confederation: in a word to form some general government for the continent, not only to comprehend its commercial concerns, but every other concern.

A convention met at Annapolis, but it consisted only of delegates from five states. The result was a recommendation for another convention at Philadelphia in 1787.

Now the question was whether this convention would ever meet. If it did meet, whether the thirteen independent states, or republics, would forego the pleasure, and privileges, and pride of separate sovereignty, for the good of the continent, and their own good, properly understood. The probability was that they would not. In the meantime, the mind of Washington, and of all wise and good men, was in a state of the utmost gloom and anxiety. It was evident that the recommendation for a convention to form a new government should have come from *congress* (from the confederated government already existing), not from any particular state, like Virginia or Maryland; and the convention, if met, could not be considered as a legal meeting. But again, it was sufficiently evident, that if some efficient government was not soon established, the licentiousness of the people would very soon terminate in perfect anarchy. Hot-headed, presumptuous, ignorant men were many of them (particularly the young) indisposed to all control whatever, and the critical situation of things was extremely increased by the number of persons who owed money, and who could see no hope or comfort for themselves, but in the absence of all the obligations of order and law.

At length commotions agitated all New England; and in Massachusetts a positive insurrection against all government actually took place. Washington wrote to his friend, Colonel Humphries, "For God's sake tell me what is the cause of all these commotions; do they proceed from licentiousness, British influence, real grievances?" "From the *information* I have received," said the colonel, "I should attribute them to all the three; but it rather appears to me, that there is a licentious spirit prevailing among many of the people, a levelling principle, a desire of change, and a wish to annihilate all debts, public and private."

General Knox said, "that high taxes were the ostensible cause of the commotions, but not the real. The insurgents never paid any, or but little taxes; they see the weakness of government; they feel at once their own poverty, compared with the opulent, and their own force; and they will use the latter to remedy the former. Their creed is (there is always one of some kind or other), that the property of the United States has been protected from confiscation by the joint exertions of all, and therefore ought to be common—ought to belong to all."

A majority of the people of Massachusetts was described by Colonel Lee after the manner of General Knox, as in open opposition to the government. "Some of the leaders avow," says he, "the subversion of it to be their object, together with the abolition of debts, the division of property, and a reunion with Great Britain. In all the eastern states the same temper prevails more or less."

"The picture you exhibit," replied Washington, "and the accounts that are published, exhibit a melancholy verification of what our transatlantic foes have predicted; and of another thing, which is perhaps still more to be regretted, and is yet more unaccountable, that mankind, when left to themselves, are unfit for their own government. I am mortified beyond expression, I am lost in amazement, when I behold what intrigue, the interested view of desperate characters, ignorance and jealousy of the *minor* part of our fellow citizens, are capable of effecting; for it is hardly to be supposed that the great body of the people can be so short sighted."

But in the midst of all the perturbations of the mind of Washington, the even tenor of its justice never forsook it, and even at this fearful moment, his letter gives a lesson to all the governments of the earth. "Know," says he, "precisely what the insurgents aim at; if they have real grievances, redress them, if possible, or acknowledge the justice of them, and your inability to do it in the present moment. If they have *not* real grievances, employ the force of government against them at once. If this is inadequate, all will be convinced that the superstructure is bad, and wants support. To be more exposed in the eyes of the world, and more contemptible than we already are, is hardly possible."

Such were Washington's sentiments, and in the history you will see that it was found necessary to subdue the insurgents by force. "But the most important effect of this unprovoked rebellion," says Marshall, "was the deep conviction it produced of the necessity of enlarging the powers of the general government, and the direction of the public mind to-wards the convention . . . that was to assemble at Philadelphia. At last it was declared in *congress* to be expedient, that a convention should be held to render the federal constitution adequate to the exigencies of government, and the preservation of the union."

This recommendation, which legalized the original scheme, added to the consideration of the rebellion, inclined at length the states of New England to favour the measure and at the time and place appointed, the representatives of twelve states assembled (Rhode Island was the exception). Washington was elected president, and the doors were closed—an important meeting for America. On the great principles which should constitute the basis of their system, not much contrariety of opinion is understood to have prevailed; but more than once there was reason to fear, that all would have been lost, by the rising up of the body without effecting the object for which it was assembled. At length the high importance of the union prevailed over local interests; and in September, 1787, the constitution was presented to the consideration of the different states of the whole continent.

But neither the intrinsic merits of the scheme of government, nor the weight of character by which it was supported (Franklin, Washington, and others), gave assurance that it would be ultimately received. Many individuals, it seems, of influence and talents, were desirous of retaining the sovereignty of the states unimpaired, and reducing the union to an alliance between thirteen independent nations. Many thought that a real opposition of interests existed between these different parts of the continent; many could identify themselves with their own state governments, but considered the government of the United States as in some respects *foreign*. Many thought that power must be abused, and were therefore persuaded, they said, that the cradle of the federal constitution would be the grave of republican liberty. Every faculty of the mind was strained on the subject of the proposed constitution to procure its reception or rejection. To decide the interest in question, men of the best talents of the several states were assembled in their respective conventions. So balanced were the parties in some of them, that even after the subject had been discussed for a considerable time, the fate of the constitution could scarcely be conjectured. In many instances, the majority in its favour was very small; in some, even of the adopting states, it is scarcely to be doubted, a majority of the people were in opposition; in all of them, the numerous amendments which were proposed, show that a dread of dismemberment, not an approbation of the system, had induced an acquiescence in it.

At length the conventions of nine (and subsequently of eleven states) assented to and ratified the constitution; and this most important question, on which it was so difficult to obtain unanimity (and which it was therefore so perilous to agitate), was thus at last settled in favour (as it must surely be thought) of America. Washington was unanimously elected president, and on the 30th of April, 1789, delivered his first speech to the Senate and House of Representatives. . . .

A love for civil liberty is so respectable at all times, and when the friends of civil liberty in any country make mistakes, those mistakes are of such importance, and operate so unfavourably to this first of national blessings, that you cannot be too well prepared against the errors into which men may fall on subjects of this nature. You cannot be rendered too expert in detecting the fallacies of popular reasonings on such questions; in seeing the manner in which *statements* may be exaggerated by feelings, honourable as well as base; the manner in which principles the most noble may be insisted upon with a disregard to *particular* circumstances, till they become subversive of themselves.

The mistakes of those who are friendly to harsh government and arbitrary power are seldom of any fatal effect to their particular cause, for their measures are still only more or less arbitrary; no advantage can commonly be hence obtained against the general cause of arbitrary power; but it is not so with the friends of the liberties of mankind. Do they relax their principles or exertions; are they careless or inert? The ground they desert is instantly occupied by their opponents, and cannot afterwards be recovered. Do they urge their principles and exertions too far; are they too active and impassioned? Their measures lead to inconvenience or calamity, to some injurious disturbance of the political machine, and moderate men join the side of their opponents. Their injudicious attempts to advance the public good are reprobated, and they are themselves accused of factious selfishness, or ridiculed for enthusiasm and folly.

The cause of civil liberty has to depend, not only on the virtues, but on the wisdom of mankind; arbitrary power, only on their necessities. The advocates for the one have always to prove, first, that their own intentions are pure; and, secondly, that their measures are calculated to advance the happiness of the community: the supporters of the other have only to show, that they are securing its peace and order: and thus it happens, as I have so repeatedly intimated in the course of these lectures, that civil liberty is of all things the most perishable and delicate; arbitrary rule, on the contrary, the most hardy and indestructible. . . .

I cannot go into the detail of the merits of Washington. In the course of his administration he had to assert the constitutional rights of the executive power against the House of Representatives. In the year 1794, he had to issue his proclamations, call forth the militias, and put down by force (every lenient measure having been tried in vain) a positive insurrection in Pennsylvania, and he had continued to maintain the proper exercise of authority, the principles of peace, of national justice, and of civil liberty, till, amid the wild effusions of virulence and folly, he was at last himself accused even of peculation, and of plundering the public in the discharge of his office: it was even thought necessary that the Secretary of the Treasury should produce his accounts.

The period, however, at length arrived when Washington thought he might retire; when the situation of America allowed him, as he conceived, to consult his own inclinations. As the last service he could offer, he drew up a valedictory address, in which he endeavoured to impress upon his countrymen those great political truths which had been the guides of his own administration, and which could alone, in his opinion, form a sure and solid basis for the happiness, the independence, and the liberty of America. This composition is not unworthy of him, for it is comprehensive, provident, affectionate, and wise. You will conceive the topics of it: gratitude to his countrymen for their confidence and support on every occasion: the necessity and the advantages of the federal system, and of a government as strong as was consistent with the perfect security of liberty. "Liberty," he observed, "was little else than a name, where the government is too feeble to withstand the enterprises of faction, to confine each member of society within the limits prescribed by the laws, and to maintain all in the secure and tranquil enjoyment of the rights of person and property; that, however useful might be the spirit of party [and he thought it might be useful in governments of a monarchical kind, and to keep alive the spirit of liberty], the contrary was the case in governments purely elective; that of the dispositions and habits which lead to political prosperity, religion and morality were the indispensable supports; that a volume could not trace all their connexion with private and public felicity; and that, whatever might be conceded to the influence of refined education on minds of peculiar structure, reason and experience both forbade men to expect that national morality could prevail in exclusion of religious principle."

He insisted that good faith and justice were to be observed to all nations. "Can it be," said he, "that Providence has not connected the permanent felicity of a nation with its virtue?" Respecting the conduct of America to the nations of Europe, his advice was impartiality, neutrality; to have as little political connexion as possible. It is but painful to observe his description of our European nations. "Why," says he, "entangle our peace and prosperity in the toils of European ambition, rivalship, interest, humour, or caprice?"

"The sentiments of veneration," says his biographer, "with which his address was generally received, were manifested in almost every part of the union. Some of the state legislatures directed it to be inserted in their journals, and nearly all of them passed resolutions expressing their respect for the person of the president, their high sense of his exalted services, and the emotions with which they contemplated his retirement from office."

I must conclude my account of Washington by observing that the behaviour of France made it necessary for America to disturb this great man once more in his retirement, and to place him at the head of her military force. Washington indeed expected that favourable alteration in the conduct of France which afterwards took place; but he lived not to see it; dying in December, 1799, after a short illness, and resigning his spirit, with a calm and untroubled mind, to the disposal of that Almighty Being in whose presence he had acted his important part, and to whose kind providence he had so often committed in many an anxious moment, in the cabinet and in the field, the destinies of his beloved country. He was not, he said, "afraid to die."

To the historian, indeed, there are few characters that appear so little to have shared the common frailties and imperfections of human nature; there are but few particulars that can be mentioned even to his disadvantage. It is understood, for instance, that he was once going to commit an important mistake as a general in the field; but he had at least the very great merit of listening to Lee (a man whom he could not like, and who was even his rival), and of *not* committing the mistake. Instances may be found where perhaps it may be thought that he was decisive to a degree that partook of severity and harshness, or even more; but how innumerable were the decisions which he had to take! how difficult and how important, through the eventful series of twenty years of command in the cabinet or the field! Let it be considered what it is to have the management of a revolution, and afterwards the maintenance of order. Where is the man that in the history of our race has ever succeeded in attempting successively the one and the other? not on a small scale, a petty state in Italy, or among a horde of barbarians, but in an enlightened age, when it is not easy for one man to rise superior to another, and in the eyes of mankind—

A kingdom for a stage,
And monarchs to behold the swelling scene.

The plaudits of his country were continually sounding in his ears, and neither the judgment nor the virtues of the man were ever disturbed. Armies were led to the field with all the enterprise of a hero, and then dismissed with all the equanimity of a philosopher. Power was accepted, was exercised, was resigned, precisely at the moment and in the way that duty and patriotism directed. Whatever was the difficulty, the trial, the temptation, or the danger, there stood the soldier and the citizen, eternally the same, without fear, and without reproach, and there was the man who was not only at all times virtuous, but at all times wise.

The merit of Washington by no means ceases with his campaigns; it becomes, after the peace of 1783, even more striking than before; for the same man who, for the sake of liberty, was ardent enough to resist the power of Great Britain and hazard every thing on this side the grave, at a later period had to be temperate enough to resist the same spirit of liberty, when it was mistaking its proper objects and transgressing its appointed limits. The American Revolution was to approach him, and he was to kindle in the general flame; the French Revolution was to reach him and to consume but too many of his countrymen, and his "*own etherial mould, incapable of stain, was to purge off the baser fire victorious.*" But all this was done: he might have been pardoned, though he had failed amid the enthusiasm of those around him, and when liberty was the delusion; but the foundations of the moral world were shaken, and not the understanding of Washington.

To those who must necessarily contemplate this remarkable man at a distance, there is a kind of fixed calmness in his character that seems not well fitted to engage our affections (constant superiority we rather venerate than love), but he had those who loved him (his friends and his family), as well as the world and those that admired.

As a ruler of mankind, however, he may be proposed as a model. Deeply impressed with the original rights of human nature, he never forgot that the end, and meaning, and aim of all just government was the happiness of the people, and he never exercised authority till he had first taken care to put himself clearly in the right. His candour, his patience, his love of justice were unexampled; and this, though *naturally* he was not patient—much otherwise, highly irritable.

He therefore deliberated well, and placed his subject in every point of view before he decided; and his understanding being correct, he was thus rendered, by the nature of his faculties, his strength of mind, and his principles, the man of all others to whom the interests of his fellow creatures might with most confidence be intrusted; that is, he was the first of the rulers of mankind.

The American Revolution is a great epoch in the history of the world, and nothing but the appearance of the French Revolution, so fitted from its tremendous circumstances and unknown consequences, to sweep away every thing else from the curiosity and anxieties of mankind, could have made men insensible, as they may now be, to an event in itself so striking and important. By the American Revolution the foundations of a new empire are laid, immense in extent, unrivalled in natural advantages, and at a safe distance from the hostilities of the old world; a new empire is to begin its course where other empires have ended, with all the intellectual, moral, and religious advantages, which other empires have only attained during the time that has elapsed since the records of history began. A receptacle is now opened for every human being, of whatever country, and whatever be his disposition or fortunes, opinions, or genius. What is to be the result of such an admixture and collision of all personal qualities and intellectual endowments?

The government too is founded not only on a popular basis, but on a basis the most popular that can well be conceived. It must even be confessed that in America is to be made a most novel and important experiment, and it is this:—with how small a portion of restraint and influence the blessings of order and Christianity can be administered to a large community. It must be observed, indeed, that this experiment is to be made under such particular advantages of a new country as must always prevent America from being a precedent for older states and empires. This is true; yet, to the reasoners of after ages, it will be useful to learn from the event what reasonably may be expected from mere human nature when placed in the *most favourable* situation, and what it is that government may properly attempt to do for mankind, and what not. This I think will hereafter be shown when all the attendant circumstances have been properly balanced and considered. What, however, will be the result?

I am much disposed to offer this subject to your reflections, and therefore, as a conjecture, though an obvious one, I should say (though I cannot allude to what may be said of a contrary nature) that the great event to be expected is that this empire should break up into two or more independent states or republics, and that at some distant period the continent of America may be destined to exhibit all the melancholy scenes of devastation and war, which have so long disgraced the continent of Europe.

This, however, must be considered as the grand calamity and failure of the whole; it can only arise from a want of strength in the federal government; i. e. from the friends of liberty not venturing to render the executive power sufficiently effective.

This is the common mistake of all popular governments: in governments more or less monarchical the danger is always of an opposite nature.

In the meantime, I know not how any friend to his species, much less any Englishman, can cease to wish with the most earnest anxiety for the success of the great experiment to which I have alluded, for the success of the Constitution of America. I see not, in like manner, how any friend to his species, much less any American, can forbear for a moment to wish for a continuance of the Constitution of England; that the Revolution of 1688 should for ever answer all its important purposes for England, as the Revolution of 1776 has hitherto done for America. What efforts can be made for the government of mankind so reasonable as these—a limited monarchy and a limited republic? Add to this that the success of the cause of liberty in the two countries cannot but be of the greatest advantage to each, a limited monarchy and a limited republic being well fitted by their comparison and separate happiness, each to correct the peculiar tendencies to evil which must necessarily be found in the other.

Successful therefore be both, and while the records of history last, be they both successful! that they may eternally hold up to mankind the lessons of practical freedom, and explain to them the only secret that exists of all national prosperity and happiness, the sum and substance of which must for ever consist in mild government and tolerant religion; i. e. (rationally understood) in civil and religious liberty.

Mark the difference between Europe and Asia. What is it, what has it ever been? Slavery in the one, and freedom in the other.

Take another view more modern and more domestic. Mist is in the valley, and sterility is on the mountain of the Highlander; his land is the land of tempest and of gloom, but there is intelligence in his looks and gladness in his song. On the contrary, incense is in the gale, and the laughing light of Nature is in the landscape of the Grecian island; but

> *Why do its tuneful echoes languish,*
> *Mute but to the voice of anguish?*

Yet where was it that once flourished the heroes, the sages, and the orators of antiquity? What is there of sublimity and beauty in our moral feelings, or in our works of art, that is not stamped with the impression of their genius?

Give civil and religious liberty, you give every thing; knowledge and science, heroism and honour, virtue and power; deny them, and you deny every thing: in vain are the gifts of nature: there is no harvest in the fertility of the soil; there is no cheerfulness in the radiance of the sky; there is no thought in the understanding of man; and there is in his heart no hope: the human animal sinks and withers; abused, disinherited, stripped of the attributes of his kind, and no longer formed after the image of his God.

Lectures
on
the History
of
the French Revolution

1. LOUIS XIV

Louis XIII came to the crown at the age of nine, and, though the son of the great Henry, remained through life only a fit object of tutelage. Louis XIV became king when only five years old. So that it is the history of the first favourites, and it is the reigns of Richelieu and Mazarin that we are to read, not of the kings of France. . . .

Richelieu, who first appears, is evidently fitted for a scene like this in many most important respects; but he either did not comprehend the whole of his high office, or did not live to perform it. The first supposition seems nearest the truth; his objects were the grandeur of France and the force of the monarchy. The permanent happiness of the great mass of the community was only secondary, if indeed it occurred at all. His great merit was that power of genius, which rules every thing around it apparently with or without the necessary means; his great fault, the want of real patriotism and enlightened benevolence. He, however, surveyed the situation of his country, had his objects, and accomplished them. He could be at no loss to perceive that abroad the great power opposed to France was the house of Austria; that at home the executive authority was constantly thwarted or controlled, and would always continue to be so, if the princes of the blood and the nobles were not broken down and subdued. And to Richelieu it must have appeared, that neither the house of Austria nor the nobles could be reduced to any tolerable state of inferiority, unless the Huguenots were first crushed; a powerful body, who could be practised upon by both, and between whom and the court there was a never-failing source of mutual jealousy and hostility in the difference of their religious tenets. Such must have been the views and reasonings of Richelieu, and therefore, without troubling himself about principles or rights, and with no other means but the resources of his own genius, and the authority which belonged to him as the representative of the crown, no leader of armies or military conqueror, he performed the achievements of those who are. He supported the Protestants in Germany, while he subdued the Protestants in France; he broke the force of the house of Austria abroad, and of the nobles at home; awed the legislative bodies, the parliaments, and all the functionaries of the state; dissipated, terrified, and subjected to his will the intriguers, the courtiers, the generals, the princes of the blood, the nobility, the queen consort, the queen mother, and the very king he served; imprisoned, ruined, proscribed, or brought to the scaffold every person of authority or respect who could be opposed to him; and, on the whole, must be considered as the greatest example of the controlling powers of a single mind in the history of any civilized country.

Peter the Great, when he visited France, embraced his statue in a transport of admiration. We may understand this in the Tamer of Russians; but it is difficult, after all, to consider Richelieu as a patriot, or the enlightened benefactor of France; he cleared away the ground, and this was no doubt a great achievement, for any edifice to be hereafter erected for the happiness of his country, but he erected none himself: he left nothing behind him but the royal authority. . . .

Had another minister succeeded with powers of genius like his own, and animated with a generous patriotism, it is possible that during the feebleness of Louis XIII and the minority of Louis XIV some provisions might have been made for the proper management of the powers and principles of the constitution, for the States-General, the parliaments, and the various acknowledged authorities of that great kingdom, and that England might not have been the only country in the world where the civil and religious liberties of mankind were to be found successfully established, amid the ruins of the papal power and of the feudal system, at the close of the seventeenth century. But no such happiness awaited France or Europe, for it was Mazarin who succeeded; a minister who assisted to build up the national grandeur of France (according to the general notions of national grandeur), and that with more skill and success than were at the time acknowledged, but not a minister with a genius like Richelieu, still less with a benevolence that could meditate upon the political situation of a great people; still less with the understanding that could revive the energies of a free constitution. . . .

Louis finished the work which Richelieu had so powerfully begun; he stepped at once, while yet a youth of fourteen, into the place which that extraordinary man had so prepared for his reception; and this great nation, most unfortunately for itself and for the world, seems from that moment to have identified its own dignity and happiness with the personal authority and aggrandisement of the monarch on the throne.

The great object on which the eyes of Europe were turned, for nearly half a century, was Louis XIV: and on this account, not only the political but even the personal character of the monarch has become a subject of history, and as such must be studied.

In like manner, a very great interest belongs to the lives and characters, the qualities and talents, of the statesmen, the generals, the men of science and literature, who adorned this remarkable age.

The subject, therefore, in all its relations, is very copious. It has attracted the genius of the celebrated Voltaire, and has given occasion to one of his most agreeable and admired productions. If in the general subject, of the reign of Louis, the literature connected with it be included, it may occupy your attention to any possible extent; and it becomes my province, as usual, to mention such works, not as *may*, but as *must* be read; and to attempt, at the same time, to give some faint description of the general importance that belongs to the whole.

But there is another reason which induces me to recommend this part of history to your consideration. It is this: the European forms of government, though originally founded on principles more or less popular, have in general lost their public assemblies, and degenerated into arbitrary monarchies; monarchies, no doubt, very easily to be distinguished from the monarchies of the East; but to be distinguished also from that particular monarchy established in our own island. Now to me it appears, that Louis XIV and his court, the French monarchy and its establishments, the king, the courtiers, and the nobles, the fleets and the armies, the laws and the police, public edifices and institutions, the arts, the sciences, the literature of France, at this renowned period, form altogether, not indeed a fair general specimen, but the most favourable specimen that can be well conceived of an arbitrary government founded upon the European model, but existing without any proper representative bodies of the people. . . .

The court of Louis XIV must always be considered as a very remarkable phenomenon in the history of the civilization of mankind; such, we may say, were our fellow-creatures once, in the most distinguished portion, at the time of improving Europe, and what a curious spectacle, it may surely be added, is here displayed! under what strange, and often whimsical forms, does our common nature here appear! our vanities, our frailties, and our follies, our noble qualities, our heroism, and our virtues, our genius, our religious feelings, all that is great in our composition, and all that is little, under what extraordinary aspects are they here presented! Who can wonder that the memoirs connected with these scenes should never want an interest, and to this hour should not want an interest to the readers in fashionable life; and even, if a real speculator on human nature, to the philosopher in the shade. But with reference to this new edition of St. Simon, the great misfortune is that it is now extended to twenty volumes, and I have therefore to observe to you with some satisfaction, that to each chapter there is a very good index, and by this means a selection of the topics that are most interesting may easily be made. The impression that was given me by the former work has been now renewed and extremely strengthened. What my first impression was, you will see in the next lecture; from the present work, what I have chiefly brought away is a more strong sense of the misery and ruin of France, produced by the victories of Marlborough and Eugene; and of the terror and subdued state not only of Louis and his court, but still more of the common people of Paris, and, at the same time, of all intelligent men in the kingdom. Again, a very strong confirmation is afforded of the accuracy of the views of the Whig party in England. All this appears very strongly marked in the present production. And again, the minute and more endless detail of the new work makes more than ever striking the extraordinary system of etiquette that was established, and all the faults and prejudices not only of Louis, the monarch, but of St. Simon, the peer of France, himself. . . .

II. LOUIS XIV

Louis was one of those rulers of the earth, who became a king while an infant, whose education was most defective, who was left ignorant, according to the account of St. Simon, to a degree that is quite astonishing; who was surrounded, not only by courtiers and sycophants, but by a nation, whose character, if analyzed, seems never to ascend beyond the merit of the second degree I have mentioned, the love of true glory, not often so high; whose character is much more generally moulded by the mere love of praise, of praise however procured.

As Louis was, unfortunately for the world, possessed also of a fine constitution and a handsome person, his moral improvement was rendered still more impossible; and the result, as seen in St. Simon, was precisely all that a speculator on human nature would have expected.

Eternally uneasy, and in action, as every man will be, who (though on a smaller scale) thinks of nothing but praise; eternally finding, or looking to find, an audience, before whom he might exhibit his performances; eternally at his levees or on his terraces, a sort of posture-master; the very rising and going to bed was with Louis a sort of drama; through the whole of the royal day he had his exits and his entrances; and whether he rode or walked, or dined or dressed, the whole world was supposed to be present, and the hero of the piece was Louis. Even at the hour of prayer, it was the *grand monarque* that was at his devotions; and no ideas, however awful, however overwhelming, could sweep away from his mind, even for a moment, the tinsel trumpery of human grandeur.

But Louis not only desired to live upon applause, but was enabled to do so. The applause was always ready; he had only to look and to receive it; and in the total absence of all that moral discipline which other human beings more or less find in the looks and words of those around them, no wonder that he became ungovernably selfish, a ridiculous egotist, so as even to join in singing his own panegyrics; no wonder that he was a slave to his passions, and that he at last conceived not only that his own people, but that the world itself was intended merely to furnish out materials for what he was pleased to denominate, his glory.

It is remarkable how completely the French nation gave in to these delusions, how thoroughly they identified themselves with their monarch. They had lost their States-General, they had no houses of representation to convey any worthier images of the nation, or to furnish them with the materials of more dignified reflection; they had just emerged from the horrors of religious wars and the miseries of domestic confusion and dispute. Independent of these political circumstances, their own merits and faults, their wisdom and their follies, were all those of the young king; their virtues the same, the same their vices. Praise is with them to be acquired; if by proper means, well, but at all events to be acquired. The cause, therefore, of both was common; their sympathies with their monarch, their excuses for his conduct were always ready; and their property, their lives, their talents, and their genius, all became the instruments of his power, and were wielded at his pleasure to the purposes of his own gratification and aggrandizement.

And this leads me to the second aspect under which he is to be viewed. What was he to his people? To them he has often been considered as a benefactor; at least it has been thought that France, as a great kingdom, is under lasting obligations to him. This may be admitted, but must then be understood in a certain limited sense.

For instance, the religious and civil wars, and long years of contest, hatred, and bloodshed, of private wrongs, and public executions, had left the French nation fierce and ferocious. Louis had the merit of civilizing them. This he did in the first place, as has been generally observed, by the arts and sciences which he encouraged and protected. But, again, he must have produced the same salutary effect in another way, one not so generally noticed. For instance, he constantly exhibited in his own person, and in the persons of his ministers and officers, the whole power of the state, regularly asserted, exercised, and diffused all over the community; maintaining, everywhere, order, tranquillity, and the due execution of the laws of civil and criminal justice. On both accounts, therefore, he contributed to civilize France. This is the most favourable point of view in which Louis can be surveyed. It is very creditable to Louis that, coming to the throne so young, and to a kingdom so situated as France then was, he was yet able to carry on the government without incurring any renewal of domestic confusion, or the apparent domination of any minister, by whose power or genius he was himself eclipsed. Again, under the influence of his personal qualities, the great feudatories of the state became no longer a dangerous description of men, ready to be themselves monarchs, but a mere court noblesse, dependent on the sovereign for their honours, distinctions, and often even their private fortunes. He could

> *Grace with a smile and ruin with a frown.*

Louis, in this respect, followed up, and indeed carried to excess, the original achievement of the great Henry and the triumphs of Richelieu; even the manners of the people were affected; and, on the whole, the kingdom, in every respect, though not without some unfavourable collateral effects, was materially civilized. He had undoubtedly, at the same time, the very important merit of choosing able men for the various departments of the state. And this is not only at all times the best criterion of the merit of every prince, but it is more particularly so of Louis; from whose ignorance, vanity, pride, and impetuosity, no conduct so rational could have been expected.

It happened that during the reign of Louis the most celebrated men appeared that have ever adorned this great kingdom. And as they all seemed to move under the influence of his protection and encouragement, their glory has, in the general apprehension of mankind, been reflected on the monarch. Nor is this entirely unjust; however soberly we may estimate the influence of the great on the talents of those around them, and however powerful the effect, which we may ascribe, in affairs of this nature, to the mere operations of chance, merit, and even considerable merit, must still be left to Louis, when we consider all those very striking and successful exertions of genius and learning which are seen, under his auspices, to have illustrated his age and nation.

This, the great praise of Louis, has been seized upon by one of his panegyrists. "Turenne," says he, "Condé, Luxembourgh, were his generals; Colbert, Louvois, Tourcy, were his statesmen; Vauban, his engineer; Perault constructed his palaces—they were adorned by Le Poussin and Le Brun; Le Notre laid out his gardens; Corneille and Racine wrote his tragedies; Molière, his comedies; Boileau was his poet; Bossuet, Bourdaloue, Massillon, were his preachers. It is in this august assemblage of men, whose fame can never die, that this monarch, whom they acknowledged as their patron and protector, presents himself to the admiration of posterity."

There is certainly something here to arrest us in the career of our censure, after travelling through all the strange and disgraceful disorders of the former reign. We see, at length, a disciplined army, public order, authority everywhere vigilant and resistless; regular government duly administered through all its departments; habits of obedience and loyalty deeply engrafted, and thoroughly introduced into the national character. To these, the solid basis of this system, and of every system of government, must be added the more ornamental part—the paintings, the statues, the splendid vases, the libraries—all the rich and massy furniture, with which the great national edifice, the work of Louis XIV, was adorned; and we thus see, altogether presented to us, that magnificent whole, which so strongly impressed, which so entirely fascinated and overpowered not only the French people, but the people of all the kingdoms of Europe; and if no more remained to be told, the admiration of posterity might not only be demanded for Louis, but allowed. There is, however, much more to be told, and we must not, like the French people themselves at the time, be insensible to the serious faults which so obscured the merits of their *grand monarque*.

The great object of the administration of Louis was, from the first, to suffer nothing of weight or dignity to exist in the state, but what immediately emanated from the throne, or was visibly dependent on his pleasure. He wished himself to direct the marine, the army, and the finances; everywhere to be the spring and principle of every movement. The people were to have no other guardian of their happiness, the empire no other security; his ministers, his generals, no other patron or protector; above all, there was to appear no representative of the national consequence and will but himself. The ancient assemblies of the community, the States-General, were, at all events, not to be summoned. "L'état, c'est moi" was his favourite phrase. He was in his own apprehension, as is very apparent from different passages in his works, a sort of divinity on earth, certainly the representative of the Divinity.

All this was but the result of his inordinate love of distinction, his total selfishness, and the contracted views which had resulted from an education originally defective. To accomplish this monopoly of all power and all consequence was the secret and entire labour of his life on every occasion—at the most frivolous entertainment as at the most important sitting of the cabinet. His ministers were therefore obliged to endeavour to direct his councils by contrivance and stratagem, and to deceive him into a belief that he was himself the origin of the plans which he only adopted. His nobility was to remain continually within the reach of his smiles or frowns, or they lost all their personal influence and weight. It was a sufficient accusation that he "never saw them," as he termed it.

Not only the nobility, but every person was to be kept in a state of constant subjection to his criticisms by an extensive system of espionage, which descended to the most disgraceful expedients, and entered into the detail of all the intrigues and silly adventures of the metropolis; he had a police that kept every person and every concern within his view; every being was to be fixed in his own exact station and office, and the movements of every mind and body that approached the court, or enjoyed any distinction there or elsewhere, were to be combined into a sort of harmony with those of the monarch, by the most widely extended and duly adjusted system of form and etiquette that was probably ever devised or executed: Louis, and the court which I have thus described, were to meet and parade in palaces, whose extent and magnificence were to rival the romances of the imagination; even Nature herself was to be insulted and overpowered, to achieve the wonders of Versailles; the sums expended are understood to have increased in so frightful a manner that the king at last threw the accounts into the fire; still, however, continuing them. They had reached more than sixty millions of our money; the very roofs of this palace would cover a surface of twenty-five French acres; similar prodigality was exhibited at Marly, and his rage for expensive buildings was quite a characteristic and a most criminal one of his reign. All this was fitted to produce what it did produce, the spectacle which I have already described, as so striking to all Europe, and as so deserving of the curiosity and reflection of every reader of history; the best specimen that can be shown of the court and the administration of an arbitrary monarch, on the European, not Asiatic model, but without any representative bodies of the people, or indeed of the nobility; the spectacle of a great kingdom advanced to a situation in some respects of an enviable, and in most respects of a very imposing appearance;—opulent cities, spacious roads, canals, and ports, and harbours, arsenals and dockyards, every apparatus, naval and military, for attack or defence;—academies, hospitals, public buildings and palaces;—manufactures, arts and sciences;— statesmen, theologians, philosophers, historians, and antiquarians, orators and poets; much of the accommodation, much of the embellishment, all the outward magnificence of civilization. All this is certainly to be found, and gave rise to what was called the Age of Louis XIV; and it seems at first sight too presumptuous to say that all this is still insufficient, to say that civilization can realize something still more valuable to the community, and more dignified to the monarch; yet such is assuredly the truth; and it is no improper indulgence of national pride to say, that in consequence of our public assemblies, and more particularly of our representative assembly, our House of Commons, more, and even far more than all this, striking and splendid as it may be, is undoubtedly to be found in this distinguished island of our own.

iv. LOUIS XV

It will readily be supposed that the opposition of the parliaments to the crown was not confined to religious matters. The finances, it will easily be conceived, were a constant subject of complaint and ill-humour.

The secret of the French constitution, as I must often repeat, lay in the power or right which the parliaments had to deny their sanction to the king's edicts, and therefore to the taxes. The power of thus legalizing the king's taxes would not have been contested with the States-General; but the parliament only claimed as the representative of the States-General, in the intervals of their sittings; and the right was therefore open to dispute.

Now, whether their claim was, or was not, well founded, still, as the right was a great constitutional question, the obvious policy of the crown was to give the parliament as few opportunities as possible of asserting it.

But this could only be done, as far as taxation was concerned, in three modes:

1st, By keeping the expenses of the crown and court as low as possible.

2dly, By abstaining from foreign wars.

Or, lastly, by persuading or obliging the clergy or nobility to pay their shares of the public burthen.

Now, it was impossible for any ministers of finance to produce any reform in the first two modes of diminishing the public expense; no system of economy, no system of peace, and avoidance of foreign wars, was possible. But neither, on the other hand, was the third mode possible; for neither the nobility nor the clergy had virtue to do what it was both their duty and ultimate interest to do, to pay their shares of the public burthen. The finances, therefore, got at length into irremediable embarrassment. The situation of a minister of finance may be easily conceived, and is not ill-described by Lacretelle.* "If one of these unhappy functionaries," says he, "endeavoured to ascertain the real situation of the public revenue, he was disgraced, he was in danger if he talked of any existing evil, and ruined if he proposed any remedy. Did he speak of any reduction in the expenses, the court were furious; of any equalizing of the imposts, the parliaments, the clergy, and the nobility were in an uproar; was he exact and methodical in conducting business, the financiers ridiculed him as a man of little mind and of no genius; did he endeavour in his edicts to disguise and conceal the new impositions which he laid, the economists denounced him not only as guilty of oppression, but of the most egregious folly. To escape from difficulties like these, what resource, but to anticipate, from year to year, the coming revenue; and yet what expedient so ruinous?" . . .

Through nearly the whole of the last century, the great kingdom of France has been seen under the direction of cabinets that continued to indulge themselves in every enterprise of ambition and injustice.

* Jean-Charles-Dominique Lacretelle (1766–1855), French journalist and historian.—Ed.

Beginning with a debt to which her revenue was unequal, and persevering still further to accumulate a weight so dangerous to her monarchy; determined always to take the same part in the politics of Europe, and incur the same expenses as if she had been possessed of funds adequate to discharge the interest of her old debts, and even to meet the interest of new ones. Unhappy country, destroying and destroyed! disturbing every potentate and neighbour, and ruled in the meantime by debauched kings, with their impudent mistresses and daring ministers, who could waste not only in wars, but in excesses of every kind of ostentation or of profligacy, the earnings that could be wrung from the hands of peasants, and from the incomes of the laborious and virtuous classes of the community. Continue the picture: the clergy and the nobility, you will remember, are in the meantime seen to refuse their contingents to the general expense; and the hereditary maxim of the privileged orders is to be this—"that they, forsooth, are not to be taxed." Every outrage is in the meantime to be offered to public opinion. The parliaments, the only images of the nation, then constitutionally existing, are to be kept by the court in a continual warfare, sometimes of a religious, sometimes of a financial nature.

v. LOUIS XVI, TURGOT, NECKER

MY FIRST OBSERVATION is a startling one. The French Revolution must be considered as having failed: in every immediate and proper sense of the word, it failed.

No beautiful system of civil and religious liberty was seen to arise in France, and they, who wished well to the happiness of mankind, and who had looked forward to the progressive improvement of the human species, saw swept from their view all the splendid visions on which they had so fondly gazed. What cause for so cruel a disappointment to the expectations of the wise and good? There had been long a conflict between the old opinions and the new; the government was lost in public estimation; the king was without energy, ill fitted for his situation; the privileged orders were too selfish; the patriots too violent; the great military powers of Europe interfered.

Such is a short explanation of this deplorable event—the failure of this great experiment.

It is a great calamity to mankind when the patriots of a country fail; they are the salt of the earth. We are placed by our Almighty Master in a world where nothing can be obtained without enterprise and effort; but the conclusion from the failure of such men is that enterprise and effort are in vain.

It may be, however, useful to allude in such passing manner as the nature of these lectures will admit, to the great scenes of this interesting history, to see what instruction can be reaped from it, and what estimate can be formed of it, asking ourselves what we could have done, what attempted in each different situation, each crisis that will be presented to us. It is easy to blame; of two different courses that might have been pursued, it is easy to see, when one has failed, that the other should have been preferred; but what we are to do is this: we are to try to place ourselves in the situation of those who had alternatives before them, and were obliged to act; we must, above all, try not to judge from the event. Mistakes were no doubt committed, but the great lesson of the whole is the wisdom, the duty in all political affairs, of moderation; a lesson that will be thought by some too trite to be worth the drawing, and by others too tame and uninteresting to be likely to be observed by such absurd and furious beings as mankind are composed of; yet it is the great lesson of the whole, and it is the lesson that by me, at least, must for ever be inculcated. . . .

The young king [Louis XVI] was grave, decorous, sensible, modest, pious, virtuous, and deeply interested in the happiness of his people—such was the young king. Louis, just twenty, was happy to call to his assistance the experience of the Count de Maurepas, a statesman that was old enough to have been a counsellor to Louis XIV. The ministers of Louis XV . . . were dismissed; among them the chancellor Maupeou, who had contrived the destruction of the parliaments. The celebrated Turgot was called into office.

A new system was therefore evidently adopted. Turgot was the favourite of the philosophers, and he was soon removed from the marine, where the old minister had originally thought proper to place him, to the situation of comptroller-general of the finances. You will now remember what I have said of the new opinions. It was in the finances that Turgot was expected to introduce the most important reforms, those to be followed by reforms in the laws, and these again, by reforms in the manners of the country and all the ancient institutions of the monarchy.

Now that such hopes should be entertained not only by men of intelligence, but by the young monarch himself, was highly natural. Benevolence was the ruling passion of his nature; this may assuredly be asserted, and must never through the whole of this history be forgotten; but he was born a king, no doubt, and had his appropriate difficulties and temptations: hitherto we see no mistake. You will find in the notes of Lacretelle an affecting letter from Turgot, addressed to the young king.

"We will have no bankruptcies," said the philosophic minister, "no augmentation of the imposts, no loans. I shall have to combat abuses of every kind; to combat those who are benefited by them, and even the kindness, sire, of your own nature. I shall be feared, hated, and calumniated; but the affecting goodness with which you pressed my hands in yours, to witness your acceptance of my devotion to your service, is never to be obliterated from my recollection, and must support me under every trial."

This letter is surely very creditable to both parties. The minister had said, you will observe, "we will have no bankruptcies"; and I will now stop for a moment to mention, that there is in the community a great looseness of thought upon this subject of a national bankruptcy. You hear people speaking "of a national sponge," of "sweeping away the stocks at once," as if the whole was a castle in the air, which might be made to disappear, and no one be affected.

It is a pity that such light reasoners do not ask themselves what must be the consequence if those who now receive their dividends were to receive them no longer? This is a very short and intelligible question. Do they not know, does not every one know, that they who receive dividends are not so much a few rich capitalists as widows and orphans—the helpless and the unprotected, particularly the female part of the community: the old and the infirm; public institutions of every description; hospitals, places of education; suppose all these without their usual means of support? a partial earthquake or a deluge would in comparison be a trifling calamity.

But to return. The finances were the great point to be considered; the minister had no doubt directed his view to the real difficulty. The revenue, through a long succession of years, had continually fallen short of the expenditure. There could be no repose for the monarch, no real security for his crown, unless some happy alteration could be effected in the management of the finances. . . . The question was what could be attempted, supposing, as was the case, that the minister was enlightened, and the monarch benevolent. Great improvements in the system of taxation; in the nature of the taxes, in the collection of them, in the expenditure of them; again, great reforms in the expenditure of the court; an active and skilful resistance, a sort of war to be waged against abuses of every kind, against profligacy and folly, wherever they might appear; these improvements were possible.

But when all this was done, all this it was evident would be insufficient unless something more could be accomplished.

The fact was that the privileged orders were exempted to a certain degree from the taxes to which the rest of the country was exposed. Now, unless they could be brought to bear their part, no real relief could be afforded to the monarchy. The accumulated deficit, the annual deficit, were each too great.

To accomplish so desirable an end was the great object, was the great hinge on which turned the happiness of the community, the authority of the monarch, the safety of the privileged orders themselves; and unless these orders could be brought to rise superior to their own views of self-interest, and the prejudices of their birth, and even their views of the constitution of their country, there could, in truth, be no chance for the improvement or even the welfare of France, in the state of things which had arisen from the expenses of government on one side, and the prevalence of the new opinions on the other.

Of all this Turgot seems to have been well aware. He had announced himself as decidedly of opinion that an impost must be fairly and equally levied upon proprietors of every description; and certainly this was a doctrine perfectly right and just. What meanness in the privileged orders to resist it! what selfishness, what guilt! but what folly, particularly when the country had evidently begun to inquire and to think! What truth so obvious as this, that nothing can be secure that is not agreeable to the moral feelings of mankind? Still the minister and the monarch were to take into their account the inherent baseness and stupidity of mankind on all such occasions; and the student should himself now consider how, in the situation of the monarch and the minister, he would have endeavoured to procure from the privileged orders so reasonable and so necessary a sacrifice.

It will not be easy for him to determine upon his measure, but certainly he will not, I think, propose the measure that really was adopted—the recall of the parliaments.

If he turns to the reign of Louis XV, he will see in what manner these bodies were superseded and destroyed. But why renew their existence? They were connected with the privileged orders rather than with the king or the people.

Their doctrine had been that a tax could not be legally levied, unless first enregistered by them. What chance for any great scheme of improvement in the finances, such as the minister contemplated, if their consent was first to be made necessary? Their proper office was the administration of justice; other courts had been, on their suppression, erected: what need of their revival?

What but opposition could be expected from them to such measures as intelligent men would have proposed, such as the minister himself no doubt meditated, and as he had probably, already, in the whole or in part, introduced to the consideration of the young monarch. The free commerce of grain, for instance; the suppression of oppressive duties—that on salt, the gabelle; the abolition of the corvées, or the repairing of the roads by the peasantry; the abolition of tyrannical feudal usages; the imposition of a land-tax, from which the nobles and clergy should not be exempt; a more merciful criminal code; a civil code, improved, and throughout the whole of France consistent and every where the same. What hope for projects like these, particularly the last, if they were to pass through the ordeals of the parliaments?

Turgot was well aware how unfavourable to his plans would be the restoration of the parliaments, and he opposed it, as did the minister of war; but the old courtier, the Count de Maurepas, prevailed, and the parliaments were in an evil hour recalled. It is not easy to say what could be the motive with Maurepas, unless jealousy of Turgot; but with the king, at least, it was surely a mistake. The measure was indeed popular— no reason this for its adoption, but rather the contrary. The king was on this account only the more likely to create a power which he could not control; Malesherbes was added to the ministry, a valuable auxiliary to Turgot; but in the event, what was the fate of this minister of reform, of Turgot? Maurepas was not faithful to him; the privileged orders were soon united against him and the parliaments and the clergy forgot their differences, the better to oppose him. The queen committed the mistake of uniting with the old minister and the noblesse against the reformers, as they were called; and when Turgot at length produced his six edicts, a clamour arose, that seemed to indicate that all the very elements of the public safety had been endangered. The five last of these edicts had reference only to the proper management of the interior traffic and business of the metropolis, more particularly the commerce of grain, but the first was the suppression of the abominable corvées; and the roads were, by the new edict, to be repaired, and the expense defrayed by a contribution, from which the privileged orders were *not* to be exempt; hinc illæ lacrymæ—the nobles and the prelates, it seems, considered themselves degraded if they were to contribute to the repair of roads; and they would no doubt have declared that their dignity and their existence, the very rights of property itself, were endangered, if they were now for the first time, they would have said, in the history of the monarchy, to be subjected to the visits of the tax-gatherer. It is in the sentiments and the conduct of these privileged orders, on this and on all similar occasions, former or subsequent, that you are to find *one* of the greatest lessons to be derived from this French Revolution. Nothing, as I must for ever repeat, that is not agreeable to the fair, obvious conclusions of the moral feelings may slumber for years, for ages, but if by any chance they are awakened, the wise and the good will conform to them in time, will conform to them with all possible expedition, will make what sacrifices are necessary, and the truth is that if sacrifices are made early, such sacrifices may be found light and be little felt; not so if delayed; no wisdom, no moral sensibility of this kind, was on *this* occasion shown by the parliaments and the privileged orders, and it never was on any subsequent occasion shown, till too late. They saw not exactly their situation, probably no one in France at the time did; but were they not calling for reforms and sacrifices from the king, from every one but themselves? Was not this at least plain? And was it not plain, also, that the peasants and the public were alone contributing to an expense which they themselves were bound in common justice to share? Were they not taking the business of reform from the king and his ministers, where alone it could be safely lodged, to be undertaken by themselves? And with whose assistance, it may be asked, if they moved not in concert with the king and his masters—with whose assistance, but as in former times of the parliaments, the assistance of the people— the assistance of the people! And this, then, was the expedient of the parliaments and the privileged orders, for the accomplishment of their own, and the happiness and prosperity of the community. In the event, you will see, that the minister Turgot was dismissed, that the excellent Malesherbes retired, and that the nobles, the parliaments, and the clergy were triumphant. But triumphant over whom? Over a benevolent monarch, and a patriotic minister. Turgot soon after died, early in 1781; his epitaph might have been the couplet of the poet:

> *Truths would you teach, or save a sinking land,*
> *All fear, none aid you, and few understand. . . .*

The situation of the king is the great point of curiosity; he is benevolent, and wishes the happiness of his people; he is calm and sensible, and therefore summons to his assistance an ancient counsellor, M. de Maurepas, and at the same time a man then celebrated for his intelligence, and for those more enlarged views which the gradual progress of civilization and knowledge had introduced to the notice of the French nation—M. Turgot. All this Louis does; but Louis was born a king, and had the feelings natural to his birth and situation; he could not mean so to alter the institutions of his country that he should appear to himself to be king no longer; and any philosopher and any patriot that required this of him was unfeeling and unjust. He was surrounded, too, by a court (the queen at his head) who could not be expected to see any merit in any minister or any system that at all disturbed their usual routine of opinions and enjoyments; beside him stood a noblesse and a clergy, among whom many men of intelligence and patriotism might be found; of more, indeed, than could be expected to belong to those bodies in their collective capacity; but the question was, whether those bodies could be persuaded to act with any feeling for the lower orders, with any due sense of the sacrifices that were now required of them; for on this depended the safety of their monarchy, the repose of their king, the real security of themselves. Their organ at this time seemed to be the parliaments, particularly the parliaments of Paris, the members of which had long been engaged in struggles with the crown, appeared to be animated with a wish to save the country from oppression, more particularly from taxation, but seemed ready to unite with the privileged orders in resistance to every measure that the king could propose, if any taxation was thus to reach the privileged orders themselves, as well as the rest of the community.

Now, I ask what more unhappy state of things can be conceived for the monarch? What is he to do, and where is his power? He is quite young; the patriotic minister Turgot would go far greater lengths than could be intelligible to him, than could be agreeable to his other minister, to an old courtier, the experienced friend on whom the king naturally depended, than could be endured by the privileged orders, or thought of with any patience by the court.

What now could the king do? What but endeavour to turn to the best advantage he could the intelligence and sentiments of all concerned, and make such attempts for the welfare of the community as might appear likely to succeed. He therefore proposes the six edicts of Turgot, which I have mentioned, to the parliaments. The privileged orders are in these edicts only required to contribute like the rest of the community to the repair of the roads, nothing more; but no, the edicts are resisted by the parliaments (the privileged orders had taken the alarm). The king then insists upon their being enregistered, and calls a bed of justice.

But the result of the whole is that the patriotic minister is dismissed, and the edicts gradually forgotten. This no doubt the king should not have submitted to; though young, he should have seen that nothing unreasonable had been proposed, and that his patriotic minister must be supported while he was only proposing what was reasonable, and while it was clear that, sooner or later, and in some way or other, sacrifices of their personal interests must be procured from the privileged orders, or the finances fall into the most irremediable confusion, his own happiness be at an end, and possibly even his crown endangered. . . .

It is probable that a monarch not only of benevolence but of decision of character, who would have insisted upon these edicts, and carried his minister through all his difficulties, might thus have prevented the Revolution; if the king could but have seen his danger at so early a period as this, all might have been well; but he did not, nor indeed did any one at the time. He was young and inexperienced, and even if he had speculated more deeply and successfully on his situation, he was not of a temperament to confront and overpower resistance.

All through the history of the Revolution, and from the very first appearance of it, this want of character in the king must be considered as the great misfortune of all; as contributing to its progress and failure, as fatal to his people, and still more fatal to himself.

On this occasion it operated most unhappily, and whatever we may say of the king in his existing situation of youthfulness and ignorance, his counsellors at least are not to be forgiven; nor is he himself, if Turgot, as probably he did, made proper representations to him, and presented to his consideration views that were reasonable, and such as were fitted somewhat to alarm him, anxious and uneasy as he already was. The case before them all, the king included, was simple, the steps few: the finances, for instance, were to be repaired; the immunities, therefore, or the privileged orders were to be disturbed, modified, more or less conceded: this could not be done without a struggle; but it was evident if the king gave up his minister, and retired from this struggle, that the struggle might then come to be, not between the privileged orders and the king, but between them and the community; the king withdrawn from the field, to be rendered insignificant, and perhaps put aside or trampled down amid the chances of the combat.

These are reflections, it may be said, only obvious from the event; the danger, it may, however, be replied, the danger might not be obvious, but the faults that the king was committing, these really were obvious; and he is not to be pardoned for the commission of them. He should have prevented Turgot from producing these edicts, or supported him in them; he did worst of all, he suffered them to be proposed; he made the parliaments, as I have already mentioned, enregister them by a bed of justice, that is, by force; and he then gradually and silently abandoned the minister and the edicts together. But the defects of the character of Louis—for defects he had—were but too important; a want of rational confidence in himself, an unwillingness to rule any one, while born the ruler of millions, born and not created by his own choice, and this is his excuse, and must always be remembered; and positive vices and outrageous faults would have been less fatal to himself and to his country than was this unhappy failing (this want of character) at this singular crisis.

What was to be his situation when both the edicts and the minister were gone? Probity and wisdom, if attempting any opposition to the privileged orders, had evidently no chance at court, even when honoured by his protection. But what hope was there then for the finances, that is, for his own repose, perhaps security? You will easily conceive the situation of the court, and what must necessarily have been the character of any *new* comptroller of the finances. How little agreeable were the sounds of economy, of reform, the total want of all real ability, that must have belonged to any minister that could now undertake, on any opposite system, the post from which Turgot had been driven.

One remark is indeed to be made; the king, amidst all the frivolity and folly, whether grave or gay, that surrounded him, had still his anxieties directed to the right point. He was never at ease about the finances; his attention was still fixed upon them—this is merit and sense. And at last, in a very singular manner, which you will see explained in the histories, a Swiss banker, M. Necker, was called to the administration of them; the old minister, Maurepas, still remaining the minister, and at the head of affairs. The maxim of Turgot was "no new loans and no new impositions." This was tolerably hardy, when the annual deficit was twenty-five millions of livres; but Necker's was even more so, "new loans, and yet no new taxes."

This system might indeed save him and the king from contests with the parliaments, the nobility, and the clergy, but how was the interest of these loans to be paid? By the suppression of offices, Necker would have replied, reforms in the expenditure of the court, in the collection of the taxes, and by all the savings of a very vigilant economy; but economy was apparently a very inadequate resource for a minister of finance, of French finance, to depend upon. The loans, however, succeeded; they were made, and they were registered by the parliaments, though not without difficulty.

But, in the midst of these transactions came on the perilous question of war with England. The North American colonies had declared themselves independent. An opportunity was offered to France of humbling her ancient rival; how was it to be resisted? how, by a French cabinet? by the French people? It is understood that the king, when he signed the treaty with the revolted colonies, could not help saying to the minister, Vergennes, "You will remember, sir, that this is contrary to my opinion." The king was surely right; it was no time for France to engage herself in a war when the finances were already in a state of confusion. She had received no offence from England; had no grounds of interference between her and her colonies; the war was unjust on the part of France, as well as impolitic; either reason should have been sufficient. No doubt it would have been difficult to have preserved a neutrality, and the king would have thus rendered himself unpopular; but his want of firmness on this second great occasion, and the want of honour and good faith to England in the ministers of France, must be considered as having mutually contributed, and most materially, to the Revolution that followed. Dodsley's Annual Register for 1789, opens with a statement of the effects produced upon the affairs of France by her interference in the American contest; the influence attributed to it is very great, and I do not conceive exaggerated. I refer you to the work itself. Those of the young French officers who distinguished themselves in America (La Fayette and others), became afterwards the patriots and heroes of the French Revolution. The appearance of Franklin at Paris was quite an event.

While the war with England continues, the history of this French Revolution seems suspended. Necker is the minister of finance, and is employed in making provision for the expenses of the war by all the possible expedients of economy. This would have surely been but a strange system of finance—loans, and the interest to be paid by particular measures of economy—even if there had been no war, and even if the court had been virtuous and patriotic; but the court was not so; it was giddy, frivolous, and expensive. The king was too easily satisfied with his own privations and sacrifices, and thought that doing this, he had done every thing; and he was too indulgent to the queen and the light troop of pleasure by which she was surrounded. The situation of Necker was indeed deplorable; the apathy of Maurepas, the facility of the king, the caprices and folly of the court. "Never shall I forget," he says in a work he published in 1791, "the long dark staircase of M. de Maurepas, the terror and the melancholy with which I used to ascend it, uncertain of the success of some idea that had occurred to me, likely, if carried into effect, to produce an increase of the revenue; but likely, at the same time, to fall severely, though justly, on some one or other; the address, the expedients, I had to make use of to succeed; the sort of hesitation and diffidence with which I ventured to intermingle in my representations any of those great fundamental truths, those maxims of justice and of right, with which my own heart was animated. I was really like the ancient Sully when he stood surrounded by the young and tittering courtiers of Louis XIII." Victories, it seems, were the hopes of Necker in this unseasonable war; and then an honourable peace, he thought, would open all the world to the French commerce, and the influx from the customs would render other taxes unnecessary.

Necker was popular with the monied men, and carried his loans and his annuities very successfully. They were enregistered, but with some difficulty, by the parliament of Paris. He met there, however, an acute and violent opponent in D'Esprémenil,* who inspired his colleagues, young and old, with an ardour and a boldness like his own; turned the grave legal court of the parliament of Paris into a political assembly, like the House of Commons in England, and at last talked of an appeal to the States-General. The words fell with little effect upon the ear of the public at this moment; but twelve years after, they were the signal of the Revolution.

Opposition of this kind from the parliaments, and many secret misgivings, must no doubt have not a little disquieted the mind of Necker. He meant well to the country, but was in the first place faithful to the king he served. He saw the wonders produced by credit in England. He

---

* Jean Jacques Duval d'Esprémenil (1746–94), who later became a resolute royalist, and was executed in the last days of the Terror.—ED.

had been in that country, and a free government must have appeared to him the secret of the whole.

Publicity of accounts, and representation of the people, these must have occurred to him as the real remedies for all the miseries of the great empire of France; for the disorders of the finances; the oppressions of the people; the vices of the nobility and of the privileged orders; the anxieties and insecurity of the monarch.

But how were such objects to be accomplished or to be approached? The kingdom of France, as you are already aware, was originally composed of a number of small and separate kingdoms, which had gradually been forced or persuaded to accumulate round one great central province. The great merit of Henry IV was that he kept them together; and, during the time of Richelieu and Louis XIV the whole kingdom got consolidated, and became at last one and indivisible; but each province had its laws and its customs; many of them . . . had made distinct bargains with the crown, which were still in full effect; and any rational system of commercial intercourse, certainly any system of uniform jurisprudence, seemed impossible. . . . How could a minister like Necker, a Protestant from Geneva, reduce to order such a chaos of feudal usages and opinions? What, again, could he effect on the subject of the representation of the people? The States-General, the original representation of the country, had been long disused, and it was evidently a most perilous experiment to revive them. The parliament was sufficiently factious and troublesome; and these difficulties, that must have presented themselves to the meditations of this philosophic minister, would only have appeared more alarming and insuperable if he had endeavoured to discuss them with his youthful sovereign; who, benevolent as he was, was neither enterprising nor resolute, was still a pupil to his ancient counsellor Maurepas, and devoted to the queen; who, like the court around her, could have little taste for reforms and improvements, and the timely counsels of prospective wisdom.

But one of the measures which Necker now adopted was of a very important nature, and in itself not a little objectionable. He published his Compte Rendû; that is, the Report he had furnished to the king, of the finances; in other words, he gave publicity to the national accounts. He unveiled every mystery that they contained; that is, he threw himself, for the support of his financial schemes, on the candour and intelligence of the community.

No doubt, what he meant by this measure was to persuade or morally oblige the privileged orders to contribute to the public burden. It was but too evident to him, as it must have always been to every thinking man, as it had been to Turgot, as it must have been to the king himself, that this contribution of the privileged orders was the great remedy, was at least the first more immediate and practical remedy for the evils that embarrassed the government.

But surely this publication of the Compte Rendû was, on the whole, a measure, the expediency of which may be very reasonably doubted, if not entirely denied. What good could have been expected to result from it, by any very sensible and sagacious man? The new opinions did not then want fresh fuel, or any new and authentic means of attack. Necker knew enough of the privileged orders to doubt the influence of reasonable motives on their minds. The great accusation against this minister has been always that of personal vanity, a love, a passion for public applause.

Materials for such an accusation may perhaps be here found. It is not very agreeable to see defects of this kind in the character of a benevolent, virtuous, and enlightened man; but if they appear, they must be noted.

But the next great measure of Necker was to improve, if possible, the constitution of the country; to introduce some representation of the community into the system of government; to create some bodies that should be the organs of the respectable and intelligent part of the people. In this manner he might have hoped gradually and silently to extinguish the political importance of the parliament of Paris, and eventually to control the selfish passions of the privileged orders. He seems to have done what alone could be done; to have availed himself of existing institutions, and to have endeavoured to modify and wield them to his purposes. Good was chiefly to be expected, he must have thought, from gradual amelioration, and training the people to better habits, and modes of political thought and government. He was, perhaps, too late; but this was his misfortune, not his fault. He revived the idea of Turgot, and formed a project of provincial administrations. According to Necker's management, these bodies would have become a sort of States-General, not collected at Paris, but established in every province, consisting of nobility, clergy, and (equal in number to the other two) of *tiers état*.

The provinces of the Pays d'Etat, Languedoc, Burgundy, &c. had assemblies already of this description. Many advantages would have been thus obtained; the vexations arising from the immediate agency of the officers of the crown, the taxgatherers, the intendants of the provinces, would have been thus avoided; the dangers to be feared from the parliament of Paris weakened; the dangers to be feared from Paris itself escaped; and a step made, an important one no doubt, yet on the whole a cautious one, towards the accomplishment of those objects which the patriotic minister and benevolent monarch had equally at heart. You will see some account of this part of our subject in the work of Mme. de Staël; it has not, I conceive, been considered with sufficient attention by the writers on the French Revolution, not even by Mme. de Staël herself. Yet what she says is valuable and curious. To me it appears among the

first measures that the king should have attempted to carry, and he should
have attached himself firmly to Necker, as the only minister fitted to
serve him. The experiment is considered by Mme. de Staël as having been
successful in the two provinces where it was tried; but a work upon the
subject, addressed to the king by Necker himself, in which his ultimate
views were displayed, having come to the knowledge of the parliament,
so much opposition was excited, that the minister was overpowered. The
minister, it seems, had no object but economy and the welfare of the
state; and no powerful friend in the court but the monarch himself, who,
in a crisis like this, was unhappily from his nature unfitted for the office.

The parliament saw from Necker's own work that their own influence,
that their own existence, as a political body, if his provincial assemblies
succeeded, would gradually cease; and the privileged orders saw, that
now powers and authorities were, according to Necker's plan, to arise in
the state, which could be of no advantage to them; but, on the contrary,
must eventually, more or less, deprive them of their immunities, and withdraw from them their prerogatives. The old minister therefore combined
with every one around him, in and about the court and his more immediate sphere, and Necker was disposed of as a common grievance, and
dismissed from the ministry.

VII. NECKER

NECKER RETURNED to power, in August, 1788, under very unfavourable
circumstances; the critical year and a half of the archbishop's administration * was for ever lost; and the time that might have been employed
by a popular minister in saving the monarchy from a revolution, had been
only used in making a revolution inevitable. . . .

You who have not exactly lived during the times of the French Revolution cannot at all imagine how long and how deeply it affected the
thoughts, the feelings, and the interests of every human being, without
any exception, that then existed in the civilized world; the lives, the
properties, the affections, the daily anxieties of millions—but you must
endeavour to conceive it; and I cannot but believe, that with a little reflection, you will be able to do so to a considerable degree; to a degree sufficient, at least, to enable you to listen to the detail of what passed in
the mind of one of the most important actors in the scene, M. Necker,
at a moment when the business of the scene was of the most critical nature.

Recollect what has been already intimated to you; the manner in which

* Etienne Charles Loménie de Brienne (1727–94), French ecclesiastic—one of
Louis XVI's most inept improvisations as chief minister.—ED.

the affairs of the kingdom have been now for some time journeying on to a state of the greatest difficulty and danger: figure to yourselves the court and the patrons of the old régime on the one side, the patriots and the patrons of the new opinions on the other; the king and his minister, Necker, between the two; the convocation of an assembly promised that was to be the image of the whole nation, the assembly consisting of three orders; of two that would be naturally leagued with the old opinions; of one that would be as naturally animated with all the ardour and en- thusiasm of the new; and the questions to be determined then are, whether the popular part was to equal in number the other two, and whether the three orders were to meet in three houses or in one; that is, as you will easily see, whether the new opinions were entirely to bear sway or not. This consequence, at least, was pretty evident even then; but to us who live after the events, it is difficult to say, what consequences, and what calamitous consequences, may not be traced up to the man- ner in which, on whatever account, these great questions were now de- termined; and as this determination seems to be the hinge on which the Revolution may be said to have turned, you can surely think no time lost that is employed in considering what were the views of M. Necker, by what circumstances he was surrounded, if misled and mistaken, how and why; and whether any instruction can be derived for ourselves from the conduct of all parties on this occasion, the minister and those whom he undoubtedly wished to serve. You will observe then, with respect to Necker and his book, that nothing can be more reasonable or manly, than all his preliminary observations and admissions. He seeks not to withdraw himself from responsibility in any part of the discussion. Add to this, he affirms, and no doubt with perfect truth, that he never ceased to speak to the king of the wants and unhappy situation of his people; nor to the people of the virtues and benevolent intentions of the king; that it was the object of all his efforts to defend the monarchy without concealing from the monarch how useful it was to have the constitu- tion of a government properly balanced; and at every turn and on every occasion through the whole of his administration, he insists, to use his own words, that so far from accelerating, as has been supposed by his ac- cusers, the descent of a car that was already running down with such velocity, he did everything he could to stop the wheels of it, and never ceased, while by the side of it, to call aloud for help.

In the first place, he says that the States-General were promised be- fore he returned to power. He shows very satisfactorily that it was then totally impossible to prevent their assembling; that this fault, at least, he did not commit. "I must declare, too," he says, "to the honour of the prince, that he never for a moment made it a question, whether he was to keep an engagement so distinctly entered into."

"Great changes are always so hazardous," he says, "that had not the States been promised, I should have made every possible effort to *serve* France by means of the provincial assemblies, and yet *save* her from disturbance and convulsion; and why should I disguise the truth? Like the nation, I was full of hope—hope that I then could not suppose vain—Alas! how can one now think, without tears, on the hopes and expectations then every where felt by all good Frenchmen, by every friend of humanity?" He then goes on to describe how the new opinions were brought to bear, in the most unfortunate manner, on every existing principle, and institution, and usage in the state; on the confused and contradictory nature of the different powers existing in the constitution; how easy were the improvements, it was thought, that must result from the assembling of the representatives of the nation; how beneficial and how certain, as it was supposed, the regeneration of the whole system: and he thus arrives at the consideration of his own particular case. . . .

Some general notion of M. Necker's views I can give you, but some general notion only; but before I give them, you will observe that I consider them as reasons not sufficient to justify him in the conduct he pursued, but rather as fitted to show that he should have done what he did not do; what we have already mentioned that he should have done; that is, decided every thing in the king's declaration, on the king's own authority. In his work on the French Revolution, to which I am all along referring, you will see him exhibit the difficulties of the case. They were very great. You will then see, that in the event, and after the States had met, he was at last obliged to propose a system of conciliation and accommodation to all the parties, as a remedy for all these difficulties. Now, it would have been better, or rather, perhaps, it would have been the only chance to have made this system, which he had afterwards to *propose*, his measure from the first, and to have announced it as the king's will in the declaration, in the instrument, by which the king did the public the favour of calling the States together at all. M. Necker's representations are of the following nature:—A long interval, he observes, had elapsed since the last assembly of the States; and, from being veiled in a distant obscurity, they were embellished by all the colours of the imagination. Almost all the former assemblies had been convoked for the mere will and purposes of the crown; an ephemeral senate, which the sovereign could dissolve at pleasure. Subsidies were demanded, and grievances brought forward, which might or might not be afterwards attended to.

But times of this nature were passed, says M. Necker. Louis XVI had scarcely ten millions of feudal revenue, and it was for the entire sum of the public expenses, of the whole interest to be provided for an immense debt, that he found himself under the necessity of having recourse to the States; a necessity imposed upon him, not only by a resolution of the sovereign courts, but even by the parliament of Paris, which declared itself incompetent legally to register either impost or loan any longer.

What power, what authority would not naturally be obtained, says M. Necker, by the deputies of the *tiers état*, the representatives of those who had chiefly to contribute, while they were called to deliberate upon all the conditions and all the reasons for which they were to make an annual sacrifice of five hundred millions.

The clergy of France, he says, were at one time so situated, that superstition combined with religion to elevate and sustain their supremacy. The nobility were *once* aided by all the consideration with which the feudal system had environed them. But these two orders, even in all the splendour of their former greatness, if they had been called to deliberate with the *tiers état* on the form and mode of collecting an immense contribution of this kind, would have found it quite impossible to maintain their ascendant; but what hope for them, when the relative importance of the two orders, and of the third, had actually changed situations, and been transferred from the one to the other. But here, it may be replied to M. Necker, if this was the case, as it certainly was, ought not M. Necker to have foreseen what must be the event, if the question of voting or any other material question was left to be decided by the States, when met together? Was he not to have tried to anticipate their decision by one from the king? Commerce alone, he continues, among other things, had entirely changed the solid importance of the *tiers état* in the social system. It was to their talents and industry that the existence of national wealth was owing; that is, the existence, as every day more and more proclaimed, of national power. Education, admission to offices in the provincial assemblies, a thousand causes had placed their intelligence and their knowledge in a rapid state of progress and improvement. There was little resemblance between the *tiers état* of 1789 and those of former periods. Once more, too, with regard to the other orders, M. Necker goes on to say, the prelates and clergy naturally owed their influence to the general respect that prevailed for religion itself: but this had unhappily been weakened. Other causes had conspired to diminish their authority.

Every thing contributed to engage them to support the royal authority, but it was no longer in their power to afford it any material assistance by their influence over the *tiers état* and the nation.

And with regard to the nobility, Necker observes, that many circumstances (which he mentions) had contributed to rob them of all their constitutional dignity and lustre, in the eyes of the nation. There were those among them, no doubt, of historic name; but the greater part consisted of those who had been ennobled only in more modern times by the crown. The whole composition of the body was altered, the most ancient and most honourable of distinctions had been made a subject of traffic; each sort of nobility had equally a right to vote; at least one-half the order consisted of families ennobled within the last two centuries. This disposition of things might do very well for Louis XIV; he had various court contrivances of ceremony, indulgence, and decoration, by which he kept the two sorts of nobility distinguished from each other; so had Louis XV: but all this was in vain when the whole body was to rally round the throne, and effect, by its political consideration, the *tiers état* and the nation.

"What a subject here for reflection," says Necker, "this relative importance of the *tiers état* and the other two orders, to suppose that it could be balanced by any contrivance of the respective numbers of the two orders!" But to this it may be surely answered, that to suppose that there was no contrivance by which it could be balanced, and no preparatory measures to be adopted, is to surrender at discretion; to give up the cause of the crown (that is, the cause of peaceful or temperate improvement) at once. It is in vain to dissemble, he continues, that the power of the crown had attained its height in the best days of Louis XIV, and had from that period declined. Louis XV himself, perhaps, had indulged but too imprudently in a taste for popularity, Louis XVI and the queen, their love of the ease and the comforts of a private station. The personal dignity of a crowned head can never equal the conventional grandeur of a monarch.

These are not trifling considerations, he says: the conduct of the court was affected by the examples of the king and queen, and the manners were changing. Great effects are produced by the union of an infinity of small causes.

A strange situation of things, says Necker: it might well be doubted, whether even the re-establishment of the States themselves could sufficiently provide for it. He then mentions a notion entertained by himself and others at the time, that all would have been well if something like the constitution of England could have been proposed and accepted. Was it unnatural for a statesman, he says, to cast his eyes on the constitution of England? The order of nobility in France, mixed as it was, could no longer discharge its office in the political system; but a House of Peers like the English might.

There were difficulties, he continues, as France then stood, with regard to the contributions of the *tiers état;* but there was an end of them, by supposing the people of property (the Peers excepted) represented in a House of Commons, as in England. It was necessary that something should be done for France immediately; but what could be expected from the discordant views and mutual disgusts of a legislature divided into three orders? Not so, if divided only into two, as in England.

"And why again should I dissemble," says Necker, "that both my first and my last thoughts have leaned in favour of a system of government like that of England, with which neither States in three orders, nor any form of monarchy, can be put in comparison?

"The king, unfortunately for any views I might have entertained of this kind, had a prejudice against whatever might resemble the usages and institutions of England. His opinion afterwards altered, but it was then too late."

At the time that the Cour Plénière was attempted by the Archbishop of Sens, a Chamber of Peers and a House of Representatives would have been received from the king with acclamations; but it is in vain to regret, says Necker, thoughts of foresight, of prevention—the generality of people have nothing to say to them; the tocsin of events must sound before they can be awakened or instructed.

There was nothing for it then, concludes Necker, but to embark upon this sea of troubles; to take the chances of these States, thus called, and their three orders; a scene of rivalry that the dispositions of men had made so dangerous. An exact line of conduct it was not possible to trace; it was evident, however, that the two orders could not sufficiently support the crown; that the crown must get assistance from public opinion; that great address would be necessary to manage the general movement in the public mind; that the love of the people was to be sought to regain for the king what royalty had on various accounts lost. . . .

There was no reconciling the respective pretensions, continues M. Necker, of the three orders; the king became quite uneasy; he required them to send commissioners to discuss them before him in council; they did so: it was in vain; long debates ensued.

I endeavoured to accommodate all difficulties, says Necker. I submitted propositions to the commissioners for that purpose; there seemed to be no objection to them. The nobility, however, made reserves and distinctions which were equivalent to a refusal, and as such were seized upon by the *tiers état*, who then declared themselves the National Assembly. The nobility afterwards wished to have recovered the false step they had made, but it was too late.

No doubt the *tiers état*, in voting themselves the National Assembly, in affecting thus to supersede the necessity of the concurrence of the other two orders, says M. Necker, were guilty of every fault that can belong to an usurping power; but the two orders, at this period, particularly the nobility, committed every error that could result from a want of policy, circumspection, and foresight.

Such are the general representations of Necker; and the two orders may have conducted themselves with the want of prudence, the *tiers état* with the spirit of encroachment he describes; but the question is, whether any of the parties acted differently from what might have been expected; and whether their subsequent ill-conduct forms any justification of his prior imprudence? M. Necker made a distinct and a reasonable effort afterwards to conciliate all parties. Now, the question is whether all the efforts he afterwards made might not have found their place in the king's declaration *originally?* Might he not have anticipated and provided some measure to prevent the difficulties which he might have foreseen would otherwise arise? And is not M. Necker to be asked whether the king, by first, and originally, pronouncing and determining what Necker afterwards proposed, would not have taken his best course? Whether this would not have been the best chance of preventing the collision, the exasperation, that afterwards ensued, and that could not but ensue; the best chance of preventing the mistakes of the privileged orders, the usurpations of the *tiers état*, the unhappy diminution of that royal authority which it was so much the wish of Necker, and of all wise and good Frenchmen at the time, to defend from disrespect and violence?

No doubt, it is easy for us, or for any one, to be wise after the event; but Necker, from the first, saw and felt the force of public opinion; no one more so; indeed too much so: it was his business, therefore, as soon as possible, to take some position, such that he might either secure the best chance of avoiding a contest with public opinion altogether, or, that he might contend with the best advantage.

Circumstances are not easily appreciated at a distance of time or place; the precise influence and effect that each or any of them ought to have upon a reasonable mind, called to decide at the moment; but Necker seems to have been of a temperament too sanguine. He had expected more wisdom, more disinterestedness, from the parties than was reasonable; more than they afterwards showed. As a man of sense and humanity, he was desirous that something should be done for France; he must have supposed that nothing would, if the double representation was not conceded to the popular party. He therefore granted it. He had expected, no doubt, to influence afterwards all parties, by showing them, from time to time, what it was just, and right, and wise to do; but he should have prescribed what was just, and right, and wise, by the royal authority in the first declaration, and he should have left nothing to be settled, that he could possibly avoid, by the result of the general fermentation and the conflict of the three orders.

VIII. TIERS ETAT

I HAVE described in the last lecture the views of Necker and his situation, referring myself in the main to his own works and to his own statement of the case, as he drew it up at a subsequent period, deliberately consider-' ing it in the calmness of his retirement. It is difficult to judge of the conduct of statesmen, no doubt; for, in politics, existing circumstances are every thing. On the present occasion, however, we judge not a little from the materials which he himself submits to our consideration; and though no mistake was of more importance to the world than his, if it was one, we may determine, as I conceive, on the nature of it in this instance, with rather more confidence than in most others.

In politics, I have just said, existing circumstances are every thing. Not that the general rules of justice and right are to be made light of or forgotten, but that wise and good men must in politics look earnestly to discover the expediency of the case, and that this can only be judged of by the circumstances. Very painful struggles are sometimes occasioned by the doubts that arise, which of two general rules of obligation it is best, that is, it is ultimately most expedient to prefer; including in the word expedient, as must never be forgotten, the importance and sanctity of all moral obligations. But a statesman, above every other moralist (he is only a moralist on a larger scale), is bound to mark well the nature of every thing around him at the moment, and to adapt well his means to his end. With him, above all others, success is included in the idea of his merit: not only must his objects be noble, but the expedients he uses to accomplish them must be adequate to their purpose. He must not injure his fellow-creatures, however good his intentions. . . .

By . . . acts of supremacy, made without the concurrence of the other two orders, and without waiting for the approbation of the king, they [the *tiers état*] not only decided the two former questions about the mode of voting, but they acted as a sort of legislature, as a complete assembly authorized of themselves and alone to reform the old government, in fact to form a new government—certainly to present themselves as such—the government of the National Assembly.

Now, certainly to me, I confess, who turn to look on this scene as a matter of history, nothing can appear more unjustifiable than the whole of a conduct like this; but it may not to others; what had the king done, or even the court, to make it necessary? Why was the king to be made so soon to repent of his calling the States together for his own and the public advantage? What indifference had he shown to the public welfare?

What measure had he rejected? What effect could usurpation on their part produce, but irritation and hostility on his, and rage and violence on the part of the court? What benefit could hence accrue to the community? Was peace no object? Was not order and regularity, and a system of conciliation and mutual sacrifices, the best, and indeed the only, chance for the permanent improvement of the constitution? It seems indeed to have been taken for granted, that unless the States were to vote by poll, no benefit could result from their meeting; but this was an assumption, and in truth a very violent assumption. The *tiers état* seem quite to have overlooked the most important circumstances of the case: the progress of the new opinions; the ferment of the public mind; the influence of public opinion; the intensity of the expectation of the community; the difficulties that the king and court would be under if they ventured often or very materially to disappoint that expectation. It might have been asked them, what measure of clear importance and benefit to the state, if pressed for by the *tiers état*, could long have been withheld by the king and the other two orders. Suppose the privileged orders had been made to contribute equally to the public taxes, and suppose provision had been made for the future meeting of the States-General, would not even this have been sufficient to secure eventually, in the existing state of the world, a complete though gradual amelioration of the whole system of the government? Why was the Assembly to rush forward in this manner, and assume to themselves the office of what they called the regeneration of France; to set aside all the existing authorities, the king included, or only to consider them as subservient to themselves, as only useful or estimable as they would contribute to forward their own particular views of political expediency; as they would or would not assist them in newly organizing society, or in giving, as they termed it, a new constitution to France?

There is no doubt that the majority of the *tiers état* meant well, there is no doubt that very wise and very good men concurred in these proceedings, there is no doubt that the greatest blessing that can be procured for a nation is civil liberty, that just allowance must be made for men who step forward in a cause so noble and so animating; but it is on these very accounts the more necessary for history to criticize such men; because the mistakes of bad men and arbitrary rulers do not necessarily lead to liberty, while those of good men and virtuous patriots inevitably do to the loss of it.

ix. TWENTY-THIRD OF JUNE *

To us who live at the present period, however sincerely we may feel the love of civil liberty, the difficulty of procuring it by violence and revolution is sufficiently apparent; the sort of hope and confidence with which we speak on such subjects is very different from what it was, on the breaking out of the French Revolution. The value of all concessions from power, of all steps to improvement, of all progressive advances to amelioration, are by this time duly estimated (I speak of men of sense and experience). We no longer talk of organizing a community afresh, of regenerating a kingdom, of giving a constitution to a great people, with all the ease and dispatch which at the breaking out of the French Revolution was thought possible. The wisest men and the best, at that period, were, no doubt, dazzled and made confident by the delusive and irrelevant example of America; and nothing was thought of but the original rights of the people, the imperfections of society as it then existed, and the dignity and the happiness to which a people might be exalted; exalted by no more difficult process, it was understood, than their own wishes. It was a favourite maxim, that a people had only to will to be free and to be so. Doctrines like these may be so modified and veiled as to be reducible to salutary practice; they may be, in secret, the principle of vitality to the free constitution of a great people; but it was a little too much to expect that they should be the maxims which should prompt the feelings and colour the language of a monarch of France, when now only for the *first time* addressing the States-General of his kingdom.

This is the unreasonableness, this is the intolerance for all old opinions, that distinguished, at that time, the holders of the new. Bristling with their logic, and confident in the superiority of their reason, everything, they thought (for they were generally young men), might be safely intrusted to the prevalence of reason among mankind; and as this will ever be the case on all such occasions, and with all such men who are also on such occasions the most effective part of the community, this becomes one of the lessons of history.

Again, and on the contrary side of the question, little less intolerance of the *new* opinions, it must be observed, was felt by the court and the holders of the old opinions; either now or at any subsequent period; "all or nothing" was always their maxim, and this is *also* the lesson of this

* We have contented ourselves with Smyth's observations upon the famous *séance royale* of June 23, 1788, when Louis XVI showed himself unable to cope with the newly shown power of the third estate.—Ed.

history. But on the present occasion, on the occasion of this royal sitting, it should be considered that concessions many and important had been made; they afforded a sufficient ground on which to have proceeded to the settlement of the kingdom, and the main blame must rest with the *tiers état*, after deducting the blame that rests with the court—for great blame certainly does rest with the court; and out of common justice to the leaders of the Constituent Assembly it must be remembered: on occasions of this kind, imprudence is fault.

You must observe then, that the concessions made by the king, considered with reference to the state of the government *de facto* for some centuries past, were, no doubt, very great, and as such, should have been felt and acknowledged, and acted upon; but whether they were so, with reference to the state of opinion and the public expectations *at the time*, is more doubtful. The royal prerogative was now so injured in general estimation, and the many experiments made with a view of avoiding the present necessity had been so unsuccessful, and had so damaged the government, that it was hardly considered to be in a situation to propose terms, still less to determine the extent of the concessions to be made. There was no longer a disposition to accept a constitution as a boon. The popular writers all agree in representing this measure as one of the most doubtful expediency; and the circumstances by which it was attended, as well as the declaration of the king respecting the voting of the orders separately, and the rights of the privileged orders, completed its unpopularity. Until this sitting of the 23rd of June, Mirabeau seems to have hesitated, and to have kept his eye upon the court. He had been against the measure of the *tiers état* constituting itself a National Assembly, but from the moment of the sitting of the 23rd, from the moment that he saw the folly of the court, he seems to have thought there was no chance for them, and threw himself headlong into popular measures. . . . Unless Necker could have obtained the concurrence of the moderate men, the measure of a royal sitting should never have been resorted to. And again, who could conceive it possible, that the king should have been advised by any one, or should have himself consented to come down to an Assembly, already exasperated and strong in popular opinion, with a scheme that had not been discussed with some of the principal leaders among them? Who could dream at that time of keeping the three orders separate, merely by a royal direction; the clergy, in fact, gone over, and the noblesse divided? What can we say of a king who could turn away from Necker, the only person near him capable of forming an estimate of all the circumstances by which he was surrounded, and who could even suffer the violent people of his court so to alter the minister's measure, that the minister could not even appear in his place lest he should seem to approve it? Surely it must be allowed, that a king and a government so unmindful of the temper and circumstances of the time, and of all the plain dictates of the most obvious common sense that belonged to the case, could not possibly avoid their ruin, and by many will be thought even to have deserved it. But it is ever thus: a court and its more immediate supporters can never see either wisdom or virtue in the feelings and opinions of moderate men, and a king but too naturally listens to those who echo his own sentiments. Such conduct, however, is not the lesson of this Revolution.*

xiv. NECESSITY OF EXECUTIVE POWER

THE FIRST events that occurred after the king had adopted the Revolution promised ill; Foullon and Berthier † were massacred in the streets of Paris by the multitude; and every where through the interior of the kingdom the people of condition saw their country-seats burnt and pillaged, and themselves and their families exposed to the most dreadful outrages. Popular victories in the Assembly seem never to have had any effect on the ferocious passions of the people. It is no light matter to withdraw a community from the influence of established authority; it is never easy, it may not be possible, to substitute for some time any new system of control. In the interval the lower orders are ready for any enormity that their own passions or the passions of designing or bad men may propose to them. It is very true that patriots must expose the faults of their rulers and the vices of their government, or they can hope for no reform in either; but every distinction should be always made, that can possibly be made, between governors and government itself, the selfish, unfeeling, odious vices of the rulers are to be resisted, but care must be taken not to pander to the base and brutal passions of the multitude. To do this, however, it will be replied, is pretty nearly to effect impossibilities. It may be so; yet such is the task to be held up to the virtuous ambition of brave and good men; and such men, the patriots of a country, must endeavour to accomplish it according to the varying opportunities of the case, and the qualities of mind and body with which they have been intrusted. Much of this task was accomplished by the patriots of America in the great revolution that separated them from this country;

* Smyth's next two lectures were concerned with the events of the 14th of July—the taking of the Bastille. Lecture XII explored the career of the benevolent Jean Sylvain Bailly (1736–93), who went to the guillotine as the result of his moderate courses. Lecture XIII concerned the "views and reasonings" of Charles Élie, Marquis de Ferrières de Marsay (1741–1804), an indiscreet and vocal royalist who was luckier than Bailly.—ED.

† Respectively an unpopular minister of state and his son-in-law.—ED.

a favourable one, totally unlike that of France or of any European country; cases with which it is so often confounded: and you may remember, even in this case of America, the confusion, the shame, the anguish with which the mind of Washington was but too often overwhelmed by the indisposition of his countrymen to the necessary restraint of regular authority, and the proper machinery of executive government.

The difficulty, you will remember, is, and it is most intelligible, how to restrain the selfish passions of mankind, how to procure any attention to the common obligations of law and justice, when the former ministers of law and justice have been displaced and lost their authority.

To return to the instance of America. One of my lectures on the American Revolution was chiefly intended to show you how much Washington suffered, how much the best interests, present and future, of the great continent of America were endangered from that absence of executive power, which necessarily took place, when the contest with Great Britain was terminated. The difficulty will always occur. In the case before us, the patriots of the French Revolution had talked of the sovereign will of the people, and had made such large references to their wisdom and their power, that the multitude seem to have taken them at their word, and to have concluded that every thing that was agreeable to them, must necessarily be right. All government is instituted for the happiness of the people; this is the first step, and one of which there can be no doubt; but the second is that of this happiness they can be themselves the only and the best judges; a position totally different, and which requires many limitations, distinctions, and explanations, and which, when thrown out to the multitude, as it continually was, by the patriotic leaders in the most unqualified manner, could lead only to those unhappy excesses, which it is the grief of every friend to the liberties of mankind to read and hear of, and which constitute so much of the history of the French Revolution.

I have now made three distinct accusations. I have accused the people of Paris (the multitude at least) of taking the law into their own hands, and in defiance of what authority yet remained, of massacring those who had offended them in the public streets. I have accused the common people all over France, when the authority of the old government was removed, of committing the most disgraceful and cruel outrages on the property and persons of the aristocracy of the country. I have accused the leaders of the Revolution of addressing such language to the people (that of their sovereignty and their sovereign will) as could only be fatal to the people and to themselves; such as was unworthy of them as statesmen; such as could never have been necessary, if they had acted during the first weeks of the Revolution in a spirit of temper and moderation, and made the best of their case with the king, who was, according to the limits of his views and feelings, as patriotic as themselves.

Now these are accusations which you must consider in the detail of the history, as you read it for yourselves. Of the two first there can be no doubt; of the last there may, and it will require your best attention. But even of this last position, that the leaders used fatal language to the people, the truth is sufficiently apparent; and after the first lessons that are given to rulers, the next are, those that are afforded to all who love freedom, and more particularly those who are ready to resist, or even overturn, a government for the sake of bettering the condition of their country. Patriots have their temptations and their mistakes, as well as those who govern; and you must keep your attention directed to the faults that were committed (and by them committed) on the subject of executive power. The great cause of the French Revolution failed for want of executive power. This is indeed a difficult subject, and one which I ought not thus to decide and anticipate—this conduct, I mean, of the Assembly with respect to the executive power; but this at least I may say, that the first and most important point of all others to be accomplished when the king had resigned himself to the Revolution, in the Hotel de Ville, was the immediate establishment (more particularly in Paris) of something like an effective power. The next point was, when the constitution came afterwards to be regularly settled, to make the executive power sufficiently strong. Now, the Constituent Assembly did neither. These are, I think, the two great lessons of instruction for you during all the earlier parts of the French Revolution, during the sitting of the Constituent Assembly; their failures on the subject of executive power. . . .

And now you will observe, that there seems to have been in Paris, all through the Revolution, a set of wretches among the multitude always ready to undertake any projects of insurrection and bloodshed: these were always considered as the followers and hired ruffians of the Duke of Orléans, though I know not with what sufficient reason: money may have been given, and a certain effect in consequence produced, but no such effect, I conceive, as was unhappily witnessed: and it is quite out of the question to suppose that such a spirit and such excesses, as were witnessed, could have been produced by money; far different, and far more awful, was the origin of such frightful phenomena in the history of our species. There was in the houses of legislature also, at all times and from the first, a party that were always urging every thing to extremes, and seemed to have no relish for any counsels but those of fury and violence. Now men of both these descriptions, whether men of bad designs and desperate characters, or men inflamed to a sort of madness by the intoxicating nature of new opinions, men both like the one and like the other, must always be expected to appear, must always be taken into account in all revolutions. They are naturally the favourites of the multitude, and it is very difficult, it is almost impossible, to save a community from their destructive influence. You will see them in action all through the Revolution; the low party of the Constituent, the republicans of the Legislative Assembly, the mountain of the Convention, the leaders of the Jacobin club, the demagogues of the Palais Royal. Observe their speeches, the decrees they propose, their conduct; these (after the first lessons have been given) are the next lessons of the Revolution. Such men will arise, will necessarily be found in public mobs, in public assemblies; but these are the men against whom real patriots, the real friends of liberty, are to be more particularly on their guard. I must now make a painful reference, in some slight and passing manner, to subjects of this nature.

M. Bailly gives a regular account of the massacre of M. de Berthier. He presided that day at the town hall. All the way to Paris, it was but too clear, as M. de Berthier was brought along, under the conduct of the civil power, that no civil power would be sufficient for his protection. The savages that had just murdered his father-in-law, Foullon, brought the head upon a pike, close to the carriage where he was sitting; M. de la Rivière, his conductor, exerted himself very humanely, made him turn aside his eyes, and told him it was the head of M. de Quesnay; but the sufferings of the unhappy man were extreme, and M. de la Rivière was unable to lodge him, according to his orders, in the prison of the Abbaye, and he could only bring him to the town hall. M. Bailly had procured a strong guard from La Fayette; it was their object to remove Berthier to prison, if possible, preparatory to his trial; but even while they were interrogating the prisoner, the blood-thirsty impatience of the crowd had become uncontrollable, and he no sooner appeared on the steps, than he was torn away from the guard, and massacred on the spot. A dragoon brought his heart to the council; he was repulsed with horror. The multitude next attempted to bring his head on a pike, and were already on the staircase; the helpless committee were obliged to send word that no admission could be allowed, as they were, at the moment, sitting and engaged in business. "In these terrible moments," says M. Bailly, "pretexts were to be made use of to escape from these atrocities; there was a real danger," he continues, "to those (it was useless to brave it) who attempted to speak the language of justice and humanity; the people could hear nothing; whoever thought not with them was supposed a traitor."

This is an awful specimen of the rude passions of mankind. The dragoon, however, it is said, was pursued to death by his indignant comrades, and was killed in the first duel with one of them. The honour of the military character was justly felt; and these, the very murderers of Foullon and Berthier, brought their money and trinkets to the Assembly. These incidents speak something in favour of human nature. But in the notes to Bailly's *Memoirs*, you will see a sort of pamphlet, or handbill, that appeared at the time, written by some bad man, but one evidently of intelligence and of literary talents. What are we to say, what are we to think of the frail nature of the peace of society, and of the danger of loosening its bands, when even such a man could deliver to his fellow-creatures a detail of the abominations of these massacres, decorated by the refined expressions of pleasantry and good writing? "But to lose no more time," says this handbill, "we strangled him; and then, as he was an ex-administrator, we took off his head, in a manner the most respectful; we took from him his heart and his entrails; the head walked off on the one side, and the body on the other,—the first time that these two intimate connections had found themselves separated from each other." Other passages, and more disgusting, occur; the whole is properly given by the present editor of Bailly, to show to what an extent the human mind may be hardened by political fury.

After all, it is very strange that no resistance could be made to such atrocious proceedings, and it seems difficult to suppose that the mere mob were alone concerned; not that, if they were, this would be any justification of the Assembly. Where was all the force of the capital? Why did not the Assembly call aloud, in the cause of everything that should have been dear to them? When the citizens of Paris, a few days before, expected their town to be attacked by Broglie and the army, the body of electors had assembled, had created a regular force, La Fayette was at the head of it; afterwards, when the king repaired to the capital, wherever he looked, he had seen the population under arms; where were they all? They must have constituted much of the respectable part of the population of Paris. Efforts were made by La Fayette and by Bailly, by the military and civil powers, all in vain. What the editors of Bailly have to say is only this, that at the time of these massacres the armed force was not properly organized; that the officers scarcely knew each other, and that their persons were scarcely known to those who were to obey them; that it was an irregular mass, divided in sentiment, over which no general influence could be exercised. Divided in sentiment, but how? on an occasion like this? To be able to say no more than this for the people of Paris is to say but little. La Fayette, it is added, had saved from popular fury, at different times, seventeen persons just before: a melancholy addition this to the crimes of the populace, and a new cause of reproach to the Assembly and the respectable part of the community.

La Fayette on every occasion, it will be found, all circumstances considered, did everything that could possibly be done by a brave and good man, often at great personal risk, often with very eminent success. In this instance, La Fayette was not wanting to his own character, or to his country; the cause of civil order and of the law was evidently at issue.

He must have been deeply mortified at this early specimen of the Revolution. He wrote to Bailly, and to the districts, to throw up his command, and he was able to write to them a calm and reasonable letter. Every effort was made to appease his just indignation, and he at last resumed the command, as he had always secretly intended, on a promise of proper obedience to him, given by the electors and deputies of the districts in the name of the citizens of Paris; "that his zeal," they said, "seconded by their common efforts, might conduct to perfection the great work of the public liberty."

How ill this promise was observed is but too well known; these massacres produced some sensation in the districts of Paris, and occasioned a seasonable proclamation, but they should have far more powerfully affected the National Assembly. It was evident how dreadful was the monster that they had unchained, while endeavouring to free their country from a system of bad government and the oppressions of a court; but no proper sentiment seems to have been awakened in the democratic party. . . .

The scenes I have alluded to are highly disgraceful to the Assembly, and all the constituted authorities of Paris. They show, no doubt, the necessity of some executive power. This is the first lesson; but more is to be considered. The two unhappy men who were massacred were literally torn in pieces by the multitude. Their heads were carried on pikes, and led in a sort of triumphal procession through the streets. A fiend in the shape of a man, as I have already mentioned, actually thrust his hand into the entrails of one of these unfortunate victims, tore out the heart, and brought it to the council table, where the committee was sitting in the town hall. These are the great facts to be remembered.

Now horrors of this kind, and they are innumerable through the French Revolution, show, as I have mentioned, in the first place, the necessity of some executive government; but in the second place, they have been always considered as the most decisive proofs that can possibly be produced to show the necessity, after all, of the Revolution itself, and the badness of the old French government. What must have been the rulers, or at least the system of government, when such were the people? What further justification can be required?—Now whether this rapid mode of reasoning be or be not entirely conclusive, one thing must, I think, be admitted; that the moral situation of the lower orders in France at the time of the Revolution, forms an eternal answer to those who would give the people no instruction and no freedom. How is the brute to be taken out of the human animal but by the influence of that moral and religious knowledge, which alone distinguish him from other animals in the desert? But give him instruction, it will be answered, and he will then be a more intelligent and discerning critic on the vices and follies of his superiors. No doubt they must behave better; and why not? Is not this in other words to say that the community will in every class and in every directon be advanced and improved?

But the community will never be safe, it will be again answered, if every man is thus to be converted into a judge of his betters and erected into a statesman. This is a gross exaggeration: the generality of mankind must be occupied in making provision for themselves and their families; the knowledge they can acquire must be very limited, little more than what may save them from the brutal vices; the political power which will sufficiently gratify them and make them respectable in their own eyes and those of their superiors is in truth, generally speaking, and in any ordinary state of the world, very little; and at all events the community can never for a moment be safe, when the multitude are degraded and despised. They will, on some opportunity or other, rise, as they did in France, first in the Jacquerie, next at the Revolution; on both occasions, but too much after the manner of slaves in a West India island. And even in regular and good governments, like our own, in times of any difficulty or danger, the visitation of a scarcity, a fall in the price of labour, a stoppage of the manufactures, to whom has a factious demagogue the best chance of successfully addressing himself—to an ignorant creature that can understand no voice but the clamour of his wants and passions, or to one that has been accustomed to consider occasionally the nature of his duties, moral and religious, occasionally to exercise his thoughts, occasionally, in the language of the poet, "to look before and after"? Again, to which of the two can a wise and good man address himself in these seasons of public calamity with the best chance of success? Which is most likely to understand what even a wise and good man can then only say—the wisdom of patience; the necessity of suffering; that governments cannot perform impossibilities; that the best will be abused; the wisest make mistakes; that perfection, that happiness, in our sublunary state, are not to be expected;—of such things, which of the two is likely to be the best auditor, the ignorant man or the more improved?

But to return to our subject of the want of executive power. The Revolution failed not a little on account of the tumultuary mobs of Paris. The student's attention should always be directed to this point; why and how it came about that there was no proper executive power in the metropolis and in the country; why the Constituent Assembly never seemed sufficiently aware of the necessity of one; why democratic principles of the most unqualified nature so uniformly prevailed.

This subject of executive power is at all times so important, and is so intimately connected with every part of the French Revolution, that I will endeavour, in the remainder of the lecture, to furnish you with such particulars of a general nature, as may give you some notion of what it was, during the period we are now considering, and long after.

A sort of slight history of it seems the following.

The first executive power that existed in France prior to the Revolution was of course the ancient power, prerogative, and authority of the crown. The king was, under the old régime, the great executive, and indeed legislative power.

But this executive power grew weaker as the Revolution proceeded, and might be said to be suspended, when the king was thought to have brought up Marshal Broglie and his troops to put down the Revolution and to subdue Paris. His authority, on the failure of this measure, was virtually at an end, and a new sort of executive power was created.

Recourse was had to the body of Parisian electors, about three hundred in number, those who originally chose the deputies that were sent to the States-General, and they became the first magistracy, or executive and civil power; and, in the revolutionary state of things then existing, were highly fitted to be so. They arranged and formed the military force, that appeared as by enchantment, and probably saved Paris, not only from Marshal Broglie, but from internal pillage and destruction at that terrible crisis.

But it was afterwards found that they and the military force, with all the assistance of La Fayette and Bailly, were insufficient to secure the peace and order of the community; they had not been able, or they had not sufficiently exerted themselves, to prevent the massacres we have lately alluded to; and the real executive power became little to be distinguished from the mere will of the multitude, the will of the sovereign people. This was in truth the law; there was no other, and none could be worse. The electors were not at ease or pleased with their situation; they seemed to have understood the nature of their fellow-citizens, the Parisians, perfectly well; they were not very desirous to retain their authority; and they therefore persuaded the sixty districts of the capital to elect each two deputies, who should constitute a temporary administration, make proper provision for a future municipal government, and being the acknowledged representatives of the community, could assume the appearance of regular legitimate authority, according to the new opinions.

These one hundred and twenty deputies then constituted the second municipal authority or acting executive power of the capital; and these might have succeeded eventually in maintaining some appearance of order in the community, but for one unfortunate circumstance: it was this; they were the immediate representatives each of their own districts; and these districts had each of them, most unhappily, General Assemblies. In these Assemblies every inhabitant was permitted to speak (each inhabitant, a Frenchman), permitted, I say, to speak and vote. These Assemblies, in this manner, framed resolutions, which were laws in their own districts, issued proclamations, and granted passports. They became themselves, rather than the deputies, the effective executive power; and the result of this was, that the great city of Paris became at once tormented with sixty republics, each with a General Assembly, where all the citizens, meeting, speaking, voting at the same time, each Assembly became a cave of Æolus, but with no master-spirit to control its inmates. This, then, was a dreadful species of executive power or municipal authority. Such Assemblies, with such representatives, the Assemblies constantly sitting, the representatives the mere organs of their will—this was a miserable specimen of the sovereignty of the people, a melancholy caricature of the doctrines of freedom. . . .

When such was the great source of executive power, that is, of the authority of the community, the next step in the progress of destruction, as the student will easily conceive, would be, that these Assemblies would fall under the management of wrong-headed, furious demagogues; that sensible people in disgust would withdraw (a constant but most lamentable consequence at all times of a disorderly public assembly); that these demagogues, in each district, would communicate and correspond with each other, and at last would fall into a great united club (as they did, the Jacobin club); be there joined by the more violent members of the National Assembly; and by forming a similar organization in the great towns and all over the kingdom, influence these Assemblies, organize these districts, and in fact constitute the real effective government of the empire, and give the law to the National Assembly itself, under whatever form or name it appeared. All this took place.

Now a more tremendous executive (or rather legislative and executive power) than this, to exist in any country, no imagination can conceive. It was highly fitted, it must be allowed, to beat off an invading enemy; to raise armies, that might be let loose upon the rest of Europe: but it was the least fitted in the world to build up the regular constitution, and lay the foundations of the future peace and prosperity of a great empire. You will often hear of the municipality of Paris, as you read the history; that is, of the body composed of the representatives of the sixty districts, each district having its own Assembly. You will often hear of the Jacobin club: bear in mind this slight sketch of these dreadful ministers of authority that I have given you; the nature of the power, its organization, and extent; and all the enormities that disgraced the Revolution, and destroyed all the efforts of good men, will not surprise you. . . .

Now I must turn for an instant to observe that the picture of general ignorance in the people of France, as you see, is very complete; and yet, as you also see, the old government was not in this way made secure, as it should have been, according to those who contend against the instruction of the lower orders: quite the contrary; there was no chance left for it. But in this general state of public ignorance the political press seems to have been active and unprincipled to the most extraordinary degree. In Paris, thirteen or even sixteen pamphlets a day were no matter of surprise. These innumerable productions were spread from the capital through every part of the kingdom with the greatest dispatch; it is said they were given away: a circumstance which, like many others, leads to the belief of an Orléans faction existing to a certain extent at least, and exercising all their abominable machinations for the propagation of disorder. Lastly, as a supereminent difficulty for good patriots to struggle with, a scarcity, a famine, was sorely felt in Paris, and more or less in other parts of France, during these earlier parts of the Revolution. Demagogues, and revolutionists, and all the artificers of confusion, can have no instrument in their hands like this—the rich man eating bread while the poor man is famished. How vain to talk to the latter of order and law! how easy, of the necessity of insurrection and a better government! Bailly mentions that he was often uncertain at midnight of the proper supply for the city the next day. To all these causes of disorder and calamity must, I conceive, after all, be added the immense fortune of the Duke of Orléans, and the manner in which he suffered it to be employed. And lastly, and above all, the nature of the new opinions, intoxicating alike to the speaker and the hearer, to the writer and the reader, to the thousands of demagogues and literary men who supposed they were already wiser than all who had gone before them, and to the crowds and multitudes, more particularly those, rising into life, who thought they were now to become so. The very nature of these opinions was to suppose that there was a new era to commence in the religion, morals, and governments of mankind; and when, in this state of things, even the wise and the people of property seemed no longer to respect any established system of conduct or opinion, and openly to avow it, what was to become of the mass of the community?

You will now, I hope, be able to form some general notion of the state of Paris and of France when the king adopted the Revolution, and for some time after; a notion sufficiently clear to enable you to understand what I am delivering on the subject of executive power in this lecture; and the question now is, What was done by the Constituent Assembly from the moment that all the regular and legitimate power was transferred from the king to them? what was done for the preservation of their own consequence; for the security of the public; for the very success of any measures they could possibly prepare; for the improvement of the constitution of their country? Are they, or are they not, to be blamed for their want of sense and spirit? . . . What has been the event is now known, and what the event *could not but be* might have been foreseen (so it must now be thought) by all intelligent men at the time. I do not deny their difficulties, but they were intoxicated with the new opinions, as men will always be; and they made no efforts, or thought none necessary, to form a proper executive power for their own defence, the protection of the community, in fact, the protection of their own Revolution.

You will of course consider the subject more thoroughly hereafter. It was on the whole a most perilous and unhappy situation of affairs, though it appeared not so at the time to the friends of liberty in this country, in America, and in Europe. The question in reality was, whether the National Assembly (for this was the only hope), consisting of so many enlightened and respectable men, could restrain the general ardour, and could by their own virtues, wisdom, and moderation, compensate for all the tendencies to evil which we have thus briefly and very imperfectly described.

xv. FOURTH OF AUGUST *

SOCIETY CANNOT exist (any state, at least, that deserves the name of society) without the institution of property, but it may without the institution of church property. The foundation, therefore, of the two is not the same—this must be admitted; the property of the individual is necessary to the very constitution of society—not so, the property of the clergyman.

It may be very possible that an establishment may be the best method of providing society with the consolations of religion, the best method of explaining its doctrines and exhibiting its evidences, of securing mankind from degrading or dangerous fanaticism on the one side, or even on the other, from licentious indifference: it is very possible, that the best method of securing these most important ends, may be the establishment of an ecclesiastical body, and the furnishing of that body with a permanent, independent, visible, real support, like that of land or its produce. All this may be very true; and as this possession is from age to age continued, it may not, in the common estimation of mankind, or in a court of law, be distinguished from any other possession or property; and an estate of land or tithes may thus be enjoyed by an ecclesiastical body, or by a minister of religion, as an estate is by any other individual:

* Again, passing by the hysteria of the night of August 4, 1789, when the Assembly all but did away with the *ancien régime* in a series of resolutions (proposed chiefly by the higher nobility and clergy), we give Smyth's meditation upon these events.—ED.

still it must be allowed, that the original nature of the possession is different; that society cannot exist without the one sort of property, but may without the other; that the one is a case of necessity, the other of legislative wisdom.

But when this sort of reasoning has been admitted, with Mirabeau, still it must be laid down, with the Abbé de Sieyes, that men must be just; and when a state has long proceeded, from age to age, on a certain system; has long suffered men to educate themselves for a specific purpose; has at all times, and in all places, dedicated, or allowed individuals to dedicate, which is the same thing, real possessions to that specific purpose, and suffered their possessions to assume the office and character of property; it surely can have no right to turn round on a sudden, to tell such a body of men, that it has altered its system, that they are no longer wanted, and that they were mistaken in supposing their land or their tithes property; that the original elementary difference of property was now to be acted upon; that they must give up the whole, or any part of it, which the legislature now found it convenient to resume, or to annul the right of. Language of this kind, the language of the revolutionists, is surely not, for a moment, to be considered as consistent with humanity or justice. A wide distinction even exists between what a state may do as regards the future, and as regards the present; a future hierarchy it may treat according to its new system and views, or it may in future dispense with an hierarchy altogether; this may be a matter of legislative wisdom, and no more; but it is not to proceed in this speculative manner with those in whom it has already raised rational expectations, and whose thoughts, opinions, feelings, and habits, whose ideas of comfort, respectability, and happiness, it has suffered to grow up and be fashioned to a particular model of its own approving or proposing. Indemnity, compensation, voluntary adjustment, these are the only sounds that can now be heard.

In these observations I have not insisted on the nature of *trust* property, that it is inviolable if the duty be performed; I have consented to take the ground which the enemies of church property propose. They may, however, be reminded, that what is now church property was never in possession of the state; that it was originally given by those who possessed it to ecclesiastical bodies and functionaries, who were thus to be supported while they dispensed the offices of religion; and that while therefore they do faithfully dispense the offices of religion, their part of the obligation is performed, and the property must remain with them according to the intention of the original possessor and giver of it; the property is trust property.

There never was, as is supposed, any gift of property made by the state; the state is only indirectly the giver, as allowing such gifts to be legal.

As far as the state has interfered, it has not been to give property, but rather to prevent the gift of it, that is, to prevent persons of religious feelings, by statutes of mortmain and other legal expedients, from giving away their property to pious uses, in a manner that became at last injurious to the community.*

xix. FIFTH AND SIXTH OF OCTOBER

IN THE THREE last lectures, I have endeavoured to draw your attention to the period that intervened between the 14th of July and the beginning of October 1789. I have endeavoured to place it before you in every point of view: the different questions that were then discussed, the different opinions that were then expressed; and I have done this at great length (reckless of any charge of tediousness and repetition), on account of what I believe to be the importance of the lessons that this period offers to all who are disposed to engage in public concerns, more especially to the friends of freedom. During this period, had Mounier †and his friends been properly supported, the Revolution might have been adjusted upon a system of mutual sacrifices, conciliation, and peace; but the opportunity was lost. No proper terms were kept with the king and with the court. The friends of freedom, some of them, still entertained their terror of the return of arbitrary power, while others of them were animated with hopes of a new order of things, more favourable, as they thought, to liberty, but evidently of a nature far too vague and unqualified, far too democratic to be admitted into a system like that of the French monarchy, without much positive injustice, great violence, the certainty of much commotion, and the hazard of a civil war.

Now these I conceive to have been serious mistakes made by the friends of freedom on this occasion in the one way and in the other; and I am now, you will observe, speaking only of those men who are entitled to our respect, those who meant well, who supposed that they were friends to their country and mankind. I speak not of daring, selfish, unprincipled men, such as always come forward on occasions of public agitation: I speak not of those; of such men it is in vain to speak; I am directing my observations to those who were too full of their own opinions to respect those of others; who expected too much from the influence of truth and reason; who considered not the perilous and uncertain nature

* Lectures XVI, XVII, and XVIII are concerned with the gradual but inevitable processes by which not only did Louis lose the last vestiges of kingly power but also by which the character of the Assembly was changed by fear of the mob.—ED.

† Jean-Joseph Mounier (1758–1806), French politician; a moderate, he dissociated himself from the radicals, and became an émigré.—ED.

of all political dissensions; who were too sanguine to be wise. Men like these will, as I conceive, always exist: nay, more; unless men of generous minds and ardent temperaments are continually found in society, freedom cannot be maintained in it. No point, therefore, can be a point of greater anxiety than to teach men like these the temptations of their situation; to warn them, by the example of a period like this in the French Revolution, that they are to keep a guard upon their very virtues and upon some of the most indispensable and highest qualities of their nature. In revolutions, the history is always much the same. There are those of warm passions, of ready eloquence, of fearless minds: these are the men who put a revolution into motion; dangerous from the very elevation of their characters, from the very purity of their enthusiasm; young men, for the most part, caught by novelty, disposed to experiment, offensive by their presumption, and who turn away with contempt from what are proposed to them as the lessons of experience. These are found on the *one* side; and on the *other* are ranged those more advanced in age, more especially those of the privileged orders, accustomed to a certain routine of duties and opinions, and too much disposed to consider, as still in existence, those sentiments and prejudices, good and bad, which, amid the changes of the world, *may* have passed away.

Now, between these descriptions of men stand the men of intelligence and reflection, too young for the one, too old for the other; who are by nature, as by wisdom, placed between the two, and whose wish and whose labour it will be to conciliate and to harmonize, to estimate and to provide at once for the past, the present, and the future. But what will naturally be the fate of such men? Belonging not to the violent on either side, they will persuade neither, they will displease both; they will fail, they will be disappointed; they will be found in the company of the first that come forward while the revolution is ripening, but they will be also among the first who will have to retire or perish, if the revolution proceeds.

Such may be in general the melancholy history of revolutions; but the question is, ought these things to be so? This may be indeed the history, but *ought* this to be the history?

Democratic writers continually speak as if there was a progress in these affairs totally inevitable. . . . That it is in vain for the men of wisdom and counsel to raise their voice when revolutions are begun; that the wind bloweth as it listeth; that the wind becomes a storm, and the storm a hurricane, raging till the air be purified: this is their excuse for the measures of violence and guilt that too often occur. But reverse the picture, and the same is the reasoning of writers whose principles are those of an opposite and arbitrary cast; and it is *their* excuse, on the contrary, for listening to *no* projects of reform, and for ruling men from the first by mere force and authority; not perceiving, that it is for them at all times to consider whether what is proposed be just and reasonable or not; to concede nothing indeed to fear, but every thing to reason.

It is for those who read history, above all, for those who comment upon history, to resist these sweeping conclusions on the one side and on the other, these doctrines of despair, these views of human nature, that can lead to nothing but slavery on the one side, or bloodshed and anarchy on the other. Men must be called upon to observe the mistakes and the crimes of those who went before them; and they must be required to avoid and fly them, as they are rational creatures, as they are beings "that look before and after." In like manner, in domestic and social life, men will be selfish, hard-hearted, licentious, wicked. It must needs be that offences will come; but it does not follow that our sages and our divines are not still to labour on, in the duties of their callings, are not still to cry aloud and spare not. The cause of human nature must never be abandoned; nor need it, it may be added, for it can never be sufficiently known or estimated what may have been even the *success* of those, who toil for the benefit of mankind; because the evils they have prevented do not appear, and cannot be brought to the credit of their account; while those they have in vain resisted, are seen but too plainly, and operate against them.

In the history of our own country, in the times of the great rebellion, Charles I was so arbitrary and obstinate, and the religious principle got so interwoven into the disputes between the monarch and his parliaments, that the moderate men, the men of wisdom and counsel (who had been always, however, far too torpid), were at last obliged to give way, and a civil war ensued; but it was not so at the period of the Revolution of 1688; in this instance they prevailed, and this is the eternal glory of the Whigs of that era. What was then done, however, may again be done; and this splendid instance in the annals of mankind must ever be of avail to encourage the friends of freedom in their virtuous struggles, must ever be sufficient to show them that efforts for the welfare of the community do not necessarily fail; that resistance to oppression is not necessarily followed by anarchy and civil war; that the friends of their country and of mankind *may* succeed, if they can but to their high virtues add other virtues that are equally indispensable, though they may at first sight appear scarcely necessary, and, indeed, to bold and generous men may always appear virtues of a very lowly and ordinary nature. Patience, moderation, modesty of temperament, candour, attention to the feelings of others, to the arguments of their opponents; a disposition to make the ground solid under them as they go along; a deep sense of the infirmities of their own nature, and of the irritable nature of the passions of mankind; these are the virtues not less necessary than those of a more popular nature, to the proper completion of their character as patriots and reformers. The union of these qualities is difficult, but a fair object of virtuous ambition; it is within the reach of human nature, and it may and ought to be produced. On the whole, then, of the case, opposite lessons must be directed to the different portions of the community. Those in the political system, who in the first place want instruction, are, on the one side, the grave and the old, and the privileged orders, who will suffer no alteration, and make no provision for the new circumstances that may have occurred, the changes that time may have operated upon their own community and the world: and, in the second place are those on the other side, who will make no allowance for what they may esteem the prejudices of others, and who forget that, at all events, reformers must proceed upon a system of conciliation and peace, for if a temperament of this sort once cease, the violent will alone succeed, and they themselves be no longer listened to; lastly, and above all, that if, when they have the power, they make their terms too hard, their opponents cannot be expected (I speak not of the point of duty, but they cannot in *practice* be expected) to keep good faith with them, and nothing durable or solid will have in reality been accomplished. So was it in France on this present occasion: the friends of freedom did not sufficiently assist Mounier, and the men of moderation and wisdom; they would not accommodate themselves to what they esteemed the prejudices of their opponents; they proceeded not sufficiently on a system of peace and conciliation; they had more splendid views, we will suppose, of the happiness of France and of mankind, and, in a word, they made their terms with the king and court too hard, and their Revolution failed: it could not but fail: and it failed, though the king was not of a temperament to resist them; was too gentle, and too benevolent: had he been of an ordinary complexion, a civil war would have ensued; and this also I should call the failure of a revolution, as I do the subsequent disorder and anarchy. . . .

We must now reverse the picture, and turn to the king and the court. On all occasions violence in one direction produces it in another. When the decision of every question in the National Assembly went unfavourably to the executive power, what were to be the feelings of those who were attached to the royal authority? When the Assembly, who were summoned by the king to assist him in reforming the state, assumed all power to themselves, and evidently set the king entirely aside, referred every thing to the sovereignty of the people, and considered themselves as its only legitimate representative;—when to those who spoke of the ancient institutions and established principles of the French monarchy, it was only replied that France was to be now regenerated, that a new constitution was to be given, and that the king was not even to concur in its formation, was not to sanction, but was only to accept it!—when these were to be the results of the experiment, which the king had made in calling the States-General, partly, no doubt, from the necessities of the state, but surely from motives of benevolence and patriotism also;—when these were to be the results of his efforts for the general happiness, with what sentiments was the king to be affected, with what sentiments but those of indignation and anger? And what were to be the feelings of his courtiers, and the court, and the privileged orders, who had neither his benevolence nor his patriotism; what but the feelings of horror at the populace, and of hatred of their leaders, rage at the patriots in the Assembly, an abjuration of all measures of change and reform, and thoughts only of an appeal to arms, the succour of foreign powers, and a civil war? How impossible was it that effects of this kind should not be produced in the one party by the hard terms that had been imposed, by the unlimited pretensions that had been advanced by the other! But what was to be done? The royal authority had been produced on the 23rd of June, and the king's system of a constitution offered, in vain. . . .

Such is but too often the unhappy progress of civil dissensions—no magnanimity, no moderation, no kindness, no peace, no opportunity for the wise and good; violence, fury alone, bearing sway; and the happiness of a community, if accomplished at all, the result rather of its good fortune than its merit. Melancholy reflections of this kind will obtrude themselves; but we must not speak thus, though not to feel thus is sometimes impossible. The lesson is everywhere and always the same; moderation—timely moderation—the despised, unpalatable lesson of moderation, disdained by the high-minded, ridiculed by the thoughtless, forgotten by all, and most so when most needed.

But we must not, I say, speak thus, but continue to note, as well as we can, the mistakes and faults of every party in its turn; the whole of our lesson being still comprised, as I have just intimated, in the single word, moderation. And now, then, what were the events that took place? what was the more immediate history? The two great parties in the state were in the situation we have described. The history was sure to become important: the adherents of the old opinions could not possibly acquiesce, with any sincerity, in the terms which the assertors of the new opinions had imposed upon them. There were very violent, unreasonable men among the former, the adherents of the old opinions; they might and did wish only for a counter revolution; but again, there were very violent and unreasonable men among the latter, the assertors of the new opinions; and to these latter also were united many daring and bad men—the lower orders of the lower fauxbourgs of Paris, and the mobs and orators of the Palais Royal—and these were determined to secure themselves and their Revolution, as they supposed, and to bring the king to Paris.

A collision could not well be escaped, the moderate men in the National Assembly having failed—and a collision *did* take place, a dreadful one —the crisis so well known in history under the general name of the events of the 5th and 6th of October, and I must consider it at some length.

The immediate causes were soon found; these were, 1st, a scarcity in Paris; and 2ndly, some imprudence on the part of the court at Versailles. Nothing is so easy as to rouse the people to acts of violence when they want bread: and in this situation they will believe any thing of their rulers or their government that is told them. What was told them, too, in this instance, of the intentions of the court to retire and prepare a civil war, was not in itself improbable.

When a train of this kind was laid, the slightest spark from the imprudence of the court was sure to produce an explosion. But this slight spark was produced by the imprudence of the court, and in the following manner.

The critical state of affairs in Paris seems to have been apprehended at Versailles, and among others by the Count d'Estaing,* who wrote a letter to the queen, on the 14th of September, detailing to her the conversation he had lately heard in the metropolis, to the effect we have just described, the rumours and suspicions that prevailed, and requesting an audience. This was granted. What passed is not known, but the result probably was that the queen satisfied the count that the machinations he talked of meant only the safety of the king and the royal family. This is, indeed, sufficiently clear from what followed. The old French guards, who had joined the popular cause, and were at Paris, talked of returning to Versailles to re-assume their post of duty around the king; La Fayette wrote to St. Priest, who was in the confidence of the court, on the 17th of September, not to be alarmed, for he was sure he had influence enough with the troops to prevent this measure of their return. But this assurance from La Fayette could not satisfy the court; there was no force to be opposed to them; four hundred body guards and one hundred chasseurs were all; the town militia of Versailles could not be depended upon; and by a decree of the National Assembly, no troops of the line could be brought up without a requisition from the municipality. Now this requisition the Count d'Estaing made it his business to procure from the municipality of Versailles, by representing to them that La Fayette was favourable to the measure; that the king was alarmed; that the royal family, that the very National Assembly would be endangered by the presence of two thousand of the French guards, who were coming to resume their post, as they called it, round the king, and that a regiment

* Jean-Baptiste-Charles-Henri-Hector, comte d'Estaing (1729–94), appointed Admiral of France (1792). He was guillotined. He had helped the cause of the American Revolution with a squadron from the French Navy.—ED.

of the line must be brought up immediately. The regiment of Flanders was fixed upon; the court thought they could best depend upon them, for they had refused the civic oath; and, on the contrary, their colonel was a member of the Assembly, and attached to the popular cause; this consideration, therefore, it was thought would tend to quiet the fears of the Assembly. The Assembly seem not to have behaved improperly on this occasion, though the measure had, on the whole (however prudent and necessary in itself), somewhat of the appearance of an intrigue.

You will immediately see how fast were now collecting together the materials of future commotion. The municipal force, or national guards, of Versailles were to be made to coalesce as much as possible with the regiment of Flanders; they had not yet been organized; the queen was to give them their colours; there was to be a day appointed for the benediction, a sort of joint review of them and the body guards to take place. This was all very well, and would have been so at any common juncture, but on the present occasion all this was interpreted by the people of Paris as the beginning and the preparations of a counter revolution; which was therefore to be prevented by sending to Versailles the old French guards disguised, and women of the town, to detach the soldiers from their allegiance. These old French guards, as I have mentioned, were not satisfied that, because they had become patriots, they were no longer to occupy their posts of honour about the palace of the king; who, on his part, could not be well disposed to those who seemed now rather to belong to the city of Paris than to him; and the Assembly itself had already proposed its decrees and votes on the future constitution of France, of a nature far too democratic to be sincerely admitted by the king, or to be at all relished by those who wished well to his authority. Lastly, and above all, it must have been well known to the court, that the popular party meant, if possible, to accomplish the removal of the king and the Assembly to Paris; and the queen and the court could not but have surveyed any project of this kind with sentiments of perfect horror.

This was a most calamitous state of things, and the slightest untoward accident, or unfortunate mistake, or offensive imprudence, might evidently lead to consequences the most important. Such an accident, or mistake, or offensive imprudence, did immediately occur. What it was is well known; it was after the following manner. The gardes du corps (the king's body guards at Versailles) gave an entertainment to the officers of the regiment of Flanders, to which they invited several officers of the national guard, of the rangers, and other military corps; the king, at their request, lent them the theatre of the palace for the purpose; the dinner was served to near three hundred guests; the lights of the house, the crowd of spectators who filled the boxes, the music of the different regimental bands gave to the repast the brilliancy and gaiety of a festival. During the first course all was decency and order; in the second, the company drank, very naturally, to the health of the king, the queen, the dauphin, and the royal family, and the cries of "Vive le Roi!" "Vive la Reine!" "Vive la Famille Royale!" of course resounded from every quarter. All this was innocent enough, but the health of the nation was feebly proposed by some one of the company, more patriotic than wise, for the present was not the precise moment for a toast like this, and the toast (though not exactly rejected) after all was not drunk. "Vive la Nation" had not as yet become a national cry. But this was the first offence committed, and it was an offence, and was afterwards not a little dwelt upon. It was but a matter of course that some of the ladies of the palace should run to the queen, to tell her how prosperously went on the banquet, and to beg her to send the dauphin. The queen was in no spirits; she was requested to come herself; the spectacle might amuse her; she hesitated, and some mysterious, inexplicable presentiment seemed to say, that sad might be the consequences of what in itself appeared so innocent and unimportant. The king returned from hunting—would he accompany her? The king complied, and with the dauphin, the royal visitors placed themselves in one of the latticed boxes; but they were soon discovered, and a thousand cries of "Vive le Roi!" "Vive la Reine!" "Vive M. le Dauphin!" resounded from all parts of the theatre. The poor king was unable to resist these testimonies of affection, they had become to him of late more than ever precious; he descended from his box, and the queen, with the dauphin in her arms, made the tour of the table amid the most loud and reiterated acclamations and applauses.

This was a sight not likely to be unaffecting to such a company, and on such an occasion. The graces and elegance of the queen's deportment had long been the subject of general admiration in a court, and amid a nation, where graces were virtues, and elegance was the ambition of all; the dauphin, too, always made the idol of the nation, was seen reposing on the bosom of his mother in all the affecting innocence and simplicity of childhood; and both were now more than ever recommended, as well as the father near them, to the courage and the loyalty of every true Frenchman—to their courage and loyalty; for the necessity of such virtues must have been deeply felt at the moment, amid a thousand apprehensions of unknown and mysterious danger, that seemed to be gathering around them, menacing with insult their dignity and honour, and threatening even the security of the throne, and the very tenure of their existence.

The swords were drawn and flourished in the air; the healths were again repeated; the acclamations again and again resounded, and the queen seemed to renew the image of her august mother, Maria Theresa, addressing herself to her Hungarian subjects, with the young emperor in her arms, and like her, appealing for compassion, and requesting their protection against the daring and unfeeling men who were going to drive her from her throne, and plunder her possessions.

At this moment, as the royal family was retiring, the bands struck up the air of Grétry, in his musical romance of Richard Cœur de Lion, the well-known air, "O Richard, O mon Roi, l'univers t'abandonne." Never were sounds that so completely convey the sentiment that is to be expressed. They are put into the mouth of the queen, addressing her song, disguised as a minstrel, to the captive king—"O Richard, O my love, by the tyrant world forgot," as the original words were translated for the English stage. It is many years since I heard them delivered at one of our own theatres, no doubt by the sweetest voice that theatre ever listened to; and to this hour I can recollect the melting of the heart, and the indignation that was excited against the oppressor and an unfeeling world, that thus abandoned the royal captive to his brutal tyrant; all this I well recollect (allow me to speak of myself), and if at the distance of so many ages from the real event, sitting only for my amusement at a public spectacle, I could thus be affected, as I remember myself to have been, by the mere delusion of the scene, what (I can readily conceive), what must have been the effect produced by the same music upon the hearts of Frenchmen, of young officers, men of honour and of arms, fearless of the future and prodigal of life, each animated by the banquet and the sympathy of surrounding minds, while they saw palpably standing before them, with his queen and dauphin, their own unhappy Richard, whom surely the world seemed to abandon; for where was he to look for aid, and how had he offended?

What followed at this unfortunate entertainment may be without difficulty imagined. Imprudences without number: "Down with the tricoloured cockade!" "Long live the white!" "The white for ever!" these were the cries that were heard. The boxes were scaled; the guests were intoxicated; uproar and noisy merriment everywhere prevailed; white cockades were noticed in the king's anti-chamber; in the evening, ladies of the court, it is said, took the white ribbons of their head-dresses, and put them into the hats of officers of the national guard, who had asked for them. . . .

Any thing and every thing was believed, and these transactions produced the most lively indignation. Other imprudences (they were now, alas! becoming follies and faults) in the meantime took place at Versailles: the banquet was repeated the next day, the 2nd of October, and the company indulged in even greater excesses of revelry; the ladies were more bold and active with their cockades, and black cockades appeared even in Paris. The people were irritated; and with perfect reason; for these were the beginnings of a civil war, after a national cockade, the tricoloured, had been once established, and the king had himself adopted it.

Follies and faults, or experiments (as they were thought) of this kind called into full activity the revolutionists in Paris; they could now perceive, that every thing was prepared for the execution of their own projects, in front of which was placed the removal of the king to Paris. Symptoms of a counter revolution at Versailles, and a populace in want of bread in the metropolis, these were sufficient hinges on which to move the metropolis and the kingdom.

You will see in the histories the gradual progress of the insurrection which was at last brought to the point desired, and "Bread!" "Bread!" "To Versailles!" "To Versailles!" became in Paris the universal cry. The town house was on the point of being burnt; the constituted authorities exerted themselves in vain; La Fayette harangued, exhorted, and conjured them, equally in vain; his life was in danger; and the Assembly of the Commune at last sent him word, that he must go with the people, as they desired, to Versailles, since there was no alternative.

As La Fayette was one of the first movers of the Revolution, no proper justice is ever done to his character by those who were unfriendly to the Revolution; it must, therefore, be mentioned that it is quite clear, from the concurring accounts of all writers, that he made every possible exertion to prevent this fatal measure, this march to Versailles, and that, with an afflicted and foreboding heart, he accompanied the populace and the soldiers, to take the chance of moderating and directing, as well as he could, a dreadful mass of men, whom he could no longer control or bring to reason.

In the meantime, the agitation was at Versailles only less than at Paris: from the first opening of the sitting, this agitation appeared not only in the Assembly but in the tribunes, and in the looks and gestures of the multitudes that surrounded the hall.

You will see a short and good account of what passed in Ferrieres. It happened that, at the time, very unfortunately, the president * had to report the answer of the king to the Constitutional Decrees and the Declaration of Rights. This answer was not sufficiently favourable and agreeable to the more ardent part of the Assembly; violent language ensued; strong allusions were made to the unfortunate fêtes that we have just described; to orgies, as they were called; to menaces uttered; to counter revolutions intended; to the national cockade trampled under foot. "It is not the cries of 'Vive le Roi,' or 'Vive la Reine,' " said Pétion, "that we complain of, they are ever welcome to our hearts; but in these military orgies, have not imprecations been vented against the National As-

* Jérôme Pétion de Villeneuve (1756–94), French revolutionist; first president of the National Convention.—ED.

sembly, and against liberty? Have the body-guards taken the oath? What means this black cockade?" One of the members of the nobility, shocked at these misrepresentations, moved that Pétion's denunciation should be signed by him, and laid upon the table. Pétion was embarrassed; but Mirabeau, formed for such conjectures, instantly started up, and cried out, that he would himself denounce and sign, if the Assembly would first declare, that all but the king were within the reach of the law. "I will then," said he, audibly enough to be heard by those around him, "denounce the queen and the Duke de Guiche [a hated royalist]."

This unexpected proposition soon made it necessary for the president, who luckily happened to be Mounier, to call for the order of the day, and get rid of such a perilous discussion. The result was that the president, at the head of a deputation, was ordered to wait upon the king, to beseech him to give his assent, pure and unconditional, to the articles of the constitution, and the Declaration of Rights, that had been just presented to him. But in the midst of this debate, four hours before the brigands arrived, Mirabeau had gone behind the president's chair, and apprized him that there were forty thousand men marching upon them from Paris—"You had better break up the sitting."

Mirabeau, it is thought, wanted a clear stage, the better to ensure the success of his operations; and this notion is somewhat strengthened by the cold and pointed reply of the president, "So much the better, they have but to kill us all—all—and the affairs of the republic [a sarcastic word] will go on better." "That's prettily said," replied Mirabeau, and retired.

It is possible, however, that Mirabeau only wished, as a well-meaning man naturally might, on the first impulse, at least, to get the Assembly out of the way, when such a storm was approaching. Bertrand de Moleville blames La Fayette for not sending off intelligence of the formidable body of men that was coming. Only women and brigands were expected; it was thought enough to shut the iron gates of the palace, and to draw out on the Place d'Armes the regiment of Flanders, the rangers, the gardes du corps, and some other military force; the national guards of Versailles were in their neighbouring barracks. About three o'clock the phalanx of the women arrived, Maillard at their head, the man who had played the chief part in the attack of the Bastile.

A disgusting scene soon ensued; Maillard presented himself at the bar of the Assembly with his retinue, and set forth, that for three days past there had absolutely been no bread in Paris; that they were come to Versailles to ask for it, and, at the same time, to have the gardes du corps punished for having insulted the national cockade; that the aristocrats wanted to starve them. The Assembly were able to pacify tolerably well this first orator and his deputation; but other women soon forced their

way into the Hall of Assembly, mounted upon the benches, crying for
bread (all at once), the dismission of the regiment of Flanders, the
punishment of the gardes du corps, and uttering, at the same time, the
most horrid imprecations against the queen; some insulted the deputies,
particularly those of the clergy. "Speak, you deputy there," they said to
one; "Silence, you deputy there," to another; and, in short, the scene
soon became so scandalous, that the Assembly had no measure left but
to charge the president to go immediately to the palace, at the head of
a deputation, and represent the calamitous situation of Paris to the king.
This was done, some of the women accompanied, and the king received
and was able to soothe and tranquillize them.

These were, indeed, the occasions on which the unfortunate monarch
appeared to such an advantage: his genuine benevolence, his ready sensibility, his calm patience, his dignified fearlessness, his anxiety to do every
thing that was or could be required of him, his gentleness, his politeness,
his humanity, lawless as these women were, women they still were, and
such qualities it was impossible should not have some effect upon them.
One of them, a girl of seventeen, fainted, and they all retired, crying in
the court, "Vive le Roi!" "God bless the king and his family!" "We
shall have bread to-morrow!"

But the situation of the king and the palace was, in truth, most unprotected and most deplorable. The regiment of Flanders seems to have been
ordered away from the palace; it had been corrupted by the municipal
force of Versailles. Most of the body guards, too, were sent to Ram-
bouillet by the king from motives of humanity, lest they should be massacred; they were gentlemen all, from the nature of the institution. The
king then sent for the National Assembly, meaning to place himself under their protection; but such part of the National Assembly as still remained in their hall was mixed up, and reduced almost to a level, with
the poissardes and first banditti that had arrived from the metropolis,
and no use could be made of them. And afterwards, while Mounier, the
president, was endeavouring, by beat of drum, to collect a proper representation of the nation, with which to surround the king, La Fayette arrived, and their protection was thought, after an interview with him, no
longer necessary.

But the disgraceful scenes to which we have just alluded in the Assembly were but the beginnings of troubles. It is impossible to give
here the slightest idea of what passed for many hours afterwards in and
about the palace. Bertrand de Moleville was on the spot, and gives a
very detailed account, and you must refer to it. You will easily see what
were the great component parts of this dreadful whole: the royal family
who were to be protected; the body guards, who were now left few in
number, and who were alone faithful, and who wanted protection also;

the old French guards who had come to resume their posts about the king; the national guards of Versailles, whose fidelity to the king and whose attachment were of a very wavering nature, or rather were extinct and void; and lastly, the military bodies that were coming up with La Fayette, the national guards or militia of Paris; these were not favourable to the king, and not favourable to the old body guards: and again, mixed up with the whole, and first making their appearance with the women, and afterwards in fresh crowds with La Fayette's army, were to be enumerated, as actors in the scene, a description of people called by the general name of brigands, the most ferocious and brutal men and women that could issue from the most desperate part of the population of Paris; supposed by most writers to have been hired for purposes of mischief, and even for the destruction of the queen, by the Duke of Orléans and his party; but at all events engaged and brought up by the revolutionists to accomplish their one great end, that of forcing the king and royal family to Paris, that they and the Assembly might be under their control, and not only all chance of a counter revolution, or the king's flight, be prevented, but the Revolution itself made to proceed according to their pleasure.

Mirabeau and the Duke of Orléans were so accused of being the prime movers of the dreadful occurrences which now took place in and about the palace, that a judicial inquiry was afterwards instituted, which ended, as such inquiries generally do, in an exhibition of evidence, which it is impossible to weigh, and fatiguing to read, and in the acquittal of the accused. Even Bertrand's account, though comprised within a couple of chapters, it is in vain to attempt minutely to understand.

But the general history of what now took place, in a word, is this: the body guards are insulted and assaulted; La Fayette appears, answers for his troops, pacifies the court, quiets the National Assembly, and tranquillizes the king and royal family; the old French guards, who had lately gone over to the nation, resume their old posts about the king, which was their particular object and wish, as guards of the palace. Every thing is at last quiet, and at a late hour, the general, overcome with the fatigues and anxieties of such a day and such a night, sinks for a short interval to rest. The brigands, the horrible wretches that we have mentioned, early in the morning get into the palace; they make for the queen's apartment; she has just time to fly for her life to the king; her guard at the door is left for dead; many of the gentlemen of the palace and distinguished officers of the different corps are murdered, or left mangled and expiring; La Fayette is roused from his unfortunate repose; by his personal courage and activity, and the exertions and steadiness of the king, the body guards (the gentlemen about the king) are saved from massacre, and at length something of the appearance of peace and good will and

order are procured, but at a most fatal price; the removal of the king to
Paris, which is the cry at last heard, and to which no refusal, it seems,
could then be given. . . .

The remainder of the history is well known. The king and the royal
family came to Paris; they were received by the mayor, by Bailly, the
man of science, who called the day of their arrival a beautiful day, a
strange and most unfortunate expression, which Bailly was not a man
to have used in its more obvious and offensive sense. It was an expression that never was or could be forgotten, apparently so completely at
variance with every sentiment and reflection that could at the time, and
on the spot, be entertained by any wise and good man like M. Bailly, who
might wish, indeed, for freedom and the fall of tyranny, but who surely
could not see a tyrant in Louis, or freedom in excesses like these.

The king was then transferred to the Tuileries, and the palace of his
ancestors became his prison.*

xxi. FROM THE FIFTH AND SIXTH OF OCTOBER TO THE FLIGHT TO VARENNES

The Assembly, for I must now return to their history, immediately after
the abolition of the titles of the nobility, proceeded to support their
Revolution by the measures I have already announced to you, the federation; a measure in itself more harmless and more adapted to the national
character. The truth was they were not quite at ease on the subject of
the military force of the country; at least, they thought it advisable to
pledge to the Revolution the national guards, everywhere dispersed over
France, and the troops of the line. They therefore formed the project of
an immense federation, to take place on the 14th of July, the anniversary
of the taking of the Bastile; and deputations were to be sent from all
the armed bodies by land and by sea, from all the different departments
of the kingdom and constituted authorities of the capital. These were all
to assist at the fête, in the presence of the National Assembly, the king,
the queen, and the court: they were to be surrounded by the greatest
possible number of spectators, three or four hundred thousand people. An
immense plain, the Champ de Mars, was to be hollowed out into an
amphitheatre; a superb altar to be erected; three hundred priests to assemble, and twelve hundred musicians; and an oath to be taken by these

* Lecture XX summarizes the views of a number of eminent personages.—Ed.

deputies, by the nation, and the king, of fidelity to the constitution, the great leading principles of which had been already sufficiently promulgated, though the constitution itself had not as yet been finally prepared and delivered. . . .

But the leading observation resulting from the whole is that the Revolution and the National Assembly must now have been most clearly and universally approved and acceptable to the French people, or such a fête could neither have been attempted nor executed. This popularity of the Revolution, and therefore of the fête in honour of it, was in different stages of it severely tried and abundantly shown. It was intended, for instance, as I have mentioned, that three hundred thousand spectators should be accommodated with seats. Twelve thousand, some say twenty-five thousand, workmen were employed; but it was reported that the necessary preparations could not thus be finished by the day appointed. This would have been a serious difficulty anywhere but in France, and even in France must have been fatal to the success of the fête, if the Revolution had not been popular. But in an instant all Paris was in motion, and citizens of every age, sex, and condition, appeared with the spade, the pickaxe, and the wheelbarrow, all mixed and mingled together, to carry on the work. The women of fashion and the poissardes, those of good repute and those of ill, courtiers and butchers, players and monks, old men and children, capuchins, academicians, chevaliers of St. Louis, and workmen from the villages, headed by their mayors and curés,—all this assemblage of voluntary labourers was fed and accommodated by people travelling with taverns and portable shops, and enlivened by songs, and shouts of joy, and the national air of "Ca ira"; and the result was, that all the preparations for the fête were ready before the time appointed; and the triumph of these apparently curious and comical groups, but in reality these striking representatives of an overwhelming and therefore very serious and almost frightful patriotic enthusiasm, was quite complete.

It was in vain, in like manner, that the rain poured down in torrents on the day of the federation; the fête still went on. Nothing could oppose resistance to the universal joy. The dances were formed, and the processions moved forwards, and the music sounded; and neither earth below, nor sky above, the wet Champ de Mars, nor the drenching coldness of the descending clouds, had been or were of the slightest avail to repress the vivacity of the multitude, excited as they were by what was to them the dearest of all objects, a magnificent spectacle; fired, too, with exultation at the visible departure of the old régime, and gazing with delight on the approach and promises of the new.

And certainly, if we could forget for a moment all subsequent events, and the stain that has been brought on the great cause of liberty by this giddy people, by many of the very individuals here assembled, certainly there was something in this spectacle, this universal expression of inter-changed happiness and affection, this apparent dedication of a whole nation to the leading principles of liberty, this resounding exultation of the people at their emancipation from the blighting and degrading influ-ence of a government that had so long ceased to be respected, this union and amalgamation of the interests and wishes of the king and of the people well fitted to overpower the imagination and awaken the sym-pathies of the benevolent, wherever they might be found, in France or in England, in Europe or in America. It seemed no time now to hesitate or to examine, no time to consider what had preceded or what was to follow this glittering and magnificent show. Altars and arches were to be seen; the inscriptions that everywhere appeared were testimonies to liberty and to law. "The country and the law: let us die to defend them," was one, for instance. "The king of a free people, he is alone the king of power," was another. "Cherish liberty; you possess it, be worthy of it." "It is not birth that makes the difference between men, it is virtue only." "It is the law that should be everywhere; before it, all are equal." These were among the mottoes and inscriptions; and where the Bastile had once stood was an esplanade, and over every entrance to it was writ-ten, in a manner, affecting no doubt, yet truly characteristic of the na-tion, "Here we now dance."

But it was fêtes and festivals in honour of liberty that this sensitive, theatric people far better understood than the nature of liberty itself; and the scene before us has been thought the most awful and extensive exhibition of perjury that the world ever saw; for it must be observed that the same scene was acted at one and the same moment in every department of France. The perjury was that of millions of human be-ings swearing to a constitution which the next moment they destroyed; and it will be a warning, it is to be hoped, to mankind, never again to have recourse to such idle expedients, or rather to such impious mock-eries. No legislation is so immoral as that which has recourse to oaths; none so unwise, as that which depends upon them. I speak not of the point of duty in those who take them. In the coarse legislation of com-merce, custom-house oaths have become a proverb; and, even in the in-stance before us, Louis XVI was a man of piety, and would not have bound himself by an oath which he did not mean to keep; but observe the temptation to which the integrity of his mind was on this occasion exposed. How could he resist the measure? How could he decline taking the oath? He was to all intents and purposes a prisoner, and had been so since the 5th and 6th of October. He had no force to oppose to that of the National Assembly; and not to assent to the oath in the general

manner in which it was worded, would have been to say that he was determined to restore the old régime, that he would have no further concern with the Revolution, and in short to leave the patriotic party no
measure but to dethrone him, or himself no measure but to resign his
crown. He stood, therefore, at the federation, under the strictest political necessity to conform to the wishes of the Assembly, and to act the
part allotted to him in this grand national performance. It is, indeed,
sufficiently clear that the king, as far as the oath went, was perfectly
sincere. No doubt the Revolution had rolled on, and far overflowed the
boundaries within which he would have thought its course ought to be
confined; still, he was desirous of the happiness of his people, he had confidence in his own good intentions, he had no wish for any authority inconsistent with the public good, and as yet he did not despair either of
the affection or the loyalty of his subjects; as yet he conceived that, if
he could but weather the storm, the storm would gradually subside, and
that he and his people might hereafter see happier days, and enjoy the
calm of mutual confidence and an improved constitution of the government. It is sufficiently probable, therefore, that the king was sincere
when he promised to uphold the constitution by all the means that
were put in his power, and that he conformed, if not with a cheerful, yet
with a general acquiescence, to what was required of him during the fête
and ceremonials of the federation. Still, the oath was imposed upon him.
But he was not entirely without his gratifications. He seems to have been
much and very naturally affected by the general testimonies of loyalty
and respect which, amidst all the fervour of revolutionary feelings, were
still paid him by many of those who came deputed from the different
provinces. But when the tumult and excitement of the fête were passed
away, when the National Assembly resumed its wonted course of proce-
dure, and when various circumstances continued to dispel the hopes and
illusions with which the king had soothed the benevolence of his nature,
different views of his situation seem gradually to have opened up his
mind, and before the end of the year he had begun to entertain thoughts
of escaping from his prison, and of neither acquiescing, nor appearing
to acquiesce, in the constitution, such as it was likely to become, or as
it was even then administered and understood, at the close of the year
1790.*

* Lectures XXII through XXV take the reader through Louis' ill-advised flight to
Varennes and the beginning of the war with Austria.—ED.

xxvi. KING'S MISSION BY MALLET DU PAN *

WITH RESPECT to the great subject of the Austrian war, the points seem
to be that though the allied powers meant only to act on the defensive,
they expressed themselves in a manner so offensive to the national dignity of France, and assumed to themselves such a power of interfering
in the government of the country, that they left the popular party in
France a right to declare war if they thought it necessary to the interests
of their country; and yet we afterwards contended that, under the circumstances of the case, the Girondists ought not to have made war, and
that by doing so they could not but bring their Revolution into the
greatest difficulties, reducing everything to the chance of despotism on
the one side, and anarchy on the other.

We next held that the king did everything in his power to prevent
the war, and was deeply affected by the calamities to which he saw
France thus exposed, as well as clearly aware of the dangers that were thus
made to threaten himself; that he was not wanting to the constitution,
or indisposed to give it a fair trial, till the Jacobin ministry, as it was
called, was forced upon him, and war declared against Austria; that from
that time he turned to other counsels . . . that not having called the
allied powers into France, he thought he might be a mediator between
them and his subjects; that a counter-revolution was now his object, but
not arbitrary power; that his intentions were still benevolent and patriotic, but that his interference, or any interference with the combined
powers, was exposed to the objection, that no foreign armies are ever
to be suffered to intermingle themselves in the concerns of a country. We
contended, however, that allowance must be made for the unhappy
monarch: his country, he must have thought, had no other chances of
escape from calamity, or himself from a scaffold; his family from assassination, or his friends from massacre.

On the whole, the great mistake seems to have been, on the one side
and on the other, that the supporters of the old régime thought they
could set the Jacobins apart, and make war upon the clubs and more
violent Revolutionists, and not on the rest of the nation,—this seems to
have been their mistake from the first; and that, on the other hand, the
supporters of the Revolution kept no bounds in their spirit of proselytism, and justly alarmed every neighbouring country, after first violating
the feelings of every one who differed from them in their own. And thus

* The lecture title is retained, though most of the matter has been omitted.

far, indeed, I see no reason to congratulate either of the parties on the wisdom or virtue of their proceedings.

In conclusion, it is truly melancholy to observe in mankind such a total want of all moderation, of all reasonable attention to the feelings and opinions of each other. The patrons of the old opinions, for instance, and the German courts, would have disliked the Revolution under any circumstances, and under any possible modifications; and the complaints and representations of the emigrants, and the sufferings of the royal family, when the Revolution turned out to be so very destructive of all established authorities and opinions, excited the strongest sympathy in all governing classes. All this was very natural, particularly the sentiment of moral indignation by which they were animated; still, when every allowance has been made for their situation, the best *manner* of interference was evidently a question of the greatest difficulty; and some more prudence and discretion might have been expected, and some more attention than was, in fact, shown to the acknowledged rights of independent nations, to those especially of a great kingdom like France, under an acknowledged state of revolutionary excitement at the time.

And again, with respect to the patrons of the new opinions, they might look down with contempt on the old governments and the prejudices that supported them: they were free, no doubt, to follow where their reasoning seemed to lead them, in making up their *own* opinions; but why were they to be animated with such a restless, offensive, revolutionary spirit of proselytism?

Their principles and notions went certainly to the disturbance and even the subversion of the other feudal governments of Europe. Why were they to proclaim them everywhere, disseminate their revolutionary writings, and establish their clubs?

It afterwards appeared that wherever the French armies went, the ground was prepared for them; the friends of the new opinions were found organized, the clubs in activity, and the foundations of society, as it had hitherto existed, subverted. But why all this aggression, this invasion, this war, this exterminating war, to be waged against all constituted authorities in the dominions of independent nations? The great truths of civil liberty, it will be said, as of religious liberty at the time of the Reformation, are everywhere to be propagated, that others may participate of the benefits we ourselves enjoy, and that the happiness of mankind may be made progressive.

This is a principle (the dissemination of truth), no doubt, of the most sacred nature, one to which we owe everything that has improved or dignified our nature; but it is a principle which, when opposed to established opinions, must always be exercised with circumspection and care. It can be exercised by no man, and by no description of men, without incurring the most awful responsibility, and a far greater responsibility than is generally supposed: certainly it must never be exercised without an examination of the new opinions, which are to be propagated, and the old opinions that are to be overthrown, far more grave and anxious than has been often exercised; without an attention to the particular circumstances of the case, far more provident and patient than has been often shown.

On this great occasion of the French Revolution, on this great crisis in the affairs of the world, the enthusiasm, the spirit of proselytism of the patrons of the new opinions, was totally ungovernable and unpardonable. They had neither sense nor patience in comparing the value of their own new opinions with the old, nor mercy nor forbearance in their conduct to those who differed from them.

With regard to the king, his case is exhibited in the memorial I have produced. What he hoped, and feared, and wished, and attempted, are all here. This document I consider as the very image and identification of his mind and nature. No doubt the general principle was against him; no communication whatever is to be held with foreign powers for the purpose of influencing the internal concerns of our own country. We dispute not a principle so universally salutary and important, so supported by experience as well as by theory. But what is to be our censure, if we consider that he had made every effort to prevent the war; that these foreign powers were approaching as enemies, whether he interfered with them or not; that the popular party in the capital were pressing forward upon him to trample him down into the dust; that he had no other hope, no other chance for his crown and dignity, but what he could derive from the assistance of the allies; that he not only saw them approaching, but had no doubts of their success? What is to be our censure, I say? Is it to be expected from human wisdom, from human feelings, that the king should, in this situation, adhere to a general principle in political science, when, by deviating from it, he only attempted to be a pacificator between his subjects and their invaders, turn his influence with the one to the best interests and purposes of the other, and endeavour to put an end to the calamities of his country, and, if possible, his own.*

---

* Lectures XXVII, XXVIII, and XXIX deal with the growing power of the extremists. They include a detailed narrative of the insurrection of June 20, 1792, when Louis XVI displayed an unwonted firmness in refusing to recall the vetoes that he had applied to certain popular measures of a radical nature. But the savage course of the Jacobins was not halted. The massacre of the Swiss Guards and the suspension of the king came on August 6.—ED.

xxx. TENTH OF AUGUST

THE MAIN events of this dreadful day of the 10th of August are sufficiently ascertained. There is some difference between the accounts of the opposite parties on one point, whether the Swiss or the assailants fired first, but on all the other leading facts they are agreed. They may be differently coloured or explained, but an inquirer will find no difficulty in satisfying himself what they really were. They are a tremendous specimen of the bloody fury of which human nature is capable, and a mortifying part of the history of mankind to have occurred in the metropolis of one of the first kingdoms of the civilized world so late as at the close of the eighteenth century.

It appears, as I have already mentioned, that through most of the month of July a regular committee had been sitting in the correspondence room of the Assembly of the Jacobins, and at Charenton, a small town near Paris, the object of which was to recall the three ministers, and depose the king; and this object was to be accomplished (as the effort on the 20th of June had failed) by a more distinct and decisive insurrection, by an attack on the Tuileries. In that palace the king and royal family remained, as in a last fortress which only waited its fall; and Barbaroux had some time before agreed to send for six hundred of the Marseillois, a desperate band, to be the life and soul of the enterprise. After traversing the kingdom from the 5th of July, they arrived at Charenton on the 30th.

"We flew," says Barbaroux, "to receive them. I cannot describe our mutual congratulations. We gave and received a thousand testimonies of affection: we had a fraternal repast."

Barbaroux, however, and his friends had no sooner retired from their fraternal repast, and held their little cabinet council, than the representations of those of the conspirators who came from Paris inspired them with a delusion, which is edifying in its way, as all instances of self-delusion are; and this was no other, than to appear themselves and their friends in Paris in such force, that the king was to be deposed, and liberty established without a struggle.

The faubourgs, it was agreed, were to march and lead on the Marseillois. Santerre had assured them that they might depend on being met by forty thousand men. They were then to take possession of the principal posts and places in the metropolis, and finally encamp in the garden of the Tuileries. Thence they were to notify to the Assembly, that the people of Paris encamped in the Tuileries would not lay down their arms till liberty had been secured by what they called grand measures, and till the departments had approved them. "It was our wish," says Barbaroux, "that this insurrection in the cause of liberty should be majestic, as is Liberty herself; holy, as are the rights which she alone can ensure, and worthy to serve as an example to every people, who, to break the chains of their tyrants, have only to show themselves."

These idle dreams, however, of Barbaroux, and perhaps of his friends, were soon dissipated; for Santerre, instead of meeting them at the time and place appointed, with forty thousand representatives of the national will, appeared with scarcely two hundred; most of them not Parisians, but Fédérés of the 14th of July, from the different departments. Nothing could exceed their astonishment. "But Santerre," says Barbaroux, "was not then known to be a heavy fellow, proud enough, but incapable of the grand. The moment was melancholy. Our hopes," he says, "were deceived; but we followed the Marseillois, who filed off to the townhouse in the most beautiful order."

Barbaroux then gives an account of the quarrel between these Marseillois and a part of the national guards in the Champs Elysées, and then interrupts an interesting narrative like this, in the most cold-blooded manner, to give descriptions of Marat and Robespierre. The remainder of the chapter is occupied with the insurrection, of which the account is neither very clear, nor fair, nor valuable. The conspirators were disposed of in different places it seems: Bertin, in the National Assembly; Aubert, at the faubourg St. Antoine; Carrière, with the Marseillois. Barbaroux and Rebecqui appear to have reserved to themselves the office of observing events from some secure point of distance, and superintending the movements of the whole.—The rise, then, the intention, and the names and characters of some of the first and chief movers of this insurrection are clear from this account, however short, of Barbaroux.

We will now turn from these memoirs, and advert to the main general results furnished us from all our other sources.

Barbaroux and the Marseillois were disappointed, in what they represent as their first notion of appearing with Santerre and his Parisians in such force, as to overcome the Assembly and the metropolis, and depose the king, by an intimation of their sovereign will. This could not be done; but force remained as a measure to be resorted to, and to the employment of such an expedient everything seemed favourable. That an insurrection was intended for the 9th or 10th of August was a matter of perfect notoriety. It was evident, from what was daily passing in the Assembly, that no resistance would be made from that quarter; Pétion (the mayor), as the conspirators knew, was heart and part in the enterprise; the department, unpopular and disorganized by the resignation of all the members of the directory, was without power; the commune and sections, who alone might have been able to restrain the populace and brigands, had joined them in demanding from the Assembly the deposition of the king; of the forty-eight battalions of the national guard, there were not more than three or four well inclined to the king, and the artillery (a most important point) were all, without exception, furious Revolutionists.

This was but a melancholy prospect for the king and royal family, and the other inhabitants of the Tuileries. They saw around them the Swiss guards, some of the national guards, and a body of noblemen and gentlemen, who came in this last extremity, and came (they could suppose no other) to die, with their swords in their hands, the last ensign of honour left them, in defence of their royal master. These were to be his protectors, evidently not sufficient for the office: the Swiss, about nine hundred; the national guard, of doubtful fidelity; the gentlemen and noblemen not properly armed, and very offensive, as decided Royalists and Aristocrats, to all the national guard, who were at best only Constitutionalists. And this was not all that was to be lamented.

This insurrection, this 10th of August, was a crisis in the king's fate for which the unhappy monarch was in no respect fitted. He feared not death; he wanted not understanding; he was not without the softer, or even many of the respectable virtues of the human character; but he was not endowed with the high and commanding qualities that his situation now, more than ever, required; with the prompt, decisive, resentful energies, that enable a man to maintain his authority against the fierce, unfeeling, unjust assaults of those who invade it. Men of gentle dispositions and mere passive courage, if they voluntarily present themselves in public situations, are to be blamed if they fail; their situation has been their choice. But it was not so with Louis: he was born a king; and his failures, therefore, are a just cause of compassion to the considerate and the good.

As this attack was every hour expected, the king spent a sleepless night; sometimes in his own room, sometimes in the council room, where the ministers were assembled, and constantly receiving fresh intelligence of what was passing out of doors: at other moments he retired with his confessor, turning away from all human hopes and aid, from all human arbiters of his motives and conduct, to that Almighty Being who could now best furnish him with courage and resignation, and of whom, as an equitable judge, he would have no reason to complain. The queen, in the meantime, who was as unconcerned for her own danger as anxious for all that might affect the king's, frequently went to his room, and to her children's, accompanied by Mme. Elizabeth, and then returned to the council chamber; while the enthusiasm and fidelity of all who saw her were animated by the presence of mind, the greatness, and the intrepidity

she displayed, in the slightest things she said; and not less affected by
the countenance of Mme. Elizabeth, where visibly were expressed, her
sisterly tenderness, her grief, her piety, and all the virtues which belonged
to a mind so eminently softened by the feelings of humanity, and
strengthened by the sentiments of religion.

But the dawn appeared, the night had worn away, and the palace had
not yet been attacked. The tocsins, however, had been sounding since
midnight, the dreadful notes of preparation had never ceased, and the
assault was not likely to be long deferred. The committee that was charged
with the insurrection had, in fact, formed itself on three points. Fournier
and others were at the Faubourg St. Marcel; Santerre and Westermann,
at the Faubourg St. Antoine; Danton, the chief agitator, Camille Desmoulins, Carra, were at the Cordeliers with the battalion from Marseilles, where
Barbaroux was also, provided with poison, if necessary, and waiting the
result of the insurrection.

Some measures, however, had been taken for the defence of the
palace: a reinforcement had arrived from the Swiss barracks at Courbevoye; some battalions of the national guard had been collected; the
cannoniers, with their artillery, were in the court; and, above all, the
commandant, Mandat, was faithful to his trust, and had disposed of his
force, which was in numbers at least very respectable, in a regular manner, occupying the proper posts, and making every provision for repelling
the invaders. It was thought advisable, therefore, early in the morning,
that the king should go down into the courts, attended by a few general
officers, and by the queen and the royal family, to review the troops, and
to animate the soldiers in his defence.

This was a scene in which the king was little formed to shine. There
had been no war on the continent during his reign; he had seen no field
of battle, had no taste for the military profession, had sacrificed little
to the Graces, was awkward in his carriage and manner, and had the air
rather of a man of thought than of energy and spirit. He descended, therefore, among the soldiers with but ill effect; he received, indeed, their
acclamations, and addressed them in a few broken sentences, which were
sensible, but no more; and on the whole, he went through the part he
was recommended to act rather as a duty he had to perform, than as
a pleasure he had to enjoy. . . . Louis, who came, not in the national
uniform, a dress he had once worn, and should now have worn, but in
his evening suit, in the ominous colour of violet, the royal mourning.
But the queen should have been the hero on this occasion. Her bosom
was observed to be labouring with contending passions: her Austrian lip,
it seems, and the turn of her features, gave her eagle countenance a
majesty which, it is said, could only be seen, not conceived.

"I was in the window," says Mme. de Campan, "that overlooks the garden. The king was pale, as if life was no longer left in him. The royal family returned to their apartments. 'All is lost!' said the queen to me; 'the king has shown no energy. A review like this has done us more harm than good.' "

I must here digress for a moment to observe that it is in general a needless office to excite in men the fierce and resentful passions; they need no instructor of this kind. But as I lose no opportunity of recommending to you the softer virtues, I must not now forget to bear my testimony to the severer and the manly virtues of the human character. Their value, their dignity, their indispensable necessity, is but too evident; it was but too evident on this critical occasion, when the unhappy king stood so much in want of them. "As it must needs be, that offences will come," we must have active courage as well as passive, spirit to contend as well as fortitude to suffer; and the world must not be abandoned to the ruffian and the oppressor; to those (and such there will ever be) who can only be brought to observe the rules of justice and right, by some mere physical force superior to their own.

I must not, however, bear too hard on the unfortunate monarch. I have mentioned to you, in a former lecture, the explanation of his character, as given by one who must have studied him thoroughly, the queen; and I have just offered to you the excuse which he has a right to claim, that his station in life was his misfortune, not his choice; that he was born a king, and would never willingly have obtruded himself into a situation, where the commanding qualities which he possessed not, were required. On the present occasion, however, I have more to say, which it is but justice to say, in mitigation of our censure. Such occurrences took place as were enough to damp and dishearten the boldest minds. It was true that the king was received with "Vive le roi!" by the Swiss guards and the national guards more immediately about the palace; but the artillery and the battalion of the croix rouge shouted only "Vive la nation!" Two more battalions of the national guard arrived while the king was in the courts, and they, too, cried out "Vive la nation! vive Pétion!" The king was afterwards persuaded to review the reserve, who were posted at the far end of the garden, at the Pont Tournant. It was not without danger that he even reached it. "Down with the veto! down with the traitor!" was the cry. Two battalions marched out of the garden through the gate facing the Pont Royal, took their cannon with them, and drew themselves up along the railing, to wait for the assailants and to join them. The same thing was done, and almost at the same moment, in the royal court before the palace by the two other battalions, who in like manner had but just arrived; they separated, and many of the soldiers fixed themselves in the Carousel, stopping the fresh battalions that were coming to reinforce the guard of the palace. "I saw," says Mme.

de Campan, "the cannoniers quit their posts, clench their fists, thrust them into the face of the king, and insult him in the grossest terms. M. de Salvert and M. de Briges exerted themselves with vigour, and kept them off." What conclusion was the king to draw from appearances like these? what but this, that from within and from without he was surrounded by enemies; that all Paris was coming to dethrone him; and that he had no adequate means of resistance? What could be done against troops of insurgents if the artillery deserted him, if it was clear that they would even turn against him? What adequate defence but artillery against the armed populace of a whole metropolis? Above all, there was no longer a master mind to superintend the whole defence, and keep every man to his duty; there was no one now in authority. Mandat, the commandant-general, was no longer to be found; he had been sent for by the common council at the Hotel de Ville, and had not returned.

Everything was, therefore, in a state of confusion, and was likely to remain so. It would have indeed required a vigorous mind and a military sovereign to have made head against circumstances like these; and they must be duly weighed when we are going to censure the dejected looks of this most unfortunate of kings.

Mandat, the commandant-general, I have just said, had been sent for, and did not return. This I must explain; and the explanation will enable you to understand how dreadful was the nature of the desperate men to whom the king was now opposed.

The conspirators did not think that the council-general of the commune of Paris was sufficiently favourable to their designs; Mandat, the commander-in-chief of the national guards, was known to be faithful and loyal: it was resolved, therefore, that the council-general and the commandant should be got rid of. In the night, therefore, while the tocsin was sounding, the générale beating, and the citizens of course under arms at the alarm posts, a few of each section, under the pretext that the present common council had lost the confidence of the people, assembled and elected new members for the council to the number of near two hundred, and these new-chosen councillors went directly to the hall where the old council had assembled, declared themselves the real council, and actually drove out all the other, except Pétion, Manuel, and Danton, and began the exercise of their functions, as if they were the true and only legitimate authority.

This was the first point. The disposal of Mandat was the second. They therefore sent for him from the Tuileries; and when he entered their hall, and was surprised and totally confounded to see a different assembly from what he expected, and people he knew not, they instantly accused him of a design to attack and slaughter the people, ordered him to the Abbaye, and had him murdered at the top of the staircase.

Such were the men the king had to contend with.

But it is now to be observed that these daring measures of these bloody demagogues had but too decisive an influence on the events of the night. The arrangements of Mandat were set aside; the party of national guards that he had placed on the Pont Neuf, to prevent the communication of the opposite sides of the river, was ordered off. The officer and the guard were withdrawn from the arsenal, and muskets were distributed amongst the people. No one knew the act of usurpation that had been committed, and the orders of the new council were obeyed as of course. When Mandat went from the Tuileries to the Town Hall, as he designed to return immediately, he left no particular directions. Various detachments of national guards, which at his requisition were assembled round the palace and in the different courts, were long in impatient expectation of seeing him. In his absence, they knew not whom to obey or how to act; were more exposed to the influence of the disaffected; and, as in every army and in every enterprise mutual confidence is the soul of it, nothing could be so fatal to the defence of the palace as the distrust, uncertainty, and confusion that now everywhere prevailed.

The king wanted not sense, and could observe these things. It can be no matter of surprise that he considered the palace as without any adequate means of defence.

This was between seven and eight in the morning. Even at a much earlier hour, and before the review, Mme. de Campan mentions that the queen came out of her room and told her that "there was no hope for them; that Mandat had gone to the Hotel de Ville to receive fresh orders, had there been assassinated, and that they were then carrying his head about the streets."

Something, however, was done to make resistance, and drive back, if possible, the assailants; and the fault of the king and court was not so much a want of presence of mind *now*, as a want of forethought and decision, which might have induced them to have made proper preparations several days before.

The noblemen and gentlemen, and the officers of the constitutional guard, which the Assembly had disbanded, formed themselves into two companies, under the command of Mareschal de Mailly. To this veteran chiefly, and to three or four other general officers, were intrusted by the king, on the loss of Mandat, the command and direction of the whole defence. Several national grenadiers joined these two companies. The queen addressed them, as did afterwards the king, and with the greatest effect. These noblemen and gentlemen had indeed only their swords in their hands, but they had loyalty in their hearts, and were ready to die. Their spirit pervaded all the national guards at the posts *within* the palace.

But here again occurs a trait, that shows the untoward nature of the circumstances by which the king and the royal family were surrounded. The national guards at the *outside* of the palace could not bear, as I have already intimated, these minions of a court, for so they thought them, men who would not wear the national uniform, these aristocrats, thus assembled for its defence: they desired that they might be dismissed, and sent a message for the purpose. It was brought by one of their commanders. "No," answered the queen, "nothing shall separate us from these gentlemen; they will share the dangers of the national guards. Do you order them," she said to the officer, "do you order them to the cannon's mouth, and they will show you how they can die for their king."

On these gentlemen, then, on those of the national guards within and without the palace that were yet faithful, and above all, on about nine hundred Swiss guards, who were, and who continued to be to the last, "without fear and without reproach," the defence now depended.

The palace was too large to be easily defended: an extensive front, large open gardens behind, and on one side the long endless gallery, by which it was united to the ancient Louvre. In front of the palace was not, as there is now, a large open area, but there were several courts, the court royal in the middle, and beyond, and separated from them, the Place de Carousel. Behind the chateau were five terraces, running round the great, open, but ornamented space of the gardens; the Terrace of the Feuillants was on that side which was connected with the ancient manège, or riding-house of the palace, where the Assembly were then sitting: and on the whole, there were twenty different posts at which it was necessary to place the Swiss: and this was a most perilous dispersion of a force originally so small, and afterwards so diminished, when all the populace of Paris were approaching, with the Marseillois at their head.

The system of defence was extended by the commandant Mandat to some distance beyond the chateau itself; and his meaning in making his dispositions may be now understood, and they were very good, on the two suppositions,—1st, that the national guards and gendarmerie would have done their duty; and, 2ndly, that he had remained to superintend the operations of the whole: but neither of these suppositions were afterwards realized. He was put out of the way by the conspirators early; and the gendarmerie, the cavalry, the national guards, were soon infected, partly through fear, partly by example, with the spirit of the crowd that surrounded them. Mandat's arrangements were broken up by the new commune of the conspirators, and destroyed; and it will be easily conceived, that if the defenders of the chateau, who had been pushed forward to the Louvre and into the city, were once passed by and left behind by the assailants, they were, under the existing circumstances of general disaffection, from that moment cut off and lost.

The army of the insurrection, that had been expected all the night, began to march about six in the morning. Every account that was now brought confirmed their approach. There were about fifteen thousand in the body which had formed in the Faubourg St. Antoine; they were armed with pikes and muskets taken from the arsenal, which, by order of the new council, you may remember, had been forced. The body from the Faubourg St. Marcel was much fewer in number, about five thousand, but both were more than doubled by the brigands and by the mobs, that were continually joining them.

This totally immense and indescribable multitude, headed by the Marseillois, advanced nearer and nearer to the palace, and at last, a little before eight, the vanguard had arrived at the Place de Carousel, within the immediate sight of it.

And now there came on another crisis in the fortunes of the king and his unhappy family; the last, and, in the event, the most fatal of all. It was this. The Procureur Syndic of the department, the chief magistrate, M. Rœderer, endeavoured in vain to convince these furious men, who came to storm the palace, that so great a multitude could not have access either to the king or the Assembly, and that they must name twenty deputies to present their petition. They would hardly listen to him. Again: on his calling upon the troops to defend their post conformably to the law, and repel force by force, he was attended to by only a small part of the national guard. The artillery, whom he only exhorted to be orderly, made him no other answer than that of actually unloading their guns before his eyes. Finding, therefore, that no dependence was to be placed on the troops stationed to guard the palace, M. Rœderer, with other officers of the department, obtained immediately a private audience of the king and queen, and declared to them that the danger was imminent and beyond expression; that the greater part of the national guard was corrupted, and would fire upon the palace; that the king, the queen, the children, and every one about them would certainly be massacred, unless the king instantly decided upon taking refuge in the National Assembly.

What was now, therefore, to be done? This is the crisis I allude to. "Go to the Assembly?" "Never!" said the queen; "no, never take refuge there!" She had before said, when such a measure had been suggested to her, "I will on no account leave the palace; I would rather be nailed to the walls of it; I will never leave it." "But, madam," expostulated Rœderer, "would you be answerable, then, for the death of the king, your children, and all the faithful servants waiting here to defend you?"

This was a cruel moment for the poor queen. She must have been conscious that the means of defence were insufficient; but to fly to the Assembly, to the very men whom she disdained and abhorred, and who had already, and even during the last few hours, treated with neglect and indifference the requests that had been made to them for protection and assistance—this was indeed a humiliation to which she found it hard to submit. And what hope of safety even after such a humiliation? Better die at once, since to die was all that remained, and death was at least not disgrace. Such were, no doubt, the suggestions of her indignant spirit; such would have been, no doubt, her resolve: nor is it clear that her resolve might not have been the best, as it certainly would have been the most elevated measure to have taken. "Is the king, then, going to the Assembly?" said an old Swiss officer; "he is lost then for ever."

What courage might have done; what turn this affair might have taken if the king had been ready to die at the head of his Swiss guards, (the witness and the rival of their virtues and their fame); what a versatile multitude, like the assailants, would have done, when they were repulsed, as they were sure to be, in the first instance, by the regular troops in the palace, and saw the king amid those troops acting the part of a hero, or even visible at the head of them; how far the disaffected might have been shamed into their duty, and how far the Assembly, who sat close at hand, might have been roused into some decency of conduct, when they heard firing from the palace, and understood that the king was defending himself, and his queen, and children, against ruffians that, from Marseilles and the Faubourg St. Antoine, had come to massacre them; what might have been the transition, the movement, the result, amid an electric people like this, on suppositions like these, and even at this moment of the insurrection, it is quite impossible to say. But it is not, I think, too much to say, that if this resolve of decided and desperate defence (at first the only proper one) had been, from the first, the resolve; had been so, many days before; and if the king, in a firm and active manner, had made proper intimations and proper preparations for the attack, the attack would have failed; and by this second outrage on the king and his palace, in addition to the day of the 20th, by a regular, determined, bloody insurrection of this kind, the army of La Fayette might have been so excited, that the general might have found no difficulty in marching them to Paris, and realizing all that he had before in vain attempted for the preservation of the monarchy, and the welfare of the state.

But far from any reasonable resolve of this kind having been made in time, and measures taken in consequence (it was always the only chance to have stood a siege till La Fayette's army came up), such an indispensable point as that of the artillery was so neglected, that, as you have seen, the cannoniers were all disaffected; of the national troops that were produced, it could not be told which were loyal and which were not—with the exception of the two battalions of Petits Pères and the Filles St. Thomas, none could be depended upon; and finally and above all, though nothing could be so clear as this, that the palace should be so provided as to be enabled to stand a sort of siege, the Swiss soldiers had only fifteen rounds a man—it is never stated that they received above thirty when they left their barracks—and the palace was, at last, lost not a little from the mere want of ammunition.

But at this dreadful moment, while the king was impressed with all he had observed and suffered during his review and his return through the garden, while the Procureur Syndic was urging him to retire, and while the vanguard of the assailants were now arrived before the palace, the natural course for him to take was to escape from the present uneasiness, at all events to avoid the immediate shedding of blood, to take the chances of the future, whatever they might be, and to retire, as he was entreated to do, to the National Assembly. This was at all events to avoid the shedding of blood, the blood of his gallant defenders and of his people.

"Be it so, then," said the queen; "it is the last sacrifice." "There is nothing more to be done here," said the king, as he was leaving the palace; and a party of about one hundred and fifty or two hundred of the Swiss guards, and another of the national guard, with the greatest difficulty and amid the insults, menaces, imprecations, and opposition of the thronging and armed populace, conducted him and the royal family along the terraces to the neighbouring hall, where the Assembly was sitting.

Here we must leave this unfortunate family. The mortifications and sufferings of every kind, mental and physical, which they had to endure while they were detained in the logographe, a sort of small room at the back of the Assembly, where they were for the time disposed of, you will see detailed in the Memoirs, and I cannot now advert to them. We must return to the palace.

The first part, as it may be called, of this afflicting history of the 10th of August we have now passed through; we must next, therefore, turn to the second,—what passed after the king had left the palace.

When it was resolved that the king should take refuge in the Assembly, I have mentioned, as you may remember, that he said, "There is nothing more to be done here; let us go." And thus occurred, at this moment, when he was parting from his palace, the most unhappy inadvertence, the greatest misfortune, perhaps, and calamity of his whole unfortunate life.

With some words, of the general nature we have mentioned, he left the palace, meaning, no doubt, that every one should follow his example and leave it too; conceiving that nothing more in the way of command was necessary, no intimation of his will more distinct, no further positive orders. Amid the anxiety, affliction, and confusion of the moment, this important point was probably not at all considered. No proper proclamation was made. It was not even known, either to the assailants or the Swiss in the courts, that the king was gone to the Assembly; and the best excuse for the king is that the point seems not to have occurred to any of his friends, or the military men around him, who certainly, if it had, would have procured from the king, what he would so readily have granted, a positive order for the evacuation of the Tuileries; that no resistance was on any account to be made, every one to retire, and the Swiss and national guards to march off instantly to their barracks. Coupled with orders like these, the measure taken, of retiring to the Assembly, was, perhaps, under the cruel circumstances of the case, and at the existing moment, the least objectionable that could have been adopted. He might retire as the king, not without dignity, from a rude and lawless combat, if the combat was thus to be prevented; but unless orders of the kind just mentioned were first distinctly given, unless the immediate chance of bloodshed was provided against (for this was the great recommendation of the measure), the measure became, on the contrary, the worst possible.

"I came here," said the king to the Assembly, "to prevent the commission of a great crime." This was very true, and the best explanation that could be given of his appearance in the Assembly at all. It was reasonable enough to suppose that he and his family would have been massacred in his palace if he had stayed there.

But, alas! it was soon perceived, that others might be massacred in the palace as well as the king; and that those who were left behind were not in a state of security, whatever the royal family might be. Dreadful firing was heard, small arms and artillery; the hall was shook, and consternation spread through the Assembly. "I gave orders for the Swiss not to fire," said the king. He had supposed so, no doubt; but the point, it was now apparent, had not been sufficiently attended to, and the confusion and misery of the royal sufferers were now more agonizing than ever.

This situation long continued. The difficulty, the impossibility, was, how to convey any order to the palace while the continued fire of the besiegers and the besieged prevented any one from approaching it.

At last one of those gallant spirits, which human nature sometimes supplies on such occasions, M. d'Hervilly, offered to carry any order which the king might wish to send. The king and queen were unwilling to expose the life of one of their most valuable and faithful servants;

they seized his arm to prevent his moving, as did the Princess Elizabeth. Distinguishing marks of regard like these only animated him the more. "It is my duty," said the soldier; "my post is amid arms and firing; it is not for me to fear these things." He received the order, and hastened to the scene of action.

Here we must awhile leave him. He lost not his life; his escapes were wonderful; but he came too late—the Swiss had been too long and too fatally engaged.

You will see in the histories the melancholy detail of these transactions. We will allude to them a little hereafter. For the present you will easily understand, that almost immediately after the king had left the palace, the assailants had so approached it, that they got into contact with the defenders of it, more particularly the Swiss, who would neither give up their arms nor resign their post, not having been regularly ordered, as they believed, by their king to do either the one or the other; and that a very unequal but very bloody conflict ensued, ending, though not immediately, yet at last ending, as you will readily conceive, in the destruction and massacre of the greatest part of them, overpowered as they were by numbers, and their ammunition failing: all this you will readily imagine. We will advert a little more to the detail hereafter.

But I must hasten first to observe that of all the personages concerned in this most melancholy drama of the 10th of August, it is these unfortunate Swiss guards that most entirely interest our sympathy, and engage our respect. Whoever were right, or whoever were wrong, *they*, at least, are without blame, and only to be admired. Their noble history can soon be told. They were soldiers to whom a post was intrusted, and they died in defence of it. Who or what were their assailants? what their numbers, or what their force? what the chances in their own favour, or what was to be their reward? These were questions not to be thought of: *there* they were, they were to do their duty, and, if necessary, they were to die —and they did die.

Men like these we would follow, if we could, through every change of their unhappy fortunes in the whole course of this disastrous day. There is not an individual among them that is not elevated into a hero, and that fills not, in our imagination, the space of the most perfect of heroes. Men have died in battle in defence of their country, Spartans have fallen at Thermopylæ, these are great passages in the history of our kind; but here we have men dying, not for their wives and their children, their firesides and their altars, but for their characters as soldiers and as men, their principle of honour and duty only; a calm and deliberate valour, indifferent to the approach of an overpowering destruction, and faithful to its promise and its pledge. We have here the triumph of everything that is elevated over all that is lowly, or recreant, or base, in our imperfect nature.

It is soothing to find that every testimony was paid by their fellow-citizens to the memory of men who were an honour to their country, and worthy to be held up as models to future ages.

At the high diet of the Swiss Cantons, it was decreed, "to hand down to posterity by inscribing in the federal archives the names of those who fell in the field of battle; of those who for their fidelity were afterwards massacred; of those lastly, their brothers in arms, who survived; and to decorate all of the regiment who still lived, and who were present at the attack of the Tuileries on the 10th of August, 1792, with an iron medal, with the inscription, 'Fidelity and honour.' "

At Lucerne is to be seen the affecting monument that has been erected to their memory: on the chapel near it are the words, "Invictis pax"; and again, the line—

*Per vitam fortes, sub iniquâ morte fideles.**

Such is the inscription which the traveller may see, and it is sufficient; he must meditate the rest. Admiration at human virtue, melancholy at the fate of it, these are the tributes he will offer; and a sigh, perhaps, for the wild conflicts of mankind, where not the base and the guilty are alone to perish, but the innocent also, the high-minded, and the brave.

We will now allude to a few of the particulars of this memorable insurrection. It is not very easy to find a very distinct account of what passed in the attack and defence of the Tuileries. We have narratives from the Swiss officers, but soldiers always tell their story in a very imperfect manner, and eyewitnesses cannot be in every place, or give a very connected or intelligible account; we can, however, easily comprehend the main events of this unhappy combat. The Swiss were materially weakened by the loss of the detachment (one hundred and fifty or two hundred strong) that escorted the king to the Assembly, were at last without ammunition, and were overpowered by numbers; having first shown, by repulsing their assailants in their first attack, and driven them from the courts before the palace, that if they had not been so unfortunately circumstanced, they would have maintained their post against the second attack, and every succeeding one. This is the general description of this unequal combat. More minute particulars are of the following nature.

The assailants having made their preparations, and their ammunition being arrived, got through the gates of the royal court, and advanced to the palace. Some efforts were made by them, according to their own account, to fraternize with the Swiss, and friendly answers and signs were returned from the palace; but it was soon clear, however these things might be, that the Swiss were to lay down their arms, and surrender their post; and it is but an idle discussion who fired first, if the assailants came

* *Unconquered living, dying faithful found.*

to get possession of the palace, and on such terms. It appears, however, that there were Swiss sentinels at the vestibule, and on the great staircase, and Swiss in the windows, and that a scuffle having ensued below, which was sure to be the case if the assailants pressed forward in the way they are admitted to have done, and a pistol having been fired at the chateau from one of the leaders of the Marseillois, then in the court below, the Swiss gave the fire from the staircase and the windows, and with such effect, that they descended into the courts, and by the regularity of their movements and their discipline, soon cleared the areas of all their opponents, and the victory was at the moment entirely on their side, and was complete; and so it might have remained if they could have served the artillery, which they seized upon, and had also been in sufficient force to present a front not only in the courts before the palace, but on the terraces in the gardens behind. This, however, with their numbers, and the disaffection of so many of the national guards, of nearly all but the two faithful battalions we have mentioned, was physically impossible. According to the last arrangement, after the king's retirement, seven hundred and fifty Swiss had actually twenty different posts to maintain; and when, therefore, the assailants at length returned, aware no doubt of these circumstances, and furnished with pieces of artillery, the combat became so unequal, that the unfortunate Swiss, their ammunition expended, had only to cry for quarter, and to be massacred, wherever they could be found, by the thronging crowds of their exasperated enemies.

It was in the midst, or at the commencement of this second attack on the palace, that M. d'Hervilly reached the combatants. You will see, in Bertrand de Moleville, his extraordinary adventures before and after he joined the Swiss; but instead of giving the king's order not to fire (it was a vain order now), he set himself to make good the defence by every effort in his power: and having, in pursuance of this plan, posted what Swiss could be found in the most advantageous manner, he proceeded to the interior of the palace, and ascended the great staircase. He was met by a Swiss soldier, who told him that an immense armed populace had penetrated into the palace by the gallery of the Louvre, and were massacring every one they met in their way. The Swiss were evidently too few to continue the defence in front on the side of the Carousel, and to repel the numbers that had rushed in on the side of the Louvre; M. d'Hervilly, therefore, produced the king's order, and ordered these brave but unfortunate men to follow him to the National Assembly, where their royal master was. This is the account given by Bertrand de Moleville.

The Swiss officers in their narratives mention M. d'Hervilly, but not exactly in this manner, and not as taking the command, but they speak of him as coming with an order from the king, before or about the com-

mencement of the second attack. M. Durler, the gallant officer who was
defending the front of the chateau, speaks of his followers as being
mowed down on the second attack by artillery, that had been brought
up by the Marseillois, and that now commanded the courts. It is clear
that the assailants multiplied about the Swiss on all sides, from the gardens of the Tuileries in the rear, as well as the courts in front; and as their
ammunition failed, even with those who survived, the defence must on
these accounts, and about the period Bertrand de Moleville speaks of, be
considered as having ceased.

We have now then to advert, as well as we can, to the fate and fortunes of all the devoted actors that yet remained of this afflicting drama.

M. Durler, seeing the defence hopeless, and receiving from M.
d'Hervilly the king's order to cease firing, submitted to retreat with his
followers to seek the presence of his royal master, and, if such was his
pleasure, to resign his arms. All the Swiss were, therefore, everywhere collected, as well as circumstances allowed, and a retreat was attempted. The
soldiers, about a dozen officers, and M. d'Hervilly were the party; but
unfortunately their only way was by the garden of the Tuileries, and
there they had no sooner appeared, than they were exposed to the fire of
the cannon that were planted in it, and of the disaffected troops that were
ranged on the different terraces. On leaving the palace their numbers
amounted to a hundred, but only sixty reached the Assembly. Arrived
at the corridor of the Assembly, the advice, the remonstrances of the
deputies were all in vain, and lost upon M. Durler; but having been
brought to the king, "Sire," said the officer, "I am desired to give up my
arms; but though there are few of us left, this cannot be done without
your orders." "Lay them down, then," replied the king; "I cannot choose
that brave men like you should all perish."

These gallant men were now soothed and rewarded by every inquiry
and attention paid them by the queen, the Princess Elizabeth, and all the
unhappy group of nobles and gentlemen around them; who, fallen as
they might now be, their royal master at their head, were still, and not
the tumultuous Assembly (their oppressors around them), were still
alone the objects of all the affection and respect of M. Durler and his
brother soldiers, their magnanimous defenders. They retired, and a note
was sent to M. Durler by the king, written to him, as he says, by the
king's own hand, and in consequence he persuaded his followers to
ground their arms; with some difficulty, for these heroes told him, that
though their ammunition was gone, they could still defend themselves
with their bayonets.

The division we have now alluded to consisted of the Swiss who had
been engaged in or about the courts. Those who were at their posts
within the palace, or who could not be collected by M. Durler at the

moment of his retiring, seem to have retreated to the great staircase, and to have gathered about the vestibule; they were in number about eighty: they defended themselves for more than a quarter of an hour, and after selling their lives most dearly, after destroying at least four hundred of their opponents, fell every man on the spot.

The assailants (who were now no longer opposed) rushed forwards into all the apartments of the palace, seeking for and butchering all the Swiss they could find, cutting them down or throwing them alive out of the windows. Seventeen who had taken refuge in the vestry, were seized and immediately massacred. A party of about one hundred attempted to escape by the Court de Marsan; they were soon in the midst of an immense and furious crowd, who called aloud, "Down arms!" Thinking to appease the people by submission, they surrendered without further resistance. Eighty of them were, however, massacred in the Rue de St. Echelle; the rest had the good fortune to escape by running into shops, hiding in cellars and under staircases, remaining some of them several days without nourishment, and furnished by humane people with clothes (for the red uniform wherever it appeared was fatal) to enable them to get away unknown. Another detachment of eighty, under the command of four of their officers, were endeavouring to return to their barracks at Courbevoye, but they were surrounded in the Champs Elysées by the base gendarmerie, the recreant cavalry who had deserted them, and there seized upon by the people, who soon came up to conduct them to the Hotel de Ville, promising to save their lives; but the moment they came to the Place de Grêve they were torn in pieces by the populace.

We hear not much in the narratives that are given us of the noblemen and others of the old court, who had repaired to the palace for the defence of their king. They had no firearms, only small swords, and had rather the air of coming to die with their master than to defend him: they could not well find an opportunity of contributing to the common defence. If the king had stayed, they might have formed a rampart around him and the royal family; but when he went, they must have thought their office at an end. It was with difficulty they could be prevented from accompanying the king, only by the representations of M. Rœderer, that they might thus occasion the destruction of the royal family, and the failure of the whole attempt to reach the Assembly. The king, the queen, the dauphin, had all to interfere. The queen dropped some words, as if she would return. They seem to have expected this, to have stayed waiting in the apartments, to have been very uncertain what to do, and at last, probably when they saw that all was lost, some of them, to have made an attempt to escape through the Louvre side of the palace; but it was an unsuccessful one: the remainder, and indeed the greater part, seemed to have determined on going, at all events, to the king. "When they left the palace," says Bertrand de Moleville, "they were three hundred; but very few escaped, for the garden and terraces through which they had to pass were in possession of their enemies." Among these noblemen and gentlemen was the Duc de Choiseul, the gallant man who is so deserving of admiration for his address and courage while the king was detained at Varennes.

"The Swiss and the gentlemen," says Bertrand de Moleville, "rallied by the Duc de Choiseul, were received at the bottom of the steps leading to the Feuillans with so brisk a discharge of small arms, that they found it impossible to get up to the terrace. The Duc de Choiseul, thinking they were following him, opened a way for himself, sword in hand, to the door of the hall. He was dismayed, as well as surprised, when he turned round and found himself there alone; but he went forward, and was thus preserved."

Such are the appalling scenes of this dreadful day. . . .

All war is dreadful, even regular and honourable war; the result, a field of battle, whatever may have been the noble qualities exhibited by the combatants, is still a scene of horror. But what are we to say of political convulsions like these, and of the enormities that attend them; not occurring at Rome under a Nero, or under the government of Turkey, where neither human wisdom nor human nature knows what course to pursue, or has any regular principle left to stand upon? I am not going to speak of such cases of despair, but speaking of European governments and of civilized men. What are we to say of convulsions like these, in the midst of such governments and such men? What are we to say of insurrections, regularly planned and brought forward as proper expedients to procure their particular ends, by men engaged in political warfare? They are no proper judges who have not been unfortunate enough to witness them.

We may be little affected while we read of them in histories and memoirs; the mind is at ease, the scene at a distance: it is repulsive, and we turn away. To estimate them properly, we should have seen with our own eyes, and heard with our own ears; we should have seen the uplifted weapon of the ruffian, and heard the terrified shriek of its victim; we should have seen men running in troops after some breathless, helpless fugitive, who totters and sinks on his knees before them, receives a thousand wounds at once, and on whom they fall, dispatching and tearing him to pieces, like savage animals worrying and devouring their prey; we should see men breaking open the doors of houses, rushing up stairs, ransacking every hiding-place, and we should see a crowd, with fury in their looks, their hands and garments covered with blood, waiting with impatience in the street, and we should ourselves wait, with whatever different feelings, till we hear the cries of those whom they, who have gone into the house, are now in the act of murdering; we should wait

till we see them thrown through the windows, to be stabbed and muti-
lated, and their fragments to be left scattered on the pavement, or carried
away upon pikes, in a sort of procession, amid unhallowed shouts of
revelry and triumph. These are the scenes we should witness; the streets,
the public places, stained with blood, and dead bodies, with all their
ghastly appearances, under our feet as we walk along, and meeting our
eyes wherever we turn them. When such horrors have been really witnessed, we shall then, and not before, for no imagination can conceive
them, we shall then only be fit to judge of scenes like these; what the
meaning of that which is called an insurrection of the people really is;
what it is to expose our fellow-creatures to be thus frightfully transformed
into beings no longer human; and we shall then be competent to estimate,
and it is on this account that I make the observation, what it is, to carry
political measures by calling in the mere physical strength of the people;
what it is, to exasperate them into fury, and urge them on to vengeance,
whether by practising on their base or appealing to their nobler feelings;
what it is to leave them to consider themselves as without law and above
it; to suppose that they have a right to make an insurrection when they
think good, while in the meantime, it is clear from all experience, that
there is nothing in savage cruelty like men exposed to the delirium of
civil or religious hate; and then, above all, we shall be fitted to judge
what is the real nature of the counsels of those who are so ready on all
occasions to urge every thing on to violence, precipitation, and force; who
turn away from all proposals of conciliation and forbearance; who despise
all sentiments of caution; who are impetuous, irritable, and daring; who
will make no sacrifices to the opinions or interests of others; and who do
not scruple about their means, if they think their end good. I speak not
of men whose proper element is tumult, who seem able, in some unnatural manner, to behold the shedding of blood without emotion. I
speak not of Danton or others; they are fiends in human shape, and we
need say no more of them. I speak of men like Barbaroux, and even
Vergniaud, and the other Girondists, men of very enlightened and very
powerful minds, and I would say of such men (and they are continually
appearing in every country, wherever their voice can be heard), that scenes
like these are to be their warning and admonition, and that they are not
to suppose, that all means are lawful to procure an end because that end
is lawful. Making the best of their case, and as far as they are actuated
by moral considerations, it is the custom for men like these to conceive
anything justifiable which may, according to their notions, ultimately
produce the general good; they resolve every thing (as do the French
popular historians) into a calculation of utility, and full of their principle,
and inattentive to its proper interpretation; they weigh, in a sort of
sacrilegious balance, present crime against future happiness; they dye the

hands of a populace in blood, that their country hereafter may have a better system of rule; they unchain the savage passions of mankind; they destroy their moral feelings, to take the chance of *future* law and order; and they regularly sit, and calmly plan and organize a bloody insurrection, of which no one can tell the result, as an allowable means of clearing away the government they see before them. Of such proceedings no one, as I have just said, can tell the result; but be the result what it may, this is not the way in which mankind can be served, this is not to understand the doctrine of utility, and it is to caricature, not exemplify it. Society can never be safe, countries can never be reformed, the cause of improvement can never be patronized, or even tolerated, by people of influence or good sense, if men in pursuit of their political ends, and under the influence of their supposed patriotism, are not to hesitate about their means; if they are to allow themselves, while they refer every thing to utility, to sink the consideration of all present crimes and horrors for the sake of future good; a future good, of which they, in their own inflamed and enthusiastic state of mind, are to constitute themselves the judges, and which, at all events, they have no right whatever, in this manner, at least, to attempt to procure.

As in private dissensions there are points at which every sane mind stops; as we do not poison our opponents, or assassinate them in the dark, whatever may have been their conduct, and however they may be the objects of our just indignation; so in public concerns—the reformation of the state, the resistance to a bad government, the management of a revolution (if any charge so awful should be at all within our competence), on all such occasions there are points, there are landmarks and boundaries, at which we must necessarily stop. Crimes we must not commit; horrors and atrocities are not to be our expedients; these are to be banished at once as pollutions, to which we are not to familiarize our thoughts for a moment. Our country, if she is to be served at all, must be served in some other manner, for she can never be served in this,—this is not the worship to be offered at the shrine of Liberty. "O Liberty!" said Mme. Roland, as she looked at the statue of Liberty, just at the moment she was to be herself executed, "O Liberty! how many crimes have been perpetrated in thy name!" It will be ever thus. She had herself heard of insurrections without reprobating them. The enlightened men, who with real aspirations after their country's welfare, the first patriots, who first allow crimes to be perpetrated, forget that they are thus setting examples which are sure to be followed by men at every turn, even more and more lawless and inhuman; they forget that crimes produce crimes, with accelerated fury and enhanced guilt; that the man who in private life becomes even a murderer, or in public life, like Robespierre, even a monster and a destroyer of his species, only becomes so, because he proceeds from step to step, because he has not originally stopped in time, because he has not had, from the first, landmarks in his mind of right and wrong, of guilt and innocence, which his mind is on no account ever to be suffered to pass.

It is idle to speak of the good intentions of men; that they endeavoured, at least, well; that their feelings were benevolent; that they were disinterested and pure; that they had hoped better of mankind. Excuses of this kind come too late. Crimes have been committed, horrors and atrocities have been witnessed; their Revolution fails; a country has been stained for ever in the annals of mankind; the sacred cause of liberty has been made an object of suspicion and terror to the wise and good, and that for ever. These are the events, these the results; and they are the guilty men, they, first and principally, who have tampered with their own moral feelings, who have not recoiled with instinctive abhorrence from the first approach and view of crimes and bloodshed, and who have adopted counsels which could only lead to scenes like these; scenes which it has been our melancholy office to shadow out thus indistinctly to your reflection; scenes which soon exhaust the sensibility of those who attempt to follow them; degradations to our common nature, sufferings, agonies, abominations, which the mind must not be permitted to conceive nor the tongue to tell.*

xxxiv. BURKE, A POLITICAL AND MORAL PROPHET

I WILL NOW allude to what I conceive to be his [Burke's] merit, as a moral prophet. I do not think, that this part of Mr. Burke's work was at the time properly understood. The English people have never much studied books and treatises on morals, though they have had great moral writers, Bishop Butler for instance: they seem, like the celebrated nation of antiquity, to have been contented to place between themselves and others, the dictinction, that they would *practise* virtue, and let *others talk* about it; morals and metaphysics have more occupied the attention of our northern neighbours. Mr. Burke must have been personally acquainted with the great Scotch writers, and understood the subjects of morals, on which they had written with such success, perfectly well; better than did his

* Lectures XXXI, XXXII, and XXXIII takes the narrative through the culminating event of January 21, 1793—the execution of Louis XVI. Then Smyth, as if horrified by the mere recital of these bloody matters, turns aside to examine the political philosophy of Burke insofar as it turned on the French Revolution.—ED.

brother statesmen in our houses of legislature, far better than did the English public; and he does not seem to me, to have made a sufficient allowance for the want of familiarity with such topics, which I conceive certainly then existed in the community. He stops not to explain and exhibit all his meaning with the distinctness which he might have done; but you will hereafter find, if you come to consider, what may be called, the moral situation of this country, and of Europe, that all the deviations from the established notions of mankind, that were afterwards to appear, were anticipated and protested against, in the passages I shall soon have to read to you: the change that was to take place, Mr. Burke saw clearly. Man, as you know, is a creature of reason and feeling: he saw distinctly that it was attempted to make him, in a word, the creature of *reason* only, and he protested against this, as unnatural, foolish, and ridiculous; as unfavourable to his happiness; at all events, as fatal to everything that was established in civilized Europe. I will allude more particularly for the present to one great and main point.

The moral system of those who patronized the new opinions was at the time founded on the doctrine of utility; this doctrine, as too many of them, indeed as they all understood it, left everything to the decision of calculation. A man was at every turn to set himself to consider, whether what he was *going* to do was likely to benefit his species, and it was to him to be right or wrong accordingly. Mr. Burke, on the contrary, had insisted on the authority of instinct and natural feelings, and the common notions of duty, that arise from them. The former system was evidently favourable to revolutions, the latter not. Men, for instance, are prevented from engaging in revolutions, by their existing associations, habits of thought and feeling, social enjoyments, domestic charities. He, on the contrary, who thinks, not of these, but only of the distant and ultimate consequences, to be calculated on every occasion of his being called to act, who has not his notions of duty prepared and arranged under general rules, is ready for any new system or enterprise that may be proposed to him by any leader of revolutions, for he has only to resolve the case into some case of utility or the general good, and no further difficulty remains.

To illustrate what I am describing—Suppose a house on fire—and according to what was then the real and what was afterwards to become the avowed morality of the followers of the new opinions (I take the instance from one of their writers, Mr. Godwin), a man was to pluck from out of it, not his mother, his wife, or his benefactor, who might be supposed not likely to benefit the world, but any philosopher, like Fénélon, who certainly *would*. According to Mr. Burke, he was to obey his natural instincts and feelings, and his established notions of duty, and save his wife, his mother, or benefactor, without speculating on the matter for a moment.

Now though you may see the propriety of Mr. Burke's system in this case, for it is a strong one, you may not, in all the cases that might be proposed, though the same in principle; and Mr. Burke might have dedicated a page to the consideration of the doctrine of his opponents, the doctrine of utility, not as it ought to be understood, but as they described it. He never condescends, however, to do so, in a single sentence, and leaves the question to be decided, if made a question at all, by the common sense and common feelings of mankind. This contempt in Mr. Burke of this part of the new philosophy has rendered this portion of his work (a short but most important one) indistinct to the general reader, and unsatisfactory; and given it an appearance of mere declamation, and vague, and even superficial reasoning; but very unjustly, as I conceive; it is his opponents that are the declaimers, and superficial reasoners, not *he*. Not only might Mr. Burke have readily explained himself, if he had chosen, but they who meditate these subjects will, I apprehend, arrive pretty nearly at Mr. Burke's system of moral opinions; surely not at the system of his opponents. For with regard to the point more immediately before us, the doctrine of utility, this doctrine may be, to a considerable extent, admitted; it may even be altogether admitted; it is the doctrine of a very respectable school of moralists, both among the ancients and the moderns—it is the system of benevolence; but then, it cannot be understood, as the patrons of the new opinions understood it, and as *at first sight* it might very naturally be understood; the very circumstance of its being so favourable to revolutions shows that it cannot, for revolutions cannot be the natural order of things, in which men are intended to live. The truth is that for the sake of utility itself, the principle cannot be interpreted in any revolutionary manner, not so interpreted that men are to neglect the common duties of life; *for it is not thus that mankind can be served. This*, therefore, is no proper system of *utility*; it cannot be *useful* to the world, for men to break through and cast from them the common ties of nature, for views of contingent happiness to their species. Men are not to stand speculating upon the possible consequences of every action, before they perform it, instead of doing instantly what they have always understood to be right. The principle of utility is, immediately after the first reception of it by the mind as a general principle, to be shaped out into general rules, to which ever after, the conduct, without further thought, is to be adapted; it is to be converted, if I may make use of such a metaphor, into great high roads, in which every man is to travel in his journey through life; and he is not on every occasion to stop and turn aside into a pathless moor, over which he is to wander in pursuit of objects, which he expects somewhere or other to find, at a distance in the horizon. This is not to understand the doctrine of utility.

Dr. Paley, in the preliminary books of his *Moral [and Political] Philos-*

ophy, comes to the conclusion, that whatever is useful is right; he therefore immediately in the subsequent chapters sets himself to show, that the principle of utility necessarily assumes the shape of the great duties of life; that the performance of these great ordinary duties is indispensable to the public good, while it is the best chance of happiness for the individual. Dr. Paley did not, however, warn his readers, as he ought to have done, that the doctrine of utility might be misinterpreted, and was liable to be so; he has a chapter on general rules, no doubt; but he should have still more distinctly said, that men were *not* on every occasion, every man for himself, to institute calculations as if no general rules existed; that such speculations on the consequences of actions should have been entered into long before, should have subsided into general rules, and then be supposed terminated for ever; that such speculations on the spur of the moment, and amid the temptations or necessities of the moment, were only fitted to afford an opportunity to every weak man to decide erroneously, and to every bad man to decide licentiously; and would in truth lead directly to the destruction of all the morality that existed in the world; existing, as it does, and ever did, and ever must, on the obedience of men to general rules. With all my most grateful remembrance of what I owe to Paley, the most sensible of all writers, I consider his work, as in this point, defective, and the two first books of his *Moral Philosophy* (with the exception of his admirable chapter on Human Happiness), as the least valuable of anything he ever wrote. There is no proper knowledge of the subject imparted to the reader, or apparently possessed by the writer. I have already mentioned that the English public had not attended to inquiries of this kind. It is remarkable that Mr. Hume saw clearly the abuse to which the doctrine of utility, which he had adopted, was liable; and provided against it, in a note to his *Treatise on Morals*. "What wonder, then," he says, in his text, "if we can pronounce no judgment concerning the character and conduct of men, without considering the tendencies of their actions, and the happiness or misery which thence arises to society?" Here we have the doctrine of utility. But he immediately subjoins a note; and in the course of it he observes, "When the interests of one country interfere with those of another, we estimate the merits of a statesman by the good or ill which results to his *own* country from his measures and counsels, without regard to the prejudice which it brings on its enemies and rivals. His fellow-citizens are the objects which lie nearest the eye, while we determine his character; and as Nature has implanted in every one a superior affection to his own country, we never expect any regard to distant nations, when a competition arises. Not to mention, that while every man consults the good of his *own* community, we are sensible, that the *general* interest of mankind is better promoted, than by any loose, indeterminate views to the good of a species, whence no beneficial action could ever result, for want of a duly limited object on which they could exert themselves." Here we have in this last sentence, the general doctrine of utility properly limited and accommodated to human practice. Mr. Hume in this treatise, laboured to show that all moral distinctions must be ultimately resolved into the principle of utility; and this particular system of morals was never before or since so completely drawn out and exhibited, nor indeed can any system of morals be constructed, in which the principle of utility must not make a very conspicuous appearance. "Utilitas justi prope mater et æqui." But Mr. Hume takes care to observe in another note, as in the former, "It is wisely ordained by Nature, that private connections should commonly prevail over universal views and considerations; otherwise our affections and actions would be dissipated and lost for want of a proper limited object." "Wisely ordained," says Mr. Hume, "by Nature"; that is, Nature itself, or rather our Creator, sanctions and establishes the authority of instincts and natural feelings, or the system of Mr. Burke, as the best mode of attaining all that is desired by the principle of utility; and the patrons of this system of utility must, therefore, admit the theory of instincts and natural feelings, and acknowledge their authority, if they mean to be faithful to their own doctrines, and really carry into practical effect the principle of utility. Let them make the experiment, and they will find that such instincts and natural feelings will be always sanctioned by the principle of utility, if they choose to appeal to it, and to admit of no other criterion.

But here it will be observed that, on this system, no changes could ever be attempted, no abuses corrected, no efforts for mankind made, no revolutions, however desirable, ever thought of; these all proceed upon the doctrine of mere expediency, and the calculation, at the time, of consequences. Undoubtedly they do, and must be left to do so; and where the expediency, or rather the necessity, can be made out, they are sufficiently sanctioned; but then it must be observed, that the great instincts and feelings of our nature having been already sanctioned by this principle of expediency, the great rules of human conduct having been already adjusted, all violence done to them, all deviations that afterwards occur, in revolutions or on whatever occasion, for the sake of our liberties, as we suppose, of our country, or mankind, must be considered as exceptions to prior general rules, exceptions to those common maxims of duty, on which all practical virtue depends, on which the welfare and security of all human society can alone be rested. These deviations from general rules may, on great occasions, sometimes lead to actions of the most exalted virtue: this is possible; still they must be considered as actions of great responsibility, and as rather coming within the province of casuistry than any ordinary system of moral obligation. And this is the important point. The new morality was a sort of revolutionary morality, springing out of revolutionary times, and fitted for revolutionary purposes.

I may appear converting my lecture into a treatise on morality; but the subject is curious, is not without its difficulty, and is in truth (strange as it may at first appear) fundamentally connected with the general subject of the French Revolution far more than those can well suppose, who lived not at the time.

I shall probably have to advert to it again before I close hereafter my remarks on that great event; what I have now said, I have only said, because I thought it necessary to enable those who have not considered these subjects properly to comprehend the extracts I am going to read from Mr. Burke. I may observe, indeed, in conclusion, that those who may hereafter address themselves to this high argument, this great subject of the theory of morals, and endeavour to consider it in an elementary manner, will not proceed far, before they will find themselves involved in metaphysical inquiries of the most subtle nature; they will perceive how little rest or satisfaction can be here obtained for their thoughts; and, with some surprise and disappointment, they will feel themselves obliged to return from their unprofitable wanderings, to join the mere vulgar in their beaten road, taking their duties as they see them understood, and as they feel them to be rightly understood, by the common mass of mankind. They will no longer labour to penetrate into the metaphysics of morals, the nature of the sentiment for instance, that is, what is the origin of the very notion of right and wrong at all; the criterion, or whether there is one and the same quality in all actions that are morally right (utility, for instance); the motive, or what is the influence by which we are urged to do what we think right.

These questions must be, no doubt, considered by the student; but after having been duly and regularly considered, a reasonable man may turn away, and adopting some system of benevolence properly understood, or of instincts and natural feelings, or both conjoined, leave such abstruse disquisitions to the schools, and be content.

All such modest and reasonable inquirers will be satisfied to perceive that the Almighty Master has so constituted us, that we cannot mistake our duties in practice, though he may not have given us faculties to understand them in their elementary theory; that we know what we are to pursue, and what to shun; know all that is necessary for our own well-being here and hereafter—our own responsibility, his awful observance of us. These great truths are surely sufficient, though the great Creator may not have thought it necessary so to gratify our curiosity as to unveil to us the secret springs and movements of that moral machinery which (if I may so presume to speak) He evidently applies, and has always applied, to the sentient and intelligent beings whom He has placed in this our portion of His universe. "The secrets of nature" is a phrase familiar to every philosopher. These secrets occur in morals as in other subjects. All knowledge imparted to finite beings must end somewhere. By the phrase "the secrets of nature," the philosopher means only to allude to that part of knowledge which the great Author of our being and of the world has, in our present state, thought proper in his wisdom to withhold from us.

I will now offer you some extracts from Mr. Burke. They describe or anticipate, as I have announced to you, the moral phenomena which were already, in 1790, beginning to appear, and which, as you will find, afterwards did appear, in a most remarkable manner, both in this country and in the rest of Europe, as the Revolution proceeded—to a degree as I have mentioned, which not living at the time, you cannot possibly conceive.

"But now," says Mr. Burke, "all is to be changed. All the pleasing illusions, which made power gentle, and obedience liberal, which harmonized the different shades of life, and which, by a bland assimilation, incorporated into politics the sentiments which beautify and soften private society, are to be dissolved by this new conquering empire of light and reason. All the decent drapery of life is to be rudely torn off. All the superadded ideas, furnished from the wardrobe of a moral imagination, which the heart owns and the understanding ratifies (as necessary to cover the defects of our naked, shivering nature, and to raise it to dignity in our own estimation), are to be exploded as a ridiculous, absurd, and antiquated fashion.

"On this scheme of things a king is but a man, a queen is but a woman, a woman is but an animal, and an animal not of the highest order. All homage paid to the sex in general as such, and without distinct views, is to be regarded as romance and folly. Regicide, and parricide, and sacrilege are but fictions of superstition, corrupting jurisprudence by destroying its simplicity. The murder of a king, or a queen, or a bishop, or a father, are only common homicide; and, if the people are by any chance or in any way gainers by it, a sort of homicide much the most pardonable, and into which we ought not to make too severe a scrutiny.

"On the scheme of this barbarous philosophy, which is the offspring of cold hearts and muddy understandings, and which is as void of solid wisdom as it is destitute of all taste and elegance, laws are to be supported only by their own terrors, and by the concern which each individual may find in them from his own private speculations, or can spare to them from his own private interests. In the groves of *their* academy, at the end of every vista, you see nothing but the gallows. Nothing is left which engages the affections on the part of the commonwealth. On the principles of this mechanic philosophy, our institutions can never be embodied, if I may use the expression, in persons; so as to create in us love, veneration, admiration, or attachment. But that sort of reason which banishes the affections, is incapable of filling their place."

And again, in another place,—"Four hundred years have gone over us, but I believe we are not materially changed since that period. Thanks to our sullen resistance to innovation, thanks to the cold sluggishness of our national character, we still bear the stamp of our forefathers. We have not (as I conceive) lost the generosity and dignity of thinking of the fourteenth century; nor as yet have we subtilized ourselves into savages. We are not the converts of Rousseau; we are not the disciples of Voltaire; Helvetius has made no progress amongst us. Atheists are not our preachers; madmen are not our lawgivers. We know that *we* have made no discoveries, and we think that no discoveries are to be made, in morality; nor many in the great principles of government; nor in the ideas of liberty, which were understood long before we were born, altogether as well as they will be, after the grave has heaped its mould upon our presumption, and the silent tomb shall have imposed its law on our pert loquacity. In England we have not yet been completely embowelled of our natural entrails; we still feel within us, and we cherish and cultivate those inbred sentiments which are the faithful guardians, the active monitors of our duty, the true supporters of all liberal and manly morals. We have not been drawn and trussed, in order that we may be filled, like stuffed birds in a museum, with chaff and rags and paltry blurred shreds of paper about the rights of man. We preserve the whole of our feelings still native and entire, unsophisticated by pedantry and infidelity. We have real hearts of flesh and blood beating in our bosoms. We fear God; we look up with awe to kings, with affection to parliaments, with duty to magistrates, with reverence to priests, and with respect to nobility. Why? Because when such ideas are brought before our minds, it is *natural* to be so affected; because all other feelings are false and spurious, and tend to corrupt our minds, to vitiate our primary morals, to render us unfit for rational liberty; and by teaching us a servile, licentious, and abandoned insolence, to be our low sport for a few holidays, to make us perfectly fit for and justly deserving of slavery, through the whole course of our lives.

"You see, sir, that in this enlightened age I am bold enough to confess that we are generally men of untaught feelings; that instead of casting away all our old prejudices, we cherish them to a very considerable degree, and to take more shame to ourselves, we cherish them because they are prejudices; and the longer they have lasted, and the more generally they have prevailed, the more we cherish them."

By a prejudice, however, we do not mean an opinion that is necessarily wrong, but only an opinion that, whether right or wrong, is held by a man without his knowing the reason of it. Mr. Burke does not stay to give this explanation.

"We are afraid to put men to live and trade each on his own private stock of reason, because we suspect that the stock in each man is small, and that the individuals would do better to avail themselves of the general bank and capital of nations and of ages. Many of our men of speculation, instead of exploding general prejudices, employ their sagacity to discover the latent wisdom which prevails in them. If they find what they seek, and they seldom fail, they think it more wise to continue the prejudice, with the reason involved than to cast away the coat of prejudice, and to leave nothing but the naked reason; because prejudice, with its reason, has a motive to give action to that reason, and an affection which will give it permanence. Prejudice is of ready application in the emergency; it previously engages the mind in a steady course of wisdom and virtue, and does not leave the man hesitating in the moment of decision, sceptical, puzzled, and unresolved. Prejudice renders a man's virtue his habit; and not a series of unconnected acts. Through just prejudice, his duty becomes a part of his nature."

Such are the sentiments to be found in the work of Mr. Burke; not only conceived and written during the spring and summer of 1790, but, as I must again and again repeat, published at the close of 1790, full two years before that stage of the Revolution at which we are now arrived, the execution of the king. It was followed immediately by another work, "A Letter to a Member of the National Assembly"; and again, soon after, by his "Appeal from the New to the Old Whigs"; a work well worthy to support his *Reflections*, and full of important wisdom. In each of them may be found matter of the same prophetic nature with what I have quoted from the *Reflections*. Of this, his greater work (the *Reflections*), the fault may be, and indeed is, that Mr. Burke did not sufficiently exhibit the prior offences of the privileged orders, and their want of political virtue and wisdom, the general disrespect into which the old government had justly fallen, by its long defiance of public opinion, and its disregard of its duties; the fault of Mr. Burke's work may be also, that he makes not sufficient allowance for the difficulties with which the members of the Constituent Assembly had to struggle, nor states the faults that were committed by the court party; but when all this has been admitted, as I think it must, such paragraphs as I have selected from the midst of many, many others of the same kind, show clearly a penetrating and philosophic mind, that saw distinctly what others did not see, the full danger of this invasion of the world by the new opinions; that, whether *politically* or *morally* considered it was impossible that these opinions should lead to practical good; that it was not for the interest of France or of mankind ever to adopt them; and still less in so headlong a manner to cast off their old opinions; that the politicians of the day everywhere were too sanguine, too daring, too experimental; that neither in morals nor in governments could men be rendered wiser, or happier, by resolving, on system, to demolish every thing and begin anew; that this was neither the tone nor the manner of those who deserved to be thought the instructors and improvers either of their own country or of mankind. These were the general views and doctrines of Mr. Burke, at a season of somewhat universal enthusiasm, running (and very violently) in a contrary direction, among the young and the intelligent more especially, wherever they were found; and this is a merit, and a very extraordinary merit, which, amidst all the faults of his mind (and they grew more striking as the Revolution proceeded), must not be denied him, and this has rendered his book (I speak of his *Reflections*, though not at all excluding, much the contrary, his *Appeal from the New to the Old Whigs*) so invaluable to the same description of most important persons in a community, the young and the intelligent, if they will but, as they are always bound to do, seize upon the wisdom of a book, and cast away such passages as may appear intemperate, and less worthy to be retained.

To them, indeed, thus considered, the reference being had to such objections as I have made, and as are sufficiently obvious, it is a work of the most eminent usefulness and weighty admonition, because the principles alluded to and enforced, are as unchangeable as Nature itself, and of an application that can never cease.

xxxv. STATE OF ENGLAND IN 1792

WE MUST NOW turn our eyes to the other side of the picture; to the effects produced by all these elements of alarm; to the conduct of the people of property, and the government. Mr. Pitt was a popular and decisive minister; his royal master had never shown any great relish for new opinions, no tolerance even for the Whig party; and the government therefore, early in the year, addressed itself to the subject, and resolved to resist the popular opinions, that were circulating in the country, by every means in their power. You must look at their proclamation, issued at the close of May, 1792, against seditious meetings and publications; this was their first measure. Again. When the King of France was driven from the Tuileries, on the 10th of August, they recalled our ambassador, which was in fact our protest against these proceedings, as putting an end to all government in France, that could be acknowledged by other nations. The sentiments of our cabinet were therefore clear in August 1792. But in the months immediately following, the horrid massacres of September occurred; the Duke of Brunswick was obliged to retreat; Dumouriez rushed after him and overran the Netherlands, the decree of November was passed in the Convention, and those who live *now* can little conceive what was then the agitation and anxiety of the public mind in England.

On the 20th of November was formed an Association at the Crown and Anchor in support of the Constitution; another, for the west end of the town, at the St. Alban's tavern. A declaration of the merchants, bankers, and traders of London was very generally signed, dated 5th December. Resolutions and manifestoes were published by these societies, and everywhere circulated through the country; proclamations were issued to call out the militia, and to assemble parliament in December instead of January. Every note of alarm that was possible, was sounded by government; the stocks fell; a correspondence began between Lord Grenville [foreign secretary] and the French ambassador [François-Bernard Chauvelin: 1766–1832] that seemed likely to terminate in war; and the general expectation was that some dreadful storm, perhaps some revolutionary convulsion, was approaching.

But the point to which you are now to direct your attention, is this: that the moment the government by their various strong measures announced their alarm, addresses flowed in from every possible quarter, manifesting the most steady attachment, and offering the most determined support to the constitution and government of these kingdoms; on the whole, very clearly showing, that however noisy and elated and presumptuous had been the clubs and societies that corresponded with France, and however wide had been the circulation of Mr. [Thomas] Paine's publications, *still* that the mind of the great mass, and majority of the people of England, was in a sound and sane state; that they were properly impressed with the value of the blessings they already enjoyed, and not disposed to political experiments in search of new. This, I must repeat to you, is a main point for you to observe, since, if this were the case, the government of England was left at liberty to act as they thought best with regard to France, and were under no necessity of rushing into a foreign war, in the usual vulgar and mistaken manner, for the sake, as it is superficially reasoned, of keeping peace at home; and I say this, because now comes before you one of the greatest questions that history presents to you since the Revolution of 1688,—the question of peace or war with France at the close of the year 1792. Peace or war, with all the consequences of either system of policy.

On this question must rest the merits of Mr. Pitt, as a minister. He was a great commercial minister, a great financial minister; but inferior spirits may act in concerns like these: this can be no praise to Mr. Pitt. The present was a crisis in human affairs; millions of the existing generation were to be affected by his determination, and posterity to the most distant ages; how then did he determine? What makes this question even still more interesting, is this: that the great rival statesman of these times (Mr. Fox), when the question came to be agitated, differed totally with Mr. Pitt on the measures to be pursued; and though an overpowering majority of the House of Commons and of the country was with Mr. Pitt, it does not at all follow, that the historical student will now concur with them in opinion. In discussing a great political question, at a subsequent period, all the subordinate discussions, all that entangled the mind and impeded its progress to the real point at issue, must be cast aside. It is impossible to escape from them at the time: people in political questions generally take their side from their feelings and their interests, and then set about finding arguments to justify them in their decision: any arguments that are offered to them, and there is always a supply, will satisfy; the most exaggerated statements, the most incorrect assumptions, the most unfounded accusations of their opponents. The question is thus spread over a large surface; a worsted disputant on one point can always fly to another, and no distinct decision can be, or at least really *is*, attained. This sort of tumult and disorder, this sort of war against all propriety and common sense and the interests of the country at the time, cannot be escaped in a free country, and we may lament what it is in vain to hope to alter. Thus it was insisted at the time, that the French went to war with us; and I shall soon have to mention a publication by Dr. Marsh,* which will fully exhibit to you the mode of reasoning that was employed. But to say this, is to lose the question entirely; the war was on our part, as on the part of the allied powers, a war against the Jacobins, or it was nothing; a war against furious and wicked men, who had got possession of the kingdom of France, and by their principles and armies were going to revolutionize Europe. It was in this point of view only, that it could be considered as a war of defence. The success of Mr. Paine's books in England, the success of Dumouriez in the Netherlands, the fury and triumphs of the Jacobins in Paris, the proselytizing spirit of the French rulers, these were motives for war that were alone worthy to influence, or that alone did or could in reality have influenced, a man of the capacity of Mr. Pitt; and to talk of insurrections at Yarmouth and Shields, or Dundee, that might have happened at any time; of the decree of November, and the opening of the Scheldt, that were matters of negotiation to be openly carried on by ministers commissioned for the purpose—to insist on topics of this nature, was to make the war a war of underhand dealing, of pretexts and deceptions; pretexts and deceptions that were very properly trampled under foot, and cast back to the minister with scorn, by his mag-

---

* Herbert Marsh (1757–1839), successively bishop of Llandaff and Peterborough, "a vigorous but coarse phampleteer" ever on the side of the status quo.—ED.

nanimous opponent Mr. Fox. This I conceive to be the fair view of the subject, the only view fit for an historical student now to entertain; and I must therefore hasten to mention to you such documents as will enable you to form your judgment in the shortest time which so important a subject admits of.

The first book you are to turn to is Marsh's *Politics:* this book was originally written in German, and published in February, 1799, six years after the crisis that is now before us. Dr. Marsh was then a resident at Leipzig, and had observed that the most unfavourable notions were entertained all over Germany of the conduct of England. He therefore drew up the present work, and had the satisfaction to find, as he says in his preface, that it had not long appeared, when the first literary reviews in Germany pronounced, that the British government was completely rescued from the charges which had been laid to it, and that the origin as well as the continuance of the war must be wholly and solely ascribed to the mad ambition of the French rulers. You will find in the work a full and elaborate enumeration of all the offences of the French Convention, and the rulers of France at the time; of all the indications their speeches and conduct exhibited of a spirit of aggrandizement and proselytism; and from the whole, at the end of his book, he considers himself as entitled to draw the following conclusions:—"That a war with Great Britain had been resolved on, in the French cabinet, not only before the negotiation was ended, but even before it was commenced; and the object of the executive council was not to produce a reconciliation, but to amuse the British government, and to deceive the nation, till the plan which had been laid for the destruction of the British empire, was fully ripe for execution." He goes on to observe—"The mad ambition of the French rulers, their determination to extirpate all kingly governments, and the confident expectation of insurrections in every part of Europe, aided by the necessity of finding employment for their turbulent armies, were their motives to war in general; and their firm belief, that the inhabitants of Great Britain were so disaffected to their government, that French assistance would induce them to an immediate revolt; the inconsiderable number of troops at that time in Great Britain, in comparison with those which could easily be spared from France; the forward state of the French navy; the persuasion that a landing on the British coast would be attended with no difficulty; and the immense advantage expected from the acquisition of the British wealth, commerce and marine, in the prosecution of their conquests on the continent; all these motives, added to the innate desire of crushing an ancient and formidable, but, at that time, despised rival, induced them to a war with Great Britain in particular." And therefore finally, Dr. Marsh infers, "that it was a war of aggression, of injury, and of insult on the part of France, as well in the motives which gave it birth,

as in the open declaration of it; and on the part of Britain, it was just
and necessary, as being strictly a war of self-defence."

To prove all this, it will probably strike you, is to prove a great deal,
and it is not very creditable to arguments to appear to prove too much;
yet such is the opinion at which Dr. Marsh arrives by a consideration of
all the circumstances and documents which he produces. And these you
must therefore also meditate, and hereafter other documents and circumstances; but in the mean time, and in the first place from the perusal of
Dr. Marsh's book, your conclusion is to be, not I think Dr. Marsh's conclusion, but that the case before Mr. Pitt was one of no ordinary difficulty, arising from a most unexampled state of the world; such as common
maxims and common notions, those alone which Dr. Marsh brings to the
subject, were totally inadequate to meet. Dr. Marsh's work is the statement of a diligent and able advocate, the statement of one side of the
question only; nothing is said on the other; as such, it may be very useful
to you. I must therefore proceed to recommend to you other materials
for the formation of your opinions; but, before I do so, I must again state
to you, what the question now before you really is. It is this—Whether
we might not have avoided the war, without any stain on our honour;
and whether, if this be found the case, peace was not our policy, as a
better means of saving England from the proselytizing spirit of France,
than war.

Now, with regard to the first part of the question, you must weigh well
the correspondence that took place between Lord Grenville and Monsieur
Chauvelin; you must then look at a very celebrated letter that was written by Mr. Fox to the electors of Westminster; and lastly, to these you
must add the due consideration of the debates in parliament; they are
necessary to the illustration of the documents I have mentioned, and of
the times: they are not long, and nothing can be more worthy of your
attention. These are the three great means of forming your opinion.
The student, when he reads the correspondence between Lord Grenville
and M. Chauvelin, is to ask himself, which is the conciliating party,
and which the haughty, the dictatorial, and therefore the hostile party;
whether a great nation, like France, could be expected, in the face of
the world, to humble itself before its great ancient rival and opponent,
more than France did on this occasion, before the cabinet of England;
and again, he is to ask himself, what possible answer can now be made
to the representations of Mr. Fox's letter. I should not occupy you improperly if I were to endeavour to argue these points, because the tendency of what I should have to say would be to produce in you magnanimity, and a love of peace—few greater objects to me than these; but I
am now, as always, too limited in time, and you must be left to judge for
yourselves. But you will be unable to judge, I must again repeat, if you

do not read the debates; read, at least, those in the Commons. No reading can be proposed to you, so interesting, or so instructive; the subject, I must repeat, is the greatest that had occurred since the Revolution of 1688; and such men have never appeared, certainly have never appeared together, in the House of Commons, as were then seen there; Mr. Pitt and Mr. Burke on the one side, and Mr. Fox and Mr. Sheridan on the other. The speeches, too, you will find, characteristic and sufficiently exemplifying the particular merits of the speakers; bare, and meagre, and inadequate, as all reports must be; still, you will see, you will be enabled to conceive at least, the merit of Mr. Pitt, the luminous statement, the imposing force, the long majestic march of his eloquence; and of Mr. Burke, the wide knowledge, the discursive wit and fancy, the philosophy, and, on this particular occasion, the irritated enthusiasm (a treacherous counsellor) of his overflowing mind. And on the other side, of Mr. Fox, you will see the simplicity, the open and generous feelings, his sincere, straightforward, powerful argumentation; and of Mr. Sheridan, the spirited, brilliant reasoning, and caustic wit, dignified and recommended by the most honourable love of liberty—liberty, whether of England or of the world. All this might be a sufficient reward to you in point of entertainment, but much more than entertainment may be derived, edification of the most important kind. As on former occasions I most earnestly recommended to you the speeches of Mr. Burke on the American war, so do I now the speeches of Mr. Fox, as showing you the manner (I concern not myself now with the opinions), but as showing you the manner in which a British statesman should think and feel. Nothing can be so admirable throughout, as the uprightness of the sentiment, and the generosity of the feeling; the disdain of everything shifting, shuffling, and base; the contempt of all the expedients of low cunning, and vulgar policy; the magnanimous frankness, the simple wisdom, the elevated love of freedom, the benevolent love of peace, the detestation of all interference with the rights of others, however imposing the form, or plausible the pretext. Mr. Fox thought that the liberties of his own country were endangered by the measures that the government were adopting, and sanctioning under the influence of alarm; Mr. Pitt thought there was no other chance of preserving these liberties. The student must decide. Mr. Fox thought that the liberties of England and mankind would be at an end, if the allied powers succeeded in putting down the Revolution in France, and that it was for England on no account to participate in the shame and guilt of so atrocious an enterprise. Mr. Pitt was not disposed to admit that we were going to be engaged in any such enterprise, but he maintained, that the proceedings and principles of the French leaders must be resisted. "They are then best resisted by peace," said Mr. Fox. "By war," said Mr. Pitt, "nor can we avoid it." "You use no proper means," rejoined Mr. Fox, "to avoid it." The student must judge between these distinguished states-men; and if he takes the trouble I have proposed to him, he may.

A question now remains behind, which will certainly be asked by those who accede to the war system of Mr. Pitt,—Could we ultimately have escaped the war? If not entered upon in the beginning of 1793, must it not have been entered into in 1794? Would the violence and revolutionary spirit of the Jacobins have left us any alternative? To this, the answer seems to be, that the uncertainty of human affairs is at all times great, and particularly during the period of the Revolution of France; that it could not be just to go to war upon presumptions like these; that the objection supposes a better case hereafter; that this case must then be waited for; that no war can be lawful, till such last and best case arrives—the case of clear and strict necessity. War is not to be made sure of, but rather the chances of peace. We were in no such situation as has sometimes occurred; when a weaker nation must anticipate war, against a stronger, even as the last and best hope of safety. Our resources were great, and we were in no fear.

It would be to partake of the party violence of the times, to accuse Mr. Pitt of being unfriendly to the liberties of mankind, still less to those of his own country; no doubt he thought he was acting in the defence of both; but the crisis was of the most singular nature, and his remedy was war; was this prudent? He meant to resist the new opinions; was war the best mode? to weaken the influence, and to destroy, if possible, the Jaco-bins; was war the best expedient? Did not war, on the contrary, throw everything into the hands of the Jacobins, who could thus identify their power and their measures with the defence of the country? He meant to support our establishments; was war the best means of doing so? What danger could they run, as the people had shown their attachment to them, but from the increase of the national debt? There might be difficulty in the case from the extraordinary nature of the times, from the folly and fury of the French Convention, passing decrees by acclamation, amid the uproar of a revolution, and the intoxication of success on the repulse of an invading enemy; but was he to accommodate himself to such extraor-dinary times or not, for the sake of peace, and of such considerations, as we have mentioned? Was he not, as Mr. Fox advised, at least to negotiate; at least, to state our wrongs, and demand redress from those who were alone competent to afford it? Is it any answer to say with Dr. Marsh, that this would have been to betray fear, and could not have been successful; or with Mr. Burke, and the furious people of these times, that it was im-possible to negotiate with ruffians and assassins? These are the questions which the student must ask himself, and Mr. Pitt's fame as a minister must depend on the answer. That his intentions were the best, there can be no doubt; but this is not sufficient. Mr. Pitt has been celebrated as the pilot that weathered the storm; but the storm is the national debt, and is not weathered. In great and perilous conjunctures, ill fares it with a land, where its rulers are men, accustomed to give the law, with haughtiness in their temperament, and eloquence in their tongue; conscious of commanding talents, with all the imposing merits, but all the dangerous faults of genius. "Nullum numen abest, si sit prudentia."—Prudence is the one thing needful in a minister. Walpole in our own country, Washington in America, men of calm minds and circumspect understandings; this is the description of men that can alone be intrusted, on critical occasions, with the interests of their own country and the welfare of mankind; the patrons of mild government, the votaries of peace.

After all, it is possible that war might have been avoided by both countries, if the popular party in France (that guilty party) could but have behaved with any tolerable moderation and justice to their fallen monarch. The Duke of Brunswick's invasion and manifestoes, no doubt, were most unfortunate. But the allied powers had been driven back; the Convention had assembled, and seized and administered all the authority of the state; the supporters of the old opinions had been overpowered, had been taught to respect the convulsive strength, at least, of the wild democracy of France; and if a pause could but have *now* ensued, if the Jacobins could but have been now wise and magnanimous and just, or if the Girondists could but have prevailed, and if the king in consequence, and the royal family, had but been dismissed (to America for instance), it is possible that France and Europe might have been saved a long and dreadful series of the most appalling calamities;—it is possible, but it was *no longer possible*, when the Convention had not only brought to trial their benevolent and well-intentioned monarch (for such virtues were never denied him), but had even, with such intolerable cruelty, deliberately shed his blood; then, indeed, no terms were any longer to be kept with the new opinions, or their defenders. That a civil war would ensue in France (it did break out in La Vendée) was the general expectation; and even in England, such was the alarm created by the proselytizing spirit of the new opinions, such the indignation, detestation, and horror naturally produced by the 10th of August, the massacres of September, and above all, by the execution of the king, that all that could be done by the popular party, Mr. Fox at their head, was to attempt, and in vain attempt, to keep the two countries from going to war, and maintain, if possible, the existence of the free spirit, and free maxims of the constitution of England. Even to make these attempts at all, required all the exertions of the most transcendent eloquence, and the most resolute devotion to the general principles of freedom, amidst the impatient and indignant hatred of the very name of freedom that now generally prevailed, and that naturally resulted from the long-witnessed licentiousness of the mobs of Paris, and from the unprincipled reasonings and atrocious conduct of this upstart and merciless Convention. "With whom shall we treat?" was the question triumphantly asked, when peace with France was proposed; "ruffians, banditti in their cave," were the only appellations that could be found for her rulers; and all Europe, as in the times of the crusades, seemed now loosened from its hold, and ready to precipitate itself upon this one detested country. The leaders of the Revolution in France had therefore to defend their Revolution against the world; the European governments were resolved, if possible, to put the Revolution down. Each party had their appropriate means of attack and defence; but the great calamity was that the dispute, like other disputes among mankind, was to be decided by arms. The Revolutionists produced everywhere their doctrines, "liberty," "equality," "the rights of man," "the abuses of government," "the miseries of mankind," which were all imputed to the tyranny of their rulers, but they also produced their armies. Their opponents in like manner, while they insisted, in their manifestoes and reasonings, upon the wild anarchy and horrors that had followed the success of the new opinions in France, on the necessity of order, of the maintenance of the existing institutions of society, the distinctions of ranks, and the rights of property, omitted not to draw out their armies also, to enforce *their* arguments; and no crisis in the affairs of mankind, since the attack of the Roman empire by the northern nations, could ever be likened to the crisis which now ensued; for even the followers of Mahomet with their Koran, and their sword, as they came with an adverse faith, and uncongenial habits and manners, were not nearly such formidable opponents to the established governments and institutions of Europe, as were the French commissioners and generals, with irresistible military science, their innumerable hosts of soldiers totally reckless and prodigal of life, and their doctrines of liberty and equality (war to the palace, and peace to the cottage); so animating to themselves, so terrifying to their opponents, so plausible, so exciting, and so flattering wherever they turned, to all the most deeply rooted prejudices and passions of the lower orders of society. This, then, is the contest, this the crisis, which you are now to consider. It was so from the *first*, in the opinion of Mr. Burke; undoubtedly it became so from the moment that the 10th of August, the invasion of the Duke of Brunswick, the massacres of September, and the execution of the king, had so entirely infuriated the contending parties, as to leave no sentiments in their bosoms, but those of mutual indignation, disgust, and terror of the success of each other, and to render all councils of moderation and peace, in their own opinion, at least, impossible.*

* Lecture XXXVI, on William Godwin's political opinions, has been omitted.—Ed.

xxxvii. FALL OF THE GIRONDISTS

It is in [the] . . . works [i. e., apologetics] of the Girondists themselves, that . . . delusions and faults, as should be avoided by men animated often with the most generous feelings, may be seen in their more striking point of view. I shall allude to a few passages of this nature. I do not think that I shall thus misuse your time; no object of ambition can be, to me, more attractive, as I must for ever repeat, than to impart, if possible, the slightest hint of instruction to those who may be destined hereafter to be the patriots of their country, who are, in truth, the noblest of their kind, those who are elevated with a love of freedom, and an interest in the happiness of others.

Observe, then, as I continue to read to you, all through the remainder of this lecture, observe the virtuous principles with which these Girondists suppose themselves animated; observe their disappointments, their lamentations over the faults of the people, their invectives against the crimes of their opponents; and then remember their own prior history; the manner in which they pandered to the furious passions of that people; the faults they themselves committed, the daring and bloody means, the insurrections to which they themselves had recourse, to accomplish their own political ends; to establish what they called liberty.

We will first allude to Mme. Roland. "On a throne to-day, in chains to-morrow." Such is the motto which she prefixed to her account of her first imprisonment. "On a throne to-day, and in chains to-morrow." "Such," she says, "is the fate of virtue in times of revolution. After the first movements of a people wearied out by the abuses to which they have been subjected, the men of wisdom (who have enlightened them on the subject of their rights, who have aided them in the recovery of them), are called into place; there they cannot, however, long remain; for the men of ambition, ardent to profit by circumstances, soon succeed in their wish, by flattering the people to lead them astray, and indispose them to their true defenders, that they may themselves become persons of power and consideration. And this has been the course of things, more particularly, since the 10th of August."

Such was the observation of Mme. Roland, taught by her own melancholy experience. Let this then be remembered in time by those who would benefit their country, that though they may be themselves men of virtue, there are those behind them who are not.

You will read on; and you will, at last, see that an order comes from the Revolutionary Committee to arrest her husband. Nothing can be so ani-

mated or so striking, as her description of the manner in which she flew
to the hall of the Assembly, to obtain a hearing,—to obtain justice; the
delays, the difficulties she met with; the noise, the confusion, the scene
that she observed, was going on, whenever the door happened to open; at
last she got a sight of Vergniaud. "In the present state of the Assembly,"
he cried, "I cannot flatter you, and there is no hope for you; if admitted
to the bar, as a woman, you might experience a little favour, but as to the
power of doing good, it is all over with the Convention now." The narrative
continues, and continues in the most interesting manner, to paint her
efforts in the cause of what yet remained of liberty and right; her sufferings, and her disappointments; the disgraceful, but memorable scenes, by
which she was surrounded. She is at last thrown into prison herself; she
describes her situation, her prison, her thoughts; she remains in this situation some little time. "At last," she says, "I waited with impatience to hear
the heavy bars of the door drawn, that I might ask for the journal. I
read it; and I read the decree for arresting the twenty-two deputies (the
Girondists);—the paper dropped," she says, "from my hands, and I cried,
in an agony of grief, 'My country is lost!' While I continued alone," she
says, "or nearly so, proud, yet tranquil under the yoke of the oppressor,
I could still form vows, I could still cherish hopes for the defenders
of liberty; but error and crime have *now* the ascendant; the national
representation is violated, its unity broken; whatever was in its bosom distinguished for probity, character, and talents, is now proscribed. The commune of Paris lords it over the legislative body; Paris is lost; the flames of
civil war are lighted; the enemy will profit by our dissensions; for the north
of France, liberty will be no more; and the whole republic will be rent and
abandoned to the most frightful disorder. Sublime illusions, generous sacrifices, O hope, happiness, my country, adieu! adieu! In the first expansion
of my youthful heart, at twelve years old, I wept that I was not born a
Spartan or a Roman. I thought I saw, in the French Revolution, the un-
hoped-for application of all the principles on which I had seemed to live.
Liberty, I said to myself, has two sources:—good morals, and then we have
wise laws; enlightened minds, and we are then led on to both, to morals
and wise laws, by the knowledge of our common rights. My soul (I said)
shall be no more desolated by the spectacle of the debasement of humanity. Mankind shall be ameliorated in their condition; and the happiness of all shall be the base and pledge of the happiness of each individual.
Brilliant chimeras! seductions that have so charmed me! you are vanished,—vanished all, before the frightful corruptions of an immense city;
—but I disdain to live; your loss has made life hateful to me, and I wish
but for the last sufferings that await me from these guilty wretches. Why
tarry you, ye anarchists and brigands? You proscribe virtue; shed then
the blood of those who profess it; shed their blood, and it shall make the

earth upon which it falls, ravenous; it shall make it open under your feet."

It will not be possible, I think, for any of you to cast your eyes over the writings of Mme. Roland, however slightly, without being sufficiently struck, to induce you to turn and read them throughout. The great moral of the whole is, no doubt, the care and caution with which early reformers should proceed; that real patriotism and prudence are inseparable: but when this moral has been well digested, and made a part of our nature, then the writings of Mme. Roland can only benefit and not mislead; can only animate us to those tasks of patriotism, which our calmer meditation has enabled us better to understand.

"Grand swelling sentiments of liberty," says Mr. Burke, in one of his many beautiful paragraphs, "I am sure, I do not despise; they warm the heart, they enlarge and liberalize our minds, they animate our courage in a time of conflict. Old as I am, I read the fine raptures of Lucan and Corneille with pleasure." He had before said, "But what is liberty without wisdom, and without virtue? It is the greatest of all possible evils; for it is folly, vice, and madness, without tuition or restraint."

So thought the statesman and philosopher, while sitting in his closet, in the middle of the year 1790. The Revolution rolls on; and three years afterwards, what are the thoughts of Mme. Roland, waiting in her dungeon for the axe of the executioner? You have heard them already; but hear more.

"A friend to liberty," she says, "on which reflection had taught me to set a just value, I beheld the Revolution with delight, persuaded that it was destined to put an end to the arbitrary power, which I detested, and to the abuses, which I had so often lamented, when reflecting, with pity, on the fate of the lower orders of mankind. I know, that in revolutions, law, as well as justice, is often forgotten; and the proof is that I am here. I owe my trial to nothing but the prejudices and violent animosities which arise in times of great agitation against those who have been placed in conspicuous situations, or are known to possess any energy or spirit. It is necessary that I should perish in my turn. But when innocence thus walks to the scaffold, every step is an advance to glory. May I be the last victim sacrificed to the furious spirit of party! I shall quit with joy this unfortunate earth, which swallows up the friends of virtue, and drinks the blood of the just. Truth! friendship! my country! objects that are so sacred, sentiments that are so dear to my heart, receive my last sacrifice. It is to you that I have dedicated my life,—it is from you that I derive pleasure and glory in my death. Just Heaven! enlighten this unfortunate people, for whom I desired liberty. Liberty! it is for the wise people that cherish humanity, practise justice, despise their flatterers, know their true friends, and respect the truth. Till you are a people like this, my fellow-citizens, it is in vain you will talk of liberty; you will have only licentiousness, of which you will each fall the victim in your turn; you will ask for bread, and dead bodies will be given you; and you will finish by being slaves." Such were the sentiments of Mme. Roland. She had furnished herself with poison against the last extremity; but, afterwards, thought it a duty she owed her country and liberty, to die on the scaffold. . . .

What shall we say to them [the Girondists]? The crimes of some of them, the faults of many of them, disappear in the midst of the greater crimes and faults of their opponents, and are forgotten while we read of their misfortunes, and the calmness with which they met their fate, or the courage with which they defied their oppressors.

It is impossible to save ourselves from an influence of this kind, while we contemplate their high qualities, and read their story. But after this has been felt, and every testimony due to them thus properly discharged, we must not turn away from what is necessary to the purposes of our own instruction, and what is due to the moral purity of our own minds; we must not forget their behaviour to the king, during the earlier sittings of the Legislative Assembly; their hostility to the Constitutionalists, and La Fayette; their resolution, at all events, to have their experiment of a republic, or of some new dynasty, which must have ended in a republic, tried; and lastly, their contrivance of the insurrection of the 10th of August; from the first, their referring all political right and wrong to the mere will of the people. These mistakes, and faults, and crimes must not be forgotten.

I consider the example of these men, in all its bearings, as very edifying, and of the highest importance, to a very interesting, very elated, but very impracticable and dangerous description of the friends of freedom, if they would but condescend to consider it; edifying and important to them in the way I have endeavoured to explain. But my doctrines are so humble in their nature, and so little captivating in their sound, that I may well fear to fatigue an audience (a youthful audience) by recurring to them too often, and insisting upon them too long. In brief, the faults of the Girondists were not a little the faults of young men, as described by Lord Bacon. "Young men," says he, "in the conduct and management of actions, embrace more than they can hold, stir more than they can quiet; fly to the end, without consideration of the means and degrees; pursue some few principles, which they have chanced upon, absurdly; care not to innovate, which draws unknown inconveniences; use extreme remedies at first, and that which doubleth all errors, will not acknowledge or retract them, like an unready horse, that will neither stop nor turn. Of the old, on the contrary," says Lord Bacon, "they object too much; they consult too long; they adventure too little; they repent too soon; and they seldom drive business home to the full period, but content themselves with a mediocrity of success." In these last words the great philosopher did not, perhaps, mean to compliment the old, but in these few words appears to me, I confess, the sum and substance of all human wisdom in practical politics—"to content ourselves with a mediocrity of success." This does not exclude, but it on the contrary supposes, enterprise and benevolence, active virtue; but it supposes also, a deep sense of the uncertainty of everything human, the respect that is due to the opinions and feelings of others, the tremendous nature, if once roused, of the collective passions of mankind.

xxxix. REIGN OF TERROR *

THE QUEEN [Marie Antoinette] can be little expected to have escaped, amidst such a promiscuous massacre as took place during this Reign of Terror. I cannot enter into her trial. You will see it in the historians. . . .

In the meantime, I know not how to avoid adverting to a particular circumstance that occurred while she stood before her tribunal; it is so descriptive of these dreadful times, and of the people that assisted at these dreadful tribunals; the circumstance you may have heard, but it is not quite accurately represented. An infamous question was asked her, with respect to herself and her own child, the young dauphin; the question was asked her in the midst of a crowd of other questions (for such is the very improper and strange manner of the examination of a prisoner in France), and she had replied to the whole mass in some general manner. The trial went on, and some time after one of the vile wretches that sat as her juror called back the attention of the president, and desired him to observe to the queen that she had made no answer to the particular question that had been asked her; and it was not until this moment, and until thus again distinctly questioned, that she deigned to reply. "If I answered not, it was because nature refused to answer to an accusation like this, made to any mother. I appeal to those mothers that may be here." The suppression of her answer had been, therefore, perfectly sincere, and when it did come, there was in it nothing of ostentation or smartness, nothing but the indignant voice of an insulted woman, addressed to wretches that were unworthy the name of men. A nation must indeed be fallen, when such a scene as this could take place in the high court of their justice; a scene to which I extremely hesitate, though it appears on the

* Smyth devoted no less than six lectures—XXXVIII through XLIII—to the Terror, the bloody convulsion of the French Revolution. We give excerpts from two: XXXIX and XLI.—ED.

face of history, even to allude in the most distant manner, lest I should pollute your minds by the approach of thoughts so foul.

The queen, when conducted to execution, like the lowest of male-factors, on a common tumbrel, and with her hands tied behind her, could little concern herself with the priest (the constitutional priest) that at-tended her, still less with the crowd by which she was surrounded: the dead paleness of her cheek was occasionally varied by a strong hectic, probably of indignation, that passed across it; but her emotion was visible when she came within sight of the gardens of the Tuileries, and her countenance changed; changed to behold that ancient palace, so long the abode of all that was once magnificent in France, of a splendour to which she had been so intimately associated, lately the scene of her own anxieties and sufferings, and now the seat of that assembly of men who had brought her king and husband to the scaffold, and were at the instant exercising the same last act of cruelty and vengeance upon herself. It was, how-ever, but a look that she cast, and it was but the thoughts of a moment that occupied her mind; yet how crowded must that moment have been with all the mingled, innumerable, indescribable emotions of the present and the past; disdain and anger, melancholy and regret, astonishment and awe: but she turned hastily away, and hurried to the scaffold, as if re-coiling indignantly from this world, and eager to be precipitated into a better.

Of the character of the queen it is not easy to speak; she had the faults of exalted rank, but she had all the merits. It would be unreasonable to have expected from her any interest in the cause of liberty, or any very enlightened view of the relative duties of princes to their subjects. She must have generally counselled the king ill, and once, in the instance of Necker's measure of the 23rd of June, perhaps fatally. The most disagree-able observation to be made is that she seems to have been almost hated by a majority of the French people: this, however, might be possible, without any correspondent demerit on her part during revolutionary times of a nature so extraordinary. Censure has been busy with her character; and though none but the vulgar consider her as generally licentious, one, and even two names have been mentioned; and an unfavourable impres-sion will descend to posterity, which, whether just or not, cannot now be removed. A suspicion of this kind might easily arise in a court like that of France, and once existing, exist for ever. The very wise, on these oc-casions, are too wise, they think, to be deceived; and not to suppose un-favourably, would be to appear to know nothing of the world. It would be unjust for us, in England at least, to try her by the standard of our own manners, one unknown to her. It is not always easy for spectators to dis-tinguish in a lively, careless woman, between the regard that is consistent with innocence and the attachment that belongs to guilt; more particularly in a queen always eager to burst through the thraldom and even the decorum of her exalted station, and apparently with no pleasure so great as the enjoyment of that social intercourse which is the privilege of happier and humbler life; a queen, in brief, who could not submit to the penalty of a throne, the misery of having no friend. She seems to have been lively and amiable, formed to be the idol of the court of a great monarch, a model of elegance and grace: "never lighted upon this orb, which she hardly seemed to touch, a more delightful vision." How, indeed, she deported herself at all times in the gay hours of her prosperity, it may now be impossible to ascertain, and she may not have been, during that treacherous season, always innocent; but when the scene changed, and all was ominous and dark, she was more worthy of herself, and the *misfortunes*, at least, of her husband she shared with truth and loyalty, with magnanimity and firmness, with patience and with hope. On all trying occasions (and they were many) she was the affectionate and faithful wife, with the intrepid heart that became a daughter of Maria Theresa. Whatever may be doubtful, whatever difficult in the estimate of her character, one thing is but too certain, that she was most unfortunate; and when affliction is in the scale (and such affliction), it is no longer possible to watch the vibrations of the balance. . . .

Nothing is so common as for men to justify their crimes by a necessity which they have themselves created. This was shown on a tremendous scale by the Jacobins in France; and it seems a constant occurrence in human nature, from the most elevated usurper of a throne down to the lowest ruffian, who murders those whom he originally intended only to rob. But reasonings of this kind are not to be endured; mark their progress in the case before us. The allied powers invade the country in the summer of 1792, and with some success; Danton, therefore, and the Jacobins immediately rushed forward, Danton more particularly, and after a furious speech from this demagogue, they massacre all the unresisting wretched creatures of every age and sex, that can be found in all the prisons of Paris—and why? that the Revolution, which they have thus made desperate, may be afterwards defended; that the whole population of Paris may be so steeped in guilt that no retreat may be possible: that the cause of the Jacobins and the rest of the inhabitants may be one and the same, and that they may be all intermingled together, and the city set on fire, rather than the allies should prevail, or any submission be made; and this is called defending the country. But again, in the event the invaders retreat, not indeed on account of these proceedings, but from causes of a very different nature; the Convention meets, and the Jacobins then suppose themselves under the necessity, as all Europe is outraged by the horrid tale of those massacres, to outrage all Europe still further, and to bring to trial and to execute the king. It was in vain represented to them that this was an act totally inhuman, totally unjustifiable; that it would make the cause of the Revolution odious in the sight of all men; that it would cause a civil war in France; that all the powers of civilized Europe would rise up in arms against such lawless and atrocious barbarity. No, no! was the answer of the Jacobins; it is necessary for the Revolution that a republic should be established, for the republic that the king should be put out of the way; it is necessary that the Revolution should roll on, not be impeded in its progress by royalists and traitors of whatever description; that all who resist it, whether at home or abroad, should be exterminated; that there was no other safety for freedom, no other success. "I mourn," said Robespierre, "over the fate of Louis; but it is necessary for the good of the people, and he must die." The act is committed, and what follows? That Europe rises up in arms against them, as was predicted: the prior necessity is made more and more apparent. But further, the Girondists are now totally revolted by one cruelty after another, by the massacre of the king, as well as the massacres of September; and though they meanly (too many of them) vote for the one, they make every effort in their power to bring to justice the perpetrators of the other. But again, No, no, no! said the Jacobins, "these excesses in a good cause are not to be too scrupulously looked into; they were conducive to the public good: it is, in short, necessary to pass them over; it is necessary to keep alive the spirit of the Revolution: none but enemies to it, and traitors to their country, would think of discrediting the Revolution, by calling the public attention to them: these are the necessary evils of a revolution; it is in vain to lament them, quite impossible to punish them." Such was the language of the Jacobins, as the necessities, which they themselves created, continually accumulated upon them.

In this, as in every other case, a sort of justification, a species of reasoning was adopted; and because this reasoning was not satisfactory to the Girondists, daring and lawless as they themselves were, Robespierre and his Jacobins were happy in this opportunity of overpowering their rivals for the public favour, and they turned round upon *them* also, as they had done upon their victims in September, and lately upon their king: and it was necessary, they cried aloud, "that the *Girondists* should, in like manner, be sacrificed on the altar of the Revolution; it was necessary that the Girondists too should be considered as royalists and federalists, and whatever might be their pretences, as traitors to the common cause; *they* too, were to be massacred in the Convention, if possible; they were at all events to be dragged out of it, and detained in prison till they could be put to death. It was necessary that such moderate men as these, with their silly cries and idle declamations about anarchy and blood, should be themselves publicly punished as traitors, who could only thus mean to betray the cause of the Revolution; that traitors they evidently were, and could not but be esteemed such by all true patriots; that it was necessary that true patriots should alone bear rule; and that it was necessary that not only federalists, like the Girondists, but traitors of every description should perish, for it was necessary to defend the country, and how else could the country be defended?" Such again was the language of Robespierre and the Jacobins.

And what, then, was the result of all these still multiplying necessities, these reasonings of enthusiasm, guilt, and cruelty, but that Robespierre and the Jacobins saw all that had been predicted, and all that they might themselves have foreseen, take place, and found their country in a state of siege, as it was called; an insurrection in the great towns and some of the departments, on account of the fate of the Girondists; a civil war in La Vendée, and all Europe leagued against them, on account of the execution of the king: and they are then to say that the country is to be defended, that a system of terror must be introduced; and because, in point of fact, the revolutionary armies not only beat off their invaders, but rush onward, and terrify and subdue half Europe, they are then again to come forward and present themselves as having defended their country, as having maintained their Revolution by this system of terror: and philosophic historians are to allow their pretensions, and even men of humanity and sense are to look upon them without detestation, and to talk, like themselves, of the defence of the country.

The truth is that this Reign of Terror was the expedient made use of by Robespierre and the Jacobins to defend themselves, not their country, to defend themselves against the Royalists in La Vendée, the Girondists and Constitutionalists in the departments and in the great towns, and against the powers of Europe, who thought their rule inconsistent with the maintenance of the established notions of society.

While they were thus defending themselves, and at the head of the government, they drove away the invaders of their country, by means of the heroic armies that thought not of them, and have therefore been sometimes considered by French historians and writers, always the apologists at all hazards of their country, as having defended the cause of the Revolution. But no Revolution in defence of freedom could be defended by any system of terror, such as in reality took place; no other consequence could possibly follow but a military government. The enemy might be kept at a distance, or great conquests be made, even while it lasted, and in defiance of it, but no cause of FREEDOM could be thus established or introduced; sooner or later the rule of the army and of some great captain was inevitable, and Robespierre and the Jacobins, though they might defend themselves, far from defending their Revolution and the cause of freedom, rendered its success, either in France or the rest of Europe, from that moment totally impossible.

The world at the time made no mistake on this subject; men saw in these massacres and proscriptions, and in this Reign of Terror, only the struggles of desperate and lawless factions, contending with each other for power. What else could they see in the triumph of Robespierre and the Jacobins over the Girondists, and of Robespierre over Danton? The scene has passed away, and we are too apt to lose the first natural and original impression, which it very properly conveyed; but this must on no account be suffered; it would be to confound all right and wrong, to be insensible to cruelty and injustice, to lend ourselves to the delusions of writers who are endeavouring to shelter their countrymen from the reproaches of mankind: it is not too much to say, it would be to find patriots in monsters, and defenders of liberty in cut-throats and assassins.

XLI. REIGN OF TERROR

ONE WORD, as I conclude my lecture, on the subject of another extraordinary man, who appeared in these extraordinary times; one word of Danton.

Something of the praise that, however late, belongs to Camille Desmoulins, belongs also even to Danton. After following him through all the scenes of the Revolution, with horror and detestation, we at last concede to him an unexpected emotion of approbation; and it is with no pleasure that we see him fall, at least fall by the hands of Robespierre. He had got rich by plunder, had been fortunate in his marriage, and had found it better happiness to serve a beautiful woman, than the grim idol he had worshipped under the abused name of liberty. He had abandoned himself to indolence and indulgence, (always his proper elements), and amid the enjoyments of the heart, his heart had been taught a lesson, and he had been awakened to the long-forgotten feelings of humanity. At the foot of the scaffold he thought of her he loved, the wife of his bosom, and, stern as he was, the moment had nigh overcome him: "No weakness, Danton!" he cried; and he prepared to die.

When Lacroix was conducted with him to the Luxembourg, "For us to be arrested!" he cried: "To arrest us! I never thought of such a thing!" "Not thought of it!" replied Danton; "I knew it, I had been told of it." "You knew it," replied Lacroix, very naturally; "you knew it, and did nothing! your usual indolence has been the destruction of us."

And such, indeed, was the secret of the fate of Danton. Nothing could be so able as the speech of Robespierre against him, or the report of St. Just; for nothing could be so difficult as to make out a plausible case, nothing so preposterous as a charge of treason to be brought against

Danton; and well might the base and cold-blooded Robespierre rub his hands with delight, when he found, as he came up through the garden of the Tuileries, that his execution had been accomplished.

Danton was formed to be the tribune of the people: a mind capable of conceiving at any exigency a measure that should carry away the fluctuating and expectant opinions of the populace, by its daring and decisive nature; a ready, intelligent, and most impressive eloquence; a voice that was likened, by those who lived at the time, to the roaring of a wild animal, certainly one that could make a street or public square re-echo; a countenance that, like the famed head of Medusa, could petrify the beholders; and a figure that seemed to belong to some Titan of old, who could seize a mountain, as a weapon of offence, and bury an enemy beneath it. It is astonishing how such a demagogue could be attacked at all, much less overcome by such a cowardly wretch as Robespierre; that the populace could suffer their hero to be dragged to execution, the idol they had so long worshipped, and whose influence they had felt on occasions, so many and so trying.

Yet all this was done. And Danton had at last only to despise the populace, the instruments he had so often wielded to the destruction of others, and despise alike the rival who now converted them to his own. Camille Desmoulins, as they went to execution, had poured out his imprecations on the base and hypocritical Robespierre. The hired mob that surrounded their tumbrel, repaid his insults in their own opprobrious manner. Camille lost all temper. "Let them alone," said Danton, casting on them a look of cold contempt; "let them alone, the vile canaille!"

"We are sacrificed," he said, on another occasion, "to a few cowardly brigands, but they will not long enjoy their victory; I drag Robespierre after me; Robespierre follows me; these brothers of Cain [he said] know nothing about government. I leave everything in a frightful disorder." When they arrived at the Conciergerie, they occupied the same dungeon which the Girondists had done before them, the Girondists whom they had sent there. This sort of retributive justice was often and amply experienced in the course of this memorable Revolution. "It was on such a day as this," he said, "that I instituted the revolutionary tribunal. I beg pardon of God and man; but my meaning was to have prevented a new September, not to have let loose such a scourge of humanity." Once, and once only, he showed a slight regret at having taken part in the Revolution. "Better far," he said, "to be poor and be a fisherman, than to be a governor of men."

A meeting took place between Robespierre and Danton, sought by the latter, for the purpose of an accommodation. "No doubt," said Danton, "we must keep down the Royalists, but we should only strike where the cause of the Republic requires; the innocent should not be confounded with the guilty." "And who told you," replied Robespierre, sharply, "that any innocent person had perished?" Danton turned to his friend who had accompanied him, and with a bitter smile, "What say you," said he, "not an innocent perished!!!" Robespierre and he then separated; and all friendship was now at an end for ever. Danton was in vain urged to exert and defend himself. "I had rather," he said, "be the one to be guillotined, than the one to guillotine." And again, "My life is not worth the trouble; I am sick of mankind."

He contented himself with insisting that Robespierre and the committee durst not attempt his life; and with no other answer than "they dare not," in a sort of morbid indifference and indolence, he was dead to the entreaties of his friends, and waited the event.

But Danton, by retiring awhile a short time before from the scene, had suffered his influence to part away from him. Robespierre had got possession of the Jacobins; the Cordeliers belonged to the Hebertists; and the Convention passive, spiritless, and fallen, could afford him no efficient support. Robespierre, too, had one virtue which Danton had not; he had remained poor. He could always, therefore, represent himself as having no object but the republic; could always obtain an audience, belief for his assertions, and turn his own purity and merits to the destruction of his opponents.

The account given of Danton is everywhere the same, but it is best given by Thiers. He was consistent to the last, and not a word or look escaped him that was not worthy of his dreadful career and terrible renown. He appalled the president and the jury, and embarrassed the hardened Fouquier [-Tinville], the public accuser. "Be calm," said the president; "it is the mark of innocence." "Calm!" said Danton, "when I see myself so basely calumniated. It is not from a man of the Revolution like me that you are to expect a cold defence. Men of my temperament are, in revolutions, above all price; on their front is stamped the Genius of Liberty." Danton, at these words, assumed the port and movement of the Jupiter Olympus of the ancients; and the well-known looks that had so often struck terror into the hearts of the spectators, lost not now their impression; and a murmur of approbation was heard.

"Me!" he cried, "accuse me of having conspired with Mirabeau, with Dumouriez, with Orléans, of having crawled at the feet of despots!" He then detailed the main incidents of his life; his resistance to Mirabeau; his stopping the royal carriage that was going to St. Cloud; his bringing the people to the Champ de Mars to protest against royalty; his proposing the overthrow of the throne in 1792; his proclaiming the insurrection of the 10th of August; and then, suffocated with indignation, to think that he had been accused of concealing himself on that day. "Who are the men who had to engage Danton to come forward," he cried, "on that occasion? Produce my accusers! Let me unmask the three miserable beings that surrounded at that moment and ruined Robespierre. Produce them, and let them appear, that I may plunge them into that annihilation, from which they shall never afterwards emerge."

Danton poured forth the thunder of his indignation till the president attempted to drown his voice by sounding his bell. Danton still went on. "Do you not understand me?" said the president. "Your bell!" said Danton. "He who is defending his honour and his life has a voice that must outsound your bell." But he had exhausted himself, and became silent.

You will read with eagerness whatever relates to Danton; indeed, there is an unworthy interest that belongs to characters of this particular description. Energy, decision, courage, contempt of death, the power of confronting dangers, and trampling upon difficulties,—these are all so useful in the warfare of life, and indicate such a superiority of character and mind over our common nature, that our respect gets inextricably associated, even when such qualities are connected with enormous vices and atrocious conduct. We are ever ready to forget the guilt, when great capacity is shown, and a fearless contempt for the common terrors of humanity; but when, as in the case of Danton, there is shown at the same time something of a nature capable of affection, of friendship, and of love, of careless gaiety, of indolence, and a taste for the relaxation of pleasure, every offensive part of the character (more particularly in cases and moments of misfortune) seems to disappear, and ruffians, and pirates, and banditti, men of desperate lives, every hour engaged in scenes of lawless outrage and bloody violence, can be rendered by a Schiller or a Byron the idols and the delight of the gentle, the generous, and the kind, of the young and the beautiful, the studious and the retired; those who would be the first to shrink from deeds of cruelty, and sights of death, and who, of all others, are most interested in the general prevalence of peace and order, of humanity and good sense.

But this must not be. Our moral feelings must not be suffered to tolerate such men, least of all Danton, the dreadful tribune of the worst stages of the French Revolution, who scrupled not, as a mode of resistance to the allies, to institute in September a regular massacre of helpless beings of every description; whose very plan was, so to defile the people of Paris with carnage, that they might be rendered desperate; who was the relentless destroyer of a benevolent king; who was not satiated with blood, nor made to pause till he had passed through the Reign of Terror; and who turned aside from his course of violence and guilt, only that he might the better enjoy his plunder, and profit by his crimes.

XLIV. CONCLUDING LECTURE

OBSERVE THE reign of Louis XIV, the wars of ambition, the profuse expenditure, the immoral conduct of this celebrated hero of vanity and ostentation, the destruction of all freedom in the government. What better way than this to endanger the existence of the monarchy? Observe next the court and privileged orders during the regency and the reign of Louis XV; their profligacy, their prodigality, their defiance of public opinion: I have dwelt upon them in these lectures. And observe again, during all this time, the writings of men of genius, of Rousseau and others, the agitators of the community; and again, the low publications of the schools of obscenity and atheism. What seeds for a harvest of destruction were here! How could all the actors in the scene perform, each their part, with more thoughtless absurdity, with more unprincipled guilt! Observe, again, when a young and benevolent monarch, the unfortunate Louis XVI, ascended the throne, how could the privileged orders have behaved with more selfishness and less political wisdom than they did? Are the maxims which courts and privileged orders then adopted, as the rules of their conduct, to be ever again admitted, after the experience of this French Revolution? Were they ever (even before it) consistent with what is considered as common sense on every other occasion? Do men manage thus their physical health, their property, or any other concern in life? Do they not take medicine, submit to operations, embank rivers, clear away nuisances, anticipate evils, provide for the future? Is there not such a thing as prudence in the world, and even exercised by these privileged orders upon every occasion, but upon questions, political questions, where their own most important interests and these of the community are concerned? It is melancholy to see the blind perverseness of men in matters of this nature; and it should seem, as if even the example of the French Revolution were to have been exhibited in vain.

Turn now the picture, and look at the patriots of the French Revolution, even those of the Constituent Assembly. Their mistakes might be natural; their faults (many of them) pardonable (men with generous intentions and noble aspirations, it is not easy to condemn); but is it too much to say, that there was scarcely a mistake or fault possible, which they did not commit? What is the main question between them and Mr. Burke? Is it not this:—that they proceeded upon a totally wrong system: that their system was not that of reform, but of entire alteration; not to improve, but to begin anew? Can it be now supposed that this was not a fundamental mistake and fault? Can it be contended that the events of the Revolution would have been the same, if the principles of it had been different? But the world, it will be said, was in a state of enthusiasm; the new opinions had inflamed the imagination of every good and intelligent man. Be it so. Let this then be the lesson of the Revolution; and let the world be on its guard in future against every species of political enthusiasm.

This part of my subject I have laboured to the utmost, and I have wearied my hearers with expostulations, entreaties, and remonstrances, from the very respect I bear to the friends of freedom, and from the deep interest that I cannot but feel in their success at all times. It is to them, I confess, as it appears to me, that the lesson of the French Revolution should be principally addressed, and for the reason I have often mentioned. Men of this generous and noble nature are not to suppose that they cannot commit the most important faults; most assuredly they can; and they are not, with these French modern historians, to destroy their moral sensibilities, and to escape from responsibility, by notions of fatalism, and of necessity; by talking of revolutionary tides, that must roll on: systems of carnage, that were the inevitable result of existing situations, of parties that could not but arise; deeds of atrocity and cruelty, that could not but be perpetrated. Men are not to soothe themselves, and pander to their own impetuous or guilty passions in this daring and unjustifiable manner. The truth is, and must be, that as patriots do, or do not act, with prudence and virtue, their Revolution does, or does not succeed; and they are justly amenable, as are their opponents, in their characters and in their fame, to the community and to posterity, for the prosperity or failure of their political projects.

What could possibly be the result, if the patriots of the Constituent Assembly were so constantly to fall back on the people, refer everything to their will, and deify their sovereign wisdom? Admit that all government is intended, not only for the coercion of the passions of mankind, but for the happiness of the community, is the community to govern, or the representatives they have appointed? There can be no doubt on this subject, it will be answered; but the Constituent Assembly were singularly situated, and could not have made head against the court, without a continual appeal to the physical strength of the people. I must deny this position. The Assembly began with usurpation; the tide was evidently running strong in their favour; the king was not against them; the minister with them. But be these points determined as they may, was it not even in those times, and in all times, a matter of mere prudence and common sense, that an Assembly was to respect itself; was not to allow its own members to be interrupted and insulted by the tribunes; was not to suffer, surely was not to encourage, as they often did, petitions and remonstrances from tumultuous and armed bodies of people, exhibiting menacing gestures, and using vehement language in the very hall of their sittings? The different turns of the Revolution, which these French historians resolve into the effect of some high and sublime principles of fatalism and necessity, is it too much to say, that they were all brought about by mobs of the lowest of the populace, which ferocious demagogues packed into the galleries for the purpose? And what but this could be the consequence of the constant habit of the popular party, to refer themselves to the people, to submit to their outrages, and to appear to have no dependence but on the multitude? Patriots may make mistakes and commit faults, but are these to be pardoned? What was the result? Before the Assembly had sat six months . . . the most virtuous and intelligent men that belonged to it, not choosing to serve the people in their own way, as the historian calls it, retired from the Revolution, and gave up the whole cause in disgust and despair.

Thus far have I to speak even of the Constituent Assembly, and of the most virtuous and enlightened members, that made, for some time, a leading part of it.

The next great lesson, and indeed the main one, as far as the friends of freedom are concerned, is the care with which men should consider their means, when they are endeavouring to accomplish an end. The great rule of morality is, that we are not to do evil, that good may come. In a world like this, and constituted as men are, general rules encounter each other, above all, in politics; and exceptions do, and will arise, and must be supposed possible. But the general rules of morality must be laid down (the great rule just mentioned, for instance), in order that human beings may elevate their virtue to the proper point, as far as the imperfections of their nature will admit, and leave circumstances and situations to enforce their own lessons. Certainly, on all occasions, and more particularly in politics, men are too much disposed to make exceptions to general rules, and to consult their convenience, or their interests, rather than do their duty. From an early period of the Revolution, the popular leaders were guilty in this respect. It is the very nature and genius of revolutions to commit this fault; this must be confessed; still it is one of the best virtues of patriots to labour to avoid it; it is even the best policy; for men, and the multitude more particularly, soon get callous to all sense of moral obligation, when general rules are once violated, and the Revolution goes inevitably to ruin, from the want of principle with which it is conducted. Thus in the Revolution before us, the mob are tolerated in their bloody outrages and processions, till at last a dreadful demagogue starts up, and as an expedient to resist the Duke of Brunswick, institutes a regular system of massacre for several days together. Even the official authority in Paris announces and recommends it to the provinces. And this again prepares the way for the system of terror, a sort of massacre for the space of nearly two years. Again, the Constituent Assembly want funds, and they fall upon the church; they plunder the members of it from the highest to the lowest. No proper regard to the rights of property is shown; not then, and consequently never after.

Again. All law and order are violated in the person of the king, and he is brought a prisoner to the Tuileries on the 6th of October; and from that time no sentiment of law or order could be found sufficiently strong to avail long for his protection. He is attacked in his palace, and his guards butchered; and he is afterwards, for no other reason, but that a republic is wanted, put to death.

These are among the more appalling specimens of the importance of steadiness of principle; the importance of observing ourselves, as legislators, of teaching the public, by our example, to observe, as citizens, the great leading obligations of humanity and justice. It is scarcely too much to say that the whole of the Revolution, from the earliest periods, was marked on the part of the popular leaders by too great a disregard of their means for the sake of their ends (no doubt, with more or less of excuse, from the different exigencies of the case, and the difficulties of their situation, which were often very great); still an attentive observer, accompanying them through the detail of their proceedings, will, for a long time, have so much to blame as well as to lament, and will, at length, as he proceeds, find himself wound up to such feelings of indignation and abhorrence, that he will be ready to impute all the evils that happened, and the loss of their cause (for it must be considered as lost when it merged in the power of Buonaparte), to the friends of freedom themselves—the friends of freedom, as they professed themselves; to their own fault and failure, in not observing this great rule of human conduct, not to neglect the means for the sake of the end.

Nor is it sufficient to reply, as it is always replied, that the faults and even crimes of the Revolution were owing to the court first, and afterwards to the invasions of the allied powers. I consider all the great measures of the popular leaders as ill judged or criminal. Their insisting upon becoming one Assembly, their usurpation of the supreme power, their lodging the king a prisoner in the Tuileries, the Austrian war, the insurrection of the 10th of August, the massacres of September, the decree of November, the execution of their sovereign, for none of these measures (and they are the leading measures) do I see any proper necessity or justification; and all of them, as I conceive, may be shown to be in the different popular leaders, to say nothing of their treatment of each other, mistakes or crimes. To say this is not at all to defend the unjustifiable invasion of the Duke of Brunswick, or the impolitic conduct of the allied powers in the spring of 1793.

But to return to the great faults, which I object to the popular leaders.

This disposition to forget every consideration, for the chance of accomplishing some favourite object, was not a little sanctioned by an abuse
of the doctrine of utility; and I therefore directed your attention to this
particular subject, this abuse of the doctrine of utility. It may be
thought, that men, acting under the influence of ambition, rivalship,
hatred, political enthusiasm, and all the stormy and all the corrupt passions of this unhappy period can little be supposed to have felt the influence of any mistakes in their moral theories, or of any moral feelings
at all. But the characters and conduct of men are of a very mixed nature;
and they are never unaffected by such notions of duty, as they in reality
entertain. Patriotism, the public good, the cause of the Revolution, which
they considered as synonymous; these were expressions that were never
absent for a moment from their speeches, addresses, and manifestoes of
every kind and on every occasion; and this abuse of the doctrine, this
practice of resolving everything into a separate calculation of consequences, at the instant, was very favourable, was indeed necessary, to all
those acts of revolutionary violence and injustice to which we have just
alluded. There was no difficulty for one of these revolutionary leaders to
carry any point he chose, when an action was to be right, just as the
reasoner himself determined the nature of the case and of the consequences. Measures of injustice, systems of confiscation and plunder, proscriptions, insurrections, the murder of the king, the murder of each other,
the destruction of a large part of the population of a whole town, of
the inhabitants of a whole district or province, all these outrages on humanity were always announced to the public, and to the world, as acts
of patriotism in the actors, as necessary to the Revolution, as evils that
would be compensated by the future freedom and happiness of France,
as calamities that must be overlooked, for the present, on account of the
future consequences; and the perpetrators of these deeds often made it
a merit with themselves, and the country, that they had been able to
overpower the influence of their private feelings of sympathy and compassion, from a regard to the public weal; and the modern historians of
France speak a language of this abominable nature to this hour. . . .

This new morality, as it was called, a sort of contradiction in terms,
extended its influence not only over the minds of men, when acting on
the most important occasions, but descended through the whole scale of
their existence, and reached the most frivolous concerns of society and
manners. Man is a creature of association, as he is of reason; and all
his ordinary associations, and indeed his associations of whatever kind,
were, according to the new notions, to be stripped from his nature. He
was to be strictly a being of reason, and he was to find, amid the cold
realities of life, the amusements and pleasures of his existence, and derive from the mere logic of his understanding, all his maxims of con-

duct, of moral and religious belief, the undisturbed security of his most ordinary rights and interests, the consolations of his state, and his hopes and dignity, here and hereafter. . . .

In this general wreck of the older notions of mankind, and triumph of the new, ample room was made for the theories of Rousseau, for visions of equality and systems of society, where government, with its restraints and terrors, was to be superseded. Rousseau was always the great writer of the Revolution. He was canonized as their saint. And it is remarkable, that Robespierre and St. Just were dreaming over plans after his manner, for the new organization of society, where "every rood of ground was to maintain its man," and Barrère had drawn out an elaborate report, as their associate minister and fellow-labourer, a very short time previous to their fall, on the 9th Thermidor. Wherever the French armies went, liberty and equality were proclaimed, and "Vive la république" was the cry. The meaning of those terms was seen to be sweeping confiscations of property, the abolition of all existing authority, and the elevation of the populace. The practice of the doctrines was fearful enough, but even the doctrines themselves, as embellished by Rousseau, as produced by the French Revolutionists, and as exhibited in our own island, by Mr. Godwin, seemed evidently to subvert all the established notions of property and government, and to leave mankind no better chance than eternal contention, and the sacrifice of all men of intelligence, consideration, and peaceful habits, to the unbridled passions of the multitude.

When to these notions on the subject of property and government was added the new morality, and again, first the public abolition of all religion, of whatever nature, next the obliteration, though not of natural religion, of Christianity, the religion of Europe for nearly two thousand years, with all its evidences, observances, hopes, and fears, the whole must be considered, as presenting a mass of hardy and desperate innovation, not only sufficient to alarm and appal, as it did alarm and appal, all the more sober and intelligent portion of civilized Europe, but as also exhibiting to the philosophers, present and future, the most astonishing example that the world has ever witnessed of the length to which human opinions may be carried. Nothing seemed too wild to be adopted, too daring, too revolting to all ordinary nature and common sense; and adopted, as I must again observe, not by any visionary in his closet (lost amidst the mazes of his metaphysics, or the wanderings of his sensibility, the fantastic subtleties of his understanding, or the delusions of his imagination), not by any dreaming enthusiast of the kind, but by legislators and public assemblies, and by large masses of mankind in one of the most distinguished communities of Europe.

And it is these frightful extravagances, of which the human mind was seen to be capable, these scenes of affliction and despair, the wide-wasting cruelties, the unutterable horrors, by which these new opinions were accompanied, that must henceforth teach their own lesson: they must show the value of every writing, usage, and institution, that can have any tendency to keep men within the paths of sobriety and duty; keep them aware of the imperfections of their nature, submissive to the dispensations and conscious of the presence of their Almighty Judge. These are the lessons, and this the permanent benefit, which, it is to be trusted, mankind will hereafter receive from this most appalling portion of the history of Europe. In addition to this first obvious, most indispensable lesson, I must mention, as another (and though inferior) yet a very important lesson to be drawn from these times, that if the friends of freedom suffered themselves to be hurried along into excesses of opinion like these, it can be matter of no surprise, that their Revolution failed, and that everything connected with them and their cause, became a word of reproach and detestation to the rest of the world.

There was, however, no necessity for such excesses of opinion: there was neither truth, nor meaning, nor sense, in such extravagances; and the first duty which the real friends of freedom owe themselves and their own better cause, the great cause of humanity, at all times, is to withdraw themselves from the mistakes and faults of the earlier and more respectable patriots of the Constituent Assembly, and utterly to denounce and abjure the tenets and practices of those that followed.

I cannot now stay to weigh differences of merit and guilt in the different parties and leaders of the Revolution: I have already done so, to the best of my power, in the course of these lectures. What I wish to maintain, what I wish you to bear away from these lectures, is, that the friends of freedom are not to identify themselves with the French Revolutionists: that they are to consider those revolutionists as eminently deficient in the great, leading, and proper virtues of patriots and reformers; that neither the cause of freedom, nor any other cause, can succeed, without the exercise of the calmer, as well as the more ardent qualities of the human character; and that no example can be drawn from the failure of these inexperienced, presumptuous, giddy, unschooled, and often unprincipled, infuriated men; no example to paralyse or even discountenance the efforts of patriots, if better worthy and if properly worthy the name, cautiously, and patiently, and modestly, and with due observance of the feelings and interests of others co-operating to improve the constitution of their country, or advance the happiness of mankind.

These observations, it is not, I conceive, unreasonable to make; for the friends of freedom, at the present period, seem to me, too many of them, not to draw the proper lessons from this dreadful drama of the

French Revolution. They appear to me, to consider the privileged orders of France as *alone* in fault. No doubt they were in fault, but not exclusively so, and they adopt the general and somewhat splendid estimates and abstractions of the late French historians. They seem ready to admit, that all of these calamities were necessary; that in revolutions one event leads on to another; that preventive wisdom, that prudence and moderation can, on such occasions, find no place. And as liberty must be purchased, be the price what it may, they are quite prepared to compound with convulsions and calamities, and to press forward with their improvements, at any risk of consequences; consequences, which, though they may lament, they consider as quite out of the reach of their control.

I must again and again protest against all such conclusions; they cannot, I think, be drawn by those who consider with due patience and minuteness, the detail of these remarkable occurrences. After coming to the first great conclusion, that soon after the accession of Louis XVI, particularly after the American war, it was necessary that some change, some distinct improvement, should be made in the constitution of France: all the rest was a question of prudence and good feeling and steady principle in all the parties concerned, and the faults that were on every side committed can be now clearly seen and stated, and were neither at the time necessary nor were even to be expected in the ordinary course of things, as the astonishment of all Europe from time to time continually manifested.

Again. The friends of freedom, the more ardent friends, I mean, of the present day, appear, in another instance, not sufficiently to have meditated the lesson of the French Revolution. They are too much disposed, after the manner of the French Revolutionists, to strip men of the associations that belong to their nature; they talk far too much of their principle of utility. We admit the existence of this principle; we admit the value of the benevolent system of morals, always found among the systems of the ancient schools: it harmonizes with and practically illustrates all the higher moral instincts and intuitions given us by our Creator; properly understood, it is in no respect inconsistent with them. But that the principle of utility should be produced as a sort of modern discovery in the moral world is somewhat ridiculous, and as far as it has received any new interpretation, or application, or extension, it has been misunderstood and misdirected, turned to revolutionary purposes, and made inconsistent with itself.

One word more. The same more ardent friends of freedom are naturally caught by the example of America. Much that the French revolutionists attempted, is here realized:—no king, no privileged orders, no religious establishment, everything emanating from, and continually referred to, the sovereign will of the people. But for the friends of freedom in European governments to think of assimilating their country to America, is to commit the very mistake of the more violent of these French Revolutionists, and it is not to draw the instruction that ought to be derived from their example. The Americans were republicans from the first; the feudal notions and usages of European governments, their monarchies and privileged orders, never existed among them (the first but little, the last not at all). The two cases never can be made the same, even in these important points; but in another and most obvious point, they are not the same. America is a young country; it is with them eternal spring; the most immeasurable tracts of land, that may be made subservient to the purposes of man, remain still unoccupied. It would take centuries that roll away from the eye of a speculator into perfect mist and darkness, before the American can become an old government, and afford a parallel case to the governments of Europe.

But to this reasoning it will be replied, "Let, however, an approach be made." If by these words be meant a conversion of European governments into republics or into constitutions, that do not materially differ, then, I say, that the example of the French Revolution has been exhibited in vain, and that such friends of freedom speak not the words of truth and soberness, but those of a political enthusiasm, the dreadful effects of which have been distinctly witnessed in France, and would infallibly be again renewed; it is to suppose, that no form of government can consist with the happiness of a community, but that of a republic.

At the close of my lectures on America, I have observed, that the republican government of America, and the limited monarchy of England, for instance, are well fitted by contrast and comparison mutually to suggest hints of improvements, and to contribute to the permanent prosperity and security, each of the other. I think so still; but only on the supposition of the warning and example held out by the French Revolution being kept distinctly in view.

In a word, comparing European governments (that of our own island included) with that of America, neither can the quantity of happiness enjoyed under the one and the other be the same, nor the quality the same.

One word more at parting to those more ardent friends of freedom. I may be aware, as well as themselves, of the imperfections and abuses of old governments, and of our own, among the rest. I can see, as well as they, that even with us improvements are very slowly introduced, that the selfish interests of bodies of men and orders of men often impede, and even defeat the efforts of those who honourably labour for the public good; I can observe, as well as they, in many places the expense, in some the corruptions of our system; all such imperfections, and abuses, and evils, I can remark as well as they; but I must declare, after making these admissions, that while reading the history of the French Revolution, I have been struck repeatedly, I had almost said, I have had eternally forced upon my consideration the very singular merits and advantages of the English constitution. I consider this constitution as binding up into one harmonious and permanent whole, all the various contending interests and opinions that can possibly belong to a collected mass of human beings, with a success that is quite marvellous; and I am quite satisfied that the more the French Revolution is considered, the more will this important truth, from the effect of contrast, be felt and acknowledged. And not only is it that this our constitution leaves everything at liberty, and yet keeps everything in its place, to a degree that is, as I have said, quite marvellous, but it is impossible for those, who read the history of the French Revolution, not to be reminded, from the same effect of contrast, how fitted this English constitution is to produce regular habits of sober thought, of probity, of decency, of steady principle, of domestic virtue, of sincere piety, and rational devotion; not the brilliant merits of the French or Italian character, but such feelings and notions as an intelligent philanthropist would be glad to observe in a people, and a legislator would consider an admirable foundation on which to build, if he meant still further to refine that people and improve them. For my own part, I have lived long under this constitution: I have seen it tried to the utmost, by times of the most unparalleled nature: I have sometimes thought, that such was its principle of vitality, that nothing could destroy it; no madness from without, no probable folly from within. The longer I have lived, the more I have admired it; certainly admired it the more, the more I have read the history of the French Revolution. I mean not to deal in general panegyrics. I have stated, as I conceive, distinct grounds for the student's love and admiration; and this conclusion of my own mind (such as it is), and this decided result, while remembering the French Revolution, and while reading the history of the French Revolution, I now leave, as a parting legacy of my lectures, to all who have heard them.

Having addressed myself to those whom I consider as the more ardent friends of freedom, I must now turn to those who would rather, perhaps, entitle themselves the friends of that very constitution I so admire, those of high notions in church and state; men with whom peace and order is the one thing needful, and who also read the history of the French Revolution, as I conceive, amiss; who draw any conclusions but the proper conclusions, from the scenes that were there witnessed. Such men are made more than ever determined in their dislike of all movement in the political world, of all inquiry and discussion, of all schemes of improvement, of all popular feelings, meetings, and privileges; and the example of the French Revolution is quoted by them, not as a reason for improving everything in time, but for keeping everything at rest.

This is the effect which has been very generally produced over our own islands by the example of the French Revolution: the recoil from all popular principles of government has been very visible and very widely extended.

But I could wish to remind all such men, the lovers of peace and order, that popular principles of government, and popular privileges, are to them, paradoxical as may to them seem the assertion, the best and only security. Where governments are arbitrary, insurrections are the usual resource; and the more arbitrary the government, the greater the chance for such calamities. Not so where popular privileges exist: patriots may there be wise, and the cause of freedom temperate; there is no movement at all, or it is of a rational nature.

Take the instance of England. A sensation is felt in the community; a tax is thought oppressive: some reform is thought desirable; some intended measure of government is deprecated: what is the consequence? A mob, an insurrection, sounds of sedition, or a tumult? Nothing of the kind. A public meeting is announced, its purposes stated, a president chosen, the speakers heard, resolutions drawn up, in a few days all the proceedings known to the government and all the kingdom; and those who have been interested in the affair discussed, having proceeded to the length appointed by the constitution, and no further, the sentiment subsides or circulates, and at last becomes successful, sooner or later, or fails, as the reason of the case requires.

If there be any one conclusion that can be drawn more clearly than another, from the history of the French Revolution, it is, the value of popular privileges. If they had existed in France, it is impossible that the people of property, and the church, and the privileged orders, and the king, should have suffered such calamities and destruction as they did. The parliaments were aristocratic bodies, and come not within our present meaning. The people in France had no legal methods of expressing their sentiments, and none of redress.

Violence, tumult, the alarming of the persons in authority by manifestations of discontent, calculated to excite their personal fears; these were the means they but too naturally resorted to. They were exposed, from this very want of popular privileges, to be the mere instruments of furious and wrong-headed demagogues. Every great step in the French Revolution was the immediate effect of some popular insurrection. No habits of constitutional freedom existed in the country. . . . All through these lectures (and the lesson is made more than ever striking from the history of the French Revolution) I have never failed to make every effort in my power to impress upon the minds of those who are not only of arbitrary but of peaceful disposition, that popular privilege, timely concessions, mild government, that these are the safety as well as the prosperity of a state; that these are the conclusions to be drawn from the records of history, and more particularly from the French Revolution; the very reverse of what men of high prerogative notions themselves draw, and would wish everywhere to be drawn by others.

Let me not be accused of having spoken all through these lectures with alternate censure, sometimes addressed to the friends of freedom, sometimes to those who are rather the friends of prerogative. This cannot be avoided: such is the nature of man, the virtues and vices run into the confines of each other; advantages are placed on the right and on the left. Neither in morals nor in politics (to a commentator on history they are the same) can a reasoner proceed a step without his balance in his hand.

Distinctions must be made, and differences weighed out. The scale will often descend with very different velocity; but weight, of some kind or other, must always be expected in each scale, however trifling in the lighter scale it may sometimes appear to be. On all occasions, through all the details of history, when different parties are to be blamed, the student, who wishes to gain wisdom from the past, should consider to which class he himself belongs, and be ready to mark not so much the faults of those who are opposed to him, as of those who are of his own peculiar temperament; for in their failings and mistakes he may consider himself as warned of the temptation that doth so easily beset him; he may receive edification where others have nothing to learn, and on the contrary, hear of faults which he is in no danger of committing.

Supplementary Lectures

I. DUMONT *

ANOTHER WORK has also appeared, respecting which, fortunately, there is no doubt—the work of M. Dumont †: every thing is known of it that can be required. M. Dumont was a very distinguished man of letters, originally of Geneva, and who lived much in London; well acquainted with some of the first men of the time, and highly estimated by them for the variety of his knowledge, the extent of his views, and his many virtues and amiable qualities; and the work is an account given by such a man of what he could recollect ten years afterwards of Mirabeau, with whom he was connected, and of the Legislative Assemblies, particularly of the Constituent Assembly, at whose debates he was often found during the earlier parts of the French Revolution. There could be no want of interest in a book like this; and it so happened, that it arrived in London in the midst of our unhappy divisions on the subject of the Reform Bill, while the instance of the French Revolution was brought forward by writers and speakers on each side with great earnestness, and often with great effect, to illustrate their reasonings and justify their conclusions. The opinions and comments of a distinguished writer and philosopher like M. Dumont, at a period such as this, had even a more than natural importance, and particularly as he was known to be a warm friend of the liberties of mankind, and as his recollections were found to be not a little disparaging to the Constituent Assembly and the popular party. Even to me this publication was an event of considerable importance. I had been acquainted with M. Dumont, seen him often, and benefited by the variety of his literary knowledge, and his sensible observations (so they appeared to me) on every subject in its turn. Being at the same time well aware how conversant he was with every thing that related to the French Revolution, I was not a little anxious to ascertain how far his views and opinions, as seen in this new publication, went to confirm, or not, what I had delivered in these lectures. I therefore applied myself to the work, with all the diligence in my power; and some of the observations that have occurred to me, I will now proceed to lay before you. In the first place, then, I must remark that this work ought not to be represented as a description of the evolution of any conspiracy in the popular leaders against the old government; no such conspiracy is here ever thought of: nor, again, is his

* Of Smyth's six Supplementary Lectures (the preface to which is dated 1832), we give excerpts from I, II, IV, and V. We omit III, which continues II without adding very much to its contents, and VI, a "General Summary," which cannot properly be called a contribution to the philosophy of history.—ED.

† Pierre Etienne Louis Dumont, Swiss publicist (1759–1829). He wrote *Souvenir sur Mirabeau*.

work any précis of the French Revolution, how it arose, or what are to be
its effects hereafter in France; it is merely a description of such faults and
errors in the popular leaders and the people, as had a tendency to prevent
the success of the Revolution: least of all, is it a work where such faults and
errors are considered, as, in revolutions, a matter of course. It is all along
taken for granted that the crimes and miseries which so often accompany
them ought to be prevented, and can be prevented by the virtue and
prudence of those who engage in them; nor would a word in the work
be altered by Dumont, as far as the popular leaders are concerned, were
he now living, or had again to write it. The faults and errors he describes
in part caused, and were enough of themselves to cause, the failure of the
Revolution; this is sufficient for Dumont. He is not a writer that would
ever have entered into any dreadful calculation, how far present crimes
and miseries are to be compensated by subsequent prosperity; his humane
effort is to prevent from the first all crimes and miseries, and to teach
political men a little sobriety of thought and conduct. He therefore exhibits and records those faults and mistakes which he had an opportunity
to observe in the popular leaders; and to these he may be said to confine
himself. In these lectures which I here deliver, indeed, I endeavour to do
more, for I attempt to describe the faults and mistakes that were committed by the court and privileged orders, and which had so powerful a
tendency to prevent the success of the Revolution. To these M. Dumont
does not direct his attention; they were taken for granted by him: he was
known to be a warm friend to the popular cause; it never occurred to him
that he was to give his reasons for being so: he was writing no history,
nor even any account of the French Revolution; he was recollecting only,
at the distance of ten years, what he had seen and felt, while an eyewit-
ness of the scene. The work is a mere collection of sketches: what he
knew of Mirabeau, what he had observed and lamented in the conduct
of the Assembly and the people; no doubt such mistakes and faults as he
thought ought to be a warning to any people struggling for its liberties,
and to all leaders of revolutions hereafter; but certainly as constituting
only one part of the case, in no respect as the whole of the lesson that
was to be drawn from the French Revolution; and surely not such faults
and mistakes as might not, and ought not to have been avoided. . . .

I will now mention to you some few of those unfavourable representations and strictures of Dumont on the popular leaders, which confirm
such as I have hazarded myself in these lectures. There was nothing, it
seems, of this prudence which I have just alluded to, at the breaking out
of the Revolution. You will see Dumont intimately acquainted with the
leading people in Paris at the time, present at their committees, and quite
disgusted at their nonsense, and at the chaos of their opinions; the wild
hopes, the contending interests, the confusion, and the cabals; the delays

that were thus occasioned in the elections that were to be made by the sections: above all, he remarked what was the great point contended for by Mr. Burke, that the past went for nothing; and while he was himself, with a good sense that was very remarkable at that period, referring always to England for his ideas of liberty, such wisdom was a perfect scorn to the popular leaders at the time, with some brilliant exceptions, however,—Mounier, Lally Tollendal, and others. In the third chapter, and in the note, an amusing account is given of the folly of the celebrated Abbé de Sieyes in this particular. He considered the English, it seems, as mere infants in the science of government, and himself as a perfect master; an ignorance and a presumption that no doubt were shared with him by many others at the time. In the eighth chapter of the work, there is a very beautiful contrast of the English and French character. "Let me stop," says Dumont, "a hundred people in the streets of Paris and of London, and propose to each, on the part of government, something to be done; there will be ninety-nine in the one place that will instantly undertake it, and as many in the other that will decline it. Romilly," he continues, "had drawn up a work of the most interesting nature, on the rules observed by the House of Commons in England—rules," he says, "the fruit of a well considered experience, and the more to be admired, the more they are examined; customs carefully preserved by an assembly very watchful against any innovation: they are not written, and it required great care and pains to exhibit them in order. This little code was to show the best way of putting the questions, of preparing the motions, of debating them, of collecting the votes, of nominating the committees, of managing business, by making it pass through different stages—in a word, all the tactic of a political assembly. This work," says Dumont, "I translated at the commencement of the States-General; it was presented by Mirabeau, and laid upon the bureau of the Commons; and when the question was, whether it was to be a rule for the National Assembly, 'We are not English, and we have no want of the English,' such was the answer that was received; not the slightest attention was paid to this document, though it was printed; no one condescended to inform himself of the proceedings of a body so celebrated as the parliament of Great Britain; the national vanity was hurt at the very idea of borrowing from the wisdom of any other nation, and they chose rather to persist to the end in a mode of deliberation of the very worst and most dangerous nature; witness the sitting of the 4th of August." Again. "There was an intention of introducing Mirabeau into the ministry, but a motion was carried upon some idle principle of democracy, that no minister should be a member of the Assembly. It was in vain," says Dumont, "that the example of England was produced; instead of making in favour of the measure, it made against it. The slightest idea of imitation wounded the vanity of these innovators; they pretended to make a monarchy without a single monarchical element."

Such are the words of Dumont. Now, I must observe, that this is from beginning to end the great drift of the book of Mr. Burke; and to perceive the truth at Beaconsfield [Burke's country seat] so early and so distinctly, whatever may be said of the unfortunate intemperance of his prejudices, is a specimen of his political sagacity never to be forgotten. The vanity, the self-conceit of the members of the Assembly, more particularly of the popular leaders, ruined every thing. This is the constant language of Dumont; it was the constant torment and terror of his thoughts while in the midst of them. Now, is it too much to say that this vanity, this self-conceit, is but too naturally allied to men of popular feelings, while young, and to all such men, whether young or old, when starting up from unexpected situations in society, and obtaining notice, by exhibiting themselves on public occasions, in addresses, meetings, and associations? "Every member of the Assembly," says M. Dumont, "supposed himself capable of any thing. Never was seen such a number of men who conceived themselves to be all legislators; who supposed that they were then to repair all the faults of the past, to remedy every error that had been committed by the human mind, and to ensure the happiness of all future ages. Doubt had never for a moment any access to their minds, and infallibility presided over all their contradictory decrees. It was in vain," says he, "that a numerous minority told them their faults, and protested against their decrees; the more they were attacked, the more they were satisfied with themselves; and when the king made some remonstrances in the most modest manner against their decree of the 4th of August, and their declaration of rights, they were astonished that ministers should have the audacity to make comments on their labours, and Necker, who was the author of them, began to decline in their favour." Such are the words of Dumont. No doubt, I may observe, personal vanity is not the character of our own English nation, and we are each of us so quick in observing it, and so readily disgusted with it in others, that it is to be hoped that many ardent men among ourselves may be kept in check by the salutary phlegm and good sense that naturally belongs to an English community; but the strong sensations of Dumont, when brought into contact with Barrère, Barnave, Pétion, the Abbé Sieyes, Brissot, Paine, and almost every public man he met, should not be lost in the way of example and admonition, to all who, like them—and they were no common men —are engaged in the task of improving the institutions of their country. There is even in human nature sometimes to be found a delight in mischief, and there are those, who, though not ferocious in disposition, are disturbers of the public peace, from mere taste and perverseness. Look at the character of Clavière, a living portrait, and the type of a thousand others, as drawn by Dumont in the twentieth chapter. "Always attacking authority," says Dumont, "though afraid of danger; fond of troubled waters, though not of the consequences; maintaining," says he, "that in a free state political agitation, though not harmless, does a great deal more good, and throws people into a much more agreeable mood than they would experience amidst what he termed the insipidity of repose. He had even his fancy," continues Dumont, "for anarchy, and produced his sophisms in defence of it; his activity knew no bounds; he would get up in the middle of the night, write fifty pages, go to rest for an hour, and totally neglect his affairs; yet was he an honest man, and disinterested; office improved him, it seems." Such is the description given by Dumont. Real business and responsibility probably taught him some lessons; this sort of busy, troublesome, wrong-headed character, not to be reasoned with, and sometimes thought fit only to amuse, is in critical times a perfect nuisance and scourge to society. It is drawn from the life by Dumont; but the character is as old as the Proverbs. "There is one that scattereth arrows and death, and says, 'Am I not in sport?' "

It is a great pleasure to me to find that the views I have taken of the French Revolution, and the characters of the principal actors in the scene, are sufficiently confirmed by the work of Dumont. He corroborates what I have said of the Constituent Assembly, and of the events that passed during its sitting; what I have said of La Fayette, of Necker, and of the king; and again, what I have said on more doubtful and difficult subjects, the subsequent conduct and character of the Girondists and the Austrian war. Hereafter, as I read my lectures, I may notice briefly such of M. Dumont's observations as may be fitted to corroborate or modify my own. You will find him not a little scandalized by the proceedings of the Assembly on the night of the 4th of August. He did not, he says, concern himself in the discussion respecting the property of the church; he had, however, his opinion, that it was unjust to despoil the clergy, to pay the national debt. The reduction of the salaries of future ecclesiastics might be compatible with justice and prudence, but it appeared to him quite essential not to diminish by a single farthing the engagements of actual possessors. He had disputes, he says, even with some of the beneficed clergy themselves; and he appealed to the practice of England, where it was always a sacred principle never to make reforms at the expense of present possessors. But in France, he observes, "no one had any ideas of this kind: the old government had violated the principle with respect to the Jesuits; Necker, when making his economical reforms, never troubled himself about the individuals who were to suffer, it was favour enough to leave them the necessaries of life; the inflexible Camus, because he did not put the spoils of the pensioners of the state into his own pocket, was supposed a perfect Cato, and this, while he was multiplying decrees that made thousands of people wretched, and not one happier: but what reformers," continues Dumont, "are men like these, who have no receipt but to sacrifice one set of people to ameliorate the condition of another? At this period one would have supposed that the ecclesiastics were not a part of the nation. The Assembly itself did not carry their prejudices so far," says Dumont, "but we know sufficiently how far they did carry them, and how the people and the demagogues improved upon the example which had been set them by the legislature." Governments, when they commit an act of injustice and wrong, never set a precedent which stops there. Indeed, all through the proceedings of the Constituent Assembly, the general looseness of principle on the subject of property is very remarkable; and this must have been not a little owing to the composition of the Assembly.

Dumont mentions, as one of the causes of the faults of the Assembly, the too great proportion of people without property and of lawyers, who run into extremes in their democracy. These were probably young men, and such as had their fortunes to make. Those, who with us in England, are our country gentlemen, almost all belonged to the noblesse: the mercantile class was little in the habit of taking a share in public discussions. In the composition of the clergy, too, there was far too large a number of the curés; this was a mistake of Necker; most of these consisted of men with little or no property. The prejudice of the people in this country in favour of persons of property is quite right; the habits of thought that belong to such men are very favourable to sound legislation and just government, and well fitted to promote and secure many of the best interests of society. The interval that elapsed during the dispute between the *tiers état* and the two orders, was fatal in its effects, by throwing every thing into the power of the former, and this power was consummated by the assumption of the title of "National Assembly." "So to call themselves was to count for nothing," Dumont observes, "the king, the nobility, and the clergy." I have held the same language. It was carried by a majority of six to one. And the fourth chapter gives some curious particulars on the subject, and is worth your attention, but more especially would I recommend to you the remainder of the chapter; it concerns the state of Versailles and Paris at one of the most critical moments of the Revolution, prior and during the sitting of the 23rd. I have represented this sitting as the hinge on which the whole turned; as the ultimatum which the court offered to the people. I have always contended, that it ought to have been accepted by the popular leaders. The American, Jefferson, I afterwards found had said the same at the time, and when on the spot. The project of the measure of the 23rd, it seems, originated with Dumont's friend, Duroverai. On this most important measure ample information is given by Necker himself, of which I have availed myself. Considered in itself, never were such concessions made by a king to his people; and at any other time they would have excited the most hearty acknowledgments. Such objections as I have made to the conduct of the court (they were but too obvious), their total want of all precaution and management, are made also by Dumont, and from this moment he dates the ruin of the monarchy. "It is in the state of parties and their violence," says Dumont, before he comes to this point of the Revolution, "it is in these that one must seek for the origin of events. One must have been witness of the fermentation that existed to comprehend what afterwards followed. Historical facts, stripped of the circumstances that prepared them, are inexplicable. The atmosphere of Versailles, so to speak, was ominous and on fire, and the explosion that was coming could not but be terrible." Such are the expressions of Dumont. We have here, you see, nothing of the fatality of Thiers and Mignet, and other modern writers and historians. I have been given to understand that Dumont, with other intelligent writers and historians, all agreed in reprobating these doctrines of fatalism, when they first appeared in a regular form, as the explanation of history, in the work of Mignet. This very measure of the 23rd, if considered in all its critical importance and attendant circumstances, as it is detailed in Necker's own account, and in his histories, is of itself a remarkable instance to show, how improper it is to introduce this doctrine of the schools into the practical affairs of the world. And finally, I have to observe, that the reflections of Mr. Burke, while sitting in his study, were, as far as the Constitutent Assembly went, in the main, the same with those that were passing through the mind of Dumont, while a witness of the scene, and personally engaged in promoting the success of the Revolution to the utmost of his power. Their opinions on the whole of the case were not, indeed, the same; but in their views of the composition of the Assembly, of the faults of the Assembly, and many other important matters, they sufficiently coincide.

Such is the short notice that for the present I can take of such views and opinions as I have found in Dumont, of a nature to corroborate what I have ventured to observe in the course of these lectures, first in the way of censure of the popular leaders, and next with regard to the bearing of some particular measures. Of the latter I may take some further notice hereafter. The great defect of the work of Dumont is that he has too much omitted all reference to the faults of the court party, while he is describing the faults of the popular party, those with whom he lived, and the members of the Assembly; and this will give an undue advantage to writers and reasoners who too much resemble that court party, and by whom this otherwise most valuable work will be always quoted and appealed to. These faults of the court party were, however, very real, and must not be forgotten; they were first in order of time, an important cir-

cumstance. It is not unjust to say that in the court and privileged orders
there was a total want of sympathy with the interests of the community.
Of the benevolence that was always so visible in the king, not a spark
was ever to be seen in those around him; all his efforts before and during
the administration of Necker were thus rendered vain. Necker's own conduct and measures were injuriously affected by it. His great measure of
the 23rd, the last that could be tried, was ruined; so were Calonne's; so
those of the first patriots and revolutionary leaders. Again, those in like
manner of the Legislative Assembly and the Girondists (I defend
neither), were unfortunately influenced by the conduct of the court and
the emigrants. The Austrian war found here its justification in the minds
of the French public, the proximate cause of all the ruin and horrors that
ensued. It is impossible not to take into account the faults of the court
and privileged orders, more particularly at the beginning of the reign, and
the earlier parts of the struggle. It is true, that with these faults Dumont
did not concern himself: in justice to him, this must be observed, though
notices of them occur which sufficiently show his opinion. His book,
never intended to be a regular work, is a description of the faults of his
own party, and it is on that account a work quite invaluable, such as no
one had ever the candour, the probity, and the philanthropy to write before. If public men, if leaders of parties and public meetings, would consider a little more their own faults, and a little less those of their opponents, the affairs of the world would go on in a much more rational manner. There is a fallacy constantly resorted to by our public speakers and
political writers, which, little as I wish to refer to our politics, I think it
my duty to warn my hearers against, most distinctly. Our debaters of
every kind, the most respectable of them, are advocates after the manner
of feed counsel, rather than senators judging of and applying an historical
case: they seize upon that part which they think to their purpose, and
that which is not, and which ought equally to be produced, is totally set
aside and passed by; and if there happen to be no adequate knowledge of
the subject in the opponents of the speaker, a victory is obtained, quite
unfair and improper. On the contrary, Dumont, who was of the popular
party, not only gives a critique on the faults and mistakes of that popular
party, but gives an unsparing one. In the course of it may be found paragraphs which the greatest hater of popular leaders, and popular assemblies, and innovators, and reformers of every description, would have been
glad to have written, and would not have written more strongly, if, like
Dumont, they had been witnesses to the scene. These form the instruction of the work; but instruction will not be derived from it unless men
will be candid and reasonable. Never, it is true, never was such a lesson
to men of popular feelings; but men of opposite feelings are not to suppose that this is the whole of the case. Do they imagine, that if M. Du-

mont had been as intimate with the Count d'Artois and the court, as he was with Mirabeau and the patriots, that he could not have drawn up a lesson of equal force and truth, to be an eternal warning to them also, and all who are hereafter to resemble them? Would not the same good sense, and enlightened sympathy with the best interests of mankind, have animated his composition in the one case as in the other? Take a paragraph that presents itself in the seventh chapter, to show the rigid justice that he administers.

"The Assembly," he says, "had such a terror of offending the people, that it regarded almost as a snare, every motion that had a tendency to repress these disorders, and to censure popular excesses; it was by the people they had triumphed, and to the people, therefore, they had no power of showing themselves severe. On the contrary, though the Assembly declared often in their preambles that they were deeply afflicted, and even indignant at the outrages committed by the banditti and brigands, who burnt the chateaux, and insulted the nobility, in secret they rejoiced over a terror which they esteemed necessary. They were placed in an alternative, either to make the nobility fear, or themselves to fear the nobility: they blamed for the sake of decency; they kept fair with those they blamed, from policy: compliments were paid to authority, and encouragement given to license: respect for the executive power was but a formulary of style; and at bottom, when the ministers came to show their weakness, and betray their nonentity, the Assembly, too ready to remember the fear that they had once entertained of them, were not very sorry to think, that the fear had now changed sides. 'Were you powerful enough,' they said, 'to make yourselves respected by the people, you would be enough so, to be a terror to us.' Such was the sentiment that appeared entirely to influence the left side; it was the reaction of fear."

Now, what a paragraph is here to show the base servility to which popular leaders may be made to descend, the guilty and dangerous cowardice into which they may fall; what a lesson of instruction, when we consider more especially the events that followed, is for ever held up to them; with what delight and triumph will such a paragraph as this be hailed by those of opposite sentiments! But should it not occur to such men to ask themselves what there is, on the other hand, to be said of those, who will never make any effort to correct abuses in time, who will never suffer them to be made by others, until the people are thus brought forward to terrify them. They know perfectly well that popular leaders are likely to act on the ordinary, paltry principles of human nature, as Dumont here reports the Assembly to have done, and yet will they never make any timely concession, never any prudent sacrifice of their own interests or opinions, to prevent their opponents from thus throwing themselves into the arms of the populace.

Many like paragraphs may be found in this posthumous and unfinished work of M. Dumont, and the work will be a perfect treasure to be delivered to mankind, if it be but fairly treated; if it be but considered as a statement, not of the whole of the case, but of that part of it only which the author had a more immediate opportunity to observe; if it be considered that the faults here described from the life are connected with antagonist faults, that might equally have been produced by Dumont, if he had been in the confidence of the inmates of the Palace of Versailles: but if, on the contrary, it is made a manual and text book for men of arbitrary opinions, a magazine where such men are to find arguments to justify their unfortunate notions, and their aversion to all men who find any fault in the institutions of their country, and propose any changes for the benefit of the people; if such be the uses to which this remarkable publication is to be turned, the work will become any thing but a treasure to mankind. The singular merit of this friend of liberty, while making his confessions, and speaking from a situation of a most extraordinary nature, will be lost, and effects will be produced, that this good man, this enlightened man, this amiable, sensible, and honourable man, would be of all others, were he now alive, the first to lament, and the most anxious to deprecate.

We have another work (a work of our own) well fitted to benefit mankind, like this work of M. Dumont; but only on the same conditions, it must be fairly used,—the *Reflections* of Mr. Burke. Never was such a mirror of instruction held up to all men of popular feelings, of whatever country and age. The great maxims, the fundamental truths it contains, are not only invaluable, but are innumerable. I must beg to observe to you that I read it over and over, and as the events of the world come changing and crowding upon me, every year with more and more admiration, at the profound philosophy which it contains, at the extraordinary powers which could have produced it. But then it is an indictment, not an estimate, of the National Assembly; an exhibition of all the faults that they had committed, and that all men of popular feelings are for ever exposed to commit; it is an eternal lesson and warning to all such men, but it is not from this, to be concluded by men of opposite opinions, that they have not also their lessons and warnings to receive, though they must not suppose they are to find them in the *Reflections* of Mr. Burke. Observe the candour and propriety with which M. Dumont speaks of this very work, though he was living at this period with those in this country and in France, who resisted both the work and its author, as opposed to all the genuine principles of liberty, and the best interests of mankind at the time. "The first considerable check," says Dumont, "that was given to the general enthusiasm in the cause of the Revolution, came from the famous publication of Burke; where he attacked, himself entirely alone, the gigantic force of the Assembly, and represented these new legislators, in the midst of all their power and glory, as maniacs, who could only destroy every thing and produce nothing. This work [he continues], beaming with genius and eloquence, though composed at an age when the imagination is on the decline, created two parties in England. Events have but too much justified it, but it remains to be determined, whether the war-cry which it raised against France has not contributed to the violence which has characterized that period. It is possible that in calling the attention of governments and people of property to the dangers which were connected with this new political religion, Mr. Burke may have been the saviour of Europe; but he mixed up so much exaggeration in his work, and made use of arguments so alarming to the cause of liberty, that he was controverted in many points in a manner not only very plausible, but very forcible. Be that as it may, this publication of Burke, this manifesto against the Assembly, had a prodigious effect in England."

Such are the sentiments of Dumont. I cannot but recommend this great work to your meditation, not as a code of instruction to men of high principles of government, such men were not in his thoughts at the time, but as a code of instruction to all men of popular feelings, who mean well. No sooner had it appeared, but it was replied to by very able men, and even hooted and ridiculed, such was the violence of that period, by most of the opposite party; a great prejudice against it has in consequence descended to the friends of liberty, even to those who are now in existence. I must counsel you not to give way to any such prejudice, and if your minds are generous and warm, to resort to this great magazine of political wisdom, which may the better enable you, and can alone enable you, to serve your country by combining such wisdom as is here found, with the wisdom that is taught by benevolent feelings and superior talents: such feelings, and such talents, are the great materials that go to the composition of a patriot; but they will be both useless, or worse than useless, if advantage be not taken of such lessons of enlightened thought and matured experience, as are to be found in the *Reflections* of Mr. Burke.

The work of M. Dumont is addressed to two main subjects: what he observed of the National Assembly, and what he could recollect of Mirabeau. On this latter part of his work I have little to say, because every thing in it is so interesting, so beautiful, and so masterly, that it is impossible you should not read every word of it with the greatest attention; and it is also so very instructive, so obviously instructive, that you can need no hints from me to enable you to benefit by it. The general character of Mirabeau, and his proceedings in the French Revolution, were sufficiently known before the appearance of Dumont's publication; but the description of him that was given, of his personal appearance and influence, his talents, speeches and measures, was so very extraordinary, that it is well to have them so fully confirmed on such unquestionable authority. Never was such an instance of the fascination of great talents. Much too is added, though of the same nature, that is very curious and very valuable. Take as an instance a very remarkable conversation that took place between Dumont and Mirabeau, which may be very edifying to the student if he will consider it as a sort of scene, to show him the difference that always, in truth, exists between a man of genius and a man of sense, when engaging in political affairs, and how indispensably necessary the latter is to the former. Mirabeau brought to Dumont, in confidence, a grand project that he had formed for the preservation of the king, and the secure establishment of the liberties of the people; and "have you considered," said Dumont, "and do you expect," and "do you suppose," and "are you sure?" Such is the sort of dialogue, and this the kind of interview that passed between the two; and if the student will but meditate on the whole affair, and what was said on both sides, it is seldom that in books he will find any thing so fitted to show him the nature and value of circumspection, forethought, caution, what is on the whole called prudence; the quality, that, little attractive or imposing in itself, happens to be that quality without which every other is vain. The part that you will see Dumont take, is infinitely creditable to his sagacity and judgment, and indeed very creditable to him in every respect.

Lastly. The student will do well to observe also the effects that were produced by Mirabeau's licentiousness and want of reputation. It is difficult to escape from the fascination of genius and talents, but it is necessary. Neither in himself nor others must the student ever for a moment suppose, that any thing can compensate for the absence of the regular virtues of the human character. Dumont, with all his idolatry of Mirabeau, felt this at last, and is obliged to confess it, even in the instance of this wonderful master of the minds of others. To say nothing of the moral part of the case, success, if attained by such a man, which it seldom can be, is after all never perfect; and to others, to his sovereign or a party, he is an instrument or weapon, never valued, never to be trusted, liable at any moment to snap short, and wound the hand that employs it. How useless was Mirabeau to Mounier, and the more virtuous part of the Assembly! With the best intentions for the monarchy, with the most ardent love of liberty, how little did he do for either! How affecting, but how instructive is it, to see him melt into tears, even in the presence of Dumont, and be suffocated with grief, while he lamented that he was so cruelly to expiate the vices of his youth, and that he had lost the empire of France from the want of virtue! Mirabeau then, you perceive, is conscious, that if he had been a man of reputation, France would have been at his feet; yet is he a patriot. And what are to be his sensations, when he

has shortly after to die, die prematurely, exhausted by his vices? Does he
see in prospect that his country is to be regenerated, does he see any
happiness that yet awaits her? Is he consoled with the success of his own
efforts for the public good? Does he look forward to the efforts of others?
"My friend," says he, on parting with Dumont, and with an emotion
that he had never before shown, "my good friend, I am dying, and we
shall probably not see each other again; when I shall be no more, they
will then know how to value me. The calamities that I have stayed will
then pour down on France from every quarter; that guilty faction, that
trembled before me, will no longer feel restraint. I have before my eyes
no visions but those of ill. Oh! my friend, how right we were when we
endeavoured at the first to prevent the commons from declaring themselves the National Assembly. It is this that has been the source of all our
evils. From the moment they carried that victory, they have never ceased
to show themselves unworthy of it; they have chosen to govern the king,
instead of governing by the king: but it will soon be the case, that neither
they nor he are to govern, and a vile faction will take the lead, and cover
France with horrors."

Such may be considered as the dying words of Mirabeau. What a lesson this, on the grander scale of human life, how striking and how complete! I press not upon more awful considerations. "Who art thou that
judgest another man's servant?"

I may say, however, of licentious men like these, that though it be allowed them, which neither in reason nor religion it can be, to have their
kingdom only of this world, and though the balance be of their own
choosing, still when weighed in it, they are found wanting, their vices
ruin their influence, and their kingdom is divided from them.

II. PRELIMINARY LECTURE, 1833

THE FIRST course of my lectures on the French Revolution was given last
year; I am now proceeding to the second and last. But before I do so, I
know not how to avoid making a few preliminary observations.

I have been, as I conceive, a friend to civil and religious liberty from
the earliest period of my life; but this, on the established principles of
the English constitution. This constitution, the more I have read and
reflected, the more I have learnt to reverence and love. And I am grieved
and mortified, I confess, in the extreme, to observe the various crude and
wild theories, the unconstitutional doctrines, and what appear to me the
shallow sophistries that are everywhere floating around us; and it would
more than ever grieve and mortify me, if I could conceive that the youth

of this University were, any of them, likely to be influenced by reasonings and views, not worthy to be entertained by the people of England, much less by those who have had the benefit of a regular education.

These mistakes and delusions, for such I deem them, are the noxious exhalations that naturally arise from those states of fermentation into which society is occasionally thrown. I have seen one of these situations of the world already, it was at the opening of the first French Revolution; and I consider myself as on that account more fitted, than those who have had no such experience, to comprehend such situations; more fitted to understand the value of new opinions, when they are offered to us; more fitted to see the exact bearings of such sentiments of benevolence and patriotism as characterize the speeches and writings of those, who are anxious to make experiments on the condition of their fellow-creatures.

New opinions are always very attractive, particularly in any highly civilized state of society, and particularly to the young; that is, to the more effective portion of the public. In the useful and in the fine arts, wherever we turn, and even at last on graver subjects, in legislation and politics, the charm of novelty is deeply felt, and it is quite irresistible to those who, rising into life, full of ardour, and with the consciousness of talents, are always eager to press forward, and are often enabled, by their superior activity, to shoulder out of the world those they find in it, to give the tone to society, and to influence the fortunes of their country.

This passion for novelty is not without its use to a community in important respects; it gives scope, and offers rewards to the exertions of industry and genius, and is the source of much of the improvement we see in society, and of the advance of civilization: so far, it is a blessing to the world. But when the same rage for novelty enters into the vital subjects I have just alluded to, of legislation and politics, the working of the principle is then of a far different and very doubtful nature, and may not be the blessing of a community, but at particular seasons, the very torment and the curse. The rage for new opinions at the close of the last century, shook the civilized world to its centre, and destroyed France. Any similar passion for change, whenever it can be observed, will always be a subject of suspicion and dread to men of reflection and good sense; and while every applause is given, and every assistance afforded to those who would improve the condition of their countrymen by introducing political changes, it is only upon one condition, which is this: that such men seem careful and provident, and heave the lead often in seas that have now been shown to be of difficult navigation, and where shoals and quicksands abound. Against men like these, it is not to be understood that I am directing any observations which you may hear in the ensuing lecture. Patriots and reformers have always their difficulties, and may and must hazard something, and allowances must be made for them. What says the most sensible of poets?—

> *Truths would you teach, or save a sinking land,*
> *All fear, none aid you, and few understand.*

Still, there is a certain spirit in which men may work, a certain air and manner in which they may march, that cannot well be mistaken by people of any thought and experience. And as you who hear me, though you may have the one, have not exactly the other, I shall proceed to direct your attention to a few of the phenomena that have appeared, and that are every day appearing, and which I think justify me, or rather require me, to leave for a moment the ordinary track of history, and put you on your guard, that your talents and good qualities may not contribute to your deception, and be an injury, instead of a blessing, to your country.

The first description of persons against whom I could wish to guard you are those whom I shall take the liberty to call the dreamers; those who would banish poverty from the world, and ignorance, and therefore all our vices and our crimes at once, by organizing the world anew. A specimen or two of these deceivers (deceivers perhaps even of themselves) I will allude to. The first that occurs to me is the philosopher of Lanark (Mr. Owen),* one of the most active and indomitable of the kind. It is many years since I had the misery of a conversation with him; it lasted nearly two hours; and were I to meet him again to-morrow, the conversation would be just the same, if the courtesy, which at a first meeting I thought his due, could be still maintained. He had hit upon a general theorem, armed with which he defied all comers; and the theorem is no doubt his panoply and shield to this moment. It was this: "that every thing I said was perfectly true, constituted as the world at present was, but could not possibly take place in the state of society which he contemplated." What could be done? It was in vain that I controverted and confuted him, as I supposed, at every turn of the argument; he was still all tranquillity and smiles, and, retired behind his intrenchment, maintained the same happy countenance of triumph and repose; the stream of words with which he had begun still continued to flow on, mellifluous and undisturbed. And why should it not? for he was talking of the state of society which he contemplated, and of a world of his own creation; and I had no resource, but vanquished and despairing, as far at least as the noise of the battle was concerned, to leave him in possession of the field; though in the meantime I was perfectly satisfied that the state of

---

* Robert Owen (1771–1858), Welsh socialist and philanthropist. He was one of the pioneers of co-operation in industry, trying out his theories in his mills at New Lanark, near Manchester, and later (1825) founding a co-operative colony at New Harmony, Indiana.—ED.

society which he contemplated was never intended to take place by the Almighty Master, and would never be found to exist amongst the beings that in His good providence He had thought proper to create and destine for our particular planet. Is it amusing, or is it melancholy, to think, that this man with his parallelograms has been ever since (it must be now twenty years ago) tormenting the earth, year after year, and has still been able to retain his place among the wholesale dealers in the happiness of mankind? Mr. Owen is the wildest of our own dreamers (though we have many, and in every class of society), but another specimen of this sort of new-modelling the world has appeared in the neighbouring country of France, which I may also mention, with all its regular apparatus of lectures and lecturers, followers and audience, treatises published, a name given, and a sect established; I allude to the St. Simonians.* I have thought it my duty to spend a week in the perusal of the lectures of these St. Simonians of France. No fatigue could be greater; for I could not but remember that the world had been already assailed by effusions of this shadowy nature, from the eloquent pen of Rousseau; I could well remember that the world had already suffered from them. The writings of Rousseau contributed most materially to produce the unhappy folly and fatal madness of many of the French revolutionists; and what was now to be witnessed in this instance of the St. Simonians? In the same city and country, of Paris, and of France, beautiful sentences were again to be poured forth; that society, for instance, was to be so adjusted that every one was to have his place and his rewards according to the measure of his capacity; and all those smoothly flowing streams that had issued from the capacious urn of the philosopher of Geneva [Rousseau] were now again to be diffused over a country that they had already saturated with blood, and left, on their departure, heaped with carnage. But the truth is that mankind have a pleasure in listening to those who describe with eloquence and force the evils of our imperfect condition; it is a sort of philosophic tragedy, to which, as in a theatre, they delight to repair. It is easy for those who are the playwrights on these occasions to find a sufficient quantity of truth to mix up and render plausible these declamatory exhibitions. The evils of society are more readily seen than the inevitable necessity of them can be understood; and artists of this kind, who often want only a good receipt at the door, can never be without encouragement and an audience. I know not whether it may be the fortune of any of you to meet with any of these lectures of the St. Simonians; though fit for nothing else, they would be perfect models to you for your declamations, where eloquence and elegance of composition are all that are required. . . .

* Followers of Claude-Henri de Rouvroy, comte de Saint-Simon (1760–1825), French socialist.—Ed.

Human nature, it is said, is always the same; in its elementary principles no doubt it is; and thus it happens, that his system of the St. Simonians appeared in this country soon after the opening of the French Revolution, and when the times first became distempered from the pen of Mr. Godwin. Considering his work (and I find rightly considering it) as one of a class from which the world could never be clear, I dedicated a lecture to the explication of it. You will shortly hear it, as it is one of the second course on the French Revolution, which I am now going to deliver. The system was regularly overthrown by Mr. Malthus, and it was some time after, in the main, virtually withdrawn by Mr. Godwin himself; yet is it now, it seems, hashed up and accommodated to the Parisian palate; nor need we despair of seeing it presented to us in England by some of the many enterprising performers that figure on our animated scene. Of all these schemes and systems, the drift and promise is the same; to new-model human nature, and banish ignorance from the world and poverty. The benevolent are thus attracted, the sanguine and all the dreamers, sometimes the student, and generally the young. I shall hope, that now and hereafter, like men of sense and real philosophy, you will take care to observe the laws which the Almighty Creator has imposed upon his creatures; the moral state of probation in which we are placed; the process by which human prosperity is to be worked out; and the play, and action, and reaction of those affections, interests, and passions from which our vices and virtues arise, and which must for ever make a part of our nature; and contenting yourselves with any effort of sympathy and practical exertion in your power, in the cause of human improvement, under all its different and often very lowly appearances, you will expect no miracles in yourselves or others. At all events, never think of stepping into the assistance of the Almighty, and of new constituting his creatures, giving them new principles of action, that shall turn a metropolis forsooth into a temple of wisdom, and the earth into a paradise.

These airy visions, the products, when not sincere, of a perverted and unprincipled ingenuity, when sincere, of a querulous and morbid temperament, might be safely left to pass away like the bubbles of a disturbed stream, if it were not that they familiarize men to vague and unsubstantial reasonings, to sweeping and contemptuous estimates of society, and particularly of the institutions of their country—in a word, prepare them for revolutions; and if it were not also, that they descend into the minds of the lower orders and working classes, particularly in the manufacturing districts, and quite derange the common machinery of society, and even threaten the national prosperity.

But our speculative statesmen and political philosophers do not always confine themselves to such unearthly reveries as I have been describing;

they do not always hover in the clouds; they descend among us, and propose measures that are certainly of a very practicable nature, and that can certainly be carried into execution, if the people of this country should be sufficiently forgetful of the past and careless of the future. Our church, for instance, is to be dealt with, and our aristocracy; and that after no ceremonious or measured manner, but in a way totally alien to the spirit and meaning of our constitution; in a way perfectly revolutionary.

I do not choose, as I have already said, to mix myself in the politics of the day. I have never done so. I never mean it; but I shall certainly take this opportunity, on account of these modern notions and revolutionary schemes, to call you with more earnestness than ever to the study of history, and even take upon myself to request you will give your attention to the lectures I am now about to deliver. That you will observe the facts of this French Revolution, the principles, the characters, the events; that you will turn the history to some account, for the preservation of yourselves and of your country, and not be led astray, as were not only the thoughtless and the inexperienced, but the grave and the good, in that great kingdom close to our own shores, and at a period immediately touching upon our own. What then is the great lesson of the whole of that Revolution? To avoid revolutions. First, to reform in time; secondly, to build upon old foundations; never to lose sight of, never to quit your hold of the institutions of your country. But old foundations! institutions of the country! What then is to become of the march of the human mind, of the progress of science, of legislation, of civil and religious liberty, the happiness of the people, the rights of mankind; what is to become of these important interests, and what of human nature? Such is the language that you will now hear, such the sentiments of the more current publications of the day, such the questions you will yourselves be many of you disposed to ask. The answer is that such important interests will be all better served, and can only be served in the humble manner proposed,—by building upon old foundations, by never losing hold of existing institutions; that any other course is an experiment of probable confusion, anarchy, and blood; that such an experiment is not necessary, and after the experience of the French Revolution, unpardonable. But is all this denied? Is it doubted? If it be, look at this history of the French Revolution. Even listen for a moment to the rapid notices of it that are now in these lectures to be offered to you. Do you suppose that there were no men of talents originally and long engaged in these scenes; that there were no men of benevolence, of patriotism, of virtue and of honour; that courage was wanting, or that genius, or men of literary accomplishments, or men that did not suppose, at least, that they had meditated the past, and could provide for the future? Were there no aspirations, do you imagine, for the future happiness of mankind; no talk of their destinies, the march of the human mind, the rights of man, the cause of civil and religious liberty all over the world? Assuredly you will hear enough of these great interests and sacred sounds (for sacred they are and ever must be to our common nature), you will hear enough of these affecting appeals to the understanding and to the heart; and you will see an ample supply of orators, and statesmen qualified to enforce such appeals, and to work out, as might have been imagined, the happiness of their country. But suppose you that you will not see anything of an opposite descrip-tion,—the vices as well as the virtues of our nature; and orators and states-men fitted only to destroy the happiness of their country? Do you sup-pose that such men will not always be found starting up in critical times? Do you suppose that you will not see literary men puffed up with vanity, upstarts intoxicated with the new possession of power, and speculatists and projectors blown up into rashness and absurdity, by enthusiasm and self-conceit; good men led away and bewildered, and made the tools of the designing, amid the hopes and visions of their benevolence; daring and bad men hurrying on the more peaceful and reflecting into measures of violence and guilt, ready to sacrifice every thing to their ambition, or even to the success of a political theory; leaders of mobs and the orators of clubs elevated into statesmen, and ruling the destinies of their country, plunging on from one violence to another, and finding their only protec-tion in still accumulating crimes of tyranny and bloodshed? And suppose you, that such men and such atrocities can ever be avoided, if patriots and reformers presume to break up the opinions and cast away the institu-tions of their country? If any man can so suppose, if any notions of this nature are indeed indulged by those who, because they mean well, seem ready to hope from themselves and others whatever they please, and treat the passions and interests of their countrymen as cards, that they may shuffle and deal as they fancy the game; if there be any such men, let them consider well this French Revolution; the different events, as I have already said, that took place; the different characters that appeared; the appropriate faults of different descriptions of men; the total impossibility, that mistakes, and faults, and crimes, should be avoided, on all unhappy occasions, that once assumed the nature of revolutions; and surely it may be hoped, that some little check will be imposed upon the hardiness of the bold, some wisdom introduced into the apprehension of the perverse, some modesty into the minds of the conceited, something like sense, and sobriety, and reflection, and humanity, and justice, and patriotism, and philosophy, in the proper meaning of these words, into the feelings and understandings of all. I must really again assume a little more than, I hope, it is my nature to do, and I must declare to you, that even in the lectures I am now going to deliver, and those I have delivered on this French Revolution, imperfect as they may be, and a mere sketch and a series of hints and observations, rather than any proper account of these memorable scenes, still I must declare to you, that you will hear enough to edify you, and you will see pass in a sort of review before you, characters striking enough in every way of talents, of virtues, of faults, and of crimes, to afford you ample lessons of instruction, if you will make the best of such notices as can here alone be given you. In the former course of lectures you had the faults of the privileged orders exhibited to you; in these you are now to hear the faults of revolutionists. In the former lectures, the gradual progress and plausible nature of new opinions; in the present, the excesses to which they are but too naturally carried. In the former you had to witness the church offending, the more particularly the nobility, and as no remedy was thought of but their degradation, you will see in the present the consequences. You will see in the former one great National Assembly formed, and you will observe in the present what must ever be experienced from any such political mistake; that no tyrant is so unprincipled and cruel as is a single assembly. You will perceive an attempt made by La Fayette and the Constitutionalists to make a free monarchy, without clergy or nobility; to leave a king in a free monarchy to depend on the love and good opinion of his people. You will now have to note well the result of so idle an effort, the folly of making the executive power weak and inefficient, the unreasonableness of this eternal jealousy of all executive authority. Republican forms of government have been much admired; they have their merits; but you will see in the present course of lectures, an ample exhibition of the evils to which such forms are exposed, more particularly when the times become difficult, that is, when government is most wanted. Of such characters as naturally appear in seasons of a revolutionary nature, the benevolent, and the sanguine, and the young, you will now have placed before you several instances to show the ruin they must generally bring upon their country; and not only this, but the misery, the disappointment, and in many cases the destruction they will occasion to themselves.

From the first and during the earliest sittings of the Constituent Assembly, you will have to remark, how loose were the notions of its members on the subject of property. From general and abstract reasonings, such as human ingenuity can never be at a loss to produce in favour of any political measure that may be convenient, they proceeded at last to dispose of property (that of the church for instance) exactly as suited their views; and you will, I hope, observe in the lectures I am going to deliver, how their philosophy was improved upon, until all property and life itself became the tenure of an hour, at the mercy of demagogues, who had no respect for either. In the Constituent Assembly you will hear of no rights but those of the people, no sounds but those of their sovereignty; that their will was not only law but wisdom, and whatever a statesman could desire as a sanction for his votes and measures; their happiness was all that was to be accomplished, and of that they were the best and only judges. You will see the consequences of such absurd and perverted theories; you will see what are the consequences, when those who should counsel for a nation listen to no counsels but those which come from the people themselves, or rather from those who, on various accounts, take a prominent part in their concerns. You will from the first be called upon to observe, how fatal are the consequences, when those who are not the members of a Legislative Assembly express their opinion from the galleries on what is passing beneath. And finally, and above all, you will learn what follows from the existence of clubs and associations, regularly meeting, discussing, and determining upon whatever they may think affects the public weal, organizing the kingdom into similar assemblies, and constituting themselves in fact the nation, to whose wisdom, and certainly to whose physical strength all other wisdom and strength were to be submitted. All these things you will have presented to your observation, and they are the lessons, the recent lessons of history; and it is to me only a matter of astonishment, that there can be any man, professing to be either a philosopher or a statesman, on whom they have not the most decided effect, in moderating his expectations, in teaching him the treachery of popular feelings, the necessary contrariety of human opinions, the incurable fury of men in maintaining their particular notions; how easy is the descent to confusion, how valuable is every form and principle and institution, that can at all be fitted, and that has hitherto been able, to maintain peace and order in any collection of human beings —human beings, such as they are, and ever must be found, with all the passions and necessities of their nature raging about them, urging them to deeds of selfishness and violence, to disregard authority and law and the rights of property, and trample down the unoffending and the weak.

But to recur to the subjects I have already mentioned.

Our church, as I have said, is to be dealt with, and our aristocracy, and that after no ceremonious or measured manner, but in a way totally alien to the spirit and meaning of our constitution—in a way perfectly revolutionary.

Now it is not for me to step out of my province and to speak upon the subject of the church; but as a reader of history, and a lecturer on history, I will leave a few observations with you, which, I hope, when you are in the world, and listening to the sweeping and irreverent observations that you may hear in it, you will not entirely forget. I must then, in the first place, remark, that whenever the times become critical, the clergy are the first to be attacked; when revolutionary altars are dressed, they are the first victims; they are naturally the representatives of peace and order; their habits, their studies, indispose them to innovation and experiment; they are necessarily in the way of those who are desirous of change, still more of those who are ready to risk confusion; and being men whose profession it is, by their expostulations, example, and interference, to disseminate piety and check licentiousness, they are naturally disagreeable, troublesome, and hateful to those who are the leaders in civil commotions. Among such men, particularly among the most daring, and therefore the most effective of them, there are always found those who are at least little interested about the doctrines of religion, valuing at no high price either its influence or its ministers. The possessions, too, of the church are an insulated species of property, very tempting to revolutionists and those who want it for political purposes. Men of the ecclesiastical order are themselves, also, an insulated description of men, neither from their numbers nor their characters qualified to defend themselves. On all these accounts they are the first to be vituperated and insulted, assaulted and plundered by revolutionists who mean ill, and by revolutionists who know not what they mean. And as these things are the preludes to civil calamities, and the ordinary prognostics and harbingers of all sorts of atrocities, men of this sacred character are the first whose rights the thoughtful and the good will set themselves to defend, and whose political consequence they will endeavour to uphold; the first whom they will step forward to support on every principle, not only of justice, generosity, and humanity, but even on the principle of common security.

Such, I must remark, will be the first impulses that will be felt by wise and good men, with respect to the existing members of any ecclesiastical establishment. How far such an establishment may be benefited by any future regulations is another question. Still the benefit of the establishment will be the great point to be regarded.

For in the same quality of a reader of history I must in the second place observe that we are not to expect to find in an establishment men of theological learning, if the establishment be poor; that an establishment is the best expedient for the religious education of the community, for the sober administration of Christianity, the explanation of its doctrines, and the exhibition of its hopes and terrors; that while an establishment is secured, toleration may be freely granted to dissentients; and again, all the various descriptions of enthusiasts and fanatics, that are always more or less found in society, may be thus rendered comparatively harmless;—a most important consideration, for all history proclaims such men to be the great enemies of the peace, the safety, and the improvement of every community, where they obtain any material influence.

But, as I have already observed, not only is our church, but our aristocracy to be dealt with. It is always thus. It may be very true that those who now vilify and threaten either the one or the other are in no great number or estimation among us; still what we see here exhibited before us is all after the manner of the pictures of history. Immediately after the clergy the aristocracy are always attacked, their usefulness questioned, their privileges thought inconsistent with the rights of the people; their artificial rank deemed unworthy of the dignity of our common nature, mocked at, and despised; and finally, in their persons they are hunted down, exiled, or destroyed. So was it in France. The first cry was, "The bishops to the Lanterne"; next, "The aristocrats." So will it be ever, where the form of government is mixed, and the clergy and aristocracy are had in honour with their appropriate places of distinction among the forms of the constitution. Of late years, there has been an unceasing persecution, an unwearied effort to write down our aristocracy. Nothing can be more unreasonable. In our free monarchy, it is the cement of the whole system; it prevents the king from being the slave of the people, it prevents the people from openly or tacitly overpowering their king; it secures the one, it checks and liberalizes the other; it refines society from the throne down to the lowest cottage. What then is the true reason why it is so persecuted by men of letters and ultra reformers? The reason is that an aristocracy is in the way of men of literary talents and philosophic acquirements; it offers to mankind other objects of affection and respect; it prevents such men from rising to the eminence they think their due—from being, if they should choose, the rulers of the kingdom; it stands directly opposed to the establishment of a republic, naturally the great object to those who depend on their intellectual talents; and again, to those who are men of ambition.

And now, before I offer a word more on the subject of our aristocracy, I must beg not to be misunderstood. I must beg to remind you what my general doctrine has been all through these lectures. It has always been, that as it is with individuals, so in the case of large bodies of men, different orders have their appropriate temptations, and that a lecturer must at all times be not a little employed, in exhibiting, for the instruction of those who hear him, the particular mistakes and faults of each in their turn. Never was such a specimen of the truth of a remark of this kind, as was exhibited to the world by the French Revolution:—first, the faults of the court and privileged orders; next, the faults of patriots and popular leaders. And though in this instance the faults of each were carried to a totally unparalleled excess, I am quite aware, and it is my general position, that these different descriptions of men can never be entirely free, not only from a tendency to commit their appropriate faults, but from the actual commission of them. And in all these cases, it is the magnitude and the particular danger at the time of these characteristic faults that is to be considered, rather than the existence of them. I shall, in the remainder of this lecture, make a few remarks on the unconstitutional and even vulgar notions that I observe circulating around us on the subject of our aristocracy, but I do not mean to represent this order of men, or any order

of men, as out of the reach of very just and grave censure; and I must take
this opportunity of warning all of you, who are likely hereafter to be men
of consideration in the country, that you are not to give way to the
temptations that beset you, that you are not to commit the faults which naturally belong to you, that you are not to look down upon your fellow creatures as beings of a different description, that you of all others are to have
the spirit of the Christian benevolence warm at your hearts, that you are
never to be indifferent to the expenditure of the public money, that you
are not to think it a matter of course to provide for your relatives and
dependents by pensions and places, and, to use a common phrase, by quartering them on the public. These things are not creditable to our aristocracy, and are on every account most injurious to the state, sometimes
even dangerous. The constitution expects you to be, and you must not
fail to be, high-minded, and honourable, and independent, and according
to your measure, accomplished and intelligent. By the laws and institutions
of your country,—primogeniture—the peerage,—you are set upon a hill,
and you must endeavour to be objects worthy to be looked up to by the
community. Above all, and which is perhaps the hardest task of all,
you are not to be systematically averse to all proposals of alteration, that
may approach you under the name of improvement or reform. The constitution certainly supposes that you are not to be carried away by every
wind of doctrine, and that your step is to be distinguished from the
precipitate march of the vulgar; it places the highest description of you in
a distinct house, and gives you privileges precisely for that purpose, to
insure deliberation and a pause; but you are to remember, all of you, the
constitutional history of your country; which history may be almost summed
up in the single observation that it is the opening, and unloosing, and accommodating the feudal system to the growing interests and happiness of
the community. Those interests and that happiness, as I shall endeavour
to show, are now inextricably and vitally interwoven with the permanence
of our aristocracy, but with its respectability also; and I admit, that this
respectability must be kept high; that it is of a moral nature, and must
therefore, as in every other instance of human virtue, be exposed to the
criticism of those around.

IV. AMERICA

*The two following Lectures were given in 1836, after the
course on the second part of the French Revolution.*

NATURE SETS her goods on the right hand and on the left; a truth this,
obvious to every man in the common concerns of life, and equally certain
on the larger scale of his political existence. Is a man, as a private individual,
desirous to be rich? He must turn from the pleasures of peaceful study.
Does he wish, as a patriot and a statesman, for the order, the security,
and the refinement of a limited monarchy? He must forego the animated
bustle, the pride, the independence, and the sense of personal consequence,
to be found in a republic. On all occasions, no folly can be greater than
inconsistency in our expectations. It is a great source of discontent and
unhappiness to men in a private station; and in public situations it often
renders them the very torments of their own age and country. It would
be improper to conceal from you, that reflections of this kind have been
more than ever impressed upon my mind by the occurrences of later years.
I am quite amazed at the careless indifference with which some men seem
to regard the political blessings by which they are surrounded; the total
unconsciousness that they seem to bear about them, of the value of the
constitution of government under which they have been born and educated; they seem struck with mental blindness, when it is the benefit of
their own system of polity that they are to contemplate; they seem to think
nothing of the security of person and property, the protection of every
man, while endeavouring to better his condition; the freedom of thought;
the advantages of safe and cheerful study; the fair license that is allowed
to every man, to display his talents and his genius, of whatever nature
they may be, in art, in science, in literature, in society, in the senate, at
the bar, in whatever manner he may wish to be useful, or hope to be
distinguished; all these things seem to be considered as things of course,
as things which can be accomplished without difficulty, when men are
once associated together; as things that may be sported with and put to
the hazard of any experiment that may be proposed; as things that may
be left behind, without ceremony or regret, by those who are hastening
on to the introduction of some other system, as they suppose, of greater
political happiness. I confess, I cannot understand the reasonableness of
views of this nature, and I know not how I can discharge my duty better,
than by protesting against them; than by endeavouring to save your minds
at the same time, from exclusive systems in politics; from supposing, that

men cannot be in a state of happiness or respect, except under one particular form of government; above all, to impress upon your minds this
great truth, that opposite advantages and disadvantages belong to different systems; and that there is no folly greater than inconsistency in our
expectations. Time was, when our constitution was never mentioned but
in terms of panegyric—"Our glorious constitution in church and state."
Such was always the phrase adopted on every occasion, on the hustings,
in the senate, in the books of lawyers, and the treatises of philosophers.
In what manner has the constitution forfeited these honourable distinctions? We have witnessed the greatest convulsion that has ever happened in Europe since the fall of the Roman empire, yet our island still survives. Every state and potentate was insulted, trampled upon, or destroyed;
the only exception was England. Nay, to England it was owing that any
one state or empire now exists, under any form or appearance of its former
independence. Whatever else may be contested, these are facts that cannot be disputed; and whatever else may be said of the absurdity of our
institutions and our unenlightened notions, we have the appearance, at
least, of a great people. The products of our skill and capital are in every
portion of the habitable globe; the business of the world is transacted on
the exchange of London; commerce in our ports; science in our factories;
activity in our streets, and affluence in our squares; intelligence in our
societies, learning in our universities, and eloquence in our senates; affection at our hearths, and piety at our altars; no slight specimens these of the
value of our constitution. Would it be too much to say, turning away from
these more modest expostulations of a calm and reasoning philosophy,
would it be too much to say, that no such magnificent spectacle of the
civilization of mankind, was ever offered to observation, as is at this day
presented to any reflecting mind by this our favoured island? What solution can be found, then, for the restless agitation, and inextinguishable discontent, of too many amongst us? I shall not, I think, employ your time
ill, if at the conclusion of this course of lectures, I now endeavour to consider this subject thoroughly; if I now try to enable you, to the best of
my power, to judge of the reasonings of those whom you will have hereafter to meet in public and in private; men not without their importance
from their talents, or influence from their situation in society. The truth
is that the convulsion to which I have alluded, the Revolution in France,
a revolution that ought to be deeply studied by the inhabitants of these
kingdoms, produced a ferment in the minds of men which has not yet
subsided, and possibly never may. Every such ferment will always give
a currency to republican principles: the daring, the low, the ambitious,
men of commanding talents, men of desperate fortunes, those who relish
not the restraints of order, those who turn from the doctrines of religion,
and I mean not to deny, that to these must be often added respectable

men of speculative minds, with wide and extended views, and ardently interested in the happiness of their fellow creatures, all these are naturally put in motion when society is disturbed; are always ready to present their projects, and fill the air with their complaints, when an audience can be obtained. Like the winds in the cave of Æolus, no sooner is an interstice opened, than out they come, "Quà data porta, ruunt"; and it were often to be wished, that there was a master-spirit, like the fabled god, to control them, and save the world from the uproar they occasion, by restoring them to their appointed place of salutary restraint.

Republics have always existed among mankind; they are founded on one of the most essential principles of our nature, the primitive equality of all men; an equality seen in a thousand affecting instances; in our common feelings, appetites, and passions; in the same process of youth, manhood, and decay: in health and sickness common to all; and in the same great undistinguishing law of our being, that consigns to the same common earth the peasant and the king. "And how dieth the wise man?" says the preacher. "As the fool." While these are indisputable truths, and matters of the most obvious experience, the distinctions of society, though equally the result of our common nature, will always be rebelled against, will always be looked upon with an evil eye by those who are placed low in the scale of human existence. Republics are the expedients resorted to, not only for the redress of the inequalities of fortune, and the injustice of the oppressor, but for the fancied evils, and the real inevitable evils, by which a speculative mind is tormented; and a fierce and proud man, and a benevolent and good man, will thus often find an equal pleasure in contemplating a state of society, where all are to be mingled and mixed together, no superior admitted, and all left to participate, in the best manner they can, in the same common privileges and blessings of their common nature. It is thus that the writings of Greece and Rome, and the minstrels of liberty, have always found an echo in our bosoms, are the delight of our youth, and not ungrateful to our age. "Old as I am," says Mr. Burke, "I read with pleasure the fine raptures of Lucan and Corneille"; and this sort of elevation of sentiment, this indefinite aspiration after a freedom of will and carelessness of action, which is to give dignity to the character, has been entertained and transmitted through every generation of mankind, from the Roman patriot to the Gothic warrior; from the English baron to the religious puritan; from the republican of America to the revolutionist in France; and finally to those amongst us, the political enthusiasts, who would now destroy our institutions as the vestiges of feudal ignorance and oppression, and elevate us, as they suppose, in the scale of thinking beings, by turning our limited monarchy into a republic. I can hold no parley with vulgar men, who are indifferent to the refinements of society, or ferocious men who recoil not from the horrors of civil confusion;

those for whom the imagination has no pleasures, and those who feel not "the compunctious visitings of our nature." I speak to those who mean well though they counsel ill; who pursue a theory reckless of difficulties and the opinions of others; who are enamoured of their own abstract notions of right; who expect a virtue and a reasonableness in others never to be found; who can see no merit in a system where they at the same time see imperfections; who, as moral and political reasoners, are contemptuous, dogmatic, and unaccommodating; who would hazard every thing rather than not reduce the laws and government of their country to some prescribed model of their own formation; and suppose that there is nothing in the world to move the world, but logic and reasoning; to men often hard and repulsive, sometimes, however, benevolent and good, to these I would now address myself, and the points I would wish to carry with them are, as I have already intimated, that they should not be exclusive, not undervalue the blessings they enjoy, nor over-estimate the advantages of others; that they should cast an equal eye on the various conditions of society, the various systems of government which the world exhibits; should see that happiness, human happiness, may be realized under an infinite diversity of forms; and that nations, like individuals, may have often very different tastes and habits, and very different expedients for accomplishing their own particular welfare; and that while great principles of political happiness may be held up by the philosopher to the consideration of mankind, each country must be left to the modification, adoption, or even rejection of them, just as their particular opinion directs or situation requires. And entertaining views like these, and wishing them to be entertained by others, the great opponents I have to meet are reasoners of the republican school; every other form of government is, by such men, considered as a perfect insult on the rights of mankind; the most moderate of them can see little merit in any other. Those, indeed, amongst them who deserve the name of statesmen, would not, I imagine, advise an established government, like our own, to be immediately pulled down, for the sake of erecting another on the model of the American; but there is a general opinion, not only amongst them but amongst all republican reasoners, that no other but that of America exhibits the perfection of the social system; that no other can be founded on principles strictly rational and just; and that as the world rolls on, and necessarily improves, no other will at length be thought worthy to exist among mankind.

I cannot accede to these opinions; and I shall, therefore, in the remainder of this lecture, and in the whole of the next lecture, endeavour thoroughly to consider such opinions; and more especially, how far they are applicable, drawn as they are from the nature and success of the American republic, to the old-established governments of Europe, and more particularly to the constitution of government established in our own country.

The later revolutionists in France, in the years 1792, 1793, and subsequently, carried these republican notions into practice, but with them the experiment totally failed. Not so in America. In America the experiment has hitherto answered, and is, of course, appealed to by all those who would display, by contrast, the defects and faults of the older governments. This instance must be, therefore, considered. I may say, indeed, in the first place, and in general terms, that it would be somewhat strange, if the advantages of the American system were not accompanied by connected disadvantages; but we will endeavour to ascertain the fact. I will refer to what I consider as proper authorities, and make quotations. This method may be a little tedious, but it will be the most unobjectionable way of procuring evidence; and the subject is important.

There has been lately published a book by M. de Tocqueville.* He is a Frenchman, not of democratic birth, but, I think, of democratic notions, and he goes over to America to judge for himself of the government and its inhabitants. In his introduction, he observes, that everything since the fall of the Roman empire has tended to establish the equality of mankind. He proceeds in a general manner, through the detail, to establish his general statement, casting a rapid glance on the past history of Europe. "The facts," he says, "have been these: the feudal property was broken up; the lower orders, in the shape of churchmen, were assimilated to the men of rank and power; the great barons and the kings weakened each other by their contentions; the commercial men came forward; the men of genius, and again, luxury, war, fashion, passions the most frivolous, passions the most profound, all and everything tending to impoverish the rich and enrich the poor; everything to the progress of democracy." And he at last concludes, that the gradual development of the equality of conditions is the work of Providence; having all the proper signs about it, universality, durability, the failure of all human efforts to resist it, and everything conspiring to produce it. There is no alternative, therefore, he insists, for existing governments, but to submit and accommodate themselves to this, as they would to any other dispensation of the Creator. He is not satisfied, he could not well be, with the march of democracy in his own country, but America presents to him a specimen of that development of the principle of equality, at which France is sooner or later to arrive; and he, therefore, repairs to that country, not merely from curiosity, but to gather up hints for the improvement of the social condition of his own, which is evidently to be rested on, not necessarily the same, but certainly on similar principles of democracy. Such is the account M. de Tocqueville gives of himself and his political sentiments. There seems, therefore, no reason to object to any representations he may make, as coming from one too much inclined to the older school of politics; and considering him,

* Smyth refers to the epochal *De la démocratie en Amérique* (1835).—ED.

therefore, as a not unfavourable critic of republicanism, I shall hereafter
quote largely from him.

And here I have to observe, that already, even in the introduction of
M. de Tocqueville's work, I find much to object to. The equality of mankind has been the object, it seems, of Providence for ages; and therefore,
democracy is to be established in obedience to the Divine will: it is in vain
to resist it. This is the sort of reasoning always adopted by revolutionists
and republican writers; . . . from the demagogues of our own low press, to
the regular reasonings of particular statesmen, and men of property, among
ourselves. A revolution must roll on; one movement necessarily leads to
another; the spirit of the times cannot be resisted; stop, they say, the falls
of Niagara with your hand, the ocean with a bulrush; and in this manner
they go on, taking everything for granted, both with regard to the wisdom
and the prevalency of their doctrines; coming to a common vote on the
part of mankind, of whom they are, forsooth, the representatives, and
carrying along with them, too often, the light and superficial mass of gazers
and listeners by the very arrogance of their language and ignorant effrontery
of their pretensions. But the affairs of mankind, in the meantime, know
but little of this concatenated logic, and necessary consequences of irresistible principles. The gradual improvement of mankind, since the Dark
Ages, is not necessarily their progress to democracy, certainly not to equality; the poor must exist as well as the rich, the labouring poor. Communities
in the whole world, at least, cannot rest their government on the will of
the mere numerical majority; the natural rulers of mankind must be
found in the aristocracies of birth, knowledge, and affluence, which arise
and attend this progress of mankind, on which so much is supposed to
depend. One man can never be the same as another, nor by any possible
education be made so. These must be the future facts in old countries,
whatever may be the generalizing visions of speculating minds. The example of America is no precedent, from the particular nature of the case.
Great principles exist, such as are seized upon by abstract reasoners, but
they are disturbed, suspended, neutralized, or destroyed by a thousand
accidents: the appearance of a man of genius, of good qualities or of bad;
a sudden epidemic, religious or political, in large classes of mankind;
Mahomet may start up from the sands of Arabia; Buonaparte from Corsica.

With what a splendid declamation, for instance, as I have in a former
lecture observed, would a revolutionary reasoner of this description have
delighted himself and others, at the breaking out of the Reformation:
with what confidence would he have asserted, that in half a century not
a vestige of what he would have called the Roman Catholic superstition
would remain; what a magnificent vision would he have exhibited of the
progress of truth, the inevitable fall of confessors and priests, the triumph
of the freedom of the mind, and the opening glories of the knowledge and

happiness of mankind! But in the meantime confessors and priests still exist, and the Roman Catholic religion exists; and yet the freedom of the mind has been established, and the knowledge and happiness of mankind essentially advanced and placed in a state of permanent progress and improvement. That is, philosophers and statesmen will be justified in their reasonings if they will be moderate in their reasonings; not exclusive, not dogmatic; resting something and not too much on the salutary, moral efficacy of great general principles, but making large allowance for what must, to human eyes at least, appear accident and chance; not supposing that the conclusions of their own minds must necessarily be those of all the world besides, present and to come; and above all, not supposing that there is only one road to political happiness, and that, the one they have themselves selected.

Proceeding onward with the book of M. de Tocqueville, it is plain from every page of it, as it is from every page of every other book on the subject of America, that they who speculate on the democratic system, and think of applying it in any respect to their own country, must remember, that this is a principle perfectly intolerant, perfectly merciless to every other; no other is allowed to exist in modification of it, much less in opposition to it in the slightest particular. Democracy

> *sits on a despotic throne,*
> *And reigns a tyrant, if it reigns at all.*

When the American constitution was first formed, after the conclusion of the Revolutionary War with England, every effort was made by Washington and Hamilton to give strength to the general executive government, and to keep the different provincial governments under the control of the general government of the Union; that America might become a great and compact nation, not a loose assemblage of different republics, each providing for its separate welfare, regardless of any other: in every way, it was the aim of those distinguished and wise men to form republics, but not democracies. Washington had suffered many a painful moment; despondency had sometimes even reached his mind, or a melancholy approaching to it, while he observed the unreasonable fancies and the unprincipled selfishness of the popular will, when the presence of the arms of Great Britain was once removed, and the dangers of the contest passed away. Edifying particulars of this kind are to be found in Marshall's *Life of Washington,* and are sufficiently intimated in the *Federalist,* a collection of papers that were addressed by Hamilton and his friends to the American people, while the adoption of the Constitution was at issue. But Jefferson was their great opponent; and when the Constitution was at last accepted by a sufficient majority of the states, the nation soon became divided into two opposite parties, the Federalists and the Antifederalists; that is, the republicans and the democrats. And what has been the result? Democracy soon began to be popular, and, since the death of Washington, has more and more prevailed, till it has become totally triumphant; as must always be the case, when the question is to be referred to the mere majority of a community, told by the head. And thus I arrive at the great leading position which you will bear in mind, while you are considering the government of America, that it produces every good and every evil that can result from the total domination of the majority; the majority told by the head. This total domination of the majority, so constituted, is the solution of all the phenomena, good or bad, attractive or repulsive, that belong to the system. And I must again repeat, that no patriot must urge his country into republican notions and situations, unless he is prepared for the consequences; unless he is content to have everything hereafter ruled and adjusted by the majority, told by the head.

But of what avail is it, to talk of the good or the evil that may result from this system? No other system is thought lawful. Every other system of government, as I have already mentioned, is denounced as a usurpation and a tyranny; contrary to the rights of man; the produce only of feudal barbarism and injustice. It were to be wished, that these democratic reasoners, in our own country and the rest of the world, would consider for a moment how artificial is the principle which they set up, when they take it for granted that the minority are bound to give way to the majority. It is quite desirable that they should consider, that when this is the case, there is an end of the rights of man for all those who are unfortunately outnumbered. And again, let us look to practice, and reflect how little this celebrated principle is attended to, whenever it can, with any convenience, be resisted. In earlier times, large sections of a nation have moved away to the left, when the larger portion thought it better to move away to the right. How often, in ordinary life, do we see minorities entering into resolutions, appealing to the public, breaking off from majorities, and insisting, often with just reason, on the superior wisdom of their views! It is evident that if you resolve everything into the rights of man, it is the natural right of every man to do what he chooses: certainly not to submit to the physical strength of others, that is, not to the majority numerically counted. This last (however insisted upon by republican philosophers) is mere brutal force, the law of savages.

But society, it will be said, cannot exist, nor the business of life be carried on, except the rule be laid down, that the minority are to submit to the majority. This may be very true; but then we have now another principle produced, not the mere naked rights of man, but the principle of expediency. "It is desirable, it is expedient, that the majority should rule." Where then are the rights of man, where are all the original elementary principles of human nature? "It is expedient," it seems; why, we are thus returned to the unenlightened, miserable, and contracted views of our poor, barbarous ancestors, whose acts of parliament generally began, as indeed they do now, with the lowly words, and always with the principle, "whereas it is expedient," &c. &c., and "be it hereafter enacted," &c. &c. Alas for the rights of man and the vapouring dogmatism of the philosophers of democracy, "quid tanto dignum feret hic promissor hiatu!" so immutable are the constitutions of nature, properly understood; so vain is it for democratic or any other writers to rest government or society upon any other foundations but those which the Creator has appointed for them; so vain to rest everything on abstractions elicited from the metaphysical recesses of original right, neglecting what is practical, palpable, and intelligible.

But again. While this great principle of the domination of the mere numerical majority is contended for as a natural ordinance, can any possible principle be so contrary to nature as this, that the vote of one man should be considered just as good as that of another? Is this the ordinance of the Creator? Has he made the conditions of human life everywhere the same? Is the earth to be tilled, and the web to be woven, and the sea to be encountered, and the ore to be manufactured, by those who are at the same time to enlighten and to improve mankind; to teach the artist the lessons of science, and their fellow-creatures their duties to each other and to their God? But no, it will be answered, we mean only to have intelligent votes, given on all public occasions, and up to this point, at least, all men may be educated. Indeed! Are these public occasions, then, so easy to be understood? I speak of old countries, and old governments, situated in Europe. Enter into the streets of our metropolis, or our great manufacturing towns, its by-streets, and its obscure and crowded tenements, not its squares and palaces; survey the inhabitants you find there; observe their occupations and their wants; their necessary habits of thought; and consider what it is, that education can here be rationally expected to accomplish. Consider what public questions are; what the candidates for public favour are; the plausible arts of a designing man; the unattractive, the retiring, and often even the fastidious manners of a man of real intelligence and virtue.

But there is no difficulty in all these points, it will be answered, in America. Perhaps not, perhaps not at present. But was ever any country so situated, in the history of the world, as is America? Can it be in any respect an example to any of the old countries in Europe? We will refer to a few particulars. I will quote largely from others, that you may not depend on any opinion of mine; and as I proceed, you will continually compare what you hear, with what you know of your own political situation, and ask yourselves whether your limited monarchy is to be changed to an American democracy; whether it is desirable that such an object should be accomplished at all; and if accomplished, what would be the cost, and what the risk. And I must again and again observe, that it is in vain for statesmen to suppose that they can adopt a middle course; that they can take as much or as little of democracy as they choose. This cannot be. Mixed governments and monarchical governments cannot be founded on democratic principles. You may rest such governments on aristocratic foundations, and then liberalize the whole by adding and interweaving popular principles: but make the government essentially and fundamentally democratic, and the democratic spirit will, from its very nature, never rest till it has totally overpowered the other two, the monarchy and aristocracy. It behoves therefore every reformer in a mixed government to consider well what he is doing; to consider on what foundation he is resting everything; what is the moving power; what are the elements of the constitution he is proposing; how these elements are tempered, modified, checked, and harmonized; birth, rank, property, intelligence, physical strength, how all these things are disposed of.

"Many leading remarks," says M. de Tocqueville, "may be made on the social state of the Anglo-Americans; but there is one paramount to all the rest. The social state of the Americans is eminently democratic; it was so from the first: in our own times, it is more so than ever. When one speaks of the laws and civil polity of the Americans, one must always begin with the great doctrine of the sovereignty of the people. This is not a doctrine disguised as in other countries, and leading to no consequences; it is recognized in the manners, it is proclaimed in the laws, and if there be a country where the value of the doctrine may be appreciated, its application to the affairs of society studied, and its advantages and dangers judged of, that country is, most assuredly, America. The people participate in the composition of their laws, by choosing their law-makers; in the application of their laws, by electing their executive officers; and they may be said to govern themselves, so feeble and limited is the power left to the administration of the laws, so distinct the influence of its popular origin, so obedient is it to the power from which it sprang. The people in America reign in the political world as the Deity does in the universe; the people are the beginning and end of everything; from them everything proceeds, and by them is everything absorbed."

"The institutions of the country," says M. de Tocqueville, in his second volume, "are not only democratic in their principle, but in all their developments; the people nominate directly their representatives, and in general, annually, that they may retain them more completely in their dependence: it is the majority that governs in the name of the people, the majority consisting of peaceable and patriotic citizens. The parties range on each side, and endeavour to bring over to them the moderate, who stand in the middle. These parties were long the federalists and the republi-

cans: but America is the land of democracy. The federalists, though count-
ing in their ranks almost all the great men of the Revolution, were at last
obliged to give way; Jefferson and the democrats triumphed, and the society has from that time become democratic. A custom is gaining ground
in America, that will, in the end, render all the guarantees of the representative government vain. The electors, when they name a deputy, often
trace out for him a line of conduct from which he is not to depart, and
except that there is no tumult, it is as if the majority met and deliberated
in the market-place."

"Many circumstances," I continue to quote from M. de Tocqueville,
"have contributed to render the power of the majority not only predominant, but irresistible: it is not only a power great in fact, but the
public opinion is with it, and when it is once formed, this power of the
majority, no obstacle can be found, I do not say to stop, but there is none
even to retard its march; none even to leave it time to hear the complaints
of those whom it tramples down, and crushes as it passes over them. The
consequences of a state of things like this have an ill omen for the future."

M. de Tocqueville, to whose testimony there can be no possible objection, after these observations, proceeds in the next chapter to state the
instability of everything that results from the manner in which the people can indulge every change in their fancies, by a correspondent change
in their representative and executive officers. Schemes for the public good,
public institutions, laws, the constitution of the government, everything
is affected by this facility of change: and he at last observes, "How is all
this? I rest the origin," says he, "of all power on the will of the people,
and yet I regard as impious and detestable, the maxim that the majority
have a right to do what they think best—how is all this? do I not contradict
myself? No; for there is a general law, which has been adopted, not only by
the majority of the people, but by the majority of the human race; and
this law is the law of justice. It is justice, then, that forms the boundary
of the right of every people to do what they choose. A nation is like a jury
of the human race, and is to apply the law by which it is bound—the law
of justice. When I refuse then to obey an unjust law, I appeal from the sovereignty of the people to the sovereignty of the human race." The chapter
becomes animated, and he observes, "When then I see a right and a faculty
allowed to any power, be it what it may, to do whatever it chooses, be it
called people or king, democracy or aristocracy, whether exercised under
a monarchy or under a republic, then I say, there is the germ of tyranny,
and for my part, I will look for another system of laws under which to
live."

M. de Tocqueville seems, therefore, not to acquiesce in the great republican axiom, that every one is to submit to the majority. He leaves

them, he runs away—abiit, evasit, erupit. "It is not," says he, "that I object, like other European writers, to the weakness of the American government, I object to its force; not to the extreme of liberty that I find there, but that there is no protection against tyranny. Is any one treated with cruelty and injustice in America, to whom shall he appeal? To the public opinion? It is that, which forms the majority. To the legislative body? It represents the majority, and obeys it blindly. To the executive power? It is named by the majority, and is a passive instrument in its hands. To the public force? Public force is only the majority under arms. To a jury? It is but the majority clothed with the power of pronouncing its decrees. The judges themselves are in some states elected by the majority; however unjust or unreasonable your treatment, you have no course but to submit. I do not say that, at this present moment, tyranny is frequent in America, but this is owing to circumstances and manners, not to laws."

And finally, he observes, "Suppose now, on the contrary, that you have a legislature, composed in such a manner that it shall represent the majority, but not necessarily be the slave of its passions; an executive power, that shall have a force assigned to it; a judiciary power, independent of both. You will then have a government, democratic indeed, but you will no longer have such grounds to expect tyranny."

These are the objections that are urged by M. de Tocqueville against the American system; and in the last paragraph I have read, you see the remedy which he proposes, and the superior system that he wishes for. But has not M. de Tocqueville in these last few words described the constitution of England? "A legislature," he says, "composed in such a manner that it shall represent the majority, but not necessarily be the slave of its passions; an executive power, that shall have a force assigned to it; a judiciary power, independent of both. You will then have a government, democratic indeed, but you will no longer have such grounds to expect tyranny."

"Consider the nature of freedom of thought," he goes on to say; "it is then that you will perceive that the domination of the majority exceeds any domination that is known in Europe. The most absolute princes cannot, with us, prevent the circulation of thought, not even in the very bosom of their courts; and thought, hostile to their authority. But it is not so in America. While it is doubtful what the majority will decide, one may speak, but not a moment longer: the opinion of the majority once known, friends and enemies all follow in the train. No monarch, like a majority, can unite the forces of society, and vanquish every resistance; the one can act upon the conduct only, the other upon the will also. I know no country where there is, in general, less independence of mind, and less

real freedom of discussion, than in America. In America a sort of circle
is drawn round the thoughts; while within it, a writer is at liberty; but
woe to him who presumes to step beyond it! It is not that he is to expect
an auto-da-fé, but that he is to be exposed to all sorts of disgusting perse-
cutions from day to day; as a public man, every avenue is shut against him,
for he has offended the only power that could open a career to him: everything is closed, even the prospect of fame. Those who differ with him
blame him openly, those who think with him say nothing, and slink away
from him. He yields at last, and gives way, exhausted by continual effort,
and sinks into silence, as if filled with remorse that he had spoken the
truth. Chains and hangmen were formerly the gross instruments of tyranny,
but civilization has, in our days, contrived a despotism far more complete,
though tyranny seemed before to have had nothing further to learn."

M. de Tocqueville continues this strain for some time, insisting upon the
thraldom in which the human mind is held; that Molière and La Bruyère
could indulge in sallies against the court, even in the palace, and in the
presence of Louis XIV, but that the slightest criticism sets an American
in a flame; that a writer is obliged eternally to offer incense to his countrymen; and that the majority live in a continued state of adoration of themselves. He even attributes the want of distinguished writers to this source.
"There can be no genius without freedom of thought, and there is no
such freedom in America. There were great men," says he, "during the
Revolution, while thought was free, but they exist no more; minds are now
reduced all to the same model; the views of all are the same. The courtiers of America do not indeed say, 'Sire,' and 'Your Majesty'; they make
it not a question by which of the virtues their prince is most distinguished; they assure their prince (the people) that they are possessed of
all; they consign not their wives and daughters to be mistresses to their
'grand monarque,' but they sacrifice their opinions and prostitute themselves. The moralists and philosophers of America no longer present their
lessons under the veil of allegory. 'We know,' they say, 'that we speak
to a people too elevated above the weaknesses of humanity, not to be
always masters of themselves; we should not address a language of our
present admonitory nature, were we not addressing men, whose virtues
and enlightened minds render them alone, of all mankind, worthy to be
free.' Could the flatterers," says he, "of Louis XIV go beyond this? If
liberty is ever to be lost," says he, "in America, the cause will be the
domination of the majority; which will hurry minorities into despair, and
make them appeal to force. Anarchy will ensue, but an anarchy the result of despotism." And at last he quotes Jefferson, as the great apostle
of democracy. "The executive power," says Jefferson, "is in our government not the sole, nor even perhaps the principal object of my anxiety;

the tyranny of our legislature is now, and will for some years be, a danger far more formidable: that of the executive power will come in its turn, but at a far distant period."

The chapters from which I have now quoted in the work of Tocqueville describe the great evil of the American system, though I should think with some exaggeration, yet I apprehend with considerable truth, for even the exaggeration indicates a mind exasperated at the case he sees before him; and the same conclusions may be drawn from the observations of intelligent travellers, and from the confidential letters of men of genius now existing in the country; all of whom feel and lament this tyranny of the majority. To this tyranny of the majority M. de Tocqueville finds a barrier in the lawyers. "The lawyers," says he, "when there is no nobility, no men of letters, and when the people are distrustful of the rich, form the superior political class and the most intellectual portion of society; they can therefore get nothing by change: they are then made conservative, and this is a feeling added to the love of order, which is so natural to them: they are the American aristocracy, and they form the most powerful, and so to speak, the only counterpoise to the democracy." An aristocracy is therefore, it seems, wanted. With this body of men, the lawyers, he seems well pleased. He finds also great safety for America in the municipal institutions, where democracy may consume its dangerous activity, and where the people may serve a sort of apprenticeship to their republican duties. These municipal institutions he dwells upon at great length, and evidently considers this as one of the most important parts of his work; and so do others.

As far as the great object of his work is concerned, the situation of his own country, his conclusions have a fearful cast—that arbitrary power, the power of one, must be established, or democracy; he means not necessarily democracy after the exact manner of America, but democracy adapted to existing circumstances; and he does not appear in this last part of his work very distinct and intelligible. He speaks in very general terms, while he talks of applying the democratic principles he finds in America, to France and the rest of Europe. But it is obvious that while a philosopher speaks in these general terms, he may say what he pleases. Let him specify, and the objections that belong to his views will present themselves—latet dolus in generalibus. But his conclusions, whatever they may be, and his hopes and plans for his own country and the arbitrary governments of the continent, are drawn from premises which we may be thankful are not to be found in our own country of England, and while our constitution is maintained, never will be found. Nor need we fly to any such extremes as M. de Tocqueville proposes for France and the rest of Europe. But as far as we are concerned, such observations are scattered over the remainder of the work, as we might naturally expect would be made by M. de Tocqueville, and have, in fact, already been made by all intelligent travellers who have visited America. I shall proceed to refer to some of these observations: such as I think may give you a general notion of the working of the American system; such as I think may enable you to compare it with your own; and such as may even afford you some instruction with respect to the general principles of government—I shall make a long quotation.

M. de Tocqueville then observes, that "there is no aristocracy in America of any kind, neither political nor intellectual; the people are everywhere the same; merchants, farmers, all alike; there is no ignorance, and there is no knowledge; the rich indeed separate themselves from the rest, and constitute a sort of aristocracy, which is somewhat anxiously maintained. Providence, it is supposed, in America has given to every individual the means of taking care of himself; the texture of society is therefore loose: the father applies this maxim to the son, the master to the servant, the commune to its functionaries, the province to the commune, the states to the provinces, the union to the states, and it is thus extended, and becomes the sovereignty of the people, for they too are to take care of themselves. In religion, it is the same." All this is very conceivable from the original history of the country; everything in America is courage and enterprise.

"One may meet," says M. de Tocqueville, "those who have been successively lawyers, agriculturalists, merchants, ministers of the gospel, and physicians; there is no state maxim, no professional prejudice, no system, habit, or method by which the American is bound"; not even the ministers of the gospel, it seems. "The love of change and enterprise never leaves the mind of the American; he carries it with him into his laws, into his religious creeds, into his social habits, and the exertions of his industry; it follows him into his woods, and it is the inmate of his bosom, while surrounded by society; it makes him the swiftest navigator and the most skilful merchant. It is thus that party violence is diminished—the ambition of men is to be rich rather than great. Men of talents convert them to the purposes of getting money; and hence it is owing to the want of good candidates, as well as the want of discernment in the electors, that such vulgar people are seen in public situations."

This point, however, is far more thoroughly discussed in another part of his work, which, on account of its importance and general application, I shall here quote. "There are many," he observes, "who say that the people may not indeed know how to govern, but that they are very sincere in their wish for good government, and that their instinct never fails to point out to them those who are animated with the same desire, and who are the fittest for power. For myself," says he, "what I have remarked in America authorized no opinion of this kind. I was struck, from the first of my arrival, with surprise, to see how much merit was commonly to be found among the governed, and how little among the governors. It is a constantly recurring fact, that the most distinguished men are, in our days, seldom called to public situations, and one is obliged to confess, that this has been more and more the case, as the democracy has more and more exceeded its former limits. For this, many reasons may be assigned. It is impossible," says he, "do what we will, to elevate the intelligence of the people above a certain level. One may facilitate the acquirement of knowledge, and make it cheap; still, one cannot make men improve themselves and develop their intelligence, unless they devote their time to the purpose. The necessity, therefore, of more or less labour for their subsistence forms for the people the limit to their intellectual progress: this limit may be more or less distant in different countries; but that it should not exist at all, it would be necessary that the people should not have to engage in the common business of life; that is, that they should not be people. It is just as difficult to imagine a society where the people shall be all well informed, as to imagine a state where all the people shall be rich. They may be sincere in their wish for the public good, they may be more disinterested, but they always want the means of judging properly. What study does it require to know the exact character of a man! what mistakes are made by the wisest! and are the multitude to succeed? They have neither the time nor the means for any task of the kind; they have to judge at the moment, and to seize upon the most striking features; and it is thus that charlatans of every description know best how to succeed with them, and that their real friends for the most part fail: not to mention that it is not always that the democracy wants nothing but the capacity, it sometimes wants a proper disposition to choose people of merit. It is not to be dissembled that democratic institutions often generate, in a very high degree, the principle of envy in the human heart: these institutions excite and flatter the passions for equality without being always able to gratify it: this equality is continually escaping from the hands, at the moment of seizure, and the people get angry, while pursuing a good, too near not to be estimated, too far removed to be tasted: they are agitated, wearied, and put out of humour. In America, the people do not hate the superior classes, but they show no kindness for them; they like nothing that does not owe its elevation to their own favour. While the natural instincts of a democracy lead the people to keep men of merit at a distance from power, the same instincts equally dispose men of merit to withdraw themselves from attempting a career, in which it is so difficult to be independent, or to move without degradation. This is candidly," he adds, "expressed by the chancellor Kent. This celebrated American author, after praising highly that part of the constitution which gives the nomination of the judges to the executive power—'It is,' says he, 'to be expected, that men, the most proper to fill these situations, would have too much reserve in their manners, and severity in their principles, ever to unite the majority of suffrages in their favour, when the election depended upon universal suffrage.' It is clear to me," says M. de Tocqueville, "that those who look upon universal suffrage as the best means of making the best choice, are in a complete delusion: there are advantages belonging to universal suffrage, but this is not one. When you enter the House of Representatives," says M. de Tocqueville, "you are struck with the vulgar aspect of this great assembly; you look in vain for any celebrated men; they are all obscure people, village lawyers, commercial men, even men belonging to the lower classes: in a country where education is nearly universal, it is said that sometimes they cannot all write correctly. Two steps distant is the hall of the Senate, and you there can scarcely see a single person to whom some celebrity does not attach. You have eloquent lawyers, distinguished generals, skilful magistrates, or statesmen well known; everything that passes in this assembly would do honour to the first debating assemblies in Europe. Whence this strange contrast? It is," says he, "that one house is elected by direct suffrage, the other by the state legislatures." The reason given here by M. de Tocqueville is no doubt sufficient; and the fact and the reasonings are worthy of our remark. He even thinks that this last mode of election, this indirect or double election, must hereafter be more resorted to, or the American republics will run no small chance of being shipwrecked among the shoals of democracy; he thinks this the only way of bringing the exercise of political power to the level of all classes of people. And in a subsequent chapter, he considers universal suffrage as, in fact, investing the poor with the government of society.

Again. "In a democracy," says he, "the love of variety becomes a perfect passion. The frequency of elections causes a constant instability in the laws. 'The instability of our legislature,' says Hamilton, in the *Federalist*, 'is the greatest blemish in the genius and character of our government.' 'The facility with which our laws are changed,' says Madison, in the same work, 'appears to me one of the greatest evils to which our system of government is exposed.' 'The instability of our laws,' says even the democratic Jefferson, 'is really a very serious inconvenience; there should be an interval of a year between the presentation of a law and its enactment,' &c. &c."

In the foregoing remarks of M. de Tocqueville, an English reader will see the value of our own institution of the House of Lords, which not only secures a second ordeal, but one, generally speaking, of superior education and more refined habits, and one by its very nature and constitution set apart from the transitory passions and epidemic movements of the public. That it is hereditary, and not responsible, as it is called, constitutes the very essence of its value.

Newspapers, it seems, form the great reading of America; the press is, of course, entirely free: everything being left to the decision of the majority, it could not be otherwise. There is no difficulty in America, the Americans feeling no interest in their institutions, that is, in their secondary institutions: the government indeed must be republican: that is their first and indispensable principle; but nothing more is necessary, nothing beyond this. M. de Tocqueville, however, is well aware of the difficulty by which this subject, the liberty of the press, is surrounded; he is struck by its virulence in America; so, indeed, are other travellers; and while discussing the subject very thoroughly, he throws out an observation, which has a sound of melancholy truth, to an European and even to an English ear, "that liberty cannot exist without this freedom of the press, and order scarcely with it." In England we must take our chance, I believe, with such imperfect, because our only expedients, as a law of libel and a jury: it is difficult, it seems, in America to make any laws that shall operate as restraints. "All our crimes," said a gentleman to M. de Tocqueville, "arise from the drinking of spirituous liquors." "Why not, then, put a tax on ardent spirits?" "Our legislators have often thought of it," was the reply; "but the law might cause an insurrection; and certainly all who voted for it would never be again returned."

Democracies are not capable, M. de Tocqueville thinks, of long efforts, and manage foreign concerns ill; on each account they are unfitted for Europe. M. de Tocqueville should, however, observe, that the American ambassadors at least have been always men of ability and address. But he holds that the advantages and disadvantages of democratic and aristocratic governments are, that the first can easily repair its faults and has always good intentions, and that the latter has larger views and more legislative wisdom. "The American," observes M. de Tocqueville, "considers everything as his own work, and is thus rendered quite intolerable in defending everything in and about his country and her institutions, admitting no evil or defect whatever." All this seems to be quite agreeable to the experience of other travellers. For myself, I have found it, on this account, the most fatiguing thing in the world to talk with an American about his country; no information can be got; he will admit nothing. It is in vain that you may make remarks: your own understanding is not of the slightest use to you. One exception only have I met with, a very intelligent man, and tolerably candid. We talked for some time about America; and I at last observed, "The truth is that government has no difficulties in America, for there is nothing to govern." He smiled, made no reply, and the conversation ended.

Notices of the kind, which I have now selected from the work of M. de Tocqueville, do not show, and are not meant to show, that civil liberty is not a blessing to a people: there is no blessing to be compared to it;

but they may show, that men are not to be exclusive and intolerant in their notions of it; and that the democratic government in America, though it is the country to which an appeal is always made by democratic writers, is not necessarily such a perfect model, that every reasonable man in every other part of the world should set himself immediately to assimilate to it the laws and institutions of his own country. That America is a country where human happiness is diffused and realized to a very extraordinary degree, need not be at all denied; its prior history and the unparalleled advantage of having wide and untouched tracts of country accessible to every adventurer, form a sufficient solution of the phenomenon just mentioned, and for the possibility of men subsisting together with that freedom from restraint, which is so delicious to men of irregular minds and proud and lofty spirit; but it is not at all the less evident on this account, that America is no example for the governments of Europe; governments established in old countries, with no such outlet for their population, and whose inhabitants, not derived from the republican adventurers of Europe, and the puritans and pilgrim fathers of England, have long inherited habits and notions, civil and religious, of a cast totally different; such as could not be reduced to the democratic model, with any chance of permanence or success, and not without the greatest violence offered, even to those principles in the human mind, which it is incumbent upon the most democratic reasoners in common consistency to respect.

v. AMERICA

THE SUBJECT of America is very inexhaustible: no country can be more interesting, not only from the novelty of the case, but from the high tone of civil and religious liberty which is there maintained, and from the example for imitation that is supposed to be there exhibited, for every other portion of mankind. It is to this last particular, this example, that I chiefly direct my attention. The manners, the morals, the religious sects, with these I do not concern myself, they are naturally the topics adverted to by our own travellers. . . . But I do not refer to the accounts that they have given; I confine myself to the French traveller, and the American orator, because to their representations, as not arising from any feelings connected with this country, there can be no possible objection, and any conclusions that can be fairly deduced from them, must be considered as decisive.

I observed at the end of my last lecture, that it was no meaning of mine, to deaden the spirit of civil liberty; that my wish was only to direct it aright and make it reasonable; that I was not therefore unwilling that you should hear the panegyrics of the American system, displayed and enforced by the most splendid of the orators which it has produced. These panegyrics will be abundantly found in every part of these two volumes of Mr. Webster's *Speeches*; * and they will at all events animate the mind to a due sense of the value of civil liberty, and of the extraordinary state of personal independence and prosperity in which every individual in America does, or at least may exist. But the question to which I am all along inviting your attention is this:—How far the American system can be realized in an old European country, and how far, even in this new country of America, certain evils are not experienced, which would be of fearful import indeed, if any system was adopted which would introduce them into the communities of Europe.

Observe, for instance, many passages in the preface in the second volume, as given by the American editors of the work. "Our government," they say, "popular in its theory, popular in its conception and in the rightful action of the system, is still more popular in its actual operations. This being the case, flattery of the people is not merely the demagogue's accustomed theme, but the temptation to espouse popular prejudices, to inveigh against even just exercises of constituted power, to disparage institutions, and to court temporary opinions, is too strong to be resisted, except by firmly balanced minds, warmed with a true patriotism. It will accordingly be found that this is the path to advancement most frequently pursued: the people have been most flattered by those who have most systematically and boldly assailed all those constitutional safeguards, originally devised to protect the people from the abuses of executive power. So artfully contrived is this plan of popularity, that the real friend of the people, the friend of the constitution and the laws, in which the safeguard of their liberties exists, is apparently thrown upon unpopular ground, and compelled at times to resist their own hasty co-operation, in measures resulting in their own injury. The discharge of this duty, in which the very heroism of politics consists, is the touchstone of the statesman; and in nothing do Mr. Webster's public character and course of political conduct appear in so noble and commanding a light. On all occasions he has been the great champion of the constitution and laws, the supporter of the institutions of the country, and of its great fundamental interests; and from his first appearance in public life to the present day, his writings may be searched in vain for a single attempt to play the demagogue; and yet who could have played it, we were about to say, with a better right? Who could have played it with a better pretence? Why are not the catchwords of a false and party republicanism for ever on his lips? Why does he not throw himself into the circle of those who are stimulating and lead-

* The title of these volumes (Vol. I, 1830; Vol. II, 1835) was *Speeches and Forensic Arguments*.—Ed.

ing on the people to a mad crusade against the people's constitution and laws? Is he so blind as not to see that that way lies the road to honour, office, and power? Is he so wanting in discernment, that he wanders from his path through ignorance? Are there so few examples to guide his choice? Not so. Mr. Webster is a patriot: he would find no pleasure in influence and place, obtained by fomenting prejudices, by sowing alienation and hatred among the members of the community, by exciting the people to tear down the fabric of their own liberty, and by making the institutions odious in which it is organized, and so to say, enshrined. It is not merely that his understanding is too just and manly to adopt and repeat these odious sophistries; but his moral sense revolts from them, as mean and treacherous. The people, we apprehend," say the American editors, "do too little justice to such a course, and do not sufficiently consider how much they owe to such a man. Suppose the power which Mr. Webster has employed to sustain and build up, had been exerted to subvert and destroy, should we have stood where we now stand? And if the country still stands unshaken on its foundations, the people should understand that they owe it partly to the irresistible power of argument, the noonday light of illustration, which have been shed upon the great principles of the constitution, in the late fearful crisis. That we have yet a country, to be the subject of these desolating experiments, is in no small degree owing to the ability with which they have been exposed and counteracted."

We have here, you see, in the preface of these American editors, many of the objections that have been always urged against government founded on a popular basis, fully exemplified; and they must be taken into account, whenever we think of assimilating our own governments to the American model. How far these editors may be consistent in their reasoning, or justified in their panegyrics, by the facts of the case, is not the question: it is the nature of the reasoning, the influence, the practices of demagogues, that are here supposed, it is these that we are to remark, the evils that have always been considered as necessarily belonging to all republican governments.

And turning now to the work itself, many notices may be found in these two volumes of Mr. Webster, that would give information with respect to the American constitution, and instruction with respect to our own. They abound, indeed, in every page; and soberly considered, and in the equal, general, and tolerant spirit, which it is the business of these two lectures to recommend, none can be more edifying. The American orator has indeed no notion of any freedom but on his own republican or rather democratic model; but you, it is to be hoped, may have views less exclusive, and more adapted to the real and practical condition of the world; and reading in this latter spirit, it is only with pleasure that we can peruse his panegyrics on his countrymen and the constitution of America;

their past struggles, their heroism, and intelligence, and the unbounded prospect of their growing prosperity. On every account, and at every moment of our perusal of the work, we can have pleasure in observing the triumphant statements of the orator, with regard to the happiness of his countrymen. What alone I wish, in the meantime, to observe, is that it is a species of prosperity and happiness which cannot be realized, or reasonably attempted, in the old governments of Europe.

These volumes open with a discourse, delivered at Plymouth, in commemoration of the first settlement of New England; and it is of course, like the orations of Pericles to the Athenians, a defence and eulogium of the constitution of the country. "Let us rejoice," says the orator, "that we behold this day, auspicious (indeed, bringing happiness beyond the common allotment of Providence to men, full of present joy, and gilding with bright beams the prospect of futurity), is the dawn that awakens us to the commemoration of the landing of the pilgrims. For ever honoured be this, the place of our fathers' refuge! for ever be remembered the day, which saw them, weary and distressed, broken in everything but spirit, poor in all but faith and courage, at last secure from the dangers of wintry seas, and impressing this shore with the first footsteps of civilized man!" The panegyric, which the subsequent pages contain, is a noble specimen of laudatory eloquence; but at present I concern myself with such paragraphs as directly or indirectly may be edifying to ourselves.

"Of our system of government [the American]," observes the orator, "the first thing to be said is that it is really and practically a free system: it originates entirely with the people, and rests on no other foundation than their assent." This is, as you may remember, the leading observation of M. de Tocqueville; a government that rests on the will of the majority, the majority told by the head: this is, you are aware, the great republican boast: intimating that no other system is a free one, no other legal in its origin, no other worthy of the intelligence of enlightened men. This doctrine pervades the whole of these volumes; and, indeed, the volumes and speeches of every American, and of every republican writer or statesman. To this democratic axiom I have already objected. I consider it entirely unfounded in the nature of things. I consider our own notions, of the existence of a legal aristocracy, of its influence under all its appearances of birth, rank, property, and intelligence, as far more agreeable to the nature of things, as far more fitted to build up the fabrics of human happiness among communities of human beings. And, in confirmation of what I am now saying, and leaving you to apply what I shall now quote from Mr. Webster, to our European systems, observe what a sensible man like this cannot but say, in the midst of his democratic maxims, on the very important subject of property.

"There is a natural influence," says he, "belonging to property, whether it exists in many hands or few; and it is on the rights of property, that both despotism and unrestrained popular violence ordinarily commence their attacks. A republican form of government rests not more on political constitutions, than on those laws which regulate the descent and transmission of property. Governments like ours," says he, "could not have been maintained, where property was holden according to the principles of the feudal system; nor, on the other hand, could the feudal constitution possibly exist with us. The situation of our New England ancestors demanded a parcelling out and division of the lands; and this necessary act fixed the future frame and form of their government. Universal suffrage," he afterwards observes, "could not long exist in a community where there was great inequality of property: the holders of estates would be obliged, in such cases, either in some way to restrain the right of suffrage, or else such right of suffrage would long before divide the property: in the nature of things, those who have not property and see their neighbours possess much more than they think them to need, cannot be favourable to laws made for the protection of property: when this class becomes numerous, it grows clamorous; it looks on property as its prey and plunder; and it is naturally ready at all times for violence and revolution." "Life," says he, in another passage, "and personal liberty, are no doubt to be protected by law; but property is also to be protected by law, and is the fund out of which the means for protecting life and liberty are usually furnished. We have no experience that teaches us that any other rights are safe, when property is not safe: confiscation and plunder are generally, in revolutionary commotions, not far before punishment, in imprisonment, and death."

At the end of the first volume there is a curious passage in this strain, which has a reference to ourselves. "If the property," says he, "cannot retain the political power, the political power will draw after it the property. If Orator Hunt * and his fellow-labourers should by any means obtain more political influence in the counties, towns, and boroughs of England, than the Marquis of Buckingham, Lord Stafford, Earl Fitzwilliam, and the other noblemen and gentlemen of great landed estates, these estates would inevitably change hands; at least, so it seems to us. And therefore, when Sir Francis Burdett, the Marquis of Tavistock, and other individuals of rank and fortune, propose to introduce into the government annual parliaments and universal suffrage, we can hardly forbear inquiring whether they are ready to agree that property should be as equally divided as political power; and if not, how they expect to sever things which to us appear so intimately connected." So much for the subject of property.

* Henry Hunt (1773–1835), English radical; he was the guiding spirit in the events that culminated in the disgraceful "Peterloo massacre."—ED.

And now, with respect to another, not entirely uninteresting to us,—
The existence of two houses of legislature; and whether they are to be
of the same nature, or not; and what may be the office of the superior,
as it may be called. A question arose in the state to which Mr. Webster
belonged, whether senators (the members of the second house in America) were to be chosen according to the population, or according to the
taxable property. This gave occasion to the following, among many
other important remarks:—"Legislative bodies," says he, "naturally feel
strong, because they are numerous, and because they consider themselves
as the immediate representatives of the people; they depend on public
opinion to sustain their measures, and they undoubtedly possess great
means of influencing public opinion. With all the guards which can be
raised by constitutional provisions, we are not likely to be too well secured
against cases of improper or hasty and intemperate legislation. If we look
through the several constitutions of the states, we shall perceive that generally the departments are most distinct and independent when the legislation is composed of two houses, with equal authority, and mutual checks.
If all legislative power be in one popular body, all other power, sooner or
later, will be there also. The Senate is not to be a check on the people, but
on the House of Representatives. It is the case of an authority, given to *one*
agent, to check or control the acts of *another*. The people having conferred on the House of Representatives powers, which are great, and
from their nature liable to abuse, require for their own security another
house, which shall possess an effectual negation on the first. If it be wise
to give one agent the power of checking or controlling another, it is
equally wise that there should be some difference of character, sentiment,
feeling, or origin in that agent, who is to possess that control; otherwise,
it is not at all probable that this control will ever be exercised. And the
great question," says he, "in this country has been, where to find or
how to create this difference, in governments entirely elective and popular." Mr. Webster then enumerates the various expedients that have been
resorted to, in the different states of America. The difficulty is evidently
very great, or rather, on the American system of representation, quite
insuperable; for, on their constant system of representation, how can this
sort of independent second house, that is wanted, be created? The whole
passage, and this whole speech, illustrates the indispensable value of our
own House of Lords, which is just the sort of second assembly that he in
vain requires.

Another subject, too, occurs to ourselves of the greatest importance,
whether the representative is to be merely a delegate or not. Mr. Webster
opened his speech on the Tariff Bill with observing, "that the subject was
surrounded with embarrassments." He enumerates some, and then adverts to a particular one, and it is this: "Different members," says he, "of

the Senate have instructions, which they feel bound to obey, and which clash with one another. We have this morning seen an honourable member from New York (an important motion being under consideration) lay his instructions on the table, and point to them, as his power of attorney, and as containing his directions for his vote." The fact thus stated by Mr. Webster, leads to no remark on the absurdity (an inevitable one on the American system of delegation), the absurdity of having a question decided by the constituents at one end of a country, and afterwards debated at the other. Of what use were Mr. Webster's reasonings and eloquence addressed to those who in the first place had to lay their instructions on the table? The attempt by our own democratic electors to turn our representation into a system of delegation has been always very properly and constitutionally resisted, by men of any sense or spirit. It is extremely to be lamented that very dishonest sacrifices are so often made to preserve a seat: and again, it is to be remarked that the lower the suffrage, the more frequently will such sacrifices be both required and made. A member suffering himself to be influenced by such considerations, as the security of his seat, whatever he may suppose, violates his duty both to his country and to his constituents. There is a beautiful and decisive train of reasoning on this subject, in one of Burke's speeches at Bristol.

Again. The subject of parties and party spirit occurs; another subject of great importance to us. In the eulogium of Washington, Mr. Webster refers to the president's farewell exhortations against the excesses of party spirit. " 'A fire,' said Washington, 'not to be quenched'; he yet conjures us [says Mr. Webster] not to fan and feed the flame." There is some difficulty, no doubt, in the question, but it has been discussed with his usual ability by the same philosophic statesman, Mr. Burke, in his "Thoughts on the present Discontents," and I think very properly adjusted. Parties cannot possibly be avoided in a free state; and they must be adopted, under the limitations and in the spirit which Mr. Burke describes. Men of talents and virtue must engage in parties and form a portion of them; but then, they ought to make it their province to influence them, to direct, rather than be dragged along with them. But the observation of Mr. Webster is very striking and valuable: "Party spirit," he remarks, "acting on the government, is dangerous enough; but acting in the government, it is a thousand times more dangerous: the government, then, becomes nothing more than organized party; and, in the strange vicissitudes of human affairs, it may come at last to exhibit the singular paradox of government itself being in opposition to its own powers; at war with the very elements of its own existence. Such cases are hopeless. As men may be protected against murders, but cannot be guarded against suicide; so government may be shielded from the assaults of external foes, but nothing can save it, when it chooses to lay violent hands on itself." Certainly, as Mr. Webster observes in another passage, the preservation of the government, that is of the Constitution, is mainly committed to those who administer it.

Again. Those political reasoners are grievously mistaken, who suppose that the American Constitution has not, like every other free constitution, its difficulties and dangers. The second volume contains a very remarkable speech from Mr. Webster on the 12th of October, 1832, a period when America was agitated by the tariff question. In this speech he goes through a regular critique on every proceeding of the government, making his objections, and on the whole, leaving an impression on the mind of an European reader, that in governments, as in poetry, and whether on this side the Atlantic or the other,

> *Whoe'er expects a faultless piece to see,*
> *Thinks what ne'er is, nor was, nor e'er will be.*

"The resolutions," he begins, "which have been read from the chair express the opinion, that the public good requires an effectual change in the administration of the general government, both of measures and of men. In this opinion I heartily concur." And afterwards, he goes on to say, "I declare that, in my opinion, not only the great interests of the country, but the Constitution itself is in imminent peril; and that nothing can save either the one or the other but that voice which has authority to say, to the evils of misrule and misgovernment, Hitherto shall ye come, but no further. The Constitution itself is but the creation of the public will, and in every crisis which threatens it, it must owe its security to the same power to which it owes its origin.

"The power of the veto," said Mr. Webster, "is exercised not as an extraordinary, but as an ordinary power; as a common mode of defeating acts of Congress, not acceptable to the executive. We hear one day, that the president needs the advice of no cabinet, that a few secretaries or clerks are sufficient for him; the next, we are informed that the Supreme Court is but an obstacle to the popular will; and the whole judicial department, but an encumbrance on government: and while, on one side, the judicial power is thus divided and denounced, on the other side arises the cry, 'Cut down the Senate'; and over the whole at the same time prevails the loud avowal, shouted with all the lungs of party strength and party triumph, that the spoils of the enemy belong to the victors. This condition of things, this general and obvious aspect of affairs, is the result of three years' administration, such as the country has experienced." The speech then proceeds through thirty pages to remark upon the principles and policy of this administration; how hostile they have been to the great interests of the country; how dangerous to the constitution and union of the states.

I have no doubt that there is a great deal of party politics in the animad-
versions of Mr. Webster; and on that account the speech might, at first
sight, seem not deserving of our notice; but on another account it appeared to me when I first read it, what it now appears to me, on a second
perusal, as in every respect worthy of attention; not indeed on account of
the question at issue, the merits of the administration, but because it
shows the loose texture of this great republican government, and ought
to operate as a warning to all those who can approve of no other; who
would introduce no other; and think no other, but one founded on similar democratic principles, an improvement of their own.

The observations of the French traveller, M. de Tocqueville, on the
very democratic nature of the American constitution and the tyranny
of the majority, are sufficiently countenanced by passages in speeches of
Mr. Webster: "Sir," says he, "those who espouse the doctrine of nullifi-
cation reject, as it seems to me, the first great principle of all republican
liberty; that is, that the majority must govern. This is a law imposed upon
us by the absolute necessity of the case. We hear loud and repeated de-
nunciations against what is called majority government. Do gentlemen
wish to establish a *minority* government? Look to South Carolina at the
present moment: how far are the rights of minorities there respected?
I confess, Sir, I have not known in peaceable times the power of the majority carried with a higher hand, or upheld with more relentless disregard
of the rights, feelings, and principles of the minority; a minority, embrac-
ing, as the gentleman will himself admit, a large portion of the wealth
and respectability of the state. How is this minority, how are those men
regarded? They are enthralled and disenfranchised by ordinances and acts
of legislature; subjected to tests and oaths, incompatible with those already taken; they are proscribed and denounced, as recreant to duty and
patriotism, and slaves to a foreign power. Both the spirit that pursues
them, and the positive measures which emanate from that spirit, are harsh
and proscriptive beyond all precedent within my knowledge, except in
periods of professed revolution." Such is the language of Mr. Webster,
analogous to that of M. de Tocqueville. The will of the majority is proclaimed by Mr. Webster to be the only possible government, and yet the
tyranny of the majority is admitted and denounced. Certainly if it be
ever so great as it is here represented to be in a public speech by so distinguished a statesman, it must be always too great; and the question with
which we have next concern, is not, whether majorities are, or are not,
to decide, but how those majorities are constituted; for if majorities are
to be constituted of the people told by the head, the question is then reduced to one of mere physical force, and we return to the original state
of savage and uncultivated man. This is so true, that at this moment, in
case of material opposition of opinion, there is no resource in America

but civil war, or a disunion of the states, a breaking up of the general government. The same too in any of the state governments—civil war, or a new constitution, or revolution.

But the whole secret of the prosperity of America, and the possibility of the existence of a form of government so fundamentally democratic, lies in the single circumstance of its being a new country; and its prosperity cannot at all be drawn into a precedent for any old country. Observe the remarks of Mr. Webster to his countrymen in June, 1833, and let any rational man reflect, how far such remarks can be applied to any other country, in the compass of the whole world, but the singular country of America. "Our political institutions," says he, "place power in the hands of all the people. To make the exercise of power in such hands salutary, it is indispensable that all the people should enjoy, first the means of education, and second, the reasonable certainty of procuring a competent livelihood by industry and labour. These institutions are neither designed for, nor suited to, a nation of ignorant paupers. To be free, the people must be intelligently free; to be substantially independent, they must be able to secure themselves against want, by sobriety and industry; to be safe depositaries of political power, they must be able to comprehend and understand the general interests of the community, and must have a stake themselves in the welfare of that community. The activity and prosperity which at present prevail among us, as every one must notice, are produced by the excitement of compensating prices to labour; and it is fervently to be hoped, that no unpropitious circumstances and no unwise policy may counteract this efficient cause of general competency and public happiness."

Now, can it be for a moment supposed, that a reasoner like this, would contend, in any country but his own, in any part of the continent of Europe, or even in England, for majorities numerically counted, and universal suffrage? Would he for a moment imagine, that an European society could be put into such a situation as he describes; "where every man should have compensating prices for his labour; where all the people should enjoy first the reasonable certainty of procuring a competent livelihood by industry and labour; secondly, the means of education, and be able to comprehend and understand the general interests of the community":—a community, it must be remembered, placed, not as in America, alone in the midst of the Atlantic Ocean, but in the midst of the other communities of Europe, and within the reach of the influence of the mistakes and follies of every one of them; and not with wide tracts of fresh land, behind the population, ready to receive them, but in countries already occupied and peopled for the last thousand years on regular systems of feudal rights and unequal property. Mr. Webster may exult in the happiness and prosperity of his own country; and when he sees with what an unexampled absence of restraint this happiness and prosperity are accomplished, he may indulge the natural pride of his patriotism, and look down on the different systems of Europe, as comparatively inferior and likely to be sooner or later assimilated to his own model:—all this may be natural in him: but it is for the statesmen and philosophers of our old world to observe the essential differences of the cases before them, and not to wish for impossibilities.

Republican institutions and a system totally democratic may be possible in a new country, where the first settlers were originally republicans, with high-wrought religious feelings, and where the land was almost equally divided; but this forms no precedent for other countries. Republics may be very favourable specimens of government with some men, but not necessarily with others. The civilization of Europe began with republican institutions, those of Greece and of Rome; the great principles of civil liberty were thus immortalized: but surely it must be thought that those communities exhibited but very imperfect specimens of human happiness; not to mention that a portion of their population, analogous to what in modern language is called the lower orders, consisted of men that were positively slaves. All the great difficulties of modern government were thus avoided; but at what a price? By an outrage of every feeling of humanity, and surely a defiance of the rights of man, and all the elementary principles of democracy. The Spartans might comb their hair, if in the meantime the Helots were their slaves. We have it upon high authority, that "the poor shall never cease from out the land." No society can exist without labourers; men doing the drudgery of life; men cultivating land not their own; men with little or no education, and without property. Good men and benevolent institutions may exert themselves very usefully and laudably, but can never so succeed, in an old country, as to make the vote per head consistent with the security of property.

Very serious disadvantages are inseparable from republican systems, and have been always noted by all political writers;—they are evidently not escaped even in America. But whatever be the advantages by which these disadvantages are accompanied in America, the advantages are to us, in Europe, inaccessible, if the prior history of our communities be attended to. The Grecian and Roman republics declined and fell; the former after being the scene of eternal discord and confusion, and the latter after being, also, the tyrant and oppressor of the world. The northern nations rushed in; the feudal system was established; the distinctions of high and low, and the inequality of property, were thoroughly interwoven and engrafted on our systems of polity. These are the facts; and these distinctions, this inequality, we cannot now obliterate and cast aside: nor can our governments be placed upon any such democratic foundations as exist in America, without such a disorganization of society, and such a fierce and bloody domination of the multitude, as would do more than renew the dreadful scenes that were so long witnessed during the fall of the Roman empire.

But even turning away from our prior history, and considering merely the nature of man, it is quite clear, that, whatever may have taken place in America, from its singular origin of the pilgrim fathers and republican adventurers taking possession of a new country, the distinctions of society have always existed in other countries, and become more and more inevitable and more and more distinctly marked, as a community grows older. The individuals naturally and necessarily fall into different aristocracies of birth; of property, landed, commercial, and manufacturing; of science; of knowledge civil or religious; and the members of these aristocracies are the natural rulers of society, not the mere numerical majority.

The original equality of man belongs to his awful relations to the Deity, the great Creator of the world, seen in the inevitable changes of his being and the events of his existence; in his birth, his growth, his decline, his diseases, and his death; in his appetites, affections, pleasures and pains; in his moral and religious duties; in his hopes of an hereafter, and his obedience to his God: in these great, paramount, and mysterious respects we are all equal; but in no other. In our relations to each other, as the members of a civil community, all personal equality disappears. We are differently constituted; we come into a community under different circumstances of birth and natural endowments—different relations, different duties and necessities, different opportunities for good or for evil arise: and all that can be done for the original equality of man, his equality in the eyes of his Creator, is, to allow every man, as far as law and civil ordinances are concerned, to do what he thinks good, if he do it without injury to others. No other equality but this sort of equality is possible: this civil and personal equality may be carried in America to an extent totally unprecedented in the history of mankind, and may present, in some most important respects, a most imposing and even enviable spectacle of civil society; but it is one, for the reasons I have mentioned, totally unattainable by the rest of the world.

It is indeed so totally unattainable that the agitators of society appear to me, to give men of any discernment, who have at all reflected on the nature of human affairs, full warning of their intentions. Let the writings and reasonings of such men be considered, and it will be found that, in France, those who are favourable to republican institutions, notwithstanding the comparative equality of fortune in that country, and the great subdivision of the land, still, never think of proposing a scheme of republican government, without at the same time looking to the destruction of religious establishments and an entire change of manners and social habits. Even the common principles of morals are to suffer the same fate.

And it is the same in this country. So was it at the breaking out of the first French Revolution. The system of Mr. Godwin appeared among us, obtained an audience, and established a school. Again, in France, at a subsequent period, the St. Simonians. All these belong to the same description of reasoners; men who, though advancing to different stages of absurdity, are all animated (the best of them) in the most unjustifiable degree, with their particular theories; and who, in pursuit of those theories, and intoxicated with any power they may acquire, are not to be stopped by any considerations from asserting them; by no future consequences, no probable mischief, no possible ruin.

But another school, and one within the reach of the respect of mankind, has of late become fashionable, not only in France but in this country: those who propose to place the power of the state, by means of political institutions, formed with that view, in the hands of the middle classes, the traders, farmers, and higher artificers; and this system is considered as both just and necessary, on account of the dissemination both of capital and knowledge which has already and may be expected still further to take place, from the gradual progress of the prosperity of the world. To this system it is not the business of these two lectures to object, any further than as it is applied to our own country of England. It is a system of republicanism, but republicanism only; it is not democracy; it is the republicanism that has more or less, and under different modifications and intermixtures of aristocracy, existed in particular portions of Europe; it is the republicanism which properly Washington, certainly Hamilton, would have wished for America; it is not the sweeping and unqualified democracy which Jefferson and the natural tendency of things introduced into that country. But in the science of government everything is a question of degree. There is no need of any exclusive system of this kind with us: those of our politicians who mean well should take care that they are not drawn aside too far by its captivating pretensions.

Our middle classes can surely have their proper weight and influence (of this there can be now no fear), without monopolizing the powers of the state; and something more may be, and has been, accomplished by our constitution than what can ever arise from the domination of the middle classes. I am approaching too near the politics of the day; and this is what I am always desirous of avoiding: and through these two lectures, and at all times, I am only anxious to throw out those general principles which I think are worthy to influence the mind and feelings of a rational Englishman.

In politics, everything, as I have said, is a question of degree. Those who insist upon the government of the middle classes would probably make a very objectionable definition of the middle classes: not to mention that, in the present condition of the world, republicanism invariably ends in democracy. The very fact that a country has very large towns and great seats of manufacturing industry, where the means of subsistence of the lower classes are fluctuating and uncertain, quite unfits it for democratic institutions. And what are we to say, if to such circumstances be added the existence of great inequalities of property in other parts of the same country; and again, a very peculiar species of property resulting from a national debt? Even Mr. Jefferson himself, in his letters from Paris, and in other parts of his Memoirs, frequently alludes to this impediment, in old countries, to what he supposes to be political freedom. He had a horror of the mobs of large capitals; M. de Tocqueville has similar apprehensions; and we already see mobs at New York and Philadelphia. What are we to conjecture of the future? The advocates for republicanism in our old countries would find nothing to sanction their views, but everything the contrary, in the writings of Mr. Jefferson, as I showed in a separate lecture, when the work first came out.

But still, it will be contended, that though we turn not our governments into democracies or republics, we may at least place them under the influence of public opinion. To this it must be observed, in the first place, that no doubt regular governments are too much disposed to be indifferent to public opinion. This is never wise, nor even just; but it is the most difficult point of all others for the rulers of such governments to ascertain when they are to concede to it, and when to resist. Arbitrary governments remain in the one extreme; democracies rush into the other. The only rule that can be proposed is that rulers should take what care they can, to have reason with them: this was the great characteristic of Washington. He viewed the subject on all sides, and then, in the first place, put himself in the right; after this, he calmly stood the consequences, and he and his character always survived the storm.

But having made these preparatory remarks, I must observe, that though the opinion of the public is a very popular phrase, and the influence which ought to belong to it is loudly contended for, still it must be allowed that it is a phrase which, in every word of it, admits very different meanings. What, for instance, is meant by the public; how far the opinion is ascertained; what is the influence required; these are matters of explanation and doubt; but one thing is certain, and one observation, which I have already made, I must now leave with you, and it is this, that no government in which monarchy is to have any part can be placed upon republican foundations; that the edifice would necessarily, in that case, be tottering and unstable. See what the Constituent Assembly, by a mistake of this kind, have made of the French monarchy; they abolished the right of primogeniture, weakened or destroyed its aristocratic elements, and what has it ever since become? What is it at this moment? But on the contrary, if a government be first placed on aristo-

cratic foundations, democratic institutions may be then introduced with
the happiest effect, and give air and light to the building; and therefore in
every mixed government, and in every government, the pretences and proposals of republican politicians must be carefully watched. There is nothing that it is so impossible to satisfy as the spirit of democracy; nothing
so encroaching, exclusive, and unreasonable; nothing so faithless: an end
accomplished, it is immediately said, that this was only a means to some
further end; and the democratic spirit always supplies a succession of those
who press on to trample down those before them. Look at the instance of
the progress of democracy in the first great revolution of France; still
more in the instance of America; for in this last case, nothing can in the
slightest manner be pretended in the way of explanation or apology. What
was the fact? It was in vain that the great man of the country, their justly-
adored Washington, it was in vain that, with the assistance of other wise
and distinguished men, he laboured to make the general government
strong: to introduce into the republican system as much executive power
as possible, to keep the union firm, and render it respectable in the eyes
of Europe, while America herself might be the better saved from the sins
that naturally beset all republican systems; nothing could properly tame
or abash the democratic spirit; and it is now entirely triumphant: everything is left to rest on the decision of the mere numerical majority, and
the system is apparently, and on the surface at least, quieted; but it is
only so, because the spirit of democracy can descend no lower, and can
have nothing further to require, from the mere physical impossibility of
collecting the people into a plain, and consulting them at every sunrise.

The American people are a great people, orderly and religious, exhibiting a high spirit of civil and religious liberty. The republican character
has great qualities, but it has important faults; it displays the severer
virtues, but not the softer; it may be admired, but cannot easily be loved;
it is courageous, enterprising, hardy, and independent, manly and erect;
but it is fierce, selfish, intractable, assuming and opiniated, hard and
arrogant: and if we cast a general glance over the northern continent of
America, the great leading description of the people, more particularly in
the northern and eastern states, will seem to be, that they are the children
of Mammon. They may have the merits, and they may attain to the happiness of those who are every moment engaged in the successful pursuit
of worldly prosperity; but speaking generally of the people, they think of
nothing else; everything with them is business; there is among them nothing of the poetry of life. This is no very elevated character. And if we
turn to the south and the west, what are we to say of the cruelties of the
slave states, or the vulgar coarseness of the Vale of the Mississippi; cruelties, far beyond the common tyrannies of slaveholders; coarseness, far
more revolting than the rudeness of uncivilized man. Of course, from the

midst of this disagreeable mass, individuals will arise, distinguished by all the intelligence and refinements of the most perfect character in European society, but I speak of the whole people, as everywhere to be seen and found; and much in the same way, I must observe, as I should have to speak of ourselves, if it were not for the aristocratic influences that everywhere circulate among us, surely to the extreme improvement and civilization of the whole.

A love of civil liberty is an ennobling principle, and one of the highest attributes of the human character, when it is really founded on a sympathy with the feelings of those below us, and on a generous indignation at the selfishness of the oppressor; but when it is in itself only selfishness, when it is mere personal pride, when it is a mere impatience of restraint, it is but the virtue of the savage, who, the moment he is interfered with, tomahawks the offender.

And now, finally, and to advert to one subject more, the restiveness of the Americans on all subjects of executive government. They are in an eternal alarm lest tyranny should approach them, after the manner, as they think, of European governments; and this idle fear has always been, and ever will be, the great difficulty and danger which the general government of America has to encounter.

The permanency of the American Constitution has always been a matter of speculation and doubt. Indeed, to all institutions of a republican nature, instability has been at all times the objection; resting on the good will of the people, their existence is naturally supposed to be feverish and uncertain; and a serious advantage is justly thought to be obtained, when such democratic materials as those of which they are composed, are pressed down by a monarchy and aristocracy, and prevented from starting from their appointed places.

Reflections of this kind were made forcibly to occur to the minds of all reasonable men in Europe, by the alarming transactions that took place during the late American war in 1812, and again still more by those that lately took place on the subject of the tariff. "During that war," said Jefferson, "four of the eastern states were only attached to the union, like so many inanimate bodies of living men"; and lately the subject of the tariff occasioned the most violent agitation, and produced all the appearances of an approaching civil war. The fact was that the influence of the northern states had prevailed so far as to carry a measure, placing a duty, amounting, in respect of some articles, almost to a prohibition, on British goods, of which the great consumption is in the southern states, and that this prohibition was intended for the encouragement of the manufactures of the north. But the measure was held by South Carolina to be partial and oppressive, and so destructive to its interests and those of the southern states, that it threatened, in fact, open rebellion, and to break up the union, rather than submit. This question gave occasion to some of the most eloquent and able of the speeches of Mr. Webster, a member from the north. I do not now enter into the subject of the tariff, and I may not agree with the opinions of Mr. Webster, as a political economist, but I can perfectly sympathise with his animated effusions on the subject of the permanency of the federal union.

The maintenance of this federal union has been always the great difficulty in the American Constitution. Provision was made to meet this difficulty by Franklin, and the other framers of the Constitution; but amidst the impatience of control that is generated by the American system, and the variety of local interests among the states, the difficulty is insuperable.

A certain analogy appears to me to exist between this great difficulty in the American Constitution, and the great difficulty in our own. In the American, you have the state governments and you have the general government, each with their separate interests, at least with their appropriate temptations to infringe upon the powers of each other. So is it in our own. We have the royal power, the House of Peers, and the Commons House, each with propensities, feelings, and prejudices of their own; but, as in the American Constitution, all, nevertheless, fitted to harmonize into a whole, for the general benefit of the community: and neither in America, nor with us, can any writer or statesman be so ill employed, as in exciting animosity, creating causes of dissension, exaggerating the faults, diminishing the reputation, or weakening the constitutional importance of either or of any of these great component and necessary parts of the whole. Such conduct on either the one side of the Atlantic or the other, can proceed only from thoughtless, giddy, irritable, superficial men, who know not what they are doing, or from wicked and unprincipled men, who know too well.

With reason did Mr. Webster exert his utmost eloquence in animating his countrymen to the maintenance of the federal union of America; and there is scarcely a sentence in this part of his address, that is not applicable to our own union of king, lords, and commons,—the established constitution of the realm of England. I will quote it at some length, and you can make the application as I read.

"I profess, sir," said Mr. Webster, "in my career hitherto, to have kept steadily in view the prosperity and honour of the whole country, and the preservation of our federal union. It is to that union we owe our safety at home, and our consideration and dignity abroad; it is to that union that we are chiefly indebted for whatever makes us most proud of our country. That union we reached only by the discipline of our virtues in the severe school of adversity. It had its origin in the necessities of disordered finance, prostrate commerce, and ruined credit. Under its benign influences, these great interests immediately awoke, as from the dead, and sprang forth with newness of life. Every year of its duration has teemed with fresh proofs of its utility and its blessings; and, although our territory has stretched out wider and wider, and our population spread farther and farther, they have not outrun its protection or its benefits. It has been to us all, a copious fountain of national, social, and personal happiness. I have not allowed myself, sir, to look beyond the union, to see what might lie hidden in the dark recess behind; I have not coolly weighed the chances of preserving liberty, when the bonds that unite us together shall be broken asunder; I have not accustomed myself to hang over the precipice of disunion, to see whether, with my short sight, I can fathom the depth of the abyss below; nor could I regard him as a safe counsellor in the affairs of this government, whose thoughts should be mainly bent on considering, not how the union should be best preserved, but how tolerable should be the condition of the people, when it should be broken up and destroyed. While the union lasts, we have high, exciting, gratifying prospects spread out before us, for us and our children. Beyond that, I seek not to penetrate the veil. God grant, that in my day, at least, that curtain may not rise! God grant, that on my vision never may be opened what lies behind! When my eyes shall be turned to behold, for the last time, the sun in heaven, may I not see him shining on the broken and dishonoured fragments of a once glorious union; on states dissevered, discordant, belligerent; on a land rent with civil feuds, or drenched, it may be, in fraternal blood!"

Such was the language, and such the sentiments of Mr. Webster. With reason did he pour out his soul in the patriotic effusion which I have just read to you; and with equal reason might a patriot, in our own country, dedicate every energy of his mind, and every feeling of his heart, to the preservation and defence of that union, which, as Mr. Webster said of his own, has been to us all, a copious fountain of national, social, and personal happiness. "And never," to use his animated language, "never may the sun be seen to shine on the broken and dishonoured fragments of a once glorious union" of king, lords, and commons; "on powers dissevered, discordant, belligerent; on a land rent," as it once was, "with civil feuds, or drenched," as it once was, "in fraternal blood!"

"Other misfortunes," says Mr. Webster, in his eulogy on Washington (the parent and protector of the American union), "other misfortunes may be borne, or their effects overcome." And we too, in England, may echo back the patriotic strain of Mr. Webster, for we too have had our misfortunes, and we too have a constitution that I trust we admire and love, as the Americans may their republic. "Other misfortunes," says Mr. Webster, "may be borne, or their effects overcome." Let us make his sentiments our own. "If disastrous war should sweep our commerce from the ocean," says he, "another generation may renew it; if it exhaust our treasury, future industry may replenish it; if it desolate and lay waste our fields, still, under a new cultivation, they will grow again, and ripen to future harvests. It were but a trifle, even if the walls of our Capitol were to crumble (and the walls of our Capitol, of our House of Parliament have so crumbled), if its lofty pillars should fall, and its gorgeous decorations be all covered by the dust of the valley. All these might be rebuilt; but who shall reconstruct the fabric of demolished government?" And well may we too say, "but who shall reconstruct the fabric of demolished government?" and with even more propriety than Mr. Webster, for his democratic government, "a breath may make it, as a breath has made." "Arbitrio popularis auræ." "Who shall rear again," continued Mr. Webster, "the well-proportioned columns of constitutional liberty?" "Who shall frame together," said Mr. Webster, and what English patriot may not say the same? "the skilful architecture, which unites national sovereignty with state rights, individual security, and public prosperity? No, gentlemen, if these columns fall, they will be raised not again. Like the Coliseum and the Pantheon, they will be destined to a mournful, a melancholy immortality. Bitterer tears, however, will flow over them than were ever shed over the monuments of Roman or Grecian art, for they will be the remnants of a more glorious edifice than Greece or Roman ever saw,—the edifice of constitutional American liberty."

"Constitutional American liberty," said Mr. Webster; and constitutional English liberty shall, in like manner, be said by me. Let each country be enamoured of its own: to each country may its own be best adapted. To me there may appear a far more refined and higher specimen of civilization in this favoured island than is or can be seen in America; but I contend only for candid estimates, for reasonable allowances in each country for the appropriate and inevitable evils of the other. I wage war only with exclusive systems, with this democratic doctrine, which first appeared in the arrogant pages of Paine, that no government can be lawful which rests not on the will of the majority, told by the head, that aristocracies of every kind, of birth, of rank, and of property, are mere usurpation and tyranny, and with the gradual civilization of the world must necessarily disappear. I look to no such revolutions in the world, or rather, in human nature: I consider such aristocracies as the great elements, materials, and results of the civilization of mankind; as the best hope, foundation, and support of that civilization; as the best protection against selfishness, vulgarity, the coarser vices, and the fierce and ruder passions of mankind; as the best promoters of every higher sentiment of benevolence, honour, and virtue, of taste, of literature, of learning, and of knowledge; of the aspirations of genius in every direction. Such aristocracies have ever existed in our island, and never may they decline or fall! They form the constitution of England, a constitution, to which, by birth, as an Englishman, by study, by gratitude, by reason, by every principle of duty and of feeling, I am, for one, deliberately but ardently attached, and I shall never cease to be attached, be the changes, and whims, and whirl-winds of opinion in this restless world, be they what they may; "non ego perfidum dixi sacramentum." Our country has had its misfortunes, the misfortunes of Europe. They were nigh fatal; they lie still heavy upon us. We may have committed our mistakes; we may have our faults. An old country cannot be without its difficulties; difficulties hard to wrestle with. In the midst of great exhibitions of affluence and prosperity, great extremes of poverty and misery cannot but arise. Different classes of men may have their appropriate temptations and be found too ready to submit to them; but the constitution itself, the ancient constitution of our hon-oured land, the constitution of king, lords, and commons, each and all with their appropriate privileges and prerogatives, "Esto perpetua" be the cry, now and for ever; "esto perpetua"; for, whatever be our political differences, this at least should be the cry of every Englishman that de-serves the name.

And I now, as my concluding effort, deliver this aspiration to you, to be the treasure of your hearts, and the maxim of your public conduct; and as far as your own country is concerned, to be considered by you, as the sum and substance of all political wisdom and all genuine patriotism.

INDEX